I0461271

RONALD J. WENDEL

ELEGANT NUMBERS

(2ND EDITION)

A Look at Methods, Patterns, and

Symmetries in Mathematics

Kravitz & Sons

INNOVATORS IN PUBLISHING, MARKETING AND ADVERTISING

Kravitz and Sons LLC
1301 Farmville Blvd, Suite 104
Greenville, NC 27834

© 2025 Ronald Wendel. All rights reserved.

No part of this book may be reproduced, stored in a retrieval system, or transmitted by any means without the written permission of the author.

Published by Kravitz and Sons LLC.

ISBN: 979-8-89639-267-5 (sc)
ISBN: 979-8-89639-268-2 (e)

Library of Congress Control Number: 2025912722

Because of the dynamic nature of the Internet, any web addresses or links contained in this book may have changed since publication and may no longer be valid. The views expressed in this work are solely those of the author and do not necessarily reflect the views of the publisher, and the publisher hereby disclaims any responsibility for them.

Table of Contents

Introduction

This is a book about number patterns. The human mind has a great ability to look for, find and interpret patterns. Sometimes these patterns are seen as superstitious occurrences, and then it appears that the destinies of individuals and nations are determined by the roll of the dice; but at other times science prevails, and we find that these patterns are actually related to physical and natural properties and processes.

This search for patterns starts when we are very young. One of the most complex sets of patterns that a young child learns to recognize and understand is language. And keep in mind that language is not just about vocabulary. It also includes grammar and the proper word order to convey the intended meaning. In addition to this, many languages either require or at least allow tones and inflections, facial expressions, hand gestures and other types of body language that accompany the spoken word.

When my oldest child was learning to speak, we would remind him to say please whenever he would ask for something. However, for some reason he thought that saying please also meant that he had to go to a certain spot in the living room to say it. Every time he wanted something, he would run to that same place in the living room and say, "Please, please, please." Somehow he recognized, and therefore thought that standing in a certain place was part of the communication process of saying "please."

Mathematics is the language of science. Formulas are nothing more than an explanation of scientific events that follow similar patterns. However, many times there are also patterns within these patterns. Formulas for differing phenomena seem to have similar structures. It is by looking for these patterns in the things we can see that gives us understanding and insight when looking at similar things that we cannot see.

For many, learning mathematics is also a journey. We learn arithmetic before algebra, then algebra before trigonometry, trigonometry before analytic geometry, and analytic geometry before calculus - each step building on previous steps. This book is meant to point out some of the scenery from that journey that you might have missed along the way. Without delving into complicated mathematics, structures and theories, this book uses basic algebra to examine various patterns, relationships and symmetries in the world of mathematics that surrounds us.

While in school, some of your peers may have found mathematics to be a boring and barren landscape. You, on the other hand, may have found that this journey through mathematics was an adventure full of discovery and surprise. In this book we will conduct our own expedition through a world of patterns and symmetry where some of these patterns appear, then reappear, and then yet reappear again in some of the least expected places. We will find formulas and fractals, repeating cycles and number patterns within patterns of numbers, some relating to other patterns through simple arithmetic and geometric combinations.

If you really want to enjoy this expedition, then you must do some of your own exploring along the way. Get out a pencil, some paper and a pocket calculator. Work through the ideas presented here, as well as any of your own. Make up your own mathematical experiments, and keep your own log. (You don't need safety glasses to do experiments in mathematics, and the lab coat is optional.)

Note that the chapters in this book can stand on their own. This means that even though you can read the book straight through from cover to cover; you can also read the chapters in any order you choose; or you can even skip a chapter or two if that suits your fancy.

And now in the spirit of this self-similar and recursive adventure, we begin our journey with a recursive and self-similar tale:

> "It was a dark and stormy night. The rain came down in torrents. The wind blew gigantic swells over the sides of the ship. The captain turned to Antonio and said, "Antonio, tell us a story." And he began:
>
>> "It was a dark and stormy night. The rain came down in torrents. The wind blew gigantic swells over the sides of the ship. The captain turned to Antonio and said, "Antonio, tell us a story." And he began:
>>
>>> "It was a dark and stormy night. The rain came down ...

"... and what we heard ..., no, what we saw, ..., no, ... what we experienced that night was self-similar and recursive. Patterns appeared and disappeared and then reappeared. There was organization within chaos, and symmetry within these recurring relationships; indeed, it was more than we had ever dreamed, yet it was just the beginning ..."

Chapter 1
Number Patterns

Number Patterns

Perhaps you've seen patterns within numbers as you've added and subtracted them, or multiplied and squared them. These patterns are everywhere. For example, we know that if we square the numbers 1 through 9 we get:

$$1, 4, 9, 16, 25, 36, 49, 64, 81$$

When we look at the last digit (the right-most digit) of each of these numbers, we have:

$$1, 4, 9, 6, 5, 6, 9, 4, 1$$

This pattern is palindromic (it reads the same forwards as it reads backwards). But did you know that if we do the same thing with the numbers 11 through 19, we again get the same pattern. Here are the numbers 11^2 through 19^2:

$$121, 144, 169, 196, 225, 256, 289, 324, 361$$

The last digits of those numbers show the same pattern:

$$1, 4, 9, 6, 5, 6, 9, 4, 1$$

And this pattern repeats itself for the numbers 21 through 29, and so on.

Another interesting pattern generates squared numbers from a sum of consecutive numbers, where the series starts with the number 1, then adds every number up to the number being squared, and then goes back down to 1. We start with 1^2 equal to 1; and continue with 2^2 equal to $1 + 2 + 1$; then 3^2 equal to $1 + 2 + 3 + 2 + 1$; and so on. The pattern looks like this:

$$
\begin{aligned}
1^2 &= 1 = & 1 \\
2^2 &= 4 = & 1 + 2 + 1 \\
3^2 &= 9 = & 1 + 2 + 3 + 2 + 1 \\
4^2 &= 16 = & 1 + 2 + 3 + 4 + 3 + 2 + 1 \\
5^2 &= 25 = & 1 + 2 + 3 + 4 + 5 + 4 + 3 + 2 + 1 \\
& \text{etc.}
\end{aligned}
$$

Yet, another interesting pattern of numbers that generates squared numbers can be seen when we look at the sums of odd numbers. Just as we started the previous series above with 1^2 equal to 1, this next series also starts the same. However, this time we continue with 2^2 equal to $1 + 3$; and then 3^2 equal to $1 + 3 + 5$. We could say that n^2 is equal to the sum of the first n odd numbers. The following listing shows what this pattern looks like:

$$1^2 = 1 = 1$$
$$2^2 = 4 = 1 + 3$$
$$3^2 = 9 = 1 + 3 + 5$$
$$4^2 = 16 = 1 + 3 + 5 + 7$$
$$5^2 = 25 = 1 + 3 + 5 + 7 + 9$$
etc.

A variation of the pattern above will generate cubed numbers. This time start with 1^3 equal to 1, and continue with 2^3 equal to $3 + 5$; and 3^3 equal to $7 + 9 + 11$, and so on. In other words, the first number cubed is equal to the first odd number, the second number cubed is equal to the sum of the next two odd numbers, the third number cubed is equal to the sum of the next three odd numbers, etc. The listing below shows this pattern that we just described:

$$1^3 = 1 = 1$$
$$2^3 = 8 = 3 + 5$$
$$3^3 = 27 = 7 + 9 + 11$$
$$4^3 = 64 = 13 + 15 + 17 + 19$$
$$5^3 = 125 = 21 + 23 + 25 + 27 + 29$$
etc.

And yet another variation will generate numbers raised to the fourth power. Again, 1^4 is equal to 1. This time, 2^4 is equal to the sum of the first four odd numbers; and 3^4 is equal to the sum of the first nine odd numbers. This pattern continues such that n^4 is equal to the sum of the first n^2 odd numbers. And here is the listing that shows this pattern:

$$1^4 = 1 = 1 \qquad (\text{1 term})$$
$$2^4 = 16 = 1 + 3 + 5 + 7 \qquad (\text{4 terms})$$
$$3^4 = 81 = 1 + 3 + 5 + 7 + \ldots + 17 \qquad (\text{9 terms})$$
$$4^4 = 256 = 1 + 3 + 5 + 7 + \ldots + 31 \qquad (\text{16 terms})$$
$$5^4 = 625 = 1 + 3 + 5 + 7 + \ldots + 49 \qquad (\text{25 terms})$$
etc.

And there are patterns like these all over in mathematics. In this chapter we'll look at some of them; beginning with some of the peculiar properties of the number nine.

The Number 9

Many numbers exhibit specific properties. Most of these properties are independent of the system or base used to describe the number (for example, a number is prime whether it is written in base 10, base 16, or base 23). Other numbers show certain properties when written in a specific base. The number 5 has certain properties in base 10, while the number 4 shows similar properties in base 8. We will see one of these properties of the number 5 (in base 10) a little later in this chapter.

A peculiar property of base 10 can be seen when multiplying any number by ten. It's easy to do, we simply add a 0 to the right side of that number. This also works in other bases. In base 8, to multiply a number by 8, simply add a 0 to the right side of that number. Likewise, in base 2, if you wish to multiply a number by 2, add a zero to the right side of it. No matter what base, if you wish to multiply by the number that is the same value as your base, just add a 0 to the end of the number.

2

The number 9 has many peculiarities because we use base 10 as our number system. Some of these peculiarities can be very useful. There are accounting tricks and magic tricks based on the number 9. For example, a powerful mind reading trick goes something like this: Ask a volunteer to write down a seven-digit number and not show it to you. Now ask that volunteer to take that number and multiply it by 9. Your volunteer now has a number that is divisible by 9 which means that if you were to add together all the digits in that number it would also be equal to a multiple of 9 (of course, you don't tell the volunteer, or the audience that little piece of information). Instead, you tell your volunteer that if there are any 0's in the number to cross them out. Then have them circle another number, and then read the rest of the numbers back to you. All you have to do is add the numbers as they are read to you. You will get a sum that is not a multiple of 9. Subtract your number from the next highest multiple of 9, and you will have the number that they circled. (i.e., If your sum is equal to 23, then subtract that from 27, and you will know that the circled number is equal to 4. And if the sum you get is a multiple of 9, then that means that the number your volunteer circled was a 9). Many people will be very impressed that you were able to divine the circled number without ever knowing what the original number was.

And the number 9 isn't the only number with special properties like this. When working in base 8, the number 7 has many of these same properties, and even the number 1 shares similar properties when working in base 2.

Another property of the number 9 can be seen when we multiply any single digit number by 9. This method can be demonstrated by lining up ten coins in a row. Now, to find the product of some number and 9, count from the left that number of coins, and remove it. There now remain two groups of coins; one group is to the left of the removed coin, and the other is on the right. The number of coins in the left group is the tens digit; and the number of coins on the right is the one's digit. The following example shows the products of 3 times 9 and 6 times 9.

First, we begin with ten coins in a row. To find the product of 3 times 9, we remove the third coin. This leaves us with 2 coins, a space, and then 7 coins, which we interpret to be 27. In other words, the product of 3 times 9 is 27. Similarly, to find the product of 6 times 9, we take the ten coins and remove the sixth coin. We are now left with 5 coins on the left and 4 coins on the right, or 54. Thus, the product of 6 times 9 is 54. We can use this method to find the product of 9 and any number between 1 and 9.

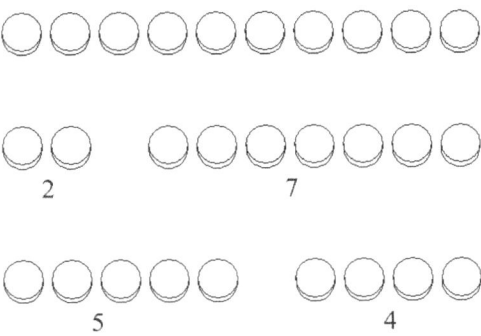

Figure 1.1   Coins show the products of 3 x 9, and 6 x 9 (in base 10).

Many school children have learned that they don't need to round up 10 coins. They can simply use their 10 fingers and achieve the same result. They hold up both hands with the fingers extended, and then lower the finger that represents the number they are multiplying by 9. The remaining fingers are in two groups and from there they can tell what the product is.

3

As mentioned earlier, this same principle holds true in other bases. In base 8, we can do the same thing for the multiples of 7. However, keep in mind that the result will be in base 8. This time we begin with eight coins in a row:

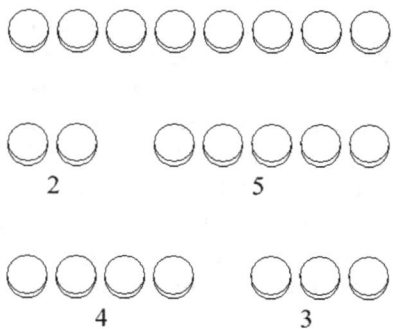

Figure 1.2   Coins show the products of 3 x 7, and 5 x 7 (in base 8).

Again, to find the product of 3 times 7, we remove the third coin. This leaves us with 2 on the left and 5 on the right, or 25, which is the product of 3 and 7 (in base 8). Likewise, the product of 5 times 7 (in base 8) is equal to 43. Again, we obtained the 43 by lining the eight coins, and removing the 5th coin.

Dividing by 9

As we continue our look at the number 9, there is a pretty slick trick that can be used to divide any number by 9. We'll first see how it is done with a three-digit number; then we'll apply it to numbers with more digits. The best way to understand this method will be by working through a few examples. For our first example we'll take 143 and divide it by 9. We start by taking the three-digit number 143 and separating the right-most digit from the other two digits.

$$14 \mid 3$$

Next, we'll take the leading 1 and add it to the 14; and then we'll take the 1 and 4 (from the left side), and add them together, and then add them to the 3 (on the right). Our next step looks like this:

$$14 \mid 3$$
$$\underline{+\quad 1 \mid 5} \leftarrow (5 = 1 + 4 \text{ from the other column})$$

The result is:

$$15 \mid 8$$

This means that 143 divided by 9 is equal to 15 and 8/9.

Now, let's try dividing 793 by 9. Again, we start by separating the right-most digit from the other two:

$$79 \mid 3$$

Next, we bring the leading digit down, and add it to the 79; then we add the 7 and 9 (from the left), and add that to the 3 (on the right). This gives us:

$$79 \mid 3$$
$$+ \quad 7 \mid 16 \leftarrow (16 = 7 + 9 \text{ from the other column})$$

Adding up the two sides gives us:

$$86 \mid 19$$

Therefore, our result is equal to 86 and 19/9. Of course, 19/9 is equal to 2 and 1/9; which means our final answer is 88 and 1/9 (which is the result of 793 divided by 9).

Now that we basically understand how this method works for three-digit numbers, let's look at a four-digit number. We'll divide 3728 by 9. Once again, we start by separating the right-most digit from the other three digits.

$$372 \mid 8$$

Next, we bring down the leading two digits and add them to the 372; then we add the 37 and 2 together, and then add that to the 8. This step looks like this.

$$372 \mid 8$$
$$+ \quad 37 \mid 39 \leftarrow (39 = 37 + 2)$$

The total equals:

$$409 \mid 47$$

Which is equal to 409 and 47/9. The fraction 47/9 reduces to 5 and 2/9; therefore, our final answer is 414 and 2/9.

The Number 9 and a Method of Subtraction Through Addition

As mentioned earlier, many of these properties of the number 9 can be carried over to other numbers in their respective bases. In this section, we'll look at a method that uses the complement of a number to perform subtraction through addition. In base 10, we use the number 9 to find the complement of a number. A complement is a number that when added to the original number gives us the number 9. For example, 1 and 8 are complements, as are 2 and 7; etc. If we have a three digit number such as 610, its complement would be 389. Notice that adding the first digit of each number gives us 9. Likewise, adding the second digits together or the third digits together also give us a 9 in each case. These complements are the key to being able to subtract two numbers by adding them together.

The way this method works is very simple. Start with two numbers, one being subtracted from the other. However, instead of subtracting, take the number being subtracted, find its complement and add one. Then add the two numbers together. Disregard the left-most carry, and the result is the difference between the two original numbers. Let's look at some examples. We'll start by subtracting 16 from 23:

$$23$$
$$- 16$$

First, find the complement of 16, and add one to it. The complement of 16 is 83. We add one to 83 to give us 84, and our original subtraction problem can now become an addition problem:

$$23$$
$$+\ 84$$

With these two numbers, we perform a normal addition and disregard the last carry. Three plus 4 is 7, 2 plus 8 is 0, carry the one (but we ignore this carry) and our result is 07, or just 7. Hence, 23 minus 16 is 7.

$$23$$
$$+\ 84$$
$$\overline{07}$$

This is a very nice process; however, to make it work all of the time, there are a few rules that we need to keep in mind. One is that the two numbers being subtracted must each have the same number of digits. This can easily be done by adding 0's to the front of the shorter number. For example:

45	this becomes	45	take the complement, add 1 and add		45
- 7		- 07	(ignore the last carry)		+ 93
					38

The second rule is that if the number being subtracted is larger than the number it is subtracted from, then after we get the sum, we must subtract 1, and take the complement of that sum. For example, look at 12 minus 26:

12			12
- 26	take the complement and add		+ 74
			86

In this case, our answer is a negative number, and we must perform our series of operations in reverse on the 86. First, we subtract 1 from 86 to get 85. Next, the complement of 85 is 14 (which is the difference between 26 and 12). And because we were taking the 26 away from 12, the result is negative, or -14.

This property is true for number systems in other bases, including the number 1 in base 2. In fact, this is the way most computers subtract two numbers. (Computers do this so that they can use the same algorithm for subtraction that they use for addition, thus conserving computing resources.) Let's use this method to subtract 17 from 23 in base 2. The number 23 in base 2 is equal to 10111, and 17 in base 2 is equal to 10001.

10111		10111
- 10001	Take the complement, add 1 then add	+ 01111
	(finally, disregard the last carry)	00110

Our result after addition is equal to 00110 which is equal to 6. Twenty-three minus 17 is equal to 6 (even in base 2).

A Second Method of Subtraction Through Addition

At this point we'll briefly take leave of our look at the properties of the number 9 in order to consider a second method of subtraction through addition. This method uses several more steps than what a person would normally use; however, it also makes it very easy to find the difference between two numbers. In a nutshell, this method starts with the number being subtracted, and then allows you to add 5's and 10's (and 100's and so on) until you arrive at the number that is being subtracted from. Let's take a look, and see how this is done. Our first example will subtract 56 from 93. Start with:

$$93 - 56 = \ ?$$

Then we ask ourselves, what number can we add to 56 to bring it up to the nearest number that ends with a 5 or 0. In this case when we add 4 to 56 we get 60:

$$56 + 4 = 60$$

Next, what multiple of 10 do we add to 60 to get us as close to 93 as we can. Adding 30 to 60 will give us 90:

$$60 + 30 = 90$$

Finally, what do we add to 90 to give us 93? As can easily be seen, adding 3 will give us 93:

$$90 + 3 = 93$$

Now we simply add together the numbers that we added throughout this process (which were the $4 + 30 + 3$) to arrive at 37. Therefore, $93 - 56$ is equal to 37.

Now that we have an idea how this works, let's look at a more condensed example. We'll subtract 43 from 132:

$$132 - 43 = \ ?$$

Start with the 43:

$$43 + 2 = 45$$
$$45 + 5 = 50$$
$$50 + 50 = 100$$
$$100 + 30 = 130$$
$$130 + 2 = 132$$

The numbers that we added within this process were 2, 5, 50, 30, 2; so now we simply add these numbers together to give us 89. And there it is, $132 - 43 = 89$. Once a person understands the concept behind this method, they find that it is very easy to use. And it can be applied equally well to large numbers, small numbers, and even numbers with decimals.

Additional Properties of the Number 9

Returning to our look at the number nine, we see some additional relationships with other numbers. For example, when we multiply nine to the numbers 1, 12, 123, 1234, etc. we get:

1	* 9 =	09
12	* 9 =	108
123	* 9 =	1107
1234	* 9 =	11106
12345	* 9 =	111105
123456	* 9 =	1111104
1234567	* 9 =	11111103
12345678	* 9 =	111111102
123456789	* 9 =	1111111101

A variation to the pattern above adds the numbers 2 through 10 to give us:

1	*	9	+	2	=	11
12	*	9	+	3	=	111
123	*	9	+	4	=	1111
1234	*	9	+	5	=	11111
12345	*	9	+	6	=	111111
123456	*	9	+	7	=	1111111
1234567	*	9	+	8	=	11111111
12345678	*	9	+	9	=	111111111
123456789	*	9	+	10	=	1111111111

These patterns are also evident in other bases. For example, in base 7, we multiply by 6 to get:

1_7	*	6_7	=	06_7
12_7	*	6_7	=	105_7
123_7	*	6_7	=	1104_7
1234_7	*	6_7	=	11103_7
12345_7	*	6_7	=	111102_7
123456_7	*	6_7	=	1111101_7

And this pattern also has the same variation as the base 10 variation listed above:

1_7	*	6_7	+	2_7	=	11_7
12_7	*	6_7	+	3_7	=	111_7
123_7	*	6_7	+	4_7	=	1111_7
1234_7	*	6_7	+	5_7	=	11111_7
12345_7	*	6_7	+	6_7	=	111111_7
123456_7	*	6_7	+	10_7	=	1111111_7

We see a similar pattern when we multiply nine to the numbers 9, 98, 987, 9876, etc. (We'll align these products in columns so that the pattern can be seen more easily.)

9	*	9	=	81
98	*	9	=	882
987	*	9	=	8883
9876	*	9	=	88884
98765	*	9	=	888885
987654	*	9	=	8888886
9876543	*	9	=	88888887
98765432	*	9	=	888888888
987654321	*	9	=	8888888889

Again, these patterns hold in other bases. For bases above base 10, we let letters of the alphabet represent our numbers. In the next example, we look at numbers in base 12; therefore, the number 10 is represented by the letter a, and the number 11 is represented by b. Here is the pattern we get when we multiply b to the numbers b, ba, ba9, ba98, etc.:

$$b_{12} \quad * \quad b_{12} \quad = \quad a1_{12}$$
$$ba_{12} \quad * \quad b_{12} \quad = \quad aa2_{12}$$
$$ba9_{12} \quad * \quad b_{12} \quad = \quad aaa3_{12}$$
$$ba98_{12} \quad * \quad b_{12} \quad = \quad aaaa4_{12}$$
$$ba987_{12} \quad * \quad b_{12} \quad = \quad aaaaa5_{12}$$
$$ba9876_{12} \quad * \quad b_{12} \quad = \quad aaaaaa6_{12}$$
$$ba98765_{12} \quad * \quad b_{12} \quad = \quad aaaaaaa7_{12}$$
$$ba987654_{12} \quad * \quad b_{12} \quad = \quad aaaaaaaa8_{12}$$
$$ba9876543_{12} \quad * \quad b_{12} \quad = \quad aaaaaaaaa9_{12}$$
$$ba98765432_{12} \quad * \quad b_{12} \quad = \quad aaaaaaaaaaa_{12}$$
$$ba987654321_{12} \quad * \quad b_{12} \quad = \quad aaaaaaaaaaab_{12}$$

Another interesting pattern can be seen when we square the numbers 9, 99, 999, etc.

$$9^2 = 81$$
$$99^2 = 9801$$
$$999^2 = 998001$$
$$9999^2 = 99980001$$
$$99999^2 = 9999800001$$
$$999999^2 = 999998000001$$
$$9999999^2 = 99999980000001$$

Similar patterns exist when we square the numbers 8, 88, 888, 8888, … in base nine, or when we square the numbers 7, 77, 777, 7777, … in base eight, and so on.

Now consider the following relationship when we divide 9 into nine 1's in base 10, and 8 into eight 1's in base 9, and 7 into seven 1's in base 8, and so forth:

$$111111111_{10} \div 9_{10} = 12345679_{10}$$
$$11111111_{9} \div 8_{9} = 1234568_{9}$$
$$1111111_{8} \div 7_{8} = 123457_{8}$$
$$111111_{7} \div 6_{7} = 12346_{7}$$
$$11111_{6} \div 5_{6} = 1235_{6}$$
$$1111_{5} \div 4_{5} = 124_{5}$$
$$111_{4} \div 3_{4} = 13_{4}$$
$$11_{3} \div 2_{3} = 2_{3}$$

The pattern above shows that if we have nine 1's written in base 10, and we divide this number by nine, our result is 12345679 (which has the numbers written in order from 1 to 7, skips 8 and then ends with a 9). Now if we take eight 1's written in base 9 and divide this number by eight, the result is 1234568_{9} (which has the numbers 1 through 8, except the 7). And so the pattern continues.

Products of Numbers

In this section we'll move away from the properties of the number 9, but still consider various patterns within the products of two numbers; for example, if we multiply a number to a second number that is four more than the first, the product is the same as (and equal to) the square of the average of the two numbers minus 4. You may have read that and said, "Huh?" But let's apply it to an example and see what it means.

We start with two numbers like 3 and 7 (where the second number is four more than the first); then the product of 3 and 7 can also be calculated by taking the average of 3 and 7 (which is 5), squaring it (to give us 25) and then finally subtracting 4 (to give us 21 which, as a matter of fact, is the product of 3 and 7). Here are a few more examples:

$$
\begin{array}{llll}
3 * 7 & \text{is the same as} & 5^2 - 4 & \text{and both are equal to} & 21 \\
4 * 8 & \text{is the same as} & 6^2 - 4 & \text{and both are equal to} & 32 \\
5 * 9 & \text{is the same as} & 7^2 - 4 & \text{and both are equal to} & 45 \\
6 * 10 & \text{is the same as} & 8^2 - 4 & \text{and both are equal to} & 60 \\
7 * 11 & \text{is the same as} & 9^2 - 4 & \text{and both are equal to} & 77 \\
8 * 12 & \text{is the same as} & 10^2 - 4 & \text{and both are equal to} & 96 \\
& \text{etc.}
\end{array}
$$

This is an interesting relationship that will work for any pair of numbers that have a difference of four. However, this relationship is not unique. If we multiply a pair of numbers together that have a difference of six, their product is equal to the average of the two numbers squared, minus nine. Here are several examples showing this relationship:

$$
\begin{array}{lllll}
3 * 9 & = & 6^2 - 9 & = & 27 \\
4 * 10 & = & 7^2 - 9 & = & 40 \\
5 * 11 & = & 8^2 - 9 & = & 55 \\
6 * 12 & = & 9^2 - 9 & = & 72 \\
7 * 13 & = & 10^2 - 9 & = & 91 \\
8 * 14 & = & 11^2 - 9 & = & 112 \\
& & \text{etc.}
\end{array}
$$

And if there is a difference of 8 between the pair of numbers multiplied together, their product is equal to the average of the two numbers squared, minus 16. Here are examples showing this relationship:

$$
\begin{array}{lllll}
3 * 11 & = & 7^2 - 16 & = & 33 \\
4 * 12 & = & 8^2 - 16 & = & 48 \\
5 * 13 & = & 9^2 - 16 & = & 65 \\
6 * 14 & = & 10^2 - 16 & = & 84 \\
7 * 15 & = & 11^2 - 16 & = & 105 \\
8 * 16 & = & 12^2 - 16 & = & 128 \\
& & \text{etc.}
\end{array}
$$

This method can be summarized with the following formula.

$$ a * b = ((b + a)/2)^2 - ((b - a)/2)^2 $$

The examples we used had a difference of 4, 6 or 8 between the numbers multiplied together. However, with this formula we can see that it doesn't matter what the difference is between the two numbers, the relationship still works. In fact, this formula is one of the methods the ancient Babylonians used to find the product of two numbers (See the chapter on Multiplication Methods for other methods of finding products).

The Product of Three Consecutive Numbers Plus the Middle Number

Another interesting pattern can be seen when we multiply three consecutive numbers together, and then add again the middle number. The result is equal to the middle number cubed.

$$
\begin{aligned}
1*2*3 + 2 &= 8 &&= 2^3 \\
2*3*4 + 3 &= 27 &&= 3^3 \\
3*4*5 + 4 &= 64 &&= 4^3 \\
4*5*6 + 5 &= 125 &&= 5^3 \\
5*6*7 + 6 &= 216 &&= 6^3 \\
6*7*8 + 7 &= 343 &&= 7^3 \\
7*8*9 + 8 &= 512 &&= 8^3
\end{aligned}
$$

etc.

This can easily be shown to be true for any three consecutive numbers by letting x equal the middle number, and multiplying $(x - 1)$, x, and $(x + 1)$ together and then adding x. The result reduces to x^3.

The Product of Four Consecutive Numbers Plus One

When we multiply four consecutive numbers together, and add one, we find that it is always equal to a square of some other number. In fact, it is equal to the square of the product of the two middle numbers minus one. For example, the product of the numbers 3, 4, 5 and 6 is equal to 360. Now, when we add one, we have 361 which is equal to 19^2. And the 19 is equal to the product of the two middle numbers, 4 and 5, minus one. This relationship is interesting by itself; however, there are also several other patterns within it. We'll list a dozen of these consecutive products and see if we can find any other kind of a pattern:

$$
\begin{aligned}
0*1*2*3 + 1 &= 1 \text{ or } 1^2 &&= [(1*2) - 1]^2 \\
1*2*3*4 + 1 &= 25 \text{ or } 5^2 &&= [(2*3) - 1]^2 \\
2*3*4*5 + 1 &= 121 \text{ or } 11^2 &&= [(3*4) - 1]^2 \\
3*4*5*6 + 1 &= 361 \text{ or } 19^2 &&= [(4*5) - 1]^2 \\
4*5*6*7 + 1 &= 841 \text{ or } 29^2 &&= [(5*6) - 1]^2 \\
5*6*7*8 + 1 &= 1681 \text{ or } 41^2 &&= [(6*7) - 1]^2 \\
6*7*8*9 + 1 &= 3025 \text{ or } 55^2 &&= [(7*8) - 1]^2 \\
7*8*9*10 + 1 &= 5041 \text{ or } 71^2 &&= [(8*9) - 1]^2 \\
8*9*10*11 + 1 &= 7921 \text{ or } 89^2 &&= [(9*10) - 1]^2 \\
9*10*11*12 + 1 &= 11881 \text{ or } 109^2 &&= [(10*11) - 1]^2 \\
10*11*12*13 + 1 &= 17161 \text{ or } 131^2 &&= [(11*12) - 1]^2 \\
11*12*13*14 + 1 &= 24025 \text{ or } 155^2 &&= [(12*13) - 1]^2
\end{aligned}
$$

Notice that the last digit of the resulting numbers (the 1, 25, 121, 361, 841, etc.) is either a 1 or a 5. In fact, the 1's and the 5's follow a pattern of four 1's between each 5. Then if we take the square root of these numbers, the last digit is either a 1, 5 or 9. These numbers have their own pattern that repeats again and again, which is a 1-5-1 followed by two 9's and then repeats:

1, 5, 1, 9, 9, 1, 5, 1, 9, 9, 1, 5, 1, 9, 9, 1, 5, 1, ...

An Interesting Product Property

There is an interesting multiplication pattern that occurs when we look at the product of two-digit numbers who share the same first digit, and whose second digits complement each other (where the complementing numbers add to 10). Examples include pairs of numbers that would be multiplied together like 32 and 38; or 53 and 57. Consider the following product list of pairs of numbers that fit this category:

23	*	27	=	621		
32	*	38	=	1216		
34	*	36	=	1224		
41	*	49	=	2009		

51	*	59	=	3009
53	*	57	=	3021
62	*	68	=	4216
74	*	76	=	5624

When multiplying two numbers together like 34 to 36, the product is obtained by taking the first digit (which is a 3 in this case) and multiplying it with its subsequent number (which would be a 4) to get 12. The 12 is then placed in front of the product of the second digits (which are a 4 and a 6 that yield 24). Therefore, the overall product of 34 and 36 is equal to 1224. If the second digits are a 1 and a 9, then their product is represented as the two-digit number 09 (as in the example of 51 and 59 above).

We can also extend this relationship to three-digit numbers and beyond. With the case of three-digit numbers, we take the first two digits of the number, treat them as a single number, and multiply it to its subsequent number; which is placed in front of the product of the last digits. For example, to find the product of 142 and 148, we multiple 14 by 15 (the first two digits which gives us 210) and place this result in front of the product of 2 and 8 (which is 16) to arrive at 21016 (which is the product of 142 and 148).

Squaring 5's

An extension of the method in the previous section can be seen when we square multiples of 5 that end with a 5 (this includes the numbers 5, 15, 25, 35, etc.). Consider the following list:

$05^2 =$	25
$15^2 =$	225
$25^2 =$	625
$35^2 =$	1225
$45^2 =$	2025

$55^2 =$	3025
$65^2 =$	4225
$75^2 =$	5625
$85^2 =$	7225
$95^2 =$	9025

Notice that the last two digits of each result ends with a 25. The number 25 will always be the last two digits of the square of any number that ends with a five. As for the digits in front of the 25, they are generated from the first digit of the number. To calculate what goes in front of the 25, we again take the first digit of the number being squared and multiply it with its subsequent number. This product is then placed in front of the 25 to obtain the final result.

Looking at 35^2 as an example, we know that because it ends with a five, it automatically has a 25 as the last two digits. We now take the 3 and multiply it with a 4 to get 12. Then we place the 12 in front of the 25 to get the final result, which is 1225. Likewise, to find 85^2, take the 8 and multiply it to 9 to get 72. Finally, place the 72 in front of 25 to get the result 7225 (which is equal to 85^2).

This works for the ten numbers listed above, but it is also true for any number that ends with a 5. Take the number 135. If we square it using this method, we would take the number in front of the 5 (which is 13) and multiply it with the following number (which is 14).

12

The product of 13 and 14 is 182. We place the 182 in front of a 25, and we get 18225 (which is equal to 135^2).

Squaring 4's in Base 8

This pattern of multiplication can also be carried over into other bases. For example, the number 4, when written in base 8, has the same property. Consider the following list (Note that the subscripted 8 means that the number is written in base eight):

$$(4_8)^2 = 20_8$$
$$(14_8)^2 = 220_8$$
$$(24_8)^2 = 620_8$$
$$(34_8)^2 = 1420_8$$
$$(44_8)^2 = 2420_8$$
$$(54_8)^2 = 3620_8$$
$$\dots, \text{etc.}$$

Four squared is equal to 16, and the number 16 written in base 8 is 20_8. If the number ends with a four, then the last two digits of the square of that number will always be 20_8. To determine the number in front of the 20, we look at the number in front of the 4. Again, simply take the number in front of the 4, multiply it to its subsequent number and place this value in front of the 20 to get the final result. Of course, throughout the whole operation, both the number being squared, and the final product are in base 8.

Squaring Selected Numbers

As we've seen so far in this chapter, some of the patterns are in the methods, and some of them are in the numbers themselves. Let's look again at patterns within the numbers themselves. Squaring repeating digits of 3's, and 6's in base 10 yields interesting patterns similar to those we saw when we squared repeating digits of 9's:

3^2	=	09	6^2	=	36
33^2	=	1089	66^2	=	4356
333^2	=	110889	666^2	=	443556
3333^2	=	11108889	6666^2	=	44435556
33333^2	=	1111088889	66666^2	=	4444355556
333333^2	=	111110888889	666666^2	=	444443555556
	etc.,			etc.	

We can also see variations of this pattern when we start with other numbers and then continue with repeating 3's or 6's in front of these numbers. Here is an example using 4:

4^2	=	16	4^2	=	16
34^2	=	1156	64^2	=	4096
334^2	=	111556	664^2	=	440896
3334^2	=	11115556	6664^2	=	44408896
33334^2	=	1111155556	66664^2	=	4444088896
333334^2	=	111111555556	666664^2	=	444440888896
	etc.,			etc.	

Another squaring pattern can be seen when we square certain numbers and then look at the reverse of those numbers. These patterns only appear where the digits of the numbers are made up from selected combinations of the numbers 0, 1, 2 and 3. For example, take the number 12 and square it to get 144. Now, reverse the 12 to get 21, and then square it to get 441. The second number along with its square is the reverse of the first number and its square. It doesn't work with every number composed of 0's, 1's, 2's, and 3's, but it does work with many of them. Here are a few more examples:

$$13^2 = 169 \qquad\qquad 102^2 = 10404$$
$$31^2 = 961 \qquad\qquad 201^2 = 40401$$

$$112^2 = 12544 \qquad\qquad 113^2 = 12769$$
$$211^2 = 44521 \qquad\qquad 311^2 = 96721$$

$$122^2 = 14884 \qquad\qquad 1012^2 = 1024144$$
$$221^2 = 48841 \qquad\qquad 2101^2 = 4414201$$

$$1103^2 = 1216609 \qquad\qquad 1301^2 = 1692601$$
$$3011^2 = 9066121 \qquad\qquad 1031^2 = 1062961$$

Palindromic Numbers with Palindromic Squares

A palindrome is a word or phrase that reads the same backward as it does forward. There are several words in the English language that have this property like "mom," "level," and "noon." You can also find this property in word pairs like "race car," and the phrase "A man, a plan, a canal: panama!" Of course you must take out the spaces and punctuation, rewrite the phrase backwards and then replace the spaces and punctuation, to get the original phrase again.

We've already seen one example of a palindromic sequence of numbers at the beginning of this chapter. In fact, if you look for them, you'll see that it is very common to find numbers that are palindromes. However, it is more difficult to find palindromic numbers that when squared are also palindromes. Here is a listing of the first ten numbers that fit into this category (see the appendix for a more extensive list of palindromic numbers with palindromic squares):

$$11^2 = 121$$
$$22^2 = 484$$
$$101^2 = 10201$$
$$111^2 = 12321$$
$$121^2 = 14641$$
$$202^2 = 40804$$
$$212^2 = 44944$$
$$1001^2 = 1002001$$
$$1111^2 = 1234321$$
$$2002^2 = 4008004$$

In the list above we see that the original numbers (the numbers in the left column) are only made of digits comprised of the numbers 0, 1 and 2. If the original number has a 3 or higher as one of the digits, it's square will not be a palindrome.

14

Also, within this set of numbers we can find a few super-palindrome numbers. These are numbers that are palindromes, and whose square is a palindrome, and then when squared again, is another palindrome. Here are some of them:

$$11^2 \quad = \quad 121$$
$$121^2 \quad = \quad 14641$$

$$101^2 \quad = \quad 10201$$
$$10201^2 \quad = \quad 104060401$$

$$1001^2 \quad = \quad 1002001$$
$$1002001^2 \quad = \quad 1004006004001$$

$$10001^2 \quad = \quad 100020001$$
$$100020001^2 \quad = \quad 1000400060004001$$

$$100001^2 \quad = \quad 10000200001$$
$$10000200001^2 \quad = \quad 100004000060000400001$$

Products of 1's Squared

Before we close this chapter, we'll look at one final relationship of numbers along with a variation to this pattern. Consider the following list of numbers:

$$1^2 \quad = \quad 1$$
$$11^2 \quad = \quad 121$$
$$111^2 \quad = \quad 12321$$
$$1111^2 \quad = \quad 1234321$$
$$11111^2 \quad = \quad 123454321$$
$$111111^2 \quad = \quad 12345654321$$
$$1111111^2 \quad = \quad 1234567654321$$
$$11111111^2 \quad = \quad 123456787654321$$
$$111111111^2 \quad = \quad 12345678987654321$$

This pattern takes an interesting twist as even more 1's are considered (the spaces were added to the listing below to help accentuate the change in the pattern):

$$1111111111^2 \quad = \quad 123456790 \ 0987654321$$
$$11111111111^2 \quad = \quad 123456790 \ 12 \ 0987654321$$
$$111111111111^2 \quad = \quad 123456790 \ 1232 \ 0987654321$$
$$1111111111111^2 \quad = \quad 123456790 \ 123432 \ 0987654321$$
$$11111111111111^2 \quad = \quad 123456790 \ 12345432 \ 0987654321$$
$$111111111111111^2 \quad = \quad 123456790 \ 1234565432 \ 0987654321$$
$$1111111111111111^2 \quad = \quad 123456790 \ 123456765432 \ 0987654321$$
$$11111111111111111^2 \quad = \quad 123456790 \ 12345678765432 \ 0987654321$$

And there is still at least one other way to look at this pattern. A variation of the pattern above (that works for the first nine repeating 1's) looks like this:

$$\frac{1 * 1}{(1)} = 1 \qquad\qquad = 1^2$$

$$\frac{22 * 22}{(1+2+1)} = 121 \qquad\qquad = 11^2$$

$$\frac{333 * 333}{(1+2+3+2+1)} = 12321 \qquad\qquad = 111^2$$

$$\frac{4444 * 4444}{(1+2+3+4+3+2+1)} = 1234321 \qquad\qquad = 1111^2$$

$$\frac{55555 * 55555}{(1+2+3+4+5+4+3+2+1)} = 123454321 \qquad\qquad = 11111^2$$

$$\frac{666666 * 666666}{(1+2+3+4+5+6+5+4+3+2+1)} = 12345654321 \qquad\qquad = 111111^2$$

$$\frac{7777777 * 7777777}{(1+2+3+4+5+6+7+6+5+4+3+2+1)} = 1234567654321 \qquad = 1111111^2$$

Again, this pattern holds true for numerators through 999999999 x 999999999 divided by the sum $(1 + 2 + 3 + 4 + 5 + 6 + 7 + 8 + 9 + 8 + 7 + 6 + 5 + 4 + 3 + 2 + 1)$, which is equal to 12345678987654321, and which is also equal to 111111111^2.

This chapter has been a mixture of many Mathematical methods, patterns and relationships. In the following chapters we will focus our look to specific relationships and methods as we examine various mathematical patterns and properties. Keep in mind that it's not only the symmetry of these patterns that makes them beautiful, but also the amazing places and ways that these patterns are found (and then found again) that make them so interesting and intriguing. But, we are getting ahead of ourselves, and yet we are just getting started.

Chapter 2
Fractal Number Sequences

Building a Fractal Sequence

In this chapter we will look at a few fractal number sequences. We'll use counting numbers to create these non-repeating fractal sequences; then later we'll use a rule based system to find other fractal sequences. But before we look at any of these, let's briefly explain the terms "non-repeating" and "fractal." A sequence of numbers is non-repeating if it never repeats the same sequence of digits in exactly the same order in a regular manner. The digits that make up the square root of 2 are an example of a non-repeating sequence of numbers.

$$\sqrt{2} = 1.41421356237309504880168887242 \ldots$$

Even though this sequence of numbers is infinite, these numbers never form a pattern that repeats itself. In contrast, the digits used to represent the fraction 1/7 form a repeating sequence of numbers.

$$1/7 = 0.142857\ 142857\ 142857\ 142857\ 142857 \ldots$$

Again we have an infinite sequence, but in this example the numbers 142857 continually repeat throughout the entire length of the sequence.

Now, for a sequence to be fractal it should be self-similar; or in other words, even though it doesn't repeat, we should still be able to find a scaled version of the sequence again within itself. This combination of characteristics (of being fractal and non-repeating) almost seems like a contradiction of terms; after all, how can a series of numbers not repeat, and yet contain a copy of itself within itself? Let's take a look.

We'll start by creating a simple fractal number sequence from a list of counting numbers where the first row of this list has the number 1; the second row has the numbers 1, 2, the third row has 1, 2, 3, and so on. Here are the first five rows:

$$
\begin{array}{l}
1 \\
1, 2 \\
1, 2, 3 \\
1, 2, 3, 4 \\
1, 2, 3, 4, 5 \\
\text{etc.,}
\end{array}
$$

Each row contains the numbers from the previous row with the addition of the next counting number. We create the fractal sequence by simply listing each row after the pervious so that we combine all the rows into a single sequence, as shown here:

$$1, 1, 2, 1, 2, 3, 1, 2, 3, 4, 1, 2, 3, 4, 5, \text{etc.,}$$

This sequence has a self-similar property that can be seen when we remove each number the first time we encounter it, so that we get the following sequence:

$$1, 1, 2, 1, 2, 3, 1, 2, 3, 4, 1, 2, 3, 4, 5, \text{ etc.,}$$
$$1, \quad 1, 2, \quad 1, 2, 3, \quad 1, 2, 3, 4, \quad \text{etc.,}$$

As we moved from left to right, in the original sequence, we removed the first 1 we encountered. Then we removed the first 2, and then the first 3, and so on. Now, when we take out the spaces, and push the numbers altogether, we find that once again we have our original sequence:

$$1, 1, 2, 1, 2, 3, 1, 2, 3, 4, \text{ etc.,}$$

This fractal sequence is infinite and non-repeating. Our next fractal sequence will also be made from counting numbers. We'll do this by building a table of numbers. The first column lists the numbers 0, 1, 2, 3, 4, 5, and so on. The second column contains construction numbers used to build the fractal sequence, and in this case are simply the numbers from the first column written in base 2. The third column is the actual fractal sequence. The numbers in this column are made by adding the digits of the number in the second column and placing that sum in the third column.

Counting Numbers	Construction Numbers	Fractal Sequence
0	0	0
1	1	1
2	10	1
3	11	2
4	100	1
5	101	2
6	110	2
7	111	3
8	1000	1
9	1001	2
10	1010	2
11	1011	3
12	1100	2
13	1101	3
14	1110	3
15	1111	4
16	10000	1

Table 2.1.   Building a fractal sequence from numbers in base 2.

For example, in the table above, where the first column has the number 5, the second column again has the number five, but written in base 2, which is the number 101. Then we sum these digits to give us $1 + 0 + 1$, or 2; and place the 2 in the third column, the fractal column. Due to the fact that the set of positive integers goes on forever, we can conclude that this sequence is infinite. The first 32 numbers in this sequence are:

$$0\ 1\ 1\ 2\ 1\ 2\ 2\ 3\ 1\ 2\ 2\ 3\ 2\ 3\ 3\ 4\ 1\ 2\ 2\ 3\ 2\ 3\ 3\ 4\ 2\ 3\ 3\ 4\ 3\ 4\ 4\ 5$$

In order to see that this sequence is non-repeating, notice the positions of the 1's in the sequence. If we say that the 0 is the zeroeth term, then the 1's appear as the first, second, fourth, eighth and sixteenth terms. In fact, the 1's only appear wherever we have a term raised to some integral power of two. Since this spacing between the 1's is non-uniform (and always increasing), we summarize that this sequence is non-repeating. Now we'll show that this sequence is fractal by generating a new sequence of numbers from this sequence by starting with the leading zero, and taking every other number.

```
0 1 1 2 . 2 2 3 1 2 2 3 2 3 3 4 1 2 2 3 2 3 3 4 2 3 3 4 3 4 4 5
0   1   .   2   1   2   2   3   1   2   2   3   2   3   3   4
```

The second row is the sequence of numbers that we get when we copy every other number from the first row. Next, we remove the spaces from the second row, and compare the first and second sequences side by side (actually top and bottom):

```
0 1 1 2 . 2 2 3 1 2 2 3 2 3 3 4 1 2 2 3 2 3 3 4 2 3 3 4 3 4 4 5
0 1 1 2 . 2 2 3 1 2 2 3 2 3 3 4
```

The second row is an exact duplicate of the first half of the first row. We have found a copy of the original sequence within itself. This characteristic of the sequence is self-similar, in other words, it is fractal. If we keep in mind that these sequences are infinite, we could also start with the leading zero and take every fourth number or every eighth number, and still get an exact copy of the original sequence:

Original sequence:	0	1	1	2	1	2	2	3	1	2	2	3	2	3	3	4	1 2 2 3 2 3 3 4 2 3 3 4 3 ...
Every 2nd number:	0		1		1		2		1		2		2		3		1 2 2 3 2 3 3 ...
Every 4th number:	0				1				1				2				1 2 2 3 ...
Every 8th number:	0								1								1 2 ...

Each of these sequences is identical to the original. However, what happens if we take the original sequence, and instead of starting with the leading zero, we start with the next digit and then take every other number.

```
0 1 1 2 1 2 2 3 1 2 2 3 2 3 3 4 1 2 2 3 2 3 3 4 2 3 3 4 3 4 4 5
  1   2   2   3   2   3   3   4   2   3   3   4   3   4   4   5
```

Now let's take the second row, remove the extra spaces and line it up with the first row (starting half way through the first row).

```
0 1 1 2 1 2 2 3 1 2 2 3 2 3 3 4 1 2 2 3 2 3 3 4 2 3 3 4 3 4 4 5
                                1 2 2 3 2 3 3 4 2 3 3 4 3 4 4 5
```

This time we see that the numbers in the second row are identical to the second half of the numbers in the first row. We can also take this same second row and line it up with the first number of the first row to find yet another relationship.

```
0 1 1 2 1 2 2 3 1 2 2 3 2 3 3 4 1 2 2 3 2 3 3 4 2 3 3 4 3 4 4 5
1 2 2 3 2 3 3 4 2 3 3 4 3 4 4 5
```

Here we see that each number in the second row is exactly one more than its corresponding number in the first row. And, as we did before, we could start with the second number in the original sequence and take every 4th number or every 8th number and continue to find copies or similar variations of our original pattern.

Original sequence:	0 1 1 2 1 2 2 3 1 2 2 3 2 3 3 4 1 2 2 3 2 3 3 4 2 3 3 4 3 ...
Every 2nd number:	1 2 2 3 2 3 3 4 2 3 3 4 3 4 ...
Every 4th number:	1 2 2 3 2 3 3 ...
Every 8th number:	1 2 2 3 ...

This property of finding the original pattern within itself over and over again demonstrates the fractal characteristics of this sequence of numbers. And there are still other ways to look at the fractal properties of this sequence. Let's rewrite our fractal sequence of numbers, and every time we come to the number one in the sequence, we start a new row.

```
0
1
1 2
1 2 2 3
1 2 2 3 2 3 3 4
1 2 2 3 2 3 3 4 2 3 3 4 3 4 4 5
```

Except for the first and second rows, every row has twice as many numbers as the row before it. Notice also that except for the first two rows, the first half of any row carries the pattern of the row before it. The second half of the row is a copy of the first half, with each number in the second half being one more than its corresponding number in the first half. Knowing this, we could construct the whole sequence from a single row. For example, say we were given the fifth row. We would have the numbers:

1 2 2 3 2 3 3 4   (the 5th row from the sequence above)

The fourth row is simply the first half of this row. The third row would be the first half of the fourth row, and so on. We can also go in the other direction, and build the sixth row from the fifth row. We know that the first half of the sixth row is a copy of fifth row, and the second half of the sixth row is the fifth row with each digit being one more than its original value.

The 5th row: 1 2 2 3 2 3 3 4
The 6th row: 1 2 2 3 2 3 3 4 2 3 3 4 3 4 4 5

In this manner, we could create the seventh row, the eighth row and so on. We can create the original sequence by starting with the first row, and listing these rows, one-after-the-other, in order. In fact, this is another interesting property of fractals. All we need is just a small subset of the original sequence (such as we saw with the fifth row), and then with that information, we create the entire infinite fractal sequence.

Building Additional Fractal Sequences

We can use this last method of looking at the fractal sequence to build an entirely different fractal sequence. In the previous example, each row held enough information to build the complete fractal sequence. We could have started with the numbers 1 2 in the third row, and built the fourth row, and then the fifth row, and so on; until we had as many digits in the sequence as we wanted. In this next example, we'll create our own variation and start with the numbers 1 3, and use that to build a different fractal sequence.

The numbers 1 3 will be the third row. The second row is the number one, and the first row is the number zero. The fourth row will be built from the third row by copying the third row for the first half of the fourth row. The second half of the fourth row will be another copy of the third row where each digit is two more than its original value. In the same way, the fifth row can then be built from the fourth row, and so on.

```
0
1
1 3
1 3 3 5
1 3 3 5 3 5 5 7
1 3 3 5 3 5 5 7 3 5 5 7 5 7 7 9
```

Now, we create the fractal sequence by listing the rows, one-after-the-other, in order.

0 1 1 3 1 3 3 5 1 3 3 5 3 5 5 7 1 3 3 5 3 5 5 7 3 5 5 7 5 7 7 9

If we take the list, start with the leading zero and take every other number, we again find our sequence.

0 1 1 3 1 3 3 5 1 3 3 5 3 5 5 7 1 3 3 5 3 5 5 7 3 5 5 7 5 7 7 9
0   1   1   3   1   3   3   5   1   3   3   5   3   5   5   7

For yet another variation, we could have started with the numbers 1 3 in the third row, and then generated the fourth row by copying those numbers for the first half, and then multiplying those same numbers by three for the second half. In this case, this is what we get:

```
0
1
1 3
1 3 3 9
1 3 3 9 3 9 9 27
1 3 3 9 3 9 9 27 3 9 9 27 9 27 27 81
```

Again, we take each row and list them in order to finally create the fractal sequence.

0 1 1 3 1 3 3 9 1 3 3 9 3 9 9 27 1 3 3 9 3 9 9 27 3 9 9 27 9 27 27 81

Notice that if we take the list, start with the leading zero and take every other number, we again find our sequence. And once again, the original pattern can be found again within itself, thus proving to ourselves that we have a fractal sequence.

0 1 1 3 1 3 3 9 1 3 3 9 3 9 9 27 1 3 3 9 3 9 9 27 3 9 9 27 9 27 27 81
0   1   1   3   1   3   3   9   1   3   3   9   3   9   9   27

Creating a Fractal Sequence Using Numbers Written in Base 3

Of course we're not done. In this next example we'll create another fractal sequence from the counting numbers written in base three. We'll use the same method that we used earlier in this chapter where the first column lists the positive numbers in base 10 starting with zero. The second column has the corresponding numbers written in base 3, and the third column contains the sum of the digits from the second column (in base 10 again).

Counting Numbers	Construction Numbers	Fractal Sequence
0	0	0
1	1	1
2	2	2
3	10	1
4	11	2
5	12	3
6	20	2
7	21	3
8	22	4
9	100	1
10	101	2
11	102	3
12	110	2
13	111	3
14	112	4
15	120	3
16	121	4
17	122	5
18	200	2
19	201	3
20	202	4
21	210	3
22	211	4
23	212	5
24	220	4
25	221	5
26	222	6
27	1000	1

Table 2.2.   Building a fractal sequence from numbers in base 3.

In other words, where we have the number 5 in the first column, that corresponds with the number 12 in the second column, and the sum of those digits are equal to 3, which is placed in the third column. (see the table above) The fractal sequence is again taken from the third column. The first 27 numbers of this fractal sequence are:

0 1 2 1 2 3 2 3 4 1 2 3 2 3 4 3 4 5 2 3 4 3 4 5 4 5 6

Even though this sequence of numbers was created in the same way as the sequence of numbers written in base 2, it's not quite a fractal in the same way. To see the self-similar characteristics in this example, we'll start with the leading zero and take every third number (instead of every second number).

0 1 2 1 2 3 2 3 4 1 2 3 2 3 4 3 4 5 2 3 4 3 4 5 4 5 6
0   1   2   1   2   3   2   3   4

Now, if we take the second row, and remove the spaces we can easily see that it is the same as the first nine digits of the fractal sequence in the first row.

22

0 1 2 1 2 3 2 3 4 1 2 3 2 3 4 3 4 5 2 3 4 3 4 5 4 5 6
0 1 2 1 2 3 2 3 4

Similarly, if we start with the second number and take every third number we get the following sequence:

0 1 2 1 2 3 2 3 4 1 2 3 2 3 4 3 4 5 2 3 4 3 4 5 4 5 6
   1   2   3   2   3   4   3   4   5

After removing the spaces from the second row, we find that we can line it up with the middle section of the line above it, and see the correspondence there.

0 1 2 1 2 3 2 3 4 1 2 3 2 3 4 3 4 5 2 3 4 3 4 5 4 5 6
         1 2 3 2 3 4 3 4 5

And we can do the same thing the third time by starting with the third number and taking every third number.

0 1 2 1 2 3 2 3 4 1 2 3 2 3 4 3 4 5 2 3 4 3 4 5 4 5 6
    2   3   4   3   4   5   4   5   6

And once again, we remove the spaces and then line up the second row with the row above it. This time it lines up with the last nine numbers of the sequence in the row above.

0 1 2 1 2 3 2 3 4 1 2 3 2 3 4 3 4 5 2 3 4 3 4 5 4 5 6
                  2 3 4 3 4 5 4 5 6

From what we just saw, it **appears that we need to perform** this "removing-every-third-number" operation three times to find three partial sequences that can then be used to create the original sequence; however, that is not the case. Let's take the three partial sequences from the example above and compare them with each other.

0 1 2 1 2 3 2 3 4
1 2 3 2 3 4 3 4 5
2 3 4 3 4 5 4 5 6

By lining them up on top of each other, we see that the numbers in the second row are one greater than the corresponding numbers in the first row; and similarly, the numbers in the third row are one greater than the numbers in the second row. Therefore, we only need to know the numbers of the first third of the sequence, and from that we generate the other two-thirds of the sequence. We could then use that sequence again as the first third of the numbers needed to generate an even longer sequence; and thus continue indefinitely.

Earlier we saw that when we created our fractal from base 2 numbers, we could then take every second number (or every 4th number, or every 8th number, etc.) to create an identical sequence from the original. The concept is similar with our fractal created from base 3 numbers; however, in this case we take every third number (or every 9th number, or every 27th number, etc.) and create identical sequences to sections of the original. With an understanding of this latest example, it now becomes intuitive that we can extend this method and create fractal number sequences using any base we desire.

Fractal Sequences within Palindromic Squares

If we look hard enough, sometimes we can even find fractal sequences hiding in interesting and unusual places. For example, in chapter 1 we saw number palindromes whose squares were also palindromes. If we look at the middle numbers of palindromes created from the squares of palindromes we see a pattern start to develop with the 4-digit and 6-digit palindromes, and by the time we get to the 8-digit and 10-digit palindromes this pattern can be seen very easily. Here are the even-number-of-digit palindromes with their squares that are also palindromes:

4-digits:	1001^2	=	1002001
	1111^2	=	1234321
	2002^2	=	4008004
6-digits:	100001^2	=	10000200001
	101101^2	=	10221412201
	110011^2	=	12102420121
	111111^2	=	12345654321
	200002^2	=	40000800004
8-digits:	10000001^2	=	100000020000001
	10011001^2	=	100220141022001
	10100101^2	=	102012040210201
	10111101^2	=	102234363432201
	11000011^2	=	121000242000121
	11011011^2	=	121242363242121
	11100111^2	=	123212464212321
	11111111^2	=	123456787654321
	20000002^2	=	400000080000004
10-digits:	1000000001^2	=	1000000002000000001
	1000110001^2	=	1000220014100220001
	1001001001^2	=	1002003004003002001
	1001111001^2	=	1002223236323222001
	1010000101^2	=	1020100204020010201
	1010110101^2	=	1020322416142230201
	1011001101^2	=	1022123226223212201
	1011111101^2	=	1022345658565432201
	1100000011^2	=	1210000024200000121
	1100110011^2	=	1210242036302420121
	1101001011^2	=	1212203226223022121
	1101111011^2	=	1212445458545442121
	1110000111^2	=	1232100246420012321
	1110110111^2	=	1232344458544432321
	1111001111^2	=	1234323468643234321
	2000000002^2	=	4000000008000000004

Each of these squares has an odd number of digits. Now, let's look at the middle numbers from each of these sets of squares.

4-digit squares:	2 4 8
6-digit squares:	2 4 4 6 8
8-digit squares:	2 4 4 6 4 6 6 8 8
10-digit squares:	2 4 4 6 4 6 6 8 4 6 6 8 6 8 8 8

We'll take the pattern from the 10-digit squares (because the pattern becomes very apparent here), and pull the fractal pattern from it by listing every second number from that pattern.

10-digit squares:	2 4 4 6 4 6 6 8 4 6 6 8 6 8 8 8
Fractal pattern 1:	2 4 4 6 4 6 6 8
Fractal pattern 2:	4 6 6 8 6 8 8 8

When we remove the spaces from the fractal patterns, we see that fractal pattern 1 is the first half of the original sequence; and fractal pattern 2 is the second half of the original sequence.

10-digit squares:	2 4 4 6 4 6 6 8 4 6 6 8 6 8 8 8
Fractal pattern 1:	2 4 4 6 4 6 6 8
Fractal pattern 2:	4 6 6 8 6 8 8 8

Until now we have found fractal sequences of numbers in natural lists of numbers; and we will yet see another fractal sequence when we look at specific numerators of Farey fractions in a later chapter. Until then, we'll continue in the next section by looking at still another type of fractal sequence.

Rule Based Fractal Sequences

There are still other methods that can be used to generate fractal sequences. In this section we will generate fractal number sequences using a set of rules to guide our construction. Each step in the process will be generated from the previous step by following predefined rules. There are only three rules in our first example. They are:

1. Start with a 0.
2. Replace every 0 with: 0 1
3. Replace every 1 with: 1 0

The rules are simple, and as we can see from the rules, this sequence will only have zeroes and ones in it. Also, in this sequence we won't append succeeding lines onto their predecessors. Instead, we'll look at each line as its own sequence of numbers, and in that way we'll compare each line with those above and below it. Let's generate a few lines:

```
0
0 1
0 1 1 0
0 1 1 0 1 0 0 1
0 1 1 0 1 0 0 1 1 0 0 1 0 1 1 0
0 1 1 0 1 0 0 1 1 0 0 1 0 1 1 0 1 0 0 1 0 1 1 0 0 1 1 0 1 0 0 1
   etc., ...
```

Notice that the length of each line doubles as each new line is generated. This is due to the fact that the rules require us to replace each digit with two digits. There are also several other patterns within these sequences. For example, the 3rd and 5th rows are palindromes. They read the same forward as they do backwards. In fact, starting with the third row all odd numbered rows are palindromes.

Another easily seen pattern is that the first half of each row is an exact copy of the row before it. Then for the 2nd and 4th rows, the second half is the inverse of the first half, such that where there is a 0 in the first half, there is a 1 in the second half, and where there is a 1 in the first half, the second half has a 0. Therefore, each line carries enough information to generate all of the preceding lines as well as any of the following lines without actually knowing the three rules that generated the original sequence.

We can also see that each line is self-similar, or fractal, by starting with the first digit and taking every other digit, we get a copy of the first half of that line. If we start with the second digit and take every other digit, we get a copy of the second half of the line.

```
6th Row:        0 1 1 0 1 0 0 1 1 0 0 1 0 1 1 0 1 0 0 1 0 1 1 0 0 1 1 0 1 0 0 1
1st digit start: 0   1   1   0   1   0   0   1   1   0   0   1   0   1   1   0
2nd digit start:   1   0   0   1   0   1   1   0   0   1   1   0   1   0   0   1
```

Of course it's easier to see the pattern if we take out the spaces and line up the numbers:

```
6th Row:        0 1 1 0 1 0 0 1 1 0 0 1 0 1 1 0 1 0 0 1 0 1 1 0 0 1 1 0 1 0 0 1
1st digit start: 0 1 1 0 1 0 0 1 1 0 0 1 0 1 1 0
2nd digit start:                 1 0 0 1 0 1 1 0 0 1 1 0 1 0 0 1
```

In the example above we started with the first digit and took every other number, giving us a series of numbers that matched the first half of the sixth row. Then by starting with the second digit and taking every other number we got a series matching the second half of the sixth row. Together, they recreated the row they came from.

Additional Rule Based Fractal Sequences

We could build other rule based fractal sequences composed of just ones and zeroes, but our possibilities increase when we add another number to our sequence. And, adding another number also requires us to add another rule. The rules of generation for our next sequence of numbers are:

      1. Start with a 0.
      2. Replace every 0 with: 0 1 2
      3. Replace every 1 with: 1 1 1
      4. Replace every 2 with: 2 1 0

These rules generate the following set of sequences:

```
0
0 1 2
0 1 2 1 1 1 2 1 0
0 1 2 1 1 1 2 1 0 1 1 1 1 1 1 1 1 1 2 1 0 1 1 1 0 1 2
   etc., ...
```

This sequence also has palindromes on the odd numbered rows, starting with the third row. It also has several self-similar properties. Let's see what we get when we start with the first digit and take every third digit, and compare that with what we get when we start with the second digit and take every third digit, and finally start with the third digit, and take every third digit.

```
       4th Row:       0 1 2 1 1 1 2 1 0 1 1 1 1 1 1 1 1 2 1 0 1 1 1 0 1 2
1st digit, every 3rd: 0   1   2   1   1   1   2   1   0
2nd digit, every 3rd:   1   1   1   1   1   1   1   1   1
3rd digit, every 3rd:     2   1   0   1   1   1   0   1   2
```

Again, if we take out the spaces and line up the numbers we see an interesting relationship:

```
       4th Row:       0 1 2 1 1 1 2 1 0 1 1 1 1 1 1 1 1 2 1 0 1 1 1 0 1 2
1st digit, every 3rd: 0 1 2 1 1 1 2 1 0
2nd digit, every 3rd:                   1 1 1 1 1 1 1 1 1
3rd digit, every 3rd:                                     2 1 0 1 1 1 0 1 2
```

As this illustrates, if we start with the first digit and take every third digit, we have the first third of the sequence. Starting with the second digit and taking every third digit gives us the middle third of the sequence; and starting with the third digit and taking every third digit produces the final third of the original sequence.

Of course, the sky is the limit when it comes to creating rule based fractal number sequences. We can make them as simple or as complicated as we like. Here's another set of rules that can be used to create a fractal sequence using the numbers 0 through 3:

1. Start with a 0.
2. Replace every 0 with: 0 1 2 3
3. Replace every 1 with: 1 1 2 2
4. Replace every 2 with: 2 2 1 1
5. Replace every 3 with: 3 2 1 0

Notice that certain guidelines are used when creating each set of rules. There must be pairs of rows that complement each other; and where there are an odd number of digits, at least one of the rules must be symmetrical with itself.

In the rule sets defined so far, the first rule always states that we start with a 0. The second rule states that every 0 is replaced with 0 1 2 ... n. Likewise, the last rule always says that n is replaced with n ... 2 1 0. These two rules don't have to list the numbers in ascending and descending order, but the second and last rule must complement each other (whatever one does, the other must do the opposite). In the example above, the third and fourth rules also complement each other. These and similar conditions must be met for the sequences to be fractal and a palindrome on every other line. As we understand these rules more, we can see that it is also possible to start with some other number besides 0. Look at the next example:

1. Start with a 2.
2. Replace every 0 with: 0 2 3 1
3. Replace every 1 with: 1 3 2 0
4. Replace every 2 with: 2 1 0 3
5. Replace every 3 with: 3 0 1 2

The first few rows of this sequence are:

```
2
2 1 0 3
2 1 0 3 1 3 2 0 0 2 3 1 3 0 1 2
etc ...
```

In this example, we started with a 2. Rule 4 then describes the set of numbers that replace the 2. The last number in this set is a 3, and therefore rule 5 (the rule describing the 3) complements the rule describing the 2. Likewise, Rules 2 and 3 describe the numbers that replace the 0 and 1. These rules (and sets of numbers) also complement each other. Now, as we create more and more rows of the sequence, these sequences will be fractal, and every other line will be a palindrome.

Building Another Type of Rule Based Fractal Sequence

In this section we change the way that we build our rule based fractal sequences. This type of fractal sequence starts with a pair of numbers, and then adds those numbers together to generate our next sequence of numbers. After repeating this process just a few times, we find that we are generating a fractal sequence of numbers. Let's look at a few examples to see exactly how this is done.

We'll start with the sequence: $\qquad$ 0, 1

Now we add each member of the sequence to itself to generate the next sequence. In other words, we'll add a 0 and a 1 to the first 0, and then add a 0 and a 1 to the 1. Here is the next step (the construction step), and the resulting next sequence:

$$(0 + 0), \ (0 + 1), \qquad (1 + 0), \ (1 + 1)$$

This is the next sequence: $\qquad$ 0, 1, 1, 2

For the next level, we repeat the process, which gives us these four numbers added to the first number, and then the same four numbers added to the second number, again the same four numbers added to the third number and finally these four numbers added to the fourth number:

$$(0 + 0), \ (0 + 1), \ (0 + 1), \ (0 + 2), \qquad (1 + 0), \ (1 + 1), \ (1 + 1), \ (1 + 2),$$
$$(1 + 0), \ (1 + 1), \ (1 + 1), \ (1 + 2), \qquad (2 + 0), \ (2 + 1), \ (2 + 1), \ (2 + 2)$$

Which gives us: $\qquad$ 0, 1, 1, 2, 1, 2, 2, 3, 1, 2, 2, 3, 2, 3, 3, 4

Of course we could continue repeating this process indefinitely, but at this point we can already see the fractal properties of this sequence begin to emerge. Let's take a look by starting with the leading 0, and keep every other number thereafter:

Our original sequence: $\qquad$ 0, 1, 1, 2, 1, 2, 2, 3, 1, 2, 2, 3, 2, 3, 3, 4
Every other number removed: $\qquad$ 0,   1,   1,   2,   1,   2,   2,   3

Finally, removing the spaces gives us: 0, 1, 1, 2, 1, 2, 2, 3

Notice that our resulting sequence is the same as the first half of the original sequence. We also could have started with the leading 0, and then kept every fourth number, which would have given us a sequence that would have been the same as the first quarter of the original sequence.

Of course, we also could have started with any pair of numbers and gotten similar results. A variation of this type of fractal sequence also starts with a pair of numbers, but this time we only add those two numbers to the growing sequence in order to generate the next level. To see how this works, let's start with the same two numbers:

We'll start with the sequence: 0, 1

Again, we add each member of the sequence to itself to generate the next sequence. And again, we have the construction step, and the resulting sequence:

$$(0 + 0),\ (0 + 1),\quad (1 + 0),\ (1 + 1)$$

Which gives us: 0, 1, 1, 2

This time we will only add the initial 0 and 1 to each member of our sequence to generate the next level of the sequence:

$$(0 + 0),\ (1 + 0),\ (1 + 0),\ (2 + 0),\quad (0 + 1),\ (1 + 1),\ (1 + 1),\ (2 + 1)$$

Which gives us: 0, 1, 1, 2, 1, 2, 2, 3

And doing it one more time, gives us:

$$(0 + 0),\ (1 + 0),\ (1 + 0),\ (2 + 0),\ (1 + 0),\ (2 + 0),\ (2 + 0),\ (3 + 0),$$
$$(0 + 1),\ (1 + 1),\ (1 + 1),\ (2 + 1),\ (1 + 1),\ (2 + 1),\ (2 + 1),\ (3 + 1)$$

Which is: 0, 1, 1, 2, 1, 2, 2, 3, 1, 2, 2, 3, 2, 3, 3, 4

Notice that this last sequence contains the same set of numbers that we had in our previous example. We just took an extra step to get here. And therefore, just like the previous example, this sequence is also fractal.

Now, without belaboring all of the details, we'll use these two methods one more time, but this time, we'll start with the numbers 1, 3. Using the first method discussed in this section gives us the follow set of sequences:

1, 3
2, 4, 4, 6
4, 6, 6, 8, 6, 8, 8, 10, 6, 8, 8, 10, 8, 10, 10, 12

Now, we'll compare that with what we'll get when we use the second method from this section. In this case, we generate this set of sequences:

1, 3
2, 4, 4, 6
3, 5, 5, 7, 5, 7, 7, 9
4, 6, 6, 8, 6, 8, 8, 10, 6, 8, 8, 10, 8, 10, 10, 12

Again, the third line from the first method is identical to the fourth line from the second method, and in both cases these sequences are fractal. Needless to say, but these results are very interesting and can also be verified with other starting numbers.

The One-One Semi-Fractal Sequence

Finally, let's look at another interesting set of number sequences. To generate this set of sequences, start with a given number (or numbers), then create the next row by reading the current row out loud, saying the quantity first, and then the number. For example, if we start with 1, then we would read this out loud as one-one, which would then be written as 1 1, and would be our second row. Now reading this row out loud gives us two-ones, which would be written as 2 1 (on the third row). Continuing on, the next row will be one-two and one-one which would be written as 1 2 1 1, etc. In spite of their apparent irregularity, these sequences still have certain properties. For example, unless you start with a number above 3, you will never have a number above 3 in the sequence. Let's look at a few examples. This first sequence starts with the number 1:

1
11
21
1211
111221
312211
13112221
1113213211
31131211131221
13211311123113112211
... , etc., ...

Beginning with the 4th line, each line ends with either a 211 or a 221. And starting with the 6th line, the number 3 is at the beginning of every third line. This next set of sequences starts with the number 2 and is generated in the same way as the last:

2
12
1112
3112
132112
1113122112
311311222112
13211321322112
1113122113121113222112
... , etc., ...

In this second example, we see that starting with the 5th row, and all subsequent rows thereafter, each row ends with a 2112. This second set of sequences shares many similarities with the first; however, what is even more interesting is that it is nearly identical to the set of sequences generated from the number 3; as can be seen in the next list of numbers:

```
3
13
1113
3113
132113
1113122113
311311222113
13211321322113
1113122113121113222113
... , etc., ...
```

From the fifth row on, each row ends with a 2113; and the 2-sequence and the 3-sequence are identical except for the last digit. Starting with a 4, 5, 6, 7, 8 and 9 and generating these sequences will also create sequences that are similar in the same way to the 2 and 3 sequences.

And what about starting with a double number? If we start with a 11, we get the 1-sequence, but shifted down one row. Starting with a 12 gives us the 2-sequence, also shifted down one row. However, starting with a 22, gives this unique, non-growing series of sequences:

```
22
22
22
22
22
22
22
22
etc...
```

And as far as I can tell, this is the only sequence that can be generated in this manner that does not continue to grow as subsequent rows are created.

Starting with a 33 gives us:
```
33
23
1213
11121113
31123113
132112132113
1113122113121113122113
311311222112311311222113
... , etc., ...
```

We can see that starting with the sixth row, and each row after that ends with a 2113 (which is very similar to the 3-sequence)

Starting with a 44 gives us this sequence:

44
24
1214
11121114
31123114
132112132114
11131221121113122114
... , etc., ...

This sequence is identical to the 33-sequence, except the last number on each row is a 4. The same is true if we start with a 55, 66, 77, 88 or 99.

These sequences have a few peculiarities (in addition to what we have already seen). For one thing, the size doesn't grow in a regular fashion as we go from row to row. In fact, within the first few rows, there are often rows that have the same length. The numbers also appear to be random; however, there is a certain amount of fractal-ness within these sequences. For example, look at the last row in the previously mentioned series. We have the following numbers:

11131221121113122114

Now, start with the second number and take every other number, we get this sequence:

1321213214

Compare this line with the line just above it (the next to the last row of numbers):

132112132114   (next to the last row in the previous example)
1321 21321 4   (generated sequence from the last row)

Except for a couple of ones that are missing, the next to the last row can be generated from the last row of numbers. The patterns are very similar. And you must remember that we were taking every other number in the last row; but the last row wasn't twice the size of the previous row. In spite of that, the similarity between these rows is very close.

A Variation to One-One

You may have noticed that as each number sequence was created in the previous section, it was done by saying the quantity of the numbers first, and then the number itself. (We did it that way because that's how normal English is spoken. We say three apples and two oranges.) For this reason the sequence 1211 was read as one-one, one-two, and two-ones, which then generated the following sequence 111221.

But what if we change the way we create each following sequence by saying the number itself first, and then its quantity second. Therefore, the sequence 1211 would be read as one-one, two-one, and one-two. This would create the sequence 112112.

Let's look at an example where we start with the number 1. The column on the left will be our variation. In this column we say the number first and the quantity second, and use that to generate the numbers on the next row. The second column will be our original sequence where we say the quantity first followed by the numbers. The following listing shows how these two columns compare with each other.

32

The One-One Variation	**Original One-One Number Sequence**
1	1
11	11
12	21
1121	1211
122111	111221
112213	312211
12221131	13112221
1123123111	1113213211
12213111213113	31131211131221
112211311321113111231	132113111231131121211
... , etc., ...	..., etc., ...

The numbers in each row of the first column (the one-one variation) are the reverse of their corresponding rows in the second column (the original one-one sequence). The result is interesting, but if you think about it, it is hardly surprising at all.

In this chapter we saw several types of number sequences, and each of them shared various fractal properties. However, there are still other types of various patterns within number sequences, as we will see in the next chapter.

Chapter 3
Decimal Number Patterns

The Pattern
Have you ever looked at the decimal value of the fraction 1/98? Most calculators only show the first eight or nine digits - hardly enough to whet your appetite; yet just enough to show the beginning of a pattern. Here are the first 20 digits to the right of the decimal point:

$$1/98 = 0.01020408163265306122 ...$$

Notice that the 01, 02, 04, 08, 16 and 32 are the first twelve digits of the decimal. These are the consecutive powers of 2; however, the pattern seems to stop after 32. The next two digits are 65. In fact, the rest of the digits in this sequence don't seem to have any relation to the powers of 2, or do they?

Building Decimal Number Series
Let's rewrite the powers of 2 so that we list them as two digit numbers. The number 01 will be just to the right of the decimal point. The number 02 will be on the next line, and shifted right two places. We continue listing each power of 2 on the following lines, with each line shifted to the right two more places. When we get to 128, we again shift it only two places to the right (even though this number is a three digit number). What we end up with looks something like this:

```
1/98 = .01
             02
                04
                   08
                      16
                         32
                            64
                               128
                                  256
       +                         512 ...
1/98 = .010204081632653061...
```

Now, when we add straight down the columns, we find that the fraction 1/98 can indeed be made from adding together the powers of 2. Interesting, but the fraction 1/98 isn't the only fraction that can be made from adding up the powers of 2. What if we repeated the procedure, but instead of shifting two places to the right each time, we only shift one place to the right? Or what if we shift three places to the right?

By shifting only one place to the right, we can use the powers of 2 to create the fraction 1/8. By shifting three places to the right, the powers of 2 will generate the fraction 1/998.

$$1/8 = 0.1$$
$$2$$
$$4$$
$$8$$
$$16$$
$$32$$
$$64$$
$$+ \quad 128 \ldots$$
$$1/8 = 0.124999\ldots$$

$$1/998 = 0.001$$
$$002$$
$$004$$
$$008$$
$$016$$
$$032$$
$$064$$
$$+ \quad 128 \ldots$$
$$1/998 = 0.001002004008016032064128\ldots$$

Compiling what we've learned so far, we see that the powers of 2 can be used to generate the decimal values of the fractions 1/8, 1/98 and 1/998 simply by shifting the powers of two one place to the right, two places to the right or three places to the right, and then adding numbers straight down the columns.

Surely this must be some fluke of nature, right? Wrong! Let's look at the powers of 3. Again, we'll write them as two digit numbers, while writing each succeeding number on the next line, and shifting two decimal places to the right. What we get is a decimal representation of the fraction 1/97.

$$1/97 = .01$$
$$03$$
$$09$$
$$27$$
$$81$$
$$243$$
$$729$$
$$2187$$
$$+ \quad 6561 \ldots$$
$$1/97 = .010309278350515\ldots$$

In a similar manner, we can create the fraction 1/7 by shifting right only one decimal place; and we can create the fraction 1/997 by shifting right three decimal places.

And it doesn't stop there. In a similar way, another set of fractions that shows an interesting pattern are 1/9, 1/99 and 1/999. Written as decimal values, they are:

$$1/9 \quad = 0.111111111111111 \ldots \qquad \text{(repeating 1's)}$$
$$1/99 \quad = 0.010101010101010 \ldots \qquad \text{(alternating 1's and 0's)}$$
$$1/999 = 0.001001001001001 \ldots \qquad \text{(alternating 1's and 00's)}$$

Up to this point we have only looked at one, two and three digit patterns. However, these patterns apply to any number of digits, and we could easily have extended them to four and five digit patterns and beyond. The fact is that we have a pattern of patterns, and we need to take a closer look at it. Let's do this by rewriting our funny-looking decimal addition as a series of fractions. The fraction 1/98, would be rewritten as:

$$\frac{1}{98} = \frac{1}{100^1} + \frac{2}{100^2} + \frac{4}{100^3} + \frac{8}{100^4} + \frac{16}{100^5} + \frac{32}{100^6} + \ldots$$

Or

$$\frac{1}{98} = \frac{2^0}{100^1} + \frac{2^1}{100^2} + \frac{2^2}{100^3} + \frac{2^3}{100^4} + \frac{2^4}{100^5} + \frac{2^5}{100^6} + \ldots$$

The numerators to these fractions are successive powers of 2. The denominators are successive powers of 100. (Notice that dividing by successive powers of 100 is the same as shifting each numerator to the right by two places.)

It is also interesting to note that not only did we used the powers of 2 to create the fraction for 1/98, but also that 98 is equal to 100 minus 2. Likewise, we used the powers of 3 to create the fraction for 1/97, and 97 is equal to 100 minus 3. Continuing this thought, we can rewrite the fraction 1/98 as 1/(100-2) and the fraction 1/97 as 1/(100-3).

$$\frac{1}{98} = \frac{1}{(100-2)} = \frac{1}{100^1} + \frac{2}{100^2} + \frac{4}{100^3} + \frac{8}{100^4} + \frac{16}{100^5} + \frac{32}{100^6} + \dots$$

$$\frac{1}{97} = \frac{1}{(100-3)} = \frac{1}{100^1} + \frac{3}{100^2} + \frac{9}{100^3} + \frac{27}{100^4} + \frac{81}{100^5} + \frac{243}{100^6} + \dots$$

And for numbers shifted only one place to the right, the fraction 1/8 is rewritten as:

$$\frac{1}{8} = \frac{1}{10^1} + \frac{2}{10^2} + \frac{4}{10^3} + \frac{8}{10^4} + \frac{16}{10^5} + \frac{32}{10^6} + \dots$$

Again, the numerators are successive powers of 2, but this time the denominators are successive powers of 10. Dividing by successive powers of 10 is the same as shifting each numerator to the right one place. We can also say the 8 is equal to 10 minus 2, and we used the powers of 2 to create the fraction 1/8. Therefore, the fraction 1/8 can then be rewritten as 1/(10-2).

$$\frac{1}{8} = \frac{1}{(10-2)} = \frac{1}{10^1} + \frac{2}{10^2} + \frac{4}{10^3} + \frac{8}{10^4} + \frac{16}{10^5} + \frac{32}{10^6} + \dots$$

We definitely have a pattern here. We've seen it work for a couple of different values in the numerator and several powers of ten in the denominator, but can we be so bold as to say that it will work for any number? In other words, could we replace the numerator and denominator with other pairs of numbers and still have it work? If so, we could have fractions like these:

$$\frac{1}{2} = \frac{1}{(3-1)} = \frac{1}{3^1} + \frac{1}{3^2} + \frac{1}{3^3} + \frac{1}{3^4} + \frac{1}{3^5} + \frac{1}{3^6} + \dots$$

Or:

$$\frac{1}{4} = \frac{1}{(8-4)} = \frac{1}{8^1} + \frac{4}{8^2} + \frac{16}{8^3} + \frac{64}{8^4} + \frac{256}{8^5} + \frac{1024}{8^6} + \dots$$

Or even:

$$\frac{1}{24} = \frac{1}{(31-7)} = \frac{1}{31^1} + \frac{7}{31^2} + \frac{49}{31^3} + \frac{343}{31^4} + \frac{2401}{31^5} + \frac{16807}{31^6} + \dots$$

Think of the possibilities. If this is true, then the general form of this formula would be:

$$\frac{1}{(B-n)} = \frac{n^0}{B^1} + \frac{n^1}{B^2} + \frac{n^2}{B^3} + \frac{n^3}{B^4} + \frac{n^4}{B^5} + \frac{n^5}{B^6} + \dots$$

And if this is true, then we could take an ordinary fraction, such as 1/3, and create practically an unlimited supply of geometric number series that each add up to 1/3.

The Proof

Now, to show that this statement is true, we will rearrange the right side of the above equation until we can get it to look like the left side. If we can do it, then we can consider the statement to be true for all values where B is greater than n.

We'll start by multiplying the terms on the right by n/n. (This has the same effect as multiplying by one which doesn't change the value of the right side.)

$$\frac{1}{(B-n)} = \left(\frac{n^0}{B^1} + \frac{n^1}{B^2} + \frac{n^2}{B^3} + \frac{n^3}{B^4} + \frac{n^4}{B^5} + \frac{n^5}{B^6} + ...\right) * \frac{n}{n}$$

We'll take the n in the numerator and multiple it to each term inside the parenthesis, and leave the 1/n outside of the parenthesis. We're doing this so that the n in the numerator will be raised to the same power as the B in the denominator.

$$\frac{1}{(B-n)} = \left(\frac{n^1}{B^1} + \frac{n^2}{B^2} + \frac{n^3}{B^3} + \frac{n^4}{B^4} + \frac{n^5}{B^5} + \frac{n^6}{B^6} + ...\right) * \frac{1}{n}$$

Next, we'll add a one and subtract a one inside the parenthesis on the right. (This has the same effect as adding a zero which again doesn't change the value of the right side.)

$$\frac{1}{(B-n)} = \left(1 - 1 + \frac{n^1}{B^1} + \frac{n^2}{B^2} + \frac{n^3}{B^3} + \frac{n^4}{B^4} + \frac{n^5}{B^5} + \frac{n^6}{B^6} + ...\right) * \frac{1}{n}$$

We take the -1 outside of the parenthesis (and we must keep in mind that by so doing, it is multiplied to the 1/n.

$$\frac{1}{(B-n)} = \left(1 + \frac{n^1}{B^1} + \frac{n^2}{B^2} + \frac{n^3}{B^3} + \frac{n^4}{B^4} + \frac{n^5}{B^5} + \frac{n^6}{B^6} + ...\right) * \frac{1}{n} - \frac{1}{n}$$

Now, we did all this work because there is a nice little relationship in many Analytical Geometry books that says that if there is a fraction greater than zero, and less than one, and if that fraction is represented by r, then the following statement is true:

$$\frac{1}{(1-r)} = 1 + r^1 + r^2 + r^3 + r^4 + r^5 + r^6 + ...$$

Therefore, if we let r = n/B, then we can substitute the infinite series (everything inside the parenthesis) on the right side of our equation with 1/(1 - n/B). By making the substitution, this is what our expression looks like now:

$$\frac{1}{(B-n)} = \left(\frac{1}{1 - n/B}\right) * \frac{1}{n} - \frac{1}{n}$$

All we have to do is simplify the right side and see if it equals the left side. First, we'll simplify the compound fraction within the parentheses. This is done by getting rid of the fraction in the denominator. The line from above, goes to this:

$$\frac{1}{(B-n)} = \left(\frac{1}{B/B - n/B}\right) * \frac{1}{n} - \frac{1}{n}$$

And then reduces to this:

$$\frac{1}{(B-n)} = \left(\frac{B}{B-n}\right) * \frac{1}{n} - \frac{1}{n}$$

Which then goes to:

$$\frac{1}{(B-n)} = \frac{B}{n(B-n)} - \frac{1}{n}$$

After combining terms we get:

$$\frac{1}{(B-n)} = \frac{B - B + n}{n(B-n)}$$

The B - B in the numerator on the right add to zero (cancel each other); and then the n in the numerator cancels with the n in the denominator. The right side finally reduces to:

$$\frac{1}{(B-n)} = \frac{1}{(B-n)}$$

The expression is true; and therefore it will work for all positive values of B and n as long as B is greater than n.

Other Examples

Now that we proved the relationship to be true, this means that we can build some very interesting fraction series. We can also create several unique fraction series that are all equal to each other. In fact, we could have a lot of fun with this. Again, here is the general formula:

$$\frac{1}{(B-n)} = \frac{n^0}{B^1} + \frac{n^1}{B^2} + \frac{n^2}{B^3} + \frac{n^3}{B^4} + \frac{n^4}{B^5} + \frac{n^5}{B^6} + \ldots$$

Here are several infinite fraction series that are all equal to ½. In this first example, B is equal to 3 and n is equal to 1 :

$$\frac{1}{(3-1)} = \frac{1^0}{3^1} + \frac{1^1}{3^2} + \frac{1^2}{3^3} + \frac{1^3}{3^4} + \frac{1^4}{3^5} + \frac{1^5}{3^6} + \ldots$$

$$= \frac{1}{3} + \frac{1}{9} + \frac{1}{27} + \frac{1}{81} + \frac{1}{243} + \ldots$$

= 0.333333333333333333333333333333333...
  0.111111111111111111111111111111111...
  0.037037037037037037037037037037037...
  0.012345679012345679012345679012346...
+ ...   ...
  _____
  0.5

In this next example, B is equal to 4 and n is equal to 2:

$$\frac{1}{(4-2)} = \frac{2^0}{4^1} + \frac{2^1}{4^2} + \frac{2^2}{4^3} + \frac{2^3}{4^4} + \frac{2^4}{4^5} + \frac{2^5}{4^6} + \ldots$$

$$= \frac{1}{4} + \frac{1}{8} + \frac{1}{16} + \frac{1}{32} + \frac{1}{64} + \ldots$$

$$= \begin{array}{l} 0.25 \\ 0.125 \\ 0.0625 \\ 0.03125 \\ 0.015625 \\ + \qquad \ldots \\ \hline 0.5 \end{array}$$

In this example, B is equal to 5 and n is equal to 3:

$$\frac{1}{(5-3)} = \frac{3^0}{5^1} + \frac{3^1}{5^2} + \frac{3^2}{5^3} + \frac{3^3}{5^4} + \frac{3^4}{5^5} + \frac{3^5}{5^6} + \ldots$$

$$= \frac{1}{5} + \frac{3}{25} + \frac{9}{125} + \frac{27}{625} + \frac{81}{3125} + \ldots$$

$$= \begin{array}{l} 0.2 \\ 0.12 \\ 0.072 \\ 0.0432 \\ 0.02592 \\ + \qquad \ldots \\ \hline 0.5 \end{array}$$

And in this final example, B is equal to 6 and n is equal to 4:

$$\frac{1}{(6-4)} = \frac{4^0}{6^1} + \frac{4^1}{6^2} + \frac{4^2}{6^3} + \frac{4^3}{6^4} + \frac{4^4}{6^5} + \frac{4^5}{6^6} + \ldots$$

$$= \frac{1}{6} + \frac{1}{9} + \frac{2}{27} + \frac{2}{81} + \frac{8}{243} + \ldots$$

$$= \begin{array}{l} 0.166666666666666666666666666\ldots \\ 0.111111111111111111111111111111\ldots \\ 0.074074074074074074074074074074\ldots \\ 0.024691358024691358024691358024691\ldots \\ 0.032921810699588477366255144032922\ldots \\ + \quad \ldots \qquad\qquad\qquad\qquad\qquad\qquad \ldots \\ \hline 0.5 \end{array}$$

If you did the math yourself, you noticed that some of these series didn't converge very fast. However, you may have also noticed that the closer B is to the original denominator (which makes n smaller), the faster the series does converge, while the further B is from the original denominator (with a larger n), the slower it converges.

Interesting Ramifications

Of course, the formula presented in the preceding pages has some very interesting ramifications. Not only are there several ways to express the same fraction (as we just saw in the section above); but we can also describe multiples of a unit fraction in terms of unit fractions, and in that way create multiple ways of describing non-unit fractions.

You may have noticed that the method used above can be used to create fractions that have a one in the numerator. If some other number is in the numerator, we factor that number, and in this way create an infinite series for this fraction. For example, to create an infinite series for the fraction 3/5, we could rewrite this fraction as 3(1/5). Now by choosing 6 for B, and 1 for n, we have the following:

$$3 * \frac{1}{5} = 3 * \frac{1}{(6-1)} = 3 * \left(\frac{1^0}{6^1} + \frac{1^1}{6^2} + \frac{1^2}{6^3} + \frac{1^3}{6^4} + \frac{1^4}{6^5} + \frac{1^5}{6^6} + \dots \right)$$

$$= 3 * \left(\frac{1}{6} + \frac{1}{36} + \frac{1}{216} + \frac{1}{1296} + \dots \right)$$

$$= \frac{3}{6} + \frac{3}{36} + \frac{3}{216} + \frac{3}{1296} + \dots$$

Which reduces to:

$$\frac{3}{5} = \frac{1}{2} + \frac{1}{12} + \frac{1}{72} + \frac{1}{432} + \dots$$

Notice that the value of the denominator in each fraction is six times the value of the preceding denominator; making it is easy to predict subsequent denominators, and thus giving us a series for the fraction 3/5. By carefully selecting values for B and n, we can create some very interesting infinite series for any fraction. **And that's not all. By selecting the same B value for a pair of fractions, we can also use these infinite series to add or subtract combinations of fractions.** For example, we could set B equal to 9 for both of the following fractions, and then add:

$$\frac{1}{5} + \frac{1}{6} \quad \text{would be the same as} \quad \frac{1}{(9-4)} + \frac{1}{(9-3)}$$

The individual fractions are equal to:

$$\frac{1}{5} = \frac{1}{(9-4)} = \frac{1}{9} + \frac{4}{81} + \frac{16}{729} + \frac{64}{6561} + \dots$$

$$\frac{1}{6} = \frac{1}{(9-3)} = \frac{1}{9} + \frac{3}{81} + \frac{9}{729} + \frac{27}{6561} + \dots$$

And the sum of these two fractions is equal to:

40

$$\frac{1}{5} + \frac{1}{6} = \frac{2}{9} + \frac{7}{81} + \frac{25}{729} + \frac{91}{6561} + \dots$$

This is a very interesting series for the fraction 11/30 (which is the sum of 1/5 and 1/6). Again, this series doesn't converge very fast, but it is possible to select other values for B where the series could converge a little faster.

More Patterns between Fractions and Their Decimals

Finally, here is another interesting relationship between fractions and their decimal equivalent. We started this chapter by noticing a number pattern in the decimal value of the fraction 1/98. The 98 we were using was obtained from 100 minus 2. Now, let's take 98 as the denominator, and compare the fraction 1/98 with the fraction 2/98. The decimal values of the two fractions have an interesting relation to each other. We'll show this relation as two lines. The top line shows the fraction 1/98. To the left of this fraction we show that 98 is equal to 100 minus 2. To the right of the fraction is the decimal equivalent of 1/98. The second line takes the 2 and places that as the numerator above 98, giving us the fraction 2/98, or 1/49. Here is a visual representation of what we are trying to look at:

$$100 - 2 = 98 \qquad 1/98 = \qquad 0.0102040816326530612244489 \dots$$
$$2/98 = \qquad 1/49 = \qquad 0.020408163265306122444489 \dots$$

Notice on the right that except for the 01 at the beginning of the decimal value for 1/98, the rest of the decimal values for the two fractions have numbers that follow the same sequence.

No big deal, you say. Well, let's do the same thing for 97. First we show on the left that 97 was obtained from 100 minus 3. On the same line we show to the right the decimal value of the fraction 1/97. On the next line, we use 3 as the numerator and divide by 97. The decimal value of 3/97 is lined up under the decimal value of 1/97 in such a way that we can easily see the similarities between these two numbers.

$$100 - 3 = 97 \qquad 1/97 = \qquad 0.0103092783505154639175025 \dots$$
$$3/97 = \qquad 3/97 = \qquad 0.03092783505154639175025 \dots$$

Still not impressed? Let's compare what we've just seen with a few other fractions where 97 is the denominator. Here are the fractions 2/97, 4/97, 5/97, 6/97, and 7/97:

$$2/97 = \qquad 0.020618556701030927835051546391753 \dots$$
$$4/97 = \qquad 0.041237113402061855670103092783505 \dots$$
$$5/97 = \qquad 0.051546391752577319587628865979381 \dots$$
$$6/97 = \qquad 0.061855670103092783505154639175258 \dots$$
$$7/97 = \qquad 0.072164948453608247422680412371134 \dots$$

Notice that none of the fractions shown above line up so nicely under 1/97 as the 3/97 does. However, you probably still have your doubts because after all, 1/97 lists all of the multiples of 3, and if you multiply the multiples of 3 (in the decimal) by 3, you still have the multiples of 3 (except, of course, for the 01 in front), where they are shifted two decimal places to the right. (We did see the same thing with the fraction 1/98. The decimal value of 1/98 listed the multiples of 2, and then after multiplying this decimal value by 2, we again had a list of the multiples of 2 but shifted two places to the right).

For this reason I can understand any skepticism on your part; however, this is actually a very interesting pattern, and it appears that we can do the same thing for at least the next seven sets of numbers – as shown below:

$100 - 4$	$=$	96	$1/96$	$=$	$0.0104166666666666666666 \ldots$
	$4/96$	$=$	$1/24$	$=$	$0.0416666666666666666666 \ldots$
$100 - 5$	$=$	95	$1/95$	$=$	$0.0105263157894736842105 26 \ldots$
	$5/95$	$=$	$1/19$	$=$	$0.0526315789473684210526 \ldots$
$100 - 6$	$=$	94	$1/94$	$=$	$0.0106382978723404255319 14 \ldots$
	$6/94$	$=$	$3/47$	$=$	$0.0638297872340425531914 \ldots$
$100 - 7$	$=$	93	$1/93$	$=$	$0.0107526881720430107526 88 \ldots$
	$7/93$	$=$	$7/93$	$=$	$0.0752688172043010752688 \ldots$
$100 - 8$	$=$	92	$1/92$	$=$	$0.0108695652173913043478 26 \ldots$
	$8/92$	$=$	$2/23$	$=$	$0.0869565217391304347826 \ldots$
$100 - 9$	$=$	91	$1/91$	$=$	$0.0109890109890109890109 89 \ldots$
	$9/91$	$=$	$9/91$	$=$	$0.0989010989010989010989 \ldots$
$100 - 10$	$=$	90	$1/90$	$=$	$0.0111111111111111111111 111 \ldots$
	$10/90$	$=$	$1/9$	$=$	$0.1111111111111111111111 \ldots$

And in fact, we can follow this same process and do it for any number under 100. Here are a few more examples using 11, 12, 51 and 76:

$100 - 11$	$=$	89	$1/89$	$=$	$0.0112359550561797752808 98 \ldots$
	$11/89$	$=$	$11/89$	$=$	$0.1235955056179775280898 \ldots$
$100 - 12$	$=$	88	$1/88$	$=$	$0.0113636363636363636363 \ldots$
	$12/88$	$=$	$3/22$	$=$	$0.1363636363636363636363 \ldots$
$100 - 51$	$=$	49	$1/49$	$=$	$0.0204081632653061224489 79 \ldots$
	$51/49$	$=$	$51/49$	$=$	$1.0408163265306122448979 \ldots$
$100 - 76$	$=$	24	$1/24$	$=$	$0.0416666666666666666666 \ldots$
	$76/24$	$=$	$19/6$	$=$	$3.1666666666666666666666 \ldots$

Notice that once we start using numbers above 50 that the second half of the process gives us numbers greater than 1. There appears to be no problem with that since we are only looking at the values to the right of the decimal point. Therefore, even with these numbers, the pattern still holds.

And since we mentioned the number 50, it may appear to be an exception (as might any other multiple of 10), but actually, these numbers aren't an exception. Here are the numbers 50 and 90 using our process:

$$100 - 50 \;=\; 50 \qquad 1/50 \;=\; 0.02000000000000000000000\ldots$$
$$50/50 \;=\; 1/1 \;=\; 1.00000000000000000000000\ldots$$

$$100 - 90 \;=\; 10 \qquad 1/10 \;=\; 0.10000000000000000000000\ldots$$
$$90/10 \;=\; 9/1 \;=\; 9.00000000000000000000000\ldots$$

In these examples, we include the 0's when we look at the numbers to the right of the decimal place, and in this way they fit into the pattern just like any other number.

So, does this process work for larger numbers? What if we subtract our number from 1000? If we then line up the second decimal number under the first by shifting the second number over three places to the right (instead of two places as in the previous examples), we see that it still does work. In the examples below, we will subtract a few numbers from 1000.

$$1000 - 122 \;=\; 878 \qquad 1/878 \;=\; 0.0011389521640091116173\,12\ldots$$
$$122/878 \;=\; 61/439 \;=\; 0.1389521640091116173\,12\ldots$$

$$1000 - 243 \;=\; 757 \qquad 1/757 \;=\; 0.0013210039630118890356\,67\ldots$$
$$243/757 \;=\; 243/757 \;=\; 0.3210039630118890356\,67\ldots$$

$$1000 - 493 \;=\; 507 \qquad 1/507 \;=\; 0.0019723865877712031558\,18\ldots$$
$$493/507 \;=\; 493/507 \;=\; 0.9723865877712031558\,18\ldots$$

$$1000 - 724 \;=\; 276 \qquad 1/276 \;=\; 0.0036231884057971014492\,75\ldots$$
$$724/276 \;=\; 181/69 \;=\; 2.6231884057971014492\,75\ldots$$

What we have done here can be applied to other examples. Proving this relationship has much to do with the concepts that we saw at the beginning of this chapter, but proving it could also take away some of the magic of the relationship; so I will leave the proof as an exercise to the curious reader. For the rest of us, the pattern is very amazing.

Chapter 4
Farey Fractions

The Farey Series

The Farey Series is a sequence of consecutive fractions between 0 and 1 that have a denominator limit, and are listed in ascending order. The following list of five fractions is an example of a Farey Series:

$$1/4, \quad 1/3, \quad 1/2, \quad 2/3, \quad 3/4$$

In this example, we list all the fractions between 0 and 1 that have as their denominator a 2, 3 or 4. These fractions are listed in lowest terms, and in ascending order, from smallest to largest.

The sequence is named after John Farey who was believed to be the first to observe these relations around 1816. Modern records now appear to show that he was not the original discoverer of many of the relationships. It appears that a man by the name of C. Haros preceded Farey by fourteen years. However, the mathematician Cauchy gave Farey the credit, and from there the credit stuck.

To create a Farey series, first select some arbitrary limit that the denominator will not exceed. Then list all the fractions between 0 and 1, in ascending order and in lowest terms that are within the denominator limit. In this next example we'll choose 5 as our denominator limit. We now list all fractions that have a 2, 3, 4 or 5 in the denominator. This is the Farey series:

$$1/5, \quad 1/4, \quad 1/3, \quad 2/5, \quad 1/2, \quad 3/5, \quad 2/3, \quad 3/4, \quad 4/5$$

At first glance the Farey series doesn't look so unusual; however, it does have some interesting properties. We can pick any fraction within the sequence, and then by adding the numerators together and then the denominators together of the fractions on either side of the selected fraction, we get the fraction in the middle. Let's take the fraction 1/4. The fractions on either side are 1/5 and 1/3. When we add the numerators together, we have $1 + 1$ which is 2; and when we add the denominators together, we get $5 + 3$ which is 8. By placing the 2 over the 8, we have the fraction 2/8 which reduces to 1/4, which is the fraction between 1/5 and 1/3. This type of addition will work for any fraction within this sequence.

You may have noticed that this is not regular fraction addition. We're not trying to get a common denominator; instead, we are simply adding numerators to numerators and denominators to denominators. There are still several other properties that this series has. The following is a listing of these properties:

- The sum of the numerators and the sum of the denominators on either side of a fraction will be equal to that fraction between them.
- All sequences have an odd number of terms.
- 1/2 is always the middle term.

- Fractions equidistant from 1/2 (on each side of 1/2) are complementary. (In other words, their sum is equal to 1)
- The difference between consecutive fractions is equal to the reciprocal of the product of their denominators.
- The cross multiplication of two consecutive fractions gives you two consecutive numbers.

We've already looked at the first property, and the next three of these six properties are fairly obvious; however, the last two are somewhat peculiar. Let's look at these properties while examining another Farey series. In this next example, we'll use 6 as the denominator limit.

$$1/6, \ 1/5, \ 1/4, \ 1/3, \ 2/5, \ 1/2, \ 3/5, \ 2/3, \ 3/4, \ 4/5, \ 5/6$$

Here we see that there are eleven terms (an odd number) and 1/2 is the middle term. Pairing the fractions that are equidistant from 1/2 on the left with those corresponding fractions on the right shows that each pair adds up to one.

Now let's take a closer look at the fifth property, the one that says, "The difference between consecutive fractions is equal to the reciprocal of the product of their denominators." If we select the fractions 1/3 and 2/5, we find that the difference between them is equal to 1/15. (15 is the common denominator with 1/3 equal to 5/15 and 2/5 equal to 6/15.) The fifth property says that we could have just as easily found the difference between these two fractions by multiplying the denominators together and taking the reciprocal. And sure enough, the product of the denominators is equal to 15 and the reciprocal is 1/15.

The sixth property says that if we take any two consecutive fractions, and multiply the first numerator with the second denominator, and then take the first denominator and multiply that with the second numerator, we will have two consecutive numbers. Let's try it with the fractions 3/5 and 2/3. The numerator of the first multiplied to the denominator of the second is equal to 9. The denominator of the first multiplied to the numerator of the second is equal to 10. And as the property stated, we have two consecutive numbers.

				1/3,				1/2,				2/3				
			1/4,	1/3,				1/2,			2/3,	3/4				
		1/5,	1/4,	1/3,		2/5,		1/2,	3/5,		2/3,	3/4,	4/5			
	1/6,	1/5,	1/4,	1/3,		2/5,		1/2,	3/5,		2/3,	3/4,	4/5,	5/6		
1/7,	1/6,	1/5,	1/4,	2/7,	1/3,	2/5,	3/7,	1/2,	4/7,	3/5,	2/3,	5/7,	3/4,	4/5,	5/6,	6/7
1/8, 1/7, 1/6, 1/5, 1/4, 2/7, 1/3, 3/8, 2/5, 3/7, 1/2, 4/7, 3/5, 5/8, 2/3, 5/7, 3/4, 4/5, 5/6, 6/7, 7/8

Table 4.1   The Farey Series with denominator limits from 3 to 8.

The preceding table shows six Farey Series (where each line is a different series), starting with a denominator limit equal to 3, and continuing sequentially to the Farey Series with a denominator limit of 8. It is also interesting to see the relative positions of the fractions with regard to each other. We will see these relative positions again when we look at Ford circles later in this chapter.

A 2nd Farey Series

Here's an interesting variation of the Farey Series:

$$0/1, \ 1/5, \ 1/4, \ 2/7, \ 1/3, \ 3/8, \ 2/5, \ 3/7, \ 1/2, \ 4/7, \ 3/5, \ 5/8, \ 2/3, \ 5/7, \ 3/4, \ 4/5, \ 1/1$$

This sequence has an 8 as the largest denominator; and yet, it is missing quite a few fractions to be a true Farey series. In spite of this, it still shares all of the properties of a true Farey series, and in addition to this, the numerators have a self-similar, fractal-type property. I'll leave it to the reader to verify that the other properties are true. Right now, we'll take a look at the self-similar property of the numerators, and then I'll explain how the series was created. We'll begin by listing the numerators:

$$0, 1, 1, 2, 1, 3, 2, 3, 1, 4, 3, 5, 2, 5, 3, 4, 1$$

As you may remember (from chapter 2), a sequence of numbers is self-similar if a part (or all) of the sequence can be found within itself. In the sequence above, we start with the leading 0 and look at every other number. The new sequence generated is:

$$0, 1, 1, 2, 1, 3, 2, 3, 1$$

This new sequence is an identical copy of the first half of the original sequence. We then take this new sequence and apply the same steps again to get another self-similar sequence that is half of the one above - in other words, we start again with the leading 0 and take every other number to get:

$$0, 1, 1, 2, 1$$

The numerator is self-similar. So, how was our second Farey series created? We started with the fractions 0 and 1 (which we actually write as 0/1 and 1/1). Then we generated the first sequence by creating exactly one fraction between the existing fractions. To create the new fraction, we added the numerators together to get the new numerator, and then we added the denominators together to obtain the new denominator. The first sequence is:

$$0/1, \ 1/2, \ 1/1$$

To get the next sequence, we repeat this process by creating a new fraction between each of the existing fractions. The next sequence is:

$$0/1, \ 1/3, \ 1/2, \ 2/3, \ 1/1$$

So far this is still a regular Farey Series; however, if we do it one more time, we start to deviate from a standard Farey series. Here is our next sequence of fractions:

$$0/1, \ 1/4, \ 1/3, \ 2/5, \ 1/2, \ 3/5, \ 2/3, \ 3/4, \ 1/1$$

This sequence is missing the 1/5 and the 4/5 terms to be a true Farey series. However, it still has all the properties of a regular Farey series, and at this point we can already see the self-similar properties of the numerators in this sequence. If we do it one more time and create a single fraction between each existing fraction we get the sequence that we started with at the beginning of this section.

$$0/1, \ 1/5, \ 1/4, \ 2/7, \ 1/3, \ 3/8, \ 2/5, \ 3/7, \ 1/2, \ 4/7, \ 3/5, \ 5/8, \ 2/3, \ 5/7, \ 3/4, \ 4/5, \ 1/1$$

This process can be continued indefinitely, and each time, we maintain all of the original properties of a Farey series along with the additional self-similar property of the numerators. Here are the first three iterations of this second set of Farey Series:

		1/3,		1/2,		2/3		
	1/4,		1/3,	2/5,	1/2,	3/5,	2/3,	3/4,
1/5,	1/4,	2/7,	1/3,	3/8, 2/5, 3/7,	1/2,	4/7, 3/5, 5/8,	2/3,	5/7, 3/4, 4/5

Table 4.2   The first three iterations of the 2nd set of Farey Series.

A 3rd Farey Series

If you were to create a regular Farey series, and use a larger number as the denominator limit, you would notice that the first few terms share an interesting property. For example, say that we set 9 as the denominator limit, and we started to create a standard Farey series. The first six terms of this sequence are:

$$1/9, \ 1/8, \ 1/7, \ 1/6, \ 1/5, \ 2/9, \ ...$$

Notice that the first five terms of this sequence all have a one in the numerator. It's not until the sixth term that we have some other number in the numerator besides a one. In a similar manner, the last five terms of this sequence all have a numerator value that is one less than the denominator:

$$..., 4/5, \ 5/6, \ 6/7, \ 7/8, \ 8/9$$

By simply extending this idea a little further, we can create a variation of the Farey series that has all one's in the numerator until we reach the fraction 1/2, and then for the second half of the series, we list all the fractions where the numerator is one less than the denominator until we reach the final term. As an example, let's set 10 as the denominator limit; therefore, our new Farey series is:

$$1/10, \ 1/9, \ 1/8, \ 1/7, \ 1/6, \ 1/5, \ 1/4, \ 1/3, \ 1/2, \ 2/3, \ 3/4, \ 4/5, \ 5/6, \ 6/7, \ 7/8, \ 8/9, \ 9/10$$

This series also shares all of the properties of a true Farey series with a fraction of the fractions (so to speak). We could even go so far as to call this a Farey series lite. The following table shows the third type of Farey series with the denominator limits going from 3 to 9:

						1/3,	1/2,	2/3						
					1/4,	1/3,	1/2,	2/3,	3/4					
				1/5,	1/4,	1/3,	1/2,	2/3,	3/4,	4/5				
			1/6,	1/5,	1/4,	1/3,	1/2,	2/3,	3/4,	4/5,	5/6			
		1/7,	1/6,	1/5,	1/4,	1/3,	1/2,	2/3,	3/4,	4/5,	5/6,	6/7		
	1/8,	1/7,	1/6,	1/5,	1/4,	1/3,	1/2,	2/3,	3/4,	4/5,	5/6,	6/7,	7/8	
1/9,	1/8,	1/7,	1/6,	1/5,	1/4,	1/3,	1/2,	2/3,	3/4,	4/5,	5/6,	6/7,	7/8,	8/9

Table 4.3   The third type of Farey Series with denominator limits from 3 to 9.

We began the last section by looking at the numerators of the second type of Farey series and we will end this section by looking at the numerators of this type of Farey series. These numerators don't create any type of fractal pattern; nevertheless, they do have an interesting and recognizable pattern. Here are the numerators to the series when we set the denominator limit to 10:

$$1, \quad 1, \quad 1, \quad 1, \quad 1, \quad 1, \quad 1, \quad 1, \quad 1, \quad 2, \quad 3, \quad 4, \quad 5, \quad 6, \quad 7, \quad 8, \quad 9$$

These numerators are all ones until the fraction ½, after which they increase sequentially until they reach a value that is one less than the denominator limit.

A Hybrid Farey Series Using the 1st Series with the 2nd Method

We now have three different methods of creating a Farey series and we can now mix and match pairs of these methods to create a few hybrid Farey series. The first one we will look at takes the standard Farey series (which we will call the first method), and create variations of it using the second method. As an example, we'll take a Farey series of the first method, with a denominator limit equal to five, and then use the second method to create the next series.

$$1/5, \quad 1/4, \quad 1/3, \quad 2/5, \quad 1/2, \quad 3/5, \quad 2/3, \quad 3/4, \quad 4/5$$

$$1/5, \quad 2/9, \quad 1/4, \quad 2/7, \quad 1/3, \quad 3/8, \quad 2/5, \quad 3/7, \quad 1/2, \quad 4/7, \quad 3/5, \quad 5/8, \quad 2/3, \quad 5/7, \quad 3/4, \quad 7/9, \quad 4/5$$

The second method creates a single fraction between each existing fraction. The resulting series is a hybrid series. It has a pair of fractions with 9's as the largest denominator, yet this fraction begins with 1/5 and ends with 4/5. This series maintains all of the properties of an original Farey series, yet it is unique from any previous series that we have so far created.

A Hybrid Farey Series Using the 3rd Series with the 2nd Method

If we take a Farey series that was created using third method above, and from that create another Farey series using the second method, we get still another Farey series that has a distinct set of fractions that we wouldn't have gotten any other way. Let's look at an example. Here is a Farey series that was created using method 3 with 6 as the denominator limit:

$$1/6, \quad 1/5, \quad 1/4, \quad 1/3, \quad 1/2, \quad 2/3, \quad 3/4, \quad 4/5, \quad 5/6$$

Now, we will create our next Farey series from this one in the same way that we created subsequent Farey series in method 2. We will take adjacent fractions and add the numerators together and then add the denominators together to come up with the fraction in between. Here is our next Farey series:

$$1/6, \quad 2/11, \quad 1/5, \quad 2/9, \quad 1/4, \quad 2/7, \quad 1/3, \quad 2/5, \quad 1/2, \quad 3/5, \quad 2/3, \quad 5/7, \quad 3/4, \quad 7/9, \quad 4/5, \quad 9/11, \quad 5/6$$

Again, this hybrid Farey series has all the same properties of a regular Farey series. And now if we continue using the second method to create subsequent Farey series, we would create still more unique sets of Farey series fractions.

Extending the Farey Series

Even though the Farey series was originally defined for the fractions between 0 and 1, the properties all hold true when 0 and 1 are included. (We used 0 and 1 as our boundary fractions, or end points, when we created our Farey series using the second method.) The boundary fractions become important when we use the second method to create subsequent Farey series. With 0 and 1 as the end points, the Farey series includes more fractions; while if we omit 0 and 1, the Farey series appears more limited. Let's compare two examples. In the first we will start with a Farey series that doesn't have the 0 and 1 on the ends. This is the series using the second method to create two subsequent generations:

1/3, 1/2, 2/3
1/3, 2/5, 1/2, 3/5, 2/3
1/3, 3/8, 2/5, 3/7, 1/2, 4/7, 3/5, 5/8, 2/3

Notice that all three series in the example above are bounded by the fractions 1/3 and 2/3. We also see that all the fractions added in subsequent series in this example have numerator values that are larger than one. Now here is the same series with the 0 and 1 on each end:

0/1, 1/3, 1/2, 2/3, 1/1
0/1, 1/4, 1/3, 2/5, 1/2, 3/5, 2/3, 3/4, 1/1
0/1, 1/5, 1/4, 2/7, 1/3, 3/8, 2/5, 3/7, 1/2, 4/7, 3/5, 5/8, 2/3, 5/7, 3/4, 4/5, 1/1

In this case, because the series is bounded by 0 and 1, we are adding unit fractions (fractions that have ones in the numerators) to the series, as well as adding the same fractions that the previous example included.

We can even expand this concept further by extending the Farey series for fractions beyond one. In fact, the many of the properties still hold true. For example, look at the following sequence of numbers:

0/1, 1/4, 1/3, 1/2, 2/3, 3/4, 1/1, 5/4, 4/3, 3/2, 5/3, 7/4, 2/1

In the example above, we set the denominator limit to 4, and we carried out the sequence from 0 to 2 (from 0/1 to 2/1). Actually, we could start our sequence at some arbitrary fraction, and end it at some other fraction, and most of the original properties would still be true. However, part of our interest in this sequence is its symmetry; therefore, we will maintain that the sequence must start at some integer (a fraction with a one in the denominator) and end at some other integer. With that in mind, we'll review the properties that we defined earlier. The first property states:

- The sum of the numerators and the sum of the denominators on either side of a fraction will be equal to that fraction.

  This property is still true just the way it stands.

- All sequences have an odd number of terms.

  This is true as long as we start at some integer, and end at another integer.

- 1/2 is always the middle term.

  We have to modify this to say that some multiple of 1/2 will always be the middle term.

- Fractions equidistant from 1/2 (on each side of 1/2) are complementary. (In other words, their sum is equal to 1)

  This also must be modified to say that fractions equidistant from the mid-point (on either side of it) are complementary in that they are equal to the sum of the start and end points.

- The difference between consecutive fractions is equal to the reciprocal of the product of their denominators.

  This is still true just the way it stands.

- The cross multiplication of two consecutive fractions gives you two consecutive numbers.

  And this is still true just the way it stands.

Notice that we had to be a little more specific with some of our definitions, but as for the main ideas, they all remained true.

Ford Circles

Ford Circles appear to be a geometric relative of the Farey Series. To create Ford Circles, start with a Farey series drawn to scale on a number line; in other words, the fractions that we use won't be equally spaced along the line; instead, they will be placed in their actual locations on a number line.

In this example, we will use a number line extending from 0 to 2, with a denominator limit of 6. The Farey Series is:

0/1, 1/6, 1/5, 1/4, 1/3, 2/5, 1/2, 3/5, 2/3, 3/4, 4/5, 5/6, 1/1, 7/6, 6/5, 5/4, 4/3, 7/5, 3/2, 8/5, 5/3, 7/4, 9/5, 11/6, 2/1

We place these points on the number line in their respective positions, and then we draw circles tangent to each of these points. The diameters of these circles are dependent upon the denominator of the corresponding fraction. For any fraction, p/q, the diameter of the corresponding circle is equal to $1/(q^2)$. In other words, the fractions 0/1, 1/1 and 2/1 each have a denominator equal to 1; therefore, the diameter of the corresponding circles is $1/1^2$ (or just 1). The fractions ½ and 3/2 each have a denominator equal to 2; therefore, the diameter of those circles is $1/2^2$ or 1/4. And so on with the other fractions.

With these circles all drawn to scale, it appears that none of them overlap. (See Figure 4.1) And in fact, adjacent circles don't overlap; instead, they are tangent to each other as we shall soon see.

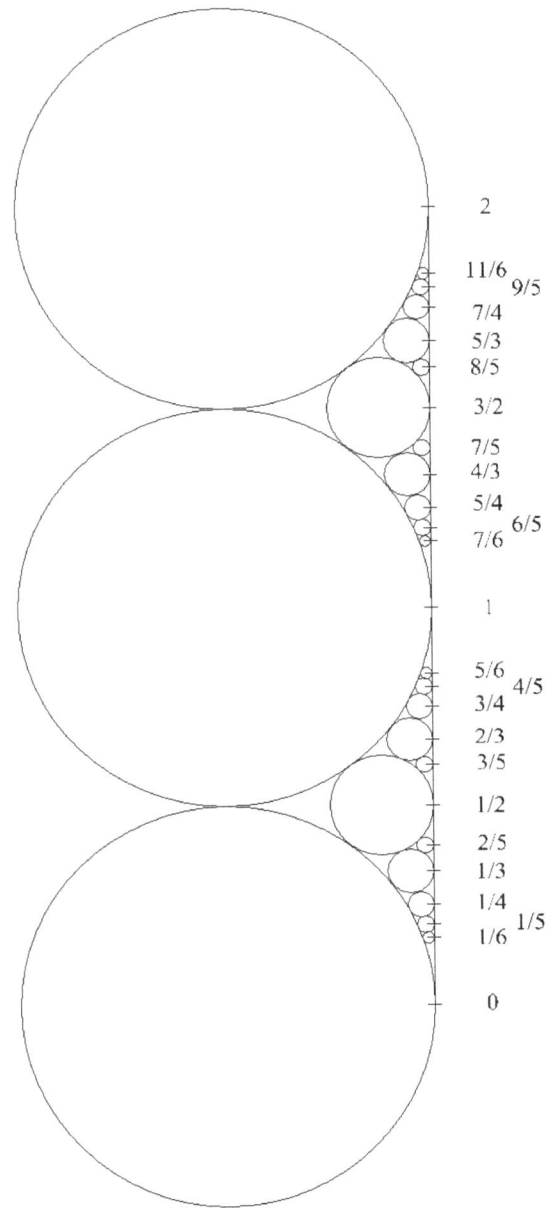

Figure 4.1   Ford Circles (drawn vertically) for fractions between 0 and 2 with a denominator limit of 6.

It is an interesting exercise to prove that these circles are tangent to each other (that they just touch without overlapping). The way to do it is to take any two adjacent circles and create a right triangle between these circles where the hypotenuse is the line between the centers of the circles, one leg is made by dropping a line perpendicular from the center of the larger circle to the number line, and the other leg is drawn from the center of the smaller circle, parallel to the number line until it intersects the first leg (the length of the first leg is actually just the line from the center of the circle to this intersection). The figure below shows this right triangle:

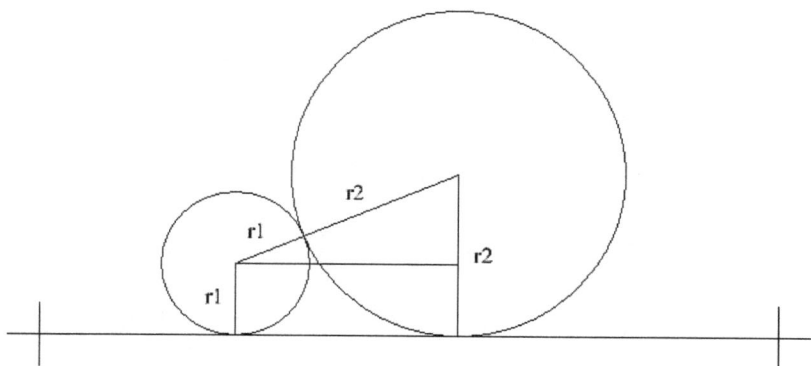

Figure 4.2   The set-up drawing to show that Ford Circles are tangent to each other.

We'll also say that the two Farey fractions used to define these circles are n/p and m/q. Therefore, the diameters of the two Ford circles would be respectively $1/p^2$ and $1/q^2$, and their corresponding radii would be half the diameters, or $\frac{1}{2}p^2$ and $\frac{1}{2}q^2$. For the sake of simplicity we'll also define "r1" as the first radius, and "r2" as the second radius.

The length of the hypotenuse (the distance between the centers of the two circles) is equal to the sum of the two radii, $\frac{1}{2}p^2$ plus $\frac{1}{2}q^2$. The length of the first leg is equal to the difference of the larger radius minus the smaller radius, or $(\frac{1}{2}p^2 - \frac{1}{2}q^2)$.

To find the length of the second leg, we go back to the definition of the original Farey fraction relationships where we saw that "the difference between consecutive fractions is equal to the reciprocal of the product of their denominators." The product of the denominator is equal to pq; and the reciprocal is then 1/pq; therefore, the distance between the fractions n/p and m/q is equal to 1/pq (and this distance is equal to the length of the second leg of our triangle).

With that, we know the length of the two legs and the length of the hypotenuse, and now we just need to use the Pythagorean theorem and a little algebra to verify that r1 and r2 are just touching each other (which would mean that the circles are tangent to each other). Here is the relationship:

$$(\tfrac{1}{2}p^2 - \tfrac{1}{2}q^2)^2 \ + \ (1/pq)^2 \ = \ (\tfrac{1}{2}p^2 + \tfrac{1}{2}q^2)^2$$

Squaring each term gives us the following:

$$1/(4p^4) \ - \ 2/(4p^2q^2) \ + \ 1/(4q^4) \ + \ 1/(p^2q^2) \ = \ 1/(4p^4) \ + \ 2/(4p^2q^2) \ + \ 1/(4q^4)$$

We now combine like terms, and in doing so we find that many terms cancel each other, leaving us with:

$$1/(p^2q^2) \ = \ 1/(p^2q^2)$$

This means that the adjacent circles are indeed tangent to each other.

Ford Circle Representations of Farey Series Variations
Ford circles are an excellent visual representation of the Farey series, so let's use them to look at some of the Farey series variations we created earlier in this chapter. Here are the Ford circles representing the first method of creating a Farey series with a denominator limit equal to 8:

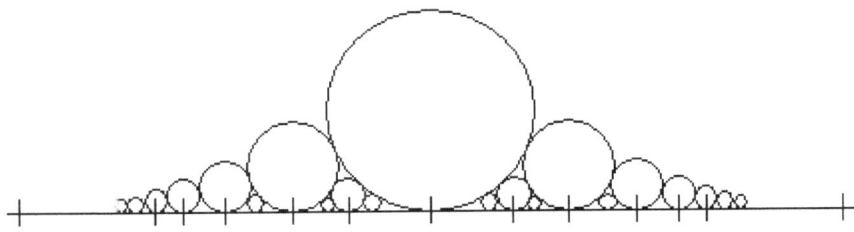

1/8, 1/7, 1/6, 1/5, 1/4, 2/7, 1/3, 3/8, 2/5, 3/7, 1/2, 4/7, 3/5, 5/8, 2/3, 5/7, 3/4, 4/5, 5/6, 6/7, 7/8

Figure 4.3   Ford Circles and Farey series using the first method with a denominator limit set to 8.

The figure above is a regular Farey series between 0 and 1; and it shows all the possible fractions in the series along with the corresponding Ford circles.

The next two figures will be the Ford circles of Farey series created using the second and the third methods (these figures also contain the corresponding fractions). Remember that the second method uses 0 and 1 to create each successive Farey series. For the purposes of clarity, we'll leave out the circles that represent the 0 and 1. Here are the Ford circles of the second method where the largest denominator is also set to 8:

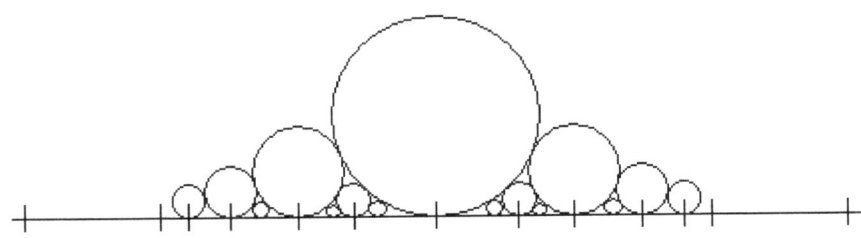

0/1, 1/5, 1/4, 2/7, 1/3, 3/8, 2/5, 3/7, 1/2, 4/7, 3/5, 5/8, 2/3, 5/7, 3/4, 4/5, 1/1

Figure 4.4   Ford Circles and Farey series using the second method with the largest denominator set to 8.

And here are the Ford circles representing the third method we looked at in this chapter (also with the largest denominator set to 8):

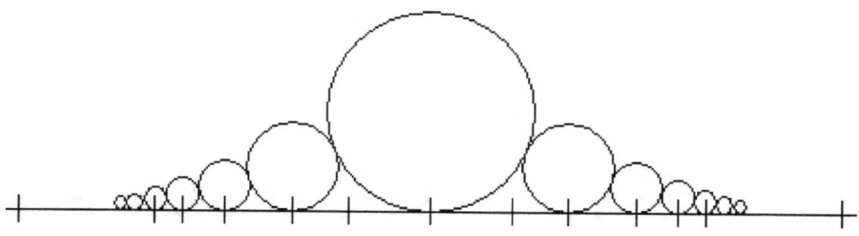

1/8, 1/7, 1/6, 1/5, 1/4, 1/3, 1/2, 2/3, 3/4, 4/5, 5/6, 6/7, 7/8

Figure 4.5   Ford Circles and Farey series using the third method with the largest denominator set to 8.

In the figures above, the Ford circles make it easy to see that using method 2, we get the inside 7th and 8th fractions (2/7, 3/7, 4/7, and 5/7; and also 3/8 and 5/8); while the third method gives use the outside 7th and 8th fractions (1/7 and 6/7; and 1/8 and 7/8). With regard to the 7th and 8th fractions, the two sets are exclusive to each other (what one has the other doesn't have, and visa-versa). Then by combining both of these figures together we get a regular Farey series.

Chapter 5
Fraction Plots

1-Digit Circular Plots

Fractions, when written in a decimal form, come in two varieties. They are either finite and non-repeating, or they are infinite and repeating. The fraction ¼ is an example of a finite, non-repeating decimal – it is written as 0.25. However, many other fractions are infinite and repeating decimals. In other words, when writing the fraction as a decimal, there is a sequence of numbers that repeats itself continuously. The fraction 1/7 is an example of such a repeating decimal.

$$1/7 = 0.142857\ 142857\ 142857\ \dots$$

Notice that the digits 142857 continuously repeat themselves. These repeating fractions can produce some very interesting graphs when we plot them.

So, you may ask yourself, "How can a person plot a single sequence of digits?" The answer is very simple; in fact, we will look at several methods of doing this over the next few pages.

The first method is a one-digit, one-dimensional circular plot. We begin by listing the numbers 0 through 9 in a circle. Then, in order to create the fraction plot, we take the decimal representation of the fraction, and simply connect the numbers as we move through the sequence.

```
        9   0
     8         1
    7           2
     6         3
        5   4
```

Figure 5.1   The template used to create a one-digit circular plot.

For example, the fraction 10/21 when written as a decimal is equal to 0.476190 476190 476190 … This fraction repeats every six digits.

To plot this fraction, we simply draw lines from number to number (kind of like connecting the dots). In other words, start at the 4 and draw a line to the 7, then from the 7 to the 6. From the 6, draw a line to the 1, then to the 9, and then to the 0. Finally, since it is a repeating fraction, close it off by returning to the 4. We now have a circular plot of the fraction 10/21. This is what it looks like (see the plot on the left in the figure below):

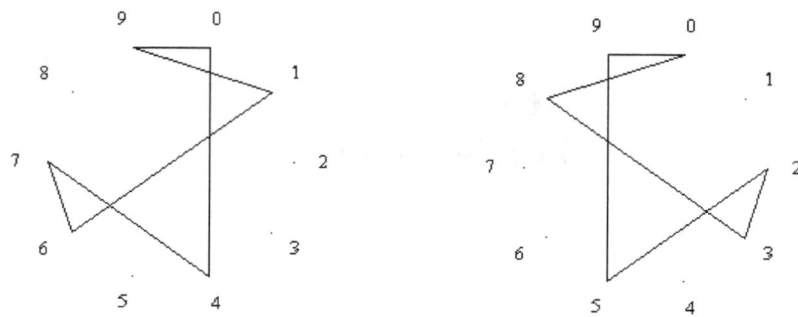

Figure 5.2   The one-digit circular plot of the fraction 10/21 (on the left) where
10/21   =   0.476190 476190 476190 476190 ...
and the one-digit circular plot of the fraction 11/21 (on the right) where
11/21   =   0.523809 523809 523809 523809 ...

The pattern for the fraction 10/21 isn't that interesting and there doesn't appear to be any symmetry to it. However, we're not quite done with this example. Let's draw a circular plot of the fraction 11/21 (as shown on the right in the figure above). Notice that the circular plot of 11/21 is a mirror image of the plot for 10/21, and when we overlay them one on top of the other, we see the symmetry created when both patterns are combined, as shown in the figure below:

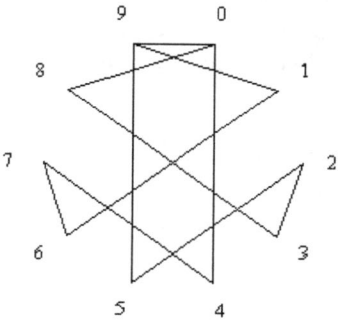

Figure 5.3   The plot pattern created when the fraction 10/21 is overlaid on top of the fraction 11/21.

Many fractions don't show any symmetry when looking at just a single circular plot, but there are also many that do. If a single fraction doesn't show any symmetry when looking at its plot, then overlaying consecutive fractions will usually bring out a symmetrical pattern. The following diagram overlays the circular plot of the fraction 10/21 on top of the plot of 11/21. We now have a symmetrical pattern.

Some fractions have different patterns with each numerator (such as the fractions 2/73, 3/73, 4/73, and 5/73 as we soon shall see). Other fractions only have one pattern for all numerators of that fraction. An example of this is the fraction 1/7. The decimal value of 1/7 is 0.142857 142857 ... If we consider the fractions 2/7 through 6/7, we find the same six numbers in the

56

same order. The only difference between each of these fractions is the start number for each cycle. Other than that, the same numbers are used, and in the same order:

$$1/7 = 0.142857\ 142857\ 142857\ldots$$
$$2/7 = 0.285714\ 285714\ 285714\ldots$$
$$3/7 = 0.428571\ 428571\ 428571\ldots$$
$$4/7 = 0.571428\ 571428\ 571428\ldots$$
$$5/7 = 0.714285\ 714285\ 714285\ldots$$
$$6/7 = 0.857142\ 857142\ 857142\ldots$$

A single fraction plot can be used to show these six fractions (1/7 through 6/7), but I will leave that to the reader. Other interesting plots can be seen from the fractions 1/17 and 1/19. The fraction 1/17 repeats every 16 digits, and 1/19 repeats every 18 digits. Each of these plots is symmetrical about a vertical axis through the middle (that's if we draw the circle with 9 and 0 at the top and 4 and 5 at the bottom).

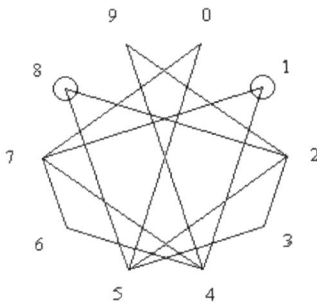

Figure 5.4   The one-digit circular plot of the fraction 1/17 where:
1/17 = 0.0588235294117647 0588235294117647 ...

Note that the fraction 1/17 has a repeating 8 and a repeating 1 in the decimal value. To show repeating numbers on these plots, we draw a circle at that point (as seen in the figure above). The following figure shows the circular plot of 1/19:

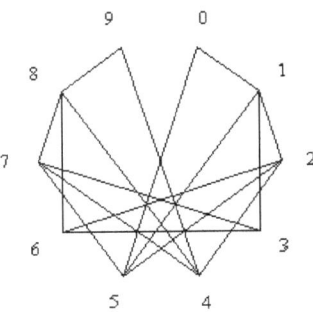

Figure 5.5   The one-digit circular plot of the fraction 1/19 where:
1/19 = 0.052631578947368421 052631578947368421 ...

Another set of interesting patterns occurs for fractions whose denominator is equal to 73. These fractions repeat every eight digits. Here we show four patterns for the fractions 2/73, 3/73, 4/73 and 5/73 respectively.

57

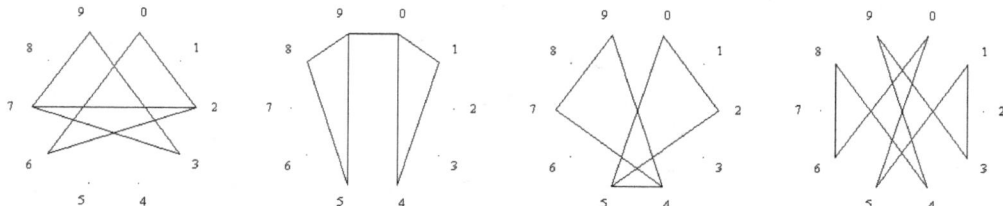

Figure 5.6   One-digit circular plots of 2/73, 3/73, 4/73 and 5/73 where:
2/73 = 0.02739726 02739726 02739726 02739726 …
3/73 = 0.04109589 04109589 04109589 04109589 …
4/73 = 0.05479452 05479452 05479452 05479452 …
5/73 = 0.06849315 06849315 06849315 06849315…

These patterns also show the same type of vertical symmetry that we've seen in other patterns. However, not all plots have this type of symmetry. Looking at fractions where the denominator is equal to 81, we see a different type of symmetry.

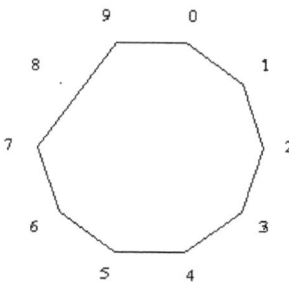

Figure 5.7   The one-digit circular plot of the fraction 1/81 where:
1/81 = 0.012345679 012345679 012345679 01234…

The fraction 1/81 connects each number in order, skipping only the number 8. It has a mirror symmetry (where one half reflects the other half) about a line passing through the eight and the three.

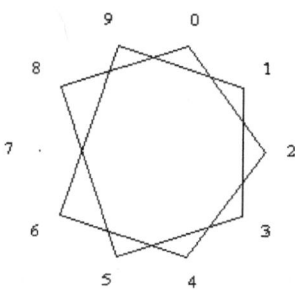

Figure 5.8   The one-digit circular plot of the fraction 2/81 where:
2/81 = 0.024691358 024691358 024691358 02469…

The fraction 2/81 skips every other number as it goes around the circle. It touches every number except the number 7. This plot is symmetrical about a line going through the 7 and the 2.

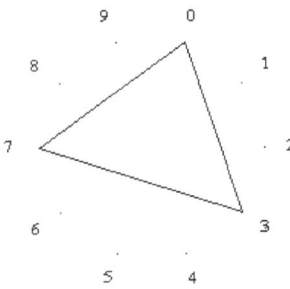

Figure 5.9   The one-digit circular plot of the fraction 3/81 where:
3/81 = 0.037 037 037 037 037 037 037 037 037...

The fraction 3/81 (shown in the figure above) is an isosceles triangle that is symmetrical about a line through the zero and the five. The fraction 4/81 is a star pattern that is also symmetrical about a line through the zero and the five.

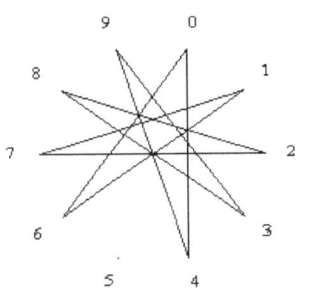

Figure 5.10   The one-digit circular plot of the fraction 4/81 where:
4/81 = 0.049382716 049382716 049382716 04938...

And there are still many other simple, yet interesting patterns. The fraction 1/121 goes through all the even numbers twice (in a non-sequential order) and then goes through all the odd numbers twice before repeating itself again. Altogether, it repeats every 22 digits. Its plot looks like this:

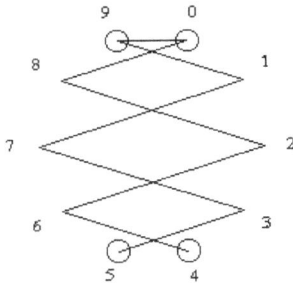

Figure 5.11   The one-digit circular plot of the fraction 1/121 where:
1/121 = 0.0082644628099173553719 0082644628099173553719 ...

In the figure above, I have again drawn circles around the numbers that repeat in the decimal sequence.

2-Digit Circular Plots

A variation of the 1 digit circular plot is a 2-digit circular plot. With the 2-digit circular plot, we list all the numbers from 0 to 99 in a circle (as we did with the numbers 0 through 9 in the previous set of plots). But this time when we create the plot, we take the decimal numbers from the fraction two digits at a time. Let's look at the 2-digit plot of 1/19.

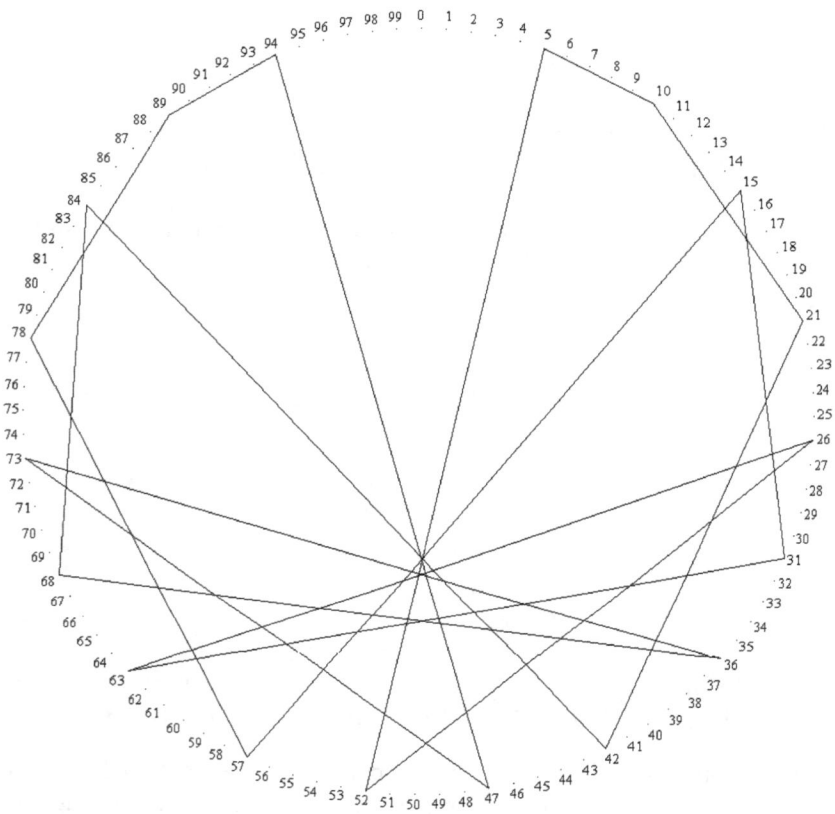

Figure 5.12   The two-digit circular plot of the fraction 1/19 where:
1/19 = 0.052631578947368421 052631578947368421 ...

Each time we take a two-digit number from the decimal, we only shift right one digit before taking the next two digit number. Therefore, the sequence of numbers that we use to create the plot are: 05, 52, 26, 63, 31, 15, 57, etc. The pattern created from this fraction also has a mirror symmetry about a vertical line through the center of the plot.

Many of the two digit plots have similarities that resemble to some degree their one-digit counterparts. By comparing the one-digit plot of the fraction 1/19 (see Figure 5.5) with its two-digit plot (shown in the figure above) we can see such a resemblance. The same can be said for the fraction 1/121. The one-digit plot (see Figure 5.11) is very similar to the two-digit plot shown below.

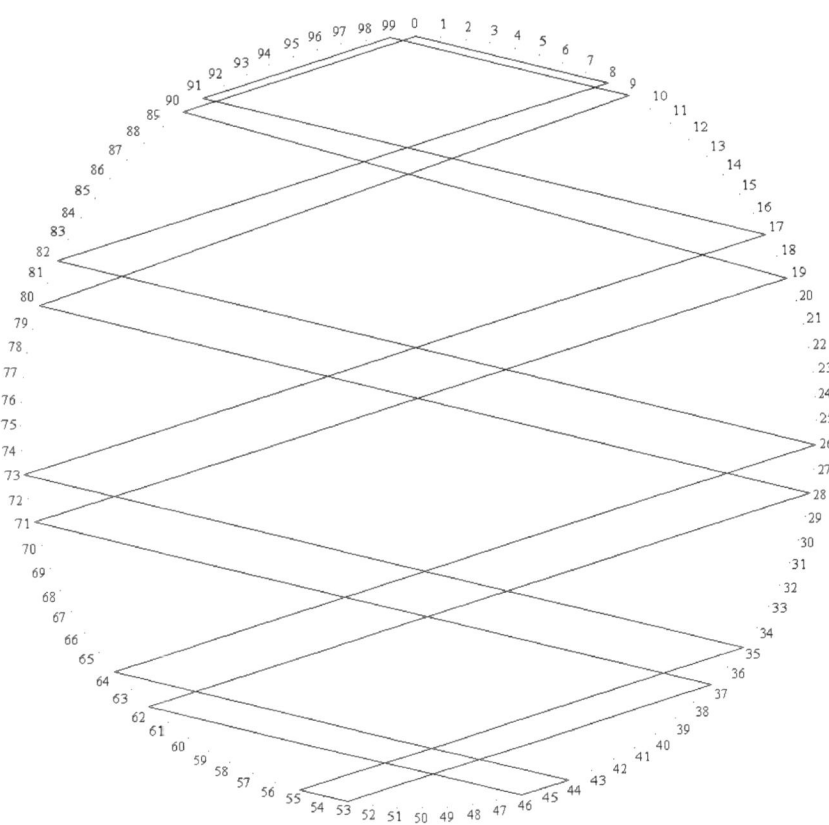

Figure 5.13   The two-digit circular plot of the fraction 1/121 where:
1/121 = 0.0082644628099173553719 0082644628099173553719 ...

Again we see the same type of mirror symmetry about a vertical line through the center of the plot. The left side of the plot mirrors the right side.

Other plots exhibit another type of symmetry. The next example displays a symmetry that we will call a repeating symmetry. Consider the circular plot for 1/243 (shown in the figure below). The pattern we see as we go clockwise around the circle can be described as a flat-side followed by a point, followed by another flat-side and a point, and so on. For example, there is a flat-side from numbers 0 to 4, and then a point at number 7; then another flat-side from 11 to 15, with the next point at 18.

This pattern repeats about every 11 digits around the circle, thus giving us 9 nearly identical patterns. Of course 9 and 11 do not divide evenly into 100 (but they do divide evenly into 99), hence the spacing between some of the flat-side-point patterns is not identical to other spacings within the circle. The points are 11 numbers apart, starting at 30 and going clockwise around the circle to 18, and only between 18 and 30 is the spacing between the points 12 numbers apart. However, in spite of this, the repeating pattern is very evident.

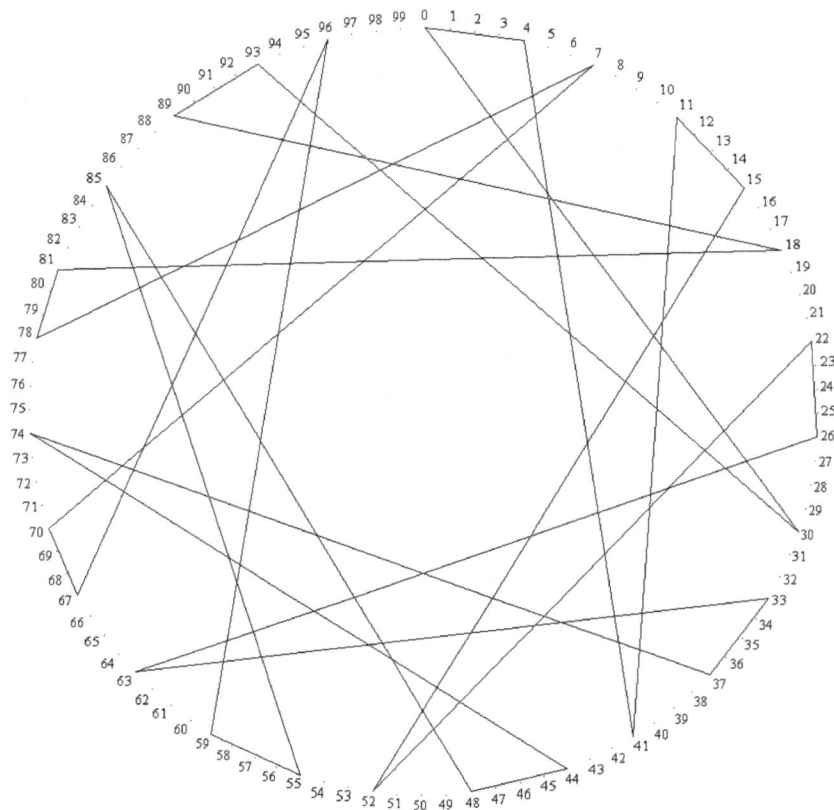

Figure 5.14   The two-digit circular plot of the fraction 1/243 where:
1/243 = 0.00411522633744855967078l893 …

Rectangular Fraction Plots

The circular plots that we looked at are one-dimensional. We didn't worry about an x and y value; instead, we simply plotted points one value at a time by connecting lines from the first value to the second, and then to the third, and so on. However, to create a rectangular graph, we need an x and a y value for each point. To do so, we will use a similar idea to that which we used with the two-digit circular plots to create these rectangular plots. We will look at two numbers at a time, the first number will be the x coordinate, and the second number will be the y coordinate. We will use these two numbers to plot an (x, y) point on the graph. Then we will shift right one digit, and then again take the first number as the x coordinate and the second number as the y coordinate and plot the next point on the graph.

To create a rectangular plot of the fraction 1/17, we start by taking the first two numbers in the decimal value of the fraction, which are 05. Then we turn this into the point (0, 5) and plot the point on our graph. Now we shift one digit to the right and take the next two numbers, which are 58. The number 58 becomes the point (5, 8). We shift right again and the next pair of numbers are 88 which become the point (8, 8), and so on. We plot all the points, drawing lines from point to point in the order they were created, and in this way we create the rectangular plot of the fraction 1/17 (as seen above).

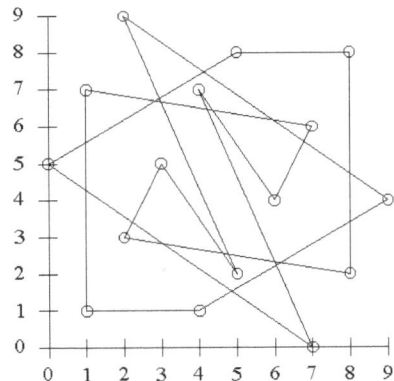

Figure 5.15   The one-digit rectangular plot of the fraction 1/17 where:
1/17 = 0.0588235294117647 0588235294117647 ...

It is surprising how much symmetry these plots also show. The next plot is the fraction 1/121. We've already seen the one and two-digit circular plots of this fraction. Here is the one-digit rectangular plot:

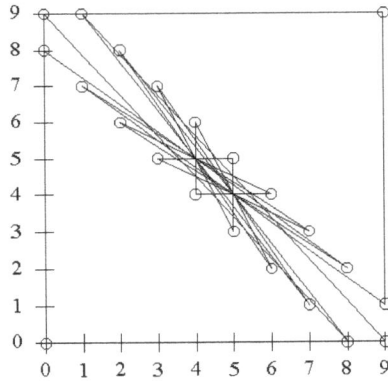

Figure 5.16   The one-digit rectangular plot of the fraction 1/121 where:
1/121 = 0.0082644628099173553719 0082644628099173553719 ...

Creating the Fraction from the Plot

Up to this point, we have taken various fractions and created one and two digit circular plots as well as rectangular plots from the decimal value of these fractions. It is also possible to go the other direction. We could create an interesting plot, and then determine what fraction would give us that plot. For example, if we plot the numbers 13681368... as a one-digit circular plot, we would have a pattern that is a rectangle. As a two-digit circular plot these numbers would give us a trapezoid, and as a rectangular plot we would get a diamond shape. So, what is the fraction that would give us these patterns? To create the fraction, we start by setting n equal to the repeating decimal:

$$n = 0.13681368 \ldots$$

Since this decimal repeats every 4 digits, we multiply each side of the equality by 10^4 (or 10,000), and then we take our original value and subtract it from the new value:

$$
\begin{aligned}
10{,}000n &= 1368.13681368 \ldots \\
- \quad n &= 0.13681368 \ldots \\
\hline
9999n &= 1368
\end{aligned}
$$

By doing this little maneuver, we eliminate the repeating decimal and we are left with a simple relationship. Next, we solve for n, and reduce the fraction to its lowest terms.

$$n = \frac{1368}{9999}$$

Converting the fraction above to lowest terms gives us:

$$n = \frac{152}{1111}$$

Therefore, the fraction 152/1111 is equal to the decimal 0.13681368..., and it will give us the various plots we described at the beginning of this section.

Chapter 6
Continuous Fractions

A continuous fraction is a fraction whose denominator is made of two parts, one of which is another fraction. This fraction (within the denominator) is also made of two parts, and again, one of those is yet another fraction. This process of having fractions within the denominator of a fraction can be finite or infinite.

Infinite continuous fractions can be messy to work with, but they also provide a unique and concise way to describe many irrational numbers (remember that an irrational number cannot be represented by a simple fraction).

Even though it takes an infinite continuous fraction to describe an irrational number, if we truncate that continuous fraction at some point, we then reduce this continuous fraction to a simple fraction that approximates the irrational number. We'll take a look at that a little later in this chapter, but for now, let's take a look at the look of a continuous fraction.

As described above, a continuous fraction has a fraction within the denominator, which in turn has a fraction within it. These fractions are also known as complex fractions, and this is one way to express the fraction:

$$a + \cfrac{b}{c + \cfrac{d}{e + \cfrac{f}{g + \cfrac{h}{i + \ldots}}}}$$

Although this method is the most accurate way to show the relationship of the various numerators and denominators, it also takes up a lot of space on a piece of paper. For convenience, the same fraction can also be written as follows (note that the +'s are in line with the denominators):

$$a + \frac{b}{c} + \frac{d}{e} + \frac{f}{g} + \frac{h}{i} + \ldots$$

For continuous fractions where the numerators are all equal to one; i.e., b = 1, d = 1, f = 1, and h = 1, etc; the continuous fraction can also written as:

$$[a;\ c,\ e,\ g,\ i,\ \ldots]$$

You may have noticed that the "a" is a whole number, and doesn't actually have to be a part of the fraction; however, it is part of the number being represented, and for this reason is included in the notation. The whole number is written with a semicolon following it while the other numbers are separated by comas.

Creating Continuous Fractions

There are several ways to create a continuous fraction. We'll look at one method and use it to create a continuous fraction from a regular fraction. Then we'll show a variation that can be used with a calculator to create a continuous fraction from an irrational number. Both of these methods create a continuous fraction where all the numerators are equal to one. For our example, we'll start with a fraction that is a good approximation for the number PI (3.1415926…):

$$\frac{355}{113}$$

To create the continuous fraction, we start by writing the fraction in lowest terms:

$$3 + \frac{16}{113}$$

Now take the reciprocal of the fraction part and write it in lowest terms:

$$\frac{113}{16} = 7 + \frac{1}{16}$$

Continue taking the reciprocal of the fraction part and writing it in lowest terms until you no longer have a fraction. In this example, our next step is the last iteration:

$$\frac{16}{1} = 16$$

Finally, use the whole numbers, the 3, 7 and 16, to create the continuous fraction. This method places the whole numbers as the denominators and uses 1's as the numerators. In this example, we get:

$$3 + \cfrac{1}{7 + \cfrac{1}{16}} \qquad \text{which is equal to the original fraction of:} \qquad \frac{355}{113}$$

This second method is practically identical to the first, except that we let the calculator do the hard work. In this example we'll find a continuous fraction that represents the square root of 5. First, we'll use a calculator to find the square root of five. My calculator shows a value of 2.236067977. Next, subtract the 2 so that the calculator now shows a value of 0.236067977. Then take the reciprocal of this number, and my calculator shows a value of 4.236067979. Now subtract the 4, and then take the reciprocal again. And again, there is another number equal to 4.2360679… Once again, take the 4, subtract it, and then take the reciprocal. These numbers that we subtract (the 2, 4, 4, 4, …) are the values of the continuous fraction. If we continued this procedure, we would subtract a few more fours, and then other numbers would appear. The other numbers are errors from the calculator working their way into the solution. If we had a perfect calculator, we would keep getting 4's indefinitely. The continuous fraction for the square root of 5 looks like this:

$$2 + \cfrac{1}{4 + \cfrac{1}{4 + \cfrac{1}{4 + \ldots}}}$$

Which also can be written like this:

$$2 + \cfrac{1}{4 + } \cfrac{1}{4 + } \cfrac{1}{4 + } \cfrac{1}{4 + } \; ...$$

And since all the numerators are all equal to one, we can also represent the continuous fraction like this:

$$[2; \; 4, \; 4, \; 4, \; 4, \; 4, \; 4, \; ...]$$

The calculator method can be used to quickly find the continuous fraction of any irrational number, including square roots, cube roots, trigonometric functions, etc. However, care must be taken when using this method because errors from the calculator can quickly work their way into the fraction, and thus into the solution (and for some numbers it happens faster than others).

Continuous Fractions of Square Roots

Continuous fractions make it easy to represent square roots as "pseudo-rational" numbers. They also reveal patterns and symmetry between the various square root values. If we examine the decimal value of a square root, the numbers appear to be random and without any pattern. (The square root of 2 is equal to 1.414213562373..., and there is no way to predict what the next digit will be in the sequence without actually going through the mathematics.) However, these same numbers when written as a continuous fraction appear to be well ordered. Earlier we saw that the square root of 5 (which is equal to 2.236067977...) appeared to be very simple when written as a continuous fraction:

$$\sqrt{5} \; = \; [2; \; 4, \; 4, \; 4, \; 4, \; 4, \; 4, \; 4, \; ...]$$

Likewise, the square root of 10 when written as a continuous fraction is:

$$\sqrt{10} \; = \; [3; \; 6, \; 6, \; 6, \; 6, \; 6, \; 6, \; 6, \; ...]$$

Notice the similar patterns between the square root of five and the square root of ten. This is because the numbers 5 and 10 are each just one number above the perfect squares 4 and 9. The continuous fraction of the numbers 17, 26, 37 and 50 also show the same type of pattern.

$$\sqrt{17} \; = \; [4; \; 8, \; 8, \; 8, \; 8, \; 8, \; 8, \; 8, \; ...]$$
$$\sqrt{26} \; = \; [5; \; 10, \; 10, \; 10, \; 10, \; 10, \; 10, \; 10, \; ...]$$
$$\sqrt{37} \; = \; [6; \; 12, \; 12, \; 12, \; 12, \; 12, \; 12, \; 12, \; ...]$$
$$\sqrt{50} \; = \; [7; \; 14, \; 14, \; 14, \; 14, \; 14, \; 14, \; 14, \; ...]$$

Each of these numbers is one more than a perfect square. Numbers that are one less than a perfect square, such as 3, 8, 15 and 24 also share a similar pattern between themselves:

$$\sqrt{3} \; = \; [1; \; 1, \; 2, \; 1, \; 2, \; 1, \; 2, \; 1, \; ...]$$
$$\sqrt{8} \; = \; [2; \; 1, \; 4, \; 1, \; 4, \; 1, \; 4, \; 1, \; ...]$$
$$\sqrt{15} \; = \; [3; \; 1, \; 6, \; 1, \; 6, \; 1, \; 6, \; 1, \; ...]$$
$$\sqrt{24} \; = \; [4; \; 1, \; 8, \; 1, \; 8, \; 1, \; 8, \; 1, \; ...]$$

Other similarities can be seen by comparing the continuous fractions of the square roots of numbers that are two less than a perfect square, such as the numbers 7, 14, 23 and 34; or by comparing the square roots of numbers that are two more than a perfect square, such as 6, 11, 18 and 27. This first listing shows numbers that are two less than a perfect square.

$$\sqrt{7} \;\; = \;\; [2;\; 1,\; 1,\; 1,\; 4,\; 1,\; 1,\; 1,\; 4,\; ...]$$
$$\sqrt{14} \;\; = \;\; [3;\; 1,\; 2,\; 1,\; 6,\; 1,\; 2,\; 1,\; 6,\; ...]$$
$$\sqrt{23} \;\; = \;\; [4;\; 1,\; 3,\; 1,\; 8,\; 1,\; 3,\; 1,\; 8,\; ...]$$
$$\sqrt{34} \;\; = \;\; [5;\; 1,\; 4,\; 1,\; 10,\; 1,\; 4,\; 1,\; 10,\; ...]$$

And the following listing show numbers that are two more than a perfect square.

$$\sqrt{6} \;\; = \;\; [2;\; 2,\; 4,\; 2,\; 4,\; 2,\; 4,\; 2,\; 4,\; ...]$$
$$\sqrt{11} \;\; = \;\; [3;\; 3,\; 6,\; 3,\; 6,\; 3,\; 6,\; 3,\; 6,\; ...]$$
$$\sqrt{18} \;\; = \;\; [4;\; 4,\; 8,\; 4,\; 8,\; 4,\; 8,\; 4,\; 8,\; ...]$$
$$\sqrt{27} \;\; = \;\; [5;\; 5,\; 10,\; 5,\; 10,\; 5,\; 10,\; 5,\; 10,\; ...]$$

There are several other ways to compare the continuous fractions of square roots. However, it is also instructive to compare the continuous fractions of a whole range of numbers between two perfect squares. This next sequence lists the continuous fractions of square roots between 16 and 25. Here we see the pattern transition from a number that is one above a perfect square to a number that is one below a perfect square.

$$\sqrt{17} \;\; = \;\; [4;\; 8,\; 8,\; 8,\; 8,\; 8,\; 8,\; 8,\; 8,\; ...]$$
$$\sqrt{18} \;\; = \;\; [4;\; 4,\; 8,\; 4,\; 8,\; 4,\; 8,\; 4,\; 8,\; ...]$$
$$\sqrt{19} \;\; = \;\; [4;\; 2,\; 1,\; 3,\; 1,\; 2,\; 8,\; 2,\; 1,\; ...]$$
$$\sqrt{20} \;\; = \;\; [4;\; 2,\; 8,\; 2,\; 8,\; 2,\; 8,\; 2,\; 8,\; ...]$$
$$\sqrt{21} \;\; = \;\; [4;\; 1,\; 1,\; 2,\; 1,\; 1,\; 8,\; 1,\; 1,\; ...]$$
$$\sqrt{22} \;\; = \;\; [4;\; 1,\; 2,\; 4,\; 2,\; 1,\; 8,\; 1,\; 2,\; ...]$$
$$\sqrt{23} \;\; = \;\; [4;\; 1,\; 3,\; 1,\; 8,\; 1,\; 3,\; 1,\; 8,\; ...]$$
$$\sqrt{24} \;\; = \;\; [4;\; 1,\; 8,\; 1,\; 8,\; 1,\; 8,\; 1,\; 8,\; ...]$$

Notice that these continuous fractions only use the number 1, 2, 3, 4 and 8. If we were to look at the continuous fractions of the square roots between 9 and 16, we would find that they only use the numbers 1, 2, 3 and 6. Likewise, the continuous fractions of the square roots between 4 and 9 only use the numbers 1, 2 and 4. It appears that the continuous fractions of all the numbers between n^2 and $(n+1)^2$ will only use the numbers 1 through n and 2n in the sequences that make up these continuous fractions. (See the appendix for more examples of continuous fractions of square roots.)

Verifying Our Continuous Fractions

These patterns are very regular; however, if you've been using a calculator to create these sets of numbers, then you've probably noticed the errors that have crept into the solution. You may be wondering if the errors are from the calculator, or on the other hand, if the conclusions in the preceding sections are wrong. For that reason, we'll look at a couple of examples and show that these values are what we say they are.

The method that we use here (to prove the value of these continuous fractions) can then be used to verify any of the patterns we've considered so far. In some examples this method can be very straight-forward, but in others the math can be a little more challenging. We will look at two examples, one where the math is easier, and the other where it is more involved. First, we'll look at the square root of 17. It appears that the following is true:

$$\sqrt{17} = 4 + \cfrac{1}{8 + \cfrac{1}{8 + \cfrac{1}{8 + \cfrac{1}{8 + \ldots}}}}$$

In order to prove that this is true, we'll set x equal to the continuous fraction, and then we'll add and subtract 4 from the continuous fraction. The equation now looks like this:

$$x = 4 + \cfrac{1}{8 + \cfrac{1}{8 + \cfrac{1}{8 + \cfrac{1}{8 + \ldots}}}} + 4 - 4$$

Next, we combine and rearrange the 4's (that we added) to get:

$$x + 4 = 8 + \cfrac{1}{8 + \cfrac{1}{8 + \cfrac{1}{8 + \cfrac{1}{8 + \ldots}}}}$$

Notice that we have an x + 4 on the left side of the equality, and the right side has a continuous fraction consisting of only 8's for all the values within the fraction. Since the continuous fraction is infinite and continually repeating itself, we can make the following substitution:

$$x + 4 = 8 + \cfrac{1}{x + 4}$$

Clearing the fraction gives us:
$$(x + 4)^2 = 8(x + 4) + 1$$

Expanding these terms produces:

$$x^2 + 8x + 16 = 8x + 32 + 1$$

And this reduces to: $\quad x^2 = 17$

Or $\quad x = \sqrt{17}$

We started by letting x equal the continuous fraction, and we ended with x equal to the square root of 17. Therefore, the continuous fraction is equal to the square root of 17. The trick to proving what a continuous fraction is equal to is to find some way to cancel out the infinite, repeating part of the complex fraction (and this is usually done by substituting the left side of the equality back into the right side in some way).

A more difficult proof is the square root of 13. We'll follow the same steps as above; however, because of the way that this continuous fraction repeats, a few of these steps become more involved.

$$\sqrt{13} = 3 + \cfrac{1}{1 + \cfrac{1}{1 + \cfrac{1}{1 + \cfrac{1}{6 + \cfrac{1}{1 + \ldots}}}}}$$

Again, set x equal to the continuous fraction. Notice also that we have a 3 at the beginning of the fraction, and a 6 imbedded within the fraction. If we change the first 3 to a 6, then we will be able to make the substitution in a later step. Therefore we will add and subtract a 3 to our continuous fraction.

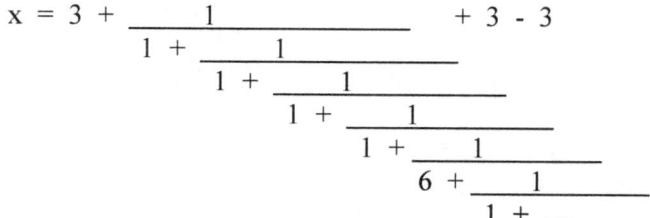

$$x = 3 + \cfrac{1}{1 + \cfrac{1}{1 + \cfrac{1}{1 + \cfrac{1}{6 + \cfrac{1}{1 + \ldots}}}}} + 3 - 3$$

Now we combine and rearrange terms so that the two positive 3's on the right add to 6, and the negative 3 on the right is moved to the left and added to the x, so that we now have:

$$x + 3 = 6 + \cfrac{1}{1 + \cfrac{1}{1 + \cfrac{1}{1 + \cfrac{1}{6 + \cfrac{1}{1 + \ldots}}}}}$$

With the 6 at the beginning of the continuous fraction, we now notice that the fraction repeats itself about 5 levels down, and since x + 3 is equal to the fraction, and since the fraction does repeat itself, we make the following substitution:

$$x + 3 = 6 + \cfrac{1}{1 + \cfrac{1}{1 + \cfrac{1}{1 + \cfrac{1}{x + 3}}}}$$

At this point we still have a very complex fraction, but at least it's not infinite anymore. Now we just need to work through the algebra until we arrive at something more manageable. In fact, the complex fraction above reduces to:

$$x + 3 = 6 + \frac{3x + 11}{5x + 18}$$

When we clear the final fraction we get:

70

$$(x + 3)(5x + 18) = 6(5x + 18) + 3x + 11$$

Expanding and combining terms on each side of the equal sign produces:

$$5x^2 + 33x + 54 = 33x + 119$$

And this reduces to:

$$5x^2 = 65$$

Or simply

$$x = \sqrt{13}$$

Again, we started by setting x equal to the continuous fraction, and we ended with x equal to the square root of 13. Therefore, this continuous fraction is equal to the square root of 13. This same method (or something similar) can be used on any other continuous fraction that has a repeating pattern.

Using Continuous Fractions to Approximate Irrational Numbers

Earlier in this chapter we mentioned that a continuous fraction can be used to approximate an irrational number. Now we'll see how this can be done. We'll use the square root of 5 as an example. We have seen earlier that the continuous fraction of the square root of 5 is equal to:

$$\sqrt{5} = 2 + \cfrac{1}{4 + \cfrac{1}{4 + \cfrac{1}{4 + \cfrac{1}{4 + \ldots}}}}$$

As it stands, this fraction is infinite. To be useful, we cut it off somewhere and make it finite. Where we truncate the continuous fraction will determine how accurate the simple fraction will be. For example, we could truncate it at any of these three places:

$$2 + \cfrac{1}{4} \qquad\qquad 2 + \cfrac{1}{4 + \cfrac{1}{4}} \qquad\qquad 2 + \cfrac{1}{4 + \cfrac{1}{4 + \cfrac{1}{4}}}$$

Each of which simplifies to:

$$\frac{9}{4} \qquad\qquad\qquad \frac{38}{17} \qquad\qquad\qquad \frac{161}{72}$$

Or, if written in decimal form:

$$2.25 \qquad\qquad\qquad 2.235294117\ldots \qquad\qquad\qquad 2.236111111\ldots$$

The first approximation is a little above the actual value of the square root of five. The second approximation is a little under the actual value; and the third is again a little above; and each approximation is more accurate than the previous.

Finally, it is possible to use our abbreviated notation to quickly (and much more easily) calculate the proper fraction that approximates the continuous fraction. For example, let's look at the square root of 24. Earlier we saw that it is equal to the following continuous fraction:

$$\sqrt{24} \quad = \quad [4;\ 1,\ 8,\ 1,\ 8,\ 1,\ 8,\ 1,\ 8,\ ...]$$

We'll use a truncated version of this continuous fraction to find a fraction that approximates the square root of 24. We'll begin by cutting off the continuous fraction after six places, so that including the integer part of the fraction, we have seven numbers:

$$\sqrt{24} \quad \approx \quad [4;\ 1,\ 8,\ 1,\ 8,\ 1,\ 8]$$

We start with the right-most number (which is 8) and take the reciprocal of it. In this case we have 1/8. Next, we add the number to its left. The 1 plus 1/8 gives us 9/8. Now, we repeat this process working our way from right to left. We take the reciprocal of 9/8 and then add the 8, which is to the left of it. This gives us 80/9. Now, we take the reciprocal of 80/9 and add the 1. This gives us 89/80. Again, we reciprocate, and then add 8; giving us 792/89. We reciprocate again, and add 1; giving us 881/792. We now reciprocate one last time, and add that to the 4 (our whole number) to give us 4 and 792/881. This is our fractional approximation for the square root of 24.

$$4 \text{ and } 792/881 \quad = \quad 4.89897843...$$

Using the square root key on my calculator gives me this value for the square root of 24:

$$\sqrt{24} \quad = \quad 4.89897949...$$

Notice that the value obtained from the continuous fraction is very close to the value we just got from the calculator.

Chapter 7
Repeated Square Roots and the Golden Ratio

The Discovery

One day, while playing with a calculator, I discovered that if I took the square root of 7, then added 7, then took the square root again, then added 7 again, and kept doing this over and over, I came up with two interesting numbers. The numbers are:

$$3.1925824... \quad \text{and} \quad 10.1925824...$$

These numbers are both irrational numbers (they can't be written as simple fractions), and the first number is the square root of the second number. But, the thing that makes them really interesting is that the irrational parts (the part to the right of the decimal) of both numbers are identical. It seemed remarkable to me that there could be two irrational numbers where one is the square root of the other, and yet their values behind the decimal point are identical so that the difference between them is a whole number (which in this case is 7).

Now, I know of one such number that has this property - it is known as the golden ratio; but I didn't know there were other numbers. However, it appears that what I had just done is find a method to create other such numbers, and being in a mood to play with my calculator, I chose the number 2, and started doing the same thing with it. I took the square root of 2, added 2, took the square root again, then added 2 again, etc. After doing this several times, and much to my surprise, I found that the two interesting numbers I was generating were:

$$2.0000... \quad \text{and} \quad 4.0000...$$

These two numbers also have the same properties as my earlier pair of numbers in that the first number is the square root of the second number, and everything to the right of the decimal for both numbers is identical (the difference between them is also a whole number); however, these two numbers are rational (not irrational).

So what was going on here? It was time to get out a pencil and paper and take a closer look at both examples. In the example with the 2 and the 4, I was performing the following sequence of operations with my calculator.

$$2 = \text{sqrt}(2 + \text{sqrt}(2 + \text{sqrt}(2 + \text{sqrt}(2 + \text{sqrt}(2 + \text{sqrt}(2 + ...))))))$$
$$4 = 2 + \text{sqrt}(2 + \text{sqrt}(2 + \text{sqrt}(2 + \text{sqrt}(2 + \text{sqrt}(2 + \text{sqrt}(2 + ...))))))$$

This is an infinitely repeating sequence. One way to understand it, and see what is going on, is to set n equal to the sequence:

$$n = \text{sqrt}(2 + \text{sqrt}(2 + \text{sqrt}(2 + \text{sqrt}(2 + \text{sqrt}(2 + \text{sqrt}(2 + ...))))))$$

And since it is an infinite sequence, we now substitute n anywhere back into the sequence. The easiest place to do this is to leave the first "sqrt(2 + " and substitute n for the rest of the sequence. This reduces our infinitely repeating sequence to something finite and manageable:

$$n = \text{sqrt}(2 + n)$$

Now all we need to do is solve for n. We'll start by squaring both sides of the equation:

$$n^2 = (2 + n)$$

We rearrange this expression, and set it equal to zero to get:

$$n^2 - n - 2 = 0$$

This equation factors to

$$(n - 2)(n + 1) = 0$$

The solutions to this equation are 2 and -1. The number 2 is the positive solution, and that is why it worked for us earlier. Now what happens if we do the same thing with the seven. In this case, I was getting this pair of numbers:

$$3.192582\ldots = \text{sqrt}(7 + \text{sqrt}(7 + \text{sqrt}(7 + \text{sqrt}(7 + \text{sqrt}(7 + \ldots)))))$$
$$10.192582\ldots = 7 + \text{sqrt}(7 + \text{sqrt}(7 + \text{sqrt}(7 + \text{sqrt}(7 + \text{sqrt}(7 + \ldots)))))$$

Again, we'll start by setting n equal to the whole sequence:

$$n = \text{sqrt}(7 + \text{sqrt}(7 + \text{sqrt}(7 + \text{sqrt}(7 + \text{sqrt}(7 + \text{sqrt}(7 + \ldots))))))$$

Then, by substituting n back within itself, we get:

$$n = \text{sqrt}(7 + n)$$

Squaring both sides, and setting everything to zero gives us:

$$n^2 - n - 7 = 0$$

This equation doesn't factor like it did with the 2's. Therefore, we'll use the quadratic formula which gives us a solution for n:

$$n = \frac{1 \pm \sqrt{29}}{2} \quad \text{with the positive solution being } n = 3.1925824\ldots$$

If we consider just the positive result from the quadratic formula, we find that n is equal to 3.1925824... This is the smaller of the two values that we saw at the beginning of this chapter. The larger value can be found by either adding seven to the smaller number, or by squaring the smaller number. (Both options give the same result.)

The Golden Ratio and Our "Square Root of 7" Number

The Golden Ratio appears frequently in mathematics, and more so in art and architecture. Earlier we mentioned that the golden ratio has properties that are similar to our "square root of 7" number. In this section we'll take a closer look at the Golden Ratio and some of its properties.

The Golden Ratio is equal to:

$$\text{Golden Ratio} = \frac{1 + \sqrt{5}}{2} \qquad \text{which is approximately} = 1.6180339...$$

If we take the golden ratio and square it, we get the same number as if we had taken the golden ratio and added one to it. In other words:

$$(1.6180339 ...)^2 = 1 + 1.6180339...$$

Notice also that with this number, the numbers to the right of the decimal place are the same in both cases. The golden ratio has an additional property that if we take its reciprocal, the resulting number is equal to the golden ratio minus 1:

$$\frac{1}{1.6180339...} = 1.6180339... - 1 = 0.6180339...$$

Again, the numbers to the right of the decimal place are identical in each case. And it turns out that the number we discovered has a similar property. If we take the number 3.1925824... and subtract the three; then the resulting number and its reciprocal have identical numbers to the right of the decimal place.

$$\frac{1}{0.1925824...} = 5.1925824...$$

And there are still other similarities between our original number and the golden ratio. Remember that we generated our number by taking the square root of seven, adding seven, then taking the square root again, and so forth. We can use this same method to generate the golden ratio. First we start with one, and take the square root. Then we add one and take the square root again. Continuing this process gives us the golden ratio:

$$\text{Golden Ratio} = \text{sqrt}(1 + \text{sqrt}(1 + \text{sqrt}(1 + \text{sqrt}(1 + \text{sqrt}(1 + ...)))))$$

And there are still other ways to express these two numbers. If we write the Golden Ratio as a continuous fractions, we have:

$$\text{Golden Ratio:} \quad 1.6180339... = 1 + \cfrac{1}{1 + \cfrac{1}{1 + \cfrac{1}{1 + \cfrac{1}{1 + ...}}}}$$

Using the short hand method for writing continuous fractions gives us:

$$1.6180339... = [1; 1, 1, 1, 1, 1, 1, ...]$$

And now, if we go back to the beginning of this chapter and look at our square root of 7 number, and write it as a continuous fraction, we have:

$$3.1925824... = 3 + \cfrac{1}{5 + \cfrac{1}{5 + \cfrac{1}{5 + \cfrac{1}{5 + ...}}}}$$

Which can be rewritten as :

$$3.1925824... = [3; 5, 5, 5, 5, 5, 5, ...]$$

Additional Interesting Irrational Numbers

So, are there more numbers that are similar to these two numbers? To some degree we can answer that question with a yes. The following is a listing of more of these numbers, along with the repeated square root method of generating them. Notice that the first of these numbers is the golden ratio.

```
1.61803399... = sqrt(1  + sqrt(1  + sqrt(1  + sqrt(1  + sqrt(1  + ... )))))
2             = sqrt(2  + sqrt(2  + sqrt(2  + sqrt(2  + sqrt(2  + ... )))))
2.30277564... = sqrt(3  + sqrt(3  + sqrt(3  + sqrt(3  + sqrt(3  + ... )))))
2.56155281... = sqrt(4  + sqrt(4  + sqrt(4  + sqrt(4  + sqrt(4  + ... )))))
2.79128785... = sqrt(5  + sqrt(5  + sqrt(5  + sqrt(5  + sqrt(5  + ... )))))
3             = sqrt(6  + sqrt(6  + sqrt(6  + sqrt(6  + sqrt(6  + ... )))))
3.19258240... = sqrt(7  + sqrt(7  + sqrt(7  + sqrt(7  + sqrt(7  + ... )))))
3.37228132... = sqrt(8  + sqrt(8  + sqrt(8  + sqrt(8  + sqrt(8  + ... )))))
3.54138126... = sqrt(9  + sqrt(9  + sqrt(9  + sqrt(9  + sqrt(9  + ... )))))
3.70156212... = sqrt(10 + sqrt(10 + sqrt(10 + sqrt(10 + sqrt(10 + ... )))))
3.85410197... = sqrt(11 + sqrt(11 + sqrt(11 + sqrt(11 + sqrt(11 + ... )))))
4             = sqrt(12 + sqrt(12 + sqrt(12 + sqrt(12 + sqrt(12 + ... )))))
4.14005494... = sqrt(13 + sqrt(13 + sqrt(13 + sqrt(13 + sqrt(13 + ... )))))
4.27491722... = sqrt(14 + sqrt(14 + sqrt(14 + sqrt(14 + sqrt(14 + ... )))))
4.40512484... = sqrt(15 + sqrt(15 + sqrt(15 + sqrt(15 + sqrt(15 + ... )))))
4.53112887... = sqrt(16 + sqrt(16 + sqrt(16 + sqrt(16 + sqrt(16 + ... )))))
4.65331193... = sqrt(17 + sqrt(17 + sqrt(17 + sqrt(17 + sqrt(17 + ... )))))
4.77200187... = sqrt(18 + sqrt(18 + sqrt(18 + sqrt(18 + sqrt(18 + ... )))))
4.88748219... = sqrt(19 + sqrt(19 + sqrt(19 + sqrt(19 + sqrt(19 + ... )))))
5             = sqrt(20 + sqrt(20 + sqrt(20 + sqrt(20 + sqrt(20 + ... )))))
5.10977222... = sqrt(21 + sqrt(21 + sqrt(21 + sqrt(21 + sqrt(21 + ... )))))
5.21699056... = sqrt(22 + sqrt(22 + sqrt(22 + sqrt(22 + sqrt(22 + ... )))))
5.32182538... = sqrt(23 + sqrt(23 + sqrt(23 + sqrt(23 + sqrt(23 + ... )))))
5.42442890... = sqrt(24 + sqrt(24 + sqrt(24 + sqrt(24 + sqrt(24 + ... )))))
5.52493781... = sqrt(25 + sqrt(25 + sqrt(25 + sqrt(25 + sqrt(25 + ... )))))
5.62347538... = sqrt(26 + sqrt(26 + sqrt(26 + sqrt(26 + sqrt(26 + ... )))))
5.72015325... = sqrt(27 + sqrt(27 + sqrt(27 + sqrt(27 + sqrt(27 + ... )))))
5.81507290... = sqrt(28 + sqrt(28 + sqrt(28 + sqrt(28 + sqrt(28 + ... )))))
5.90832691... = sqrt(29 + sqrt(29 + sqrt(29 + sqrt(29 + sqrt(29 + ... )))))
6             = sqrt(30 + sqrt(30 + sqrt(30 + sqrt(30 + sqrt(30 + ... )))))
```

Table 7.1   Repeated square roots of the numbers 1 through 30.

In the table above, the number on the left of the equal sign has the amazing property that if you add the integer used to create it, the result is equal to the square of that number. Another way to look at this relationship would be to say that we let the integer part of the number be represented by some letter such as r, s, or t, and the decimal part of the number to be represented by the letter y, then these numbers have a pattern that looks like this:

$$(r.y)^2 \ = \ s + r.y \quad \text{(which is equal to t.y)} \quad \text{and} \quad \sqrt{(t.y)} \ = \ r.y$$

Here is this relationship shown (in the following listing) with the actual numbers:

$(1.61803399...)^2 \ = \ 1 + 1.61803399...$ and $\sqrt{(2.61803399...)} \ = \ 1.61803399...$

$(2.30277564...)^2 \ = \ 3 + 2.30277564...$ and $\sqrt{(5.30277564...)} \ = \ 2.30277564...$
$(2.56155281...)^2 \ = \ 4 + 2.56155281...$ and $\sqrt{(6.56155281...)} \ = \ 2.56155281...$
$(2.79128785...)^2 \ = \ 5 + 2.79128785...$ and $\sqrt{(7.79128785...)} \ = \ 2.79128785...$

$(3.19258240...)^2 \ = \ 7 + 3.19258240...$ and $\sqrt{(10.19258240...)} \ = \ 3.19258240...$
$(3.37228132...)^2 \ = \ 8 + 3.37228132...$ and $\sqrt{(11.37228132...)} \ = \ 3.37228132...$
$(3.54138126...)^2 \ = \ 9 + 3.54138126...$ and $\sqrt{(12.54138126...)} \ = \ 3.54138126...$
$(3.70156212...)^2 \ = \ 10 + 3.70156212...$ and $\sqrt{(13.70156212...)} \ = \ 3.70156212...$
$(3.85410197...)^2 \ = \ 11 + 3.85410197...$ and $\sqrt{(14.85410197...)} \ = \ 3.85410197...$

$(4.14005494...)^2 \ = \ 13 + 4.14005494...$ and $\sqrt{(17.14005494...)} \ = \ 4.14005494...$
$(4.27491722...)^2 \ = \ 14 + 4.27491722...$ and $\sqrt{(18.27491722...)} \ = \ 4.27491722...$
$(4.40512484...)^2 \ = \ 15 + 4.40512484...$ and $\sqrt{(19.40512484...)} \ = \ 4.40512484...$
$(4.53112887...)^2 \ = \ 16 + 4.53112887...$ and $\sqrt{(20.53112887...)} \ = \ 4.53112887...$
$(4.65331193...)^2 \ = \ 17 + 4.65331193...$ and $\sqrt{(21.65331193...)} \ = \ 4.65331193...$
$(4.77200187...)^2 \ = \ 18 + 4.77200187...$ and $\sqrt{(22.77200187...)} \ = \ 4.77200187...$
$(4.88748219...)^2 \ = \ 19 + 4.88748219...$ and $\sqrt{(23.88748219...)} \ = \ 4.88748219...$

$(5.10977222...)^2 \ = \ 21 + 5.10977222...$ and $\sqrt{(26.10977222...)} \ = \ 5.10977222...$
$(5.21699056...)^2 \ = \ 22 + 5.21699056...$ and $\sqrt{(27.21699056...)} \ = \ 5.21699056...$
$(5.32182538...)^2 \ = \ 23 + 5.32182538...$ and $\sqrt{(28.32182538...)} \ = \ 5.32182538...$
$(5.42442890...)^2 \ = \ 24 + 5.42442890...$ and $\sqrt{(29.42442890...)} \ = \ 5.42442890...$
$(5.52493781...)^2 \ = \ 25 + 5.52493781...$ and $\sqrt{(30.52493781...)} \ = \ 5.52493781...$
$(5.62347538...)^2 \ = \ 26 + 5.62347538...$ and $\sqrt{(31.62347538...)} \ = \ 5.62347538...$
$(5.72015325...)^2 \ = \ 27 + 5.72015325...$ and $\sqrt{(32.72015325...)} \ = \ 5.72015325...$
$(5.81507290...)^2 \ = \ 28 + 5.81507290...$ and $\sqrt{(33.81507290...)} \ = \ 5.81507290...$
$(5.90832691...)^2 \ = \ 29 + 5.90832691...$ and $\sqrt{(34.90832691...)} \ = \ 5.90832691...$

Table 7.2   Relationship between the squared and square root numbers.

The table above, for example, shows that if you took the number generated from the square root of 5, (which is 2.79128...) and add 5 to it, the result would be 7.79128... And the square root of 7.79128... is equal to 2.79128... (which is right back to where we started).

A few of these numbers have the added property that if you remove the integer part of the number and then take the reciprocal, the resulting part of the number to the right of the decimal place will be identical to the original number. For example, take the number 2.30277... (which is generated from the square roots of 3's), and remove the leading 2.

The resulting number and its reciprocal have identical values to the right of the decimal point:

$$1/(0.30277...) = 3.30277...$$

This property appears to work with the numbers found right after the whole numbers in the first table shown above. Therefore, it also works with the numbers 3.19258... (which is generated from the square roots of 7's) and 4.14005... (which is generated from the square roots of 13's):

$$1/(0.19258...) = 5.19258...$$
$$1/(0.14005...) = 7.14005...$$

Another way to consider these numbers is to look at their continuous fractions. Doing so shows us other interesting patterns and similarities.

1.61803399...	= sqrt(1 + sqrt(1 + ...))	= [1; 1, 1, 1, 1, 1, 1, 1, 1, 1, 1, ...]
2	= sqrt(2 + sqrt(2 + ...))	
2.30277564...	= sqrt(3 + sqrt(3 + ...))	= [2; 3, 3, 3, 3, 3, 3, 3, 3, 3, 3, ...]
2.56155281...	= sqrt(4 + sqrt(4 + ...))	= [2; 1, 1, 3, 1, 1, 3, 1, 1, 3, 1, ...]
2.79128785...	= sqrt(5 + sqrt(5 + ...))	= [2; 1, 3, 1, 3, 1, 3, 1, 3, 1, 3, ...]
3	= sqrt(6 + sqrt(6 + ...))	
3.19258240...	= sqrt(7 + sqrt(7 + ...))	= [3; 5, 5, 5, 5, 5, 5, 5, 5, 5, 5, ...]
3.37228132...	= sqrt(8 + sqrt(8 + ...))	= [3; 2, 1, 2, 5, 2, 1, 2, 5, 2, 1, ...]
3.54138126...	= sqrt(9 + sqrt(9 + ...))	= [3; 1, 1, 5, 1, 1, 5, 1, 1, 5, 1, ...]
3.70156212...	= sqrt(10 + sqrt(10 + ...))	= [3; 1, 2, 2, 1, 5, 1, 2, 2, 1, 5, ...]
3.85410197...	= sqrt(11 + sqrt(11 + ...))	= [3; 1, 5, 1, 5, 1, 5, 1, 5, 1, 5, ...]
4	= sqrt(12 + sqrt(12 + ...))	
4.14005494...	= sqrt(13 + sqrt(13 + ...))	= [4; 7, 7, 7, 7, 7, 7, 7, 7, 7, 7, ...]
4.27491722...	= sqrt(14 + sqrt(14 + ...))	= [4; 3, 1, 1, 1, 3, 7, 3, 1, 1, 1, ...]
4.40512484...	= sqrt(15 + sqrt(15 + ...))	= [4; 2, 2, 7, 2, 2, 7, 2, 2, 7, 2, ...]
4.53112887...	= sqrt(16 + sqrt(16 + ...))	= [4; 1, 1, 7, 1, 1, 7, 1, 1, 7, 1, ...]
4.65331193...	= sqrt(17 + sqrt(17 + ...))	= [4; 1, 1, 1, 7, 1, 1, 1, 7, 1, 1, ...]
4.77200187...	= sqrt(18 + sqrt(18 + ...))	= [4; 1, 3, 2, 1, 1, 2, 3, 1, 7, 1, ...]
4.88748219...	= sqrt(19 + sqrt(19 + ...))	= [4; 1, 7, 1, 7, 1, 7, 1, 7, 1, 7, ...]
5	= sqrt(20 + sqrt(20 + ...))	
5.10977222...	= sqrt(21 + sqrt(21 + ...))	= [5; 9, 9, 9, 9, 9, 9, 9, 9, 9, 9, ...]
5.21699056...	= sqrt(22 + sqrt(22 + ...))	= [5; 4, 1, 1, 1, 1, 4, 9, 4, 1, 1, ...]
5.32182538...	= sqrt(23 + sqrt(23 + ...))	= [5; 3, 9, 3, 9, 3, 9, 3, 9, 3, 9, ...]
5.42442890...	= sqrt(24 + sqrt(24 + ...))	= [5; 2, 2, 1, 4, 4, 1, 2, 2, 9, 2, ...]
5.52493781...	= sqrt(25 + sqrt(25 + ...))	= [5; 1, 1, 9, 1, 1, 9, 1, 1, 9, 1, ...]
5.62347538...	= sqrt(26 + sqrt(26 + ...))	= [5; 1, 1, 1, 1, 1, 9, 1, 1, 1, 1, ...]
5.72015325...	= sqrt(27 + sqrt(27 + ...))	= [5; 1, 2, 1, 1, 2, 1, 9, 1, 2, 1, ...]
5.81507290...	= sqrt(28 + sqrt(28 + ...))	= [5; 1, 4, 2, 2, 4, 1, 9, 1, 4, 2, ...]
5.90832691...	= sqrt(29 + sqrt(29 + ...))	= [5; 1, 9, 1, 9, 1, 9, 1, 9, 1, 9, ...]
6	= sqrt(30 + sqrt(30 + ...))	

Table 7.3 Continuous fraction representations for the repeated square roots of the numbers 1 through 30.

The Golden Ratio Raised to Higher Powers

As interesting as these other numbers are, the golden ratio still reigns supreme; so, let's take a look at a few of the other properties of the Golden Ratio. Earlier we saw that if we took the golden ratio and squared it, or if we took its reciprocal, that in both cases, the values to the right of the decimal place are identical. The reciprocal is equal to the golden ratio minus 1, and the square is equal to the golden ratio plus 1.

The reciprocal of the golden ratio = 0.618033989...
The golden ratio = 1.618033989...
The golden ratio squared = 2.618033989...

The golden ratio has some other interesting properties when raised to higher powers. For example, let's take the golden ratio and cube it, and compare it with the reciprocal of its cube. For both of these values, the numbers to the right of the decimal place are identical.

$$(1.618033989...)^3 = 4.236067977...$$
$$1/(1.618033989...)^3 = 0.236067977...$$

In fact, if we take the golden ratio and raise it to any odd power, and then take the reciprocal of that number, the values to the right of the decimal in both numbers will be the same. Here we have the golden ratio raised to the 5th and 7th powers, along with their respective reciprocals. First, the golden ratio raised to the 5th power.

$$(1.618033989...)^5 = 11.09016994...$$
$$1/(1.618033989...)^5 = 0.09016994...$$

And here is the golden ratio raised to the 7th power:

$$(1.618033989...)^7 = 29.03444185...$$
$$1/(1.618033989...)^7 = 0.03444185...$$

The even powers of the golden ratio have a similar relationship. When raising the golden ratio to an even power, the digits to the right of the decimal are identical to the reciprocal of this number subtracted from one.

$$(1.618033989...)^2 = 2.618033989...$$
$$1 - 1/(1.618033989...)^2 = 0.618033989...$$

$$(1.618033989...)^4 = 6.8541019...$$
$$1 - 1/(1.618033989...)^4 = 0.8541019...$$

$$(1.618033989...)^6 = 17.9442719...$$
$$1 - 1/(1.618033989...)^6 = 0.9442719...$$

A variation of these two relationships takes the golden ratio and raises it to successive powers. Where the powers are odd, we'll subtract the reciprocal of that value; and where the powers are even we'll add the reciprocal. In each case we get an integer result.

$$(1.618033989...)^1 - 1/(1.618033989...)^1 = 1$$
$$(1.618033989...)^2 + 1/(1.618033989...)^2 = 3$$
$$(1.618033989...)^3 - 1/(1.618033989...)^3 = 4$$
$$(1.618033989...)^4 + 1/(1.618033989...)^4 = 7$$
$$(1.618033989...)^5 - 1/(1.618033989...)^5 = 11$$
$$..., \text{etc.}$$

The numbers 1, 3, 4, 7, 11, ... are known as Lucas numbers. Lucas numbers start with the numbers 1 and 3, and then each succeeding number is equal to the sum of the two preceding numbers. (Lucas numbers are very closely related to Fibonacci numbers; and several patterns and relationships with both of these numbers will be considered in the following chapter.)

The golden ratio has one other interesting relationship that we will consider. Take the golden ratio and raise it to some power. Add to that the golden ratio raised to the next power, and the sum of these two numbers is equal to the golden ratio raised to the next power still. For example:

$$\begin{array}{lll} (1.618033989...)^2 & & 2.618033989... \\ + (1.618033989...)^3 & = & + \;\; 4.236067977... \\ \hline (1.618033989...)^4 & & 6.854101966... \end{array}$$

As can be seen in the example above, we start with the golden ratio raised to the second power. We add to that the golden ratio raised to the third power; and the sum of these two numbers is equal to the golden ratio raised to the fourth power. And this will work with any two consecutive powers of the golden ratio. Here is another example:

$$\begin{array}{lll} (1.618033989...)^{23} & & 64079.00001561... \\ + (1.618033989...)^{24} & = & + \;\; 103681.99999036... \\ \hline (1.618033989...)^{25} & & 167761.00000597... \end{array}$$

This time we started with the golden ratio raised to the 23rd power and added to it the golden ratio raised to the 24th power, and our result is equal to the golden ratio raised to the 25th power.

Chapter 8
Fibonacci and Lucas Numbers

Fibonacci Numbers

Fibonacci numbers are full of interesting patterns and relationships. To create a Fibonacci number sequence, start with the numbers 0 and 1. Add these together to get a second 1. Now, each of the following numbers in the sequence are created by adding together the previous two numbers of the sequence. To get the next Fibonacci number, add the 1 and 1 to get 2. Continue the process by adding 1 and 2 to get 3, etc.. The first 10 numbers of the sequence are:

$$0, 1, 1, 2, 3, 5, 8, 13, 21, 34$$

In the sequence above, each number is the sum of the two number before it. In this chapter we will use F_n to represent Fibonacci numbers. Specifically, the n is a subscript that will denote the nth Fibonacci number. This way we can specifically identify which Fibonacci number we are looking at. Having defined this notation, we can use a formula to show that any Fibonacci number is equal to the sum of the two preceding Fibonacci numbers:

$$F_n = F_{n-1} + F_{n-2}$$

The following is a list of the Fibonacci numbers F_0 through F_{18}:

$$0, 1, 1, 2, 3, 5, 8, 13, 21, 34, 55, 89, 144, 233, 377, 610, 987, 1597$$

Not all Fibonacci numbers will divide evenly into other Fibonacci numbers. Notice that if we start with the 2, every third number in the sequence is even (or divisible by 2). Likewise, starting with the 3, every fourth number is divisible by three; and starting with the 5, every fifth number is divisible by five, and starting with the 8, every sixth number is divisible by eight. We continue this way with the rest of the Fibonacci sequence.

```
every 3rd number: x  x  2  x  x  8  x  x 34  x  x 144 x  x 610 x  x ...
every 4th number: x  x  x  3  x  x  x 21  x  x  x 144 x  x  x 987 x ...
every 5th number: x  x  x  x  5  x  x  x  x 55  x  x  x 610 x  x ...
every 6th number: x  x  x  x  x  8  x  x  x  x  x 144 x  x  x  x  x ...
                         etc.,
```

In the example above, each row is a listing of the Fibonacci sequence. The x's are place holders that represent other Fibonacci numbers in the sequence. Here we're only showing the numbers that illustrate the point.

From this we can say that F_m will divide evenly into F_n if the subscript m divides evenly into the subscript n. For example, F_6 (which is 8) will divide evenly into F_{12} (which is 144) because the subscript, 6, divides evenly into the subscript 12.

We can even go one step further and say that the greatest common divisor between two Fibonacci numbers, F_m and F_n, will be a Fibonacci number, and it will be the Fibonacci number that has the greatest common divisor between the subscripts m and n. As an example, the greatest common divisor between F_8 and F_{12} is equal to the Fibonacci number that has the greatest common divisor between the subscripts 8 and 12, which is 4. Therefore, F_4 is the greatest common divisor between F_8 and F_{12}.

$$\gcd(F_8, F_{12}) = \gcd(21, 144) = F_4 = 3$$

Sums of Fibonacci numbers also have interesting relationships. If we take any six consecutive Fibonacci numbers and add them together, the sum of these six numbers is equal to 4 times the fifth number. In a similar manner, the sum of any ten consecutive Fibonacci numbers is equal to 11 times the seventh number.

Six Consecutive Fibonacci Numbers		**Ten Consecutive Fibonacci Numbers**	
2		5	
3		8	
5		13	
8		21	
13	13	34	
+ 21	x 4	55	
52	52	89	
		144	
		233	89
		+ 377	x 11
		979	979

Another property of the Fibonacci numbers has to do with how numbers from the sequence relate to each other. If you take any Fibonacci number and square it; then take the preceding and following numbers and multiply them together; the difference between these two products will be plus or minus one. Let's look at the Fibonacci numbers 3, 5 and 8. Take the middle number, 5, and square it to get 25. Now multiply together the two numbers on either side of the 5. Those numbers are 3 and 8, and their product is 24. The difference between 25 and 24 is one. If we write this as a formula, it is:

$$(F_{n-1})(F_{n+1}) - F_n^2 = (-1)^n$$

As the formula shows, selecting the second, fourth, sixth, … Fibonacci number will cause the product of the two surrounding numbers to be one more than the number squared; while selecting the first, third, fifth, … Fibonacci number will cause the product of the two surrounding numbers to be one less than the number squared.

And yet another property of these numbers is that we sum the first n Fibonacci numbers together, add one, and this will be equal to the n+2 Fibonacci number. In other words, we can say that given the Fibonacci sequence:

$$1, 1, 2, 3, 5, 8, 13, 21, 34, 55, 89, 144, 233, 377, 610, 987, 1597$$

The following relationship is true:

$$
\begin{aligned}
(1+1) + 1 &= 3 \\
(1+1+2) + 1 &= 5 \\
(1+1+2+3) + 1 &= 8 \\
(1+1+2+3+5) + 1 &= 13 \\
(1+1+2+3+5+8) + 1 &= 21 \\
(1+1+2+3+5+8+13) + 1 &= 34 \\
(1+1+2+3+5+8+13+21) + 1 &= 55 \\
\ldots \text{etc.},&
\end{aligned}
$$

And we can sum this up in the following way:

$$ F_{n+2} = (F_n + F_{n-1} + F_{n-2} + \ldots + F_2 + F_1) + 1 $$

At the beginning of this chapter we defined a Fibonacci number to be the sum of the two previous Fibonacci numbers, or in other words: $F_n = F_{n-1} + F_{n-2}$. Actually, there are many other ways to mathematically define Fibonacci numbers. For example, we take the second pervious and third previous Fibonacci numbers, multiply the second by two and add it to the third, and that will give us the nth Fibonacci number.

$$ F_n = 2F_{n-2} + F_{n-3} $$

Similarly, we can take the third previous and fourth previous Fibonacci numbers and use them to create the nth Fibonacci number using this relation:

$$ F_n = 3F_{n-3} + 2F_{n-4} $$

The following table shows these and other pairs of coefficients that can be multiplied to previous pairs of Fibonacci numbers which can then be added together to generate the nth Fibonacci number.

	F_{n-1}	F_{n-2}	F_{n-3}	F_{n-4}	F_{n-5}	F_{n-6}	F_{n-7}	F_{n-8}
$F_n =$	1	1						
$F_n =$		2	1					
$F_n =$			3	2				
$F_n =$				5	3			
$F_n =$					8	5		
$F_n =$						13	8	
$F_n =$							21	13

Table 8.1   Coefficients used on preceding Fibonacci numbers to generate the nth Fibonacci number.

Again, the numbers in the table are the coefficients that would be used with their corresponding Fibonacci number. For example, if we look at the third row in the table, we find the coefficients 3 and 2 under the headings F_{n-3} and F_{n-4} respectively. With these coefficients and their respective Fibonacci numbers we generate the following formula.

$$ F_n = 3F_{n-3} + 2F_{n-4} $$

In other words, we can take an example and say that the 10th Fibonacci number is equal to the sum of three times the 7th Fibonacci number and two times the 6th Fibonacci number.

$$F_{10} = 3F_7 + 2F_6$$

Which is:

$$55 = 3(13) + 2(8)$$

By listing the formulas shown in the table, we can more easily see a Fibonacci pattern between the several formulas themselves. Here is the listing we get from the table:

$$F_n = 1F_{n-1} + 1F_{n-2}$$
$$F_n = 2F_{n-2} + 1F_{n-3}$$
$$F_n = 3F_{n-3} + 2F_{n-4}$$
$$F_n = 5F_{n-4} + 3F_{n-5}$$
$$F_n = 8F_{n-5} + 5F_{n-6}$$
$$F_n = 13F_{n-6} + 8F_{n-7}$$
$$F_n = 21F_{n-7} + 13F_{n-8}$$

Showing the formulas this way allows to quickly see the Fibonacci pattern that the coefficients make with each other. And there are still many other ways to create the nth Fibonacci number. The following table shows a series of relationships with fractional coefficients.

	F_{n-1}	F_{n-2}	F_{n-3}	F_{n-4}	F_{n-5}	F_{n-6}	F_{n-7}	F_{n-8}
$F_n =$	3/2			1/2				
$F_n =$		5/2			1/2			
$F_n =$			8/2			2/2		
$F_n =$				13/2			3/2	
$F_n =$					21/2			5/2

Table 8.2   Fractional coefficients used on preceding Fibonacci numbers to generate the nth Fibonacci number.

As with the first table, the numbers in the table above are the coefficients that would be used with their corresponding Fibonacci numbers to generate the nth Fibonacci number. Again, if we look at the fifth row, we find the coefficients twenty one-halves and five-halves under the headings F_{n-5} and F_{n-8} respectively. With these coefficients and their respective Fibonacci numbers we generate the following formula.

$$F_n = \frac{21F_{n-5}}{2} + \frac{5F_{n-8}}{2}$$

And again, we see the series of Fibonacci numbers as a part of the coefficients – in this case, they are the numerators of the fractions. The Fibonacci sequence is generated as we go down the table.

Fibonacci Number Formulas
Until now, we've looked at formulas that add a multiple of a Fibonacci number to some other multiple of a Fibonacci number with the result being a third Fibonacci number.

There are also several formulas that take the products or powers of Fibonacci numbers and obtain other Fibonacci numbers. Without wishing to belabor the point, we'll list several formulas along with a few examples for each formula.

Formula 1: $F_n^2 + F_{n+1}^2 = F_{2n+1}$
Examples:
$$3^2 + 5^2 = 34$$
$$5^2 + 8^2 = 89$$
$$13^2 + 21^2 = 610$$
. . ., etc.

Formula 2: $F_n^2 - F_{n-2}^2 = F_{2n-2}$
Examples:
$$5^2 - 2^2 = 21$$
$$8^2 - 3^2 = 55$$
$$13^2 - 5^2 = 144$$
. . ., etc.

Formula 3: $(F_n)(F_{n-1}) + (F_n)(F_{n+1}) = F_{2n}$
Examples:
$$(8)(5) + (8)(13) = 144$$
$$(13)(8) + (13)(21) = 377$$
$$(21)(13) + (21)(34) = 987$$
. . ., etc.

Formula 4: $(F_n)(F_{n+1}) - (F_{n-1})(F_{n-2}) = F_{2n-1}$
Examples:
$$(8)(13) - (5)(3) = 89$$
$$(13)(21) - (8)(5) = 233$$
$$(21)(34) - (13)(8) = 610$$
. . ., etc.

Formula 5: $(F_{n-1})(F_n)(F_{n+1}) \pm F_n = F_n^3$
Examples:
$$(2)(3)(5) - 3 = 3^3 = 27$$
$$(3)(5)(8) + 5 = 5^3 = 125$$
$$(5)(8)(13) - 8 = 8^3 = 512$$
. . ., etc.

Formula 6: $F_n^3 + F_{n-1}^3 - F_{n-2}^3 = F_{3n-3}$
Examples:
$$3^3 + 2^3 - 1^3 = 34$$
$$5^3 + 3^3 - 2^3 = 144$$
$$8^3 + 5^3 - 3^3 = 610$$
. . ., etc.

Formula 7: $(F_{n-2})(F_{n-1})(F_n)(F_{n+1})(F_{n+2}) + F_n = F_n^5$
Examples:
$$(2)(3)(5)(8)(13) + 5 = 5^5 = 3125$$
$$(3)(5)(8)(13)(21) + 8 = 8^5 = 32768$$
$$(5)(8)(13)(21)(34) + 13 = 13^5 = 371293$$
. . ., etc.

Lucas Numbers

Several variations of the Fibonacci sequence can be created from the Fibonacci sequence itself. One of these variations takes the first and third numbers from the Fibonacci sequence and adds them together to generate the first number of the new sequence. The second number is equal to the sum of the second and fourth Fibonacci numbers. The third number is equal to the sum of the third and fifth Fibonacci numbers, and so on. These numbers are called Lucas numbers. If we were to write this as a formula, we would have:

$$L_n = F_n + F_{n+2}$$

Even though our formula is based on Fibonacci numbers, we could also say that Lucas numbers use the numbers 1 and 3 as their initial numbers, and then the sequence is generated in the same way as Fibonacci numbers with the next number in the sequence equal to the sum of the two preceding numbers.

$$L_n = L_{n-1} + L_{n-2}$$

The following is a listing that compares the first fifteen Fibonacci numbers with the first fifteen Lucas numbers:

Fibonacci numbers: 1, 1, 2, 3, 5, 8, 13, 21, 34, 55, 89, 144, 233, 377, 610, ...
Lucas numbers: 1, 3, 4, 7, 11, 18, 29, 47, 76, 123, 199, 322, 521, 843, 1364, ...

Even though Lucas numbers are created in the same way as Fibonacci numbers, they don't quite have the same properties although many properties are very similar. For example, take any Lucas number and square it. Then take the preceding and following Lucas numbers and multiple them together. The number squared and the product of the two surrounding numbers will always have a difference of plus or minus five. With the Fibonacci numbers the difference was plus or minus one.

$$(L_{n-1})(L_{n+1}) - L_n^2 = 5(-1)^{n-1}$$

And when we sum the first n Lucas numbers together, we need to add three to this sum to get the n+2 Lucas number.

$$
\begin{aligned}
(1 + 3) + 3 &= 7 \\
(1 + 3 + 4) + 3 &= 11 \\
(1 + 3 + 4 + 7) + 3 &= 18 \\
(1 + 3 + 4 + 7 + 11) + 3 &= 29 \\
(1 + 3 + 4 + 7 + 11 + 18) + 3 &= 47 \\
(1 + 3 + 4 + 7 + 11 + 18 + 29) + 3 &= 76
\end{aligned}
$$
... etc.,

And we sum this up in the following way:

$$L_{n+2} = (L_n + L_{n-1} + L_{n-2} + \ldots + L_2 + L_1) + 3$$

Another property that Fibonacci and Lucas numbers share is the property that the sum of six consecutive Lucas numbers is equal to 4 times the fifth number; and the sum of ten consecutive Lucas numbers is equal to 11 times the seventh number. Again, it doesn't matter where we start in the sequence, as long as we select consecutive Lucas numbers, we see that this pattern will hold true (and at the end of this chapter we'll see why). Here is an example of the sum of six consecutive Lucas Numbers:

Six Consecutive
Lucas Numbers

4	
7	
11	
18	
29	29
+ 47	x 4
116	116

There are also several different ways to define Lucas numbers. Earlier in this chapter we created a table showing several different possibilities of generating a given Fibonacci number from coefficients multiplied to previous Fibonacci numbers. We can use this same type of table to show the various options we have for generating Lucas numbers.

	L_{n-1}	L_{n-2}	L_{n-3}	L_{n-4}	L_{n-5}	L_{n-6}	L_{n-7}	L_{n-8}
L_n =	1	1						
L_n =		2	1					
L_n =			3	2				
L_n =				5	3			
L_n =					8	5		
L_n =						13	8	
L_n =							21	13

Table 8.3   Coefficients used on preceding Lucas numbers to generate the nth Lucas number.

Just as we saw with the Fibonacci table (earlier in this chapter), the table above illustrates the following Lucas number formulas.

$$L_n = 1L_{n-1} + 1L_{n-2}$$
$$L_n = 2L_{n-2} + 1L_{n-3}$$
$$L_n = 3L_{n-3} + 2L_{n-4}$$
$$L_n = 5L_{n-4} + 3L_{n-5}$$
$$L_n = 8L_{n-5} + 5L_{n-6}$$
$$L_n = 13L_{n-6} + 8L_{n-7}$$
$$L_n = 21L_{n-7} + 13L_{n-8}$$

An interesting characteristic of the table above is that even though we are creating Lucas numbers, the coefficients within these formulas are still Fibonacci numbers. However, these formulas make sense because the Lucas numbers are created in the same way as the Fibonacci numbers.

And it doesn't stop there. The second table that we saw earlier in this chapter for Fibonacci numbers also works for Lucas numbers. Here we repeat it again, but this time as they define Lucas numbers:

	L_{n-1}	L_{n-2}	L_{n-3}	L_{n-4}	L_{n-5}	L_{n-6}	L_{n-7}	L_{n-8}
$L_n =$	3/2			½				
$L_n =$		5/2			½			
$L_n =$			8/2			2/2		
$L_n =$				13/2			3/2	
$L_n =$					21/2			5/2

Table 8.4   The same fractional coefficients can be used on preceding Lucas numbers to generate the nth Lucas number.

The two tables above show that there are many ways to create the nth Lucas number (just as there are with the Fibonacci numbers).

Lucas Number Formulas

In spite of the many similarities between Fibonacci numbers and Lucas numbers, the similarities end when we begin to consider the formulas. The formulas that we saw earlier in this chapter with the Fibonacci numbers don't work for the Lucas numbers, but Lucas numbers still have some interesting relationships of their own. The following listing shows four related formulas:

Formula 1: $(L_n)(L_{n+1}) = L_{2n+1} + ((-1)^n)L_1$
Examples: 3 * 4   =   11 + 1
                4 * 7   =   29 - 1
                7 * 11 =   76 + 1
                11 * 18 =   199 - 1
                . . ., etc.

Formula 2: $(L_n)(L_{n+2}) = L_{2n+2} + ((-1)^n)L_2$
Examples: 3 * 7   =   18 + 3
                4 * 11 =   47 - 3
                7 * 18 =   123 + 3
                11 * 29 =   322 - 3
                . . ., etc.

Formula 3: $(L_n)(L_{n+3}) = L_{2n+3} + ((-1)^n)L_3$
Examples: 3 * 11 =   29 + 4
                4 * 18 =   76 - 4
                7 * 29 =   199 + 4
                11 * 47 =   521 - 4
                . . ., etc.

Formula 4: $(L_n)(L_{n+4}) = L_{2n+4} + ((-1)^n)L_4$
Examples: 3 * 18 =   47 + 7
                4 * 29 =   123 - 7
                7 * 47 =   322 + 7
                11 * 76 =   843 - 7
                . . ., etc.

Other Number Sequences

Fibonacci and Lucas numbers are built in the same way (each number in the sequence is equal to the sum of the two preceding numbers) and for this reason we saw in many of the examples above that they share several properties and characteristics that were either identical or at least similar to each other. Yet, as we have seen with the formulas, they also have several properties that are different between the two, and only unique to themselves.

However, one property that will work on any sequence that is created like a Fibonacci or Lucas sequence is that the sum of six consecutive numbers will always be equal to four times the fifth number; and the sum of any ten consecutive numbers will always be equal to eleven times the seventh number. We can easily show this with a simple proof.

We'll start by selecting two random numbers, a and b. Therefore, the third number is equal to a + b, and the next number is equal to a + 2b. Each time we add the two previous numbers together to generate the next number. The following is a listing of the first six numbers in this sequence.

$$a, \quad b, \quad a+b, \quad a+2b, \quad 2a+3b, \quad 3a+5b$$

Now when we add these numbers together, we get the following total:

$$
\begin{array}{r}
a \\
b \\
a + b \\
a + 2b \\
2a + 3b \\
+ \; 3a + 5b \\
\hline
8a + 12b
\end{array}
$$
which is equal to: $4(2a + 3b)$ or 4 times the 5th number.

Notice that the sum of these six numbers is equal to four times the fifth number. It doesn't matter what two numbers we start with. They can be Fibonacci numbers, Lucas numbers, or any other pair of numbers. The total of the first six numbers will always be equal to four times the fifth number. We can also use this same type of reasoning to show that the sum of any ten consecutive numbers will always be equal to eleven times the seventh number.

Finally, as an example, we'll randomly select the numbers 4 and 19. Neither one of these is a Fibonacci number, or a Lucas number. We'll use these two numbers to initialize our sequence such that each succeeding number is equal to the sum of the two preceding numbers. Here are the first six numbers in the sequence:

$$4, 19, 23, 42, 65, 107$$

The sum of these six numbers is equal to 260, which is also equal to four times the fifth number (4 * 65).

Fibonacci Numbers, Lucas Numbers and Pi

There is an interesting relationship between the arctangent of the reciprocal of Fibonacci Numbers and Pi; and the arctangent of the reciprocal of Lucas Numbers and Pi. We start with:

$$\pi/4 \;=\; \arctan(1)$$

We also know that:

$$\arctan(1) = \arctan(1/2) + \arctan(1/3)$$
$$\arctan(1/3) = \arctan(1/5) + \arctan(1/8)$$
$$\arctan(1/8) = \arctan(1/13) + \arctan(1/21)$$

Notice that the denominators of each of these fractions are Fibonacci Numbers; and in fact, we can write a general relationship that says:

$$\arctan(1/F_n) = \arctan(1/F_{n+1}) + \arctan(1/F_{n+2})$$

And looking closely, we see that we can also substitute the last arctangent in each series for two more arctangents, giving us the following pattern:

$$\pi/4 = \arctan(1)$$
$$\pi/4 = \arctan(1/2) + \arctan(1/3)$$
$$\pi/4 = \arctan(1/2) + \arctan(1/5) + \arctan(1/8)$$
$$\pi/4 = \arctan(1/2) + \arctan(1/5) + \arctan(1/13) + \arctan(1/21)$$
$$\pi/4 = \arctan(1/2) + \arctan(1/5) + \arctan(1/13) + \arctan(1/34) + \arctan(1/55)$$

In other words, starting with 2 in the Fibonacci series, we can use Fibonacci numbers to create either an infinite series of arctangents that add up to $\pi/4$; or we can create a finite series (of any length we want) that will also be equal to $\pi/4$. The infinite series uses just the odd numbered Fibonacci numbers (i.e. F_3, F_5, F_7, etc.) to give us an expression equal to $\pi/4$. It goes on indefinitely and looks like this:

$$\pi/4 = \arctan(1/F_3) + \arctan(1/F_5) + \arctan(1/F_7) + \arctan(1/F_9) + \arctan(1/F_{11}) + \text{etc.}$$

Of course, we can end this sequence at any time by simply adding the arctangent of the reciprocal of the next Fibonacci number (instead of the next odd Fibonacci number). Which gives us this series of relationships:

$$\pi/4 = \arctan(1/F_3) + \arctan(1/F_4)$$
$$\pi/4 = \arctan(1/F_3) + \arctan(1/F_5) + \arctan(1/F_6)$$
$$\pi/4 = \arctan(1/F_3) + \arctan(1/F_5) + \arctan(1/F_7) + \arctan(1/F_8)$$
$$\pi/4 = \arctan(1/F_3) + \arctan(1/F_5) + \arctan(1/F_7) + \arctan(1/F_9) + \arctan(1/F_{10})$$
. . ., etc.

We also see a similar arrangement with Lucas numbers. Again, we create either an infinite series from the arctangent reciprocals of even numbered Lucas numbers, or we can create a finite series that ends with a Fibonacci number. Here is the infinite series for Lucas numbers:

$$\pi/4 = \arctan(1/L_2) + 2*\arctan(1/L_4) + 2*\arctan(1/L_6) + 2*\arctan(1/L_8) + \text{etc.}$$

The finite series follows the same pattern by starting with the arctangent of the reciprocal of L_2, then doubling the even reciprocals, and then ending with the arctangent of the reciprocal of an even Fibonacci number. Here is an example of these relationships showing how the reciprocals of the Lucas numbers and Fibonacci numbers are used together:

$$\pi/4 = \arctan(1/L_2) + \arctan(1/L_4) + \arctan(1/F_4)$$
$$\pi/4 = \arctan(1/L_2) + 2*\arctan(1/L_4) + \arctan(1/L_6) + \arctan(1/F_6)$$
$$\pi/4 = \arctan(1/L_2) + 2*\arctan(1/L_4) + 2*\arctan(1/L_6) + \arctan(1/L_8) + \arctan(1/F_8)$$
. . ., etc.

90

Notice that Lucas numbers are used for each of the terms in these series, except for the last term, which is a Fibonacci number.

Fibonacci Numbers, Lucas Numbers and the Golden Ratio

Let's look again at the first fifteen Fibonacci and Lucas numbers:

Fibonacci numbers: 1, 1, 2, 3, 5, 8, 13, 21, 34, 55, 89, 144, 233, 377, 610, ...
Lucas numbers: 1, 3, 4, 7, 11, 18, 29, 47, 76, 123, 199, 322, 521, 843, 1364, ...

When we divide the nth Lucas number by the nth Fibonacci number, we get an interesting ratio as n gets larger. Let's look at a few of these ratios and their decimal values:

$$
\begin{aligned}
L_5/F_5 &= 11/5 &= 2.2 \\
L_6/F_6 &= 18/8 &= 2.25 \\
L_7/F_7 &= 29/13 &= 2.23076923076\ldots \\
L_8/F_8 &= 47/21 &= 2.23809523809\ldots \\
&\ \ \ \ \cdots &\cdots \\
L_{15}/F_{15} &= 1364/610 &= 2.23606557377\ldots
\end{aligned}
$$

As we use larger and larger Lucas numbers and Fibonacci numbers the ratio starts to get closer and closer to the square root of five. My calculator show the square root of 5 is equal to:

$$\sqrt{5} = 2.236067977499789\ldots$$

This is interesting because in the previous chapter we looked at the Golden Ratio, and we saw that the Golden Ratio was an irrational number equal to the following:

$$\text{Golden Ratio} = \frac{1 + \sqrt{5}}{2} \qquad \text{which is approximately} = 1.6180339\ldots$$

We see that the square root of five is related to the ratio between Fibonacci numbers and Lucas numbers, and the square root of five is used to generate the Golden Ratio. We cement this relationship even further by showing that we can use two sequential Fibonacci or Lucas Numbers to create a fraction that approximates the golden ratio. Simply select a pair of adjacent numbers, divide the larger number by the smaller one, and this will give us a ratio that is approximately equal to the Golden Ratio. Again, as we use larger Fibonacci or Lucas numbers, the ratio we generate gets closer and closer to the Golden Ratio. Let's look at a few pairs of numbers and see how this works. Here are a few ratios and their decimal values:

Fibonacci Numbers			Lucas Numbers		
Ratio		**Decimal Equivalent**	**Ratio**		**Decimal Equivalent**
3/2	=	1.5	7/4	=	1.75
5/3	=	1.6666666 . . .	11/7	=	1.5714285 . . .
8/5	=	1.6	18/11	=	1.6363636 . . .
13/8	=	1.625	29/18	=	1.6111111 . . .
21/13	=	1.615384 . . .	47/29	=	1.6206896 . . .
. . .		. . .	. . .		. . .
610/377	=	1.618037135 . . .	1364/843	=	1.6180308 . . .

We can see in the listing above that as we select larger numbers, the ratios gradually come closer and closer to the actual value of the Golden Ratio. In addition to this, the first ratio in the listing above has a value that is less than the Golden Ratio, the second ratio is greater, the third is less than it again, and the forth is greater than it again. And so they continue to alternate as they continue to get closer and closer to the actual value.

Finally, it should be mentioned that this is true for any sequence of numbers that are generated in the same way that Fibonacci Numbers and Lucas Numbers are generated. In other words, we could start with two random numbers, like 16 and 23, and we can use these two numbers to create a sequence of numbers, where the next number is equal to the sum of the two previous numbers. Here are the first twelve numbers in this series:

$$16, \ 23, \ 39, \ 62, \ 101, \ 163, \ 264, \ 427, \ 691, \ 1118, \ 1809, \ 2927$$

Now, if we divide the last number by the next to the last number we get:

$$2927 \ / \ 1809 \ = \ 1.61802100608 \ldots$$

Which is very close to the actual value of the golden ratio.

Chapter 9
Triangular Numbers

Numbers can be placed in various categories. For example, numbers can be either odd or even; positive or negative, or even rational or irrational. Another of these is the polygonal number category. By this we mean that we can arrange a sequence of numbers to make shapes that resemble polygons, such as a triangle, square, or pentagon. We see examples of this all over; for example, at a bowling alley, there are ten pins arranged in the shape of a triangle. At the top of the triangle is a single bowling pin. Behind it are two pins, then three pins, and finally, the fourth row has four pins, making for a total of ten bowling pins. The number ten is a triangular number. In fact, if we just considered the first row with one pin, or the first two rows with three pins, or the first three rows with 6 pins, we have the numbers 1, 3 and 6, which are also triangular numbers. From this example we see that the first four triangular numbers are 1, 3, 6 and 10.

What about other geometric shapes? What if we made a square using bowling pins? We could use 4 pins arranged as a square, or 9, or even 16 pins each arranged as a square. These are square numbers, and the first four square numbers are 1, 4, 9 and 16. We could continue and do the same thing to create pentagons, hexagons, and beyond. These shapes are polygons, and hence the numbers that make up these shapes are called polygonal numbers. In this chapter we will mainly focus our attention on triangular numbers; and then towards the end we'll look at some other polygonal number relationships.

Defining Triangular Numbers

Triangular numbers can be created by performing an "addition factorial." Returning to our bowling pin example, the first row has one pin on it, the second row has two, the third has three, etc. We simply add the numbers one through n to get the nth triangular number. The following list of equations demonstrates this characteristic:

1	=	1	Triangular numbers are created from an
1 + 2	=	3	"addition factorial" where the nth
1 + 2 + 3	=	6	triangular number is equal to the sum of
1 + 2 + 3 + 4	=	10	the first n numbers. The triangular
1 + 2 + 3 + 4 + 5	=	15	numbers are 1, 3, 6, 10, 15, . . .
... etc			

There is also a simple equation that calculates the nth triangular number.

$$T_n = \tfrac{1}{2}n(n + 1)$$

Where T_n is the nth triangular number.

If we want the fourth triangular number, this equation says that we take the number 4 and the next number (which is 5), multiply them together and then take half of that product to get the number 10 (which is the fourth triangular number). Similarly, if we want the eighth triangular number, we take the numbers 8 and 9; multiply them together (to get 72) and then take half of that number to arrive at 36 (which is the eighth triangular number).

We can also check ourselves by adding the first eight numbers. We add the numbers $1 + 2 + 3 + 4 + 5 + 6 + 7 + 8$ which also gives us 36. The first fifteen triangular numbers are:

$$1, 3, 6, 10, 15, 21, 28, 36, 45, 55, 66, 78, 91, 105, 120$$

(See the appendix for a larger listing of triangular numbers.) Now let's look at some relationships within these triangular numbers.

Triangular Number Relationships

We'll begin our study of triangular number relationships by noting that two consecutive triangular numbers added together equal a square number. For example, 6 and 10 equal 16, which is 4^2. It turns out that the nth triangular number added to the preceding triangular number is equal to n squared. We write this as the following formula:

$$T_n + T_{n-1} = n^2 \qquad \text{(eq 1)}$$

We also observe that since a triangular number is equal to an "addition factorial," then it is also easy to see that when we subtract the preceding triangular number from the nth triangular number, then all we have left is the number n. From this relationship we get the following formula:

$$T_n - T_{n-1} = n \qquad \text{(eq 2)}$$

Of course we can write both of these relationships in terms of the nth triangular number:

$$T_n = n^2 - T_{n-1} \qquad \text{(eq 1a)}$$

$$T_n = n + T_{n-1} \qquad \text{(eq 2a)}$$

And from these two equations, we can derive several other relationships. For example, if we add equations (1) and (2) together, we get:

$$
\begin{aligned}
T_n + T_{n-1} &= n^2 \\
+ \quad T_n - T_{n-1} &= n \\
\hline
2(T_n) &= n^2 + n
\end{aligned}
\qquad \text{(eq 3)}
$$

Equation 3 tells us that any number squared, plus that number again is equal to twice that triangular number. (We can also rearrange the equation above to arrive at our original equation that defines Triangular numbers, namely: $T_n = \frac{1}{2}n(n + 1)$) And because triangular numbers are equal to an "addition factorial", we could just as easily say that if we add the numbers one through n and multiply that by two, it is equal to n squared plus n again. The relationship looks like this:

$2(1)$	$= 1^2 + 1$	which is the	$2(1)$		$= 1^2 + 1$
$2(3)$	$= 2^2 + 2$	same as:	$2(1 + 2)$		$= 2^2 + 2$
$2(6)$	$= 3^2 + 3$		$2(1 + 2 + 3)$		$= 3^2 + 3$
$2(10)$	$= 4^2 + 4$		$2(1 + 2 + 3 + 4)$		$= 4^2 + 4$
$2(15)$	$= 5^2 + 5$		$2(1 + 2 + 3 + 4 + 5)$	$= 5^2 + 5$
..., etc.			..., etc.		

94

In a similar way, we can subtract equations (1) and (2) and get the following relationship:

$$
\begin{aligned}
T_n + T_{n-1} &= n^2 \\
-\quad T_n - T_{n-1} &= n \\
\hline
2(T_{n-1}) &= n^2 - n
\end{aligned}
$$
(eq 4)

Here we see that any number squared minus that number again is equal to twice the preceding triangular number.

We now have four basic equations, and from these, we can derive many other relationships. For example, let's take equation (1), and multiply both sides by n. This gives us:

$$(T_n + T_{n-1})n = n^3$$

From equation (2) we'll make a substitution for the n on the left side of the equation to get:

$$(T_n + T_{n-1})(T_n - T_{n-1}) = n^3$$

Now, when we multiply the left side of the equality, we get:

$$T_n^2 - T_{n-1}^2 = n^3$$
(eq 5)

In other words, any number cubed is equal to that triangular number squared minus the preceding triangular number squared. This relationship by itself is nice, but it also creates an interesting pattern when we plug in actual numbers and show how the relationship expands with larger numbers:

$$
\begin{aligned}
1^3 &= (1)^2 - (0)^2 \\
2^3 &= (1+2)^2 - (1)^2 \\
3^3 &= (1+2+3)^2 - (1+2)^2 \\
4^3 &= (1+2+3+4)^2 - (1+2+3)^2 \\
5^3 &= (1+2+3+4+5)^2 - (1+2+3+4)^2 \\
&\ldots, \text{etc.}
\end{aligned}
$$

We can also go back to equation (3) and multiply both sides by n to give us:

$$2n(T_n) = n(n^2 + n)$$

Which simplifies to: $\quad 2n(T_n) = n^3 + n^2$
(eq 6)

On the right side of the equation, we have an n^2. We can make a substitution again, and replace the n^2 with its equivalent from equation (1)

$$2n(T_n) = n^3 + T_n + T_{n-1}$$

Again, we simplify by moving the triangular numbers to the left side of the equality and combine terms, giving us another relationship defining n^3:

$$(2n - 1)T_n - T_{n-1} = n^3$$

The expression (2n - 1) is actually just another way to say the nth odd number. So what we have here is that n^3 is equal to the nth odd number multiplied to the nth triangular number with the preceding triangular number subtracted from that product.

We see the pattern very clearly when we look at a few examples:

$$1^3 = (1)\,1 - 0$$
$$2^3 = (3)\,3 - 1$$
$$3^3 = (5)\,6 - 3$$
$$4^3 = (7)\,10 - 6$$
$$..., \text{etc.}$$

As you can see, we can have a lot of fun with this. It is possible to combine equations together, rearrange them, and then simplify them and come up with other interesting relationships. However, now let's look at a little trick that will expand our possibilities even further. Let's take equation (5) and work with it a little. We begin by rearranging it so that we have this:

$$T_n^2 = n^3 + T_{n-1}^2 \qquad\qquad (\text{eq 5a})$$

The above implies that the following is also true:

$$T_{n-1}^2 = (n-1)^3 + T_{n-2}^2 \qquad\qquad (\text{eq 5b})$$

Now, we can substitute T_{n-1}^2 from equation (5b) back into equation (5a) to arrive at this relationship:

$$T_n^2 = n^3 + (n-1)^3 + T_{n-2}^2 \qquad\qquad (\text{eq 7})$$

Similarly, we can use equation (5a) to write T_{n-2}^2 in relation to T_{n-3}^2 as:

$$T_{n-2}^2 = (n-2)^3 + T_{n-3}^2$$

Which we substitute back into equation (7) to give us:

$$T_n^2 = n^3 + (n-1)^3 + (n-2)^3 + T_{n-3}^2$$

In fact, we can keep digressing in this manner all the way back to T_0:

$$T_n^2 = n^3 + (n-1)^3 + (n-2)^3 + ... + 2^3 + 1^3 + T_0^2$$

And since T_0 is equal to 0 we can simply write:

$$T_n^2 = n^3 + (n-1)^3 + (n-2)^3 + ... + 2^3 + 1^3 \qquad\qquad (\text{eq 8})$$

This means that the nth triangular number squared is equal to the sum of the first n numbers cubed. And if we replace our triangular numbers with "addition factorials" we see an interesting relationship with the actual numbers:

1^2	is the same as	$(1)^2 = 1^3$
3^2	is the same as	$(1+2)^2 = 1^3 + 2^3$
6^2	is the same as	$(1+2+3)^2 = 1^3 + 2^3 + 3^3$
10^2	is the same as	$(1+2+3+4)^2 = 1^3 + 2^3 + 3^3 + 4^3$
	..., etc.	
T_n^2	is the same as	$(n + (n-1) + ... + 1)^2 = n^3 + (n-1)^3 + ... + 1^3$

The nth triangular number squared is equal to the sum of n numbers squared which is also equal to the sum of each of these individual numbers cubed.

Triangular Triples

In a later chapter we will look at Pythagorean Triples. A Pythagorean triple is a set of three whole numbers (or integers) where the sum of the first two numbers squared is equal to the third number squared. This characteristic appears to be a property of all polygonal numbers. There are triangular triples, square triples (a.k.a. Pythagorean triples), pentagonal triples, and so on; however in this section we will only look at triangular triples where the sum of two triangular numbers is equal to a third triangular number.

We'll start by using the trial and error method of finding some triangular triples; and from there we'll derive a couple of formulas for these triples. The trial and error method means that we'll take a list of triangular numbers, and then manually find which pairs, when added together give us a third. Here is a list of the first 20 triangular numbers:

$$1, 3, 6, 10, 15, 21, 28, 36, 45, 55, 66, 78, 91, 105, 120, 136, 153, 171, 190, 210$$

After just a few minutes of playing around with these numbers we find the following triples:

$$T_3 + T_5 = T_6$$
$$T_4 + T_9 = T_{10}$$
$$T_5 + T_6 = T_8$$
$$T_6 + T_9 = T_{11}$$

And there are more that we could find if we wanted to take the time, but this will do for now. We have two kinds of triples listed above. One kind of triple has the largest number one triangular number above the middle number of the triple (T_6 is one above T_5), and the second kind has the largest number two triangular numbers above the middle number (T_8 is two above T_6). We'll use this observation to create a couple of relationships.

First, let's derive a relation that finds triangular triples where the largest triangular number is one above the middle triangular number. To do this, we'll define our relationship as:

$$T_a + T_b = T_{b+1}$$

Using our definition for triangular numbers, at the beginning of the chapter, this formula can be rewritten as:

$$\tfrac{1}{2}a(a+1) + \tfrac{1}{2}b(b+1) = \tfrac{1}{2}(b+1)(b+2)$$

Now, we remove the $\tfrac{1}{2}$'s, combine terms and simplify:

$$(a^2 + a) + (b^2 + b) = b^2 + 3b + 2$$
$$a^2 + a = 2b + 2$$
$$a^2 + a = 2(b + 1)$$
$$(a^2 + a)/2 - 1 = b$$

What we derived isn't pretty, but it works. This relation gives us values for the two triangular numbers that when added together will give us the third triangular number. Keep in mind that a and b are our generating numbers. All we need to do is select a value for a, and then calculate what the corresponding b would be. (The numbers a and b have a dual role here: they are the generating numbers, and they represent the ath and b^{th} triangular numbers.) The sum of these two triangular numbers gives us the third one.

For example, the two columns on the left are the generating numbers for the triangular triple on the right (the three columns on the right):

if a equals:	then b equals	T_a equals	T_b equals	T_{b+1} equals
3	5	6	15	21
4	9	10	45	55
5	14	15	105	120
7	27	28	378	406
etc., . . .				

And now that we understand how this works, we can do it again where the largest triangular number is two above the middle triangular number. This relationship is defined as:

$$T_a + T_b = T_{b+2}$$

Which can be rewritten as:

$$\tfrac{1}{2}a(a + 1) + \tfrac{1}{2}b(b + 1) = \tfrac{1}{2}(b + 2)(b + 3)$$

Again we combine terms and simplify:

$$(a^2 + a) + (b^2 + b) = b^2 + 5b + 6$$
$$a^2 + a = 4b + 6$$
$$(a^2 + a - 6)/4 = b$$

Once again we have a formula for our generating numbers a and b. From these we can determine the ath and b^{th} triangular numbers; and finally, the sum of these two gives us the third triangular number. Here is a table for this set of generating numbers and their corresponding triangular numbers:

if a equals:	then b equals	T_a equals	T_b equals	T_{b+2} equals
5	6	15	21	36
6	9	21	45	66
9	21	45	231	276
10	26	55	351	406
etc., . . .				

Just like the Pythagorean triples that we will look at in a later chapter, we have developed a method here that can create triangular triples; and just like the Pythagorean triples, there also appears to be a never ending supply of triangular triples.

Other Triangular Number Relationships

We began an earlier section by saying that the sum of two consecutive triangular numbers is equal to some number squared. Now, we'll go a step further and say that any number raised to an even power is equal to the sum of two consecutive triangular numbers. For example, 2^4 is equal to the sum of 6 and 10; and 3^4 is equal to the sum of 36 and 45. Here is a sampling of numbers raised to even powers and the corresponding consecutive triangular numbers used to create them:

$$2^4 = T_3 + T_4 \qquad 2^6 = T_7 + T_8 \qquad 2^8 = T_{15} + T_{16}$$
$$3^4 = T_8 + T_9 \qquad 3^6 = T_{26} + T_{27} \qquad 3^8 = T_{80} + T_{81}$$
$$4^4 = T_{15} + T_{16} \qquad 4^6 = T_{63} + T_{64} \qquad 4^8 = T_{255} + T_{256}$$
$$5^4 = T_{24} + T_{25} \qquad 5^6 = T_{124} + T_{125} \qquad 5^8 = T_{624} + T_{625}$$
$$\text{... etc.}$$
$$n^4 = T_{(n*n)-1} + T_{n*n} \qquad n^6 = T_{(n*n*n)-1} + T_{n*n*n} \qquad n^8 = T_{(n*n*n*n)-1} + T_{n*n*n*n}$$

Using our triangular number notation, it is easy to see the patterns within these relationships and how these patterns apply to higher powers.

Another interesting relationship says that any triangular number squared is equal to the product of the preceding and following triangular numbers added again to that triangular number. Written out as a formula, it looks like this:

$$T_n^2 = T_{n-1}(T_{n+1}) + T_n$$

As some examples, we have:

$$3^2 = 1(6) + 3$$
$$6^2 = 3(10) + 6$$
$$10^2 = 6(15) + 10$$
$$15^2 = 10(21) + 15$$

And finally one other relationship that we will mention is an expanding series of triangular numbers. It looks like this:

$$T_1 + T_2 + T_3 = T_4$$
$$T_5 + T_6 + T_7 + T_8 = T_9 + T_{10}$$
$$T_{11} + T_{12} + T_{13} + T_{14} + T_{15} = T_{16} + T_{17} + T_{18}$$
$$\text{... etc.}$$

Using Triangular Numbers to Find the Product of Two Numbers

In a later chapter we will look at several methods of multiplying numbers together. One of these methods finds the product of two numbers by simply adding and subtracting a few triangular numbers together. The formula is very simple and straightforward:

$$a(b) = T_a + T_{b-1} - T_{a-b}$$

The formula states that the product of a and b is equal to the ath triangular number plus the $(b-1)^{th}$ triangular number minus the $(a-b)^{th}$ triangular number. This can easily be seen to be true by plugging in a few triangular numbers. However, even more instructive is a simple proof that shows this relationship is true. We'll start with our initial definition for the nth triangular number:

$$T_n = \tfrac{1}{2}n(n+1)$$

We'll use that to define the ath, $(b-1)^{th}$ and $(a-b)^{th}$ triangular numbers:

$$T_a = \tfrac{1}{2}a(a+1)$$
$$T_{b-1} = \tfrac{1}{2}(b-1)((b-1)+1)$$
$$T_{a-b} = \tfrac{1}{2}(a-b)((a-b)+1)$$

Now we'll enter the values above into our relationship at the beginning of this section, and see what falls out:

$$
\begin{aligned}
(a)(b) &= T_a + T_{b-1} - T_{a-b} \\
&= \tfrac{1}{2}a(a+1) + \tfrac{1}{2}(b-1)((b-1)+1) - \tfrac{1}{2}(a-b)((a-b)+1) \\
&= \tfrac{1}{2}[(a^2 + a) + (b^2 - b) - (a^2 - ab + a - ab + b^2 - b)] \\
&= \tfrac{1}{2}[2ab] \\
&= ab
\end{aligned}
$$

We have just shown that there is a simple method of finding the product of two numbers by simply adding and subtracting three triangular numbers.

Triangular Roots

At the beginning of this chapter we discussed how triangular numbers are also polygonal numbers, just as squares and pentagonal numbers are polygonal. When we look at squares, we can take the square root of a number. In some cases the square root of a number is a whole number, in other cases it isn't. Yet, we have ways to determine that square root whether or not it is a whole number. This now begs the question as to whether we can do the same thing with triangular numbers. Is there such a thing as a triangular root, and can we find it?

The answer is yes and yes. In fact, we can derive a nice little formula that will give us the triangular root of any number. We'll start with our original equation where we have T_n defined in terms of n:

$$T_n = \tfrac{1}{2}n(n+1) \qquad \text{Where } T_n \text{ is the } n^{th} \text{ triangular number.}$$

We now want to solve this equation for n. So we begin by rearranging the terms a little:

$$2T_n = n^2 + n$$

On the right side of the equality we want to complete the square:

$$2T_n = n^2 + n + \tfrac{1}{4} - \tfrac{1}{4}$$

Next, we'll multiply both sides of the equation by 4 so that we clear the fractions:

$$8T_n = 4n^2 + 4n + 1 - 1$$

Now we finish completing the square, and solving for n:

$$
\begin{aligned}
8T_n &= (4n^2 + 4n + 1) - 1 \\
8T_n &= (2n + 1)^2 - 1 \\
8T_n + 1 &= (2n + 1)^2
\end{aligned}
$$

Finally, we take the square root of both sides, and then solve for n on the right side of the equality to obtain the following equation:

$$\frac{-1 \pm \sqrt{(8T_n + 1)}}{2} = n$$

100

Using the positive square root of the equation above, we can verify that the triangular root of 6 is 3, and the triangular root of 10 is 4. We would expect that; however, we can also find the triangular root of any number. The table below lists the triangular roots of the numbers 1 through 28.

Tri #	Tri Root
1	1
2	1.56155281280883…
3	2
4	2.37228132326901…
5	2.70156211871642…
6	3
7	3.27491721763537…
8	3.53112887414928…
9	3.77200187265877…
10	4
11	4.2169905660283…
12	4.42442890089805…
13	4.6234753829798…
14	4.81507290636733…
15	5
16	5.17890834580027…
17	5.35234995535981…
18	5.52079728939615…
19	5.68465843842649…
20	5.84428877022476…
21	6
22	6.15206734782504…
23	6.30073525436772…
24	6.4462219947249…
25	6.58872343937891…
26	6.7284161474…
27	6.865459931328…
28	7

Now, let's continue with a look at the continuous fractions of these triangular roots.

Continuous Fractions of Triangular Roots

Now that we have a formula that will give us triangular roots; this begs the question: "Do the continuous fractions of triangular roots have patterns and symmetries similar to those we found with the continuous fractions of square roots?" We don't have to examine them very closely to see that there are patterns and symmetries within and between the various continuous fractions.

Let's take a look. Here are the continuous fractions for the non-integral triangular roots between 1 and 28:

$^t\sqrt{1}$ = 1
$^t\sqrt{2}$ = 1.561552812809 = [1; 1, 1, 3, 1, 1, 3, 1, 1, 3, 1, 1, 3, 1, ...]
$^t\sqrt{3}$ = 2
$^t\sqrt{4}$ = 2.372281323269 = [2; 2, 1, 2, 5, 2, 1, 2, 5, 2, 1, 2, 5, 2, ...]
$^t\sqrt{5}$ = 2.701562118716 = [2; 1, 2, 2, 1, 5, 1, 2, 2, 1, 5, 1, 2, 2, ...]
$^t\sqrt{6}$ = 3
$^t\sqrt{7}$ = 3.274917217635 = [3; 3, 1, 1, 1, 3, 7, 3, 1, 1, 1, 3, 7, 3, ...]
$^t\sqrt{8}$ = 3.531128874149 = [3; 1, 1, 7, 1, 1, 7, 1, 1, 7, 1, 1, 7, 1, ...]
$^t\sqrt{9}$ = 3.772001872659 = [3; 1, 3, 2, 1, 1, 2, 3, 1, 7, 1, 3, 2, 1, ...]
$^t\sqrt{10}$ = 4
$^t\sqrt{11}$ = 4.216990566028 = [4; 4, 1, 1, 1, 1, 4, 9, 4, 1, 1, 1, 1, 4, ...]
$^t\sqrt{12}$ = 4.424428900898 = [4; 2, 2, 1, 4, 4, 1, 2, 2, 9, 2, 2, 1, 4, ...]
$^t\sqrt{13}$ = 4.62347538298 = [4; 1, 1, 1, 1, 1, 9, 1, 1, 1, 1, 1, 9, 1, ...]
$^t\sqrt{14}$ = 4.815072906367 = [4; 1, 4, 2, 2, 4, 1, 9, 1, 4, 2, 2, 4, 1, ...]
$^t\sqrt{15}$ = 5
$^t\sqrt{16}$ = 5.1789083458 = [5; 5, 1, 1, 2, 3, 2, 1, 1, 5, 11, 5, 1, 1, ...]
$^t\sqrt{17}$ = 5.35234995536 = [5; 2, 1, 5, 5, 1, 2, 11, 2, 1, 5, 5, 1, 2, ...]
$^t\sqrt{18}$ = 5.520797289396 = [5; 1, 1, 11, 1, 1, 11, 1, 1, 11, 1, 1, 11, ...]
$^t\sqrt{19}$ = 5.684658438426 = [5; 1, 2, 5, 1, 5, 2, 1, 11, 1, 2, 5, 1, 5, ...]
$^t\sqrt{20}$ = 5.844288770225 = [5; 1, 5, 2, 2, 1, 2, 2, 5, 1, 11, 1, 5, 2, ...]
$^t\sqrt{21}$ = 6
$^t\sqrt{22}$ = 6.152067347825 = [6; 6, 1, 1, 2, 1, 3, 1, 2, 1, 1, 6, 13, 6, ...]
$^t\sqrt{23}$ = 6.300735254368 = [6; 3, 3, 13, 3, 3, 13, 3, 3, 13, 3, 3, 13, ...]
$^t\sqrt{24}$ = 6.446221994725 = [6; 2, 4, 6, 1, 2, 1, 1, 1, 1, 2, 1, 6, 4, ...]
$^t\sqrt{25}$ = 6.588723439379 = [6; 1, 1, 2, 3, 6, 1, 3, 1, 6, 3, 2, 1, 1, ...]
$^t\sqrt{26}$ = 6.7284161474 = [6; 1, 2, 1, 2, 6, 1, 6, 2, 1, 2, 1, 13, 1, ...]
$^t\sqrt{27}$ = 6.865459931328 = [6; 1, 6, 2, 3, 4, 1, 1, 1, 1, 1, 4, 3, 2, ...]
$^t\sqrt{28}$ = 7

Midway Numbers

The triangular roots of 2, 8, 18, 32, ... are midway between the roots that are perfect triangular numbers; and these midway triangular roots have an obvious pattern within their continuous fractions. Each of these fractions has a three digit cycle where the first two numbers of that cycle are 1, 1, and the third number is what we'll call the cycle termination number. Here is a listing of the first seven triangular roots that are midway between the whole number roots:

$^t\sqrt{2}$ = 1.561552812809 = [1; 1, 1, 3, 1, 1, 3, 1, 1, 3, 1, 1, 3, ...]
$^t\sqrt{8}$ = 3.531128874149 = [3; 1, 1, 7, 1, 1, 7, 1, 1, 7, 1, 1, 7, ...]
$^t\sqrt{18}$ = 5.520797289396 = [5; 1, 1, 11, 1, 1, 11, 1, 1, 11, 1, 1, 11, ...]
$^t\sqrt{32}$ = 7.515609770941 = [7; 1, 1, 15, 1, 1, 15, 1, 1, 15, 1, 1, 15, ...]
$^t\sqrt{50}$ = 9.51249219725 = [9; 1, 1, 19, 1, 1, 19, 1, 1, 19, 1, 1, 19, ...]
$^t\sqrt{72}$ = 11.510412149464 = [11; 1, 1, 23, 1, 1, 23, 1, 1, 23, 1, 1, 23, ...]
$^t\sqrt{98}$ = 13.508925726122 = [13; 1, 1, 27, 1, 1, 27, 1, 1, 27, 1, 1, 27, ...]

Continuous Fraction Cycles

The non-whole number (or non-integral) triangular roots appear to have certain characteristics and properties. Each of these continuous fractions follows a cyclic pattern followed by a cycle termination number (and then the cycle repeats). The numbers within the cycle are palindromic; and all of the roots between two integral roots share the same cycle termination number.

For example, the triangular numbers 6 and 10 have integral roots (3 and 4). The numbers between 6 and 10 have non-integral roots, and the continuous fractions of these roots each end their cycle with a 7. The continuous fractions of the roots between 10 and 15 have a cycle termination number equal to 9; and the continuous fractions of the roots between 15 and 21 have a cycle termination number equal to 11. The listing below shows these roots, their continuous fractions with each cycle length, and the cycle termination number:

$$^t\sqrt{6} = 3$$
$$^t\sqrt{7} = 3.274917217635 = [\,3;\ 3,\ 1,\ 1,\ 1,\ 3,\ 7,\ ...] \qquad \text{cycle of } 6$$
$$^t\sqrt{8} = 3.531128874149 = [\,3;\ 1,\ 1,\ 7,\ ...] \qquad \text{cycle of } 3$$
$$^t\sqrt{9} = 3.772001872659 = [\,3;\ 1,\ 3,\ 2,\ 1,\ 1,\ 2,\ 3,\ 1,\ 7,\ ...] \qquad \text{cycle of } 9$$
$$^t\sqrt{10} = 4$$
$$^t\sqrt{11} = 4.216990566028 = [\,4;\ 4,\ 1,\ 1,\ 1,\ 1,\ 4,\ 9,\ ...] \qquad \text{cycle of } 7$$
$$^t\sqrt{12} = 4.424428900898 = [\,4;\ 2,\ 2,\ 1,\ 4,\ 4,\ 1,\ 2,\ 2,\ 9,\ ...] \qquad \text{cycle of } 9$$
$$^t\sqrt{13} = 4.62347538298 = [\,4;\ 1,\ 1,\ 1,\ 1,\ 1,\ 9,\ ...] \qquad \text{cycle of } 6$$
$$^t\sqrt{14} = 4.815072906367 = [\,4;\ 1,\ 4,\ 2,\ 2,\ 4,\ 1,\ 9,\ ...] \qquad \text{cycle of } 7$$
$$^t\sqrt{15} = 5$$
$$^t\sqrt{16} = 5.1789083458 = [\,5;\ 5,\ 1,\ 1,\ 2,\ 3,\ 2,\ 1,\ 1,\ 5,\ 11,\ ...] \qquad \text{cycle of } 10$$
$$^t\sqrt{17} = 5.35234995536 = [\,5;\ 2,\ 1,\ 5,\ 5,\ 1,\ 2,\ 11,\ ...] \qquad \text{cycle of } 7$$
$$^t\sqrt{18} = 5.520797289396 = [\,5;\ 1,\ 1,\ 11,\ ...] \qquad \text{cycle of } 3$$
$$^t\sqrt{19} = 5.684658438426 = [\,5;\ 1,\ 2,\ 5,\ 1,\ 5,\ 2,\ 1,\ 11,\ ...] \qquad \text{cycle of } 8$$
$$^t\sqrt{20} = 5.844288770225 = [\,5;\ 1,\ 5,\ 2,\ 2,\ 1,\ 2,\ 2,\ 5,\ 1,\ 11,\ ...] \qquad \text{cycle of } 10$$
$$^t\sqrt{21} = 6$$

Note that each cycle starts after the semicolon, and then repeats after the cycle termination number. We can also see in the listing above that the numbers within each cycle are symmetrical and palindromic. For example, looking at the triangular root of 19 we find the following cycle:

$$[\,...,\ 1,\ 2,\ 5,\ 1,\ 5,\ 2,\ 1,\ 11,\ 1,\ 2,\ 5,\ 1,\ 5,\ 2,\ 1,\ 11,\ 1,\ 2,\ 5,\ 1,\ 5,\ 2,\ 1,\ 11,\ ...]$$

The cycle consists of seven numbers [1, 2, 5, 1, 5, 2, 1] followed by an 11, and then it repeats again. These seven numbers are palindromic, they read the same forward as they do backwards. And this palindromic pattern appears to hold true for all of the non-integral triangular roots.

Predicting the Cycle

In the section above you may have noticed that the cycles tend to get longer as the triangular root considered gets larger. The software I wrote to calculate the continuous fraction has its limitations. Machine errors start to creep into the calculations. However, after looking at the characteristics of many of the cycles, it is possible to make some assumptions and predictions about some of the longer cycles. For example, my software calculates the following for the triangular root of 94:

$$^t\sqrt{94} = 13.220422734012 = [\,13;\ 4,\ 1,\ 1,\ 6,\ 3,\ 3,\ 1,\ 1,\ 1,\ 1,\ 13,\ 9,\ 13,\ 1,\ ...]$$

This listing hasn't reached the cycle termination number, but from the roots of numbers with shorter cycles that are before and after 94, I know that the cycle termination number is 27. I also know that the listing of numbers between each 27 is palindromic, and since the numbers in the part of the continuous fraction that I have appear to be more than half way through their cycle (because it appears that 9 is the halfway number), I can predict that the entire continuous fraction for the triangular root of 94 is:

$$^t\sqrt{94} \;=\; [\,13;\; 4, 1, 1, 6, 3, 3, 1, 1, 1, 1, 13, 9, 13, 1, 1, 1, 1, 3, 3, 6, 1, 1, 4, 27, \,...]$$

Of course due to the limitations of my software I don't have an accurate method of checking this number, but with a fair amount of certainty I can assert that this continuous fraction is accurate.

Polygonal Numbers

Polygonal numbers share many interesting relationships both within themselves and between themselves. For example, here is a listing of the equations used to find the nth triangular, square, pentagonal, and hexagonal numbers:

$$
\begin{aligned}
\text{Tri}_n &= \tfrac{1}{2}n(1n + 1) \\
\text{Sqr}_n &= \tfrac{1}{2}n(2n + 0) \;=\; n^2 \\
\text{Pen}_n &= \tfrac{1}{2}n(3n - 1) \\
\text{Hex}_n &= \tfrac{1}{2}n(4n - 2)
\end{aligned}
$$

Within these formulas we can see how each is related to the other. Below we have a listing of the first ten numbers within each sequence:

Triangular:	1, 3, 6, 10, 15, 21, 28, 36, 45, 55, ...
Square:	1, 4, 9, 16, 25, 36, 49, 64, 81, 100, ...
Pentagonal:	1, 5, 12, 22, 35, 51, 70, 92, 117, 145, ...
Hexagonal:	1, 6, 15, 28, 45, 66, 91, 120, 153, 190, ...

By arranging these numbers in columns and then comparing them with each other, we see an interesting relationship. The difference between the nth triangular and the nth square number is equal to the $(n-1)^{th}$ triangular number. Similarly, the difference between the nth square number and the nth pentagonal number is again the $(n-1)^{th}$ triangular number (as is the difference between the nth pentagonal number and the nth hexagonal number).

For example, the eighth triangular, square, pentagonal and hexagonal numbers are 36, 64, 92 and 120, and the difference between each sequential pair is equal to 28, which is the seventh triangular number. This bit of information will come in handy in just a few minutes.

At the beginning of this chapter we saw that triangular numbers can be created by performing an "addition factorial." The following list of equations demonstrates this:

1	= 1	The numbers 1, 3, 6, 10, 15, ... etc., are
1 + 2	= 3	triangular numbers.
1 + 2 + 3	= 6	
1 + 2 + 3 + 4	= 10	
1 + 2 + 3 + 4 + 5	= 15	
..., etc.		

In a similar way, square numbers are created by adding consecutive odd numbers. The following list demonstrates this:

$$1 \qquad\qquad = \quad 1$$
$$1 + 3 \qquad\qquad = \quad 4$$
$$1 + 3 + 5 \qquad = \quad 9$$
$$1 + 3 + 5 + 7 \quad = \quad 16$$
$$1 + 3 + 5 + 7 + 9 \ = \ 25$$
$$\ldots, \text{etc.}$$

The numbers 1, 4, 9, 16, 25, … etc., are square numbers.

So how does this pattern continue for pentagonal numbers and beyond? You may have noticed that with the triangular numbers each number that is added is one more than the previous number. We started with the number one, then added two, and then three, and so on. With the squares, each number that is added is two more than the previous number; i.e., we started with one, then added three, and then five, etc.

Pentagonal numbers continue this pattern. These numbers start with the number one, and then each number that is added is three more than the previous number. We can see this in the following listing:

$$1 \qquad\qquad = \quad 1$$
$$1 + 4 \qquad\qquad = \quad 5$$
$$1 + 4 + 7 \qquad = \quad 12$$
$$1 + 4 + 7 + 10 \quad = \quad 22$$
$$1 + 4 + 7 + 10 + 13 \ = \ 35$$
$$\ldots, \text{etc.}$$

The numbers 1, 5, 12, 22, 35, … etc., are pentagonal numbers.

This pattern continues for hexagonal numbers, heptagonal numbers and any other type of polygonal number. Because of this, we say for example, that the nth pentagonal number can be found by adding the nth square number with the $(n-1)^{th}$ triangular number. That gives us this relation:

$$P_n \ = \ S_n \ + \ T_{n-1}$$

And we continue by saying that the nth hexagonal number can be found by adding the nth pentagonal number with the $(n-1)^{th}$ triangular number:

$$H_n \ = \ P_n \ + \ T_{n-1}$$

Of course we can't really call ourselves a Mathematician, Scientist, or Engineer if we leave it as it is, so let's substitute what we derived for P_n into the relation above, and the combine terms:

$$H_n \ = \ (S_n \ + \ T_{n-1}) \ + \ T_{n-1}$$
$$H_n \ = \ S_n \ + \ 2(T_{n-1})$$

This gives us a definition for the nth hexagonal number in terms of a square and a triangular number. But we can go even one step further because we also have a definition for the nth square number in terms of just triangular numbers. Making that substitution give us:

$$H_n \ = \ (T_n + T_{n-1}) \ + \ 2(T_{n-1})$$
$$H_n \ = \ T_n \ + \ 3(T_{n-1})$$

We can now find the nth hexagonal number from triangular numbers alone. Of course this same type of substitution can be applied to any polygonal number so that we can represent any polygonal number in terms of triangular numbers alone.

Polygonal Number Patterns

In this final section of the chapter I wish to show a few relationships that I "stumbled" across between the various types of polygonal numbers. I won't try to explain how these relationships were derived; I only wish to show the patterns within these relationships. Earlier within this chapter we saw the following triangular number relationship:

1^2	is the same as	$(1)^2$	$=$	1^3
3^2	is the same as	$(1+2)^2$	$=$	$1^3 + 2^3$
6^2	is the same as	$(1+2+3)^2$	$=$	$1^3 + 2^3 + 3^3$
10^2	is the same as	$(1+2+3+4)^2$	$=$	$1^3 + 2^3 + 3^3 + 4^3$
	..., etc.			

And what we will do is take the number pattern above, and manipulate it to get the following:

$$1(1)^2 - 0(1) = 1^3$$
$$1(1+2)^2 - 0(1+2) = 1^3 + 2^3$$
$$1(1+2+3)^2 - 0(1+2+3) = 1^3 + 2^3 + 3^3$$
$$1(1+2+3+4)^2 - 0(1+2+3+4) = 1^3 + 2^3 + 3^3 + 4^3$$
..., etc.

All I did above is add zero to the left side of the equal sign (in a round-about way). It didn't change the value of any of the relationships, but they now fit a pattern that we see with the squares, pentagonal, and hexagonal numbers (and this pattern continues for higher polygonal numbers also). Here is the relationship for the squares:

$$2(1)^2 - (1) = 1^3$$
$$2(1+3)^2 - (1+3) = 1^3 + 3^3$$
$$2(1+3+5)^2 - (1+3+5) = 1^3 + 3^3 + 5^3$$
$$2(1+3+5+7)^2 - (1+3+5+7) = 1^3 + 3^3 + 5^3 + 7^3$$
..., etc.

And here it is for the pentagonal numbers:

$$3(1)^2 - 2(1) = 1^3$$
$$3(1+4)^2 - 2(1+4) = 1^3 + 4^3$$
$$3(1+4+7)^2 - 2(1+4+7) = 1^3 + 4^3 + 7^3$$
$$3(1+4+7+10)^2 - 2(1+4+7+10) = 1^3 + 4^3 + 7^3 + 10^3$$
..., etc.

And this is it for the hexagonal numbers:

$$4(1)^2 - 3(1) = 1^3$$
$$4(1+5)^2 - 3(1+5) = 1^3 + 5^3$$
$$4(1+5+9)^2 - 3(1+5+9) = 1^3 + 5^3 + 9^3$$
$$4(1+5+9+13)^2 - 3(1+5+9+13) = 1^3 + 5^3 + 9^3 + 13^3$$
..., etc.

From what we have seen above, we summarize these relationships here:

$$1T_n^2 - 0T_n = 1^3 + 2^3 + 3^3 + 4^3 + ... + n^3$$
$$2S_n^2 - 1S_n = 1^3 + 3^3 + 5^3 + 7^3 + ... + n^3$$
$$3P_n^2 - 2P_n = 1^3 + 4^3 + 7^3 + 10^3 + ... + n^3$$
$$4H_n^2 - 3H_n = 1^3 + 5^3 + 9^3 + 13^3 + ... + n^3$$
..., etc.

And there are still other patterns and relationships that we can find within these polygonal numbers. Here is yet, another one. **We'll start with this relationship that** we saw earlier in the chapter:

$$[T_n]^2 = [T_{n-1}]^2 + n^3$$

And we'll modify it so that now it looks like this:

$$[T_n]^2 = [T_{n-1}]^2 + (1n - 0)^3 + 0(1n - 0)$$

And the only reason why I would do this is so that it will fit a similar pattern for square, pentagonal, and higher polygonal numbers. Here are the various number sequences. First, the triangular number relation:

$$1(1)^2 = 1(0)^2 + 1^3 + 0(1)$$
$$1(1+2)^2 = 1(1)^2 + 2^3 + 0(2)$$
$$1(1+2+3)^2 = 1(1+2)^2 + 3^3 + 0(3)$$
$$1(1+2+3+4)^2 = 1(1+2+3)^2 + 4^3 + 0(4)$$
..., etc.

Now the square number relation:

$$2(1)^2 = 2(0)^2 + 1^3 + 1(1)$$
$$2(1+3)^2 = 2(1)^2 + 3^3 + 1(3)$$
$$2(1+3+5)^2 = 2(1+3)^2 + 5^3 + 1(5)$$
$$2(1+3+5+7)^2 = 2(1+3+5)^2 + 7^3 + 1(7)$$
..., etc.

The pentagonal number relation:

$$3(1)^2 = 3(0)^2 + 1^3 + 2(1)$$
$$3(1+4)^2 = 3(1)^2 + 4^3 + 2(4)$$
$$3(1+4+7)^2 = 3(1+4)^2 + 7^3 + 2(7)$$
$$3(1+4+7+10)^2 = 3(1+4+7)^2 + 10^3 + 2(10)$$
..., etc.

And the hexagonal number relation:

$$4(1)^2 = 4(0)^2 + 1^3 + 3(1)$$
$$4(1+5)^2 = 4(1)^2 + 5^3 + 3(5)$$
$$4(1+5+9)^2 = 4(1+5)^2 + 9^3 + 3(9)$$
$$4(1+5+9+13)^2 = 4(1+5+9)^2 + 13^3 + 3(13)$$
..., etc.

And here is the summary of these polygonal number relations:

$$1[T_n]^2 = 1[T_{n-1}]^2 + (1n-0)^3 + 0(1n-0)$$
$$2[S_n]^2 = 2[S_{n-1}]^2 + (2n-1)^3 + 1(2n-1)$$
$$3[P_n]^2 = 3[P_{n-1}]^2 + (3n-2)^3 + 2(3n-2)$$
$$4[H_n]^2 = 4[H_{n-1}]^2 + (4n-3)^3 + 3(4n-3)$$
..., etc.

The patterns that we have seen in this last section are complicated, and don't really have any particular significance except that they do show that there is a deeper relationship between the various types of polygonal numbers.

Math, science, and engineering have found many useful applications for squares and square roots; however, that cannot be said for triangular numbers, triangular roots, or any of the other polygonal numbers. Maybe that day is just over the horizon in the not-to-distant future (and maybe not). In the meantime, we're having so much fun here that maybe this would be a good time to take a break, get a soda, and even say "Hi" to your kids (just so that they know you are alright), before continuing on.

Chapter 10
Pascal's Triangle

Building Pascal's Triangle

Pascal's triangle has an amazing variety of number patterns within this pattern of numbers. To create Pascal's triangle, we start with 3 ones distributed in a triangular pattern on two rows. The first row has 1 one, and the second row has the other two ones. To create the third row, place a one to the left of the left-most one from the second row, and place another one to the right of the right-most one from the second row. Finally, add the two one's from the second row, and place their total between the two ones on the third row. The first three rows of Pascal's triangle look something like this:

```
        1
      1   1
    1   2   1
```

For each succeeding row, we use the same procedure that we just used to create the third row. The next row will have a one to the left of the left-most one and another one to the right of the right-most one from the row above it. The numbers between the ones will be spaced midway between the numbers from the preceding row, and they will be equal to the sum of the two numbers above it.

As each row is added, it will have one more number than the preceding row, and each number between the 1's will be the sum of the two numbers above it. If continued for 11 rows, we get something that looks like this:

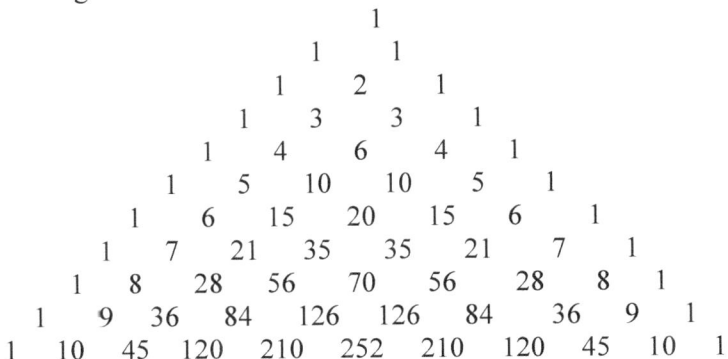

Figure 10.1   The first ten rows of Pascal's triangle.

Even though the figure above shows 11 rows, the top row is counted as the 0th row, and is sometimes omitted. In this discussion, we will show the top row and include it in our diagrams, and we will also refer to it as the zeroeth row. By counting the rows in this way, the row number will always be equal to the second number in that row. Pascal's triangle is symmetrical about its center because of the way it is constructed. If a vertical line is drawn down the center of the triangle, the left side will mirror the right side.

The Diagonals within Pascal's Triangle

There are many patterns within Pascal's triangle. We will spend the rest of this chapter looking at several of these patterns. We'll start by looking at the diagonals.

The outer most diagonal (on either side) consists of ones. The next diagonal (parallel to the edge) is the sequence of counting numbers (the numbers 1, 2, 3, 4, etc.); and the diagonal next to that is the sequence of triangular numbers (the numbers 1, 3, 6, 10, etc.). Continuing inward, the next diagonal is the sequence of tetrahedral numbers, or three dimensional triangular numbers (the numbers 1, 4, 10, 20, etc.) and the diagonal after that consists of the fourth dimensional triangular numbers (the numbers 1, 5, 15, 35, etc.)

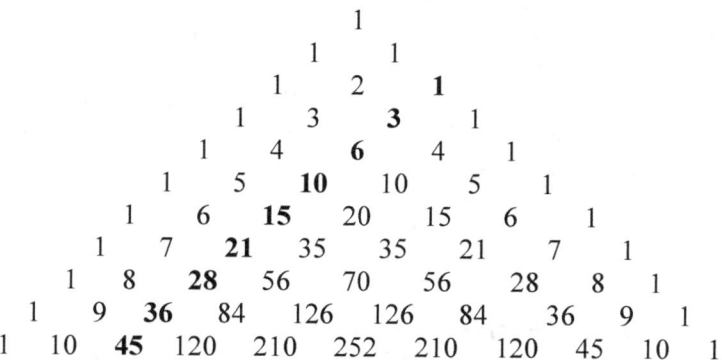

Figure 10.2   Pascal's triangle with the triangular numbers highlighted.

Fibonacci Numbers

If we construct Pascal's triangle so that each row is left justified along the side margin, we can then add the numbers along these new diagonals and create the Fibonacci sequence (as shown in the figure below).

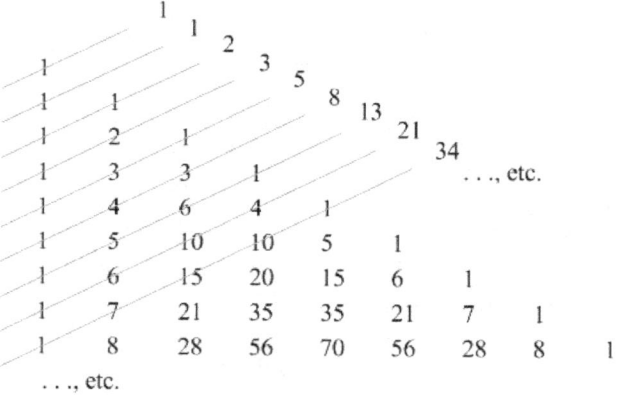

Figure 10.3   Using Pascal's triangle to create the Fibonacci sequence.

The diagonals that create the Fibonacci numbers run from the lower left to the upper right. Notice that the first and second diagonals have one number in them. The next two diagonals have two numbers, and the following two diagonals each have three numbers in them, etc. By adding

Diagonal Number	1	2	3	4	5	6
Number sequence	1	1	(1+1)	(2+1)	(1+3+1)	(3+4+1)
Total (Fibonacci No)	1	1	2	3	5	8

Binomial Coefficients

Coefficients are numbers that are multiplied to a variable. In the expression 3x, the x is the variable and 3 is the coefficient. The binomial coefficients are the coefficients we get when we expand the expression $(x + 1)^n$, where n represents some integer power. For example, if n is 1, then $(x + 1)^1$ is equal to x + 1, and the coefficients are 1 and 1. If we let n equal 2, then $(x + 1)^2$ is equal to $x^2 + 2x + 1$, and the coefficients for this equation are 1, 2, 1. And, if n = 3, then expanding $(x + 1)^3$ gives us $x^3 + 3x^2 + 3x + 1$, and these coefficients are 1, 3, 3, 1. The formula we use to calculate each of these coefficients is:

$$\frac{n!}{r!(n - r)!}$$

In this formula, the n is equal to the power that (x + 1) is being raised to, and r is equal to the number of the specific coefficient that we are trying to find. If we wish to find all of the coefficients, then r will range from 0 to n.

In order to find all the coefficients of $(x + 1)^3$, we would use this formula four times with n equal to 3, and r ranging from 0 to 3. These are the expressions that we would have:

$$\frac{3!}{0!(3-0)!} \qquad \frac{3!}{1!(3-1)!} \qquad \frac{3!}{2!(3-2)!} \qquad \frac{3!}{3!(3-3)!}$$

These expressions evaluate to 1, 3, 3, 1. Notice that these are the same numbers that we find on the third row of Pascal's triangle. Pascal's triangle contains the information required to find the coefficients of (x + 1) raised to any power.

The Sum and Product of Each Row

The sum of each row in Pascal's triangle is equal to 2 raised to that power. If we add all the numbers on the fourth row, that sum is equal to 2^4 or 16. Let's look at rows 0 through 5 and consider their sums.

$$
\begin{array}{llll}
1 & = 1, \text{ or } 2^0 \\
1 + 1 & = 2, \text{ or } 2^1 \\
1 + 2 + 1 & = 4, \text{ or } 2^2 \\
1 + 3 + 3 + 1 & = 8, \text{ or } 2^3 \\
1 + 4 + 6 + 4 + 1 & = 16, \text{ or } 2^4 \\
1 + 5 + 10 + 10 + 5 + 1 & = 32, \text{ or } 2^5
\end{array}
$$

Figure 10.4   The sum of each row of the first 5 rows within Pascal's triangle.

If we alternate the signs in front of each number, with the sign between the first and second number on each row always being negative, then starting with the first row, the sum of each row is equal to zero.

$$
\begin{array}{rcl}
1 - 1 & = & 0 \\
1 - 2 + 1 & = & 0 \\
1 - 3 + 3 - 1 & = & 0 \\
1 - 4 + 6 - 4 + 1 & = & 0 \\
1 - 5 + 10 - 10 + 5 - 1 & = & 0
\end{array}
$$

Figure 10.5   Alternating sums and differences of values within each row of Pascal's triangle.

Considering the symmetry of the triangle, it isn't surprising that the odd numbered rows equal 0. On the first row we start with a one and subtract a one. On the third row we have a positive one and three, and a negative one and three; and so the pattern continues for all of the odd rows. The interesting part of this pattern is that the relationship holds true even with the even numbered rows as well.

Looking at the product of each row (where we multiple each number on the row to the other numbers on the same row), we see that these numbers become huge very rapidly. There doesn't appear to be much of a pattern within these numbers except that the product of every odd row is a perfect square.

$$
\begin{array}{rclcl}
1 & = & 1 & & \\
1 * 1 & = & 1 & = & 1^2 \\
1 * 2 * 1 & = & 2 & & \\
1 * 3 * 3 * 1 & = & 9 & = & 3^2 \\
1 * 4 * 6 * 4 * 1 & = & 96 & & \\
1 * 5 * 10 * 10 * 5 * 1 & = & 2500 & = & 50^2 \\
1 * 6 * 15 * 20 * 15 * 6 * 1 & = & 162000 & & \\
1 * 7 * 21 * 35 * 35 * 21 * 7 * 1 & = & 26471025 & = & 5145^2
\end{array}
$$

Figure 10.6   The sum of each row within Pascal's triangle.

Of course, it makes sense that the product of the numbers on the odd rows is a perfect square since each of the odd rows has pairs of the same number multiplied together. The first row has two 1's multiplied together. The third row has two 1's and two 3's; the fifth row has two 1's, two 5's, and two 10's; etc. Hence, we get perfect squares on these rows.

The Powers of Eleven

Compare the powers of 11 with the numbers in each row of Pascal's triangle. Looking at the first few rows, we have Pascal's triangle on the left, and the powers of 11 on the right.

$$
\begin{array}{ccccc}
& & 1 & & \\
& 1 & & 1 & \\
1 & & 2 & & 1 \\
\end{array}
$$

$$
\begin{array}{rcl}
1 & = & 11^0 \\
11 & = & 11^1 \\
121 & = & 11^2 \\
1331 & = & 11^3 \\
14641 & = & 11^4
\end{array}
$$

The numbers are identical through the fourth row; yet, the pattern seems to break down when we get to the fifth row. However, let's take a closer look at these numbers. It is possible to make the fifth row of Pascal's triangle equate with eleven raised to the fifth power.

112

The fifth row of Pascal's triangle

   1   5   10   10   5   1

Eleven to the fifth power

$161051 = 11^5$

To do this, we'll start on the right side of the fifth row, and move from right to the left. We'll say that any number that has a single digit (in the triangle) will be left as such. For numbers in the triangle that have two or more digits, the least significant digit will remain, and the other digits will be added to the number on the left. In this example, the 1 and the 5 on the right side of the row are left as they are. The 10 on the right is a two digit number; therefore, the 1 and 0 are split. The 0 (being the least significant digit) is kept as such, while the 1 is added to the 10 on its left. This 10 becomes an 11. Again, the least significant digit remains while the other 1 is added to the 5 on its left. Finally, the left-most 1 remains unaffected. This is what we have:

1	5	10	10	5	1	
1	5+1	0+1	0	5	1	
1	6	1	0	5	1	which is 161051 or 11^5

We can see the same type of pattern in the sixth row as well as any of the following rows. Here's the sixth row.

1	6	15	20	15	6	1	
1	6+1	5+2	0+1	5	6	1	
1	7	7	1	5	6	1	which is 1771561 or 11^6

Using this technique, we can determine 11^n simply by looking at the nth row of Pascal's triangle.

Prime Numbers

Another property of Pascal's triangle is that prime numbers will evenly divide every number in their row (except for the 1's on the ends), while a composite number will not evenly divide every number in its row. (Remember that a composite number has several factors that divide into the number while a prime number can only be divided by one and the number itself. The numbers 2, 3, 5, 7, 11, etc. are prime while numbers like 4, 6, 8, 9, 10, and 12 are composite.) Let's take the prime number seven as an example. The seventh row from Pascal's triangle looks like this:

      1   7   21   35   35   21   7   1

The number seven divides evenly into each number between the one's on this row. Now let's compare this with a composite number. The eighth row looks like this:

      1   8   28   56   70   56   28   8   1

In this example we see that eight does not divide evenly into 28 or 70. This relationship is true for all prime and composite numbered rows throughout the triangle. This would be a valid check to determine if a number is prime; however, in real life this method has a few practical problems. Say that we wanted to check a large number to see if it was prime, and say that this large number had over 1000 digits in it. Within Pascal's triangle there would be over 1000 numbers that we would need to check, and each of these numbers would be much, much larger than the original number. This test would easily become a nightmare to try and perform in a practical sense.

The Sum of a Diagonal to the Edge

Another apparent pattern is that any number within the triangle is equal to the sum of either of the diagonals, from that number, out to the edge. For example, look at the 56 towards the left side of the 8th row. Now, find the number to the right and above the 56 which is 35. Follow this diagonal to the left, and we have the numbers 35, 15, 5 and 1. Add these numbers together, and the sum is 56.

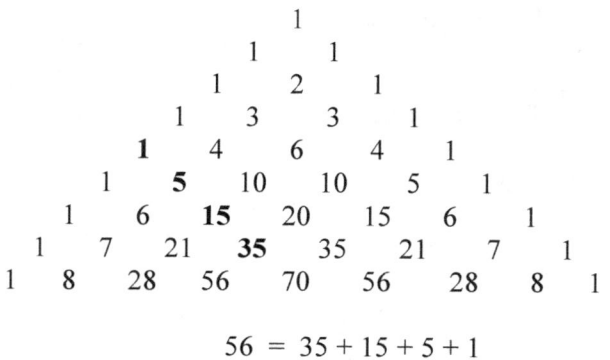

$$56 = 35 + 15 + 5 + 1$$

Figure 10.7   The sum of a diagonal to the edge.

We can also follow the diagonal starting on the other side of the 56, and go in the other direction:

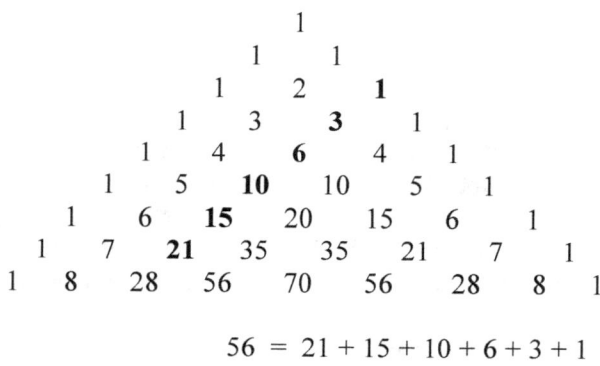

$$56 = 21 + 15 + 10 + 6 + 3 + 1$$

Figure 10.8   The sum of a diagonal to the edge.

The number to the left and above the same 56 is the number 21. Now, follow this diagonal to the right and we have the numbers 21, 15, 10, 6, 3 and 1. Add them together, and we again get a total of 56.

This relationship will hold true for any number within the triangle. Simply pick a number and then either start with the number that is above and left of the original number and sum the diagonal to the right; or start with the number that is above and right of the original number, and sum the diagonal to the left. In either case, the sum will be equal to the original number.

A variation to this pattern is that as you follow the diagonal to the top, you can stop at any point and add the number to the left (if you are following the diagonal on the right) or add the number to the right (if you are following the diagonal on the left). Let's look at an example:

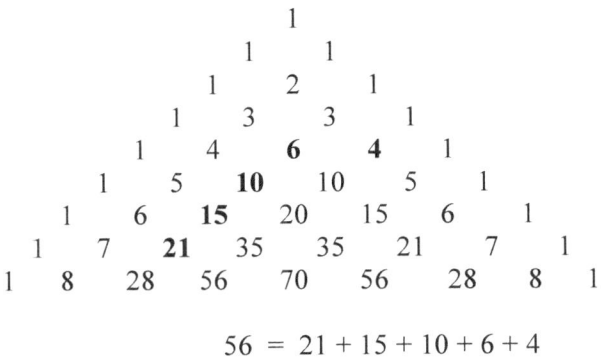

$$56 = 21 + 15 + 10 + 6 + 4$$

Figure 10.9   The sum of a diagonal to the edge.

Again, looking at the 56, we'll take the diagonal on the left, starting with the 21, and follow it up to the right. The numbers we are adding together are 21, 15, 10, 6, and this time instead of including the 3 and the 1, we'll simply stop at the 6 and go right and include the next number, which is 4. Of course, we could have also stopped at the 10 and gone right to include the next 10. In other words, some of the variations that we could have followed include:

$$
\begin{aligned}
56 &= 21 + 15 + 10 + 6 + 3 + 1 \\
&= 21 + 15 + 10 + 6 + 4 \\
&= 21 + 15 + 10 + 10 \\
&= 21 + 15 + 20
\end{aligned}
$$

Of course, what we are doing here is simply applying this rule twice. If you were to look at the 20 (in the example above), we see that the number above and to the left is the 10, and if we follow that diagonal to the edge, we have the numbers 10, 6, 3, and 1. Combining that with the 56, gives us:

$$
\begin{aligned}
56 &= 21 + 15 + 10 + 6 + 3 + 1 \\
20 &= 10 + 6 + 3 + 1
\end{aligned}
$$

The last four numbers that give us the sum to 56, are the same four numbers that give us the sum to 20. All we are doing is substituting the 20 for the last four numbers of those that sum to 56.

The Sum of a Rectangle of Numbers

A Pascal's Triangle pattern that is similar to the previous pattern takes a rectangle of numbers, adds them together, and their sum plus one is equal to the number just below the rectangle. The rectangle of numbers is parallel to the sides and extends to the top of the triangle. In the example below, we have a 2 x 6 rectangle of numbers. Summing the twelve numbers in the rectangle gives us 27. We add one and we get 28, which is also the number below the rectangle.

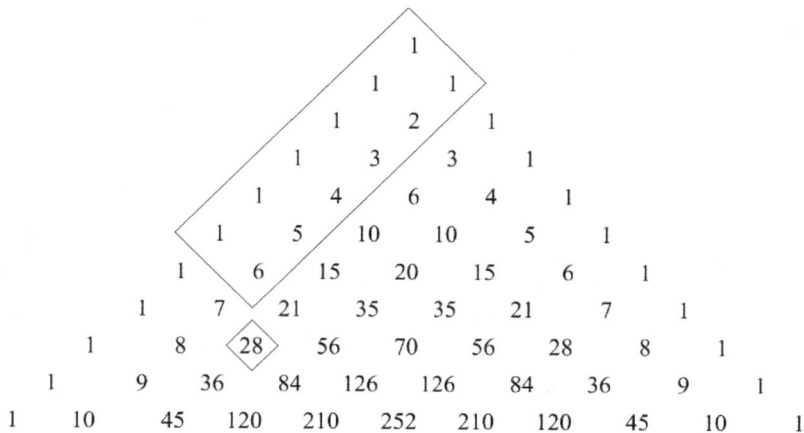

Figure 10.10   The sum of a 2 x 6 rectangle of numbers plus 1 equals 28.

In this next example, we have a 4 x 4 rectangle. Adding together these 16 numbers gives us 69. Then adding one to that gives us 70, which again is the number located below the rectangle.

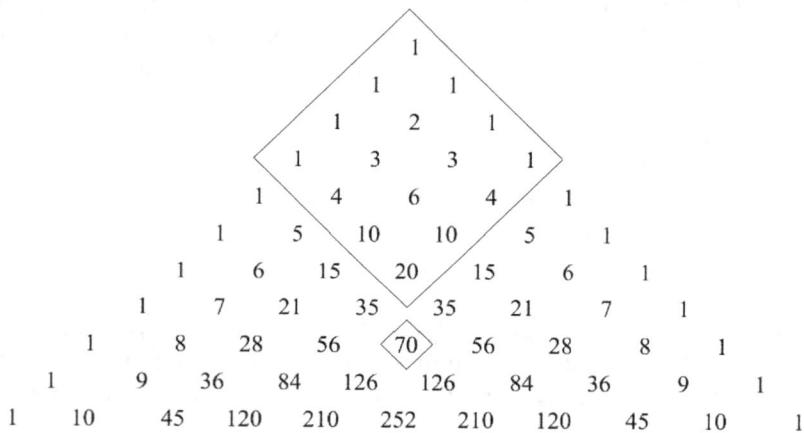

Figure 10.11   The sum of a 4 x 4 rectangle of numbers plus 1 equals 70.

The Sum of Each Sub-Triangle

Earlier we saw that if we considered each row, and summed up the numbers on that row, we would get a power of 2. We can continue this same thought a little further by adding all the numbers down to a specific row. The sum of all the numbers down to our selected row is equal to one less than 2 raised to the power of the row-plus-one. For example, if we go down to the first row, the sum of all the numbers in that row and above is equal to $2^2 - 1$, which is 3.

$$1$$
$$1 \qquad 1$$

The sum of this sub-triangle is equal to 3

Going down to the second row, the sum of the numbers in that row and above is equal to $2^3 - 1$, which is 7.

116

```
            1           The sum of this sub-triangle
        1       1       is equal to 7
    1       2       1
```

And, going down to the third row, the sum of the numbers in that row and above is equal to $2^4 - 1$, which is 15.

```
            1           The sum of this sub-triangle
        1       1       is equal to 15
    1       2       1
1       3       3       1
```

Of course, we can select any number of rows, and this property will hold true. So if we go down to the seventh row, then the sum the numbers in that row and above is equal to $2^8 - 1$, which is 255.

```
                    1
                1       1
            1       2       1
        1       3       3       1
    1       4       6       4       1
1       5      10      10       5       1
1   6      15      20      15       6       1
1   7      21      35      35      21       7       1
```

Figure 10.12   The sum of a sub-triangle is equal to $2^{row+1} - 1$.

The Hexagon Property

Another property within Pascal's triangle is called the hexagon property. As you look at Pascal's triangle, each number within the triangle is surrounded by six numbers: two on the top, two on the bottom, and one on either side. These six numbers form a hexagon. If you take the three alternating numbers around the hexagon, and multiply them together, that product is equal to the product of the other three numbers multiplied together.

```
                    1
                1       1
            1       2       1
        1       3       3       1
    1       4       6       4       1
1       5      10      10       5       1
1   6      15      20      15       6       1
1   7      21      35      35      21       7       1
1   8      28      56      70      56      28       8       1
```

Figure 10.13   An example of the hexagon property around the number 21.

Look at the number 21 on the seventh row (there are two of them, and either one will work). The six numbers surrounding the twenty-one are 6, 15, 35, 56, 28 and 7. If our first set of numbers starts with the 6 and takes every other number, we end up multiplying the 6, 35 and 28 together to get a product of 5880. Now, if we take the other three numbers, the 15, 56 and 7, and multiply them together, we find that they also have a product equal to 5880.

Of course this can easily be seen for the numbers that run down the middle of the triangle, because the numbers are symmetrical on both sides of these central numbers. For example, the 6 on the fourth row is surrounded by the numbers 3, 3, 4, 10, 10 and 4. If we multiple one set of alternate numbers, we are multiplying a 3, 4 and 10 together. The other set of alternate numbers also consist of a 3, 4 and 10, so it is no wonder that it works in this case. However, this property is true for any number that is surrounded by six other numbers.

A variation to this property only works on the numbers within the "counting number" diagonal (the diagonal made up of counting numbers). Select a number within this diagonal. Now, go around the hexagon and multiply every other number together. Add that to the product of the other, every other number, and then finally add that to the number itself, and what you have is that number cubed. Let's look at a couple of examples:

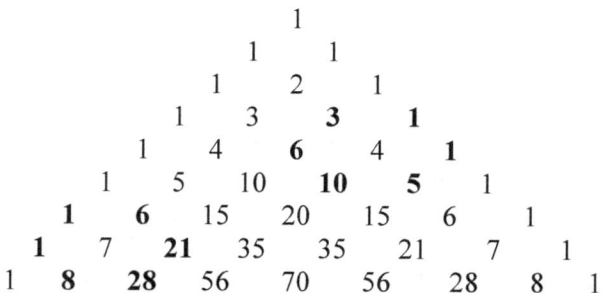

Figure 10.14   A variation to the hexagon property around the numbers 4 and 7.

The numbers that surround the 4 are 3, 1, 1, 5, 10, and 6. The product of the first set of every-other-numbers gives us 3(1*10) = 30; and the product of the other, every-other numbers is 1(5*6) = 30. Add these two numbers together, as well as the number they surround, and we have 30 + 30 + 4 which is equal to 64. And 64 is equal to the number they surround, raised to the third power.

Similarly, the numbers surrounding the 7 are 1, 6, 21, 28, 8, and 1. The product of the first set of every-other numbers is 1(21*8) = 168. The product of the other, every-other numbers is 6(28*1) = 168. Adding these two numbers together, along with the number they surround, gives us 168 + 168 + 7 which is equal to 343. And finally 343 is also equal to 7 raised to the third power.

Highlighting a Number's Multiples

The final pattern we will consider can be seen when multiples of a number within the triangle are highlighted. What we find are various sized triangles of highlighted numbers, positioned in such a way that interesting and even intricate patterns begin to emerge. For example, if all the multiples of two are highlighted, we have something that looks like this:

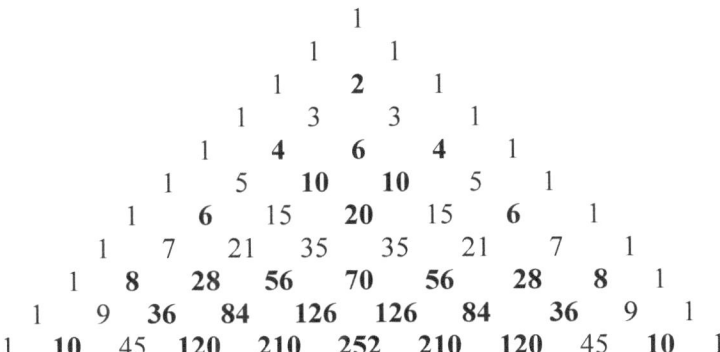

Figure 10.15   The first ten rows of Pascal's triangle with the even numbers highlighted.

In the figure above we can see the beginning of a pattern. The fourth and eighth rows have even numbers all the way across the row (except of course for the ones on the ends). The rows just beneath have one less even number; and the rows below that have an even number next to the ones, and then one less even number than the row above it. If we were to extend the triangle so that we could examine 50 rows, we could see a more fully developed pattern. However, it's not practical to list the numbers of 50 rows in the limited space we have here. Instead, we will let each number be represented as a small rectangle. Now, if we want to highlight a number in the triangle, we will do so by filling in the rectangle. The first 50 rows of Pascal's triangle with all the multiples of two highlighted looks like this:

Figure 10.16   50 rows of Pascal's triangle with the darkened blocks representing the even numbers (or multiples of two).

On the second row, and every second row after that there is an even number, except on the fourth row, and every fourth row after that, where there is the beginning of a small triangle comprised of three even numbers. Except on the eighth row, and every eighth row after that where there is the beginning of a larger triangle comprised of seven even numbers. Except on the sixteenth row and every sixteenth row after that where there is the beginning of an even larger triangle comprised of fifteen numbers; and so on.

This same type of pattern is evident for all prime numbers. For example, if we look at the multiples of five, we find on the fifth row, and every fifth row after that there is the beginning of a small triangle comprised of four numbers (that are multiples of five). Except on the twenty-fifth row and every twenty-fifth row after that where there is the beginning of a larger triangle; and so on. (see the figure below)

Figure 10.17   The first 50 rows of Pascal's triangle with the darkened blocks representing the multiples of five.

If we highlight the multiples of a composite number (a number that has two or more primes as its factors), we see a more complex pattern. However, a closer examination of the pattern would reveal that it is composed of the intersection of the prime numbers that make up the composite. For example, if we highlight the multiples of ten, we find that its pattern is equivalent to the intersection of the patterns created from the multiples of two and the multiples of five. (see the figure below)

Figure 10.18   The first 50 rows of Pascal's triangle with the darkened blocks representing the multiples of ten.

Of course, these patters become even more amazing when we look at more rows. The final four figures of this chapter show the first 150 rows of Pascal's Triangle for various multiples. The first figure highlights the multiples of 32, the second highlights the multiples of 46, the third highlights multiples of 82, and the fourth highlights multiples of 94. (See the appendix for additional figures of Pascal's Triangle with highlighted multiples.)

Figure 10.19   The first 150 rows of Pascal's triangle with the black blocks representing the multiples of 32.

Figure 10.20   The first 150 rows of Pascal's triangle with the black blocks representing the multiples of 46.

Figure 10.21   The first 150 rows of Pascal's triangle with the black blocks representing the multiples of 82.

Figure 10.22   The first 150 rows of Pascal's triangle with the black blocks representing the multiples of 94.

Chapter 11
The Sierpinski Triangle

Building a Sierpinski Triangle

A Sierpinski's triangle is a fractal-like design made within a triangle. Lines are added within the triangle that divide the triangle into smaller and smaller sections. Some of these sections are then removed, and this is done in such a way that if the process is continued indefinitely, the total length of the lines added becomes infinite, while the total area removed from the triangle is equal to the area of the triangle itself. The pattern is considered fractal because small sections of the pattern resemble the overall pattern.

A Sierpinski's triangle is made by starting with an ordinary triangle (we'll use an equilateral triangle), and placing midpoints on each of the three sides. The midpoints are connected with lines, thus creating four new triangles, one in the middle, and one at each of the vertices. The area of the middle triangle is removed (by coloring it black), and then the process is repeated with the three remaining triangles.

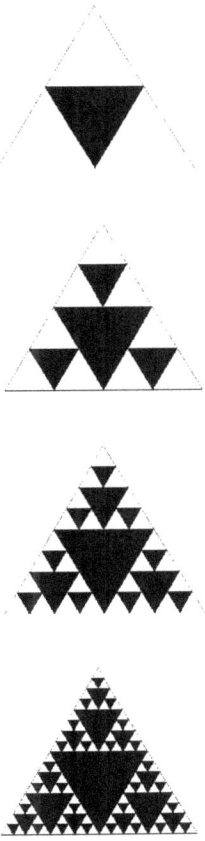

Figure 11.1   Successive steps showing the construction of a Sierpinski's triangle.

In other words, we take the remaining triangles, place midpoints on each of the sides, use lines to connect these midpoints, and then remove each of the middle triangles. Again, if we continue this process indefinitely, we have a fractal-like pattern where any section of the triangle resembles any other section of the triangle as well as the triangle itself. This process holds true and can work on any type of triangle, although it is easiest to show it on an equilateral or isosceles triangle. The figure above shows the first four iterations of our Sierpinski Triangle.

Zero Area

Now, let's take a look at the math, and see how the area goes to zero while the perimeter surrounding these areas becomes infinite. We'll begin by calculating how much area we're removing from the triangle in each iterative step of the process. If we say that the original triangle has an area of one square unit (even though we are talking about triangles, area is still measured in "square" units), then the first step divides the triangle into four equal sub-triangles, and removing the middle triangle subtracts 1/4 of the original area.

Now, if we connect midpoints and create four more triangles within each of the three remaining triangles, we find that each of these 12 triangles is 1/16th the total area of the original triangle. At this step we are removing three inside triangles with the total area removed equal to 3/16 of the original triangle. The next step removes 9 triangles that each have an area of 1/64 the total area of the original triangle. A number series is beginning to emerge, and writing this series shows that the total area removed is equal to:

$$1/4 \ + \ 3/16 \ + \ 9/64 \ + \ 27/256 \ + \ ...$$

This series is infinite, so it is next to impossible to add together all the terms and arrive at an exact value. However, this is a geometric series, and as such there is an algebraic formula that states that if r is equal to some fraction, and the absolute value of this fraction is greater than zero and less than one, then the sum of successive powers of that fraction create the following relationship:

$$r^0 \ + \ r^1 \ + \ r^2 \ + \ r^3 \ + \ ... \ = \ 1/(1 - r)$$

The left side of this relationship is an infinite series while the right side is something manageable. The series of fractions we have doesn't quite look like this, but we can work with it and make it so that it will. Notice that the numerators to all of our fractions are powers of three, while all the denominators are powers of four. Therefore, we can rewrite our infinite series with terms just using 3's and 4's.

$$3^0/4^1 \ + \ 3^1/4^2 \ + \ 3^2/4^3 \ + \ 3^3/4^4 \ + \ ...$$

In our series the numerators and corresponding denominators are not raised to the same power; however, in each case the numerator is one power less than the denominator. Therefore, multiplying the series by three will cause the numerators to be raised to the same power as the denominators. However, keep in mind that if we multiply the series by three, then we must also multiply it by 1/3 so that we don't change the actual value of the series. We'll do this by multiplying each term by three, and then we'll place parentheses around the entire series and multiply it by 1/3. We now have the numerators of each fraction in the series raised to the same power as the denominator.

$$1/3*(3^1/4^1 \ + \ 3^2/4^2 \ + \ 3^3/4^3 \ + \ 3^4/4^4 \ + \ ...)$$

At this point it is easy to see that r is equal to 3/4. The final term we need is an r raised to the zero power that we can add to the series inside the parentheses giving us something that resembles the formula we are trying to match. Adding and subtracting a one fulfills that requirement. We do it by adding another level of parentheses like this:

$$1/3*[(1 + 3^1/4^1 + 3^2/4^2 + 3^3/4^3 + 3^4/4^4 + ...) - 1]$$

We now replace the infinite series with its algebraic equivalent:

$$1/3*[(1/(1 - 3/4)) - 1]$$

This simplifies to:

$$1/3*[(4) - 1]$$
$$1/3*[3]$$

Which is equal to one. Again, what we just calculated is the total area removed, and as we just saw, the area removed is equal to the total area of the original triangle. In other words, if we carry out the removal process indefinitely, the remaining area within the triangle is equal to zero.

An Infinite Perimeter

Now, let's find the length of the lines that we use as borders to the areas being removed (that are added to the triangle with each iteration). For the sake of simplicity, we'll begin by saying that the triangle we are starting with is an equilateral triangle where the length of each side is equal to one. (We simplified the previous section by saying that the triangle had an area equal to one square unit. We could have used triangles with other areas and perimeters, and the principles would still be the same, but the Math would be more complex.)

Adding the lengths of the sides of our equilateral triangle will give us a perimeter equal to three. Now, when we perform the first "removal," by connecting the midpoints and drawing lines between the midpoints, we are adding three more lines within the triangle, where the length of each line is equal to 1/2. The internal perimeter has now increased by 3/2. The next iteration adds 9 more lines each with a length equal to 1/4. With this iteration the perimeter increases by 9/4. And as we continue, we see the following pattern emerge:

$$3 + 3/2 + 9/4 + 27/8 + 81/16 + ...$$

While we could try and find some formula that would approximate the series total, at this point it is important to notice that each term in this series is greater that one. Since every term is greater than one, and since this is an infinite series, the sum of this series is also infinite. To sum it up, we have a triangle that has an infinite perimeter surrounding removed areas, and when we add together all of the area that has been removed, it is equal to the total area of the original triangle. Quite an interesting combination of characteristics.

The Koch Curve and the Sierpinski's Triangle

Another object with an infinite perimeter is the Koch curve. A Koch Curve is a type of Lindenmayer System (we will look at these in more detail in a later chapter). To create a Koch curve, we start with a simple object consisting of a few line segments between two points. Next, we replace each segment with a scaled-down copy of the original object. Then repeat the process of replacing each segment again with a further-scaled-down version of the original object. If the original object consists of the three sides of a trapezoid, we can use this process of creating a Koch curve and turn a 3-sided trapezoid into a Sierpinski's triangle.

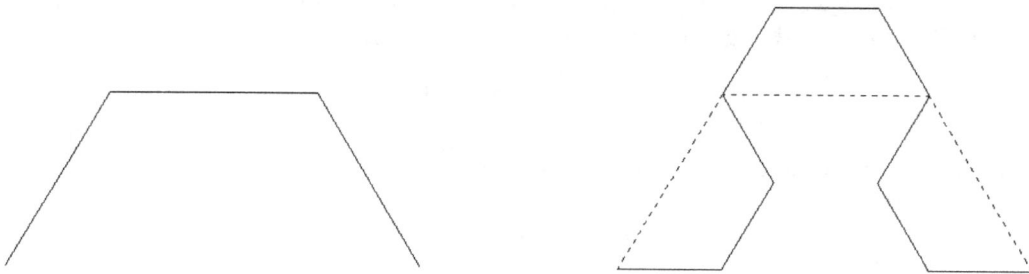

Figure 11.2   The initial pattern and the first iteration of a Koch curve.

The three lines on the left (in the figure above) are the original object. The diagram on the right has dotted lines representing the original object. Notice that each line segment from the left has been replaced with a scaled-down copy of the original object from the left.

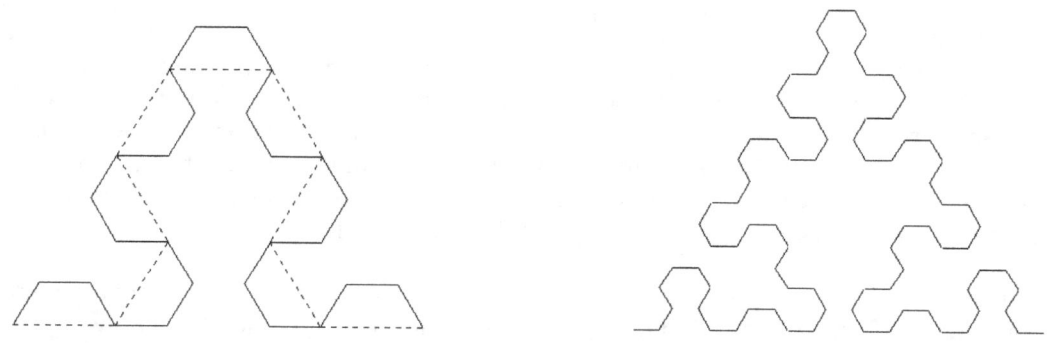

Figure 11.3   The next two iterations of this Koch curve.

The dotted lines in the diagram on the left represent the previous diagram. Again, each line segment from the previous diagram is replaced with a scaled-down copy of the original three-line object. The diagram on the right takes the diagram on the left and replaces each of its line segments with a further scaled-down copy of the original three-line object.

This process of replacing each line segment from the previous diagram with a scaled-down copy of the original object can be continued indefinitely. The next figure shows the next two iterations of this process. Notice how the image of a Sierpinski's triangle is becoming more and more defined.

Figure 11.4   Additional iterations of the Koch curve make the Sierpinski triangle more apparent.

A Third Method of Creating a Sierpinski's Triangle

The Sierpinski Triangle appears unexpectedly in several other places in mathematics. In the next few sections of this chapter, we will look at a few other unrelated methods of creating a Sierpinski's triangle. The next method we'll consider starts with a row of o's and a single X placed within that row. (We'll use little o's in order to make it easier to see the pattern created with the X's.) The first row looks like this:

o o o o o o o o o o o o o o o o o X o o

To create the next row, we look at each pair of characters, and where the pair of characters are the same, we place an o, and where the pair of characters are different, we place an X. Then after examining the pair, we shift right one character, and then consider the next pair. Therefore, in the row above, the first 17 characters are o's; which means that the first 16 pairs are all the same, and they produce an o on the next row. When we get to the o in front of the X, this pair of characters is "o X", and that will give us an X on the next row. Then, shifting right one character, the next pair of characters is "X o" which will again give us an X.

The first row ends with two zeroes as the last pair which will give us a zero as our next to the last character in the second row. If we stop here, then each succeeding row will have one less character than the row before. In order to create our desired pattern, we will simply add a zero as the last character on each row. Thus, each row will always have some combination of 20 X's or o's in it. The second row looks like this:

o o o o o o o o o o o o o o o o X X o o

We now use the same rules on the second row to generate the third row. (Remember that the two X's will yield an o; and after considering all of the pairs, we add a final zero at the end of the row.) The third row looks like this:

o o o o o o o o o o o o o o o X o X o o

And the fourth row looks like this:

o o o o o o o o o o o o o o X X X X o o

127

The sequence of X's continues to grow with each row added, and except for the first row there will always be at least two X's on any given row. The individual rows can be very interesting; however, to see the Sierpinski pattern, we need to look at several rows at a time. Here are the first 16 rows:

```
o o o o o o o o o o o o o o o o X o o
o o o o o o o o o o o o o o o XX o o
o o o o o o o o o o o o o o o X oX o o
o o o o o o o o o o o o o o XXXX o o
o o o o o o o o o o o o o X o o oX o o
o o o o o o o o o o o o XX o oXX o o
o o o o o o o o o o o X oX oX oX o o
o o o o o o o o o o XXXXXXXX o o
o o o o o o o o o X o o o o o o oX o o
o o o o o o o o XX o o o o o oXX o o
o o o o o o o X oX o o o o oX oX o o
o o o o o o XXXX o o o oXXXX o o
o o o o o X o o oX o o oX o o oX o o
o o o o XX o oXX o oXX o oXX o o
o o o X oX oX oX oX oX oX o o
o o XXXXXXXXXXXXXXXX o o
```

Figure 11.5   Building a Sierpinski pattern from the previous row.

If you look closely at the figure above, you can see the triangle has been right-justified (or you could say that it is on its side with the top in the lower right corner). As more rows and more characters are included the Sierpinski pattern becomes even more defined and pronounced.

Boolean OR Logic and the Sierpinski Triangle

We can also create a Sierpinski Triangle-like pattern using the Boolean logic OR operator. To do this, we'll begin by defining a few sets. We could actually define as many sets as we want; however for this example, we will only use four. The first one we'll call A, and it contains a 0 1 0 1, which repeats four times. The B set has 0 0 1 1, which also repeats four times. The C set has four 0's followed by four 1's and repeats that pattern once; and the D set has eight 0's followed by eight 1's:

```
Let:    A =  0  1  0  1  0  1  0  1  0  1  0  1  0  1  0  1
        B =  0  0  1  1  0  0  1  1  0  0  1  1  0  0  1  1
        C =  0  0  0  0  1  1  1  1  0  0  0  0  1  1  1  1
        D =  0  0  0  0  0  0  0  0  1  1  1  1  1  1  1  1
```

Lining these sets on top of each other (as shown above) creates columns that represent the binary numbers 0 through 15. Now, with that ground work complete, we'll combine these sets using the OR operator. This first group will only use the A and B sets. Here, we'll show the zero set, the A set, the B set, and finally the A OR B set. With these four lines on top of each other, we see the beginning of our Sierpinski Triangle (made up of the 1's). Since we are only showing four rows, the pattern is easier to see if we also only show four columns (showing additional columns only repeats the earlier pattern):

```
(    )  =      o  o  o  o
(A   )  =      o  1  o  1
( B  )  =      o  o  1  1
(AB  )  =      o  1  1  1
```

You'll notice that within the group above, I changed the 0's to o's, and made the 1's bold. This was done to make the pattern easier to see. Now, let's add the C set. Doing so adds four more lines because we are essentially OR'ing the C set with each of the four previous sets. With eight lines, we will now also show eight columns, and our Sierpinski Triangle-like pattern becomes more defined:

```
(     )  =     o  o  o  o  o  o  o  o
(A    )  =     o  1  o  1  o  1  o  1
( B   )  =     o  o  1  1  o  o  1  1
(AB   )  =     o  1  1  1  o  1  1  1
(   C )  =     o  o  o  o  1  1  1  1
(A  C )  =     o  1  o  1  1  1  1  1
( BC  )  =     o  o  1  1  1  1  1  1
(ABC  )  =     o  1  1  1  1  1  1  1
```

Finally, we add the D set. By adding this fourth set, we are again essentially OR'ing this set with the eight previous sets. This again doubles the number of lines that we will have (and along with that the number of columns we'll be showing). With the addition of this step, the Sierpinski Triangle-like pattern is even more apparent:

```
(       )  =   o o o o o o o o o o o o o o o o
(A      )  =   o 1 o 1 o 1 o 1 o 1 o 1 o 1 o 1
( B     )  =   o o 1 1 o o 1 1 o o 1 1 o o 1 1
(AB     )  =   o 1 1 1 o 1 1 1 o 1 1 1 o 1 1 1
(   C   )  =   o o o o 1 1 1 1 o o o o 1 1 1 1
(A  C   )  =   o 1 o 1 1 1 1 1 o 1 o 1 1 1 1 1
( BC    )  =   o o 1 1 1 1 1 1 o o 1 1 1 1 1 1
(ABC    )  =   o 1 1 1 1 1 1 1 o 1 1 1 1 1 1 1
(    D  )  =   o o o o o o o o 1 1 1 1 1 1 1 1
(A   D  )  =   o 1 o 1 o 1 o 1 1 1 1 1 1 1 1 1
( B  D  )  =   o o 1 1 o o 1 1 1 1 1 1 1 1 1 1
(AB  D  )  =   o 1 1 1 o 1 1 1 1 1 1 1 1 1 1 1
(   CD  )  =   o o o o 1 1 1 1 1 1 1 1 1 1 1 1
(A  CD  )  =   o 1 o 1 1 1 1 1 1 1 1 1 1 1 1 1
( BCD   )  =   o o 1 1 1 1 1 1 1 1 1 1 1 1 1 1
(ABCD   )  =   o 1 1 1 1 1 1 1 1 1 1 1 1 1 1 1
```

You may have noticed that the pattern above isn't a triangle, it is a square. But it does display the features of a Sierpinski Triangle pattern within the upper left diagonal of the square. Notice also that this pattern would continue to grow as more sets are added.

Another Method of Creating a Sierpinski's Triangle

Another method of creating a Sierpinski Triangle starts by defining three vertices of a triangle. Next, we randomly place our first point within the triangle and then randomly pick one of the three tvertices of the triangle. We then place a point half way between our original point and the selected vertex. We now use this new point as our starting point and randomly select another vertex and place another point half way between our current position and the selected vertex. The process continues where the most recently placed point becomes the next start point; a vertex of the triangle is then randomly selected, and a new point is placed midway between the start point and the selected vertex.

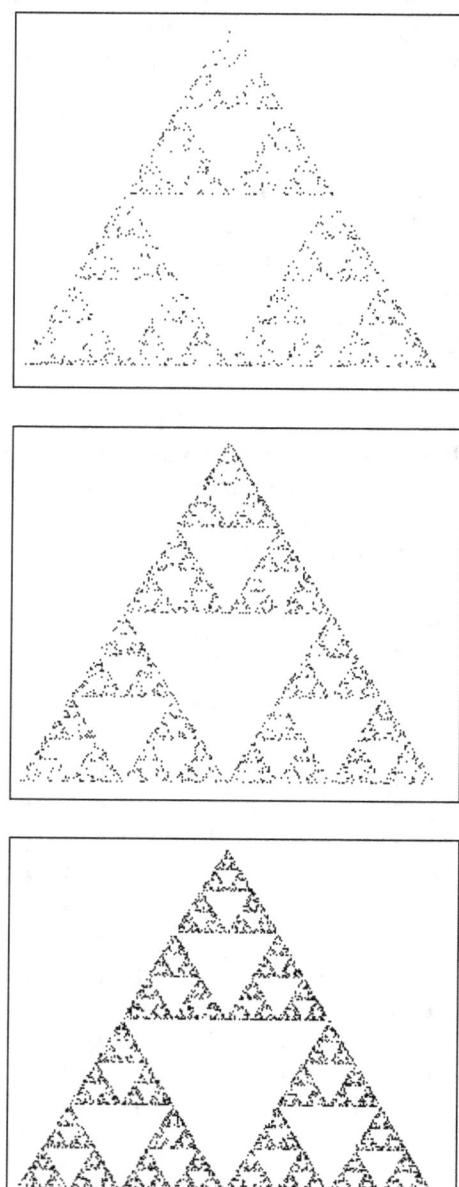

Figure 11.6   Sierpinski's triangle after 1000, 2000 and 5000 iterations.

After several iterations (more like several thousand iterations) the Sierpinski triangle pattern becomes very apparent. The three plots above show what we get after 1000, 2000, and 5000 iterations.

The Sierpinski Triangle within Pascal's Triangle

There is also a Sierpinski triangle within Pascal's triangle. If we take Pascal's triangle, and highlight (or remove) all the even numbers from the triangle, the remaining numbers create a Sierpinski triangle pattern.

Figure 11.7   A Sierpinski's triangle from Pascal's triangle.

In the diagram above, we represent each number in Pascal's triangle as a rectangle. The even numbers in Pascal's triangle are the filled in rectangles. This diagram shows the first 50 rows of Pascal's triangle.

The Sierpinski Square

After considering the various methods of creating a Sierpinski's triangle, we will close this chapter by looking at a variation to the triangle itself. Analogous to Sierpinski's triangle is the Sierpinski square (also known as a Sierpinski's gasket).

The gasket is made by taking a square, dividing it into nine equal areas, and then removing one of the areas. Each of the remaining eight areas is then divided into nine equal areas, and again one of the areas within each of these eight remaining areas is removed. If this process is continued indefinitely, we again find (just as we did with the Sierpinski Triangle) that all of the area of the square will ultimately be removed; and that the perimeter surrounding the removed areas has an infinite length.

The figure below shows four iterations of two examples of a Sierpinski square. The series on the left has the center area removed with each iteration while the series on the right has the lower left area removed with each iteration.

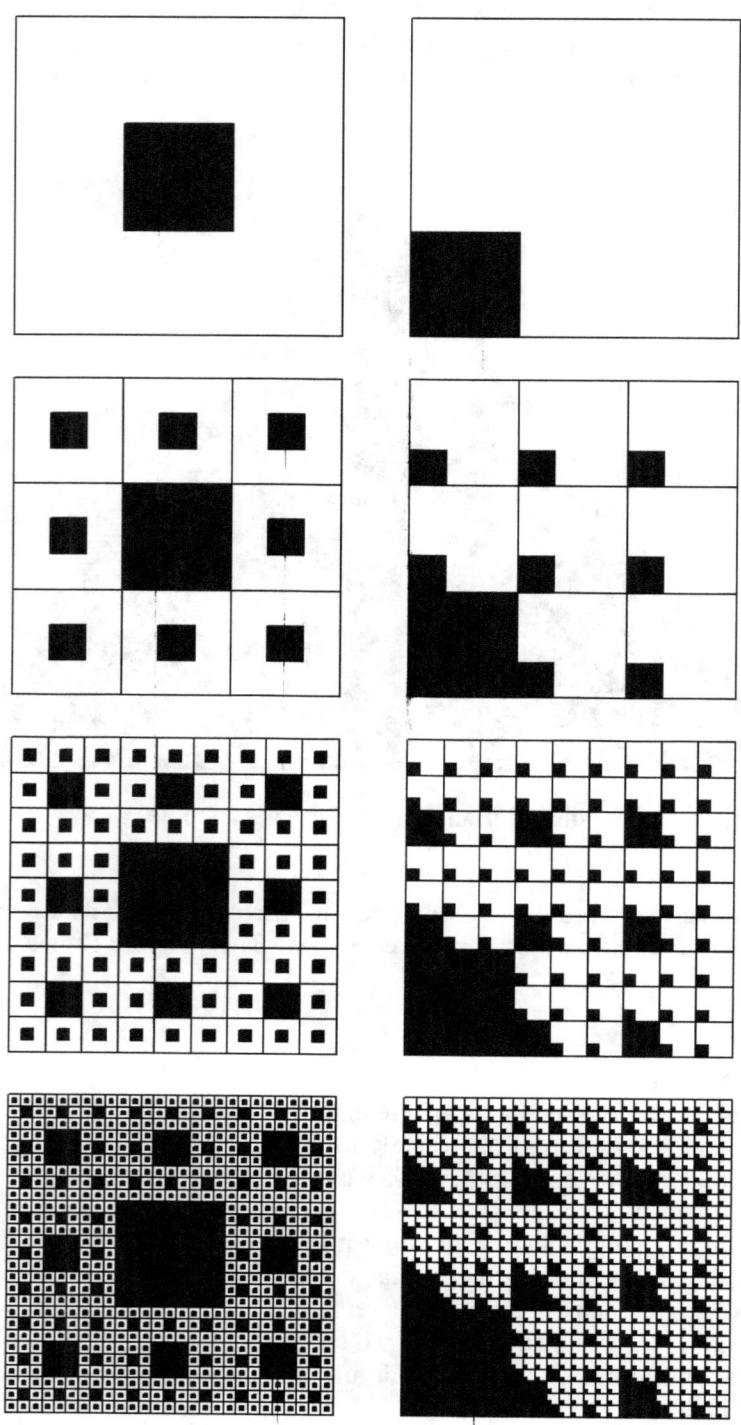

Figure 11.8   The first four successive iterations within two variations of a Sierpinski's square.

Chapter 12
Multiplication Methods

Most of us learn one way to multiply larger numbers together. Often it is the method we were taught in elementary school. Then we go throughout the remainder of our school years thinking it is the only way.

In this chapter we will look at several methods of multiplying numbers together. Some of these methods were practiced anciently in other parts of the world, and some are still practiced in foreign lands today. Most of these methods require you to still learn your multiplication tables, but some of them don't. Some of these methods create interesting patterns while performing the multiplication. Some are just for show, some are easy to check, and some are designed for speed with large numbers. Yet, all of these are valid methods of finding the product of two numbers.

The Traditional Method

Soon after learning the multiplication table, most elementary schools teach a method for multiplying larger numbers together. The method taught in American schools looks something like this:

```
      758
    x 342
     1516        (2 is multiplied to 758)
     3032        (4 is multiplied to 758, the product is shifted left one place)
   + 2274        (3 is multiplied to 758, the product is shifted left again)
   259236        (the three products are totaled to give the final result)
```

This method consists of multiplying the top number (758 in this example) by each of the digits in the bottom number. We start with the right-most digit on the bottom row, and as each successive digit of the bottom number is multiplied to the top number, the corresponding product is shifted one column to the left. The final result is calculated from the sum of each of these products. This method is one of the quickest, but, as we will see in this chapter, it isn't the easiest way to multiply two larger numbers together.

The Old English Method

This method takes the two numbers that will be multiplied together, and arranges them around the sides of a box. If, for example, the two numbers being multiplied are each two-digits, one of the numbers is written horizontally, and placed on top of the box, while the other number is written vertically and placed on the right side of the box. Lines are then drawn within the box such that one line divides the box in half vertically, and another line divides the box in half horizontally, giving us four squares within the box. (The idea is to have squares under each number on top of the box, and squares to the left of each number on the right of the box.) Finally, a diagonal line is drawn through each of these squares. This sets up the two numbers that will be multiplied together.

To understand this method better, we will look at a specific example to explain this process. In this case, we will look at the product of 36 and 49. Notice below, that we have placed the 36 on top of the box, and the 49 to the right of the box, and we already have all the lines drawn within the box.

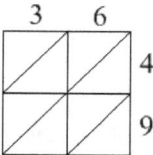

Figure 12.1   Setting up the Old English method of multiplication.

Next, we start to fill in the box. We do this by multiplying a number on the top with a number on the side and writing that product in the corresponding square. For example, 3 times 4 is equal to 12. The 12 is written in the box that is under the 3 and across from the 4 with the first digit of the 12 (the 1) in the left diagonal, and the second digit (the 2) written in the right diagonal. The same thing is done for each of the other combinations of numbers. After the box is all filled in, we have something that looks like this:

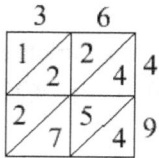

Figure 12.2   The Old English method with the box filled in.

To get the final product of 36 and 49, we add up the numbers along the diagonals, starting with the bottom-right diagonal. The first diagonal has only one number in it, the number 4, so it is written below the first box on the right. The second diagonal has the numbers 4, 5 and 7 in it. Adding these together gives us a total of 16. We write down the 6, and carry the 1 to the next diagonal. The third diagonal has the numbers 2, 2 and 2 in it. Adding these numbers together, plus the one that was carried from the previous diagonal gives us a 7. The 7 is written to the left of the bottom row of squares. The final diagonal has only the number 1 in it. This one is written to the left of the top row of squares. Our square with the numbers around it now looks something like this:

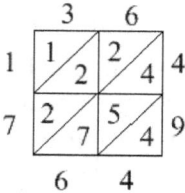

Figure 12.3   The Old English method with the final result.

The numbers written around the left side and bottom of the box are equal to the final product of 36 and 49. In other words, 36 times 49 is equal to 1764. This method is very easy to learn, and it is easy to adapt this method to the product of larger numbers.

A variation of this method draws the box as a diamond so that the diagonals in the figure above are run vertically. The two numbers being multiplied together are placed along the top, one number on one side and the other on the other side. The diagram below uses the numbers from the previous example to show how this is done.

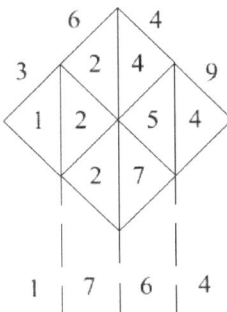

Figure 12.4   An alternate approach to using the Old English method.

The advantage to this variation is that when you do the addition, you add the numbers straight down. The disadvantage is that if you are multiplying two numbers that aren't the same size, such as a four-digit number and a two-digit number, the diamond is lop-sided and somewhat easier to get mixed up. However, with a little practice, this minor obstacle can be easily overcome.

A Variation on the English Method

This third method is a variation of the old English method, but it is a little quicker to use because we don't have to draw the box. It also has the advantage of being just as easy to check your results. We'll explain this method by looking at an example. We'll multiply 27 by 34:

$$
\begin{array}{rr}
 & 21 \\
27 & 0628 \\
\underline{\times\,34} & \underline{+\ 08} \\
 & 918
\end{array}
$$

This method uses a combination of cross and inline multiplications. We begin by writing 27 times 34 just as we normally would; however, we will write our products to the right of our original numbers instead of below them. The first row that we generate is the middle row. We create it by inline multiplications: staring with the left digits, the 2 is multiplied with the 3, and then the 7 is multiplied with the 4. Each of these products is written as a two-digit number, and that gives us the middle row, 0628. The top and bottom rows are the result of a cross multiplication. The top row is equal to 3 times 7 and the bottom row is equal to 2 times 4. Both of these products are shifted one digit to the right, and again, each product is written as a two-digit number. Finally, we add straight down the columns to get the final product of 27 times 34, which is 918.

To get a better feel for this, let's look at a couple of other examples. In one example we'll multiply 19 and 71 together, and in the other we'll multiply 44 to itself.

$$
\begin{array}{rr}
 & 01 \\
71 & 0709 \\
\underline{\times\ 19} & \underline{+\ \ 63\ \ \ } \\
 & 1349
\end{array}
\qquad
\begin{array}{rr}
 & 16 \\
44 & 1616 \\
\underline{\times\ 44} & \underline{+\ \ 16\ \ \ } \\
 & 1936
\end{array}
$$

Again, the center row is made from inline multiplications and the top and bottom rows are made from cross multiplications. On the left the multiplication is simplified because of the 1's; and on the right, we get an interesting pattern from the 4's.

So how does this method work when the two numbers multiplied together each have three digits? We'll consider another example to better under-stand this method. This time we'll multiply 246 to 753. This is what we get:

$$
\begin{array}{rr}
 & 06 \\
753 & 1012 \\
\underline{\times\ \ 246} & 142018 \\
 & 2830 \\
 & \underline{+\ \ \ 42\ \ \ \ \ } \\
 & 185238
\end{array}
$$

Once again, the center row is made from inline multiplications. The row just above the center row is made from cross-multiplications where the 2 is multiplied with the 5, and the 4 is multiplied with the 3 to give us respectively 10 and 12. Likewise, the row just below the center row is made from cross-multiplications where the 7 is multiplied with the 4 and the 5 is multiplied with the 6 to give us 28 and 30 respectively. The top and bottom rows are made from the cross multiplications of the 2 and the 3 to give us 06 on the top; and the 7 and the 6 to give us 42 on the bottom. Finally, the numbers are added straight down their respective columns to arrive at the final answer. Thus, the product of 753 and 246 is equal 185,238.

A Node Counting Method

This method doesn't really require a knowledge of multiplication; in fact, all a person needs to do is draw lines, count nodes and then add numbers together. Lines are drawn at 45 degree angles with one set of lines (representing the first number) running diagonally from lower left to upper right at a positive 45 degree angle; and the second set of lines running diagonally at a negative 45 degree angle, from upper left to lower right. The lines are also drawn in such a way that the lines from the two numbers intersect each other. The nodes of intersection are counted, and combined in such a way that they give the result of the product of the original two numbers. Here is an example.

To find the product of 21 and 34, we begin by drawing lines that represent these two numbers. First draw the lines for the number 21 with these lines running from the lower left to upper right. The two lines representing the 2 are drawn first, with the single line representing the one drawn to the right of the first number. Next we draw lines for the number 34 with these lines running from the upper left to the lower right. The three lines representing the 3 are drawn first, with the four lines representing the 4 again drawn to the right of the first number. When finding the product of two, two-digit numbers, the lines of each number can be thought of as opposite sides of a diamond (as seen in the figure on the following page).

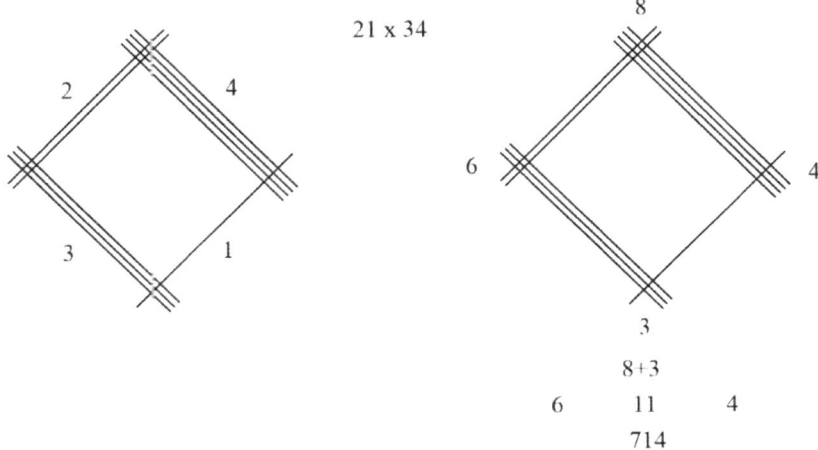

21 x 34

8+3
6   11   4
714

Figure 12.5   An method that counts the nodes of intersecting lines.

In the figure above, on the left we show the two numbers, 21 and 34, as represented by the two sets of lines. On the right, we show the node counts of the intersections from each pair of lines (at each of the corners of the diamond). Where the corners line up on top of each other, the node counts are added together (in this case, the 8 and 3 are added together to give us 11). The node counts are lined up. In this example we have 6, 11, and 4; and then they are combined together to give us the final result. The 4 is written first. Then we take the right most digit of the 11 and write it next to the 4 and then take the left most digit and carry it to the number on the left. The carry and the number on the left are added together to give us 7; thus the result of product of 21 and 34 is 714.

The same principles are followed when multiplying numbers with more digits. In this next example we'll find the product of 452 and 31:

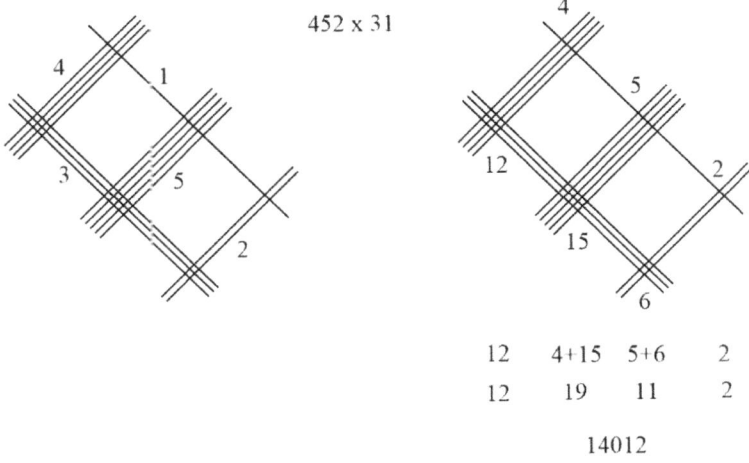

452 x 31

12   4+15   5+6   2
12   19   11   2
14012

Figure 12.6   The product of 452 and 31 using the method of counting nodes of
             intersecting lines.

The left-side diagram in the figure on the preceding page shows the numbers drawn as lines. In the diagram on the right we have the same figure, with the numbers showing the intersection counts. Where these nodes line up on top of each other, we add the numbers together, such that 5 and 6 line up and are added to give us 11; and also 4 and 15 line up and are added together to give us 19. The node counts are then lined up, giving us 12, 19, 11, and 2. Finally, we take the right-most digit of each number, and write it down, and where there is a left-most digit, it is carried to the number to the left. Therefore, the 2 on the right is written and there is no carry. Next, the left 1 from the 11 is written, and the right 1 is carried (and added) to the 19, making it 20. The 0 from the 20 is written, and the 2 is carried (and added) to the 12, making it 14. Since there are no more numbers to the left, there isn't another carry, and the number 14 is written. Thus, the final result is 14012.

A Method from India

This method has been used in India. It combines several cross multiplications and inline multiplications to arrive at the final result. The multiplications are performed from right to left, and with a little practice it is possible to use this method to learn to multiply two and three digit numbers together in your head. We'll explain this method as we look at a few examples. We'll start by finding the product of 43 and 27.

$$
\begin{array}{r}
43 \\
\times\ 27 \\
\end{array}
$$

$$8 \quad 28+6 \quad 21 \qquad (2 \times 4 = 8, \quad 7 \times 4 \text{ and } 2 \times 3 \text{ yields } 28 + 6, \quad 7 \times 3 = 21)$$
$$+\ \underline{\quad 34 \quad} \qquad (\text{note that the } 28 + 6 \text{ is written as } 34)$$
$$1161$$

When multiplying a pair of two-digit numbers together, the first and last products are inline multiplications where the top number is multiplied with the number directly below it. The middle product is the sum of the two cross multiplications. In the example above, 21 is the result of 7 times 3; and 8 comes from 2 times 4. The middle number, 34, is obtained by adding the result of 2 times 3 with the result of 7 times 4.

We now have the three products 8, 34 and 21. The final result is obtained by starting with the number on the right, writing the least significant digit and then carrying any other digits to the next product to the left. In this case, the number 21 is on the right, so we write the 1 and carry the 2. The 2 is added to the 34 with the result being 36. The 6 is written and the 3 is carried to the left. Finally, the 3 is added to the 8 to give us 11, and since there are no more numbers to the left of this number the 11 is written down. The final result is 1161, which in fact is the product of 43 and 27.

With practice, it is very easy to learn this method and become proficient with it. There are also some interesting patterns that develop when numbers with repeating digits are multiplied together as these next two examples demonstrate.

$$
\begin{array}{r}
44 \\
\times\ 55 \\
\end{array}
\qquad\qquad
\begin{array}{r}
77 \\
\times\ 77 \\
\end{array}
$$

$$20 \quad 20+20 \quad 20 \qquad\qquad 49 \quad 49+49 \quad 49$$
$$+\ \underline{\quad 40 \quad} \qquad\qquad\qquad +\ \underline{\quad 98 \quad}$$
$$2420 \qquad\qquad\qquad\qquad 5929$$

So how do we find the product of a pair of three digit numbers? The pattern is very similar to that used with two-digit numbers. Let's look at the following example:

$$\begin{array}{c} 273 \\ \times\ 845 \end{array}$$

16	8 + 56	10 + 28 + 24	35 + 12	15
+	64	62	47	

230685

Again, the first and last products are the result of inline multiplications. The 8 and 2 are multiplied together to give us the 16 on the far left; while the 5 and 3 are multiplied together to give us 15 on the far right. The 64 is obtained from the sum of the cross products of 2 times 4 and 8 times 7. Similarly, the 47 is obtained from the sum of the cross products of 5 times 7 and 4 times 3. The middle term, 62 is the sum of the cross products of 2 times 5 and 8 times 3, as well as the inline product of 4 times 7.

We now have the numbers 16, 64, 62, 47 and 15. Again, the final result is generated when we write down the least significant digit of the right-most term and then carry any remaining digits to the next term to the left. In this example we start with the 15, write down the 5 and carry the 1 to the 47. This gives us 48, where we write the 8 and carry the 4 to the 62. Here we have 66. We write the 6 and carry the other 6 to the 64. This gives us 70, so we write the 0 and carry the 7. Finally, 7 plus 16 is 23 so we place the 23 in front of the other numbers we have written, and the final result is 230685.

In order to multiply a 2-digit number with a 3-digit number, we treat the 2-digit number as a 3-digit number with a 0 in front and then follow the same procedure used for the product of two 3-digit numbers.

A Variation to the Method from India

This method is a variation to the preceding method in that it creates a series of similar intermediate products while determining the final product. Because of the way that this method is set up, there are no cross multiplications, only inline multiplications are performed; and like the preceding method, with a little practice, it is possible to perform two and three digit multiplications in your head. This is how this method works.

Take the second number (that is being multiplied to the first), and write it backwards and below the first. Take care to line up the left-most digit of the second number with the right-most digit of the first number, and perform an inline multiplication. If the result is a two-digit number, write down the least significant digit, and carry the most significant digit to the next operation. Now, shift the second number one place to the left, and then perform an inline multiplication with the two numbers that are now lined up. Add these two products together and then also add the carry (if there was one) from the previous operation. Again, write down the least significant digit, and carry the most significant digit to the next operation. Continue this process until you've run through the series of possible inline multiplications. The final product is determined from the numbers that you wrote throughout the process.

Now that we've gone through the explanation, let's look at an example, and see how it works. We'll start by finding the product of 43 and 27 (these are the same pair of numbers that we used as our first example in the previous method).

43	start by reversing the 27 and	43
x 27	lining up the 7 under the 3, and	x 72
	then inline multiply the 3 and 7:	21

Now, we take the 21, record the 1, and carry the 2 to the next operation. In order to perform the next operation, shift the bottom number one place to the left, perform the next inline multiplication, and finally add the product and the carry from the previous operation. This is what the next step looks like:

$$43$$
$$\underline{x \; 72}$$
$$28 + 6 \;\; (+ 2 \text{ from the previous operation}) \;\; \text{gives us} \;\; 36$$

In the step above, the inline multiplications are 4 times 7 and 3 times 2, which gives us 28 and 6 respectively. Add those together, and we have 34, and then add the 2 that was carried from the previous operation to give us 36. Again, we take the 36, record the 6, and carry the 3 to the next operation. In this example, the next operation will be our last one. To do so, we again shift the bottom number one place to the left, and perform our last inline multiplication. This is what we have:

$$43$$
$$\underline{x \; 72}$$
$$8 \;\; (+ 3 \text{ from the previous operation}) \;\; \text{gives us} \;\; 11$$

The in-line multiplication in the step above is 4 times 2. This gives us 8; then adding 3 from the previous operation gives us 11. Since there are no more multiplications and therefore no more operations, we don't worry about additional carries, and 11 is the final number we write down. Putting it all together gives us our final result of 1161 (which is the product of 43 and 27).

Now, if we compare this method with the previous method, the method from India, we see that the three intermediate products are the same in both methods. (The intermediate products are 21, from the first inline multiplication, 28 + 6, from the second inline multiplication, and 8, from the third inline multiplication). The method of determining the final result from the intermediate products is also the same for both methods. Therefore, the only difference between these two methods is how the intermediate products were produced.

Now, let's look at another example, and we'll do it in such a way that it goes horizontally across the page (from right to left) instead of vertically down it. We'll multiple 23 and 57 together. This is how we'll set up our multiplication:

23	becomes	23	23	23
x 57		x 75	x 75	x 75

When multiplying two, two-digit numbers together, there will be three possible inline multiplications that will take place. In the listing above, our initial multiplication problem is on the left, and the three inline multiplications are on the right. Also notice that when the 57 is reversed, it becomes 75, and the first inline multiplication with the 75 is on the right. Now, we proceed with the example:

23	becomes	23	23	23
x 57		x 75	x 75	x 75
		10	14 + 15	21

Going from right to left, the inline multiplications give us the intermediate products, which are 21 (from 3 times 7), 14 − 15 (from 2 times 7 and 3 times 5), and 10 (from 2 times 5). Now, let's determine the final product:

23	becomes	23	23	23
x 57		x 75	x 75	x 75
		10	14 + 15	21
			29 (+ 2)	
		10 (+ 3)	1	1
			1 3 1 1	

Starting on the right, we keep the 1 (from the 21), and carry the 2 to the left. In the middle we have 14 and 15, which are added together, along with the 2 from the carry to give us 31. Again, we keep the 1 and carry the 3 to the left. Finally, the 10 is added to the 3 from the carry to give us 13. The final result are the numbers that we kept, the 13 (on the left), the 1 (in the middle), and the 1 (on the right), which give us 1311 (which is the product of 23 and 57).

Even though this method is similar to the method from India, it has an advantage over that method because it only uses inline multiplications (and no cross multiplications). This advantage becomes readily apparent when multiplying larger numbers (numbers with more digits); or when multiplying numbers with uneven digits together, like a 2-digit number with a 4-digit number. In each case, the method is the same and can be easily adapted to whatever special circumstances may apply.

The Vedic Method

This method is also taught in India, and is very interesting. The method itself is easy to understand, but it has several rules and special cases that you must be aware of. These special cases give a lot of flexibility to the method, but they also open the door to possible errors. Let's look at an example, and see how this method works. We'll begin by multiplying 8 and 9 together. First we'll determine a base that we are working in, which in this case will be 10. We write the ten in parentheses above the problem, and then write out the problem normally, as shown on the left, below:

(10)	becomes	(10)	
9		9	- 1
x 8		x 8	- 2

Next, we take each of the numbers in our problem, and subtract the base from them. This gives us a -1 (from 9 minus 10) and a -2 (from 8 minus 10) as shown above on the right.

We now have two columns of numbers. The column on the left consists of the numbers from our original problem, and the column on the right has the numbers derived from the difference between the left column and the base number. To get our intermediate result on the left we perform a cross addition where we add either the 9 with the -2, or the 8 with the -1. It actually doesn't matter which cross addition we use, because both will give the same result, which in this case is 7. On the right, we simply multiply these two numbers together to get 2 (-1 times -2 gives us a positive 2).

$$
\begin{array}{cc}
(10) & \\
9 & -1 \\
\underline{\times 8} & \underline{-2} \\
7 & 2 \quad \text{or just } 72
\end{array}
$$

The final result is determined by placing these two numbers next to each other. Therefore, the product of 9 times 8 is equal to 72.

Now, let's try it again with one more example. This time we'll multiply 7 and 4 together:

$$
\begin{array}{ccccc}
(10) & \text{becomes} & (10) & & \\
7 & & 7 & -3 & \\
\underline{\times 4} & & \underline{\times 4} & \underline{-6} & \\
& & 1 & 18 & \text{or } 28
\end{array}
$$

To create the column on the right, we subtract 10 from 7 to give us -3, and we subtract 10 from 4 to give us -6. The intermediate result for the left column is equal to 1 which can be determined from the sum of either 7 and -6, or the sum of 4 and -3. The intermediate result of the right column is equal to the product of -3 and -6 which is 18. However, in this case, we have an additional step. The 18 is greater than the base number; therefore, we keep the 8 on the right, and carry the 1 to the left, where it is added to the 1, to give us a 2. The final answer is created by placing the 2 and 8 next to each other to get 28.

Now, let's look at an example where we are finding the product of two numbers that are larger than the base. Here, we'll find the product of 12 times 13. First, we create the right column by subtracting the base from each number. Then we determine our intermediate results. The intermediate result on the left is equal to 15 (which is derived from either the 13 + 2, or the 12 + 3). The intermediate result on the right is equal to 6 (which is the product of 2 and 3). The final result is the 15 placed next to the 6, which is 156, as shown below:

$$
\begin{array}{ccccc}
(10) & \text{becomes} & (10) & & \\
12 & & 12 & 2 & \\
\underline{\times 13} & & \underline{\times 13} & \underline{3} & \\
& & 15 & 6 & \text{or } 156
\end{array}
$$

We also use numbers such as 100, or 1000, as our base number. The following example uses 100 as the base, and finds the product of 93 and 86:

$$
\begin{array}{ccccc}
(100) & \text{becomes} & (100) & & \\
93 & & 93 & -7 & \\
\underline{\times 86} & & \underline{\times 86} & \underline{-14} & \\
& & 79 & 98 & \text{or just } 7998
\end{array}
$$

In the example above, the intermediate result for the left column is 79 (which we get from either 93 – 14, or 86 – 7), and the intermediate result for the right column is 98 (which is equal to the product of -7 times -14). The final result is derived by simply placing these two numbers next to each other to get 7998.

In the example below, we multiply 83 and 57 together, and this time we have to carry from the right column to the left column.

```
(100)        becomes              (100)
   83                        83    - 17
 x 57                      x 57    - 43
                             40     731     or 4731
```

To determine the final result in this case, we take the 731 from the right column, keep the 31, and carry the 7 to the left column where it is added to the 40 to get 47. The final result is created by simply placing the 47 next to the 31 to get 4731.

Of course, things become a little trickier if we multiply two numbers together where one number is larger than the base, and the other is smaller. Let's look at some examples where we have this situation so we can see how problems like this would be solved. We'll start by finding the product of 8 and 12 and we'll use 10 as our base. This is what we get:

```
(10)         becomes              (10)
   12                        12      2
  x 8                       x 8     - 2
                             10     - 4
```

The intermediate result for the left column is 10, but the intermediate result for the right column is a negative 4. To get the final result, we need to do a reverse carry: we need to subtract 1 from the 10 (to give us a 9), and then that 1 becomes a 10 that is then added to the - 4. This next step looks like this:

```
                   (10)
                      12      2
                     x 8     - 2
                      10     - 4
                      -1    + 10
                       9      6      or  96
```

And that is how we get 96, which is the product of 8 and 12. Now, let's find the product of 7 and 18. We have:

```
                   (10)
                      18      8
                     x 7     - 3
                      15    - 24
                      -3    + 30
                      12      6      or  126
```

This time we had to add 30 to the - 24 in order to get a positive number. this means that we also needed to subtract 3 form 15 in order to perform our reverse carry. However, again after getting a positive number under the right column, all we had to do was place the left and right columns together to get our final result.

The Ethiopian Method

This method is one of the easiest to use because it only requires a knowledge of doubling and halving numbers to find the product between two numbers. In order to multiply two numbers together, we place each number at the top of a column. The first column is the doubling column and the second column is the halving column. The number in the first column is doubled with each step while the number in the second column is halved. Only whole numbers are considered in the halving column, and the process of doubling and halving continues until the second column reaches one. After the second column reaches one, the second column is reviewed, and any even number appearing in the second column is crossed out, along with its corresponding number in the first column. The remaining numbers in the first column are then added together to arrive at the final sum (which is then equal to the product of the original two numbers).

Let's look at an example. Say we want to find the product of 7 and 22. This is how we would do it:

$$
\begin{array}{cc}
\cancel{7} & \cancel{22} \\
14 & 11 \\
28 & 5 \\
\cancel{56} & \cancel{2} \\
+\ 112 & 1 \\
\hline
154 &
\end{array}
$$

Either number can be placed in the first or second column. In this case we placed the 7 in the first column and the 22 in the second. The numbers in the 7 column are doubled each time while the numbers in the 22 column are halved. Notice that when we take half of an odd number we don't worry about any remainders or fractions. Half of 11 is simply 5, and half of 5 is simply 2. After reaching 1 in the second column we go back and cross out all the even values in the second column and the corresponding value in the first column. The remaining values in the first column are added together, and the result is 154, which by the way, is equal to the product of 7 and 22.

As this next example shows, it doesn't matter which number is doubled and which one is halved.

$$
\begin{array}{cccc}
23 & 41 & 41 & 23 \\
\cancel{46} & \cancel{20} & 82 & 11 \\
\cancel{92} & \cancel{10} & 164 & 5 \\
184 & 5 & \cancel{328} & \cancel{2} \\
\cancel{368} & \cancel{2} & +\ 656 & 1 \\
+\ 736 & 1 & 943 & \\
\hline
943 & & &
\end{array}
$$

Above, we have the product of 23 and 41. On the left we double the 23 and halve the 41, and on the right we switch the two. Notice that if you take the halves of the smaller number (instead of the larger), the process can be carried out in fewer steps:

This method can be adapted very easily to base two multiplication. In order to double a number in base two you simply add a zero to the right of the number. For example, the number 9 in base two is 1001. Add a zero to the end of this number and we have 10010, which is equal to 18. Likewise, to take half of a number (and not worry about the remainder) you simply remove the last digit on the right. The number 12 in base two is equal 1100. When we remove the last digit we are left with 110, which is equal to 6. In order to see how easy this is, let's multiply the numbers 23 and 13 together in base 2. 23 is equal to 10111, and 13 is equal to 1101. This is what we get:

$$
\begin{array}{cc}
10111 & 1101 \\
\cancel{101110} & \cancel{110} \\
1011100 & 11 \\
+\ 10111000 & 1 \\
\hline
100101011 &
\end{array}
$$

Again, we cross out the even rows, and then add the remaining rows. (In base 2, even numbers have a zero as their least significant digit.) The result is 100101011 which is equal to 299. So what happens when we square a number like 16? (I chose 16 because it evenly divides all the way down to one.) Here it is in base 10, and in base 2:

~~16~~	~~16~~	~~10000~~	~~10000~~
~~32~~	~~8~~	~~100000~~	~~1000~~
~~64~~	~~4~~	~~1000000~~	~~100~~
~~128~~	~~2~~	~~10000000~~	~~10~~
+ 256	1	+ 100000000	1
256		100000000	

This is pretty nice; however, before moving on to the next method, let's extend the concept of this method. What we'll look at here probably isn't practical for everyday use, but it does give us a better understanding of how the Ethiopian method works. When we half each number in the right column of our examples, we are of course, dividing each number by two. Then when we cross out the even numbers, we are simply crossing out the numbers that have a remainder of zero. In other words, if we were to find the product of 77 and 53, the Ethiopian method could actually look like this:

77	53	r.	1	(1 *	77)	=	77
154	26	r.	0	(0 *	154)	=	0
308	13	r.	1	(1 *	308)	=	308
616	6	r.	0	(0 *	616)	=	0
1232	3	r.	1	(1 *	1232)	=	1232
2464	1	r.	1	(1 *	2464)	=	+ 2464
							4081

The magic is in the column that we are halving, which in this case is the 53 column. When we divide 53 by two, we will have a remainder of one, which we write to the right of the 53. The result of 53 divided by two is equal to 26, which we place below the 53. We now repeat the process with the 26. 26 divided by two has a remainder of zero (so we write that to the right of the 26), and 26 divided by two is equal to 13 (which we write below the 26), and we continue this process until we reach one. When we get to the one, we still need to acknowledge that one divided by two has a remainder of one.

Of course, all the time that we were halving the 53 column, we were also doubling (or multiplying by two) the 77 column. Now to find the actual product of 77 and 53, we take the remainder of each of our halves, and multiply it with the corresponding number in the 77 column. All the numbers that had a remainder of zero are essentially crossed out, so that when we take the sum of all of these products, the even numbers are not included.

That explanation may seem excessive, and it even appears to complicate the simplicity of this method; however, it makes us look at this method in such a way that we can now apply it with other divisors/multiples For example, we will now repeat our example, but this time we will multiply the 77 column by three while at the same time divide the 53 column by three. This is what we now get:

77	53	r.	2	(2 *	77)	=	154
231	17	r.	2	(2 *	231)	=	462
693	5	r.	2	(2 *	693)	=	1386
2079	1	r.	1	(1 *	2079)	=	+ 2079
							4081

In the first column, we have 77 multiplied by three to get 231; then 231 multiplied by three gives us 693, and so on. In the 53 column, 53 divided by three has a remainder of two (which we write to the right of the 53), and then the result, which is 17, we write below the 53. We then repeat the process with the 17, and so continue until we get to the one. We end this process by noting that one divided by three has a remainder of one.

Now, to find the actual product of 77 and 53, we multiply the remainders from the second column with their corresponding numbers in the first column, and then we add each of these results together to arrive at the final result.

Of course, this is all very interesting. And now to "drive the point home," let's do it one last time, but this time we will multiply the 77 column by four while at the same time dividing the 53 column by four. This time, we get:

$$
\begin{array}{llll}
77 & 53 \text{ r. } 1 & (1 * 77) = & 77 \\
308 & 13 \text{ r. } 1 & (1 * 308) = & 308 \\
1232 & 3 \text{ r. } 3 & (3 * 1232) = & +\ 3696 \\
& & & 4081
\end{array}
$$

Again, in the first column we have 77 multiplied by four to get 308, and 308 multiplied by four is equal to 1232. In the 53 column, we divide each number by four, and also record each remainder. Then to arrive at the final result, we multiply each remainder from the second column with its corresponding number in the first column, and then add them together.

Of course, the larger the number used to multiply and divide the 77 and the 53 gives us fewer intermediate steps in the process; however, using larger numbers also means that we still have another multiplication to take care of when we find the product of the remainder and its corresponding number in the first column. In fact, if you are trying to simplify this method of multiplication, the easiest way to do it is to use the doubling and halving variation that makes up the original Ethiopian method.

The Russian Peasant Method

A variation of the Ethiopian method is the Russian peasant method. Two columns are also used with this method; however, this time both columns are doubling columns. The first column starts with one of the numbers that will be multiplied, and the second column starts with the number one. Both columns continue doubling until the second column is about to exceed the second number of the product. At this point the second column is examined to find those numbers that when added together will total the second number in the product. The corresponding numbers from the first column are then added together to find the actual product. Let's look at an example to clarify our understanding. We'll use this method to find the product of 23 and 41.

$$
\begin{array}{ll}
\underline{23} & \underline{41} \\
23 & 1 & \qquad 41 - 32 = 9 \\
\cancel{46} & \cancel{2} & \qquad 9 - 8 = 1 \\
\cancel{92} & \cancel{4} & \qquad 1 - 1 = 0 \\
184 & 8 \\
\cancel{368} & \cancel{16} \\
+\ 736 & 32 \\
\hline
943 &
\end{array}
$$

146

We start by labeling our columns: we have a 23 and a 41 column. Under the 23 columns we start with 23 and double it each time. Under the 41 column we start with 1 and double it each time. We continue doubling both columns until the second column is about to pass 41. In this case the number 32 is our stopping point (because if we double 32 we get 64 which is larger than 41). Now, we review the second column and look for those numbers that add to 41. If we take the largest number that we have, which is 32 and subtract it from 41, we are left with 9. The next largest number that will go into 9 is 8, so we subtract 8 from 9 to get 1. And in this way we find that the numbers 32, 8 and 1 add together to give us 41. The other numbers in the second column, the 2, 4 and 16 are crossed out, along with their corresponding numbers in the first column. The remaining numbers in the first column are added together, and the sum of those numbers is equal to the product of 23 and 41.

If we compare the product of 23 and 41 in this method along with the product of 23 and 41 from the Ethiopian method, we find that the same numbers are crossed out in the first column even though the method of generating and eliminating numbers in the second column is different.

The Fibonacci Variation

This method is a second variation of the Ethiopian method. It is called the Fibonacci method because we use the Fibonacci method of generating subsequent numbers in the two columns. Again, we start with the numbers we are going to multiply together as the head of each column. In the first column we place the number and the double of that number as the first two entries in that column. In the second column we place the number 1 and its double (the number 2) as its first two entries in that column. The remaining numbers in each column are created by adding the previous two numbers together. Notice that this will give us numbers from the Fibonacci sequence in the second column. The process of generating numbers continues until the number in the second column is about to pass the number at the head of the column. The second column is then reviewed to find numbers whose sum are equal the number at the head of the second column. The corresponding numbers in the first column are added together and this result is equal to the product of the original two numbers. Let's again look at the product of 23 and 41, and see how it compares using this method.

23	41	
~~23~~	~~1~~	41 - 34 = 7
46	2	7 - 5 = 2
~~69~~	~~3~~	2 - 2 = 0
115	5	
~~184~~	~~8~~	
~~299~~	~~13~~	
~~483~~	~~21~~	
+ 782	34	
943		

We start by labeling our columns. Under the 23 heading we'll place the numbers 23 and its double, 46, as the first two entries in that column. Under the 41 heading we start with 1 and 2 as the first two entries. Now we generate the next numbers in each column by adding together the two preceding numbers. This process continues until the second column is about to pass 41. Now, we review the second column to find those numbers that will add to 41. Here we find that the numbers 34, 5 and 2 will give us a total of 41, so the corresponding numbers in the first column are added together. To make it easier on ourselves, we cross out the numbers that we aren't using. We add together the numbers in the first column that aren't crossed out, and we have the product of 23 and 41.

The Babylonian Method

The ancient Babylonians were very adept with their mathematical skills. Among other things, they developed a sexagesimal (base 60) numbering system, and they developed the ability to manipulate numbers and formulas within that system. Our modern world has kept some of their influence, and to this day we still measure angles and time in base 60. A circle has 360 degrees, which is 6*60. Each degree is broken into 60 minutes, and each minute is further divided into 60 seconds of an arc. Time has the same divisions, where each hour is divided into 60 minutes, and each minute is sectioned into 60 seconds.

The Babylonians also developed a formula like method for multiplying two numbers together. Using only a table of squares and one of two formulas, they could find the product of any two numbers. The formulas are:

$$ab = ((a + b)^2 - a^2 - b^2)/2$$

And

$$ab = (a + b)^2/4 - (a - b)^2/4$$

Both formulas work equally well. The strength of this method comes from having a table handy; and with a table close by, there is no need to perform any other multiplications. Simply look up the squares of a few numbers, add or subtract the required numbers, and then divide by either 2 or 4. Let's look at an example and find the product of 3 and 7:

Formula 1
$ab = ((a + b)^2 - a^2 - b^2)/2$
$7*3 = ((7 + 3)^2 - 7^2 - 3^2)/2$
$\quad = (100 - 49 - 9)/2$
$\quad = 42/2$
$\quad = 21$

Formula 2
$ab = (a + b)^2/4 - (a - b)^2/4$
$7*3 = (7 + 3)^2/4 - (7 - 3)^2/4$
$\quad = 100/4 - 16/4$
$\quad = 25 - 4$
$\quad = 21$

To use this method as the Babylonians, we would get our table of squares, and from it we find that $(7 + 3)$ squared is equal to 100, 7 squared is 49 and 3 squared is 9, and $(7 - 3)$ squared is 16. We can then enter these values in the appropriate places, and using either formula we can quickly determine the product of 3 and 7.

The second formula from the Babylonian Method is also known as the Quarter Square method, and if you play around with it a little, you'll notice that some products will cause you to work with fractions (or decimals). For example, 9 times 4:

Formula 2
$\qquad ab = (a + b)^2/4 - (a - b)^2/4$
$\qquad 9*4 = (9 + 4)^2/4 - (9 - 4)^2/4$
$\qquad\quad = 42.25 - 6.25$
$\qquad\quad = 36$

The fractions (or decimals) cancel out in the end, so they really aren't a problem; however, an alternate approach is to use a table of quarter squares. An interesting property of this table is that there are no fractions in it, only the integer part of the quarter square is used. The table is created

148

by taking our list of numbers, squaring each one, dividing by four, and then only keeping the integer part of that division, like this:

$$1^2 = 1, \text{ divided by 4 gives us } 0$$
$$2^2 = 4, \text{ divided by 4 gives us } 1$$
$$3^2 = 9, \text{ divided by 4 gives us } 2$$
$$4^2 = 16, \text{ divided by 4 gives us } 4$$
$$5^2 = 25, \text{ divided by 4 gives us } 6$$
$$6^2 = 36, \text{ divided by 4 gives us } 9$$
$$7^2 = 49, \text{ divided by 4 gives us } 12$$

..., etc.

Here are the first 20 numbers along with their corresponding quarter squares:

Number		Quarter Square			Number		Quarter Square		
1^2	=	1/4	$\rightarrow$	0	11^2	=	121/4	$\rightarrow$	30
2^2	=	4/4	$\rightarrow$	1	12^2	=	144/4	$\rightarrow$	36
3^2	=	9/4	$\rightarrow$	2	13^2	=	169/4	$\rightarrow$	42
4^2	=	16/4	$\rightarrow$	4	14^2	=	196/4	$\rightarrow$	49
5^2	=	25/4	$\rightarrow$	6	15^2	=	225/4	$\rightarrow$	56
6^2	=	36/4	$\rightarrow$	9	16^2	=	256/5	$\rightarrow$	64
7^2	=	49/4	$\rightarrow$	12	17^2	=	289/4	$\rightarrow$	72
8^2	=	64/4	$\rightarrow$	16	18^2	=	324/4	$\rightarrow$	81
9^2	=	81/4	$\rightarrow$	20	19^2	=	361/4	$\rightarrow$	90
10^2	=	100/4	$\rightarrow$	25	20^2	=	400/4	$\rightarrow$	100

Table 12.1   A Quarter Square listing for numbers 1 through 20

Using the Quarter Square table, this is what we get when computing 9 times 4:

$$9*4 = (9 + 4)^2/4 - (9 - 4)^2/4$$
$$= 13^2/4 - 5^2/4$$
$$= 42 - 6 \qquad \leftarrow \text{ (from the table of quarter squares)}$$
$$= 36$$

The Triangular Number Method

With the possible exception of the Fibonacci method, the methods shown up to this point have been taught in several regions and societies, and used in various cultures throughout the world – with some of these methods dating back hundreds if not thousands of years. However, the Fibonacci method is used more for demonstration and is meant to show that there are still other methods that are similar to the Ethiopian and Russian Peasant methods of multiplication.

The same thing can be said of the Triangular Number method. It is also a table look-up method, and even though it is as easy to use as the other table look-up methods (i.e. the Babylonian methods), it probably has never been used as a practical method, except maybe as an instructional method to show that there are reasonable variations to the existing table look-up methods.

With that introduction, let's look at the triangular number method. To use this method, all we need is a table of triangular numbers. Triangular numbers can be created in several ways. Probably the easiest is to define them as addition factorials. The first triangular number, T_1, is

149

equal to 1, the second, T_2, is equal to $1 + 2$, the third, T_3, is equal to $1 + 2 + 3$, etc. In other words, a listing of triangular numbers gives us this:

$$
\begin{aligned}
T_1 &= 1 & &= 1 \\
T_2 &= 1 + 2 & &= 3 \\
T_3 &= 1 + 2 + 3 & &= 6 \\
T_4 &= 1 + 2 + 3 + 4 & &= 10 \\
T_5 &= 1 + 2 + 3 + 4 + 5 & &= 15
\end{aligned}
$$
… etc …

Now that we know this relation, we can create a table of triangular numbers, which we can then use as a look-up table with the following formula:

$$ab = T_a + T_{(b-1)} - T_{(a-b)}$$

The formula says that the product of a and b is equal to the ath triangular number plus the $(b-1)^{th}$ triangular number minus the $(a-b)^{th}$ triangular number. Of course we should mention that when using this method, a should be selected so that it is greater than b. Now, as a quick example, let's find the product of 9 times 4. Using the formula, we have:

$$
\begin{aligned}
9 * 4 &= T_9 + T_{(4-1)} - T_{(9-4)} \\
&= T_9 + T_3 - T_5
\end{aligned}
$$

At this point we use our table to substitute in the corresponding triangular numbers:

$$
\begin{aligned}
9 * 4 &= 45 + 6 - 15 \\
&= 36
\end{aligned}
$$

And as a final point of interest, let's look at what we get when we square a number. Our formula becomes:
$$a^2 = T_a + T_{(a-1)} - T_{(a-a)}$$

Notice that the last term on the right drops out, and we are left with the following:

$$a^2 = T_a + T_{(a-1)}$$

Which says that the sum of two consecutive triangular numbers is equal to a squared number; and more specifically, the sum of the ath and $(a-1)^{th}$ triangular numbers is equal to a^2. This is the same relationship that we saw in an earlier chapter about triangular numbers.

The Algebraic Method

A variation of the Babylonian method is the Algebraic method. This method takes the two numbers that are being multiplied together and breaks each of these numbers into two separate numbers. It then uses the following formula to calculate the product:

$$(a + b)(c + d) = ac + ad + bc + bd$$

At first this may look complicated, but this is simply the FOIL method that many of us learned in Algebra (where FOIL describes the multiplication process: F stands for first to first; or a times c,

O stands for outside to outside, or a times d; I stands for inside to inside, or b times c; and L stands for last to last, or b times d; which altogether gives us: ac + ad + bc + bd).

All that we are actually doing is simply multiplying the different parts of the numbers together and then performing an addition - just as we have done with several of the other methods previously mentioned. The trick to making this method easy to use is to break apart the numbers in such a way that the multiplication and addition are easy to handle. For example, if we want to find the product of 12 and 18, we can say that 12 is equal to 6 + 6, and 18 is equal to 9 + 9. We would then have:

$$(6 + 6)(9 + 9) = 54 + 54 + 54 + 54$$
$$= 216$$

In this example, the multiplication was easy, but we still had to add 54 four times (which wasn't really that bad either). We could have also broken the 12 and 18 differently so that 12 is equal to 10 + 2 and 18 is equal to 10 + 8. Now, the product becomes:

$$(10 + 2)(10 + 8) = 100 + 80 + 20 + 16$$
$$= 216$$

Not only is the multiplication easy in this case, but so is the addition. Usually (but not always) the easiest way to use this method is to break the number into a multiple of 10 plus the unit number that remains. In other words, the product of 43 and 37 would be broken up as 40 + 3 and 30 + 7. This would give us:

$$(40 + 3)(30 + 7) = 1200 + 280 + 90 + 21$$
$$= 1591$$

This algebraic method also has several other variations. For example, the formula we started with could have a difference between two of the terms instead of a sum. This would change the formula to be:

$$(a + b)(c - d) = ac - ad + bc - bd$$

And if we carry this one step further and let a equal c and b equal d, the formula becomes:

$$(a + b)(a - b) = a^2 - ab + ab - b^2$$
$$= a^2 - b^2$$

Which is known as the relationship between the difference of squares. As an example, we'll use the previous example where we found the product of 43 and 37. There we could have rewritten 43 as 40 + 3 and have 37 rewritten as 40 - 3. This would give us:

$$(40 + 3)(40 - 3) = 40^2 - 9^2$$
$$= 1600 - 9$$
$$= 1591$$

With the option to use any one of these three formulas, a person has quite a bit of latitude in finding a set of numbers that will make the multiplication easy to use and easy to understand. In fact, it is possible to spend as much or even more time trying to break the numbers apart as is actually spent multiplying and adding the parts to get the final product. As a final example, we will look at the product of 42 and 18 and compare these three formulas side by side:

$$42 \times 18 \begin{aligned} &= (40+2)(10+8) &&= 400+320+20+16 &&= 756 \\ &= (40+2)(20-2) &&= 800-80+40-4 &&= 756 \\ &= (30+12)(30-12) &&= 900-144 &&= 756 \end{aligned}$$

These algebraic methods aren't used so much with regular numbers as they are to find the products of polynomials. However, there is a very close relation to these polynomial methods that can also be used to improve the efficiency of current methods. As an example, in this next section we will look at a simplified variation to an algebraic method that makes the multiplication a little more efficient.

A Simplified Variation to the Algebraic Method

For this method we will find the product of two large numbers, a and b, by first finding some round number, N, that is close to a and b. Next, we define two smaller numbers, x' and y' such that

$$a = N + x'$$
$$b = N + y'$$

Now we'll go through a little exercise here and derive the following:

$$\begin{aligned} a(b) &= (N+x')(N+y') \\ &= N^2 + N(x'+y') + x'(y') \\ &= N(N+x'+y') + x'(y') \quad \text{(here we substitute a for } N+x'\text{)} \\ &= N(a+y') + x'(y') \quad \text{(this is the formula that we will use)} \end{aligned}$$

What we end up with is a method that will improve the efficiency of finding the product of two larger numbers by allowing us to multiple the large number, (a + y'), to a round number of our choosing, N, and then add to that the product of a pair of smaller numbers, x' and y'. Let's look at an example to see how this works.

Say that we want to find the product of 93*88. We choose 100 as our round number, N. This also means that x' = -7, and y' = -12. Now, let's enter these numbers into our formula:

$$\begin{aligned} a(b) &= N(a+y') + x'(y') \\ &= 100(93-12) + (-7)(-12) \\ &= 8100 + 84 \\ &= 8184 \end{aligned}$$

This method easily shows that the product of 93 and 88 is equal to 8184. With this introduction, the next few methods that we review in this chapter will also use algebraic shortcuts to find products of very large numbers.

The Karatsuba Method

A variation of the algebraic method is the Karatsuba method. This method was developed to be used recursively with very large numbers, and has the added benefit of reducing the number of multiplication operations by 25% . In fact, with this method, it is possible to multiply large numbers together in a way that is much quicker than most other methods. Let's take a look at how it works.

We'll start by showing how a pair of 2-digit numbers can be multiplied together using this method. We'll multiply 43 to 27. This method uses four variables that we will call k_1, k_2, k_3 and k_4. The variable k_1 is equal to the product of first digit of each number, and k_2 is equal to the product of the last digit of each number. This gives us:

$$k_1 = 4*2 = 8$$
$$k_2 = 3*7 = 21$$

The next variable, k_3, is equal to the sum of the digits from the first number multiplied to the sum of the digits from the second number:

$$k_3 = (4+3)*(2+7)$$
$$= \quad 7 * 9$$
$$= \quad\quad 63$$

Finally, k_4 is equal to k_3 minus k_1 minus k_2, or

$$k_4 = k_3 - k_1 - k_2$$

And from our example:

$$k_4 = 63 - 8 - 21$$
$$= 34$$

After we determine these four variables, the product is quickly determined using the following formula:

$$Result = k_1 * 100 + k_4 * 10 + k_2$$

For our example, we get:

$$Result = 8 * 100 + 34 * 10 + 21$$
$$= \quad 800 + \quad 340 + 21$$
$$= 1161 \quad \text{(this is the product of 43 and 27)}$$

So where is the speed with this method? When finding the product of a pair of 2-digit numbers, traditional methods of multiplication take the last digit of one number and multiply it to both digits of the other number (giving us two multiplication operations). Then it takes the first digit of that number and multiplies it to both digits of the other number (for two more multiplication operations and a total of four multiplication operations altogether). However, this method only performs three multiplication operations (to obtain the variables k_1, k_2, and k_3). And although this doesn't seem like very much of a savings, if we were multiplying two 100-digit numbers together, the time savings would be very significant. To understand this better, let's see how this might be done with a larger number. Let's look at this method again by multiplying two 4-digit numbers together.

In this example, we'll multiply 4358 to 2716. We'll start by splitting each number into two parts so that we can build our variables k_1, and k_2. Since we are using 4-digit numbers:

$$k_1 = 43 * 27$$
$$k_2 = 58 * 16$$

At this point we notice that our k_1, and k_2 are now the product of a pair of 2-digit numbers. This is where we could use the method recursively to find these products. If we did, this would give us a 25% savings on these calculations also. However, we will find k_1, and k_2 using the division above such that:

$$k_1 = 43 * 27 = 1161$$
$$k_2 = 58 * 16 = 928$$

Next we find k_3, which is:

$$k_3 = (43 + 58)*(27 + 16)$$
$$= 101 * 43$$
$$= 4343$$

Finally, k_4 is equal to:
$$k_4 = 4343 - 1161 - 928$$
$$= 2254$$

After finding our four variables, we can now find the actual product of our original numbers; however, this time the formula is a little different. Since we started with 4-digit numbers, we need to multiply by 100^2 and 10^2 respectively (instead of 100 and 10 like we did with the 2-digit numbers):

$$\text{Result} = k_1 * 10000 + k_4 * 100 + k_2$$

Therefore, the product of 4358 and 2716 is:

$$\text{Result} = 1161 * 10000 + 2254 * 100 + 928$$
$$= 11610000 + 225400 + 928$$
$$= 11836328$$

Again, this method becomes much more powerful when used recursively with larger numbers that are multiplied together.

The Toom-Cook Method

Like the Karatsuba method, the Toom-Cook method was also developed to reduce the actual number of multiplications between two large numbers, thus giving the potential to make this method very fast for very large numbers. However, to do so, this method requires even more number manipulations both before and after the actual multiplications take place. This method starts by separating each number that we are multiplying into three parts and assigning those parts as coefficients to a function. To make this method easier to understand, we'll demonstrate it first by finding the product of a pair of 3-digit numbers, and then we'll use the method again on a pair of 6-digit numbers.

For our first example, we'll find the product of 527 and 346. Separating each of these numbers and assigning them to coefficients give us:

$$527 \rightarrow \quad \begin{aligned} a_2 &= 5 \\ a_1 &= 2 \\ a_0 &= 7 \end{aligned} \qquad\qquad 346 \rightarrow \quad \begin{aligned} b_2 &= 3 \\ b_1 &= 4 \\ b_0 &= 6 \end{aligned}$$

Next, we'll define two functions G and H, such that:

$$G(x) = a_2x^2 + a_1x + a_0$$
$$H(x) = b_2x^2 + b_1x + b_0$$

Then we substitute the values in place of the coefficients to give us the following:

$$G(x) = 5x^2 + 2x + 7$$
$$H(x) = 3x^2 + 4x + 6$$

We now enter into our functions the values 0, 1, -1, -2, and a "max" value:

$$
\begin{array}{llll}
G(0) & = & 5(0)^2 + 2(0) + 7 & = & 7 \\
G(1) & = & 5(1)^2 + 2(1) + 7 & = & 14 \\
G(-1) & = & 5(-1)^2 + 2(-1) + 7 & = & 10 \\
G(-2) & = & 5(-2)^2 + 2(-2) + 7 & = & 23 \\
G(max) & = & a_2 & = & 5
\end{array}
$$

Similarly:

$$
\begin{array}{llll}
H(0) & = & 3(0)^2 + 4(0) + 6 & = & 6 \\
H(1) & = & 3(1)^2 + 4(1) + 6 & = & 13 \\
H(-1) & = & 3(-1)^2 + 4(-1) + 6 & = & 5 \\
H(-2) & = & 3(-2)^2 + 4(-2) + 6 & = & 10 \\
H(max) & = & b_2 & = & 3
\end{array}
$$

Next, we perform the actual multiplications, such that:

$$
\begin{array}{llll}
P(0) & = & G(0) \times H(0) & = & 42 \\
P(1) & = & G(1) \times H(1) & = & 182 \\
P(-1) & = & G(-1) \times H(-1) & = & 50 \\
P(-2) & = & G(-2) \times H(-2) & = & 230 \\
P(max) & = & G(max) \times H(max) & = & 15
\end{array}
$$

Finally, we start to calculate the results:

$$
\begin{array}{llll}
r_0 & = & P(0) & & = & 42 \\
r_1 & = & [P(1) - P(-1)] / 2 & = (182 - 50)/2 & = & 66 \\
r_2 & = & P(-1) - P(0) & = (50 - 42) & = & 8 \\
r_3 & = & [P(-2) - P(1)] / 3 & = (230 - 182)/3 & = & 16 \\
r_4 & = & P(max) & & = & 15
\end{array}
$$

However, we're not quite there yet — we still have a little more to do. Using the latest values of r_1, r_2, r_3, and r_4, we now calculate the final values for r_1, r_2, and r_3:

$$
\begin{array}{llll}
r_3 & = & (r_2 - r_3)/2 + 2r_4 & = (8 - 16)/2 + 2(15) & = & 26 \\
r_2 & = & r_2 + r_1 - r_4 & = 8 + 66 - 15 & = & 59 \\
r_1 & = & r_1 - r_3 & = 66 - 26 & = & 40
\end{array}
$$

Notice that when we calculate the final value for r_1, we are using the final value of r_3, and not the earlier value of r_3. Now to get the final answer, we must multiply each r value by the appropriate power of 10. The final answer is:

$$
\begin{array}{lll}
527 \times 346 & = & r_4 (10000) + r_3 (1000) + r_2 (100) + r_1 (10) + r_0 \\
& = & 150000 + 26000 + 5900 + 400 + 42 \\
& = & 182342
\end{array}
$$

This method, as well as the Karatsuba method assumes that the most time consuming part of the operation is the actual multiplication (and for very large numbers, it is). The time spent adding and subtracting numbers is minimal in comparison. Now, let's try this method again by finding the product of two six-digit numbers, namely 329745 and 165278. First, we separate each of these numbers and assign them to a coefficient:

$$329745 \quad \rightarrow \quad a_2 = 32 \qquad\qquad 165278 \quad \rightarrow \quad b2 = 16$$
$$a_1 = 97 \qquad\qquad\qquad\qquad\qquad b1 = 52$$
$$a_0 = 45 \qquad\qquad\qquad\qquad\qquad b0 = 78$$

Again, the G and H functions are defined such that:

$$G(x) = a_2x^2 + a_1x + a_0$$
$$H(x) = b_2x^2 + b_1x + b_0$$

And, substituting the values in for the coefficients gives us the following:

$$G(x) = 32x^2 + 97x + 45$$
$$H(x) = 16x^2 + 52x + 78$$

We now input the following values into our functions:

$G(0)$	=	45	$H(0)$	=	78
$G(1)$	=	174	$H(1)$	=	146
$G(-1)$	=	-20	$H(-1)$	=	42
$G(-2)$	=	-21	$H(-2)$	=	38
$G(max)$	=	32	$H(max)$	=	16

And again, this is where the actual multiplications take place, such that:

$P(0)$	=	$G(0) \times H(0)$	=	3510
$P(1)$	=	$G(1) \times H(1)$	=	25404
$P(-1)$	=	$G(-1) \times H(-1)$	=	-840
$P(-2)$	=	$G(-2) \times H(-2)$	=	-798
$P(max)$	=	$G(max) \times H(max)$	=	512

Finally, we begin to calculate the results:

r_0	=	$P(0)$	=	3510
r_1	=	$[P(1) - P(-1)] / 2$	=	13122
r_2	=	$P(-1) - P(0)$	=	-4350
r_3	=	$[P(-2) - P(1)] / 3$	=	-8734
r_4	=	$P(max)$	=	512

However, we're not quite there yet – we still have a little more to do:

r_3	=	$(r_2 - r_3) / 2 + 2r_4$	=	3216
r_2	=	$r_2 + r_1 - r_4$	=	8260
r_1	=	$r_1 - r_3$	=	9906

This time we multiple each r value by the appropriate power of 100. Thus, the product of 329745 and 165278 is equal to:

$$329745 \times 165278 =$$
$$= r_4 (100000000) + r_3 (1000000) + r_2 (10000) + r_1 (100) + r_0$$
$$= 51200000000 + 3216000000 + 82600000 + 990600 + 3510$$
$$= 54499594110$$

Notice that in the first example we multiplied each r value by a power of 10 because we initially separated the 3-digit numbers into 1-digit coefficients. In this second example we separated the 6-digits numbers into 2-digit coefficients; and therefore, the r values in the second example are multiplied by powers of 100. This same pattern is followed for larger numbers.

The Fast Fourier Transform (FFT) Method

This method performs a Fourier transform on each number, multiplies the numbers together, and then performs an inverse Fourier transform on that product to get the final result. The transform and the inverse transform are somewhat involved; but the multiplication is very easy and requires fewer steps than regular multiplication. However, because the transforms are labor intensive, it is much more work to multiply a couple of 2-digit numbers together than it would be to use practically any other method we've seen. But, as the numbers become larger and larger, this method justifies itself; the transform and inverse transform do not become significantly more difficult, and the simplicity of the multiplication makes this method very desirable to use on numbers that have hundreds or even thousands of digits or more.

While we won't take the time to show how to apply this method to a 1000-digit number, it is very instructive to see how this method does work on the product of a pair of 2-digit numbers. Therefore, as an example, we'll demonstrate how to use the fast Fourier transform to find the product of 32 and 78.

We begin by creating a single dimension array for each number, and placing the number in the array. To determine the size of the arrays, we look at the size of the numbers that are being multiplied together. Since we are multiplying two 2-digit numbers together, the most digits that the final product will have is 4-digits. Therefore, each of these arrays will have four elements where the first two elements will be the number, written with the least significant digit first, and the last two digits will be zeroes. Here are the arrays:

32 becomes [2, 3, 0, 0]   and 78 becomes [8, 7, 0, 0]

Next, we create the transform matrix. Since each number is a 4-element array, we use the four complex roots of 1 in the matrix. In our example we can represent this as a 4 x 4 matrix comprised of i raised to successive powers. This is the transform matrix that we will use:

$$\begin{bmatrix} i^0 & i^0 & i^0 & i^0 \\ i^0 & i^1 & i^2 & i^3 \\ i^0 & i^2 & i^4 & i^6 \\ i^0 & i^3 & i^6 & i^9 \end{bmatrix} = \begin{bmatrix} 1 & 1 & 1 & 1 \\ 1 & i & -1 & -i \\ 1 & -1 & 1 & -1 \\ 1 & -i & -1 & i \end{bmatrix}$$

Now, we perform a Fourier transform on our numbers. The transform is performed through a regular matrix multiplication between the transform matrix (the 4 x 4 matrix) and the number matrix (the 4 x 1 matrix) to give us a resulting 1 x 4 matrix:

$$\begin{bmatrix} 1 & 1 & 1 & 1 \\ 1 & i & -1 & -i \\ 1 & -1 & 1 & -1 \\ 1 & -i & -1 & i \end{bmatrix} \times \begin{bmatrix} 2 \\ 3 \\ 0 \\ 0 \end{bmatrix} = [\ 5,\ 2+3i,\ -1,\ 2-3i\ ]$$

$$\begin{bmatrix} 1 & 1 & 1 & 1 \\ 1 & i & -1 & -i \\ 1 & -1 & 1 & -1 \\ 1 & -i & -1 & i \end{bmatrix} \times \begin{bmatrix} 8 \\ 7 \\ 0 \\ 0 \end{bmatrix} = [\ 15,\ 8+7i,\ 1,\ 8-7i\ ]$$

Now that we have the transformed numbers (in the two 1 x 4 arrays on the right), we next perform the actual multiplication. With these transformed numbers, the multiplication is very straight-forward. We simply multiply the first element (or number) of one array to the first element (number) of the other array; we then multiply the second number to the second number, and so on:

$$[\ 5,\ 2+3i,\ -1,\ 2-3i\ ]$$
$$[\ 15,\ 8+7i,\ 1,\ 8-7i\ ]$$

This gives us:

$$[\ 75,\ -5+38i,\ -1,\ -5-38i\ ]$$

Finally, we perform an inverse Fourier transform, using an inverse matrix. In our example, the inverse matrix is practically identical to the original transform matrix except that the sign in front of the i's changes to their opposite values. Then we do the matrix multiplication and divide each number by four to transform the number back to our base 10 number.

$$\begin{bmatrix} 1 & 1 & 1 & 1 \\ 1 & -i & -1 & i \\ 1 & -1 & 1 & -1 \\ 1 & i & -1 & -i \end{bmatrix} \times \begin{bmatrix} 75 \\ -5+38i \\ -1 \\ -5-38i \end{bmatrix} = [\ 64/4,\ 152/4,\ 84/4,\ 0\ ]$$

$$= [\ 16,\ 38,\ 21,\ 0]$$

Finally, we convert this array back into a regular number. Remember that the first number in the array is the least significant "digit," followed by the next significant digit, and so on. The easiest way to combine these numbers together is to arrange them in columns where each succeeding number is shifted left one digit, and then the numbers are added together. Like this:

$$
\begin{array}{r}
16 \\
38 \\
21 \\
+\ \ 0 \\
\hline
2496
\end{array}
$$

Therefore, 2496 is the product of 32 and 78. Again, the trickiest part of this method is determining the transform matrices, and then performing the transform at the beginning and the inverse transform toward the end of the process. The in between steps (where the multiplication takes place) are very fast and straight forward.

The Similar Triangle Method

This method uses a compass, a straight edge and similar triangles to determine the product of two numbers. The principle behind this method is very simple. Say we have two similar triangles, where ABC and A'B'C' are the corresponding vertices to these two triangles. Because the triangles are similar, we know that the length of side AB divided by the length of side A'B' is equal to side AC divided by A'C'. The relationship looks like this:

$$
\frac{AC}{A'C'} = \frac{AB}{A'B'}
$$

Clearing the fractions, the relationship becomes:

$$
AC(A'B') = AB(A'C')
$$

Now, if we set the length of side AB equal to one, then the formula simplifies to:

$$
AC(A'B') = A'C'
$$

Finally, if we overlay these two similar triangles on top of each other so that they share the same vertex at A and A' (in other words, A and A' are on top of each other), then the formula shown above can be written in a simpler form using just A:

$$
AC(AB') = AC'
$$

This last relation simply says that the product of the two lengths of the sides AC and AB' are equal to the length of a third side, AC', of the similar triangle; or in other words, the product of two numbers gives us a third.

Now, let's see how this formula can be applied by looking at an example. We'll use a compass and a straight edge to multiply 3 and 4 together. We start by drawing a point A and two lines extending from this point. We'll draw one line straight down, and the second line extending at some angle to the right.

Next, we'll use the compass to mark off a length of one unit on the line going straight down and label that point B. (The one-unit is some arbitrary length decided by the owner of the compass.) Now, mark off another point along the same line, and three units from point A. This will be the point B'.

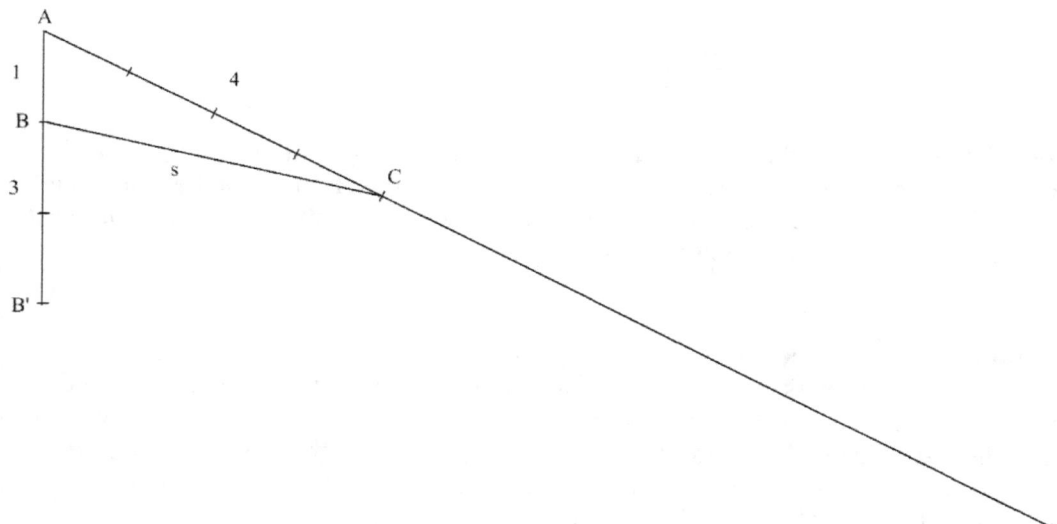

Figure 12.7   Setting up the Similar Triangle method of finding a product.

Go to the other line and mark off four units from point A, and label this point C. By drawing a line from point B to point C, we have the triangle ABC. Next, we draw a line through point B', and parallel to BC. Where this line intersects the angled line we'll call point C' (see the figure below).

We now have two similar triangles drawn on top of each other, triangle ABC and triangle AB'C'. We created these triangles so that the length of side AC is equal to 4, and the length of side AB' is equal to 3. The length of side AC' is equal to the product of 3 and 4. We now use our compass to measure the length of AC' to get our final result.

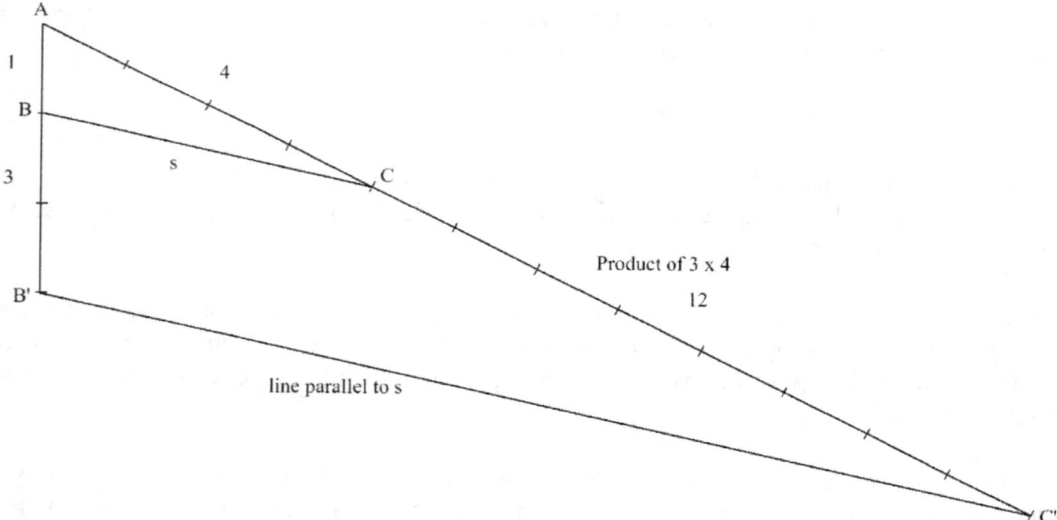

Figure 12.8   Using the Similar Triangle method to find the product.

This method is as accurate as your measurements; however, it is not very practical. As the numbers become larger, a choice must be made between using larger triangles, or scaling down the triangles and loosing accuracy.

A Practical Variation of the Similar Triangle Method

This method is a variation of the Similar Triangle method, and could almost be a practical variation of that method. This method uses two rulers, 10 units long, where both are attached to each other with a pivot point at the zeroes.

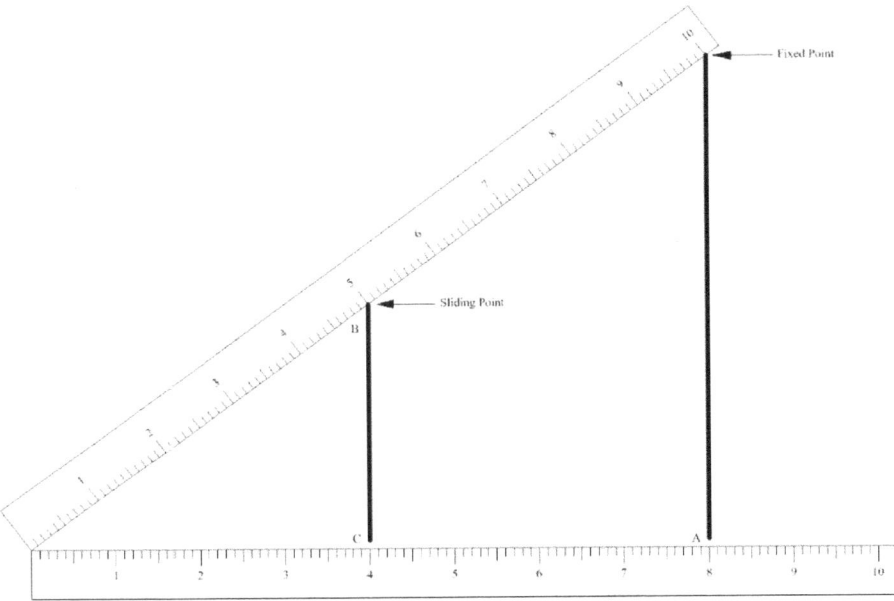

Figure 12.9   A diagram of the variation to the Similar Triangle method.

There are also two strings attached to the top ruler. One string is fixed, and is attached at the 10, and the other can slide along the ruler anywhere between the 0 and 10. The way this method works is that the bottom ruler is held horizontal, and the top ruler is pivoted up until the fixed string (hanging from the 10) falls over one of the numbers that you wish to multiple by (which, in the figure above is the 8). The second string is then slid along the top ruler until it is over the second number that will be multiplied (which, in this case is the 5). The second string will then fall over $1/10^{th}$ of the result on the bottom ruler (which is the 4, and since this is $1/10^{th}$ of the result, the actual result would be 40).

Let's use the figure above to see why this is so. First, notice that the two rulers (with the two strings) create two similar triangles laid on top of each other with a common vertex at the pivot point. Next, also notice in the figure above that we have four line segments, two on each ruler, where all four lines segments are measured out from the pivot point. On the top ruler, the two segments have lengths 10 and B; and on the bottom ruler, the two segments have lengths A and C. We now set up the following similar triangle relationship:

$$\frac{B}{10} = \frac{C}{A}$$

Clearing the fraction gives us: 10C = AB

Which means that C is equal to :   C = (AB)/10

C is equal to one tenth of the product of A and B. Therefore, to get the actual product of A and B, we must multiple C by 10. In the example above, A was set equal to 8, and B was set equal to 5. The result was C, which was equal to 4, and when multiplied by 10 gave a final result of 40. Let's look at one more example where we multiple 8 by 4:

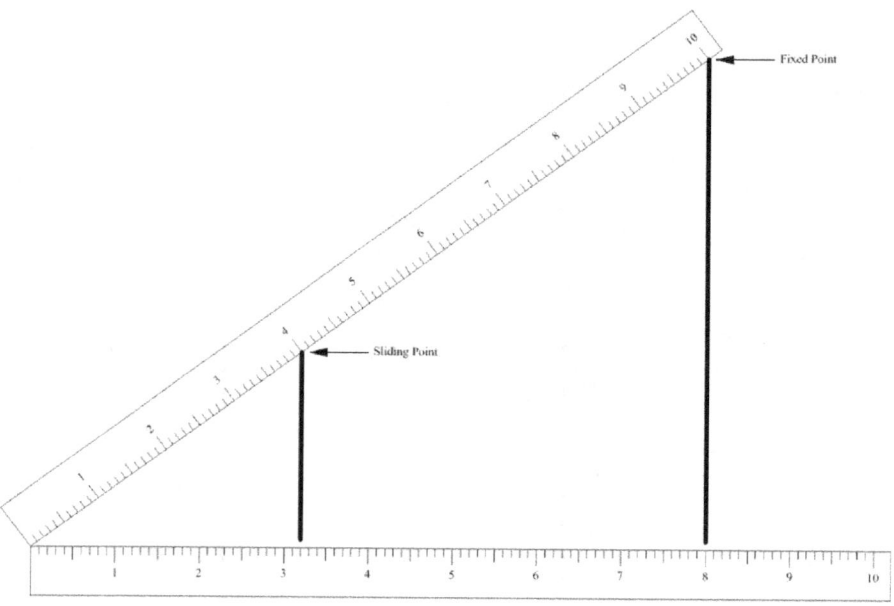

Figure 12.10 A variation to the Similar Triangle method using two rulers.

In the figure above, the top ruler is pivoted up until the string hangs over the 8 on the bottom ruler. The second string is then slid along the top ruler until it is at the 4. This is how we show 8 times 4. The second string is left to hang, and it hangs over 3.2. We multiply this result by 10 to get 32, which is the final result.

The Logarithmic Method and Slide Rules

This method could also be called the slide rule method. However, with the introduction of the calculator, the slide rule is not only obsolete, but also seems to be all but forgotten. The principle behind this method uses the fact that the product of two numbers is equal to the sum of the logarithm of those numbers. In other words, say that we want to find the product of 57 and 86. First, we take the log of these two numbers. The $\log_{10}$ of 57 is 1.7559, and the $\log_{10}$ of 86 is 1.9345. The sum of the logs of these numbers is 3.6904. And finally, we take the antilog of 3.6904 to get 4902, which is the product of 57 and 86.

It might seem like a lot of work to transform two numbers to their log, add the two numbers together, and then find the antilog to get the result; however, when dealing with large numbers (or numbers with many decimal places), this method is actually very quick. But let's also look at one more concept. Two rulers can be used to add numbers together. The rulers are placed side-by-side with one ruler sliding against the other. Now, if we want to add two numbers together like 3 and 6. We slide the first ruler so that the zero lines up with the 3 on the second ruler.

162

Next, we find the 6 on the first ruler, and we see that it lines up with the 9 on the second ruler. Therefore, 9 is equal to the sum of 3 and 6.

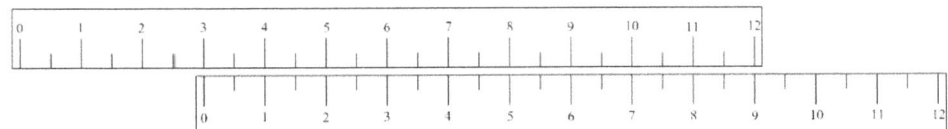

Figure 12.11 Using two rulers to find the sum of two numbers.

If the scale on these rulers is marked logarithmically, then we can easily multiply two numbers together by simply adding their logs. By marking the scales logarithmically, the numbers we wish to multiply are automatically transformed to their respective logarithms. Also, if you have a slide rule, you'll notice that there are no 0's on the scale. The 1 is used to line up the sliding scale. (Actually, the log of 1 is 0.)

To use the slide rule, take the sliding scale and line the 1 across from one of the numbers that you will multiply on the fixed scale. Now find the second number on the sliding scale that you are multiplying and find what number it lines up with on the fixed scale. This number is the product of the number on the sliding scale and the first number on the fixed scale.

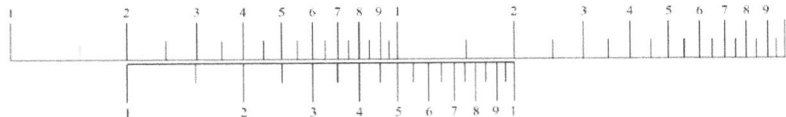

Figure 12.12 Using two logarithmic scales to find the product of two numbers.

In the figure above, the 1 on the sliding scale (the lower scale) is lined up with the 2 on the fixed scale (the upper scale). Doing so multiplies the numbers on the lower scale by 2; which means that each number on the lower scale is lined up with its double on the upper scale.

Of course, a slide rule has limits with its accuracy; but on the other hand, large numbers can be multiplied together very quickly. And keep in mind that before the advent of the hand calculator, the slide rules and log tables were used to do much of the engineering that built roads, bridges, dams and skyscrapers that are still with us today.

The Product of Cosines Method

Before John Napier invented the logarithm, a method using the product of cosines was often used to find the product of two numbers. Like the logarithm, the two numbers being multiplied together are transformed to another system where they are simply added together, with the resulting sum being the product of the two numbers. This method was known in some circles but became obsolete with the invention of the logarithm.

Trigonometry has several identities where the sum and difference of two angles is equal to the product of two numbers (two cosines, two sines, etc.) Therefore, there are actually several formulas that we could use, but for this method we will focus on just one of them:

$$\cos(a)\cos(b) = \tfrac{1}{2}\cos(a+b) + \tfrac{1}{2}\cos(a-b)$$

The way to use this formula is like this. We want to find the product of 43 times 78. First, we change 43 to 0.43 and 78 to 0.78 (we move the decimal for each number two places to the left). We do this because we need to find angles such that the cosines of these angles are equal to 0.43 and 0.78. In other words, we are finding the inverse cosine of 0.43 and 0.78 (And we can only find the inverse cosine of numbers between 0 and 1.)

$$\cos(a) = 0.43 \qquad \text{therefore} \qquad a = 64.5324°$$
$$\cos(b) = 0.78 \qquad \text{therefore} \qquad b = 38.7394°$$

Using our formula, we have:

$$\cos(a)\cos(b) = \tfrac{1}{2}\cos(a+b) + \tfrac{1}{2}\cos(a-b)$$
$$(0.43)(0.78) = \tfrac{1}{2}\cos(64.5324° + 38.7394°) + \tfrac{1}{2}\cos(64.5324° - 38.7394°)$$

Now, we simply take the cosine of the sum and difference of these angles, multiply them by one half and add them together to get the result:

$$(0.43)(0.78) = \tfrac{1}{2}\cos(64.5324° + 38.7394°) + \tfrac{1}{2}\cos(64.5324° - 38.7394°)$$
$$= \tfrac{1}{2}\cos(103.2718°) + \tfrac{1}{2}\cos(25.793°)$$
$$= -0.11478536 + 0.45018596$$
$$= 0.3354006$$

Finally, since we had to convert 43 to 0.43, and 78 to 0.78 by moving each decimal two places to the left, we must now take our result and move the decimal four places to the right to get our final answer. Therefore:
$$43(78) = 3354$$

The answer we got in this example was fairly accurate. This is because I could use a calculator to find my cosines and inverse cosines. Several centuries ago, when this method was actually used, the accuracy of your result depended upon the accuracy of the trigonometry tables that you used.

Location Arithmetic and Napier Bones (2 Other Methods by John Napier)
John Napier (1550 to 1617) developed the logarithm (and the logarithmic method of multiplication that we saw earlier). He also developed at least two other methods of multiplying numbers together. In this section we will look at his methods known as Location Arithmetic and Napier's Bones.

Location Arithmetic
The location arithmetic method uses an array of squares as a background surface. The squares along the bottom list the powers of two, going from right-to-left. Likewise, the squares along the right list the powers of two going from bottom-to-top. If we color the squares in a checkerboard pattern, it makes it easier to look at the board and use it.

An interesting property of this array is that if we multiply the numbers along the bottom to those numbers on the right, we find that numbers along the diagonals going from lower left to upper right are all equal to each other. In other words, 32 times 1 is equal to 16 times 2 which is also equal to 8 times 4, and so on. We will use this property to find our products.

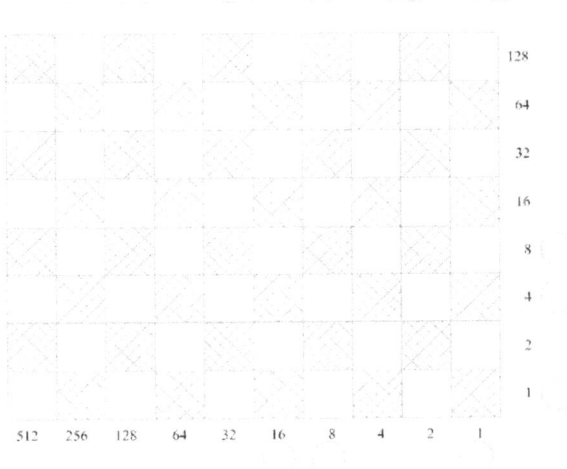

Figure 12.13   Location Arithmetic setting up for the product of 25 times 13.

The easiest way to understand this method is to see it used with an example. Say that we want to find the product of 25 times 13. We start by placing one number (in base 2) along the bottom, and the other number (also in base 2) along the right. In the diagram above, we have the number 25 along the bottom, and the number 13 along the right.

With the rows and columns thus identified, we repeat the bottom number on the board for every row where we have an indicator to the right of the board. This essentially gives us a checker (or marker) on the board every place where there is an intersection between the indicators from the bottom with the indicators from the right of the board. Our board should now look like the illustration below.

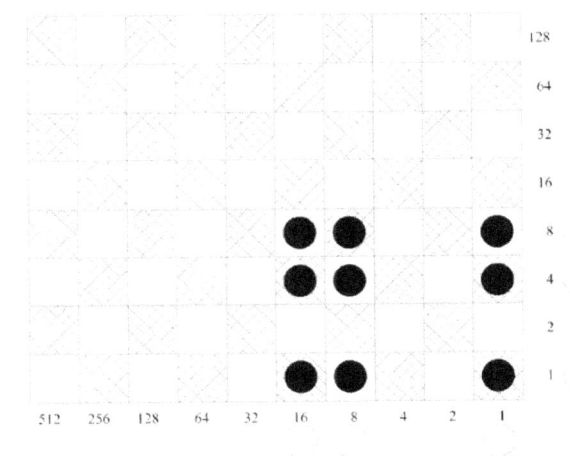

Figure 12.14   The numbers from the product are represented on the board.

The next step is to move the checkers diagonally until they are all on the bottom row. This may mean that some squares on the bottom row will have more than one checker on them. That is alright for now.

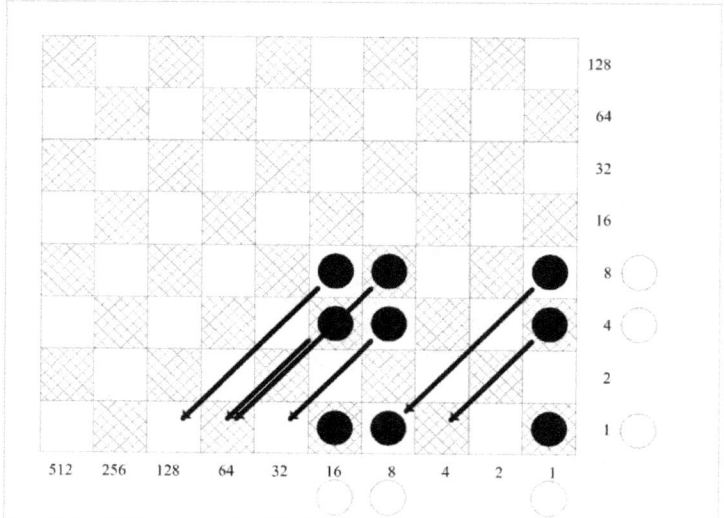

Figure 12.15   All the markers are moved diagonally to the bottom row.

Moving a checker along the diagonals does not change its value since each square along the diagonal (from lower left to upper right) is equal to the others within the same diagonal. Therefore, sliding all of the checkers diagonally down to the bottom row has maintained their actual value.

To get the final result, we need to take care of all the squares that have more than one checker on them. Starting at the right, and moving left, for every two checkers in a square, we remove them, and place (or carry) one checker to the square on the left.

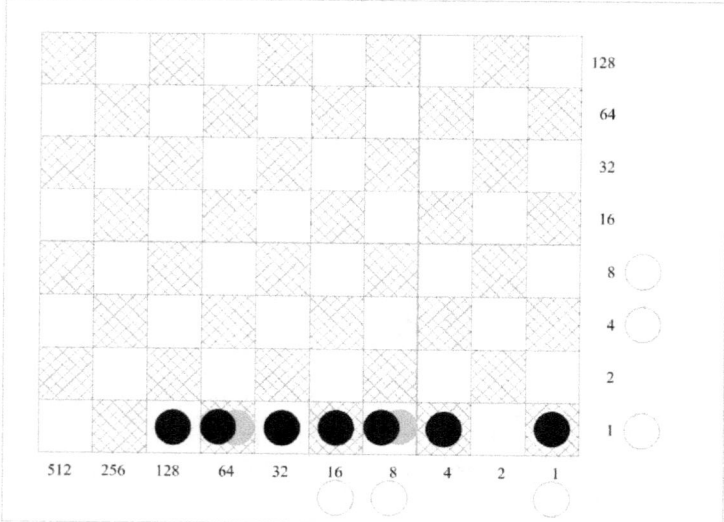

Figure 12.16   With the markers on the bottom row, the final result can now be found.

In the example above, we see that we are fine until we get to the square above the 8. There are two checkers in the square above the 8, so we remove these two checkers and place one checker in the square to the left. This gives us two checkers in the square above the 16. We remove them and place a checker in the square to the left of it. We again have two checkers in the square above the 32. We repeat the process and place a checker in the square above the 64. This time we have three checkers in this square. Here we remove two of the checkers and leave the third.

Since we removed the two checkers, we again place one in the square to the left, giving us two checkers in the square above the 128. We finally remove those two and place a checker to the left in the square above the 256. The remaining checkers represent our final result in base two. We are left with a checker in the squares above the 256, the 64, the 4 and the 1. Adding these numbers together gives us 325 which indeed is the product of 13 times 25. The figure below illustrates what our final result looks like.

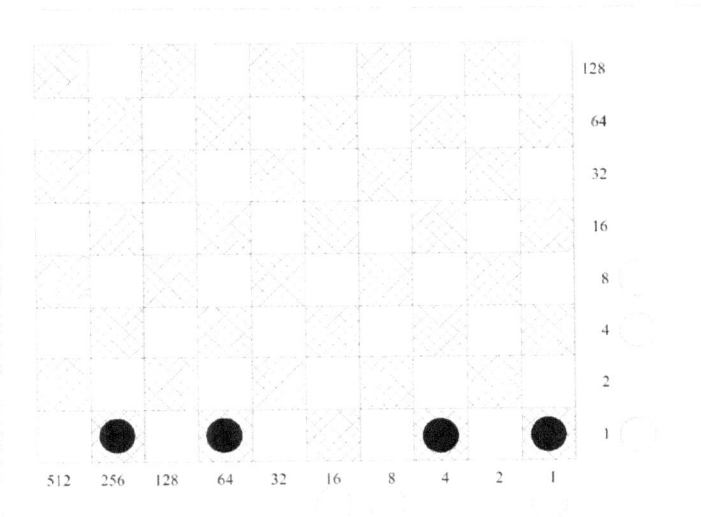

Figure 12.17   The product of 25 times 13 is represented in base 2 on the bottom row.

Napier's Bones

This is another method of multiplying numbers together that was developed by John Napier. This method uses ten strips as shown in the figure on the next page. These strips are numbered zero through nine and are divided into nine squares (each strip below actually has ten squares; however, the top square is a label used to identify the strip). The nine squares have a diagonal that runs from the lower left corner to the upper right. And within each of these squares are placed the products of 1 thru 9 for that number. The first strip has the multiples of zero on it; the second has the multiples of 1; the third has the multiples of 2; and so on.

If we look at the 7th bone (for example), we see that it has the multiples of the number 7. The first square has the product of 7 times 1, with the 7 placed in the lower diagonal of the square. The next square has the product of 7 times 2 with the number 14 divided so that the 1 is placed in the upper diagonal, and the 4 is placed in the lower diagonal. The third square has the product of 7 times 3 with the number 2 in the upper diagonal, and the 1 in the lower diagonal. In this way, the multiples of 7, from 1 times 7 to 9 times 7 is represented on this bone. With all ten bones, we have the entire multiplication table.

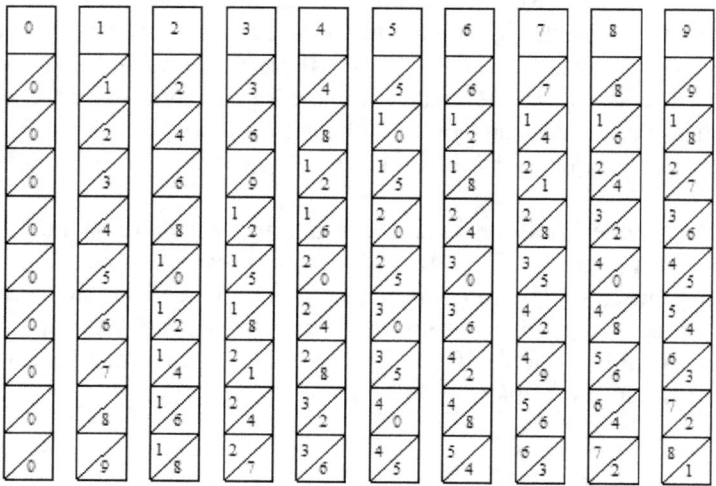

Figure 12.18   A set of Napier Bones (consisting of bones 0 thru 9).

The way to use these bones is very straight-forward. Say we wanted to find the product of 37 times 7. We start by taking the "3" bone and the "7" bone and place the two bones next to each other so that the labels on top show the number 37. We now go down to the seventh row, and there we have what we need to arrive at the product of 7 times 37. To get the answer, we add along the diagonals. In other words, the result is equal to 2, 1 + 4, and 9; or, the number 259. Therefore, the product of 7 times 37 is equal to 259.

In fact, the figure of the Napier bones below readily give us the products of 1 times 37 through 9 times 37 and we can quickly determine any of these results by simply going to the appropriate row and adding along the diagonals.

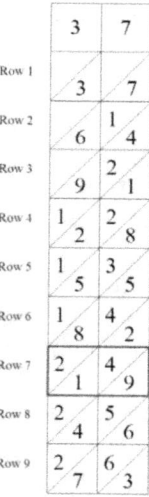

Figure 12.19   Napier Bones showing the product of 7 times 37.

168

This method will work for any two-digit number, any three-digit number, and so on. We simply place the appropriate bones next to each other, go to the corresponding row and add along the diagonals.

Now, suppose we want to know the product of some two-digit number multiplied to some other two-digit number. We use the same method; with the addition of a couple of more steps.

In this next example, let's look at the product of 94 times 46. We start by taking the "9" bone and placing it next to the "4" bone. Each of the nine rows is equal to the corresponding product of 1 times 94 through 9 times 94. To get the product of 94 times 46, we will use the numbers from the 4th row and the 6th row. Adding along the diagonals, the 4th row gives us the number 376, and the 6th row gives us the number 564.

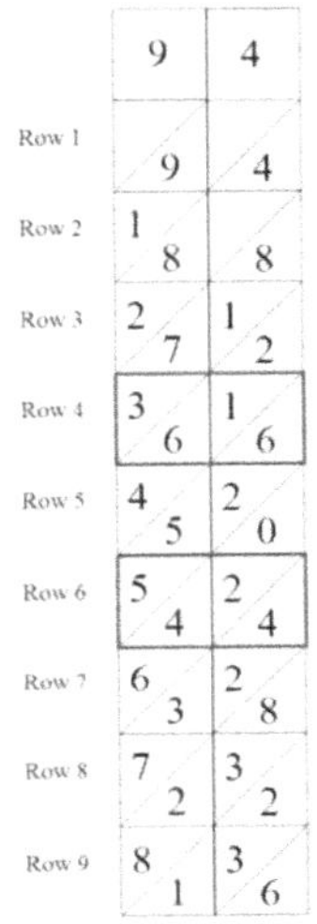

Figure 12.20   Napier Bones showing the product of 46 times 94 (and 64 times 94).

Since the number we are multiplying is 46, this is the same as 40 + 6. Since the 40 has a zero behind it, we will take the product from the 4th row and place a zero behind it. This gives us 3760. We now add these two numbers together: 3760 and 564 to get the number 4324 which is the product of 46 times 94.

We can also use the same numbers to find the product of 64 times 94. Again, we need the numbers from the 4th and the 6th rows, which are 376 and 564. This time, we see that the number 64 is equal to 60 + 4, so now we place the zero behind the number from the 6th row and add it to the number from the 4th row. Therefore, we are adding the numbers 5640 and 376 together to get the number 6016 which is equal to the product of 64 times 94. Of course, we can extend this concept so that we are able to find the product of any combination of two or three-digit numbers (and even larger numbers).

Genaille – Lucas Rulers

The Genaille – Lucas Rulers are a "second-generation" set of Napier Bones. These work in a way that is very similar to Napier Bones; yet also in such a way that it simplifies the method of finding the final result.

In this case we have eleven rulers altogether: ten of the rulers are labeled 0 thru 9, and the final ruler is an index ruler. Each of the rulers is divided into two columns. The numbered rulers (labeled 0 thru 9) have various sets of numbers in the right column, and funnels in the left column. The funnels remove the need for "carries" that you would have with the regular Napier Bones (as we will soon see). The index ruler will always be the left-most ruler used during a multiplication operation, and it will always give us the left-most digit of the final product.

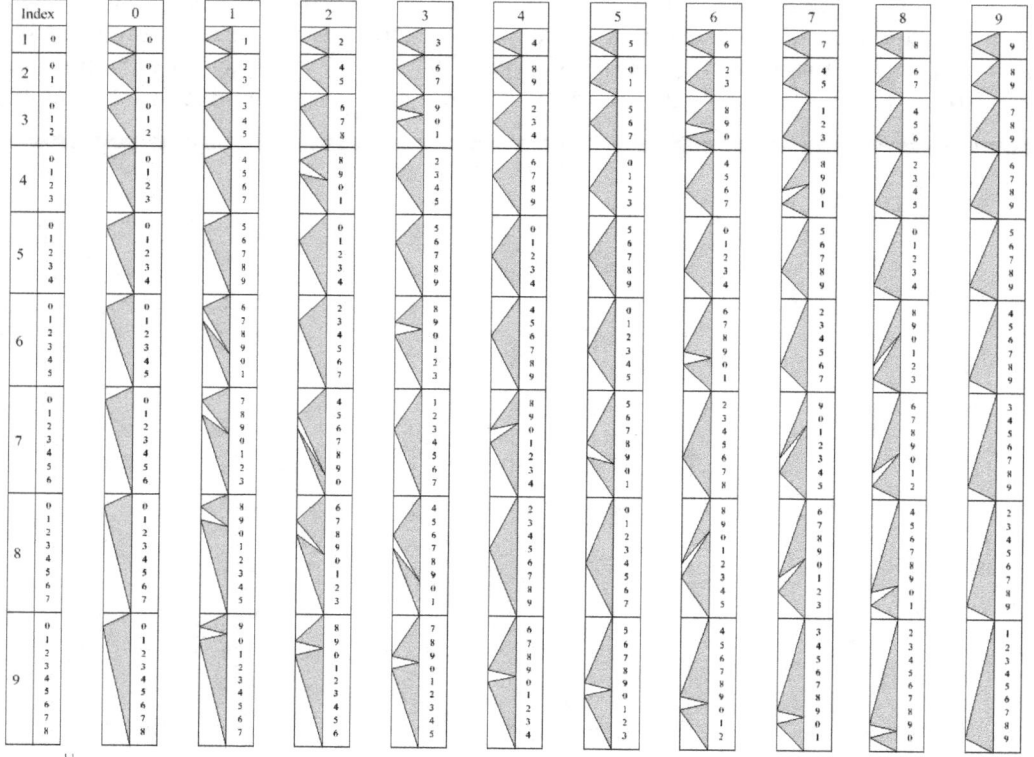

Figure 12.21   A set of Genaille – Lucas Rulers.

Let's look at a few examples using the Genaille – Lucas Rulers. We'll find the product of 3 times 9386, and also the product of 8 times 9386. And then we'll show how we would use those two results to find the products of 38 times 9386 and the product of 83 times 9386.

As with the Napier Bones, we start by selecting the 9, 3, 8, and 6 rulers, and place them in this order with the index ruler to the left of the 9-ruler. The figure below and on the left, shows how we would arrange these five rulers.

Since we are finding the product of 3 times 9386 first, we will be working along the third row (we use the index ruler to show us where the third row is).

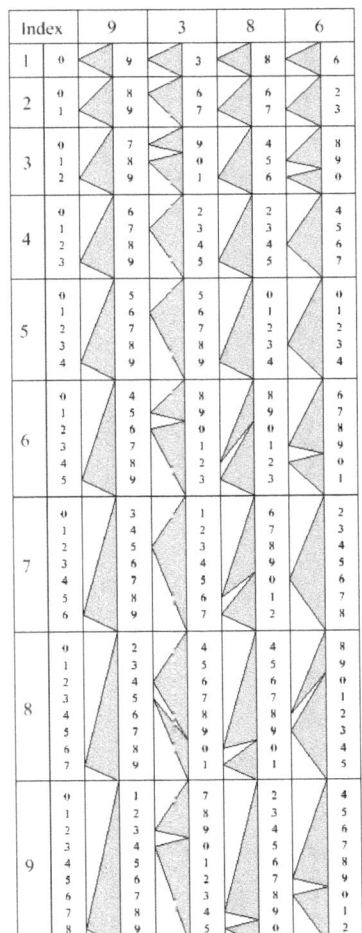 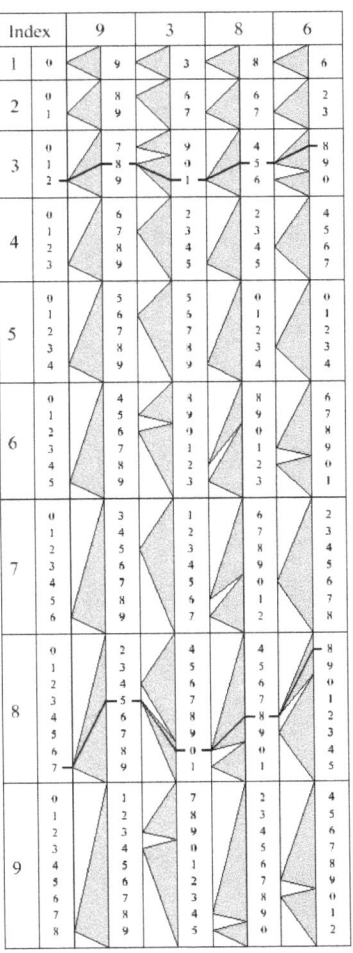

Figure 12.22   The products of 3 times 9386 and 8 times 9386 using the Genaille –
Lucas Rulers.

To find the product of 3 and 9386, we start with the product of 3 and 6 (the 6 being the last digit of 9386). The product of 3 and 6 is 18, but we'll just look at the 8 and let the rulers take care of all the carries for us. We start by finding the 8 (on the 6-ruler and the third row), and follow the funnels to the left. The funnel from the 6-ruler points to the 5 on the 8-ruler which then funnels us to the 1 on the 3-ruler. From there we are funneled to the 8 on the 9-ruler, and finally we are funneled to the 2 on the index ruler. Reading the numbers that we were funneled through (from left to right) gives us 28158, which is the product of 3 times 9386.

To find the product of 8 and 9386, we repeat the same process. We start on the eighth row, and find the last digit of the product of 8 and 6 (the 6 being the last digit of 9386). This product is equal to 48, but we only need the 8. So we find the 8 on the 6-ruler and eighth row, and then follow the funnels to the left. The first funnel takes us to 8 on the 8-ruler. Next we are directed to the 0 on the 3-ruler, and then we go to the 5 on the 9-ruler, and finally to the 7 on the index ruler. Therefore, the product of 8 and 9386 is 75088.

171

The funnels are nice, and as mentioned earlier, they take care of the carries for us. All we have to do is start at the appropriate place on the right-most ruler, and follow the funnels to the left. Now let's continue.

To find the product of 38 times 9386, we start by first finding the product of 3 times 9386, and the product of 8 times 9386, which are 28158 and 75088 (from above). Since the 3 times 9386 is actually 30 times 9386, we place a 0 behind the 28158 to give us 281580. Now we add those two numbers together to get 356668, which is the product of 38 and 9386:

9386	is the	281580
x 38	same as	+ 75088
		356668

To find the product of 83 times 9386, we again take the products of 3 times 9386, and 8 times 9386; but this time we place the 0 behind the 8 times 9386 product, and then add these two numbers together.

9386	is the	28158
x 83	same as	+ 750880
		779038

And we get 779038, which indeed is the product of 83 times 9386.

The Abacus

Along with the Napier Bones and the Genaille – Lucas Rulers, the abacus is another tool that has been around for centuries. The abacus is ideal for addition, subtraction, and multiplication. There are several types of abacuses. All types are divided into two sections, and have an upper scale and a lower scale. Some types have two beads in the upper scale, while others only have one. Similarly, some types have four beads in the bottom scale and others have five. In each case, the concept is the same – each column is used to represent any number from 0 to 9.

The way that this is done is that each bead in the upper scale represents a unit of 5 while the beads in the lower scale represent a unit of 1. A minimal amount of beads would be to have only one bead in the upper scale and four beads in the lower scale. With this arrangement, the numbers 0 through 9 can be represented. By having an extra bead in the top and/or bottom scales makes it is easier to handle carries in addition and subtraction, but it also means that several numbers can be represented in more than one way. In this section we will look at an example of multiplication using an abacus with one bead in the top scale and five beads in the lower scale.

The figure below shows how the numbers 0 through 10 are represented on our abacus. A number is represented by the number of beads touching the center bar. Note also that I have labeled the columns as A through L. A regular abacus doesn't have such a labeling. I have done it here to aid in my explanation. The number 0 is shown in column L, 1 is shown in column K, and so on moving from right to left. Also, notice that with this abacus there are two ways to represent the number 5. One way is shown in column G where the five lower beads are touching the center bar, and the second way is shown in column F where only the upper bead is touching the center bar. The six columns on the left show the numbers 5 thru 10, while the six columns on the right show the numbers 0 thru 5.

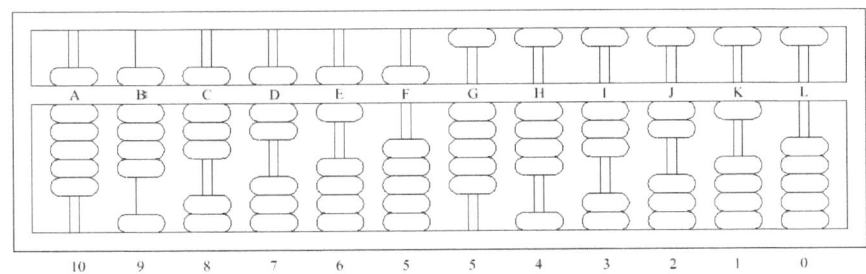

Figure 12.23   An Abacus showing how the numbers 0 through 10 are represented.

In order to multiply with an abacus, you need to already know your 0 through 9 multiplication tables. The abacus can then be used as a tool to help you multiply larger numbers quickly and efficiently. In our example we will use the abacus to find the product of 47 and 83. First, we start by zeroing out the abacus, as shown in the figure below:

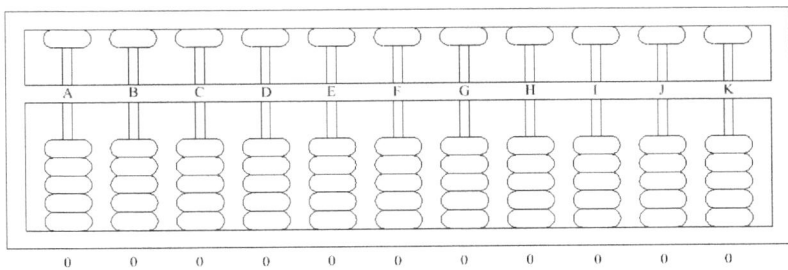

Figure 12.24   The Abacus with all the place holders set to 0.

Next, we'll place the numbers, 47 and 83 on the left side of the abacus. It doesn't matter which number is placed first, however, if there is enough space on the abacus, it is a good idea to leave a column of zeroes between the two numbers. In the figure below, we have the number 47 in columns A and B; column C is our separator column, and the number 83 is in columns D and E:

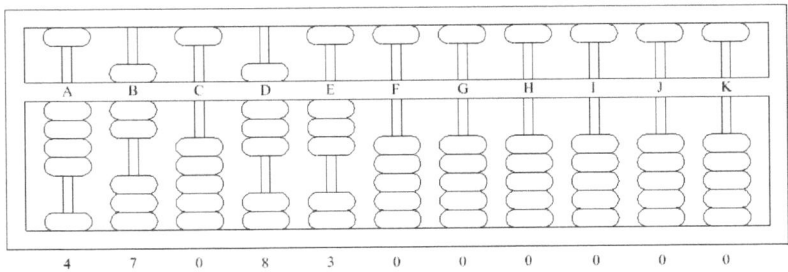

Figure 12.25   The Abacus set up to multiple 47 and 83.

Now we begin the multiplication. The method that we use is actually similar to several other methods that we have seen earlier in this chapter. The difference is that here we have a physical tool in our hands that helps us quickly go through all the steps. First we multiple the 7 and 3 together, and place their product on the right side of the abacus. The product is 21, and we place that number in columns J and K of the abacus.

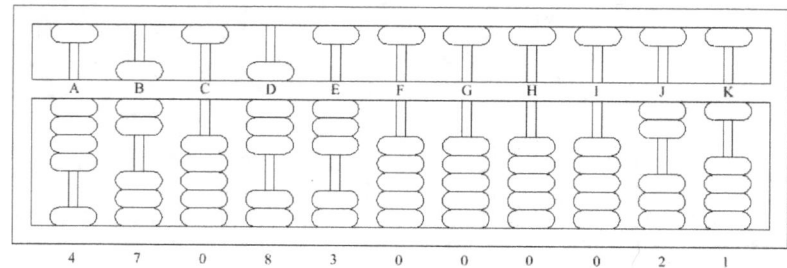

Figure 12.26   The first step in using an abacus to find the product of 47 and 83.

Notice that the 7 is from the ones-digit from the number 47 and the 3 is from the ones-digit from the number 83; therefore the product of these two numbers starts with the least significant digit of 21 at the ones-digit of the abacus (starting at column K on the right).

Next, we'll multiply the 7 and 8 together. Their product is 56, and since the 7 is from the ones-digit of 47, and 8 is from the tens-digit of 83, we add the 56 to the numbers in columns I and J (in other words, we are actually adding 560 to 21). This gives us 581 as shown in the figure below:

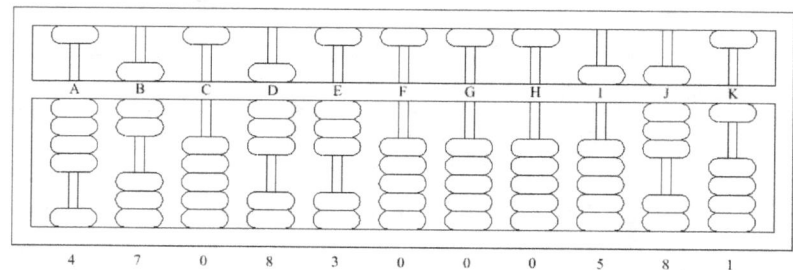

Figure 12.27   The second step in using an abacus to find the product of 47 and 83.

Now, we'll multiply the 4 and 3 together. Their product is 12, and this time the 4 is from the tens-digit of 47 while the 3 is from the ones-digit of 83. The 12 will also be added to the numbers in columns I and J (which actually means that we are adding 120 to 581).

Adding 120 to 581 gives us 701; however, that's not quite what the abacus shows. As we see in the figure below, we have a 6 in the hundreds-column (column I), with a 10 in the tens-column (column J), and a 1 in the ones-column (column K). We need to change the 10 to a zero in the tens-column and carry a one over to the hundreds-columns.

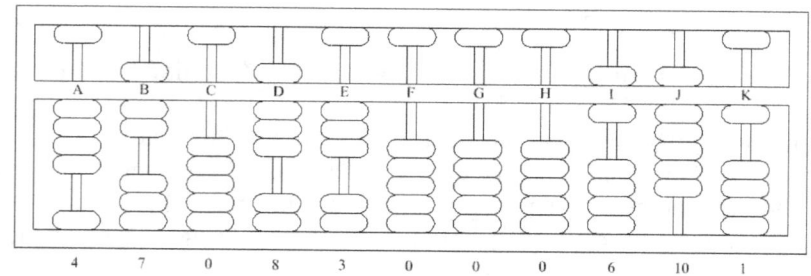

Figure 12.28   The third step in using an abacus to find the product of 47 and 83.

The figure below shows our updated abacus (after taking care of the carry) with the number 701 on the right side. We now proceed with the last step of our multiplication.

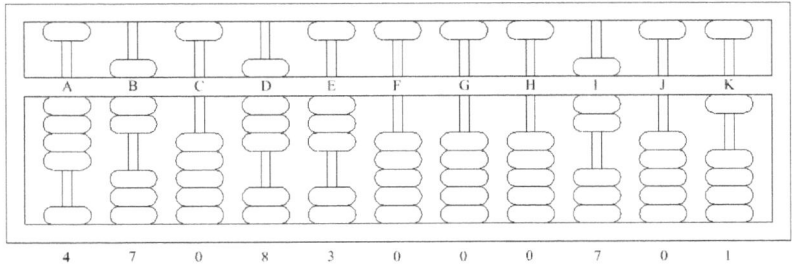

Figure 12.29   Taking care of a carry.

Finally, we multiply the 4 and the 8 together to give us 32. Since the 4 is from the tens-digit of 47, and the 8 is from the tens-digit of 83 we add the 32 to columns H and I. Therefore, we are effectively adding 3200 to 701. This gives us our final result of 3901, which is the product of 47 and 83.

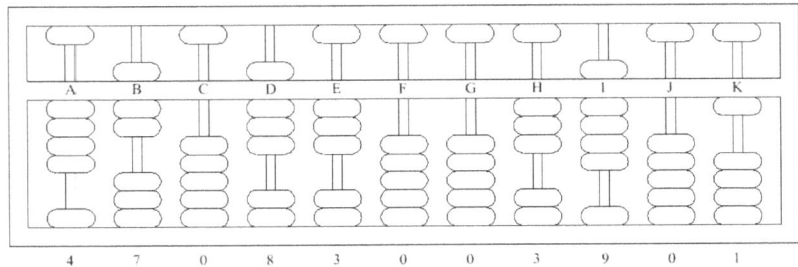

Figure 12.30   The final step in using an abacus to find the product of 47 and 83.

Just to sum up what we've done, in multiplying 47 to 83, we used the abacus to take us through the following steps:

$$47 \times 83 \quad = \quad \begin{array}{rcr} 7 \times 3 & = & 21 \\ + \ 7 \times 80 & = & 560 \\ + \ 40 \times 3 & = & 120 \\ + \ 40 \times 80 & = & \underline{3200} \\ & & 3901 \end{array}$$

Again, the abacus is very similar to other methods that we previously saw in this chapter; however, its uniqueness lay in the fact that we have a physical tool to help us multiply larger numbers together.

The Booth Algorithm

With the Booth Algorithm we now come full circle in our look at various multiplication methods. The Booth Algorithm is a variation of the traditional method that we looked at in the first section of this chapter. What makes it different from the traditional method is that it uses a property of the base you are working in to speed up the multiplication. In base 10, if we want to multiply 2481 by 999, we would line up the numbers like so:

$$\begin{array}{r} 2481 \\ \times \ 999 \\ \hline \end{array}$$

And multiple 2481 by 9 three times, where each time we shift our sub-result one place to the left. Then finally, we add the three sub-results together to get the final result. Altogether, the operation looks like this:

$$
\begin{array}{r}
2481 \\
\times\ \underline{999} \\
22329 \\
22329 \\
+\ \underline{22329} \\
2478519
\end{array}
$$

However, we could have gotten the same result (and much more quickly) if we would have taken into account that 999 is the same as 1000-1. Now, we only need to multiply 2481 by 1000, and then subtract 2481 from that product to get our final result. And, the multiplication is simplified even more because when we multiple any number by 1000, all we have to do is add three zeroes to the end of our number. Summing it up, we now have

$$
\begin{array}{rcr}
2481 & \text{is equal to} & 2481000 \\
\times\ \underline{999} & & -\ \underline{2481}
\end{array}
$$

And from this we can quickly obtain the result of 2478519 (which is the same answer that we got above). Now that we've explained this principle, we're going to take it just a little further to better understand the Booth Algorithm. This time we are going to multiple 2481 by 79992. In this example our number isn't made of just 9's; however, we do have a string of 9's in the middle of the number. If we were to take 79992 and add 10 to this number, we would get 80002. We now multiple 2481 by 80002 and then subtract 10 times 2481 to get our final result.

$$
\begin{array}{rcr}
2481 & \text{becomes} & 2481 \\
\times\ \underline{79992} & & \times\ \underline{80002}
\end{array}
$$

The product of 2481 and 80002 is 198484962; and while the multiplication was very easy, this isn't our final answer. When we added 10 to 79992, we were actually adding 10 times 2481 to the result that we want. Therefore, to get the final result, we must take 198484962 and subtract 10 times 2481. Our final result is:

$$
\begin{array}{r}
198484962 \\
-\ \underline{24810} \\
198460152
\end{array}
$$

If you had to do all of these calculations by hand, Booth's Algorithm is actually a little shorter and easier to use than the traditional method.

However, you may be thinking that this is a nice trick, but it is very limited because it only works when one of the numbers you are multiplying has a string of nines in it. And if we are working in base 10, then you are right. But if we are working in base 2 then it will work on any number that has a string of ones in it. Let's look at an example where we will multiple 19 by 94 in base 2.

$$
\begin{array}{rcr}
19 & = & 10011 \\
94 & = & 1011110
\end{array}
$$

Notice that the 94 has a string of four one's in it. If we add 10 to this number, it becomes 1100000. (Keep in mind that adding 10 to the number in base 2 is not the same thing as adding

10 to a number in base 10. Since we are working in base 2, everything that we do is in base 2.) Now we multiply 10011 to 1100000:

$$
\begin{array}{r}
10011 \\
\times\,1100000 \\
\hline
10011 \\
+\,10011 \\
\hline
11100100000
\end{array}
$$

To get our final answer, we must subtract 10011 times 10 from the answer above. There are several ways to subtract one number from another. In chapter one we saw a method of converting a number to its complement and then adding. The end result is a subtraction, and this is in fact how many computers perform subtraction. However, in this example we will perform a simple straight-forward subtraction in base 2:

$$
\begin{array}{r}
11100100000 \\
-\qquad 100110 \\
\hline
11011111010
\end{array}
$$

And when we convert that answer back to base 10, we get 1786, which in fact is the product of 19 and 94. Of course, it would be very tedious to use this method in base 2, unless you were a computer; then it becomes a method that can save several steps in most multiplication processes.

Multiplying by 11

In chapter one we saw an easy method of multiplying the numbers one through nine by nine. Now, we'll take a look at a quick and easy way to multiply any large number by 11. The concept is very easy. Simply take the number that you wish to multiply by 11, and re-write the first and last digits of that number (with plenty of room in between them). Then, starting on the right side, add the number pairs, and write down the result of that sum. And if the sum is greater than 9, only write the least significant digit of that sum, and then carry the 1 to the left. By the time you've reached the left-most digit, you have the product of that number times 11. Let's look at an example. We'll multiply 9315724 by 11:

$$
\begin{array}{r}
9315724 \\
\times\qquad 11
\end{array}
$$

The first and last digits are 9 and 4, so we re-write them with plenty of space in between:

9   4

Next, start adding the pairs of numbers (going from right to left, and including the first and last digits):

9+3   3+1   1+5   5+7   7+2   2+4

Write down these sums (notice that the sums are bounded by the first and last digits and placed between them):

9   12   4   6   12   9   6   4

Now, starting on the right, and moving left, where ever a sum is greater than 9, subtract 10 from that value, write the result, and carry the 1 to the left:

$$9^{+1} \quad 2 \quad 4 \quad 6^{+1} \quad 2 \quad 9 \quad 6 \quad 4$$

Finally, take out the spaces and we have the product of 9315724 times 11:

$$102472964$$

And with a little practice, this can practically be done in your head.

An Interesting, Roundabout, Long Method of Multiplying Numbers

This final method is reminiscent of the Vedic method (that we saw earlier in this chapter) and is also taught in India. I hesitate to count it as an actual method of multiplying numbers because of its roundabout approach, but it does show an interesting relationship that isn't obvious when multiplying two numbers together. To see what I mean, let's first look at a few single digit examples. We'll start by finding the product of 3 times 5:

$$
\begin{array}{r}
3 \\
\times 5 \\
\end{array}
\quad \text{first we'll add these numbers together to get} \quad
\begin{array}{r}
3 \\
+5 \\
\hline
8
\end{array}
$$

Then we'll take each number and subtract it from 10, and then multiply those numbers together to get a product:

$$
\begin{array}{l}
(10 - 3) = 7 \\
(10 - 5) = 5 \\
\end{array}
\quad \text{we multiply them together} \quad
\begin{array}{r}
7 \\
\times 5 \\
\hline
35
\end{array}
$$

Finally, we take our sum (the 8), shift it left one space, and add it to our product (the 35). What we have is:

$$
\begin{array}{r}
35 \\
+ \ 8 \ \ \\
\hline
115
\end{array}
$$

Our final result is the two right-most digits of 115, which is 15, and which is equal to the product of our original two numbers, 3 and 5.

If you followed that, you probably thought that it looked like a lot of hocus-pocus; but let's look at a few more examples before you pass judgment on this process. And now that I've explained the process above, I will condense it to a single line so that it will be easier to follow. Here's the product of 4 times 7 (start on the left, and move right):

$$
\begin{array}{r}
4 \\
\times 7 \\
\end{array}
\ \text{goes to} \
\begin{array}{r}
4 \\
+7 \\
\hline
11
\end{array}
\ \text{we now take} \
\begin{array}{l}
(10 - 4) = 6 \\
(10 - 7) = 3 \\
\end{array}
\ \text{multiply them} \
\begin{array}{r}
6 \\
\times 3 \\
\hline
18
\end{array}
\ \text{then add} \
\begin{array}{r}
18 \\
+11 \\
\hline
128
\end{array}
$$

And the final result is 28 (the two right-most digits of 128), and 28 is the product of our two original numbers (4 times 7). Now let's look at 2 times 6:

178

```
  2  goes to   2   we now  (10 − 2) = 8  multiply  8   then        32
x 6           + 6   take    (10 − 6) = 4  them    x 4  add       +  8
              ___                                 ___            ____
               8                                   32             112
```

And the result is 12. Finally, we'll look at 8 times 9 before moving to another concept:

```
  8  goes to   8   we now  (10 − 8) = 2  multiply  2   then        02
x 9           + 9   take    (10 − 9) = 1  them    x 1  add       + 17
              ___                                 ___            ____
               17                                   2             172
```

Which gives us a final result of 72. We've now seen enough examples to believe that this must be some fluke of nature; however, let's go to the next level and look at examples where we multiply two-digit numbers together.

When multiplying two-digit numbers there are a few things in our algorithm that we will need to change. Instead of subtracting the numbers from 10, we will now subtract them from 100. Then, when we add our product and sum together, we must shift the sum two places to the left, and then our final result will be the four right-most digits of the result (instead of the two right-most digits). This is what 78 times 51 looks like:

```
  78  goes to   78   we now  (100 − 78) = 22  multiply  22   then       1078
x 51           + 51   take    (100 − 51) = 49  them    x 49  add      +  129
               ____                                    ____          _____
                129                                     1078          13978
```

The product of 78 times 51 is equal to 3978. This is very interesting, isn't it!

Here's another example, 37 times 23:

```
  37  goes to   37   we now  (100 − 37) = 63  multiply  63   then       4851
x 23           + 23   take    (100 − 23) = 77  them    x 77  add      +   60
               ____                                    ____          _____
                 60                                     4851          10851
```

Looking at the four right-most digits, the product of 37 and 23 is 851.

And as a last example before we close this chapter, let's take a pair of single digit numbers, and treat them as two digit numbers. Here is the product of 6 times 7:

```
  6  goes to   6   we now  (100 − 6) = 94  multiply  94   then       8742
x 7           + 7   take    (100 − 7) = 93  them    x 93  add      +   13
              ___                                    ____          _____
               13                                     8742          10042
```

Again, we only look at the last four digits and we get 42 as the product of 6 times 7 (which of course, is right). As you can see, a person can have a lot of fun with this interesting, roundabout, long method of multiplication.

So, why would anyone ever use this method, after all, you still need to perform a multiplication to find the product of your two numbers? However, the multiplication uses two different numbers other than the ones you started with. In fact, if the original numbers that you are multiplying together are small numbers, then the actual numbers that you will use in the multiplication will be large numbers; on the other hand, if the original numbers are large numbers, then the actual numbers used in the multiplication will be small numbers, and this may be the advantage.

For example, say you wanted to find the product of 92 and 86. This method would give you the following:

$$
\begin{array}{ccccccccc}
86 & \text{goes to} & 86 & \text{we now} & (100-86) & = & 14 & \text{multiply} & 14 & \text{then} & 112 \\
\underline{x\,92} & & \underline{+\,92} & \text{take} & (100-92) & = & 8 & \text{them} & \underline{x\ 8} & \text{add} & \underline{+\,178} \\
& & 178 & & & & & & 112 & & 17912 \\
\end{array}
$$

And looking at the last four digits gives us 7912, which is the product of 92 and 86. Therefore, even though the actual problem was to multiply two large numbers together; in reality, all that we had to actually multiply together were 14 and 8.

Another question is why does this work? I'll leave that as something to think about when you have little else to do. Of course, maybe this really is some sort of hocus-pocus, or some other fluke of numbers in nature.

Chapter 13
Pythagorean Triples

What is a Pythagorean Triple

The Pythagorean Theorem states that for every right triangle, the hypotenuse squared is equal to the sum of the length of the two legs squared. This relation can be written as:

$$a^2 + b^2 = c^2$$

In the expression above, a and b are the legs and c is the hypotenuse. Because of this simple fact, anytime we have a right triangle, and we know any two sides of the triangle, we can use this formula to find the third side.

For the most part, if two whole numbers are entered into the formula, the third number will not be a whole number. However, where all three values are whole numbers, these values are called a Pythagorean triple. Some examples of Pythagorean triples include:

3, 4, 5	where:	$3^2 + 4^2 = 5^2$
5, 12, 13		$5^2 + 12^2 = 13^2$
8, 15, 17		$8^2 + 15^2 = 17^2$

Pythagorean triples have some interesting properties. For example, one of the three sides is always divisible by 3. One of the three sides is also always divisible by 5 (sometimes it's the same side as the one that is divisible by 3). The product of the two legs is always divisible by 12, and the product of all three sides is always divisible by 60. But even more interesting than the properties are some of the methods of finding Pythagorean triples. In this chapter we'll look at several of these methods.

Finding Pythagorean Triples, the First Method

Pythagorean triples seem to have a special charm about them. Maybe it's because we like working with whole numbers; or maybe it's because they appear to be such a rare commodity. Maybe it's because some of the methods for finding these triples are just as interesting as the triples themselves.

The first method we'll examine starts with two consecutive odd (or even) numbers. We take the reciprocal of these numbers and then add the fractions together. The numerator and denominator of the resulting fraction are the two legs of a Pythagorean triple. Finally, the third side (the hypotenuse) is found by using the Pythagorean theorem itself. For example, the numbers 2 and 4 are consecutive even numbers. Their reciprocals are 1/2 and 1/4. Add them together, and we have 3/4. The numbers 3 and 4 are the two legs of the right triangle. We then use the Pythagorean theorem to find the hypotenuse, which is 5. The following listing shows several examples of Pythagorean triples using this method.

Consecutive Even Numbers	Sum of the Reciprocals	Pythagorean Triples
2, 4	$\frac{1}{2} + \frac{1}{4} = \frac{3}{4}$	3, 4, 5
4, 6	$\frac{1}{4} + \frac{1}{6} = \frac{5}{12}$	5, 12, 13
6, 8	$\frac{1}{6} + \frac{1}{8} = \frac{7}{24}$	7, 24, 25
8, 10	$\frac{1}{8} + \frac{1}{10} = \frac{9}{40}$	9, 40, 41

Consecutive Odd Numbers	Sum of the Reciprocals	Pythagorean Triples
3, 5	$\frac{1}{3} + \frac{1}{5} = \frac{8}{15}$	8, 15, 17
5, 7	$\frac{1}{5} + \frac{1}{7} = \frac{12}{35}$	12, 35, 37
7, 9	$\frac{1}{7} + \frac{1}{9} = \frac{16}{63}$	16, 63, 65
9, 11	$\frac{1}{9} + \frac{1}{11} = \frac{20}{99}$	20, 99, 101

At the beginning of this section I said that Pythagorean triples appear to be a rare commodity. They really are rare; however, we can see from this example alone that there is still an endless supply of them.

An interesting characteristic of this method is that the two consecutive even numbers will always give a Pythagorean triple where the hypotenuse is one number greater than the longest leg; while the two consecutive odd numbers will always give a Pythagorean triple where the hypotenuse is two greater than the longest leg.

A Second Method of Finding Pythagorean Triples

We will use a derivation of the first method to generate a second method of finding Pythagorean triples. We started out the last section by saying that a Pythagorean triple can be created from the sum of the reciprocals of two consecutive odd (or even) numbers. For this method, we will let x and x+2 represent our consecutive even (or odd) numbers. The reciprocal of each would be represented as

$$\frac{1}{x} \quad \text{and} \quad \frac{1}{x+2}$$

If we find a common denominator, and add them together, we get:

$$\frac{2x + 2}{x^2 + 2x}$$

According to the first method, the numerator and the denominator of this fraction make up the two legs of a right triangle. To find the hypotenuse, we take each leg and square it, and then add them together, and then take the square root.

$$4x^2 + 8x + 4 \qquad + \qquad x^4 + 4x^3 + 4x^2$$
(numerator squared) (denominator squared)

Combining terms we get: $x^4 + 4x^3 + 8x^2 + 8x + 4$

Which factors to: $(x^2 + 2x + 2)^2$

In other words, we now have a formula, in terms of x for each of the legs and the hypotenuse. The first leg is equal to $2x + 2$; the second leg is equal to $x^2 + 2x$; and the hypotenuse is equal to $x^2 + 2x + 2$. With this formula, we plug in whole numbers for x, and get whole number solutions for Pythagorean triples. Here is a listing of a few Pythagorean triples created in this way:

Pythagorean Triples

x	2x + 2	$x^2 + 2x$	$x^2 + 2x + 2$
1	4	3	5
2	6	8	10
3	8	15	17
4	10	24	26
5	12	35	37
…, etc.			

This relation has an interesting property in that except for the 3, 4, 5 triple, the hypotenuse is always 2 units larger than the largest leg. Because of this, we can get an interesting set of Pythagorean triples if we let x = 10, 100, 1000, etc.

Pythagorean Triples

x	2x + 2	$x^2 + 2x$	$x^2 + 2x + 2$
10	22	120	122
100	202	10200	10202
1000	2002	1002000	1002002
10000	20002	100020000	100020002
100000	200002	10000200000	10000200002
…, etc.			

And we get another interesting set of triples when we let x = 9, 99, 999, etc.

Pythagorean Triples

x	2x + 2	$x^2 + 2x$	$x^2 + 2x + 2$
9	20	99	101
99	200	9999	10001
999	2000	999999	1000001
9999	20000	99999999	100000001
99999	200000	9999999999	10000000001
…, etc.			

This second method used a single number, x, to generate a Pythagorean triple. In the next example, we will see a method that uses two generating numbers.

A Third Method of Finding Pythagorean Triples

This method uses two generating numbers, m and n, to create Pythagorean triples. The two legs of the triangle are equal to $m^2 - n^2$ and $2mn$. Squaring these two legs, and adding them together give us a hypotenuse equal to $m^2 + n^2$. The numbers m and n can be any two arbitrary whole numbers; however, to keep our values positive, we will say that m must be larger than n. Let's look at a few examples:

Generating Numbers		Pythagorean Triples		
m	**n**	$m^2 - n^2$	**2mn**	$m^2 + n^2$
2	1	3	4	5
4	1	15	8	17
7	3	40	42	58
5	2	21	20	29
3	2	5	12	13
…, etc.		…, etc.		

This method of creating Pythagorean triples also has some interesting properties. If we use consecutive numbers for m and n (with m being the larger value), then the larger leg and the hypotenuse will always be consecutive numbers. (See the table below.)

Generating Numbers		Pythagorean Triples		
m	**n**	$m^2 - n^2$	**2mn**	$m^2 + n^2$
2	1	3	4	5
3	2	5	12	13
4	3	7	24	25
5	4	9	40	41
7	6	13	84	85
…, etc.		…, etc.		

Now, if we use the legs of any of these triangles as the generating numbers m and n, then the hypotenuse of the resulting Pythagorean triple will be a perfect square. This is easily seen because the hypotenuse is equal to $m^2 + n^2$.

Generating Numbers		Pythagorean Triples		
m	**n**	$m^2 - n^2$	**2mn**	$m^2 + n^2$
4	3	7	24	25
12	5	119	120	169
24	7	527	336	625
40	9	1519	720	1681
…, etc.		…, etc.		

Likewise, if we use the hypotenuse and a leg of any Pythagorean triple for m and n, then the first leg of the new Pythagorean triple will also be a perfect square. This also is easily seen because the first leg is equal to $m^2 - n^2$.

Generating Numbers		Pythagorean Triples		
m	**n**	$m^2 - n^2$	**2mn**	$m^2 + n^2$
5	4	9	40	41
13	12	25	312	313
25	24	49	1200	1201
41	40	81	3280	3281
…, etc.		…, etc.		

Notice in the previous example that not only did we use the hypotenuse and the leg of a Pythagorean triple for our m and n values, but we also selected them so that they were consecutive numbers. Therefore, the largest leg and the hypotenuse of the resulting Pythagorean triples were also consecutive numbers.

Finally, if the generating numbers m and n consist of consecutive triangular numbers, then the first leg of the resulting triple will be a perfect cube.

Generating Numbers		Pythagorean Triples		
m	**n**	$m^2 - n^2$	**2mn**	$m^2 + n^2$
6	3	27	36	45
10	6	64	120	136
15	10	125	300	325
21	15	216	630	666
…, etc.		…, etc.		

Other interesting Pythagorean triples can be found with this method by simply defining other relationships between the generating numbers m and n.

A Fourth Method of Finding Pythagorean Triples

This method uses complex numbers to generate a Pythagorean triple. As you may recall, a complex number consists of two parts, a real part, and an imaginary part; and it is usually written in the form: a + bi. The "a" is the real part, and the "bi" is the imaginary part, with the "i" representing the square root of negative one.

To generate a Pythagorean triple from a complex number, we simply square the complex number, and the result will be the legs of the triple. The only catch is that the values for a and b must be whole numbers. Let's look at the number (2 + i) as an example:

$$
\begin{aligned}
(2 + i)^2 = (2 + i)(2 + i) &= 2^2 + 2i + 2i + i^2 \\
&= 4 + 4i + -1 \\
&= 3 + 4i
\end{aligned}
$$

The complex number $(2 + i)^2$ is equal to 3 + 4i, and as we already know, the numbers 3 and 4 are the legs of a Pythagorean triple (3, 4, and 5). For a second example, we'll square the complex number 5 + 2i:

$$
\begin{aligned}
(5 + 2i)^2 = (5 + 2i)(5 + 2i) &= 5^2 + 10i + 10i + 4i^2 \\
&= 25 + 20i + -4 \\
&= 21 + 20i
\end{aligned}
$$

The numbers 20 and 21 are the legs for the Pythagorean triple 20, 21 and 29.

This fourth method may seem pretty amazing, but it is actually our third method in disguise. To see this relationship, let's square the imaginary number m + ni. Doing so gives us:

$$(m + ni)^2 \;=\; (m + ni)(m + ni) \quad\; = \;\; m^2 + mni + mni + n^2 i^2$$
$$= \;\; m^2 + 2mni + -n^2$$
$$= \;\; m^2 - n^2 + 2mni$$

The real part of our result is equal to $m^2 - n^2$, and the imaginary part is equal to 2mn. This is the same formula that we used in the third method to generate the two legs of the Pythagorean triples.

A Fifth Method of Finding Pythagorean Triples

A fifth method uses the following two equations to construct Pythagorean triples:

$$x^2 + y^2 \;=\; 1$$
$$my \;=\; n(x + 1)$$

These two equations represent a circle and a line respectively. And, depending on the numbers that we choose for m and n, the line will either be tangent to the circle at the point (-1, 0), or the line will intersect the circle at two points. If the line intersects the circle at two points, one of those points is the point (-1, 0), and the other point will give us the values we can use to find a Pythagorean triple. Let's look at some examples.

Suppose we let m = 4 and n = 3. The second equation above becomes:

$$4y \;=\; 3(x + 1)$$

or

$$y \;=\; \tfrac{3}{4}(x + 1)$$

Now, we take this equation, substitute it for y in the first equation, and get:

$$x^2 + [\tfrac{3}{4}(x + 1)]^2 \;=\; 1$$

Finally, when we solve for x, we get two solutions. One of them is x = -1, and the other is the fraction x = 7/25. We'll now enter this second value for x into the equation $y = \tfrac{3}{4}(x + 1)$ to determine the value for y. Solving for y we get 24/25. These two fractions contain the three numbers of our Pythagorean triple. The numerators of the fractions are the two legs of the triangle, and the denominator is the hypotenuse. Our Pythagorean triple is 7, 24, 25.

It will always be the case when using this method that the two numerators will be the legs of the triangle, and the denominator will be the hypotenuse.

There was a reason why I chose m and n as the variables in the construction equation. If we solve the second equation for y and plug it into the first equation, and then solve it for x, we get:

$$x \;=\; \frac{m^2 - n^2}{m^2 + n^2}$$

Then if we plug that back into either equation and solve for y, we get:

186

$$y = \frac{2mn}{m^2 + n^2}$$

Once again we see that the two legs of the triangle are equal to $m^2 - n^2$ and $2mn$, and the hypotenuse is equal to $m^2 + n^2$. And, once again, we have the third method, but this time from a geometric perspective.

A Sixth Method of Finding Pythagorean Triples

This method will also be derived from a formula. However, this time we'll start with the equation for a right triangle, $a^2 + b^2 = c^2$, but we'll rewrite it as:

$$a^2 = c^2 - b^2$$

Next, we'll define the hypotenuse to be one more than one of the legs. This gives us the relation:

$$c = b + 1$$

We'll take this relation, and square both sides so that c^2 is equal to

$$c^2 = b^2 + 2b + 1$$

Now, we substitute this expression for c^2 into the first equation, and then simplify:

$$a^2 = (b^2 + 2b + 1) - b^2$$
$$a^2 = 2b + 1$$

Finally, we arbitrarily set a equal to $2x + 1$. By squaring a and plugging it into the previous equation, we create a relation for b in terms of x, and from there we generate a relation for c in terms of x. As a result, we have:

Arbitrarily let:	$a = 2x + 1$
Use this to find b:	$a^2 = 2b + 1$
	$(2x + 1)^2 = 2b + 1$
So that	$b = 2x^2 + 2x$
And	$c = 2x^2 + 2x + 1$

This formula appears to be very similar to the formula we derived for our second method, but even though it is similar, it is not the same. This set of equations will give us an entirely distinct set of Pythagorean triples than we would get from the set of equations from method two.

By selecting some x, we can generate values for a, b and c. Notice that a (the shorter leg) will always be an odd number; while the longer leg, b, will always be even. And the hypotenuse, c, will always be one more than b.

As with the previous methods, it is very easy to generate some very interesting sets of Pythagorean triples with these relations. For example:

Pythagorean Triples

x	2x + 1	$2x^2 + 2x$	$2x^2 + 2x + 1$
10	21	220	221
100	201	20200	20201
1000	2001	2002000	2002001
10000	20001	200020000	200020001
100000	200001	20000200000	20000200001
…, etc.			

A Seventh Method of Finding Pythagorean Triples

This method uses three construction numbers, x, y and z; and starts with the relationship:

$$yz = \frac{x^2}{2}$$

We simply select values for x, y and z that make this statement true. Then once we have these values, we plug them into the following equations and generate our Pythagorean Triple, where $a^2 + b^2 = c^2$.

$$a = x + y$$
$$b = x + z$$
$$c = x + y + z$$

Now, let's return to the first equation in this section (where we have $yz = x^2/2$). The easiest way to use this method is to start by selecting a value for x. Since we know that x^2 will be divided by two, and since we are only working with whole numbers, x must be even. After choosing x, we can easily find values for y and z. For example, if we let x equal 6, then we know that the product of y and z must equal half of six squared. In other words, the product of y and z must be equal to 18. In this case there are several pairs of numbers that will work. We could use 6 and 3; or 9 and 2; or 18 and 1. If we use all three pairs, we have three sets of construction numbers, which in turn generate three sets of Pythagorean Triples.

Construction Numbers			Pythagorean Triple		
x	y	z	a	b	c
6	6	3	12	9	15
6	9	2	15	8	17
6	18	1	24	7	25

As you can see, this method has a lot of flexibility. Because of this flexibility, we also have a certain amount of control. For example, we can always ensure that y is equal to one. If we do this, then the c value of the Pythagorean Triple will always be one more than the b value. Here are a few examples:

Construction Numbers			Pythagorean Triple		
x	y	z	a	b	c
2	1	2	3	4	5
4	1	8	5	12	13
6	1	18	7	24	25
8	1	32	9	40	41
10	1	50	11	60	61

In a similar manner, if we always keep y equal to 2, we see that the z value is always equal to $(x/y)^2$ and the c value of the Pythagorean Triple will always be two more than the b value.

Construction Numbers				Pythagorean Triple		
x	y	z		a	b	c
2	2	1		4	3	5
4	2	4		6	8	10
6	2	9		8	15	17
8	2	16		10	24	26
10	2	25		12	35	37

Of course, this method is also very easy to prove. We'll simply take the relationship mentioned above:

$$a = x + y$$
$$b = x + z$$
$$c = x + y + z$$

and plug it into the Pythagorean Theorem so that we have:

$$a^2 + b^2 = c^2$$
$$(x + y)^2 + (x + z)^2 = (x + y + z)^2$$

Expanding this gives us:

$$(x^2 + 2xy + y^2) + (x^2 + 2xz + z^2) = (x^2 + y^2 + z^2 + 2xy + 2xz + 2yz)$$

Removing the parentheses, combining, and rearranging terms gives us the following:

$$2x^2 + y^2 - z^2 + 2xy + 2xz = x^2 + y^2 + z^2 + 2xy + 2xz + 2yz$$

By further combining and canceling like terms, the equation above miraculously reduces to

$$x^2 = 2yz$$

Or

$$yz = \frac{x^2}{2}$$

This equation shows the relationship between the generating numbers x, y, and z; and is the one that we started with at the beginning of this section.

An Eighth Method of Finding Pythagorean Triples

Most of the methods that we've considered so far have used some sort of generating numbers to create the Pythagorean triple (like m and n, or x, y, and z). However, for this method, we will simply select the value of a, and then use it to generate the b and c values for use in the equation $a^2 + b^2 = c^2$.

To begin, let's consider these two relations:

$$(a^2 + 1)^2 = a^4 + 2a^2 + 1$$
$$(a^2 - 1)^2 = a^4 - 2a^2 + 1$$

By subtracting the second relation from the first, we find that they have a difference equal to $4a^2$.

$$(a^2 + 1)^2 - (a^2 - 1)^2 = a^4 + 2a^2 + 1 - (a^4 - 2a^2 + 1)$$
$$= 4a^2$$

Now, if we divide by 4, then the difference between $\frac{1}{4}(a^2 + 1)^2$ and $\frac{1}{4}(a^2 - 1)^2$ is equal to a^2 :

$$\frac{1}{4}(a^2 + 1)^2 - \frac{1}{4}(a^2 - 1)^2 = a^2$$

Using this bit of information, we assign each of these to b^2 and c^2 such that:

$$c^2 = \frac{1}{4}(a^2 + 1)^2 \quad \text{and} \quad b^2 = \frac{1}{4}(a^2 - 1)^2$$

Which gives us: $\qquad c^2 - b^2 = a^2$

Now, if we take the square root of each of the terms above, we get:

$$c = \frac{1}{2}(a^2 + 1) \quad \text{and} \quad b = \frac{1}{2}(a^2 - 1)$$

We now have a method where we can select the value for a, and then use it to generate the b and c values of our Pythagorean triple. This method has the characteristic that the b and c values will always have a difference of one; however, we must keep in mind that since we are multiplying $(a^2 + 1)$ and $(a^2 - 1)$ by $\frac{1}{2}$ that the a value must be an odd number in order for b and c to be whole numbers.

It is also interesting to note that this method of finding Pythagorean triples is attributed to Pythagoras himself, and is most likely the method that he used to find the triples that now bare his name. Now, let's see what a few values of a will give us:

a	$b = \frac{1}{2}(a^2 - 1)$	$c = \frac{1}{2}(a^2 + 1)$
3	4	5
5	12	13
7	24	25
9	40	41
11	60	61
13	84	85
15	112	113

An interesting observation about this eighth method brings us full circle in our discussion of Pythagorean Triples. At the beginning of this chapter we pointed out that Pythagorean Triples can be created from the sum of the reciprocals of two consecutive odd (or even) numbers. Then, for the second method we let x and x+2 represent our consecutive numbers. The reciprocal of each would be represented as:

$$\frac{1}{x} \quad \text{and} \quad \frac{1}{x + 2}$$

However, another approach we could have taken would have let $x - 1$ and $x + 1$ represent our two consecutive numbers. The reciprocal of these would then be represented as:

190

$$\frac{1}{x-1} \quad \text{and} \quad \frac{1}{x+1}$$

Then, if we find a common denominator, and add them together, we get:

$$\frac{2x}{x^2-1}$$

And, as we discussed at the beginning of this chapter, the numerator and the denominator of this fraction make up the two legs of a right triangle. To find the hypotenuse, we take each leg and square it, and then add them together, and then take the square root.

$$4x^2 \qquad + \qquad x^4 - 2x^2 + 1$$
(numerator squared)   (denominator squared)

Combining terms gives us:

$$x^4 + 2x^2 + 1$$

Which factors to:

$$(x^2 + 1)^2$$

Meaning that the hypotenuse is:

$$x^2 + 1$$

Again, we have a formula, in terms of x for each of the legs and the hypotenuse. The first leg is equal to $2x$; the second leg is equal to $x^2 - 1$; and the hypotenuse is equal to $x^2 + 1$. Now, if we divide each of these terms by 2, and set them to a, b, and c we have:

$$
\begin{array}{rcl}
a & = & x \\
b & = & \tfrac{1}{2}(x^2 - 1) \\
c & = & \tfrac{1}{2}(x^2 + 1)
\end{array}
$$

Which is exactly what we derived at the beginning of this section as our eighth method of finding Pythagorean Triples.

Within this chapter we have now seen eight methods of creating Pythagorean triples, as well as several patterns and relationships within many of these methods as well as interesting relationships between the numbers themselves. And there are still many other formulas and relationships that can generate various Pythagorean triples and each of these have patterns and properties of their own. However, before we close this chapter, let's look at an interesting method of generating a series of squares using Pythagorean triples.

A Ninth Method, Using Fibonacci Numbers to Find Pythagorean Triples

We noted in the previous section that that last method brought us full circle and tied back in with the first method that was introduced. The method in this section goes even further, and ties all the previous methods together.

First, let's review what we learned about Fibonacci numbers in a previous chapter. Fibonacci numbers are a sequence of numbers where each succeeding number is created from the sum of the previous two numbers. The first two Fibonacci numbers are both 1's. The third Fibonacci number is equal to the sum of the first two numbers, and is equal to 2. The fourth Fibonacci number is equal to the sum of the previous two numbers, and is equal to $1 + 2$, or 3; and so on. Here are the first 15 numbers of the Fibonacci sequence:

$$1, \ 1, \ 2, \ 3, \ 5, \ 8, \ 13, \ 21, \ 34, \ 55, \ 89, \ 144, \ 233, \ 377, \ 610, \ ...$$

When using these numbers in formulas, it is often easier to represent these numbers as F_1, F_2, etc.; where F_1 represents the first Fibonacci number, F_2 represents the second Fibonacci number, and so on. Using this notation, the nth Fibonacci number would be F_n. With this introduction, the following formula uses Fibonacci numbers to generate Pythagorean triples:

$$[\ (F_n)(F_{n+3}), \ 2(F_{n+1})(F_{n+2}), \ (F_{n+1})^2 \ + \ (F_{n+2})^2 \ ]$$

Now, let's use this formula and look at some examples:

If F_n is equal to F_1, then the formula gives us: $[\ (1)(3), \ 2(1)(2), \ 1^2 + 2^2 \ ]$
which is equal to the Pythagorean triple: $[\ 3, \ 4, \ 5 \ ]$

If F_n is equal to F_2, then the formula gives us: $[\ (1)(5), \ 2(2)(3), \ 2^2 + 3^2 \ ]$
which is equal to the Pythagorean triple: $[\ 5, \ 12, \ 13 \ ]$

And

If F_n is equal to F_3, then the formula gives us: $[\ (2)(8), \ 2(3)(5), \ 3^2 + 5^2 \ ]$
which is equal to the Pythagorean triple: $[\ 16, \ 30, \ 34 \ ]$

Even though this method is defined with Fibonacci numbers, it actually works with any sequence of numbers that are generated in the same way as Fibonacci numbers. For example, Lucas numbers start with the numbers 3, and 4 as L_1 and L_2. All subsequent numbers in the sequence are then equal to the sum of the previous two numbers. Here are the first ten Lucas numbers:

$$3, \ 4, \ 7, \ 11, \ 18, \ 29, \ 47, \ 76, \ 123, \ 199, \ ...$$

Now, if we modify the Fibonacci formula to show Lucas numbers, we get:

$$[\ (L_n)(L_{n+3}), \ 2(L_{n+1})(L_{n+2}), \ (L_{n+1})^2 \ + \ (L_{n+2})^2 \ ]$$

And here are a few examples using Lucas numbers to generate Pythagorean triples:

If L_n is equal to L_1, then the formula gives us: $[\ (3)(11), \ 2(4)(7), \ 4^2 + 7^2 \ ]$
which is equal to the Pythagorean triple: $[\ 33, \ 56, \ 65 \ ]$

If L_n is equal to L_2, then the formula gives us: $[\ (4)(18), \ 2(7)(11), \ 7^2 + 11^2 \ ]$
which is equal to the Pythagorean triple: $[\ 72, \ 154, \ 170 \ ]$

Notice that the formula uses any four consecutive Fibonacci (or Lucas) numbers. And since we can actually use any set of four numbers that are generated in the same way that Fibonacci numbers are generated, we can define these four numbers in terms of a and b. Such that a is the first number, b is the second number. The third number would be equal to $a + b$, and the fourth number would be $a + 2b$ (where both the third and the fourth numbers are equal to the sum of the previous two numbers). Here are the four numbers of the sequence:

$$a, \ b, \ a + b, \ a + 2b$$

192

Plugging these numbers into the formula gives us:

$$[(F_n)(F_{n+3}), \; 2(F_{n+1})(F_{n+2}), \; (F_{n+1})^2 + (F_{n+2})^2]$$
$$[(a)(a+2b), \; 2(b)(a+b), \; b^2 + (a+b)^2]$$

Which simplifies to:

$$[a^2 + 2ab, \; 2ab + 2b^2, \; a^2 + 2ab + 2b^2]$$

We can plug any two numbers in for a and b, and we will get a Pythagorean triple. Now, this is where it gets very interesting. If we take our Fibonacci relationship above (which we now have defined in terms of a and b), and set a equal to 1, and b equal to x, (and rearrange the order of the individual terms) we get:

$$[a^2 + 2ab, \; 2ab + 2b^2, \; a^2 + 2ab + 2b^2]$$
$$[2x + 1, \; 2x^2 + 2x, \; 2x^2 + 2x + 1]$$

This is the same relationship for generating Pythagorean triples as the one that we defined in method 6.

We've also already seen how methods 1 and 2 are related to each other. Now, if we take our Fibonacci relationship above, and set a equal to x, and b equal to 1, we get:

$$[a^2 + 2ab, \; 2ab + 2b^2, \; a^2 + 2ab + 2b^2]$$
$$[x^2 + 2x, \; 2x + 2, \; x^2 + 2x + 2]$$

This is the relationship that we defined in method 2. Then in method 8 we also showed that it is related to method 2. And within the method 8 section, we also showed (among other things), that Pythagorean triples can be generated from this relationship:

$$[2x, \; x^2 - 1, \; x^2 + 1]$$

In method 3 (which we also showed was related to methods 4 and 5), we used the following Pythagorean triple relationship:

$$[2mn, \; m^2 - n^2, \; m^2 + n^2]$$

Using that relationship, if we let m = x, and n = 1, then we get the same Pythagorean triple relationship that we found in method 8.

Thus, the Fibonacci method is directly related to methods 1, 2, 6, and 8. And method 8 is related to methods 3, 4, and 5. Now, it only remains to show how method 7 is related to the Fibonacci method. Note that in method 7, we saw that:

$$\begin{aligned} 1^{st} \text{ leg} &= x + y \\ 2^{nd} \text{ leg} &= x + z \\ \text{hypotenuse} &= x + y + z \end{aligned}$$

And now if we simply say that $x = 2ab$, $y = a^2$; and $z = 2b^2$, and make these substitutions in the relationship above, we get:

$$\begin{aligned} 1^{st} \text{ leg} &= a^2 + 2ab \\ 2^{nd} \text{ leg} &= 2ab + 2b^2 \\ \text{hypotenuse} &= a^2 + 2ab + 2b^2 \end{aligned}$$

Which is the Fibonacci relationship for generating Pythagorean triples.

A Multitude of Methods that Find Pythagorean Triples

Now that we have a general method of finding Pythagorean triples that we derived from the Fibonacci numbers; and now that we've seen how several other methods relate to each other, we are now in a position where we can derive a few methods of our own. All we need to do is start with our a and b relationship, assign some number to a, and then we have a new relationship in terms of b (or we could assign some number to b, which would then give us a relationship in terms of a). Here is our a and b Fibonacci relationship that we derived in the previous section:

$$[\ a^2 + 2ab,\ 2ab + 2b^2,\ a^2 + 2ab + 2b^2\ ]$$

Now, we let a = 4 within this relationship, for example, and then our a and b relationship would become:

$$[\ 16 + 8b,\ 8b + 2b^2,\ 16 + 8b + 2b^2\ ]$$

And then using various values for b, we could generate Pythagorean triples, such as:

when	b = 1	we get	[24, 10, 26] or [5, 12, 13]
	b = 2		[32, 24, 40] or [3, 4, 5]
	b = 3		[40, 42, 58] or [20, 21, 29]
		..., etc.	

Or if we let b = 5 within the original Fibonacci relationship, we get a different relationship that also generates Pythagorean triples:

$$[\ a^2 + 10a,\ 10a + 50,\ a^2 + 10a + 50\ ]$$

And by substituting numbers in for a, we then get these corresponding Pythagorean triples:

when	a = 1	we get	[11, 60, 61]
	a = 2		[24, 70, 74]
	a = 3		[39, 80, 89]
		..., etc.	

And this is just the tip of the iceberg (so to speak). There are still many other formulas and relationships that will generate Pythagorean triples.

Generating a Series of Squares from Pythagorean Triples

It is possible to take several selected Pythagorean triples and use them to create a series of squares that when summed, are equal to another square. For example, we'll begin with the following two Pythagorean triples:

$$9^2 + 12^2 = 15^2$$
$$8^2 + 15^2 = 17^2$$

Note that the first relation has 15 as the hypotenuse, and the second has 15 as a leg in the triple. We take the second relation and write it in terms of 15 so that we now have:

$$15^2 = 17^2 - 8^2$$

And we substitute this into the first equation:

$$9^2 + 12^2 = 17^2 - 8^2$$

And rearranging terms (so that they are all positive) gives us:

$$8^2 + 9^2 + 12^2 = 17^2$$

Which is the sum of three squares equal to a fourth square. We can now go another step further by taking the following expression and rearranging its terms. Notice that the 17^2 is to the right of the equal sign in the expression above; and below, the 17^2 is one of the legs of the right triangle:

$$17^2 + 144^2 = 145^2$$
$$17^2 = 145^2 - 144^2$$

And replacing it in our previous series to get an even longer series:

$$8^2 + 9^2 + 12^2 = 145^2 - 144^2$$

Which, after rearranging terms, then becomes:

$$8^2 + 9^2 + 12^2 + 144^2 = 145^2$$

And, doing this one more time, We note that the 145^2 is to the right of the equal sign in the expression above; and below, the 145^2 is one of the legs of the right triangle:

$$145^2 + 408^2 = 433^2$$
$$145^2 = 433^2 - 408^2$$

And now we'll place this in our previous expression to get:

$$8^2 + 9^2 + 12^2 + 144^2 = 433^2 - 408^2$$

Which we can now rearrange to become:

$$8^2 + 9^2 + 12^2 + 144^2 + 408^2 = 433^2$$

We now have the sum of five squares equal to a sixth square. As can be seen from this example, the possibilities can become simply amazing. Of course, there is even more that we can do with the sums of squares; however, we will save that for the next chapter.

Chapter 14
Sums of Squares and Higher Powers

Single Digit Sums of Squares

In this chapter we'll begin by looking at a very interesting relationship between sums of squares that are set equal to other sums of squares. Let's start with the three numbers 4, 5 and 6. Squaring each of these numbers and adding them together gives us a sum equal to 77. It just so happens that when the numbers 2, 3 and 8 are squared and added together they also equal 77. We could say that we have a sum of squares relationship where:

$$4^2 + 5^2 + 6^2 = 2^2 + 3^2 + 8^2$$

Now we're going to use this relationship to build another "sum-of-squares" relationship. We'll pair up a number on the left with a number on the right to create three new numbers. It doesn't matter which number on the left is combined with which number on the right, so for this example, we'll create the numbers 48, 53 and 62. We'll square each of these numbers and place them on the left side of the equality. For the right side of the equality, we'll reverse each of the three numbers and square them. (The reverse of 48 is 84, the reverse of 53 is 35 and the reverse of 62 is 26). We now have this sum of squares relationship:

$$48^2 + 53^2 + 62^2 = 26^2 + 35^2 + 84^2$$

In this case, each side of the equality is equal to 8957.

Since it didn't matter which numbers on the left were paired with which numbers on the right, there are actually five other relationships that we could have created from our original relationship. They are:

$$48^2 + 52^2 + 63^2 = 36^2 + 25^2 + 84^2$$
$$43^2 + 58^2 + 62^2 = 26^2 + 85^2 + 34^2$$
$$43^2 + 52^2 + 68^2 = 86^2 + 25^2 + 34^2$$
$$42^2 + 58^2 + 63^2 = 36^2 + 85^2 + 24^2$$
$$42^2 + 53^2 + 68^2 = 86^2 + 35^2 + 24^2$$

Keep in mind that the numbers on the right are the reverse of their corresponding numbers on the left; and in each case we have a valid relationship where the left side of the equality is equal to the right side.

So, is this some fluke of nature? Not so my fine mathematical friend. This method of creating a sum of squares from an existing sum of squares will work for any valid relationship. Let's look at another example. This time we'll start with a relation that has four numbers squared and added together, and set equal to four other numbers that are squared and added together:

$$8^2 + 5^2 + 3^2 + 2^2 = 7^2 + 6^2 + 4^2 + 1^2$$

Matching numbers on the left with numbers on the right gives this relation:

$$87^2 + 56^2 + 34^2 + 21^2 = 78^2 + 65^2 + 43^2 + 12^2$$

And since we can match any number on the left with any number on the right, we also have these possibilities:

$$86^2 + 54^2 + 31^2 + 27^2 = 68^2 + 45^2 + 13^2 + 72^2$$
$$84^2 + 51^2 + 37^2 + 26^2 = 48^2 + 15^2 + 73^2 + 62^2$$
$$81^2 + 57^2 + 36^2 + 24^2 = 18^2 + 75^2 + 63^2 + 42^2$$

And there are still 20 more possibilities, making a total of 24 combinations altogether.

And if that's not enough, we can also use zeroes in the original relation. Therefore, if one side of the relationship has one more number than the other, we can simply add a 0^2 to the side that is short a number. This makes it possible to use the 3, 4, 5 Pythagorean triple.

$$3^2 + 4^2 = 5^2 + 0^2$$

This Pythagorean triple will generate these equalities:

$$35^2 + 40^2 = 53^2 + 04^2$$
$$30^2 + 45^2 = 03^2 + 54^2$$

The possibilities are amazing! And it doesn't matter if we have two numbers or twenty numbers (or more) on each side of the equal sign. As long as the original expression is true, we can use it to generate other expressions that are also valid.

Two Digit Sums of Squares

And it doesn't stop there, we can extend this idea further. Up to this point we have only used single digit numbers, but we can also do this with two-digit numbers. We treat each two-digit number as a single entity, and then we pair a left side entity with a right side entity. The sum of each of these terms squared is equal to the sum of the left-right pair reversed and squared. Let's look at an example:

$$12^2 + 56^2 + 64^2 = 24^2 + 32^2 + 76^2$$

Now we take a number on the left and pair it with a number on the right. Matching all of the numbers in this way creates the terms for the left side of our relationship. Then to create the numbers on the right, we reverse each of the pairs that were on the left. From the example above, we can create the following relationships:

$$1224^2 + 5632^2 + 6476^2 = 2412^2 + 3256^2 + 7664^2$$
$$1232^2 + 5676^2 + 6424^2 = 3212^2 + 7656^2 + 2464^2$$
$$1276^2 + 5624^2 + 6432^2 = 7612^2 + 2456^2 + 3264^2$$
$$\dots, \text{etc.}$$

Knowing this, we can take any Pythagorean triple and the number zero and create a valid pair of numbers. However, we must keep in mind that if one of the numbers is a two-digit number, then all of the numbers must be represented as two digit numbers. For example:

$$5^2 + 12^2 = 13^2 + 0^2$$

Will actually become:

$$05^2 + 12^2 = 13^2 + 00^2$$

Which will generate the following relationships:

$$0513^2 + 1200^2 = 1305^2 + 0012^2$$
$$0500^2 + 1213^2 = 1312^2 + 0005^2$$

Palindromic Sums of Squares

A palindrome is a word (or in our case, a number) that reads the same backwards as it does forwards. By applying the Sum of Squares relationship a second time on the same set of numbers, we can create sums of squares where all the numbers in that sum are palindromic numbers. Let's return to an earlier sum where we used $3^2 + 4^2 = 5^2 + 0^2$ to create the following relationships:

$$35^2 + 40^2 = 53^2 + 04^2 \qquad \text{and} \qquad 30^2 + 45^2 = 03^2 + 54^2$$

We can now take either of these results and perform the same pairing operation, and create a sum of squares where all the numbers on both sides of the equality are palindromes. Let's take the equation on the left. By pairing the 35 and the 53 for one number, and the 40 and the 04 for the second number, we get the following relationship:

$$3553^2 + 4004^2 = 5335^2 + 0440^2$$

In a similar manner, we could have used the equation on the right to give us:

$$3003^2 + 4554^2 = 5445^2 + 0330^2$$

It is very easy to take any other set of sum of squares, and create sums of squares that are entirely composed of numbers that are palindromes.

A Simple Proof

At first glance, this relationship seems to be very amazing (almost magic), and it definitely is something you can use to impress your friends, but how do you know if it will always be true? Even though we looked at several variations of this formula in this chapter, we will content ourselves with just proving the basic relationship. Other variations to this proof would be extensions of this example.

We'll start with: $\qquad\qquad a^2 + b^2 = c^2 + d^2$

Where a, b, c and d are all single digit numbers. Given that this statement is true, we want to show that the following is also always true:

$$(a*10 + c)^2 \ + \ (b*10 + d)^2 \ = \ (c*10 + a)^2 \ + \ (d*10 + b)^2$$

Expanding the squares gives us:

$$100a^2 + 20ac + c^2 + 100b^2 + 20bd + d^2 = 100c^2 + 20ac + a^2 + 100d^2 + 20bd + b^2$$

We combine similar terms, and the expression reduces to:

$$99a^2 \ + \ 99b^2 \ = \ 99c^2 \ + \ 99d^2$$

Finally, we divide the expression by 99, and it reduces to our original equation.

$$a^2 \ + \ b^2 \ = \ c^2 \ + \ d^2$$

As we mentioned above, similar proofs can be devised for multi-digit numbers and the other examples we've already seen in this chapter.

How Far Can We Go?

Using the methods we just devised, we can come up with some pretty big numbers in a short amount of time. For example, if we start with a simple expression like the following:

$$6^2 \ + \ 7^2 \ = \ 2^2 \ + \ 9^2$$

The next step will give us:

$$62^2 \ + \ 79^2 \ = \ 26^2 \ + \ 97^2$$

Applying the method again, we get a palindromic sum of squares:

$$6226^2 \ + \ 7997^2 \ = \ 2662^2 \ + \ 9779^2$$

And applying it again, we get:

$$62269779^2 \ + \ 79972662^2 \ = \ 26627997^2 \ + \ 97796226^2$$

And one more time gives us this palindromic sum of squares:

$$6226977997796226^2 \ + \ 7997266226627997^2 \ = \ 2662799779972662^2 \ + \ 9779622662269779^2$$

The numbers double in size with each step, and with every other step we have the potential to generate palindromic numbers. How far could we go? It all depends on how much time, patience, and paper we have.

Multigrades

A multigrade is a sum-of-squares relationship that isn't limited to just squares. We could say that it is the sum of a series of numbers raised to a power that is also equal to the sum of another series of numbers raised to the same power; and in addition to this, the relation is true for more than one power. Let's look at an example of a multigrade:

$$1^n \ + \ 4^n \ + \ 5^n \ + \ 5^n \ + \ 6^n \ + \ 9^n \ = \ 2^n \ + \ 3^n \ + \ 3^n \ + \ 7^n \ + \ 7^n \ + \ 8^n$$

This expression works for n = 1, 2 and 3. In other words, each of the following expressions is also true:

$$1^1 + 4^1 + 5^1 + 5^1 + 6^1 + 9^1 = 2^1 + 3^1 + 3^1 + 7^1 + 7^1 + 8^1 \quad (= \quad 30)$$
$$1^2 + 4^2 + 5^2 + 5^2 + 6^2 + 9^2 = 2^2 + 3^2 + 3^2 + 7^2 + 7^2 + 8^2 \quad (= \quad 184)$$
$$1^3 + 4^3 + 5^3 + 5^3 + 6^3 + 9^3 = 2^3 + 3^3 + 3^3 + 7^3 + 7^3 + 8^3 \quad (= 1260)$$

A shorthand method of writing the same thing is:

$$1, 4, 5, 5, 6, 9 =^3= 2, 3, 3, 7, 7, 8$$

Multigrades that work through the 5th power are called fifth order multigrades, or pentagrades. The following three pentagrades share an interesting relationship with each other: Adding the corresponding terms together from the first two pentagrades, gives us the third pentagrade.

$$0, \; 5, \; 6, 16, 17, 22 =^5= 1, 2, 10, 12, 20, 21$$
$$1, 11, 13, 33, 35, 45 =^5= 3, 5, 21, 25, 41, 45$$
$$1, 16, 19, 49, 52, 67 =^5= 4, 7, 31, 37, 61, 64$$

The following is a general expression to create an unlimited number of pentagrades. This expression will work with a, b and c equal to any number.

$$a, a+4b+c, a+b+2c, a+9b+4c, a+6b+5c, a+10b+6c =^5=$$
$$a+b, a+c, a+6b+2c, a+4b+4c, a+10b+5c, a+9b+6c$$

The values a, b and c can even represent the same number. If we let a = 1, b = 1 and c = 1 we get the following pentagrade:

$$1, 6, 4, 14, 12, 17 =^5= 2, 2, 9, 9, 16, 16$$

And if we let a = 0, b = 1 and c = 2 we get:

$$0, 6, 5, 17, 16, 22 =^5= 1, 2, 10, 12, 20, 21$$

Building Multigrades

So, how can we find our own multigrades? There is a method that is actually very simple. First, start with a true expression. We'll start with:

$$1 + 9 = 4 + 6$$

You'll notice that this is not a multigrade, but we will use it to build a multigrade. We'll now take a constant, like 2, and add it to each term in our expression to obtain a second expression:

$$3 + 11 = 6 + 8$$

Finally, we take the right side of our second expression and add it to the left side of our first expression; and we take the left side of our second expression and add it to the right side of the first. This gives us the following which is a second order multigrade:

$$1 + 6 + 8 + 9 =^2= 3 + 4 + 6 + 11$$

200

In other words, the following is true:

$$1^1 + 6^1 + 8^1 + 9^1 \ = \ 3^1 + 4^1 + 6^1 + 11^1 \quad (\text{both sides} = \ 24)$$
$$1^2 + 6^2 + 8^2 + 9^2 \ = \ 3^2 + 4^2 + 6^2 + 11^2 \quad (\text{both sides} = \ 182)$$

The constant we used to create our second expression could have been any number. Therefore, a general form of our first two expressions would look like this:

$$1 + 9 \ = \ 4 + 6$$
$$(1 - k) + (9 + k) \ = \ (4 + k) + (6 + k)$$

And combining these two expressions as we mentioned above gives us the following general expression for a second order multigrade:

$$1 + (4 + k) + (6 + k) + 9 \ =^2= \ (1 + k) + 4 + 6 + (9 + k)$$

By letting $k = 2$, we have the multigrade shown above. If $k = 3$, 4, and 5, we get the following multigrades:

$k = 3$:	$1 + 7 + 9 + 9 \ =^2= \ 4 + 4 + 6 + 12$
$k = 4$:	$1 + 8 + 9 + 10 \ =^2= \ 4 + 5 + 6 + 13$
$k = 5$:	$1 + 9 + 9 + 11 \ =^2= \ 4 + 6 + 6 + 14$

One requirement for this method is that the original expression must have the same number of values on both sides of the equality. If they are not equal, zeroes can be used to make up the difference. Then simply enter values for the k's to create the multigrade.

Building Multigrades from Multigrades

Once we find a multigrade, there are two ways that we can create other multi-grades from our existing one. In the first case, we can use the method above to build a higher order multigrade. For example, let's start with a basic multigrade that works through the second power:

$$2, 3, 7 \ =^2= \ 1, 5, 6$$

In order to create another multigrade from this one, we take some number k, and add it to each term in the relation to create a second relation. Now, we combine the first and second relations so that the left side has the original left-side numbers 2, 3 and 7 as well as the numbers from the right side added to k. On the right side we also place the original right-side numbers, which are 1, 5 and 6 and also the three left-side numbers added to k. With this, we now have a formula that will create an unlimited supply of third order multigrades:

$$2, 3, 7, (1+k), (5+k), (6+k) \ =^3= \ 1, 5, 6, (2+k), (3+k), (7+k)$$

Where we started with a second order multigrade, we now have a formula for a third order multigrade. The value of k now can be equal to any integer, and by letting k equal 1, 2 and 3, we get these third order multigrades:

$k = 1$	$2, 3, 7, 2, 6, 7 \ =^3= \ 1, 5, 6, 3, 4, \ 8$
$k = 2$	$2, 3, 7, 3, 7, 8 \ =^3= \ 1, 5, 6, 4, 5, \ 9$
$k = 3$	$2, 3, 7, 4, 8, 9 \ =^3= \ 1, 5, 6, 5, 6, 10$

In the example above we took a second order multigrade, and applied our method of building multigrades to create any number of third order multigrades. We can now take any of these third order multigrades, apply our method once again, and create an infinite number of fourth order multigrades. And we can continue in the same way to create fifth order and higher order multigrades. The possibilities are virtually limitless.

The second method of creating a multigrade from a multigrade is to simply add a constant to all the terms of the multigrade. This method won't give us a higher order multigrade, but it will give us another unique multigrade. For example, here's our initial multigrade from the previous section:

$$2, 3, 7 =^2= 1, 5, 6$$

Adding two to each term gives us this multigrade:

$$4, 5, 9 =^2= 3, 7, 8$$

Again, the possibilities are limitless (even though in this case the order of the multigrade doesn't increase).

An Interesting Multigrade

Here is an interesting multigrade that has some very unique properties:

$$123789, \ 561945, \ 642864 =^2= 242868, \ 323787, \ 761943$$

If we remove the first digit from each term in this series, the expression is still a multigrade. Then, if we remove the first two digits, or the first three, or all but the last digit, the expression is still a valid multigrade.

$$
\begin{array}{rcrcrclcrcrcr}
123789 &+& 561945 &+& 642864 &=& 242868 &+& 323787 &+& 761943 \\
23789 &+& 61945 &+& 42864 &=& 42868 &+& 23787 &+& 61943 \\
3789 &+& 1945 &+& 2864 &=& 2868 &+& 3787 &+& 1943 \\
789 &+& 945 &+& 864 &=& 868 &+& 787 &+& 943 \\
89 &+& 45 &+& 64 &=& 68 &+& 87 &+& 43 \\
9 &+& 5 &+& 4 &=& 8 &+& 7 &+& 3
\end{array}
$$

And:

$$
\begin{array}{rcrcrclcrcrcr}
123789^2 &+& 561945^2 &+& 642864^2 &=& 242868^2 &+& 323787^2 &+& 761943^2 \\
23789^2 &+& 61945^2 &+& 42864^2 &=& 42868^2 &+& 23787^2 &+& 61943^2 \\
3789^2 &+& 1945^2 &+& 2864^2 &=& 2868^2 &+& 3787^2 &+& 1943^2 \\
789^2 &+& 945^2 &+& 864^2 &=& 868^2 &+& 787^2 &+& 943^2 \\
89^2 &+& 45^2 &+& 64^2 &=& 68^2 &+& 87^2 &+& 43^2 \\
9^2 &+& 5^2 &+& 4^2 &=& 8^2 &+& 7^2 &+& 3^2
\end{array}
$$

But it doesn't stop there. If we start on the other side of these numbers, and remove the last digit, or the last two digits and so on we again have a valid multigrade for each instance.

123789	$+\,561945$	$+\,642864$	$=$	242868	$+\,323787$	$+\,761943$
12378	$+\,56194$	$+\,64286$	$=$	24286	$+\,32378$	$+\,76194$
1237	$+\,5619$	$+\,6428$	$=$	2428	$+\,3237$	$+\,7619$
123	$+\,561$	$+\,642$	$=$	242	$+\,323$	$+\,761$
12	$+\,56$	$+\,64$	$=$	24	$+\,32$	$+\,76$
1	$+\,5$	$+\,6$	$=$	2	$+\,3$	$+\,7$

And:

123789^2	$+\,561945^2$	$+\,642864^2$	$=$	242868^2	$+\,323787^2$	$+\,761943^2$
12378^2	$+\,56194^2$	$+\,64286^2$	$=$	24286^2	$+\,32378^2$	$+\,76194^2$
1237^2	$+\,5619^2$	$+\,6428^2$	$=$	2428^2	$+\,3237^2$	$+\,7619^2$
123^2	$+\,561^2$	$+\,642^2$	$=$	242^2	$+\,323^2$	$+\,761^2$
12^2	$+\,56^2$	$+\,64^2$	$=$	24^2	$+\,32^2$	$+\,76^2$
1^2	$+\,5^2$	$+\,6^2$	$=$	2^2	$+\,3^2$	$+\,7^2$

Unexpected Multigrades

We've now learned a few tricks about building multigrades, and we've seen a few interesting and unusual multigrades. But multigrades can still turn up in unusual and unexpected places. For example, multigrades can be found in Magic Squares. As you may recall, a magic square is a square of numbers where the sums of the numbers in the rows, columns, and diagonals all add up to the same number. Here is a third order (3 x 3) magic square:

```
8  1  6
3  5  7
4  9  2
```

Notice that the sum of the numbers within each row, column and diagonal add up to 15. Within this magic square we also have two sets of second order multigrades. One multigrade consists of the right column set equal to the left column:

$$3, 4, 8 \;=^2= \; 2, 6, 7$$

And the other consists of the top row set equal to the bottom row:

$$1, 6, 8 \;=^2= \; 2, 4, 9$$

Now, let's look at a fourth order (4 x 4) magic square. In the following magic square, each row, column and diagonal adds up to 34:

```
 1  15  14   4
12   6   7   9
 8  10  11   5
13   3   2  16
```

Within this magic square we can find four sets of second order multigrades. We can create two sets from the columns, and two sets from the rows. In the case of the columns, one multigrade is made from the two outside columns set equal to each other, and the second is made from the two inside columns:

$$1, 8, 12, 13 \;=^2= \; 4, 5, 9, 16$$
$$3, 6, 10, 15 \;=^2= \; 2, 7, 11, 14$$

203

To create the multigrades from the rows, we set the top and bottom rows equal to each other for the first multigrade, and set the two inside rows equal to each other for the second multigrade:

$$1, 4, 14, 15 \quad =^2= \quad 2, 3, 13, 16$$
$$6, 7, 9, 12 \quad =^2= \quad 5, 8, 10, 11$$

An interesting aspect of these four multigrades is that we are using the numbers one through 16 to create the first pair of multigrades, and then to create the second pair of multigrades (which are unique from the first pair), we again use the same numbers, one through 16. Not all magic squares have this kind of symmetry where they create multigrades in this manner; however, as we will soon see, magic squares do appear to order the numbers so that they are conducive to creating multigrades.

Reverse Engineering the Multigrade

Earlier, we looked at a method of building multigrades from the sum of two numbers set equal to the sum of two other numbers. With a little trial and error, we can take the four multigrades from the fourth order magic square (show above), and find the two sums of two numbers that were set equal to each other. For example, here is the first multigrade we'll consider:

$$1, 8, 12, 13 \quad =^2= \quad 4, 5, 9, 16$$

We know that the sum of two numbers on each side of this multigrade must be equal to each other. We also know that if we add a single constant to each of these numbers, we will get the other four numbers. After looking at these numbers for just a little, we find that our four numbers are 1, 13, and 5, 9 (where both pairs add to 14); and if the constant, k, is equal to 3, the other four numbers are 4, 16, and 8, 12. Therefore, working backwards, we started with the multigrade and we created the expression that generated the multigrade. Here is the original expression, and the multigrade generating expression:

$$1 + 13 = 5 + 9$$
$$1 + (5+k) + (9+k) + 13 = 5 + (1+k) + (13+k) + 9$$

and by letting k = 3 we get one of the magic square multigrades:

$$1, 8, 12, 13 \quad =^2= \quad 4, 5, 9, 16$$

In a similar way we can create the other three original expressions and their corresponding multigrade generating expressions from the original magic square multigrade. In each of these cases if we let the constant equal 1, we get the multigrade from the magic square. Here are the other three original expressions, the multigrade generating expressions, and the corresponding magic square multigrade:

Original expression: $\qquad 6 + 10 = 2 + 14$
$$6 + (2+k) + (14+k) + 10 = 2 + (6+k) + (10+k) + 14$$

when k = 1, we get: $\qquad 3, 6, 10, 15 \quad =^2= \quad 2, 7, 11, 14$

Original expression: $\qquad 1 + 15 = 3 + 13$
$$1 + (3+k) + (13+k) + 15 = 3 + (1+k) + (15+k) + 13$$

204

when k = 1, we get: $\qquad$ 1, 4, 14, 15 $=^2=$ 2, 3, 13, 16

Original expression: $\qquad$ 7 + 9 = 5 + 11
$$7 + (5 + k) + (11 + k) + 9 = 5 + (7 + k) + (9 + k) + 11$$

when k = 1, we get: $\qquad$ 6, 7, 9, 12 $=^2=$ 5, 8, 10, 11

More Multigrades from Magic Squares

There is still more we can do with these magic squares. Let's look a little closer at a different 4 x 4 magic square. In the table below, we have our magic square along with two additional columns to the right of the magic square, and two additional rows beneath the magic square (these columns and rows are shaded). The first column to the right shows the sum of each row, and the next column to the right shows the sum of the squares of the numbers within each row. Similarly, the first row beneath the magic square shows the sum of each column, and the row beneath that shows the sum of the squares of the numbers within each column.

4 x 4 Magic Square				Sum of Row	Row Sum of Squares
1	12	14	7	34	390
15	6	4	9	34	358
8	13	11	2	34	358
10	3	5	16	34	390
Sum of Column	34	34	34	34	
Column Sum of Squares	390	358	358	390	

Table 14.1 $\quad$ A 4 x 4 magic square along with the sums of the rows and columns and the sums of the squares of the rows and columns.

We see that the sums of the squares of the top and bottom rows are both equal to 390. We can also see that the sums of the squares of the first and last columns are also both equal to 390. From what we've seen earlier in this chapter, we can generate the following second order multigrades from this magic square:

$\qquad$ 1, 7, 12, 14 $=^2=$ 3, 5, 10, 16 $\qquad$ (from the top and bottom rows)
$\qquad$ 1, 8, 10, 15 $=^2=$ 2, 7, 9, 16 $\qquad$ (from the first and last columns)

And we can go even further with this. We can set the top row equal to the first column; and we can set the bottom row equal to the last column to give us these two multigrades:

$\qquad$ 1, 7, 12, 14 $=^2=$ 1, 8, 10, 15 $\qquad$ (from the top row and first column)
$\qquad$ 3, 5, 10, 16 $=^2=$ 2, 7, 9, 16 $\qquad$ (from the bottom row and last column)

Notice that the first multigrade above shares a 1 on the right and left side, while the second multigrade shares a 16 on the right and left side. This means that we can condense both of these multigrades so that there are only three numbers on right and left sides instead of four:

$$7, 12, 14 \ =^2= \ 8, 10, 15 \qquad \text{(from the top row and first column)}$$
$$3, 5, 10 \ =^2= \ 2, 7, 9 \qquad \text{(from the bottom row and last column)}$$

Similarly we can set the top row equal to the last column and the bottom row equal to the first column to again create two other multigrades that each share a common number, and which can then be further reduced to multigrades with only three numbers on the right and left. Without going through all the steps, here are those resulting multigrades:

$$1, 12, 14 \ =^2= \ 2, 9, 16 \qquad \text{(from the top row and last column)}$$
$$1, 8, 15 \ =^2= \ 3, 5, 16 \qquad \text{(from the bottom row and first column)}$$

And that is only half of the possibilities with this magic square. This 4 x 4 magic square also has two rows (the second and third row) and two columns (the second and third column) whose sum of squares each add up to 358. We can do the same thing by setting these rows and columns equal to each other and thus creating even more second order multigrades.

Things get even more interesting when we look at 5th order magic squares. In the following table, we have a 5th order magic square. This table is similar to the previous table, except that we have also added a column to the right that shows the sum of the cubes for each row, and we've added an additional row at the bottom of the table that shows the sum of the cubes for each column.

5 x 5 Magic Square					Sum of Row	Row Sum of Squares	Row Sum of Cubes
1	24	17	15	8	65	1155	22625
14	7	5	23	16	65	1055	19475
22	20	13	6	4	65	1105	21125
10	3	21	19	12	65	1055	18875
18	11	9	2	25	65	1155	23525
Sum of Column	65	65	65	65	65		
Column Sum of Squares	1105	1155	1005	1155	1105		
Column Sum of Cubes	20225	23525	17225	22625	22025		

Table 14.2   A 5 x 5 magic square along with the sums of the rows and columns, the sums of the squares of the rows and columns, and the sums of the cubes of the rows and columns.

In this table we see that sums of the squares of the first and last rows are both equal to 1155; and the sum of the squares of the second and fourth columns are also equal to 1155. This means that we can pair these rows and columns in various ways to create second order multigrades just as we did in the previous example with the 4th order magic square. We can also do the same thing with the second and fourth rows and the first and last columns whose sums of squares are all equal to 1105.

206

What I would like to do with this magic square is draw your attention to the sums of cubes of the columns and rows. Notice that the second column and the fifth row both have a sum of squares equal to 1155, and a sum of cubes equal to 23525. This means that we can create a 3rd order multigrade from this column and row, which would be:

$$3, 7, 11, 20, 24 \quad =^3= \quad 2, 9, 11, 18, 25 \qquad \text{(from the second column and fifth row)}$$

And since there is an 11 on both sides of this multigrade, we remove it from both sides to get this third order multigrade:

$$3, 7, 20, 24 \quad =^3= \quad 2, 9, 18, 25 \qquad \text{(from the second column and fifth row)}$$

And in a similar way we also notice within the magic square that the sum of cubes of the first row and the fourth column are both equal to 22625. And since their sum of squares are also equal to each other, we can create this 3rd order multigrade from that row and column:

$$2, 6, 15, 19, 23 \quad =^3= \quad 1, 8, 15, 17, 24 \qquad \text{(from the fourth column and first row)}$$

And after removing the number that is common on both sides we have this 3rd order multigrade:

$$2, 6, 19, 23 \quad =^3= \quad 1, 8, 17, 24 \qquad \text{(from the fourth column and first row)}$$

Before we leave this topic, let's briefly look at two more magic squares, a 5th order magic square, and a 7th order magic square.

5 x 5 Magic Square					Sum of Row	Row Sum of Squares	Row Sum of Cubes
1	12	20	23	9	65	1155	22625
8	19	22	5	11	65	1055	19475
24	10	13	16	2	65	1105	21125
15	21	4	7	18	65	1055	18875
17	3	6	14	25	65	1155	23525
Sum of Column							
65	65	65	65	65			
Column Sum of Squares							
1155	1055	1105	1055	1155			
Column Sum of Cubes							
22625	18875	21125	19475	23525			

Table 14.3   A second 5 x 5 magic square along with the sums of the rows and columns, the sums of the squares of the rows and columns, and the sums of the cubes of the rows and columns with five unique 3rd order multigrades.

First, the 5th order magic square (as shown above). This magic square is unique in that each of the five sums of cubes for the rows corresponds to a sum of cubes from the columns. This means that in addition to the many 2nd order multigrades that can be created from the magic square, we can also generate five unique 3rd order multigrades from this magic square. Here are the 3rd order multigrades:

$$1, 9, 12, 20, 23 \ =^3= \ 1, 8, 15, 17, 24 \qquad \text{(1}^{st}\text{ row and 1}^{st}\text{ column)}$$
$$4, 7, 15, 18, 21 \ =^3= \ 3, 10, 12, 19, 21 \qquad \text{(4}^{th}\text{ row and 2}^{nd}\text{ column)}$$
$$2, 10, 13, 16, 24 \ =^3= \ 4, 6, 13, 20, 22 \qquad \text{(3}^{rd}\text{ row and 3}^{rd}\text{ column)}$$
$$5, 8, 11, 19, 22 \ =^3= \ 5, 7, 14, 16, 23 \qquad \text{(2}^{nd}\text{ row and 4}^{th}\text{ column)}$$
$$3, 6, 14, 17, 25 \ =^3= \ 2, 9, 11, 18, 25 \qquad \text{(5}^{th}\text{ row and 5}^{th}\text{ column)}$$

And after removing the common number from each side of these multigrades, we get the following 3rd order multigrades:

$$9, 12, 20, 23 \ =^3= \ 8, 15, 17, 24 \qquad \text{(1}^{st}\text{ row and 1}^{st}\text{ column)}$$
$$4, 7, 15, 18 \ =^3= \ 3, 10, 12, 19 \qquad \text{(4}^{th}\text{ row and 2}^{nd}\text{ column)}$$
$$2, 10, 16, 24 \ =^3= \ 4, 6, 20, 22 \qquad \text{(3}^{rd}\text{ row and 3}^{rd}\text{ column)}$$
$$8, 11, 19, 22 \ =^3= \ 7, 14, 16, 23 \qquad \text{(2}^{nd}\text{ row and 4}^{th}\text{ column)}$$
$$3, 6, 14, 17 \ =^3= \ 2, 9, 11, 18 \qquad \text{(5}^{th}\text{ row and 5}^{th}\text{ column)}$$

And here is the 7th order magic square that I promised. If you look closely at the sums of cubes for each row, and compare them with the sums of cubes for the columns, you will see that there are four numbers that correspond between the two lists of numbers. Since their sums of squares also correspond with each other, we follow the same process used in the preceding example and generate four 3rd order multigrades from this magic square.

7 x 7 Magic Square							Sum of Row	Row Sum of Squares	Row Sum of Cubes
1	27	46	16	42	12	31	175	5971	226723
39	9	35	5	24	43	20	175	5677	204379
28	47	17	36	13	32	2	175	5775	212317
10	29	6	25	44	21	40	175	5579	199675
48	18	37	14	33	3	22	175	5775	216433
30	7	26	45	15	41	11	175	5677	209671
19	38	8	34	4	23	49	175	5971	231427
Sum of Column 175	175	175	175	175	175	175			
Column Sum of Squares 5971	5677	5775	5579	5775	5677	5971			
Column Sum of Cubes 226723	209671	214081	199675	214699	204379	231427			

Table 14.4   A 7 x 7 magic square along with the sums of the rows and columns, the sums of the squares of the rows and columns, and the sums of the cubes of the rows and columns with five unique 3rd order multigrades.

The reader can use this magic square as an exercise to create various 2nd order multigrades as well as the four 3rd order multigrades as previously mentioned.

And as higher order magic squares are inspected in this way (by comparing the sums of squares of the rows and columns, and then also comparing the sums of cubes of the rows and columns), it is possible to see many more 2nd and 3rd order multigrades within these magic squares.

Expanding Series

In an earlier chapter we discussed that a number series is a sum of numbers. An expanding series is a sum of numbers that increases in length as we progress through some type of sequential relationship. Here are two interesting sets of expanding series:

$$1 + 2 = 3$$
$$4 + 5 + 6 = 7 + 8$$
$$9 + 10 + 11 + 12 = 13 + 14 + 15$$
$$16 + 17 + 18 + 19 + 20 = 21 + 22 + 23 + 24$$

... etc.,

$$3^2 + 4^2 = 5^2$$
$$10^2 + 11^2 + 12^2 = 13^2 + 14^2$$
$$21^2 + 22^2 + 23^2 + 24^2 = 25^2 + 26^2 + 27^2$$
$$36^2 + 37^2 + 38^2 + 39^2 + 40^2 = 41^2 + 42^2 + 43^2 + 44^2$$

... etc.,

Besides having a similar appearance, both of these patterns also share other similarities. Both use consecutive numbers on each line, and both add a term to each side of the equality for each successive row. Also, both of these expanding series can also be carried on indefinitely.

The key term in each of these number series is the number located immediately to the left of the equal sign. In the first pattern, the numbers to the left are 2, 6, 12, 20, etc. These numbers satisfy the equation $n(n + 1)$ for $n = 1, 2, 3$, etc. (where n is equal to the row number). In the second pattern, the numbers immediately to the left of the equal sign are 4, 12, 24, 40, etc and they satisfy the equation $2n(n + 1)$ for $n = 1, 2, 3$, etc.

This pattern only works for these two sets of number series. However, if we were to continue the pattern to the next set of number series, the numbers just to the left of the equality would have to satisfy the equation $3n(n + 1)$. Of course, one obvious problem with this series is that if it did work, the first equation would have two numbers cubed equal to a third number cubed, and that would contradict Fermat's last theorem. In spite of this realization, let's indulge ourselves anyway, and look at the next series.

$$5^3 + 6^3 = 7^3 \qquad -2$$
$$16^3 + 17^3 + 18^3 = 19^3 + 20^3 \qquad -18$$
$$33^3 + 34^3 + 35^3 + 36^3 = 37^3 + 38^3 + 39^3 \qquad -72$$
$$56^3 + 57^3 + 58^3 + 59^3 + 60^3 = 61^3 + 62^3 + 63^3 + 64^3 \qquad -200$$

... etc.,

The sum of the numbers on the right side of the equality is larger than the sum on the left. The column of numbers to the far right is the difference between the right and left sides of the series (they are the numbers that need to be subtracted from the right side to maintain the equality of the relationship).

It is interesting to note that the numbers 2, 18, 72, 200, etc are related to each other. They are equal to $2(1^2)$, $2(3^2)$, $2(6^2)$, $2(10^2)$, etc. And as you may recall from an earlier chapter, the numbers 1, 3, 6, 10, etc. are triangular numbers. The number needed on each row to make the relationship true is equal to $2(T_n^2)$, where T_n is the nth triangular number, and where n is the row number.

And as luck would have it, we can continue this pattern at least one more time. Let's look at the next set of expanding series. Again, using our pattern, the number immediately to the left of the equality should be equal to $4n(n + 1)$, and this gives us the following expanding series:

$$7^4 + 8^4 = 9^4 \qquad\qquad\qquad - 64$$
$$22^4 + 23^4 + 24^4 = 25^4 + 26^4 \qquad\qquad - 1728$$
$$45^4 + 46^4 + 47^4 + 48^4 = 49^4 + 50^4 + 51^4 \qquad - 13,824$$
$$76^4 + 77^4 + 78^4 + 79^4 + 80^4 = 81^4 + 82^4 + 83^4 + 84^4 \qquad - 64,000$$
$$\text{... etc.,}$$

Again, the right side of the equality is greater than the left side, and this time, that difference is quite a bit more. However, there is still a relationship between these differences. Notice that the numbers 64, 1728, 13824, 64000, etc. are equal to $64(1^3)$, $64(3^3)$, $64(6^3)$, $64(10^3)$, etc. And once again, we find triangular numbers within this relationship.

Ratios of Sums of Squares
It is worthwhile to note that it is not possible to have two integers such that if they are both squared, that one of those numbers squared is twice the other number squared. In other words, the equality $2a^2 = b^2$ can never be true where a and b are both integers. Because, if it were true, then we could rearrange that relationship, and say that this is also true:

$$\frac{b^2}{a^2} = 2$$

So far that looks pretty harmless, but if this were so, we could take the square root of both sides, and we would have:

$$\frac{b}{a} = \sqrt{2}$$

This would mean that the square root of 2 is a rational number, and could be written as a fraction (which is the ratio of two integers). However, the square root of 2 is not a rational number, so we will not spend any time looking for one number squared that is twice a second number squared. I might also add that it was this type of reasoning that allowed the ancient Greeks to discover that there are numbers that are irrational.

In a similar manner, there are no two numbers such that when squared, the one number squared is three times the second number squared. However, it is possible to have two numbers such that when one number is squared, it is four times the second number squared. One example is:

$$\frac{36}{9} = \frac{6^2}{3^2} = 4$$

Another example are the squares of 5 and 10. Five squared is equal to 25 and ten squared is 100; and 100 is four times 25. In fact, we can take any two numbers where the second number is twice the first number, and that will give us a ratio where their squares are 4 to 1.

Even though we can't have one number squared divided by another number squared equal to 2, we can have the sum of two numbers squared divided by the sum of two other numbers squared equal to 2. Our fraction looks something like this:

$$\frac{a^2 + b^2}{c^2 + d^2} = 2$$

One example is:

$$\frac{2^2 + 4^2}{1^2 + 3^2} = 2$$

The ratio of the sum of squares in the numerator to that in the denominator is equal to 2 to 1. So how common is something like this? There is, in fact, an infinite number of these fractions, and they follow a similar pattern. Let's look at a few of them:

$$\frac{4^2 + 6^2}{1^2 + 5^2} \qquad \frac{5^2 + 7^2}{1^2 + 6^2} \qquad \frac{6^2 + 8^2}{1^2 + 7^2} \qquad \frac{7^2 + 9^2}{1^2 + 8^2} \qquad \frac{8^2 + 10^2}{1^2 + 9^2}$$

All of these fractions can be reduced to 2 over 1. And the pattern is very simple. The two numbers in the numerator have a difference of two. The two numbers in the denominator are made up of the numbers 1, and the number that falls between the two numbers in the numerator.

Of course, we can see why this is so by simply taking the following relationship, and expanding the numerator and the denominator

$$\frac{x^2 + (x + 2)^2}{1^2 + (x + 1)^2}$$

Expanded, gives us:

$$\frac{x^2 + x^2 + 4x + 4}{1 + x^2 + 2x + 1}$$

Or:

$$\frac{2x^2 + 4x + 4}{x^2 + 2x + 2}$$

Which is the same as:

$$\frac{2(x^2 + 2x + 2)}{1(x^2 + 2x + 2)} = \frac{2}{1}$$

After combining terms in the numerator and denominator, it can easily be seen that the top is twice the bottom, and therefore any fraction created in this way will always be equal to 2 over 1.

Here is another fraction made from two consecutive sums of numbers squared. This fraction also can be reduced to the ratio of 2 over 1.

$$\frac{3^2 + 4^2 + 5^2 + 6^2 + 7^2 + 8^2 + 9^2}{1^2 + 2^2 + 3^2 + 4^2 + 5^2 + 6^2 + 7^2} = 2$$

Other Interesting Formulas Using Squares

Here's an interesting relationship that comes in two varieties. Either expression can be used, and though slightly different, they give the same result.

Or

$$(a^2 + b^2)(c^2 + d^2) = (ac + bd)^2 + (ad - bc)^2$$

$$(a^2 + b^2)(c^2 + d^2) = (ac - bd)^2 + (ad + bc)^2$$

The difference between the two formulas is that the right side of the equation contains a minus sign that either can be within the first set of parentheses, or within the second.

On the surface, it is a little difficult to see how the left side of the equation can be equal to the right side; and if you expand the left side, it isn't very apparent that the left side is equal to the right. However, by expanding the right side of either expression, and using the distributive law of multiplication, it is possible to show that the right side is equal to the left. Here are a few examples that use both formulas to demonstrate these equations.

Equation 1, where a = 1, b = 2, c = 3, and d = 4:

$$(1^2 + 2^2)(3^2 + 4^2) = (1*3 + 2*4)^2 + (1*4 - 2*3)^2$$
$$(5)(25) = (11)^2 + (-2)^2$$
$$125 = 125$$

And, where a = 2, b = 7, c = 5, and d = 8:

$$(2^2 + 7^2)(5^2 + 8^2) = (2*5 + 7*8)^2 + (2*8 - 7*5)^2$$
$$(53)(89) = (66)^2 + (-19)^2$$
$$4717 = 4717$$

Equation 2, where a = 1, b = 2, c = 3, and d = 4:

$$(1^2 + 2^2)(3^2 + 4^2) = (1*3 - 2*4)^2 + (1*4 + 2*3)^2$$
$$(5)(25) = (-5)^2 + (10)^2$$
$$125 = 125$$

And, where a = 2, b = 7, c = 5, and d = 8:

$$(2^2 + 7^2)(5^2 + 8^2) = (2*5 - 7*8)^2 + (2*8 + 7*5)^2$$
$$(53)(89) = (-46)^2 + (51)^2$$
$$4717 = 4717$$

212

Chapter 15
Square Root Methods

In an earlier chapter we saw several methods of multiplying numbers together. In the chapter following this one we'll look at several methods of dividing one number into another. As fun as the one was, and as the other will be, this chapter looks at various methods of finding square roots. We'll look at two arithmetic methods, a geometric method, a trigonometric method, a few iterative methods, a logarithmic method, and a method using Napier Bones. Then we'll end this chapter by revisiting some of these methods to see how they can be used to find higher roots.

The Arithmetic Method

This first method is very easy to learn and use; however, it uses a lot of space on a piece of paper. We'll describe it by looking at an example. Say we want to find the square root of 123,904. We begin by grouping the number in pairs, starting with the first two numbers next to the decimal place, and working left. I like to draw a bar between the numbers, but a single space will work just as well.

$$12 \mid 39 \mid 04.$$

Then we start with the left most set of numbers. Because we are pairing from right to left, the left most set of numbers may have one or two digits in that set. In this example, there are two numbers, the digits 12. We now begin subtracting pairs of numbers from this first number. We start by subtracting the numbers 0 and 1. Then we subtract 1 and 2, and then 2 and 3. We continue until we can't subtract any more pairs of numbers.

```
  12|39|04
  - 0
  - 1          Subtract 0 and 1 from 12 to get 11.
  ----
   11
  - 1
  - 2          Subtract 1 and 2 from 11 to get 8.
  ----
    8
  - 2
  - 3          Subtract 2 and 3 from 8 to get 3.
  ----
    3
```

At this point we could subtract another 3, but we can't subtract the next pair of numbers, which would be 3 and 4. So we stop here and bring down the next pair of numbers and put them behind our remainder. The next two numbers from the original number are 39. We place them behind the 3 to get 339.

We note that the last number we subtracted was a 3, so in order to continue, we place a 0 behind the 3 and now begin subtracting the pairs of numbers 30 and 31; then 31 and 32; and then 32 and 33, and so forth from the number 339. Here is the process:

```
12|39|04
- 0
- 1                    Subtract 0 and 1 from 12
 11
- 1
- 2                    Subtract 1 and 2 from 11
  8
- 2
- 3                    Subtract 2 and 3 from 8
339                    Bring down the 39 from the original number
- 30
- 31                   Subtract 30 and 31 from 339 to get 278.
278
- 31
- 32                   Subtract 31 and 32 from 278 to get 215.
215
- 32
- 33                   Subtract 32 and 33 from 215 to get 150.
150
- 33
- 34                   Subtract 33 and 34 from 150 to get 83.
 83
- 34
- 35                   Subtract 34 and 35 from 83 to get 14.
1404                   Bring down the 04 from above.
- 350
- 351                  Subtract 350 and 351 from 1404.
703
- 351
- 352                  Subtract 351 and 352 from 703.
  0
```

We continued subtracting our "thirty" numbers until we got to the point where we were subtracting 34 and 35 from 83. At that point we were left with 14 so we brought down the 04 from our original number and placed it behind the 14 to give us the number 1404.

The last number that we subtracted was 35, so we place a 0 behind the 35 and we begin again by subtracting 350 and 351 from 1404. This gives us a result of 703. The next pair of numbers that we subtract is 351 and 352, and we notice that the result is 0. This means that the last number we subtracted, which was 352, is the square root of 123,904.

It is often very beneficial to look at a second example to help clarify some of the points of the method. In this next example, we'll eliminate a wordy explanation and replace it with just the highlights as we find the square root of 2,024,929:

```
 2|02|49|29
- 0
- 1                    Subtract 0 and 1 from 2
 102                   Bring down the 02 from the original number
- 10
- 11                   Subtract 10 and 11 from 102
  81
- 11
- 12                   Subtract 11 and 12 from 81
  58
- 12
- 13                   Subtract 12 and 13 from 58
  33
- 13
- 14                   Subtract 13 and 14 from 33
 649                   Bring down the 49 from the original number
- 140
- 141                  Subtract 140 and 141 from 649
 368
- 141
- 142                  Subtract 141 and 142 from 368
8529                   Bring down the 29 from above
- 1420
- 1421                 Subtract 1420 and 1421 from 8529
 5688
- 1421
- 1422                 Subtract 1421 and 1422 from 5688
 2845
- 1422
- 1423                 Subtract 1422 and 1423 from 2845
    0
```

Again we end with a zero after our final subtraction. This means that 1423 is the exact square root of 2,024,929. If we didn't get an exact solution, we would simply continue our process by bringing down the first two zeroes after the decimal place and continuing our method just as before.

A Second Arithmetic Method

In this section we'll look at another arithmetic method of finding the square root of a number. We'll use the same two numbers from the previous section as our examples in this section. First, we'll find the square root of 123,904.

We begin by pairing the numbers from the decimal place to the left (just as we did in the previous method), and then placing the number under a square root radical.

$$\sqrt{12|39|04}.$$

Next, we find the largest square that is less than the left-most set of numbers. (Since we are pairing the numbers from the decimal point to the left there may be one or two digits in the left-most set of numbers.) In this example, 12 is the left-most set of numbers and 9 is the largest square that will go into 12. We place the square root of 9 above the 12, and then we subtract the 9 from 12. At the same time we bring down the next pair of digits (which is 39) and place it next to the result of 12 minus 9 (which is 3, giving us 339).

$$
\begin{array}{r}
3 \\
\sqrt{12|39|04.} \\
-9 \\
\hline
339
\end{array}
$$

We have a 3 on the top of the radical, so we double it and put a temporary zero behind it to give us 60. Now we need to figure out how many times 60 will go into 339.

$$
\begin{array}{r}
3 ? \\
\sqrt{12|39|04.} \\
-9 \\
\hline
60 \,)\, 339
\end{array}
$$

It goes in five times, so we take the five and place it on top of the radical, and then we also replace the temporary zero with the five. Next, we take five times 65 (which gives us 325) and subtract that from 339 to get 14. And at the same time we bring down the next pair of digits (which is 04) and place it next to the 14.

$$
\begin{array}{r}
3 5 \\
\sqrt{12|39|04.} \\
-9 \\
\hline
65 \,)\, 339 \\
-325 \\
\hline
1404
\end{array}
$$

Now we repeat the previous step. We have a 35 on top of the radical, so we double it and put a temporary zero behind it to give us 700. Then we figure out how many times 700 will go into 1404.

$$
\begin{array}{r}
3 5 ? \\
\sqrt{12|39|04.} \\
-9 \\
\hline
65 \,)\, 339 \\
-325 \\
\hline
700 \,)\, 1404
\end{array}
$$

Since it will go in twice, we place a 2 on top of the radical and then replace the temporary zero with the two. Finally we take two times 702 (which gives us 1404) and subtract it from 1404 to get zero.

$$
\begin{array}{r}
3 5 2 \\
\sqrt{12|39|04.} \\
-9 \\
\hline
65 \,)\, 339 \\
-325 \\
\hline
702 \,)\, 1404 \\
-1404 \\
\hline
0
\end{array}
$$

216

Therefore, the square root of 123,904 is 352. And since we got a 0 at the bottom, this means that 352 is the exact square root of 123904. If the problem wouldn't have worked out evenly, we would simply bring down the first two zeroes to the right of the decimal and then repeated the previous step. For square roots that go on forever, we can repeat this process indefinitely and obtain whatever precision we desire.

We'll now look at a second example, and this time we'll briefly outline the steps involved with finding a solution. Here is the square root of 2,024,929.

$$
\begin{array}{r}
\underline{1\ \ 4\ \ 2\ \ 3} \\
\sqrt{2|02|49|29.} \\
\underline{-\ 1} \\
24\ )\ 102 \\
\underline{-\ 96} \\
282\ )\ 649 \\
\underline{-\ 564} \\
2843\ )\ 8529 \\
\underline{-\ 8529} \\
0
\end{array}
$$

Step 1: Pair the numbers from the decimal point going left; and then place this number under a radical. Going from left to right, the 2 is by itself, then we have an 02, a 49 and a 29.

Step 2: Find the largest square that is less than the left-most number pair. In this case, 1 is the largest square less than 2. We subtract the 1 from 2, and then place the square root of 1 (which is also 1) on top of the radical.

Step 3: Bring down the next number pair (which is 02), and place it next to the 1 to give us 102.

Step 4: Take the 1 on top of the radical, double it and place a temporary 0 behind it to estimate how many times 20 will go into 102. 20 will go into 102 five times but if we replace the temporary 0 with the five, our new number will not go five times into 102. Instead, we will use a four. We place the four above the 02 number pair in the radical. Then we replace the temporary 0 with a four and then multiply 4 times 24 to give us 96, which we subtract from 102 to give us 6.

Step 5: Repeat steps 3 and 4 for the remaining number pairs.

As we can see in this example, and as we have shown with the previous method, the square root of 2,024,929 is equal to 1423.

I purposely used the same numbers to demonstrate these first two methods. Comparing these methods side-by-side shows the same numbers appearing as the methods are worked. Both of these arithmetic methods are actually related algorithms that do the same thing.

The Geometric Method

The geometric method is very simple and straight-forward; although, it is not practical to use. Say for example, that we want to find the square root of some number that we'll call x. To use this method we begin by drawing a horizontal line that is x units long. On one end of this line (we'll use the left side), we'll place the point P, and then we'll extend the line one more unit past P to the left.

The total length of this line is x + 1 units long. Next, we'll use the total length of the line as a diameter and draw a half circle from one end of the line to the other. Finally, we'll draw a vertical line through P and extend it up until it reaches the half circle. We'll call this vertical line segment k. The length of k is equal to the square root of x.

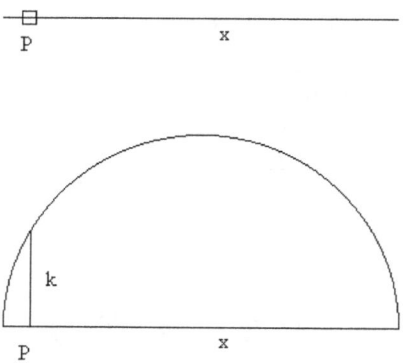

Figure 15.1   The first two steps of setting up the Geometric Method.

This method is very easy to construct. And as we saw, it seems that we barely start making our drawing, when all of a sudden we're done, and we have the answer. This method is also very easy to prove. We begin by creating a right triangle where one leg of the triangle runs from the center of the circle to point P, and the second leg of the triangle is the vertical line that goes from P to the arc (this segment is k). The hypotenuse of that triangle is equal to the radius of the circle and runs from the other end of k back to the center of the circle.

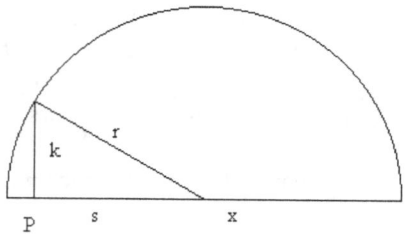

Figure 15.2   Finding the square root using the geometric method.

We keep in mind that we are trying to show that k is equal to the square root of x. The diameter of the circle was constructed so that it is equal to x + 1. Therefore, the radius, r, is half that

218

length, or (x + 1)/2. The length of s is equal to one unit less than r, or [(x + 1)/2 - 1], which simplifies to (x - 1)/2. Using the Pythagorean theorem, we know that

$$k^2 + s^2 = r^2$$

And substituting our values for r and s we have:

$$k^2 + (x - 1)^2/4 = (x + 1)^2/4$$

Multiplying this equation by 4, and expanding the squares give us:

$$4k^2 + x^2 - 2x + 1 = x^2 + 2x + 1$$

By combining like terms and then simplifying we get:

$$4k^2 = 4x$$

And simplifying further we get k equal to the square root of x.

A Trigonometric Method

We can use what we learned from the geometric method to derive a trigonometric method of finding square roots. We begin by using the r and s (which we defined in the geometric method) and finding the angle between them. The angle, which we'll call a, is equal to the cosine inverse of s divided by r:

$$a = \cos^{-1}(s/r)$$

We then use r and a to find k, and as we proved earlier, k is equal to the square root of x.

$$k = r \sin(a)$$

We write this as a single equation which would be:

$$k = r \sin(\cos^{-1}(s/r))$$

We can even go one step further and write this equation in terms of x, which becomes:

$$k = [(x + 1)/2] \sin(\cos^{-1}((x - 1)/(x + 1)))$$

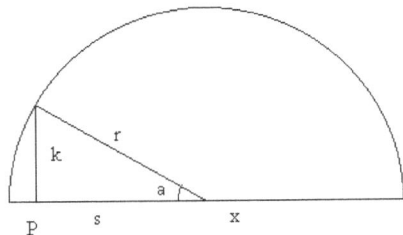

Figure 15.3   Finding the square root using the trigonometric method.

Although the geometric method wasn't very practical, the trigonometric method almost is. If for some reason the square root button on your calculator stopped working, it would be much easier to use this trigonometric formula than it would be to draw lines and half circles. But even still, if the square root button did stop working on your calculator, the easiest alternate method of finding square roots would be to use the logarithmic method. But before we look at that, let's look at a few iterative methods first.

The Bisection Method

The bisection method is an iterative method. This means that we apply the same steps over and over again to narrow in on a final answer. The way this method works is like this:

1. Determine an upper and a lower bound of the square root of the number.
2. Find the mid-point between the upper and lower bound.
3. Test the mid-point (by squaring it) to see if it is more or less than the number you're finding the square root of.
4. The mid-point becomes one of the new boundaries.
   a. If the mid-point squared is greater than the number, then the mid-point is the new upper bound.
   b. If the mid-point squared is less than the number, then the mid-point is the new lower bound.
5. Repeat steps 2 through 4 until the desired accuracy is achieved.

Let's use this method on an example, and see how it works. We'll use this to find the square root of 14. We start by finding an upper and lower bound to the square root of 14. Since 3^2 is 9 and 4^2 is 16, and 14 lies between 9 and 16, this means that the square root of 14 will lie between 3 and 4. Therefore, we'll use 3 and 4 as our initial lower and upper bounds, respectively.
Next, we find the mid-point between 3 and 4, which is 3.5. We then square 3.5 and check it, where 3.5^2 is equal to 12.25. Since 12.25 is less than 14, it means that 3.5 will become our new lower bound. Now we repeat these steps with our new lower bound and our original upper bound. The new mid-point is 3.75. Squaring this gives us 14.0625 which is greater than 14. So now 3.75 becomes our new upper bound.

The third time through, our lower bound is 3.5, and our upper bound is 3.75. The mid-point between these two numbers is 3.625. If this answer is accurate enough, we can stop here. Otherwise we can continue repeating these steps until we have an answer that is close enough to suit our purposes.

The easiest way to check your accuracy is to square the mid-point. As you square the mid-point, you should see that value getting closer and closer to the original number.

If you've worked out this example (or a similar example) by hand, you should have noticed that this method converges on the answer very slowly. Of the iterative methods that we will look at, this one converges the slowest. However, if you write this method into a computer program, you can easily go through 100 iterations or more in a relatively short amount of time, and have a very accurate answer.

The Averaging Method

Of all the iterative methods that we will consider in this chapter, this one is the easiest to use with a calculator. Start with the number you're trying to find the square root of, and an initial guess. Divide the guess into the number to get a result. Now, add the guess and the result together, and divide by two. This is the new guess you use as you repeat the process. Divide the new guess into the number to get a new result. Add the new guess and new result together and divide by two to get a newer result, and so continue. After several iterations, the guess and the result start to get closer and closer to the same number. This number is the square root of the original number. Let's go through an example:

We want to find the square root of 14, and we will use 3 as our initial guess. We start by dividing 14 by 3 to get 4.6666667. Adding these two numbers together, and dividing by 2 gives us 3.833333. Now, we repeat the process by dividing 14 by 3.8333333 to get 3.6521740. Next, we add these two numbers together, and divide by 2 to gives us 3.7427536. For our third iteration, we divide 14 by 3.7427536 to get 3.7405615. Again, we add these two numbers together and divide by 2 to get 3.7416576. A fourth iteration would give us a value of 3.7416574. And after four iterations, we find that our number is already very close to the accuracy that can be achieved with a regular hand held calculator.

A Babylonian Method

This method appears to have been first devised by the ancient Babylonians. Many hundreds of years later Sir Isaac Newton used the calculus that he invented to derive this same formula. For this reason it is known as either the Babylonian method, or Newton's method. In the next section we will look at a variation to this method, known as the Newton-Raphson method.

This method is very easy to understand conceptually, and it isn't that hard to implement; however, it is much easier to use with a calculator than it is to do by hand. This method is an iterative method that starts with an approximate value for the square root of a number, and as we apply the process over and over again, the result becomes more refined and exact. By controlling the number of iterations, we control how accurate our final result will be.

The Babylonian/Newton's method uses the following formula:

$$x_{n+1} = 0.5 \, (\, x_n \, + \, (\, a \, / \, x_n \,) \,)$$

Note that an alternate version of the Babylonian method uses the following formula:

$$x_{n+1} = 0.5 \, ((\, x_n^2 \, + \, a \,) \, / \, x_n \,)$$

Either formula can be used; and in fact, with just a little algebra you can manipulate one method to create the other. We will use the first version mentioned above in the example below.

The value of a is equal to the number we are trying to find the square root of. Also set the initial x equal to this same value (the initial x could also be set to some approximation or initial guess for the square root of a). Then calculate the right side of the equality to determine the next value for x. This new value is entered into the right side for x and the next value for x on the left is then determined again. This process is continued, and each iteration brings x closer to the exact value of the square root of a. If the process is continued indefinitely, x would equal the square root of a; instead, the process is continued only until you reach your desired level of accuracy.

Let's look at an example. Say we want to find the square root of 3. We set a equal to 3, and we also set our initial x equal to 3. Our equation starts out like this:

$$x_1 = 0.5 (x_0 + a / x_0)$$
$$x_1 = 0.5 (3 + 3 / 3)$$
$$x_1 = 2.0$$

After the first iteration, we have x_1 equal to 2.0. Now, we repeat the process by substituting 2 in for x:

$$x_2 = 0.5 (x_1 + a / x_1)$$
$$x_2 = 0.5 (2.0 + 3 / 2.0)$$
$$x_2 = 1.75$$

After the next iteration, x_2 is equal to 1.75. Continuing on, we have:

$$x_3 = 0.5 (x_2 + a / x_2)$$
$$x_3 = 0.5 (1.75 + 3 / 1.75)$$
$$x_3 = 1.7321428571...$$

Now, our results are starting to get closer; and if we consider one more iteration , we get:

$$x_4 = 0.5 (x_3 + a / x_3)$$
$$x_4 = 0.5 (1.7321428571 + 3 / 1.7321428571)$$
$$x_4 = 1.7320508100...$$

Notice how close this comes to the actual value of the square root of 3, which is equal to 1.732050807... And each iteration improves the accuracy of the result.

The Newton-Raphson Method

Both this method and the previous method can be derived using calculus; however, deriving these equations is beyond the scope of this book. But we won't let that stop us from showing the formula and how it can be implemented to find the square root of any number.

The Newton-Raphson method uses the following formula to find the square root of a number:

$$x_{n+1} = x_n - 0.5 ((x_n^2 - a) / x_n)$$

Again, we follow the same procedure that we used in the previous section. The value a is the number we are trying to find the square root of. We begin by setting x_n to some approximation of the square root of a; and then we plug these values into the right side of the equation, and get a value that will be equal to x_{n+1} for our next iteration through the equation.

As an example, let's find the square root of 3 again, and compare how this method works with the example in the previous section. However, this time we will let our initial estimate x_0, be equal to 2. For the first time through we get:

$$x_1 = x_0 - 0.5 ((x_0^2 - a) / x_0)$$
$$x_1 = 2 - 0.5 ((2^2 - 3) / 2)$$
$$x_1 = 1.75$$

After the first iteration we have x_1 equal to 1.75. We now plug that in for x on the right side of the equation, and repeat the step.

$$x_2 = x_1 - 0.5 ((x_1^2 - a) / x_1)$$
$$x_2 = 1.75 - 0.5 ((1.75^2 - 3) / 1.75)$$
$$x_2 = 1.7321428571...$$

And after this iteration we have x_2 equal to 1.7321428571... We again repeat our process for the next iteration.

$$x_3 = x_2 - 0.5 ((x_2^2 - a) / x_2)$$
$$x_3 = 1.7321428 - 0.5 ((1.7321428^2 - 3) / 1.7321428)$$
$$x_3 = 1.7320508100...$$

You'll notice that this method converges just as quickly as the previous method. So what is the benefit? By using calculus, we find that this method lends itself very nicely for finding roots of practically any type of polynomial function, and it's strength lies in that ability. We're only using a version of this method in this example to find square roots.

The Secant Method

A variation of the Newton – Raphson method is the secant method. But before we discuss the secant method in more detail, let's first back up a little and take a closer look at the Newton – Raphson method. The generic form of the Newton – Raphson method divides a function by its derivative, and it can be used to find almost any kind of root (not just square roots). In the section above, we simply adapted the Newton – Raphson method to square roots and left out any and all references to functions and their derivatives.

However, if you have taken a course in Calculus, you may remember that a derivative is also a fancy name for the slope of a curve at a single point. If we now replace the derivative part of the Newton – Raphson method with the actual calculation of a slope between two points, we have the secant method. Here is the generic formula for finding roots using the Newton – Raphson method. Notice that the function is divided by the derivative of the function:

$$x_{n+1} = x_n - f(x_n) / f'(x_n)$$

And here is the generic formula for finding roots using the secant method:

$$x_{n+1} = x_n - f(x_n) [(x_n - x_{n-1}) / (f(x_n) - f(x_{n-1}))]$$

Normally, the function is divided by the slope, but dividing by a number is the same as multiplying by its reciprocal; therefore, we simplified the relation above by inverting the slope and then multiplying it to the function.

Just like the Newton – Raphson method, the secant method is also an iterative method. The function that we will use is the same that we used in the previous method. The a represents the number that we are finding the square root of, and the x will become the actual square root as we iterate through the function. Here is the relation in its function form:

$$f(x) = x^2 - a$$

And here it is as it is applied in the secant method (note that there is some reduction of terms that takes place as the function is entered in the denominator; i.e., most of the a's cancel each other out within the formula):

$$x_{n+1} = x_n - (x_n^2 - a) \left[(x_n - x_{n-1}) / (x_n^2 - x_{n-1}^2) \right]$$

Let's look at an example of this method by finding the square root of 3. First, a is set equal to 3. Next, because we are calculating a slope, this method requires that we begin with two initial points. We'll let $x_n = 2.0$, and $x_{n-1} = 1.5$. This is what we get after the first iteration:

$$x_{n+1} = 2.0 - (2.0^2 - 3) \left[(2.0 - 1.5) / (2.0^2 - 1.5^2) \right]$$
$$x_{n+1} = 2.0 - (1.0) \left[(0.5) / (1.75) \right]$$
$$x_{n+1} = 1.7142857 \ldots$$

For the next iteration, our previous x_n is now x_{n-1}, and the x_{n+1} that we just calculated is the next x_n. Therefore, x_{n-1} is equal to 2, and x_n is equal to 1.71428:

$$x_{n+1} = 1.71428 - (1.71428^2 - 3) \left[(1.71428 - 2.0) / (1.71428^2 - 2.0^2) \right]$$
$$x_{n+1} = 1.71428 - (-0.06124) \left[(-0.28572) / (-1.06124) \right]$$
$$x_{n+1} = 1.7307677 \ldots$$

Again, we let x_n become x_{n-1}, and x_{n+1} becomes x_n, so that x_n is equal to 1.73077, and x_{n-1} is equal to 1.71428. The next iteration gives us:

$$x_{n+1} = 1.73077 - (1.73077^2 - 3) \left[(1.73077 - 1.71428) / (1.73077^2 - 1.71428^2) \right]$$
$$x_{n+1} = 1.73077 - (-0.00443521) \left[(0.01649) / (0.0568089) \right]$$
$$x_{n+1} = 1.73205511 \ldots$$

Notice that each iteration brings us closer to the actual value of the square root of 3. Of course this is a little tedious if you are doing each step by hand; yet, if we program a calculator or computer to do the tedious work for us, this method is not bad at all.

So, this begs the question that if a derivative is much more precise than a secant, then those of you who know and love Calculus may be asking yourselves why anyone in their right mind would even consider using the secant method when a derivative can give a much better slope to work with? Yet, if you truly know and love Calculus (but still have to work in the real world), then you'll understand that the answer to this question lies with the implementation of certain excruciating applications. For example, the secant method is much more practical to use whenever the derivative of a function is difficult, labor intensive, or even impossible to calculate. Hence the secant method remains a valuable tool in our collection of root-finding methods for other roots besides square roots.

Steffensen's Method

Having said all that about the secant method (and how practical it is when derivatives are difficult), we'll now look at a method that is even nicer than the secant method. This method is called Steffensen's method, and it is also an iterative method; however, it only needs a single initial point, and it only uses the function itself to calculate the next value of x. In this way it shares the advantages of both the Newton – Raphson method and the secant method.

And like both of those methods, the Steffensen's method has a generic form that can be used to find almost any type of root; however, in this section we will adapt that method to only finding square roots. But first, let's take a look at the generic form of this method:

$$x_{n+1} = x_n - f(x_n) / g(x_n)$$
$$\text{where} \quad g(x) = [f(x + f(x)) - f(x)] / f(x)$$

Notice the similarity that this method has with the Newton − Raphson and secant methods. The $g(x)$ in this method is where we would find the derivative in the Newton − Raphson method, and where we would find the slope in the secant method. However, as we take a closer look at the $g(x)$ function, we see that it is defined in terms of $f(x)$. Then by substituting the $g(x)$ expression back into the original expression (and after we invert the $g(x)$ fraction and multiply) we get the following:

$$x_{n+1} = x_n - [f(x_n)]^2 / [f(x + f(x)) - f(x)]$$

Of course, this is the generic form of our relation. To make it specific to our application, we substitute what $f(x)$ is equal to (in our case it is equal to $x^2 - a$). Doing so, and once again simplifying the denominator gives us this expression:

$$x_{n+1} = x_n - (x_n^2 - a)^2 / [(x_n + (x_n^2 - a))^2 - x_n^2]$$

As with the previous methods, a is the number we are trying to find the square root of, and x_n is our initial guess. Each iteration generates a value for x_{n+1}, which is then plugged back into x_n for the next iteration.

Applying this method to find the square root of 3 requires us to make an initial guess, which we will do by setting x_0 equal to 2. The first iteration gives us the following:

$$x_1 = x_0 - (x_0^2 - a)^2 / [(x_0 + (x_0^2 - a))^2 - x_0^2]$$
$$x_1 = 2.0 - (2.0^2 - 3)^2 / [(2.0 + (2.0^2 - 3))^2 - 2.0^2]$$
$$x_1 = 1.8$$

The second iteration gives us:

$$x_2 = 1.8 - (1.8^2 - 3)^2 / [(1.8 + (1.8^2 - 3))^2 - 1.8^2]$$
$$x_2 = 1.7375$$

And after the third iteration we get:

$$x_3 = 1.7375 - (1.7375^2 - 3)^2 / [(1.7375 + (1.7375^2 - 3))^2 - 1.7375^2]$$
$$x_3 = 1.73208879$$

Notice that by the end of the third iteration we have already started to hone in on a reasonable value for the square root of 3.

The Logarithmic Method

The easiest method of finding square roots without pressing the square root button on your calculator is to take the log of a number, divide it by 2, and then take the inverse log, or antilog. If you have log tables, you can use them; however, most calculators have a log key.

In fact, not only do most calculators have a log key, most calculators have two log keys, which means there are two ways readily available to take the log of a number. They are the $\log_{10}x$ (log base 10 of x) and the $\log_{e}x$ (log base e of x, or ln x). It doesn't matter which one you use, as long as you use the corresponding antilog after dividing by two. The antilog of $\log_{10}x$ is 10^x, and the antilog of $\log_{e}x$ is e^x.

As an example, let's find the square root of a number using both types of logarithms. In this example we'll find the square root of 723. The $\log_{10}$ of 723 is 2.85913830. We divide this by 2 to get 1.42956915. Then we take the antilog of this number (which means we are raising 10 to this power), or $10^{1.42956915}$ to give us 26.8886593…

Using natural logs, the ln of 723 is 6.58340922. Dividing this number by 2 gives us 3.29170461. Finally, we take the antilog of this number (which means we are raising e to this power), $e^{3.29170461}$ to give us 26.8886593… In both examples we have found the square root of 723 to be equal to 26.8886593…

A Method Using Napier's Bones

In the chapter showing multiple methods of multiplication, we saw a method that used Napier Bones to multiply numbers together. With the addition of a square root bone, we can use these same bones to find the square root of a number.

The square root bone is a little different than the other bones. Our square root bone consists of two columns. The first column has the square of the row number, and the second column has the double of the row number. For example, on the seventh row of the square root bone, you will see a 49 in the first column and a 14 in the second column.

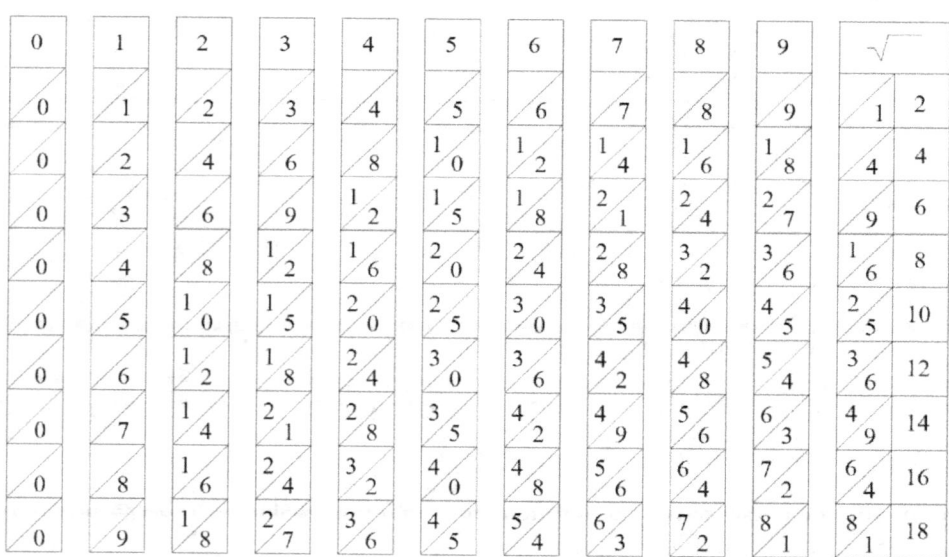

Figure 15.4 Napier Bones with the square root bone.

The Napier Bones will not directly find the square root of a number. Instead, they are used as a tool that will assist us as we determine the square root of a number. We will still do most of the work on a piece of paper. The best way to explain how to use the Napier Bones is by going through an example. In this example, we will find the square root of 162,409. We begin by writing the number so that the digits are paired in groups of two (starting from the decimal point on the right and moving left). Our number now looks like this: 16 24 09

We take the square root Napier Bone and find the largest square that is less than or equal to the left-most pair of digits, which in our example is 16. Of course the fourth row has 16 as the square. This means that the first digit of our solution is equal to 4. We write down the 4, and then also subtract the 16 from the first two digits of our number, and bring down the next two digits. At this point, the following (or something similar) is what we should have written on a piece of paper.

$$\sqrt{16\ \ 24\ \ 09} \quad = \quad 4$$
$$\underline{-\ 16}$$
$$0\ \ 24$$

Now, we go back to the square root Napier Bone, and go to the second column of the 4th row, which shows the number 8; therefore, for the next step in the process we will use the 8-bone along with the square root bone.

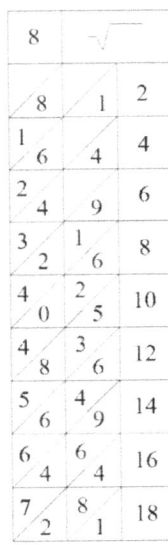

Figure 15.5 The 8-bone next to the square root bone.

Here, we add the numbers on each row (using the 8-bone and the square root bone) to find the largest number that is still less than 24. In our example, the first row is equal to 81, the second row is equal to 164, and so on. We quickly see that all of these numbers are greater than 24; therefore, the next digit in our result is equal to 0. So we write down the 0 next to the 4 (of our result), and we subtract 0 from 24 and bring down the next two digits. Our piece of paper should now look something that looks like this:

$$\sqrt{16\ \ 24\ \ 09} \quad = \quad 40$$
$$\underline{-\ 16}$$
$$24$$
$$\underline{-\ 0}$$
$$24\ \ 09$$

Currently, our result is equal to 40. We double this number to find what bones we use to place to the left of the square root bone. Since 40 doubled is equal to 80, we'll place the 8 and 0 bones next to the square root bone. Our bones should now look like this:

8	0	$\sqrt{}$	
8	0	1	2
1 6	0	4	4
2 4	0	9	6
3 2	0	1 6	8
4 0	0	2 5	10
4 8	0	3 6	12
5 6	0	4 9	14
6 4	0	6 4	16
7 2	0	8 1	18

Figure 15.6   The 8-bone and 0-bone next to the square root bone.

Again, we add up the numbers on each row (using the 8-bone, 0-bone and square root bone), trying to find the largest number less than or equal to 2409. As we check the rows, we find that the first row is equal to 801, the second row is equal to 1604, and the third row is equal to 2409. Because the third row matches the number we are looking for, it means that 3 is the final digit of our result, and our math looks like this:

$$
\begin{array}{r}
\sqrt{16\ 24\ 09} \quad = \quad 403 \\
-\underline{16} \\
24 \\
\underline{-\ 0} \\
24\ \ 09 \\
\underline{-\ 24\ \ 09} \\
0
\end{array}
$$

Notice that this method is practically identical to the second arithmetic method that we saw earlier in this chapter, except we are using the Napier bones as a tool to do the multiplication for us. We still have to keep track of what is going on by writing each step on a separate piece of paper. Therefore, we can easily sum up this method by saying that if you understand the second method, it is very easy to learn and use this Napier Bone method.

The Taylor Series

The square root of a number can also be obtained from a Taylor series expansion. If we were to derive the Taylor series for square roots, we would find ourselves using calculus; however, since Calculus is outside the scope of this book, we'll just limit our look to the particular Taylor series for square roots. It is:

$$\sqrt{N^2 + d} \; = \; N \; + \; \frac{d}{2N} \; - \; \frac{d^2}{8N^3} \; + \; \frac{d^3}{16N^5} \; - \; \frac{5d^4}{128N^7} \; + \; \frac{7d^5}{256N^9} \; - \; \ldots$$

N is equal to the highest perfect square less than the number we are trying to find the square root of, and d is equal to the difference between N and the number we are finding the square root of. Therefore, if we were finding the square root of 32, N would be equal to 5 and d would be equal to 7. Replacing N and d in the equation above gives us:

$$\sqrt{5^2 + 7} \; = \; 5 \; + \; \frac{7}{2(5)} \; - \; \frac{7^2}{8(5^3)} \; + \; \frac{7^3}{16(5^5)} \; - \; \frac{5(7^4)}{128(5^7)} \; + \; \frac{7(7^5)}{256(5^9)} \; - \; \ldots$$

Calculating the square root of 32 using the first six terms above gives me a value of 5.656894798 which is very close to the value that the square root key on my calculator gives, which is 5.65685424949.

The Bakhshali Approximation

Finally, do you sometimes find that your life is nothing but a frazzled mess? Do you often find yourself running from appointment to appointment, or meeting to meeting? Does one child come asking for this, while another is begging for that? And then as if things weren't bad enough already, you need to find the square root of a number, and you can't find your calculator. What you need my friend is the Bakhshali approximation. This approximation was developed hundreds of years ago, when life was slower, and the common pace was a little more relaxed. No, it can't promise to ease your stress, but maybe you can use it to remind yourself of a time when life was a little less hectic. Here is the Bakhshali approximation:

$$\text{Result} \; = \; a + (b/2a) - (b/2a)^2 / 2(a + (b/2a))$$

This method isn't meant to be an iterative formula, but instead a single, one-shot approximation (although it could be adapted to be used iteratively). The values for a and b are set values (there is no guessing involved). And as you examine this relation closer, you'll see that (b / 2a) is used throughout the expression. The values for a and b are integers, which means that you can calculate the expression and leave the result in its fractional form, or you can use decimal approximations to get a closer approximation to the approximation.

As with previous methods, the best way to understand this method is to see it used in an example; so let's say that we want to find the square root of 27. The value of a is equal to the largest integer squared that is still less than 27. In this example a is equal to 5. The value of b is equal to the difference between 27 and a^2, which means that our b is equal to 2. We now enter the values for a and b into the formula, or we could first calculate b/2a and then enter that into the appropriate places within the formula (as a type of a short cut). Since I have my calculator right here, I'll just plug in the numbers, and find the result:

$$\text{Result} \; = \; 5 + (2 / 10) - (2 / 10)^2 / 2(5 + (2 / 10))$$
$$= \; 26 / 5 \; - \; 1 / 260$$
$$= \; 1351 / 260$$

or

$$= \; 5.196153846 \ldots$$

This result is actually a very reasonable approximation to the square root of 27.

In Search of Higher Roots

Several of the square root methods that we've seen in this chapter also lend themselves very well to finding cube roots and higher roots. For example, when we used the logarithmic method to find the square root of a number, we simply took the log of that number, divided by two, and then took the inverse log to arrive at the square root. To find the cube root, we would follow the same procedure except that we would divide by three instead of two; and to find a fourth root we would divide by four; etc. In this way we can see the power of logs even though we are still bound by the accuracy of the log table or calculator that we are using.

The iterative methods mentioned in this chapter will also find cube roots and higher roots, and they will find them to any desired accuracy. These methods include the bisection method, the Newton-Raphson method, the secant method, and Stephenson's method.

The adaptation of the bisection method requires us to determine an upper and lower bound of the root we are finding, and then to find the mid-point between the bounds. We then raise this mid-point value to the appropriate power (raise it to the third power for cube roots, fourth power for fourth roots, etc.) and test the value to see if it is more or less than the number we are finding the root of. If it is more, then that mid-point becomes the new upper bound, and if it is less it becomes the new lower bound. The process is then repeated with the new upper or lower bound being used to find the next mid-point, and so on.

The Newton-Raphson method, the secant method, and Stephenson's method each define a function, f(x), and then use that function to find the root of the number. For square roots, f(x) is defined as:

$$f(x) = x^2 - a$$

Where x is the initial guess, and a is the number we were trying to find the square root of. To find a cube root, we would define our function as:

$$f(x) = x^3 - a$$

With x again being the initial guess, and this time a being the number we are trying to find the cube root of. And from here it is easy to see how to continue to find even higher roots.

While it would be very interesting to look at examples using each of these methods; I believe it would be more instructive to spend the rest of our time looking at a variation of the second arithmetic method and how it can be used to find higher roots.

To begin, we'll take the steps that we used to define how to find a square root, and modify them a little so they outline how to find a cube root. They are:

Step 1: Place the digits from the number in groups of three going left from the decimal point; and then place this number under a radical.

Step 2: Find the largest cubed value that is less than the left-most number grouping, and place it on top of the radical, and its cubed value under that left-most number, and then subtract.

Step 3: Bring down the next group of three numbers and place it next to the result of the subtraction that was just performed.

Step 4: Take the number on top of the radical, add a zero behind it, and use it as x in the following formula: $3x^2 + 3x$. Now use this result and divide it into the number obtained in step 3. The result of this division will be placed on top of the radical and it will be used as n in the following formula: $3x^2 + 3nx + n^2$ Now use the same x that you used at the beginning of this step along with the n value that you just obtained to arrive at a value from this second formula. Finally, place this value to the left of the value from step 3; multiply it by the n on top of the radical, and place this product under the number from step 3. Now subtract this number from the number from step three.

Step 5: Repeat steps 3 and 4 for the remaining number groups of three located under the radical.

If that process sounds like the instructions you follow to calculate your taxes, it might be because the IRS may actually use derivations similar to this. However, don't lose heart, we'll work through an example to see exactly how this is done.

First, we'll find the cube root of 146,363,183. As step 1 indicates, we'll take this number, group the digits in groups of three moving left from the decimal point, and then place this number under the cube root radical. This is what our first step looks like:

$$\sqrt[3]{146|363|183.}$$

Next we find the largest cube that is less than 146. In our example, the largest cube is 125, so we place the 125 under the 146 and subtract. We also place a 5 on top of the radical (because 5 cubed equals 125). This is what we have after completing the second step:

$$
\begin{array}{r}
5 \\
\sqrt[3]{146|363|183.} \\
-\ 125 \\
\hline
21
\end{array}
$$

Step three is the easiest. We bring down the next three digits:

$$
\begin{array}{r}
5 \\
\sqrt[3]{146|363|183.} \\
-\ 125 \\
\hline
21\ 363
\end{array}
$$

And now step four is the heart of the process. First we take the number on top of the radical, add a zero behind it; and use it as x in the following relationship: $3x^2 + 3x$. Plugging 50 in for x gives us 7650. Now we divide 21,363 by 7650 to give us 2.7925... We round this number down to the lowest integer, (which is 2), and use that as our value for n in this equation: $3x^2 + 3xn + n^2$. Entering 50 in for x, and 2 in for n gives us 7804.

We now have all the information we need to complete step 4. The 2 is placed on top of the radical and over the second group of three digits, and the 7804 is placed to the left of the 21,363 (as shown below):

$$\begin{array}{r} \underline{\quad 5 \quad 2 \quad} \\ ^3\sqrt{\ } \ 146|363|183. \\ \underline{-\ 125} \\ 7804\ )\ 21363 \end{array}$$

Finally, we multiply the 7804 by 2 (from the top of the radical) to get 15608, and subtract that from the 21,363 to give us 5755, and thus complete step 4.

$$\begin{array}{r} \underline{\quad 5 \quad 2 \quad} \\ ^3\sqrt{\ } \ 146|363|183. \\ \underline{-\ 125} \\ 7804\ )\ 21363 \\ \underline{-\ 15608} \\ 5755 \end{array}$$

Now, we repeat steps 3 and 4 again. For step 3 we simply bring down the next three digits from the next group to the right.

$$\begin{array}{r} \underline{\quad 5 \quad 2 \quad} \\ ^3\sqrt{\ } \ 146|363|183. \\ \underline{-\ 125} \\ 7804\ )\ 21363 \\ \underline{-\ 15608} \\ 5755183 \end{array}$$

And for step 4, we take the number on top of the radical, add a zero behind it and use it as x in the relationship $3x^2 + 3x$. Plugging 520 in for x gives us 812760. Next, we divide 5755183 by 812760 to get 7.081... We round this number down, and use it as our value for n. In other words, we use 520 as x and 7 as n in the equation: $3x^2 + 3xn + n^2$. This gives us 822169.

We place the 7 on top of the radical, and the 822169 is placed to the left of the 5755183 (as seen here):

$$\begin{array}{r} \underline{\quad 5 \quad 2 \quad 7 \quad} \\ ^3\sqrt{\ } \ 146|363|183. \\ \underline{-\ 125} \\ 7804\ )\ 21363 \\ \underline{-\ 15608} \\ 822169\ )\ 5755183 \end{array}$$

Finally, we multiple 822169 by 7 to get 5755183, which is then subtracted from 5755183. And in this case, the result of that subtraction is equal to 0, which means that the cube root of 146,363,183 is exactly equal to 527 (as shown below):

$$\begin{array}{r} \underline{\quad 5 \quad 2 \quad 7 \quad} \\ ^3\sqrt{\ } \ 146|363|183. \\ \underline{-\ 125} \\ 7804\ )\ 21363 \\ \underline{-\ 15608} \\ 822169\ )\ 5755183 \\ \underline{-\ 5755183} \\ 0 \end{array}$$

232

If we were to abbreviate the notation we used in step 4 we could say that the first equation takes an approximate value for x and uses that to find a value for n. The second equation is then used to complete step 4, so that we iterate back to step 3 (and continue the process). Here are the two equations from step 4:

$$3x^2 + 3x \qquad \text{and} \qquad 3x^2 + 3xn + n^2$$

You may not have noticed, but earlier in the chapter when we found the square root using this method, we also used two equations. The first was an approximation using just x to help us find the n value. The second equation then used both the x and the n to get an exact value. These two equations were:

$$2x \qquad \text{and} \qquad 2x + n$$

And actually, if we wanted to find the fourth root of a number, we would use the following two equations. Again, the first just uses an x value to help find the n value. And the second uses both the x and the n values to determine an exact value.

$$4x^3 + 6x^2 + 4x \qquad \text{and} \qquad 4x^3 + 6x^2n + 4xn^2 + n^3$$

Now, if we take these equations, and place them so that the equations used for square roots are on top, followed by the equations for cube roots on the line below, and the equations used for fourth roots on the line below that, we see a pattern beginning to emerge:

$$2x \qquad \text{and} \qquad 2x + n$$
$$3x^2 + 3x \qquad \text{and} \qquad 3x^2 + 3xn + n^2$$
$$4x^3 + 6x^2 + 4x \qquad \text{and} \qquad 4x^3 + 6x^2n + 4xn^2 + n^3$$

We've seen these numbers before; they are the same numbers in Pascal's triangle. Below is a listing of the first few rows of Pascal's triangle. The underlined numbers in the bold font are the same numbers as the coefficients in the equations above:

```
                  1
               1     1
            1     2     1
         1     3     3     1
      1     4     6     4     1
   1     5    10    10     5     1
```

Understanding this relationship means that we now have an arithmetic method of finding any whole number root of any number. Of course step four for larger roots becomes much more complicated and involved, but the process is there and it works.

Chapter 16
Divisibility and Methods of Division

Testing for Divisibility

Are there any methods or tools that we can use to break a large number into its pieces, and find its factors? For example, is there any way we can tell whether 9 divides evenly into 123,456? We could quickly perform the division with a calculator, but what if we were working with a number that was too large to use with a calculator. It would be nice to have a trick to quickly figure out if 123,456 (or any other number) is divisible by 9.

So, the question remains: does 9 divide evenly 123,456? The answer is no, but 3, 6 and 12 do divide evenly into 123,456. (Could you easily tell without a calculator?) What about 9 dividing evenly into 123,456,789,987,654,321? Here, the answer is yes, and so does 3, but 6 and 12 do not. So, how can we quickly find these answers without a calculator? Let's begin by looking at some of the rules and tricks that determine when a given number is divisible by another number. We'll start with the number 2 and go up:

2 - All even numbers are divisible by 2.

3 - A number is divisible by 3 if the sum of its digits is also divisible by 3. For example: to find if 122,355 is divisible by 3, add the digits together and see if the sum is divisible by 3. The sum of $1 + 2 + 2 + 3 + 5 + 5$ is 18. The number 18 is divisible by 3, therefore 122,355 is also divisible by 3.

4 - A number is divisible by 4 if the last 2 digits of the number are divisible by 4. (The number 325,793,811,524 is divisible by 4)

5 - A number is divisible by 5 if the last digit of the number is a 5 or a 0. (The numbers 715,893,445 and 839,834,210 are divisible by 5)

6 - A number is divisible by 6 if it is even and is divisible by 3. (The number 132,244,716 is even and is divisible by 3; therefore, it is also divisible by 6)

8 - A number is divisible by 8 if the last 3 digits of the number are divisible by 8. (The number 325,793,811,024 is divisible by 8)

9 - A number is divisible by 9 if the sum of its digits is divisible by 9. (The number 122,355 is also divisible by 9.)

10 - A number is divisible by 10 if the last digit of the number is a 0.

11 - To determine if a number is divisible by 11, take the first digit of the number and subtract the second digit; then add the third, subtract the forth, add the fifth, etc.

If the sum (after going through all the digits) is equal to 0, or is divisible by 11, then the number is divisible by 11.

12 - A number is divisible by 12 only if it is also divisible by 3 and 4.

You can use similar rules, or a combination of these rules to check if a number is divisible by 15, 16, 18, etc. For example, to be divisible by 15, the number must be divisible by 3 and 5; to be divisible by 16, the number 16 must divide evenly into the last four digits of the number, and to be divisible by 18 it must be even and divisible by 9, etc.

Testing for Numbers Divisible by 7

You may have noticed that we skipped the number 7. The number 7 is more difficult to work with. And probably for that reason, there are several tests that we could use. Some of these tests are just as cumbersome as dividing the original number by 7. For example, one method suggests that you take the right-most digit, remove it from the number, double the digit, and then subtract it from the remaining number. Continue this process until you are down to one number. If that remaining number is a 0 or a 7, then the original number is **divisible by 7**. For example, let's look at the number 61,671,141.

```
  61671141
-        2          remove the 1, double it and subtract it from the number.
  6167112
-        4          remove the 2, double it and subtract it from the number.
   616707
-       14          ... continue this process until there is one digit left.
    61656
-      12
     6153
-       6
      609
-     18
       42
-      4
        0           if the remainder is equal to 0 or 7, the original number is
                    divisible by 7.
```

The number 61,671,141 is divisible by 7. However, it is just as fast to divide the original number by 7 as it is to use this method. Also, the problem with this method is that if the number is not evenly divisible by 7, the remainder that you get has no relation to the actual remainder.

A Second Method of Testing for 7

A second method that appears similar in several ways to the previous method takes the left-most digit, multiplies it by 3, and then adds this value to the next digit to the right. This process is continued until you reach a number that you know is divisible by seven. Using the number from the previous example, we can see how this method works. Again, start with the number 61,671,141

61671141	Take the leading 6, multiply it by 3 and add to the next leading number (which is the 1).
61671141 + 18 —————— 19671141	Take the leading 1, multiply it by 3 and add to the next leading number (which is the 9)
19671141 + 3 —————— 12671141	Take the leading 1, multiply it by 3 and add to the next leading number (which is the 2)
12671141 + 3 —————— 5671141	Take the leading 5, multiply it by 3 and add to the next leading number (which is the 6)
5671141 + 15 —————— 2171141	Continue the process . . .
2171141 + 6 —————— 771141	
771141 + 21 —————— 281141	
281141 + 6 —————— 141141	

After about eight more iterations we would arrive at the number 91. And since 91 is divisible by 7, then so is our original number. In fact, every number in the each of the intermediate steps is also divisible by 7. So, if the original number is divisible by 7, then so is the number after the first iteration, and also the number after the second iteration, and so forth. Of course this method **doesn't whittle down the initial number as fast as the first method did; and with large numbers** this method can seem to go on forever. In this case, it is much easier to simply divide the initial number by 7 and be done with it.

However, both the first and second methods show an interesting property of numbers that are divisible by 7. In the case of the first method, we remove the least significant digit, double it, and then subtract it from the rest of the number, and the resulting number is still a multiple of 7. In the case of the second method, we can remove the most significant digit, multiply it by three, and then add that to the next most significant digit; and again, the resulting number is still a multiple of 7.

A Third Method that Tests Divisibility for 7, and also Works for 13

This next method takes the number to be tested and breaks it apart into six digit numbers. These six digit sections are then added together. If the resulting number is still greater than six-digit long, the process can be repeated as often as necessary. Once we arrive at our final six-digit

236

number, we simply check it to see if it is divisible by 7. If it is, then our original number was also divisible by 7. Let's test this by checking the following eleven-digit number: 10,840,846,422.

10840 | 846422   First, divide the number into 6-digit sections

846422
+ 10840
857262   Next, add the sections together.

857262 / 7 = 122466   If the resulting sum is evenly divisible by 7, the original number is also divisible by 7.

Since the sum (which was 857262) is divisible by 7, this means that the original number is also divisible by 7. This method is probably the easiest method to test whether a number is divisible by 7; however, as this method readily shows, it can only be used on numbers that consist of more than six-digits.

This method can also be used to test whether a number is divisible by 13. Again, divide the original number into 6-digit sections. Add the sections together, and then divide this sum by 13. If 13 divides evenly into this number, then 13 will also divide evenly into the original number.

A Fourth Method that Works for 7, 11 and 13

Another method takes the number to be tested, and divides it into 3 digit sections. Alternate sections are then added and subtracted. If the resulting number is divisible by 7 then the original number is also divisible by 7. When adding and subtracting the alternating sections, it doesn't matter if you start by subtracting first, or adding first. Let's see how this works by looking at the number 10,840,846,422.

10 | 840 | 846 | 422   First, divide the number into 3 digit sections

-10 + 840 - 846 + 422   Next, add and subtract alternating sections

406 / 7 = 58   If the resulting sum is evenly divisible by 7, the original number is also divisible by 7.

The number 406 can be evenly divided by the number 7; therefore, the original number, 10,840,846,422 is also divisible by 7.

This method can also be used to check if the number is divisible by 11 or 13. Again, divide the number into 3 digit sections. Add and subtract the alternating sections, and if the resulting sum is divisible by 11 or 13, then the original number is also divisible by the respective number 11 or 13.

A Fifth Method that Works with any Prime Number

This method will work with any prime number. We'll first show how it works when checking the divisibility of 7. We start by taking the remainders from successive powers of 10 divided by 7, and then we will use these numbers to determine if a number is divisible by 7. First we'll determine the remainders:

$10^0 / 7$	$= 1/7$	which has a remainder of 1
$10^1 / 7$	$= 10/7$	which has a remainder of 3
$10^2 / 7$	$= 100/7$	which has a remainder of 2
$10^3 / 7$	$= 1000/7$	which has a remainder of 6
$10^4 / 7$	$= 10000/7$	which has a remainder of 4
$10^5 / 7$	$= 100000/7$	which has a remainder of 5

We can stop here because for higher powers of 10, the sequence of numbers, 132645 repeats.

Now take the number we want to check, write it in reverse order and multiply the first digit by 1 the next digit by 3, the third digit by 2, and so on (we're getting these numbers from the sequence we generated above). If there are more than six digits in the number, then we start through the sequence again. Finally, take each of these products and add them together. If the resulting sum is divisible by 7 then the original number is also divisible by 7. Let's look at an example using the number 308,959:

959803   first, write the number in reverse order.

$9 \times 1 = \ \ 9$ now, take the digits and multiply them to the
$5 \times 3 = 15$ sequence of remainders that we generated from
$9 \times 2 = 18$ the powers of 10 divided by 7.
$8 \times 6 = 48$
$0 \times 4 = \ \ 0$
$3 \times 5 = \underline{\ 15}$
$\qquad\quad 105$ add the products together.

$105 / 7 = 15$ if the sum evenly divides by 7, then the original number is
                            also divisible by 7.

This method can be very cumbersome; however, as mentioned earlier, this test of divisibility can be adapted to work with any prime number. For example, let's check the number 308,959 to see if it is divisible by 19. First, we find the remainders from successive powers of 10 divided by 19. They are:

$10^0 / 19$ has a remainder of 1
$10^1 / 19$ has a remainder of 10
$10^2 / 19$ has a remainder of 5
$10^3 / 19$ has a remainder of 12
$10^4 / 19$ has a remainder of 6
$10^5 / 19$ has a remainder of 3

Since we are dealing with a 6 digit number, we don't need to go any further. Now we take the number we want to check, write it in reverse order and multiply the successive digits by the remainders that we obtained. Then we add the products together:

$9 \times \ \ 1 = \ \ 9$ take the digits in reverse order, and multiply
$5 \times 10 = 50$ them to the sequence of remainders that we
$9 \times \ \ 5 = 45$ generated from the powers of 10 divided by 19.
$8 \times 12 = 96$
$0 \times \ \ 6 = \ \ 0$
$3 \times \ \ 3 = \underline{\ \ 9}$
$\qquad\qquad 209$ add the products together.

The resulting sum is equal to 209, and since it is divisible by 19, the original number is also divisible by 19:

$$209 / 19 = 11 \qquad \text{the sum is evenly divisible by 19, therefore the original number is also divisible by 19.}$$

The number 308,959 is evenly divisible by 19. Actually, the number 308,959 was selected because it is evenly divisible by 7, 19, 23 and 101, and the curious reader can use this method to check this number with those factors also.

Factoring Larger Numbers

Now, suppose we want to factor a large number. Suppose also that the number we are checking is an odd number, and we have already used the methods outlined above to check if 3, 5, 7 or 11 were factors, and they were not. We could start by dividing other primes to see if any of those numbers will go evenly into the number. However, there are still other things we can do.

We'll illustrate this next method by looking at an example. Suppose we have a number like 2993. We're not sure if it is prime or not, so we begin by selecting a number that is the smallest integer just greater than the square root of 2993. The square root of 2993 is 54.708317...; therefore, the smallest integer greater than the square root is 55. We start by taking 55, squaring it and subtracting 2993 from it. We are looking for a difference that is also a perfect square.

$$55^2 - 2993 \;=\; 3025 - 2993 \;=\; 32$$

Since 32 is not a perfect square, we go back to the 55 and increase it by one. We now try 56. We square it and then subtract our original number from it. The result is 143:

$$56^2 - 2993 \;=\; 3136 - 2993 \;=\; 143$$

The number 143 is not a perfect square, so now we try 57:

$$57^2 - 2993 \;=\; 3249 - 2993 \;=\; 256$$

We have found what we're looking for. The number 256 is a perfect square. We now take this last relation (which was):

$$3249 - 2993 \;=\; 256$$

and rearrange the numbers so that it looks like this:

$$3249 - 256 \;=\; 2993$$

The left side of the equality is a difference of squares which we rewrite as:

$$57^2 - 16^2 \;=\; 2993$$

And the difference of two squares can be factored to:

$$a^2 - b^2 \;=\; (a - b)(b + a)$$

Therefore, $57^2 - 16^2 = 2993$

Factors to, and is the same as:

$$(57 - 16)(57 + 16) = 2993$$

In other words, 2993 has two factors (57 - 16) or 41, and (57 + 16) or 73. In this way we have found the two numbers (41 and 73) that evenly divide into our original number.

The Greatest Common Divisor

Another factoring trick is to find the greatest common divisor (GCD) between two numbers (the GCD is also known as the greatest common factor – GCF). As the name implies, the greatest common divisor is the largest number that will divide evenly into a pair of numbers. An interesting aspect of the method in this section is that it doesn't use division to find this value. Instead, the greatest common factor is found through a series of subtractions, thus giving us the largest number that divides into both numbers.

The way it works is to start with the two numbers, and subtract the smaller from the larger. If the result is still larger than the number subtracted, then we take the number that was subtracted, and subtract it again. Otherwise, if the result is smaller than the number subtracted, then we subtract the result from the number that was just used to subtract. We continue this process until the result is equal to the number being subtracted. When they are equal, this number is the GCD of the two original numbers.

Let's look at an example that will make this more clear. We'll find the greatest common divisor between 119 and 85. We begin by subtracting the smaller number from the larger number:

$$\begin{array}{r} 119 \\ - \ 85 \\ \hline 34 \end{array}$$

The number 34 is smaller than 85, so we use it, and subtract it from 85.

$$\begin{array}{r} 85 \\ - \ 34 \\ \hline 51 \end{array}$$

This time the 51 is larger than the 34, so we use the 34 again and subtract it from 51.

$$\begin{array}{r} 51 \\ - \ 34 \\ \hline 17 \end{array}$$

Now the 17 is smaller than 34, so we use the 17 and subtract it from 34

$$\begin{array}{r} 34 \\ - \ 17 \\ \hline 17 \end{array}$$

At this point, the result is equal to the number we were using to subtract; therefore, we have found our greatest common divisor between 119 and 85, and it is 17; and this means that 17 is the largest number that will divide evenly into both 85 and 119.

The Least Common Multiple

The least common multiple (LCM) is the smallest number that a set of given numbers will divide evenly into. For example, if we are given the numbers 6 and 8, the least common multiple between these two numbers is 24, because it is the lowest number that both 6 and 8 will divide into evenly.

One way to find the least common multiple between two numbers is to break each number into its prime factors; find pairs of prime factors that are common to each number; represent the number from that pair only once; and then finally multiply these factors together. For example, we calculate the LCM between 60 and 126 like this. First, find the prime factors for each number:

$$60 = 2 * 2 * 3 * 5 \qquad \text{prime factors of } 60$$
$$126 = 2 * 3 * 3 * 7 \qquad \text{prime factors of } 126$$

Next, we pair (and cross) out the prime factors that are common to both 60 and 126; then, represent each paired factor only once. In this case, both numbers have a 2 and a 3 in common.

$$60 = 2 * 2 * 3 * 5 \qquad \text{Cross out a 2 and 3 from both}$$
$$126 = 2 * 3 * 3 * 7 \qquad \text{sets of prime factors, and}$$
$$2 \qquad 3 \qquad \text{represent the 2 and 3 once.}$$

Now, take the factors that haven't been crossed out (from both numbers), and multiply these factors together. The product of these factors is equal to 1260:

$$2 * 2 * 3 * 3 * 5 * 7 = 1260$$

Therefore, the number 1260 is the lowest number that both 60 and 126 divide into evenly.

The least common multiple and the greatest common divisor are related to each other in the following way:

$$LCM (a, b) = \frac{a * b}{GCD(a, b)}$$

In other words, once we have either the least common multiple or the greatest common divisor, we can easily find the other. In the example above, we found the LCM of 60 and 126. Now, we use this relation to find the GCD between 60 and 126:

$$1260 = \frac{60 * 126}{GCD}$$

Solving for the GCD, we find that it is equal to 6. This means that 6 is the largest number that will divide evenly into both 60 and 126. Unfortunately, the relationship above only works with pairs of numbers. However, this brings us back to another method of finding the greatest common divisor between two numbers. The GCD can be found by breaking both numbers into their prime factors, and then finding the product of the prime factors that are shared between both numbers.

As we saw above, the numbers 60 and 126 shared a 2 and a 3 as common factors; and the product of 2 and 3 is 6; thus giving us again the GCD between 60 and 126.

As we have seen in the examples above, the key to finding the least common multiple and the greatest common divisor is in the prime factors. Knowing this, we can find the LCM and the GCD for multiple numbers (and not just pairs of numbers). Let's look at another example. Let's find the LCM and the GCD for 180, 420, and 1470. First we'll break these numbers into their prime factors:

$$180 = 2 * 2 * 3 * 3 * 5 \qquad \text{prime factors of } 180$$
$$420 = 2 * 2 * 3 * 5 * 7 \qquad \text{prime factors of } 420$$
$$1470 = 2 * 3 * 5 * 7 * 7 \qquad \text{prime factors of } 1470$$

Notice that all three numbers share the factors of 2, 3, and 5. Therefore, the GCD between these three numbers is equal to the product of 2 * 3 * 5, which is equal to 30. In other words, 30 is the largest number that will divide evenly into all three numbers.

$$180 = \cancel{2} * 2 * \cancel{3} * 3 * \cancel{5} \qquad \text{prime factors of } 180$$
$$420 = \cancel{2} * 2 * \cancel{3} * \cancel{5} * 7 \qquad \text{prime factors of } 420$$
$$1470 = \cancel{2} * \cancel{3} * \cancel{5} * 7 * 7 \qquad \text{prime factors of } 1470$$

Now, in order to find the least common multiple between these three numbers, we eliminate factors that are in common between the three numbers, and represent them only once. First, we have a 2, a 3, and a 5 that is common between all three numbers – so extra numbers are eliminated, and are represented only once. But, we can also eliminate numbers that are in common between pairs of numbers; therefore, we can also eliminate another 2 between the first and second numbers, and we can eliminate a 7 between the second and third numbers (remember that eliminating a number means that it will only be represented once). After eliminating shared factors, our factors reduce to the following set of numbers:

$$2 * 2 * 3 * 3 * 5 * 7 * 7 = 8820$$

The numbers 180, 420, and 1470 will each divide evenly into 8820; and the number 8820 is the least common multiple between our three numbers.

The Traditional Method of Division
We'll spend the remainder of this chapter looking at various methods of division. But before we do that, let's make sure we understand the terminology related to division. When we divide a smaller number into a larger number, the smaller number is called the divisor, and the larger number is the dividend. The result that we get is called the quotient. In other words, these words relate to each other like this:

$$\text{divisor } \overline{)\, \text{dividend}}^{\text{quotient}}$$

Soon after learning the basics of multiplication and division, we learn how to do long division. The method currently taught in public schools allows us to divide any smaller number into a larger number. (We can also divide larger numbers into smaller numbers; the principles and methods are the same, but for the sake of simplicity, we will limit ourselves to just dividing a smaller number into a larger number.)

242

We'll begin our look at the traditional method with an example. We'll divide 37 into 195,989. The number 37 is the divisor and 195,989 is the dividend. We start by writing the numbers next to each other so that they look something like this:

$$37 \overline{)\,195,989}$$

We then perform a series of estimates (or guesses), multiplications and subtractions until we arrive at the final answer. Since 37 is a two-digit number, we look at the first two digits of the dividend, which is 19, and since 37 will not go into 19, we then consider the first three digits of the dividend, which is 195.

We estimate that 37 will go 5 times into 195, so for the first step, we write the 5 above the last digit of the 195, then we multiply 5 times 37 to get 185. We place the 185 under the 195, and subtract. This gives us 10, and we bring down the next digit from the dividend to give us 109. At the end of this step, we have something that looks like this:

```
           5
37 ) 195,989
   - 185
     109
```

Now, we repeat this process. We estimate how many times 37 will go into 109. Since 37 goes twice into 109, we place the 2 next to the 5 (in the quotient), and then multiply 37 by 2 to get 74. The 74 is placed below the 109, and subtracted from it. The result of this subtraction is 35. We bring down the next digit from the dividend, which is 8, and place that next to the 35. After our second iteration, we have the following:

```
           5,2
37 ) 195,989
   - 185
     109
    - 74
     358
```

We repeat the process of estimating, multiplying, and then subtracting two more times to arrive at our final result in this example.

```
           5,297
37 ) 195,989
   - 185
     109
    - 74
     358
   - 333
     259
   - 259
       0
```

In the example above, 37 went evenly into 195,989; in other words, there was no remainder. Had there been a remainder, we could have continued the process by bringing down 0's after the last 9, place a decimal point in the quotient, and then continue as long as we need to (or want to).

A Simplified Traditional Method

There is a simplified traditional method that is also known as "Double Division" or the "1-2-4-8 Division" method. This method is similar to the traditional method, but it trades some of the guess-work of the traditional method for a few extra steps. We'll look at an example to show what we mean.

We'll use the example above, and start again by writing the divisor next to the dividend. And since we will be dividing by 37, we will also create a list of several products of 37; specifically: one times 37, two times 37, four times 37 and eight times 37, and we will place these products to the side of our division problem. Notice that each of these values is easily found by doubling the previous value. We will use these products as our "estimates" as we determine how many times 37 will go into 195,989. As we begin this method, we should have something that looks like this:

$$
\begin{array}{ll}
1 \text{ x } = & 37 \\
2 \text{ x } = & 74 \\
4 \text{ x } = & 148 \\
8 \text{ x } = & 296 \\
\end{array}
\qquad 37 \overline{) 195,989}
$$

For the first step, we look at our products on the left to see which of these most easily goes into the left-most part of our dividend (which is 195,989). 37 won't go into 19, and neither will 74, but 148 will go into 195, so we write 148 under the 195, and then we add three zeroes to give us 148,000. Since we are using the 4x number, we write the 4 along with the three zeroes to the right of our problem so that we have the number 4000 off to the side. Finally, we subtract 148,000 from our dividend. At the end of the first step, we have something that looks like this:

$$
\begin{array}{ll}
1 \text{ x } = & 37 \\
2 \text{ x } = & 74 \\
4 \text{ x } = & 148 \\
8 \text{ x } = & 296 \\
\end{array}
\qquad
\begin{array}{r}
37 \overline{) 195,989} \\
- 148,000 \\
\hline
47,989 \\
\end{array}
\qquad 4000
$$

Now, we repeat the process. 37 will go into 47, so we write it down along with three zeroes behind it. This time we used the 1x number with three zeroes, so off to the side we write the number 1000 (a one with three zeroes behind it). Finally, we subtract 37,000 from 47,989. This is what we have at the end of the second step:

$$
\begin{array}{ll}
1 \text{ x } = & 37 \\
2 \text{ x } = & 74 \\
4 \text{ x } = & 148 \\
8 \text{ x } = & 296 \\
\end{array}
\qquad
\begin{array}{r}
37 \overline{) 195,989} \\
- 148,000 \\
47,989 \\
- 37,000 \\
\hline
10,989 \\
\end{array}
\qquad
\begin{array}{l}
4000 \\
\\
1000 \\
\end{array}
$$

Again, we repeat the process. None of our numbers can go into the first two digits of 10,989; but 74 is the largest number that can go into the first three digits of that number. So we'll place the 74 under the 109, and then we'll add two zeroes behind the 74. This allows us to subtract 7400 from 10989, giving us 3589. Since 74 is the 2 x number, we will place a 2 to the right, and since we added two zeroes behind the 74, we will also add two zeroes behind the two (to give us 200).

```
1 x =   37        37 ) 195,989
2 x =   74           - 148,000        4000
4 x = 148             47,989
8 x = 296           - 37,000          1000
                     10,989
                    - 7400             200
                      3589
```

We continue the process over and over until our final subtraction either gives us a zero, or gives us a number that is less than 37. In our example, the next step gives us an 80; and the step after that gives us a 10, followed by a 4, then a 2, and finally a 1.

```
1 x =   37        37 ) 195,989
2 x =   74           - 148,000        4000
4 x = 148             47,989
8 x = 296           - 37,000          1000
                     10,989
                    - 7400             200
                      3589
                    - 2960             80
                      629
                    - 370              10
                      259
                    - 148              4
                      111
                    - 74               2
                      37
                    - 37             +  1
                       0             5297
```

The final step is to add the numbers on the right. Adding them together gives us 5297, and this is our answer. In other words, 195,989 divided by 37 is equal to 5297.

In the example above, the divisor went evenly into the dividend; however, if we would have ended with a number less than 37, that would have been our remainder. We could have stopped with that, or we could have brought down zeroes from the other side of the decimal point, and then continued the same process using decimal points in the values that we placed on the right.

A Method from India
This next method is one that has been taught in India. At first this method can seem a little unusual; however, with a little practice, this method is as easy, and can be even easier than the traditional method currently taught in many Western schools. Of course, the best way to understand this method is to try it on a few examples. For this first example, we will divide 23504 by 52. We'll begin by writing down our problem with a lot of spaces in the dividend.

$$2 \quad 3 \quad 5 \quad 0 \quad 4 \quad \div \quad 52 \quad =$$

The number we are dividing by (the divisor) is broken into two parts, a leading part, and a following part. Since we are dividing by a two digit number, the leading part is the 5 while the following part is the 2. The leading part is always divided into the part of the number we are working with, while the following part is always multiplied to a part of the quotient (our result) and then subtracted from the part of the number we are working with. We start by trying to divide the 5 into the first digit (the 2). Since that doesn't work, we then look at the first two digits, which are 23. The 5 goes into 23 four times with a remainder of 3. So, we write the 4 in the quotient, and the remainder (the 3) in front of the next number (which is 5), like so:

$$2 \ 3 \ {}^{3}5 \ 0 \ 4 \ \div \ 52 \ = \ 4$$

We take the 2 (from 52, the divisor), multiply it by 4 (in our quotient), and subtract that from 35:

$$2 \ 3 \ {}^{3}5 \ 0 \ 4 \ \div \ 52 \ = \ 4$$
$$\underline{\ -8\ }$$
$$27$$

Now divide the 27 by 5 (from the 52). This gives us 5 with a remainder of 2. The 5 is placed in the quotient behind the 4, and the 2 is placed in front of the next number in the dividend, like so:

$$2 \ 3 \ {}^{3}5 \ {}^{2}0 \ 4 \ \div \ 52 \ = \ 45$$
$$\underline{\ -8\ }$$
$$27$$

We again take the 2 (from the 52), multiply it by the 5 (in the quotient), and subtract that from the 20:

$$2 \ 3 \ {}^{3}5 \ {}^{2}0 \ 4 \ \div \ 52 \ = \ 45$$
$$\underline{\ -8 \ -10\ }$$
$$27 \quad 10$$

Now divide 10 by 5 (the 5 from the 52) to get 2 with a remainder of 0. The 2 is placed behind the 5 in the quotient, and the remainder of 0 is placed in front of the last digit of the dividend:

$$2 \ 3 \ {}^{3}5 \ {}^{2}0 \ {}^{0}4 \ \div \ 52 \ = \ 452$$
$$\underline{\ -8 \ -10\ }$$
$$27 \quad 10$$

For the final step (in this case), we take the 2 (from the 52), and multiply it to the 2 (from the 452), and then subtract this from the last digit in the dividend:

$$2 \ 3 \ {}^{3}5 \ {}^{2}0 \ {}^{0}4 \ \div \ 52 \ = \ 452$$
$$\underline{\ -8 \ -10 \ -4\ }$$
$$26 \quad 10 \quad 0$$

After we subtract, we get a remainder of 0 which means that 52 divides evenly into 23504 with a result equal to 452.

Now, let's try another example that doesn't work out evenly. This time we'll divide 23493 by 32. Again, we'll begin by writing down our problem with a lot of spaces in the dividend.

$$2\ 3\ 4\ 9\ 3\ \div\ 32\ =$$

And again, the 3 (from the divisor, 32) won't go into the first digit (the 2 from the dividend), so we'll begin by dividing 3 into the first two digits, the 23. The 3 goes into 23 seven times with a remainder of 2. We write the 7 in the quotient, and the remainder of 2 in front of the next number (which is 4), like so:

$$2\ 3\ {}^2 4\ 9\ 3\ \div\ 32\ =\ 7$$

We take the 2 (from the 32), multiply it by 7 (in our quotient), and subtract that from 24:

$$2\ 3\ {}^2 4\ 9\ 3\ \div\ 32\ =\ 7$$
$$\underline{-\ 14}$$
$$10$$

Now divide the 10 by the 3 (from the 32). This gives us 3 with a remainder of 1. The 3 is placed in the quotient behind the 7, and the 1 is placed in front of the next number in the dividend, like so:

$$2\ 3\ {}^2 4\ {}^1 9\ 3\ \div\ 32\ =\ 73$$
$$\underline{-\ 14}$$
$$10$$

We again take the 2 (from the 32), multiply it by the 3 (in the quotient), and subtract that from the 19:

$$2\ 3\ {}^2 4\ {}^1 9\ 3\ \div\ 32\ =\ 73$$
$$\underline{-\ 14}\ \underline{-\ 6}$$
$$10\ \ 13$$

Now divide 13 by 3 (the 3 from the 32) to get 4 with a remainder of 1. The 4 is placed behind the 3 in the quotient, and the remainder of 1 is placed in front of the last digit of the dividend:

$$2\ 3\ {}^2 4\ {}^1 9\ {}^1 3\ \div\ 32\ =\ 734$$
$$\underline{-\ 14}\ \underline{-\ 6}$$
$$10\ \ 13$$

For the final step, we take the 2 (from the 32), and multiply it to the 4 (from the 734), and then subtract this from the last digit in the dividend:

$$2\ 3\ {}^2 4\ {}^1 9\ {}^1 3\ \div\ 32\ =\ 734$$
$$\underline{-\ 14}\ \underline{-\ 6}\ \underline{-\ 8}$$
$$10\ \ 13\ \ 5$$

This time we got a remainder of 5 which means that 23493 divided by 32 is equal to 734 and 5/32.

This method is easy to get used to, and it is fairly straight-forward most of the time. However, there is an adjustment that must be made if you get a negative number when performing the subtraction. We'll look at that next. Here, we will divide 7571 by 23:

$$7\ 5\ 7\ 1\ \div\ 23\ =$$

This time, the 2 (from the 23) divides into the first digit (which is 7). It does so three times with a remainder of 1. The 3 is placed in the quotient, and the 1 is placed in front of the 5. We write the first step like this:

$$7 \ ^{1}5 \ 7 \ 1 \ \div \ 23 \ = \ 3$$

Now we take the 3 (from the 23) and multiply it to the 3 (from the quotient) to give us a 9 which we subtract from the 15 to get a 6:

$$7 \ ^{1}5 \ 7 \ 1 \ \div \ 23 \ = \ 3$$
$$\underline{-9}$$
$$6$$

Dividing the 6 by 2 (from the 23) gives us a 3 with a remainder of 0. This 3 goes in the quotient behind the first 3, and the 0 is placed in front of the next 7:

$$7 \ ^{1}5 \ ^{0}7 \ 1 \ \div \ 23 \ = \ 33$$
$$\underline{-9}$$
$$6$$

Now, when we take the 3 (from the 23) and multiply it to the second 3 in the quotient, we again get 9; however, subtracting 9 from 7 gives us a negative 2:

$$7 \ ^{1}5 \ ^{0}7 \ 1 \ \div \ 23 \ = \ 33$$
$$\underline{-9 \ -9}$$
$$6 \ -2$$

This won't work, so we have to back up a step, and reduce the quotient by one. This means that even though the 6 can be divided by 2 (from the 23) to give us our second 3 in the quotient; instead, we will say that 6 divided by 2 is equal to 2 with a remainder of 2. Therefore, our next step looks like this:

$$7 \ ^{1}5 \ ^{2}7 \ 1 \ \div \ 23 \ = \ 32$$
$$\underline{-9}$$
$$6$$

And continuing on with the rest of the step, we have the 3 (from the 23) multiplied with the 2 from the quotient to give us 6 which is then subtracted from 27:

$$7 \ ^{1}5 \ ^{2}7 \ 1 \ \div \ 23 \ = \ 32$$
$$\underline{-9 \ -6}$$
$$6 \ 21$$

And finally, the 2 (from the 23) is divided into the 21. This actually gives us 10 with a remainder of 1, but the highest number we can use is 9, therefore, we get 9 with a remainder of 3. The 9 is placed in the quotient, and the 3 is placed in front of the 1 in the dividend:

$$7 \ ^{1}5 \ ^{2}7 \ ^{3}1 \ \div \ 23 \ = \ 329$$
$$\underline{-9 \ -6}$$
$$6 \ 21$$

Now, to finish the final step, take the 3 (from the 23), and multiply it to the 9 from the quotient. This number is then subtracted from the 31 to give us a result of 4:

$$7 \ {}^{1}5 \ {}^{2}7 \ {}^{3}1 \ \div \ 23 \ = \ 329$$
$$\underline{-9 \ -6 \ -27}$$
$$6 \quad 21 \quad 4$$

Therefore, 7571 divided by 23 is equal to 329 and 4/23. The same procedure is followed when dividing by a three digit number; however, the leading part will consist of the first two digits of the divisor, and the following part will use only the last digit. Similarly, when dividing by a four digit number, the leading part will consist of the first three digits of the divisor, and the following part will again use the last digit.

The Ethiopian Method of Multiplication Applied to Division
In an earlier chapter we saw a method of multiplication that doubled one number and halved another number, and then after eliminating certain numbers, the remaining numbers in the doubled column were added together, and in this way the product of the two original numbers was found (see the section on the Ethiopian Method under the chapter of Multiplication Methods). This method didn't require any other knowledge of multiplication other than the knowledge of doubling and halving numbers.

We can apply a similar tactic of doubling numbers, and then subtracting and adding to ultimately divide one number into another. Let's see how this would be done. Again, we'll use the numbers from the previous sections to work through this example. We'll divide 195,989 by 37. In this method, we'll start with two columns, both of which will be doubling columns. The first column will start with our divisor, the number 37 (since that is what we are dividing into the dividend, 195,989), and the second column will start with the number 1.

37	1
74	2
148	4
296	8
592	16
1184	32
2368	64
4736	128
9472	256
18944	512
37888	1024
75776	2048
151552	4096

We stop doubling when the column on the left is about to pass (or exceed) the dividend: in our example, if we double our column on the left one more time, we will exceed the number we are dividing into (which is 195989).

Now, we simply subtract the largest numbers from the left column, while at the same time taking the corresponding numbers from the right column, and add them together. Like this:

```
   195989
 - 151552                              4096
    44437
  - 37888                              1024
     6549
   - 4736                               128
     1813
   - 1184                                32
      629
    - 592                                16
       37
     - 37                           +    1
        0                               5297
```

In the left column we subtract numbers from the 37 column, and in the right column we add the corresponding numbers from the 1 column. Our result in this example is 5297, which indeed is equal to 195989 divided by 37.

As with the Ethiopian method of multiplication, this method of division doesn't require any other knowledge than an ability to double numbers, and then add and subtract.

The Fibonacci Method of Multiplication Applied to Division

The Fibonacci method of multiplication is very similar to the Ethiopian method; and in a similar way, we can apply this method to division. An advantage of this method is that you don't need to have any knowledge of multiplication (not even doubling) to perform the division. This method carries out the division solely thru additions and subtractions. The problem with this method is that the numbers in the columns increase at a much slower rate, causing us to go through several more iterations before arriving at our final result. For this reason we will choose a smaller number for our example. Here we will divide 8103 by 37

37	1
37	1
74	2
111	3
185	5
296	8
481	13
777	21
1258	34
2035	55
3293	89
5328	144

Again, we'll start by creating the same two columns. The column on the left will have the number 37 at the top, and the column on the right will start with the number 1. The second row of each column will repeat the same numbers from the first row. Each subsequent row will be the sum of the two numbers from the two previous rows. In the first column we generate the numbers by taking 37 + 37 to equal 74; then we have 37 + 74 to give us 111; and so on.

The second column follows the same pattern. We start with 1 + 1 to give us 2; then 1 + 2 to give us 3, etc. (The numbers in the column on the right are Fibonacci numbers.)

We continue this addition until our number on the left is about to exceed the number we are dividing into. Notice that if we were to add the last two numbers in the left column, we would see that their sum would be greater than 8103, so we can stop our addition at this point.

Now we do the subtractions. Again, we simply subtract the largest numbers from the left column, while at the same time taking the corresponding numbers from the right column, and add them together. Like this:

```
    8103
  - 5328              144
    2775
  - 2035               55
     740
   - 481               13
     259
   - 185                5
      74
    - 74             +  2
       0              219
```

The total from the column on the right is our result. In other words, 8103 divided by 37 is equal to 219.

A Method of Division Using Napier Bones

In the previous two methods we took a method of multiplication and then used a series of subtractions to derive the numbers we needed to ultimately find the solution of one number divided by another. In a similar way, we can use Napier Bones to derive a series of numbers that we will then use to find our result. Let's look at an example where we take 18414 and divide it by 27.

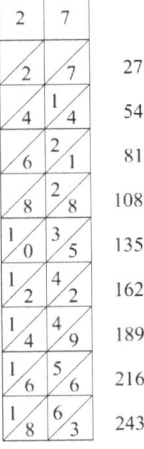

Figure 16.1 The 2 and 7 Napier Bones used to find the 9 products of 27.

Since we are dividing by 27, we take the 2 and the 7 Napier bones, place them next to each other (to give us 27). With these two bones together, we can easily see a list of all nine products of 27. In the figure above, the products are listed to the right of the bones.

We start at the left side of the number we are dividing, and find the largest number from our nine products that will subtract from our number. We don't have anything that will go into the 18 (of the 18414), but we do have a number that will go into the 184 (of the 18414). This is the number 162, which is the sixth of the nine products. We write the 6 on the right hand side, and then subtract the 162 and get 22. Then we bring down the next number to the right (which is the 1) to give us 221.

$$
\begin{array}{r}
18414 \\
-\ \underline{162} \qquad\qquad 6 \\
221
\end{array}
$$

Now, we repeat the process. This time, the largest number that we can subtract from 221 is 216, which is the eighth of the nine products. We subtract it, and bring down the 4 to give us 54.

$$
\begin{array}{r}
18414 \\
-\ \underline{162} \qquad\qquad 6 \\
221 \\
-\ \underline{216} \qquad\qquad 8 \\
54
\end{array}
$$

Once again, we repeat the process, and now the largest number that we can subtract from 54 is 54. This is the second of the nine products, and subtracting it gives us 0.

$$
\begin{array}{r}
18414 \\
-\ \underline{162} \qquad\qquad 6 \\
221 \\
-\ \underline{216} \qquad\qquad 8 \\
54 \\
-\ \underline{54} \qquad\qquad 2 \\
0
\end{array}
$$

Therefore, 18414 divided by 27 is equal to 682, and since the last subtraction gave us a 0 we know that 27 divides evenly into 18414.

The Galley Method of Division

This next method of division is called the galley method, or scratch method. It was actually the most popular method for centuries, and only in the last 150 years or so has been replaced by what we now call the traditional method. It starts out by placing the divisor below the dividend. We also place a bar to the right of the dividend, and to the right of this bar we will write the quotient, or answer, as we calculate it. We will demonstrate this method by looking at a few examples. In the first example we'll divide 21 into 7329. We start by placing the divisor and dividend like this:

$$
\begin{array}{l}
7329\ | \\
21
\end{array}
$$

Two will go into 7 three times, so we'll place a 3 to the right of the bar, and then multiple 3 times 2 and subtract it from 7. This leaves a 1 which we place above the 7. We now cross out the numbers we just finished working with (the 7 and the 2), and we have something that looks like this (the number on top is now 1329):

```
1
7329 | 3
21
```

To complete this step, we multiply the 1 in the divisor by the 3 (in the quotient), and subtract it from the 13 in the dividend (the 13 is the first two digits of 1329 which is the current dividend). Our result is 10, so we write this number above the dividend, and we cross out the numbers we just finished working with, leaving us with 1029 as the next current dividend:

```
10
7329 | 3
21
```

For the next step, we again write 21 under the dividend, but shifted one place to the right.

```
10
7329 | 3
21
   21
```

Now we look at how many times the 2 will go into the 10. It will go in 5 times, so we place a 5 next to the 3 (in the quotient), and then multiple the 2 times 5 and subtract it from 10 (the first two digits of the divisor). After crossing out the numbers we just used (the 10 on top and the 2 on the bottom), we have the following (the top number is 29):

```
10
7329 | 35
21
   21
```

To finish the step, we multiply the 1 (that isn't crossed out) by the 5 (in the quotient) and subtract it from 2 (in the dividend). Whoops! We have a problem here. This will give us a negative number. To fix this we need to back up to the beginning of this step, and use a 4 instead of a 5 in the quotient. So we uncross-out the 10 on top and the 2 on the bottom, and now we multiply the 2 on the bottom with the 4 to give us 8 and then subtract that from 10. The remainder is placed above the 10, and the 10 is again crossed out. Likewise, the 2 on the bottom (that we just used) is also crossed out. Midway through this step we now have (with 229 as the top number):

```
2
10
7329 | 34
21
   21
```

Now we multiply the 1 (on the bottom) with the 4 and subtract that from the 22 (on top) to give us 18. We write the 18 above the 22 and then cross out the numbers we just finished using (the 1 on the bottom and the 22 on top), giving us 189 on top:

1

~~2~~

~~108~~

~~7329~~ | 34

~~21~~

~~21~~

Now to begin our third (and in this case final step) we again write the 21 under the dividend and shifted to the right one place.

1

~~2~~

~~108~~

~~7329~~ | 34

~~21~~

~~21~~

21

Here we have the 2 (from our divisor) under the 18 (from our dividend). Two will go into 18 nine times, so we place a 9 in the quotient, and then multiply 2 times 9 and subtract it from the 18. Since it goes in evenly, we simply cross out the numbers we just used and then move on to the final part of this step.

~~1~~

~~2~~

~~108~~

~~7329~~ | 349

~~21~~

~~21~~

~~21~~

All we have left is a 1 in the divisor, and a 9 in the dividend. We take the 9 from the quotient, multiply it with the 1 and then subtract that from the 9 in the dividend. This also goes to 0; therefore, 349 is the result of 7329 divided by 21.

This method seems confusing; however in the example above, the point to keep in mind is that since we are dividing by 21, each step requires the 21 to be placed under the number we are dividing into, and shifted one place to the right. At the same time, the number on top consists of the numbers not crossed out as read from left to right.

For our second example, we'll divide 72 into 38592. As mentioned above, we start by listing the numbers something like this:

38592 |

72

The number 7 will go into 38 five times so we place the 5 to the right of the bar, and then multiply 7 by 5 and subtract it from 38. This leaves 3. We cross out the 38, place the 3 above it, and then also cross out the 7 (to show that we are done with it). Our dividend now is 3592.

3

~~38~~592 | 5

~~7~~2

254

For the second part of this step we take 5 times 2 , which is 10, and subtract it from the first two digits of the dividend. This gives us 2592 as the current dividend. We cross out the 3 on top and place the 2 above it, and then we also cross out the 2 on the bottom (from the 72).

$$
\begin{array}{l}
2 \\
\cancel{3} \\
\cancel{38}592 \mid 5 \\
\cancel{72}
\end{array}
$$

Now, we repeat the process where our new dividend is 2592 (the dividend is always read left to right from the top numbers that aren't crossed out); and our divisor, 72, is placed below the dividend, and shifted to the right one place, like this:

$$
\begin{array}{l}
2 \\
\cancel{3} \\
\cancel{38}592 \mid 5 \\
\cancel{72} \\
\quad 72
\end{array}
$$

As we begin the next step, it looks like 7 will go into 25 three times, so we place the 3 after the 5 (which is on the right side of the bar), and then take 3 times 7 and subtract that from 25 (where 25 are the first two digits of the dividend), leaving a 4. We cross out the numbers that we used, and this leaves us with our new dividend of 492 (on top).

$$
\begin{array}{l}
\cancel{2} \\
\cancel{3}4 \\
\cancel{385}92 \mid 53 \\
\cancel{72} \\
\quad \cancel{72}
\end{array}
$$

To complete this step, we now multiply the 2 (from the divisor) and the 3 (from the quotient) to give us 6, which we subtract from the first two digits of the divisor (49). This gives us 43, so that the current dividend is now 432. Again, after crossing out the numbers that we just used, we are left with the following:

$$
\begin{array}{l}
\cancel{2} \\
\cancel{34}3 \\
\cancel{3859}2 \mid 53 \\
\cancel{72} \\
\quad \cancel{72}
\end{array}
$$

To begin the third step, we estimate how many times 7 will go into 43. It goes in six times, so we place a 6 after the 53 (in our quotient) and repeat the process one last time. We again place a 72 below the dividend, and shifted to the right one place. As we begin this step, our problem looks like this:

$$
\begin{array}{l}
\cancel{2} \\
\cancel{34}3 \\
\cancel{3859}2 \mid 536 \\
\cancel{72} \\
\quad \cancel{72} \\
\qquad 72
\end{array}
$$

We multiply 6 times 7, and subtract it from 43. This gives us a 1, so we place it above the 43, cross out the numbers we have just used, and we now have something that looks like this:

$$
\begin{array}{l}
\cancel{2}\ 1 \\
\cancel{343} \\
\cancel{38}5\cancel{9}2 \mid 536 \\
\cancel{72} \\
\quad\cancel{72} \\
\quad\ \cancel{72}
\end{array}
$$

The remaining dividend is 12. Fortunately, 6 times 2 is equal to 12 (the 6 is from the quotient, the 2 is from the divisor, and we subtract that from 12, the dividend). We cross out the remaining digits, and we have our solution. Had there been a remainder, the final value of the dividend would have been equal to the remainder.

$$
\begin{array}{l}
\cancel{2}\ \cancel{1} \\
\cancel{343} \\
\cancel{38592} \mid 536 \\
\cancel{72} \\
\quad\cancel{72} \\
\quad\ \cancel{72}
\end{array}
$$

We have just shown that 38592 divided by 72 is equal to 536 using the galley method of division. With a little practice this method can be easy to use, and from it we can readily see why it was used for centuries before our present method of division.

The Logarithmic Method of Division

Just as we are able to use logarithms to find the product of two numbers, we can also use logarithms to divide one number into another. This is done by first converting the two numbers into their corresponding log values; subtracting the second number from the first; and then converting the result back to its base 10 equivalent. When we divide two numbers, the divisor is divided into the dividend. When these numbers are converted to logs, it is the divisor that is subtracted from the dividend.

For example, if we divide 798 by 14, we begin by taking the log of each number. The log of 798 is 2.902003. The log of 14 is 1.146128. We subtract the second number from the first to get 1.755875. Finally, we convert this number back to base 10, and we get 57.

It is worth mentioning that the logarithms we used in the example above were in base 10, or we could say $\log_{10}$. It is possible to generate logarithms in any base; however, the two most common bases are $\log_{10}$ and $\log_{e}$. Logarithms written in base e are called natural logarithms and are more commonly written as ln.

Repeating the example above, the ln of 798 is 6.682109; and the ln of 14 is 2.639057. Subtracting the second from the first gives us 4.043051. And when we take the antilog of this number and convert it back to base 10 we again get 57.

The Newton-Raphson Method of Division
Just as we saw a Newton-Raphson method of finding square roots, there is also a Newton-Raphson method of division. Like the square root method, this method is iterative and has the advantage of only using multiplication and subtraction to zero in on the answer.

To understand this method, recall that a fraction has a numerator and a denominator where the denominator divides into the numerator. Anytime we divide one number into another, we can represent this division as a fraction. We usually only use integers in our fractions, but we could also use real numbers (numbers with a decimal point). These iterative methods use a fractional notation where the N represents the numerator, and the D represents the denominator, but the actual values will be real numbers, and not just integers.

The way this method works is that we are trying to find an equivalent decimal value for N/D. Notice that the N is our dividend, and the D is the divisor. Again, N can be any real number, and D can be any number as long as it isn't equal to 0. The formula that we use to perform this division is:

$$x_{n+1} = x_n (2 - D x_n)$$

After iterating through this equation several times, we essentially generate a value for x where x = 1/D. We then multiply N and x together, which is the same thing as N/D, and this is just another way of saying that our result is equal to N divided by D.

To show how this works, let's divide 82 by 13; or in other words, let's find the decimal value of 82/13. Therefore, our N will be equal to 82, and our D is 13. We start by first finding a decimal value for our denominator. We ultimately want x to be equal to 1/13, but since we don't know yet what the decimal value of 1/13 is equal to, we will make an initial guess of 0.1. Therefore, we plug this value in for x_0 to give us the following as our initial equation:

$$x_1 = x_0 (2 - D x_0)$$
$$x_1 = 0.1 (2 - 13(0.1))$$
$$x_1 = 0.07$$

The number 0.07 is our new value for x that we plug back into the right side of the equation. Our second time through gives us:

$$x_2 = x_1 (2 - D x_1)$$
$$x_2 = 0.07 (2 - 13(0.07))$$
$$x_2 = 0.0763$$

Now we have the number 0.0763 as our next value for x. Plugging that into the right side of the equation gives us the following for the third time through:

$$x_3 = x_2 (2 - D x_2)$$
$$x_3 = 0.0763 (2 - 13(0.0763))$$
$$x_3 = 0.07691803$$

Each iteration brings the value of x closer to the actual value of 1/13. Our original problem was to find the value of 82 divided by 13 (which is the same as 82/13). Since x is (or will be) equal to 1/13, we simply have to multiply our x by 82, and we will have a decimal equivalent for 82 divided by 13. With what we have so far:

$$x_3 * N = 0.07691803*82$$
$$= 6.30727846$$

Which is very close to the answer I get with my calculator:

$$6.30769231$$

And if I were to go through a few more "denominator" iterations before multiplying my x value to the numerator, my answer would be just as accurate as the one I get with my calculator.

If you were to write a computer program that divides one number by another, the method outlined above is much easier to put into practice than trying to devise a method that follows the traditional method that we saw earlier in this chapter. However, the method we will look at next is even easier to put into a computer program.

The Goldschmidt Method of Division

This method is also an iterative method; however, it operates on both the numerator and the denominator at the same time. The difference with this method is that as the iterations proceed, the denominator will approach one while the numerator approaches the decimal value of N/D. This method iterates through the following three formulas:

$$N_{i+1} = R_i * N_i$$
$$D_{i+1} = R_i * D_i$$
$$R_{i+1} = 2 - D_{i+1}$$

Let's look at an example to see how this method works. As in the previous example, let's find the value of 82/13. In this example, N is equal to 82, D is equal to 13, and R will be our initial guess, which we will set at 0.1. The first time through gives us these values:

$$N_1 = 0.1 * 82 = 8.2$$
$$D_1 = 0.1 * 13 = 1.3$$
$$R_1 = 2 - 1.3 = 0.7$$

The next time through gives us these values:

$$N_2 = 0.7 * 8.2 = 5.74$$
$$D_2 = 0.7 * 1.3 = 0.91$$
$$R_2 = 2 - 0.91 = 1.09$$

Our third time through gives us the following:

$$N_3 = 1.09 * 5.74 = 6.2566$$
$$D_3 = 1.09 * 0.91 = 0.9919$$
$$R_3 = 2 - 0.9919 = 1.0081$$

A few more iterations produces a value for N that is very close to the actual value of 82/13. Notice also that as N gets closer to the final result, D and R both get closer to one. In fact, how close D and R are to one is an indicator of how close N is to the actual value.

A Goldschmidt Variation

The Goldschmidt method is also very easy to incorporate into a computer program; and it converges very quickly to a very accurate answer. However, there are universities and other institutions that are trying to improve this method further still. One variation iterates through the following three formulas:

$$N_{i+1} = N_i + R_i * N_i$$
$$D_{i+1} = D_i + R_i * D_i$$
$$R_{i+1} = 1 - D_{i+1}$$

These equations are set up the same as they were in the original Goldschmidt method (with N equal to the numerator, D equal to the denominator, and R equal to our initial guess at D). As we go through this method, it looks like it has a few more steps within each iteration, and it does, but it also has an important advantage. In this variation, the R value goes to zero instead of going to one. In some instances, this allows N to converge in fewer iterations to the final answer. (Note that this method still has D converging to a value of one.)

The Goldschmidt method (or one of its variations) is in fact the method that many computer programs use to divide one number by another. It is so easy to use, and it converges to an accurate answer so quickly, that it is often incorporated into the hardware part of a computer processor (instead of being done through a software process).

Dividing by 11

At the beginning of this chapter we discussed a method of determining whether a number is divisible by 11. Now, we'll end this chapter by looking at an easy way to divide any number by 11. Of course the easiest way to see how this method works is to use an example. We'll look at a couple. Let's start by dividing 25429 by 11. First, write down the number, and then take the leading number (which is 2) place it below the second digit (which is 5), and subtract. Then we'll place the result of that subtraction to the right of the 2.

```
    25429        (the leading number is placed below the 5,
    23           (subtract, and the result is placed below the 4)
```

Next, we subtract the 3 from the 4, and place that result to the right of the 3:

```
    25429        (the 3 is subtracted from the 4, and the
    231          (result is placed below the 2)
```

We repeat the procedure and subtract the 1 from the 2, and place its result to the right of the 1. We now perform our final subtraction by subtracting the second 1 from the 9. This gives us an 8, which is our remainder.

```
    25429        (the 1 is subtracted from the 2, and the
    2311  r. 8   (result is placed below the 9 and subtracted)
```

In other words, 25429 divided by 11 is equal to 2311 and 8/11.

That was nice, but sometimes the division doesn't always work out that easily. This time we'll divide 19385 by 11. Again, we write the number, and start by placing the leading 1 under the 9, and subtracting. The 8 is then placed next to the 1 to give us:

$$19385$$
$$18$$

It is at this point that we have a problem. We cannot subtract 8 from 3 without getting a negative number, so we must back up and make a change. We will take the 9 and change it to an 8, and then add a 10 to the 3. We'll rewrite our original number so that it now looks like this:

$$18^1385 \qquad \text{(instead of 19385)}$$

Now, we'll start again by placing the leading 1 under the 8, and subtracting. The 7 is now placed under the 13:

$$18^1385$$
$$17$$

We continue by subtracting the 7 from 13, and place that result under the second 8.

$$18^1385$$
$$17\ 6$$

We finish by subtracting the 6 from the 8, and placing that result under the 5. The final subtraction is then performed with a 3 left over.

$$18^1385$$
$$1762 \quad r.\ 3$$

And here we have shown that 19385 divided by 11 is equal to 1762 and 3/11.

In an earlier chapter we saw a quick and easy method of multiplying a number by 11. This method of dividing by 11 is basically a reverse algorithm of that earlier method of multiplying by 11. We can easily see this with another example. First, let's find the product of 11 times 24713. Our earlier method of multiplication showed that this product is equal to:

Or:

$$2 \quad (2+4) \quad (4+7) \quad (7+1) \quad (1+3) \quad 3$$

$$2 \quad 6 \quad 11 \quad 8 \quad 4 \quad 3$$

And reading from right to left (so we can appropriately handle any carries), this becomes:

$$2 \quad 6^{+1} \quad 1 \quad 8 \quad 4 \quad 3$$

Which gives us 271843 as the product of 11 and 24713.

Now, going backward, we perform subtractions (instead of additions) in order to divide 271843 by 11. And instead of going from right to left, this time we work from left to right, and each time we take the result from the previous subtraction, and subtract it from the number to the right:

2	write the leading 2
$(7-2)$	which is equal to 5
$(1-5)$	which doesn't work, so we back up

When we get a negative number during a subtraction, we must back up a step, and perform a reverse carry; therefore, the number 271843 is now 26 ^{1}1843, and the division goes like this:

2	write the leading 2
(6 – 2)	which is equal to 4
(11 – 4)	which is equal to 7
(8 – 7)	which is equal to 1
(4 – 1)	which is equal to 3

And the result is 24713; which indeed is what we get when we divide 271843 by 11.

Dividing by Zero

As we've seen in many of the methods in this chapter, the concept of division (the act of dividing one number into another) can be thought of in two different ways: It can be considered as the inverse of multiplication, or it can be considered as a count of the number of subtractions.

When looking at division as the inverse of multiplication, we could, for example say that finding what number is equal to 8 divided by 2 is essentially the same as saying what number multiplied by 2 will give us 8; or likewise, finding what number is equal to 21 divided by 7 is the same as saying what number multiplied by 7 will give us 21?

$$8/2 = ? \quad \text{is the same as} \quad 2(?) = 8$$
$$21/7 = ? \quad \text{is the same as} \quad 7(?) = 21$$

So now, when we take 8 and divide it by 0, we could also say what number multiplied with 0 will give us 8?

$$8/0 = ? \quad \text{is the same as} \quad 0(?) = 8$$

There isn't a number that we can multiply to 0 that will give us 8, and that is one reason why division by 0 is undefined.

Now, consider division as a series of subtractions. Eight divided by 2 is the same as subtracting 2 from 8, and counting how many times we do it. I can subtract 2 from 8 four times, and therefore, 8 divided by 2 is equal to 4. Likewise, 21 divided by 7 is the same as subtracting 7 from 21 and counting how many times I can do it. In this case, I can subtract 7 from 21 three times and therefore, 21 divided by 7 is equal to 3.

8	21
– 2	– 7
– 2	– 7
– 2	– 7
– 2	0
0	

Four 2's can be subtracted from 8,   and three 7's can be subtracted from 21.

Now, using this reasoning, let's divide 21 by 0. How many times can I subtract 0 from 21? I can do it an infinite amount of times, and still keep going. Here again we see another perspective of why anything divided by 0 is undefined.

Chapter 17
Prime Number Tables

What is a prime number? A prime number is any number that has no factors other than the number 1 and itself. The numbers 2, 3 and 5 are examples of prime numbers. Numbers that are divisible by other numbers are called composite numbers. Examples of composite numbers include 10, 12 and 15.

A Pattern Within the Primes

In 1963, during a scientific meeting that apparently wasn't very interesting, Stanislaw Ulam was doodling on some paper when he started to write numbers in a spiral pattern. He noticed that many prime numbers appeared to align along the diagonals. The pattern he generated looked something like this:

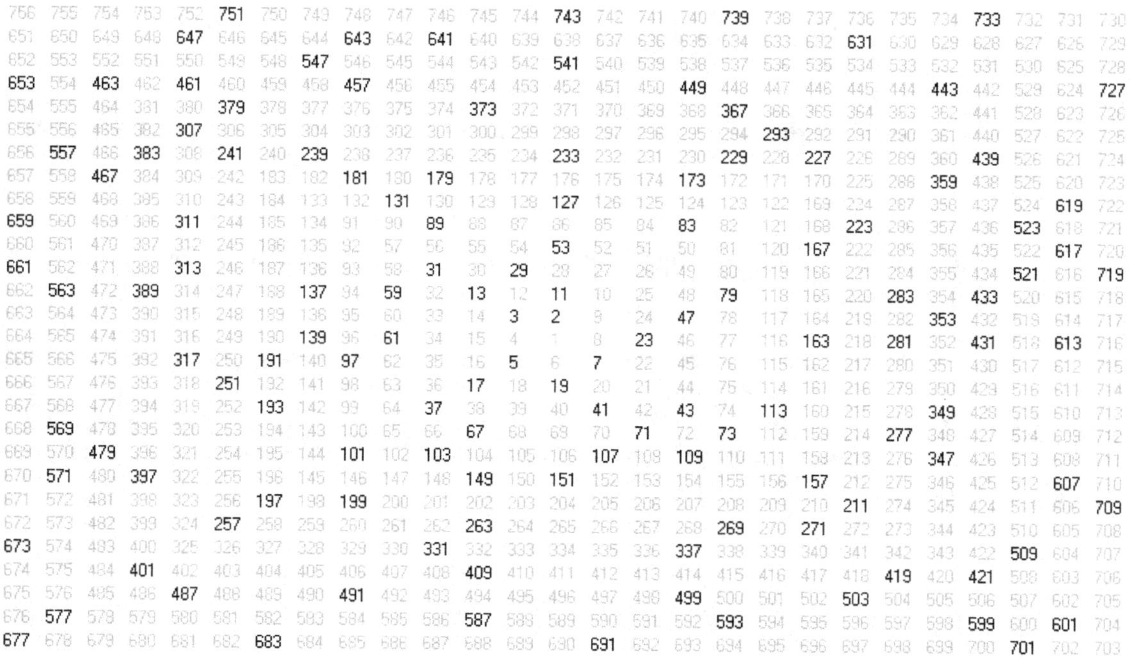

```
756 755 754 753 752 751 750 749 748 747 746 745 744 743 742 741 740 739 738 737 736 735 734 733 732 731 730
651 650 649 648 647 646 645 644 643 642 641 640 639 638 637 636 635 634 633 632 631 630 629 628 627 626 729
652 553 552 551 550 549 548 547 546 545 544 543 542 541 540 539 538 537 536 535 534 533 532 531 530 625 728
653 554 463 462 461 460 459 458 457 456 455 454 453 452 451 450 449 448 447 446 445 444 443 442 529 624 727
654 555 464 381 380 379 378 377 376 375 374 373 372 371 370 369 368 367 366 365 364 363 362 441 528 623 726
655 556 465 382 307 306 305 304 303 302 301 300 299 298 297 296 295 294 293 292 291 290 361 440 527 622 725
656 557 466 383 308 241 240 239 238 237 236 235 234 233 232 231 230 229 228 227 226 289 360 439 526 621 724
657 558 467 384 309 242 183 182 181 180 179 178 177 176 175 174 173 172 171 170 225 288 359 438 525 620 723
658 559 468 385 310 243 184 133 132 131 130 129 128 127 126 125 124 123 122 169 224 287 358 437 524 619 722
659 560 469 386 311 244 185 134  91  90  89  88  87  86  85  84  83  82 121 168 223 286 357 436 523 618 721
660 561 470 387 312 245 186 135  92  57  56  55  54  53  52  51  50  81 120 167 222 285 356 435 522 617 720
661 562 471 388 313 246 187 136  93  58  31  30  29  28  27  26  49  80 119 166 221 284 355 434 521 616 719
662 563 472 389 314 247 188 137  94  59  32  13  12  11  10  25  48  79 118 165 220 283 354 433 520 615 718
663 564 473 390 315 248 189 138  95  60  33  14   3   2   9  24  47  78 117 164 219 282 353 432 519 614 717
664 565 474 391 316 249 190 139  96  61  34  15   4   1   8  23  46  77 116 163 218 281 352 431 518 613 716
665 566 475 392 317 250 191 140  97  62  35  16   5   6   7  22  45  76 115 162 217 280 351 430 517 612 715
666 567 476 393 318 251 192 141  98  63  36  17  18  19  20  21  44  75 114 161 216 279 350 429 516 611 714
667 568 477 394 319 252 193 142  99  64  37  38  39  40  41  42  43  74 113 160 215 278 349 428 515 610 713
668 569 478 395 320 253 194 143 100  65  66  67  68  69  70  71  72  73 112 159 214 277 348 427 514 609 712
669 570 479 396 321 254 195 144 101 102 103 104 105 106 107 108 109 110 111 158 213 276 347 426 513 608 711
670 571 480 397 322 255 196 145 146 147 148 149 150 151 152 153 154 155 156 157 212 275 346 425 512 607 710
671 572 481 398 323 256 197 198 199 200 201 202 203 204 205 206 207 208 209 210 211 274 345 424 511 606 709
672 573 482 399 324 257 258 259 260 261 262 263 264 265 266 267 268 269 270 271 272 273 344 423 510 605 708
673 574 483 400 325 326 327 328 329 330 331 332 333 334 335 336 337 338 339 340 341 342 343 422 509 604 707
674 575 484 401 402 403 404 405 406 407 408 409 410 411 412 413 414 415 416 417 418 419 420 421 508 603 706
675 576 485 486 487 488 489 490 491 492 493 494 495 496 497 498 499 500 501 502 503 504 505 506 507 602 705
676 577 578 579 580 581 582 583 584 585 586 587 588 589 590 591 592 593 594 595 596 597 598 599 600 601 704
677 678 679 680 681 682 683 684 685 686 687 688 689 690 691 692 693 694 695 696 697 698 699 700 701 702 703
```

Figure 17.1   A spiral pattern of prime numbers with the number 1 in the center.

In the figure above, the prime numbers are in black, while composite numbers are in gray. We can also create the same pattern with the help of a computer. Starting with the number 1 in the center, this is the pattern of primes we get when we look at the first 50,625 numbers (each black dot represents a prime number).

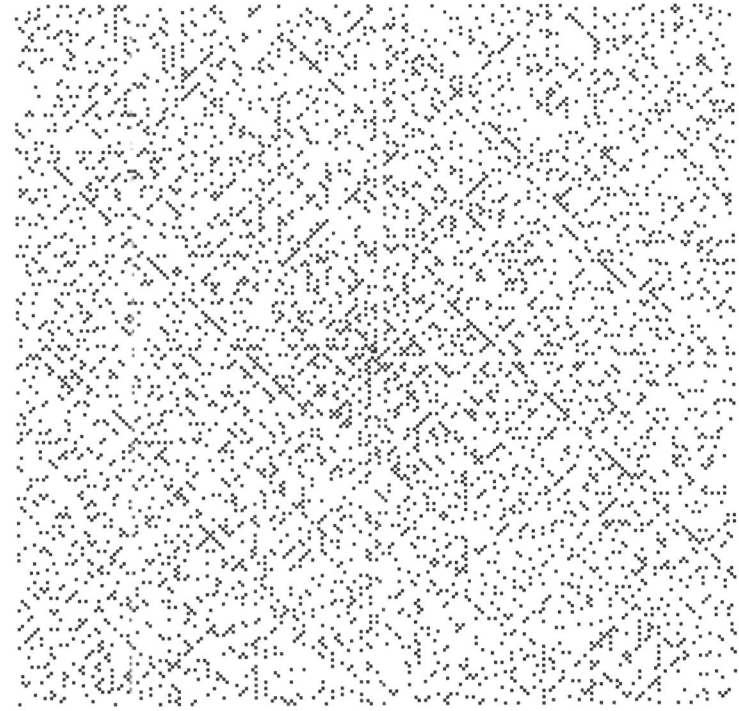

Figure 17.2   A spiral pattern of prime numbers with the number 1 in the center.

This pattern becomes even more interesting when we start with other numbers as the center number. For example, the following figure starts with the number 41 in the center.

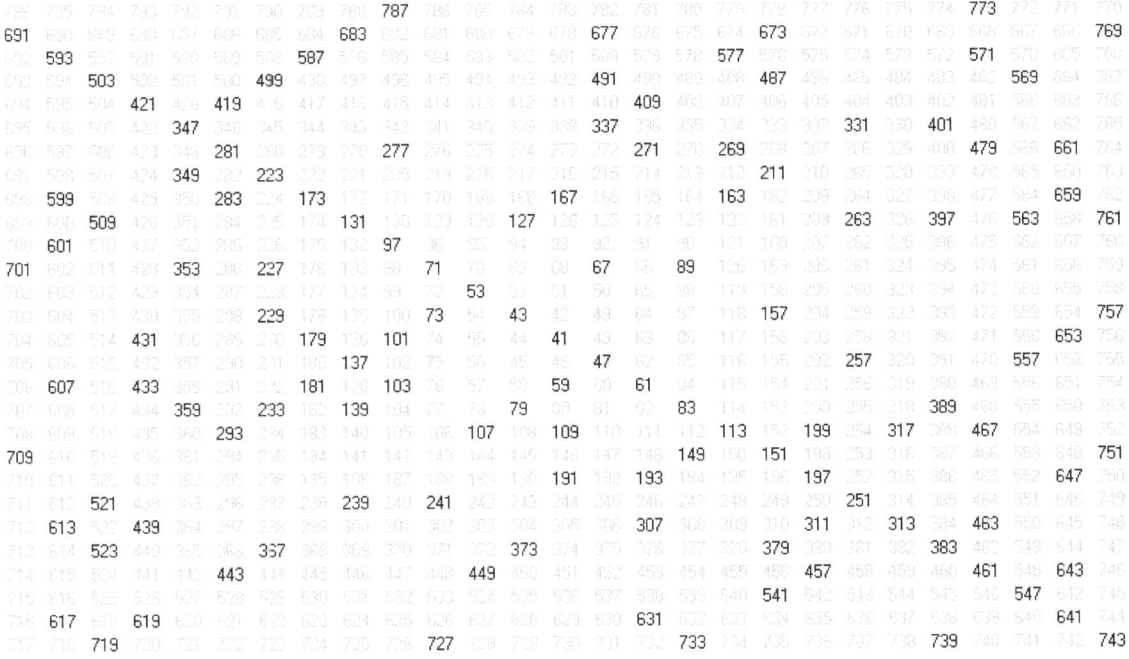

Figure 17.3   A spiral pattern of prime numbers with the number 41 in the center.

The figure becomes more impressive when we again let black dots represent prime numbers. Here is the figure from above showing some 50,000 numbers, with 41 as the initial number in the center.

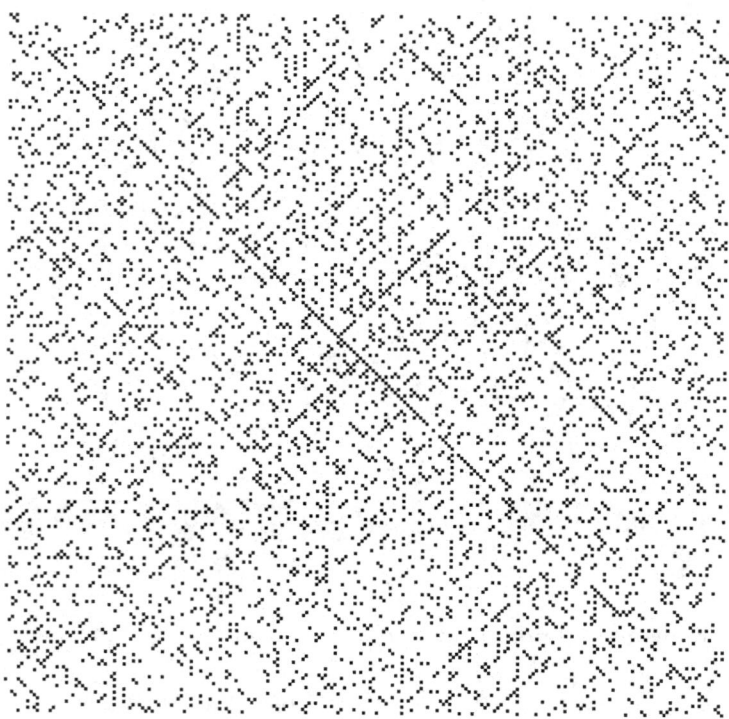

Figure 17.4   A spiral pattern of prime numbers with 41 as the number in the center.

The first feature in this figure that catches most people's attention is the diagonal of prime numbers stretching from the upper-left corner to the lower-right corner. This diagonal can be described by the following equation:

$$\text{numbers along the diagonal} \;=\; x^2 + x + 41$$

We can easily see that if we let x equal 0, the first prime we get is 41. Letting x equal 1 gives us 43. With x equal to 2 we get 47. In fact, entering any number from 0 to 39 will give us a prime number; and as can be seen above, entering many numbers above 39 into this equation will also yield a prime number.

Prime numbers, considered individually, are a set of pattern-less numbers. There are no single or simple sets of rules that will allow us to determine whether some given number is a prime or not. In spite of this, prime numbers considered as a whole still have many interesting properties. We'll look at one of them a little later in this chapter; but before we do that, let's look at some methods of finding prime numbers.

The Sieve of Eratosthenes

The oldest known method of finding prime numbers uses a process of elimination to determine if a number is prime. This method is known as the sieve of Eratosthenes, and like a sieve, it filters out all the composite numbers so that the remaining numbers are prime numbers. To create this sieve, we start with a list of numbers that begin with the number one, and extends however high we want to go. First, we cross out the number one (since by definition it isn't considered a prime number). The next number that isn't crossed out is the number 2. It is a prime, and in fact, it is the first prime number, and the only even prime. Now cross out all of the multiples of 2 that are greater than 2. In other words, starting with the number 4, all of the remaining even numbers are crossed out.

The next number that isn't crossed out is 3. This is our next prime number. From here, cross out all the multiples of 3 that are greater than three (and that haven't already been crossed out). The next number that hasn't been crossed out is 5. Again, this is our next prime number, and we continue by crossing out all the multiples of 5 greater than 5. We continue by leaving the next number uncrossed out, and crossing out all of the multiples of that number until we've gone through the list. The numbers that remain are prime numbers.

~~1~~ 2 3 ~~4~~ 5 ~~6~~ 7 ~~8~~ ~~9~~ ~~10~~ 11 ~~12~~ 13 ~~14~~ ~~15~~ ~~16~~ 17 ~~18~~ 19 ~~20~~
~~21~~ ~~22~~ 23 ~~24~~ ~~25~~ ~~26~~ ~~27~~ ~~28~~ 29 ~~30~~ 31 ~~32~~ ~~33~~ ~~34~~ ~~35~~ ~~36~~ 37 ~~38~~ ~~39~~ ~~40~~
41 ~~42~~ 43 ~~44~~ ~~45~~ ~~46~~ 47 ~~48~~ ~~49~~ ~~50~~ ~~51~~ ~~52~~ 53 ~~54~~ ~~55~~ ~~56~~ ~~57~~ ~~58~~ 59 ~~60~~
61 ~~62~~ ~~63~~ ~~64~~ ~~65~~ ~~66~~ 67 ~~68~~ ~~69~~ ~~70~~ 71 ~~72~~ 73 ~~74~~ ~~75~~ ~~76~~ ~~77~~ ~~78~~ 79 ~~80~~
~~81~~ ~~82~~ 83 ~~84~~ ~~85~~ ~~86~~ ~~87~~ ~~88~~ 89 ~~90~~ ~~91~~ ~~92~~ ~~93~~ ~~94~~ ~~95~~ ~~96~~ 97 ~~98~~ ~~99~~ ~~100~~

Table 17.1   The Sieve of Eratosthenes.

In the table above, using the Sieve of Eratosthenes, we found these primes: 2, 3, 5, 7, 11, 13, 17, 19, 23, 29, 31, 37, 41, 43, 47, 53, 59, 61, 67, 71, 73, 79, 83, 89, and 97. This method works very well, but it is impractical if we are trying to find whether a very large number is prime or not.

The Visual Sieve

The visual sieve is a graphic example of the sieve of Eratosthenes. With this method we start by plotting the equation $x = y^2$. (This is a parabola that opens up to the right.) Next, we label the integer points on the plot. The point (1, 1) is 1 and (1, -1) is -1; the point (4, 2) is 2 and (4, -2) is -2; the point (9, 3) is 3 and (9, -3) is -3, and so on. Note that these points are on the parabola. We also need to label the integer points along the x-axis. The point (1, 0) is 1, the point (2, 0) is 2, the point (3, 0) is 3, etc.

Now we draw lines. Starting from the 2 on the parabola, we draw lines to the -2, -3, -4, etc. on the opposite side of the parabola. We then go to the 3 on the parabola and draw lines to the -3, -4, -5, etc. on the opposite side of the parabola. As we draw these lines, they cross the x-axis at the absolute value of the product of the two numbers. In other words, the line from the 2 to the -3 crosses the x-axis at the 6. The line from the 2 to the -4 crosses the x-axis at the 8. If we extend this plot out infinitely, then the lines will cross the x axis on every composite number leaving the prime numbers without a line going through them. In theory, the prime numbers can readily be found using this method; however, in reality, the plot is quickly covered with lines that are very close to each other, making it difficult to see which numbers have lines over them, and which do not.

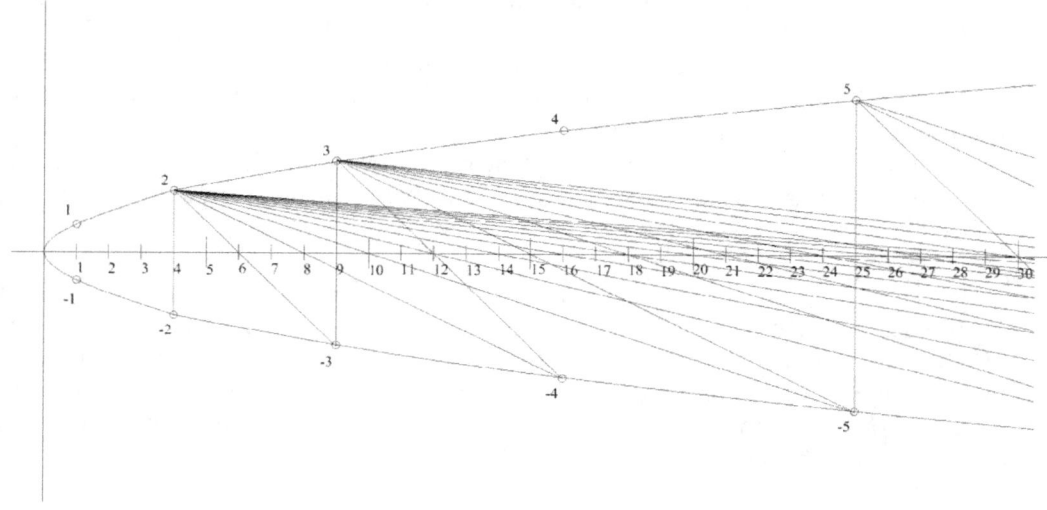

Figure 17.5   The visual sieve of finding prime numbers.

In the figure above we can easily see that the numbers 2, 3, 5, 7, 11, and 13 are prime; but it becomes much more difficult to see that 17, 19, 23 and 29 are prime numbers. We can reduce the number of lines on the plot by only drawing lines from the prime numbers on the top of the parabola to all of the numbers on the bottom of the parabola. (Which is what we did in the figure above, but it only helps a little.) This method is also very impractical for finding whether a larger number is prime or not, but it is a nice visual representation of the sieve of Eratosthenes.

The Sundaram Sieve

A third method of filtering out composite numbers is the Sundaram Sieve. This method starts by building a table of numbers where the first row starts with the number 4 and then increments each additional number by three.

$$4, \quad 7, \quad 10, \quad 13, \quad 16, \quad 19, \quad 22, \quad 25, \quad \ldots$$

The second row starts with the number 7 and increments each additional number by five.

$$7, \quad 12, \quad 17, \quad 22, \quad 27, \quad 32, \quad 37, \quad 42, \quad \ldots$$

The third row starts with the number 10 and increments each additional number by seven.

$$10, \quad 17, \quad 24, \quad 31, \quad 38, \quad 45, \quad 52, \quad 59, \quad \ldots$$

The pattern for this table should now start to become apparent. The first number of the nth row is the same as the nth number of the first row. And each succeeding number in that row increments by a value of $2n + 1$ (where n is the row number), such that the first row is incremented by 3, the second row by 5, the third row by 7, and so on. Putting it all together, our table looks something like this:

266

```
 4,   7,  10,  13,  16,  19,  22,  25, ...
 7,  12,  17,  22,  27,  32,  37,  42, ...
10,  17,  24,  31,  38,  45,  52,  59, ...
13,  22,  31,  40,  49,  58,  67,  76, ...
16,  27,  38,  49,  60,  71,  82,  93, ...
19,  32,  45,  58,  71,  84,  97, 110, ...
...
```

Table 17.2   Construction numbers for the Sundaram Sieve.

The first row is made up of the same numbers as the first column; the second row is the same as the second column, etc. In other words, the table is diagonally symmetrical with itself. Notice also that the smaller numbers are in the upper left corner, and the numbers increase in value as we move to the right and down.

Now we use this table to indirectly find prime numbers. We simply take a number not in the table above, multiply it by two, and add one, and we have a prime number. For example, the number 5 is not in the table above. So we take 5, multiply it by two and add one, and we get 11, which is a prime number. Another number that isn't in the table is 18; so we take 18, double it and add one, to get 37, which is another prime number.

If we use this same formula on numbers in the table, we'll find that we get a number that isn't prime. The number 22 is in the table. If we double 22 and add one we get 45, which isn't prime.

This method appears tedious but it has the potential of providing a practical way of checking whether a large number is a prime or not. We simply take the number in question, subtract one and divide it by two. If the resulting number can be found within the table above, then the original number isn't prime; otherwise, it is. While this method works for many primes, it hasn't been proven to work for all primes.

Varying the Widths of Prime Number Tables

In the sieve of Eratosthenes example we built a table of prime numbers that was 20 columns wide. In this section, we will look at tables of prime numbers and how their patterns change when the width of the table varies. As we look at each table, we'll notice that the prime numbers only find themselves within certain columns. Then as we vary the number of columns in our table, the columns that contain prime numbers will also vary. In most cases the primes will only be in a limited number of columns. Let's see how this works.

We'll start by making our table 6 columns wide (see the table below). Except for the first row, only the first and fifth columns have prime numbers in them while the second, third, fourth and sixth columns don't have any primes in them. (The first row of the table has exceptions and will always contain exceptions as we look at various table widths. In this case, the numbers 2 and 3 are the exceptions.)

To help see the columns that have primes and the ones that don't, we will show the pattern by placing X's and spaces below the table. Where there is a column with primes in it, we will place an X under that column; and where there is a column with no primes, we will place an underline there. A table that is six columns wide has a pattern that looks like this: " X __ __ __ X __ ".

Notice that the last column is made of multiples of the width of the column. In other words, within a table that is six columns wide, the numbers in the sixth column are the multiples of six (6, 12, 18, 24, etc.). We know that there will never be a prime in this column. Therefore, if we remove this column from our pattern, we find that our pattern is symmetrical and that it now looks like this: " X __ __ __ X ".

```
 1   2   3   4   5   6
 7   8   9  10  11  12
13  14  15  16  17  18
19  20  21  22  23  24
25  26  27  28  29  30
31  32  33  34  35  36
37  38  39  40  41  42
43  44  45  46  47  48
49  50  51  52  53  54
55  56  57  58  59  60
```

Pattern: X __ __ __ X

Table 17.3   Table of prime numbers that is 6 columns wide.

Again, keep in mind that the exceptions to this pattern are found on the first row, and for this reason, we are not considering the first row of numbers when we look for the pattern. In this example, the numbers under the 2 are all even numbers, and the numbers under the 3 are all multiples of three. There are no other primes in either of these columns. Likewise, as we look at other table widths, we will see other columns that have prime numbers in the first row and then never have another prime number within that column. Therefore, as we consider these patterns, the first row of the table will not be included when determining the overall pattern.

The next table we'll consider is 8 columns wide. Notice that this table has primes in the first, third, fifth and seventh columns, and if we exclude the last column, the pattern again is also symmetrical.

```
 1   2   3   4   5   6   7   8
 9  10  11  12  13  14  15  16
17  18  19  20  21  22  23  24
25  26  27  28  29  30  31  32
33  34  35  36  37  38  39  40
41  42  43  44  45  46  47  48
49  50  51  52  53  54  55  56
57  58  59  60  61  62  63  64
65  66  67  68  69  70  71  72
73  74  75  76  77  78  79  80
81  82  83  84  85  86  87  88
89  90  91  92  93  94  95  96
```

Pattern: X __ X __ X __ X

Table 17.4   Table of prime numbers that is 8 columns wide.

The next table is 10 columns wide and it also has only four columns of primes. They are in the first, third, seventh and ninth columns. And again, excluding the last column that consists of multiples of 10, we have a symmetrical pattern.

```
 1   2   3   4   5   6   7   8   9  10
11  12  13  14  15  16  17  18  19  20
21  22  23  24  25  26  27  28  29  30
31  32  33  34  35  36  37  38  39  40
41  42  43  44  45  46  47  48  49  50
51  52  53  54  55  56  57  58  59  60
61  62  63  64  65  66  67  68  69  70
71  72  73  74  75  76  77  78  79  80
81  82  83  84  85  86  87  88  89  90
91  92  93  94  95  96  97  98  99 100
```

Pattern: X __ X __ __ __ X __ X

Table 17.5   Table of prime numbers that is 10 columns wide.

You may have noticed that we are only considering tables with an even number of columns. If we consider tables with a prime number of columns, the primes fall under every column except the last column. (The last column will always contain numbers that are multiples of the width of the column.) And in fact, when we do have tables that have a prime number of columns, the primes appear to be arranged along diagonals. We'll briefly look at these types of tables toward the end of this chapter.

If our table is twelve columns wide, we once again have four columns with primes in them. They are the first, fifth, seventh and eleventh columns. Notice again the symmetry of our pattern.

```
 1   2   3   4   5   6   7   8   9  10  11  12
13  14  15  16  17  18  19  20  21  22  23  24
25  26  27  28  29  30  31  32  33  34  35  36
37  38  39  40  41  42  43  44  45  46  47  48
49  50  51  52  53  54  55  56  57  58  59  60
61  62  63  64  65  66  67  68  69  70  71  72
73  74  75  76  77  78  79  80  81  82  83  84
85  86  87  88  89  90  91  92  93  94  95  96
```

Pattern: X __ __ __ X __ X __ __ __ X

Table 17.6   Table of prime numbers that is 12 columns wide.

Again, keep in mind that we are not considering the primes on the first row as we determine the prime columns. In this last example, the numbers two and three are prime numbers; however, there are no other prime numbers that appear within their columns.

Let's look at a few more tables, and then we'll compile these patterns together. The next table is 14 columns wide, and in this next table there are six columns of primes and they are in the first, third, fifth, ninth, eleventh and thirteenth columns.

~~1~~ 2 3 ~~4~~ 5 ~~6~~ 7 ~~8~~ 9 ~~10~~ 11 ~~12~~ 13 ~~14~~
~~15~~ ~~16~~ 17 ~~18~~ 19 ~~20~~ ~~21~~ ~~22~~ 23 ~~24~~ ~~25~~ ~~26~~ ~~27~~ ~~28~~
29 ~~30~~ 31 ~~32~~ ~~33~~ ~~34~~ ~~35~~ 36 37 ~~38~~ ~~39~~ ~~40~~ 41 ~~42~~
43 ~~44~~ ~~45~~ ~~46~~ 47 ~~48~~ ~~49~~ ~~50~~ ~~51~~ ~~52~~ 53 ~~54~~ ~~55~~ ~~56~~
~~57~~ ~~58~~ 59 ~~60~~ 61 ~~62~~ ~~63~~ ~~64~~ ~~65~~ ~~66~~ 67 ~~68~~ ~~69~~ ~~70~~
71 ~~72~~ 73 ~~74~~ ~~75~~ ~~76~~ ~~77~~ ~~78~~ 79 ~~80~~ ~~81~~ ~~82~~ 83 ~~84~~
~~85~~ ~~86~~ ~~87~~ ~~88~~ 89 ~~90~~ ~~91~~ ~~92~~ ~~93~~ ~~94~~ ~~95~~ ~~96~~ 97 ~~98~~

Pattern: X __ X __ X __ __ __ X __ X __ X

Table 17.7   Table of prime numbers that is 14 columns wide.

With the table 16 columns wide, we find that every other column has primes in it. The last time that we had a table where every other column was a prime is when there were eight columns in the table. The next time it happens is when the table has 32 columns; and then it happens again when the table is 64 columns wide (a very interesting pattern of patterns). Here is the table and pattern with 16 columns:

~~1~~ 2 3 4 5 ~~6~~ 7 ~~8~~ 9 ~~10~~ 11 ~~12~~ 13 ~~14~~ ~~15~~ ~~16~~
17 ~~18~~ 19 ~~20~~ ~~21~~ ~~22~~ 23 ~~24~~ ~~25~~ ~~26~~ ~~27~~ ~~28~~ 29 ~~30~~ 31 ~~32~~
~~33~~ ~~34~~ ~~35~~ ~~36~~ 37 ~~38~~ ~~39~~ ~~40~~ 41 ~~42~~ 43 ~~44~~ ~~45~~ ~~46~~ 47 ~~48~~
~~49~~ ~~50~~ ~~51~~ ~~52~~ 53 ~~54~~ ~~55~~ ~~56~~ ~~57~~ ~~58~~ 59 ~~60~~ 61 ~~62~~ ~~63~~ ~~64~~
~~65~~ ~~66~~ 67 ~~68~~ ~~69~~ ~~70~~ 71 ~~72~~ 73 ~~74~~ ~~75~~ ~~76~~ ~~77~~ ~~78~~ 79 ~~80~~
~~81~~ ~~82~~ 83 ~~84~~ ~~85~~ ~~86~~ ~~87~~ ~~88~~ 89 ~~90~~ ~~91~~ ~~92~~ ~~93~~ ~~94~~ ~~95~~ ~~96~~

Pattern: X __ X __ X __ X __ X __ X __ X __ X

Table 17.8   Table of prime numbers that is 16 columns wide.

The previous table had eight columns of prime numbers. With the table 18 columns wide we find again that it only has six columns with prime numbers in them.

~~1~~ 2 3 ~~4~~ 5 ~~6~~ 7 ~~8~~ ~~9~~ ~~10~~ 11 ~~12~~ 13 ~~14~~ ~~15~~ ~~16~~ 17 ~~18~~
19 ~~20~~ ~~21~~ ~~22~~ 23 ~~24~~ ~~25~~ ~~26~~ ~~27~~ ~~28~~ 29 ~~30~~ 31 ~~32~~ ~~33~~ ~~34~~ ~~35~~ ~~36~~
37 ~~38~~ ~~39~~ ~~40~~ 41 ~~42~~ 43 ~~44~~ ~~45~~ ~~46~~ 47 ~~48~~ ~~49~~ ~~50~~ ~~51~~ ~~52~~ 53 ~~54~~
~~55~~ ~~56~~ ~~57~~ ~~58~~ 59 ~~60~~ 61 ~~62~~ ~~63~~ ~~64~~ ~~65~~ ~~66~~ 67 ~~68~~ ~~69~~ ~~70~~ 71 ~~72~~
73 ~~74~~ ~~75~~ ~~76~~ ~~77~~ ~~78~~ 79 ~~80~~ ~~81~~ ~~82~~ 83 ~~84~~ ~~85~~ ~~86~~ ~~87~~ ~~88~~ 89 ~~90~~

Pattern: X __ __ __ X __ X __ __ __ X __ X __ __ __ X

Table 17.9   Table of prime numbers that is 18 columns wide.

Now that we have a good idea of what is going on, we can compile the patterns of several of these tables together. In the diagram below, we have the patterns for the even table widths as they vary from six columns to 30 columns.

```
X _ _ _ X
X _ X _ X _ X
X _ X _ _ _ X _ X
X _ _ _ X _ X _ _ _ X
X _ X _ X _ _ _ _ _ X _ X _ X
X _ X _ X _ X _ X _ X _ X _ X _ X
X _ _ _ X _ X _ _ _ X _ X _ _ _ _ _ X
X _ X _ _ _ X _ X _ X _ X _ _ _ X _ X
X _ X _ X _ X _ X _ _ _ X _ X _ X _ X _ X
X _ _ _ X _ X _ _ _ X _ X _ _ _ X _ _ _ _ _ X
X _ X _ X _ X _ X _ X _ _ _ X _ X _ X _ X _ X _ X
X _ X _ X _ _ _ X _ X _ X _ X _ X _ X _ _ _ X _ X _ X
X _ _ _ _ _ X _ _ _ X _ X _ _ _ X _ X _ _ _ X _ _ _ _ _ X
```

Table 17.10   Left-justified column patterns from prime tables that range from 6 columns wide through 30 columns wide.

Another way to look at the patterns above would be to represent each "X" with a black square, and each "_" with a white square. Such a representation would allow us to include more rows in the limited space we have, and thus allow us to see other patterns within this tabular listing.

Table 17.11   Left-justified even numbered column patterns from prime tables ranging from 6 columns wide through 100 columns wide.

With the rows left-justified, we see interesting patterns in the table above; however, due to the increasing width of each row it also makes sense to center-align the rows. This is the pattern we get when we do that:

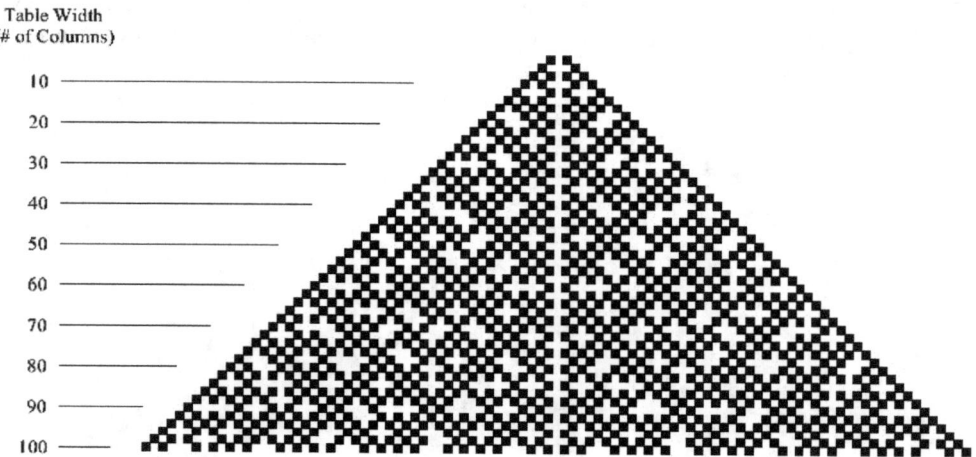

Table 17.12   Center-aligned even numbered column patterns from prime tables ranging from 6 columns wide through 100 columns wide.

With the patterns represented in this way, the center space down the middle of the table becomes very apparent. There are also many diagonal patterns of primes as well as "+" patterns of non-primes that stand out within this figure.

Another interesting characteristic of the tables above is that if we start with the pattern on the sixth row and look at every sixth row, we find the lowest ratios of columns-with-primes per column-count. The tables below start with the pattern for a six-column table, and then increase by six up through 96 columns. This first table shows these columns left justified:

Table 17.13   Left-justified column patterns from prime tables ranging from 6 columns wide through 96 columns wide (in steps of 6).

And here is the same pattern, only this time it is center-aligned:

Table 17.14   Center-justified column patterns from prime tables ranging from 6 columns wide through 96 columns wide (in steps of 6).

It is very easy to see that the two tables above have much more white spaces within them as compared to the two tables that precede them. It is also interesting to note that when the table is 30 columns wide, it has the lowest ratio of columns with primes per total number of columns out of all the columns considered to that point. However, the ratio is even lower when the table is 210 columns wide. So, is there anything special about the numbers 30 and 210? Yes, they do have one thing in common: 30 is the product of the first three prime numbers (2, 3 and 5) while 210 is the product of the first four prime numbers (2, 3, 5, and 7). The figure below shows how nicely the prime numbers line up when the table is 210 columns wide.

Note also that in the following figure, the first 42,000 numbers were checked, and 4392 primes were found within that range.

Table 17.15   Table of prime numbers that is 210 columns wide and 200 rows high.

It appears that these column patterns could be a valid characteristic of primes, and if they really are, then when the table is 2310 columns wide, we would expect the ratio of prime columns to total columns to be even smaller (because 2310 is equal to the product of the first five primes: 2, 3, 5, 7, and 11).

Before we look at a few other pattern within these tables of primes, we'll briefly look at two other tables of prime number. In these tables, the black dots represent prime numbers. It can clearly be seen in both of these tables (below) that there are several groups of columns where there are no prime numbers within them. And yet, each pattern of prime/no-prime columns have the same type of symmetry that we saw with even number columns earlier in this chapter. The first table is 154 columns wide and 200 rows high. This table has 3319 prime numbers out of a total of 30,800 numbers that were checked.

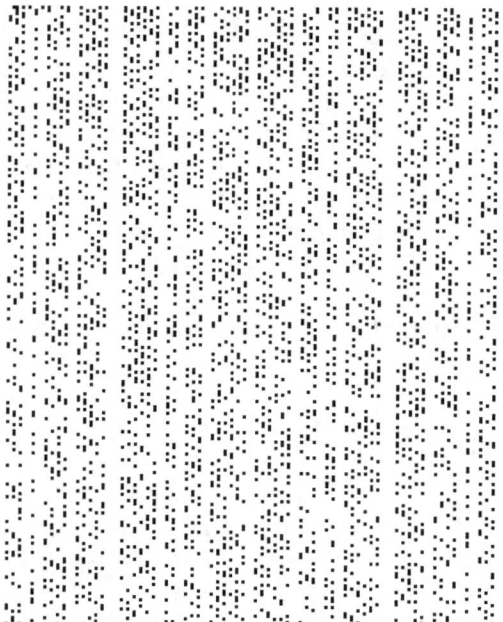

Table 17.16   Table of prime numbers that is 154 columns wide and 200 rows high.

The following table is 168 columns wide, 200 rows high, and has 3598 prime numbers within the first 33,600 numbers checked.

Table 17.17   Table of prime numbers that is 168 columns wide and 200 rows high.

ODD Table Widths

So far we have only considered tables that have an even number of columns. What about tables that have an odd number of columns? As mentioned earlier, if the table has some prime number of columns (like if it is 11 or 13 columns wide), we find prime numbers in every column except the last column. But even more interesting, if the table has a prime number of columns, many of the prime numbers appear to align themselves along diagonals. The figure below is the pattern we get when the table is 211 columns wide.

Table 17.18   Table of prime numbers that is 211 columns wide and 200 rows high.

And what if we look at odd table widths that aren't prime numbers? Here are the patterns for table widths that have 9, 15, 21 and 27 columns (these columns have been center justified):

```
                     X X _ X X _ X X
                 X X _ X _ _ X X _ _ X _ X X
             X X _ X X _ _ X _ X X _ X _ _ X X _ X X
         X X _ X X _ X X _ X X _ X X _ X X _ X X _ X X _ X X
```

Table 17.19   Center-justified column patterns from prime tables that have 9, 15, 21 and 27 columns.

Each of these patterns is also symmetrical about the center (the first half of the pattern mirrors the second half). It is also interesting to note the similarities between the patterns. For example, the tables with nine and 27 columns (the first and last patterns listed above), each have two columns of primes followed by a space and then two more primes and a space, and so on.

It should be noted that tables that have a prime number of columns always appear to have a diagonal pattern (and we will look at a few more prime number column tables a little later in this section). There are also many other odd-number column tables also appear to have a diagonal pattern, but they also have a vertical pattern. We see this in the next two examples.

The following table is 155 columns wide and 200 rows high. The diagonal patterns can be seen going in both directions. What is harder to see are the vertical patterns in this table (but they are still there). This table has 3340 prime numbers out of 31,000 numbers checked.

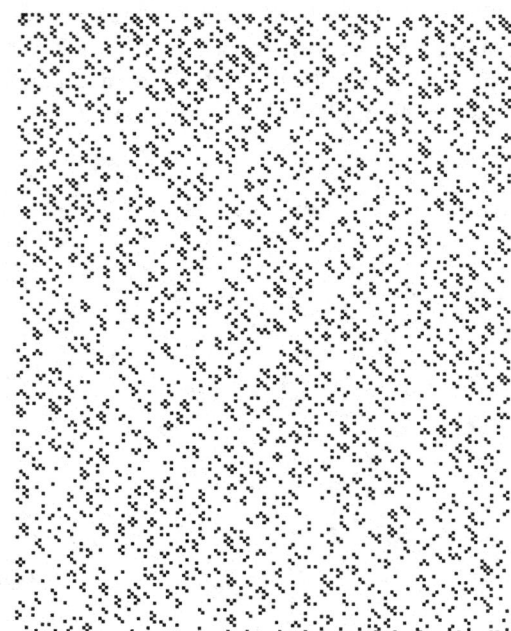

Table 17.20   Table of prime numbers that is 155 columns wide and 200 rows high.

The following table has 165 columns, yet even though there are an odd number of columns in this table, it is fairly easy to see the vertical pattern. On the other hand, there doesn't appear to be a diagonal pattern in this table.

Table 17.21   Table of prime numbers that is 165 columns wide and 200 rows high.

Altogether, the preceding table has 200 rows along with the 165 columns. That means that there are 33,000 numbers represented within this table, and of those, 3538 are prime.

In the previous section we saw that when the table was 30 columns wide, it had the fewest number of prime-columns per total-number-of-columns (out of the first 30 columns checked). And out of that same group, it appeared that the 9 and 27 column tables have the most columns with primes (but actually they didn't). If we set the number of columns in a table to 25, we find that it has the most prime number columns out of any patterns that we considered in that group. Remember, 25 is equal to a prime number squared, specifically 5 squared. Its pattern looks like this:

X X X X _ X X X X _ X X X X _ X X X X_ X X X X

Table 17.22   Pattern of prime numbers where the table is 25 columns wide.

This pattern has four columns of primes followed by a space and then four more columns of primes followed by a space and so on. The next table with a large number of prime columns is the table that is 49 columns wide (and 49 is equal to the next prime number squared). The 49 column table has six columns of primes followed by a space and then six more columns of primes followed by a space, and so on. Knowing this, we have a good idea of what the pattern would look like if it were 121 columns wide or 169 columns wide, or even 289 columns wide. In fact, let's look at the table that is 169 columns wide.

The following table is 169 columns wide and has 200 rows. There are 3620 prime numbers within this table, which are represented as black dots. As we look at this table, it appears to have a mix of left and right diagonals; however it still follows the pattern above. There are 12 columns with primes followed by an empty column, and then 12 more columns of primes, and then another empty column, etc.

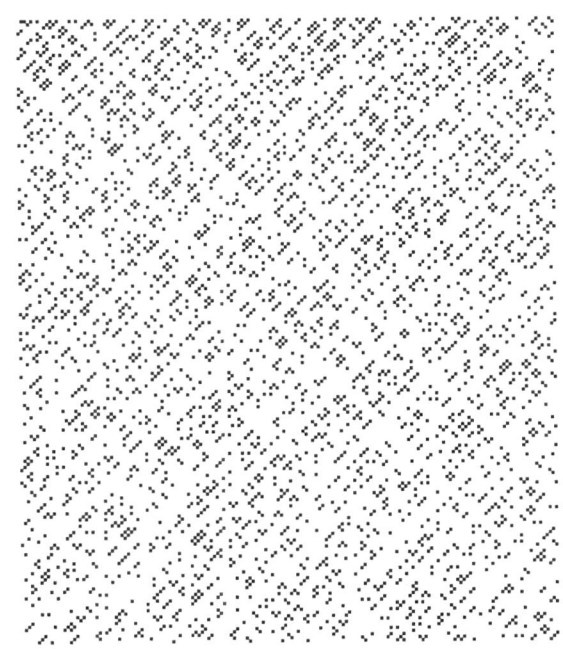

Table 17.23   Table of prime numbers that is 169 columns wide and 200 rows high.

The next three tables are very interesting. They have been scaled down and placed side-by-side in order to make it easier to see their patterns in relation to each other. The first table on the left is 149 columns wide (a prime number of columns) and there we see that the prime numbers in the table form diagonals that slant to the left. The table in the middle is 150 columns wide. Here the prime numbers in the table form vertical columns (as do all tables that have an even number of columns). The table on the right is 151 columns wide (another prime number of columns), and this time the prime numbers in the table form diagonals that slant to the right.

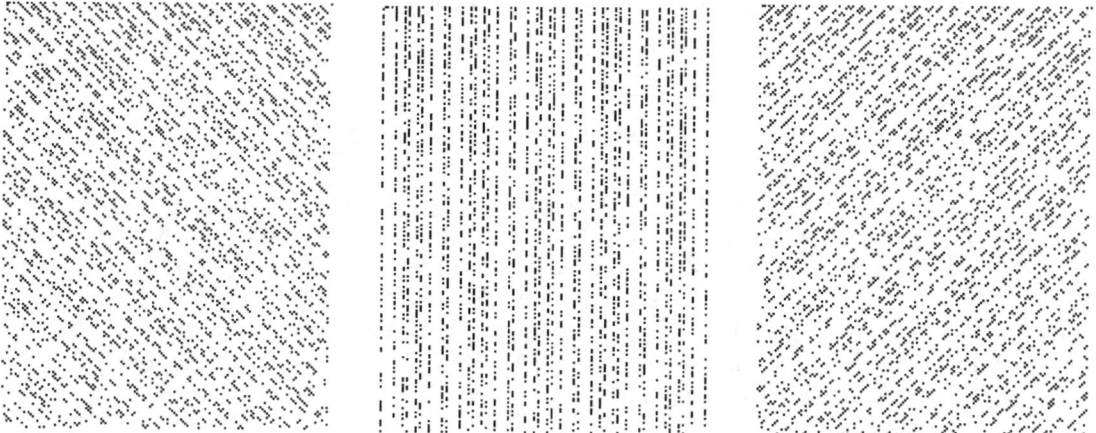

Table 17.24   Tables of prime numbers that are 200 rows high and 149 columns wide on the left, 150 columns wide in the middle, and 151 columns wide on the right.

Similar patterns can be found whenever we look at tables where there are double primes (two prime numbers separated by a single composite number). See the appendix for more examples of prime number tables with various column widths.

Chapter 18
MOD Table Patterns

The Multiplication Table

In this chapter we'll take a look at the MOD operator and in particular we'll consider its application to the multiplication table, and a few other similar tables. And once again we'll create some interesting and symmetrical patterns. For our purposes, we'll construct the multiplication table with counting numbers along the top, and along the left side. Each entry in the table will be equal to the product of the corresponding number above it and to the left of it. This table has several properties. For example, the numbers become larger as we move to the right and down within the table. And except for the row and column that are multiplied by one, there are no prime numbers within the table.

*	0	1	2	3	4	5	6	7	8	9	10
0	0	0	0	0	0	0	0	0	0	0	0
1	0	1	2	3	4	5	6	7	8	9	10
2	0	2	4	6	8	10	12	14	16	18	20
3	0	3	6	9	12	15	18	21	24	27	30
4	0	4	8	12	16	20	24	28	32	36	40
5	0	5	10	15	20	25	30	35	40	45	50
6	0	6	12	18	24	30	36	42	48	54	60
7	0	7	14	21	28	35	42	49	56	63	70
8	0	8	16	24	32	40	48	56	64	72	80
9	0	9	18	27	36	45	54	63	72	81	90
10	0	10	20	30	40	50	60	70	80	90	100

Table 18.1   A 10 by 10 multiplication table.

The table above shows a ten-column by ten-row multiplication table. (We're not counting the zero row and column.) And since we are dealing with a 10 by 10 multiplication table, we will perform a MOD 10 operation on the table. The MOD 10 operation is the same as dividing each entry in the table by 10 and then placing the remainder of that division back in the table.

By using the MOD operator, the numbers now don't become increasingly larger as we move to the right and down through the table. In fact, several new patterns start to become apparent as the MOD operator is applied.

The following table shows our 10 by 10 multiplication table after the MOD 10 operator has been applied to each entry.

*	0	1	2	3	4	5	6	7	8	9	10
0	0	0	0	0	0	0	0	0	0	0	0
1	0	1	2	3	4	5	6	7	8	9	0
2	0	2	4	6	8	0	2	4	6	8	0
3	0	3	6	9	2	5	8	1	4	7	0
4	0	4	8	2	6	0	4	8	2	6	0
5	0	5	0	5	0	5	0	5	0	5	0
6	0	6	2	8	4	0	6	2	8	4	0
7	0	7	4	1	8	5	2	9	6	3	0
8	0	8	6	4	2	0	8	6	4	2	0
9	0	9	8	7	6	5	4	3	2	1	0
10	0	0	0	0	0	0	0	0	0	0	0

Table 18.2   A 10 by 10 multiplication table after applying a MOD 10 operator.

It becomes easier to see patterns within this table if we just concentrate on certain numbers, or certain pairs of numbers. For example, if we look at just the 4's and the 6's within the table we see that together they make a circular pattern.

*	0	1	2	3	4	5	6	7	8	9	10
0											
1					4		6				
2			4	6				4	6		
3			6						4		
4		4			6		4			6	
5											
6		6			4		6			4	
7			4						6		
8			6	4				6	4		
9					6		4				
10											

Table 18.3   The 4's and 6's within a MOD 10 multiplication table.

The 4's by themselves create a pattern that is symmetrical with itself about the diagonals; and the 6's by themselves also form another symmetrical pattern about the diagonals. Together they form a pattern that is not only symmetrical about both diagonals, but also symmetrical about horizontal and vertical lines running through both of the 5's.

The 2's and 8's have the same kind of symmetry as the 4's and 6's even though their pattern is different. In the table below, we see that the 8's are symmetrical about the diagonals; while the 2's are also symmetrical about the diagonals. Together they form a pattern that is also symmetrical about the horizontal and vertical axes running through both 5's.

*	0	1	2	3	4	5	6	7	8	9	10
0											
1			2						8		
2		2			8		2			8	
3					2		8				
4			8	2				8	2		
5											
6			2	8				2	8		
7					8		2				
8		8			2		8			2	
9			8						2		
10											

Table 18.4   The 2's and 8's within a MOD 10 multiplication table.

We can also find symmetrical patterns when we consider the 3's and 7's, the 9's and 1's and the 0's and 5's. Keep in mind that these patterns aren't unique to the MOD 10 function. We can find symmetrical patterns with any MOD value. However, as we build these tables, we need to consider the correct number of rows and columns to consider. The correct number of rows and columns depends on the MOD value being used. In the previous examples we used a MOD 10 value. Therefore, in order to get a complete pattern for those examples, we needed to consider ten rows and ten columns (not counting the initial 0 row and column). If we use more than 10 rows and columns, we find that the pattern begins to repeat itself. In contrast to that, if we have less than 10 rows or columns, the pattern appears to be incomplete, and lacking. We use the MOD value to determine the number of rows and columns that will be considered.

Now let's look at some of the patterns we get when we use a MOD 14 operator on the multiplication table. In this case, to get a complete pattern we need to look at 14 rows and 14 columns of the multiplication table. The following is the multiplication table after we perform a MOD 14 operation on each member within the table.

*	0	1	2	3	4	5	6	7	8	9	10	11	12	13	14
0	0	0	0	0	0	0	0	0	0	0	0	0	0	0	0
1	0	1	2	3	4	5	6	7	8	9	10	11	12	13	0
2	0	2	4	6	8	10	12	0	2	4	6	8	10	12	0
3	0	3	6	9	12	1	4	7	10	13	2	5	8	11	0
4	0	4	8	12	2	6	10	0	4	8	12	2	6	10	0
5	0	5	10	1	6	11	2	7	12	3	8	13	4	9	0
6	0	6	12	4	10	2	8	0	6	12	4	10	2	8	0
7	0	7	0	7	0	7	0	7	0	7	0	7	0	7	0
8	0	8	2	10	4	12	6	0	8	2	10	4	12	6	0
9	0	9	4	13	8	3	12	7	2	11	6	1	10	5	0
10	0	10	6	2	12	8	4	0	10	6	2	12	8	4	0
11	0	11	8	5	2	13	10	7	4	1	12	9	6	3	0
12	0	12	10	8	6	4	2	0	12	10	8	6	4	2	0
13	0	13	12	11	10	9	8	7	6	5	4	3	2	1	0
14	0	0	0	0	0	0	0	0	0	0	0	0	0	0	0

Table 18.5   A 14 by 14 multiplication table after applying a MOD 14 operator.

Just by looking at the table as it is we can see many patterns beginning to emerge. However, once again it will be easier to see these patterns after we remove some of the other numbers. For example, let's remove everything but the 2's and the 4's. This is what we get.

*	0	1	2	3	4	5	6	7	8	9	10	11	12	13	14
0															
1			2		4										
2		2	4						2	4					
3							4				2				
4		4			2				4			2			
5							2						4		
6				4		2					4		2		
7															
8			2		4					2		4			
9			4						2						
10				2			4				2			4	
11					2				4						
12						4	2						4	2	
13											4		2		
14															

Table 18.6   The 2's and 4's within a MOD 14 multiplication table.

The following is the pattern that we get when all the numbers are removed except the 1, 3, 11 and 13. Notice the symmetry in the patterns when we chose pairs of numbers that add up to the MOD value (see the figure below) as compared to the type of pattern when the numbers chosen don't add up to the MOD value (see the figure above).

*	0	1	2	3	4	5	6	7	8	9	10	11	12	13	14
0															
1		1		3								11		13	
2															
3		3				1				13				11	
4															
5				1		11				3		13			
6															
7															
8															
9				13		3				11		1			
10															
11		11				13				1				3	
12															
13		13		11								3		1	
14															

Table 18.7   The 1's, 3's, 11's and 13's within a MOD 14 multiplication table.

By using larger numbers we have more combinations of numbers to choose from, and hence we can create a wider variety of more complex patterns.

Looking at Multiples of a Number

We add another dimension to these figures when we highlight multiples of a number, as well as the number itself. For example, here are the multiples of 3 within our original MOD 10 table:

*	0	1	2	3	4	5	6	7	8	9	10
0											
1				3			6			9	
2				6					6		
3		3	6	9							
4					6					6	
5											
6		6					6				
7								9	6	3	
8		6					6				
9		9		6			3				
10											

Table 18.8   A 10 by 10 multiplication table, MOD 10 showing multiples of 3.

If we represent each number as a dot, we can show even larger patterns. The following figure shows a 100 by 100 multiplication table, MOD 100 with the multiples of 3 highlighted. Keep in mind that we are showing the multiples of 3 after the MOD operator has been applied. For example, 9 x 12 = 108. The number 108 is divisible by 3, but 108 MOD 100 = 8, and 8 is not divisible by 3.

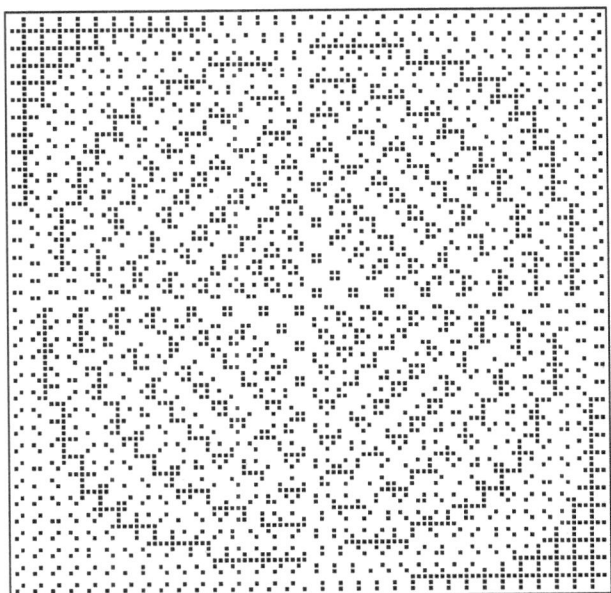

Table 18.9   A 100 by 100 multiplication table, MOD 100 showing multiples of 3.

A simple variation to the figure above is to substitute the MOD 100 with a MOD 50 operator. The following table shows what we get:

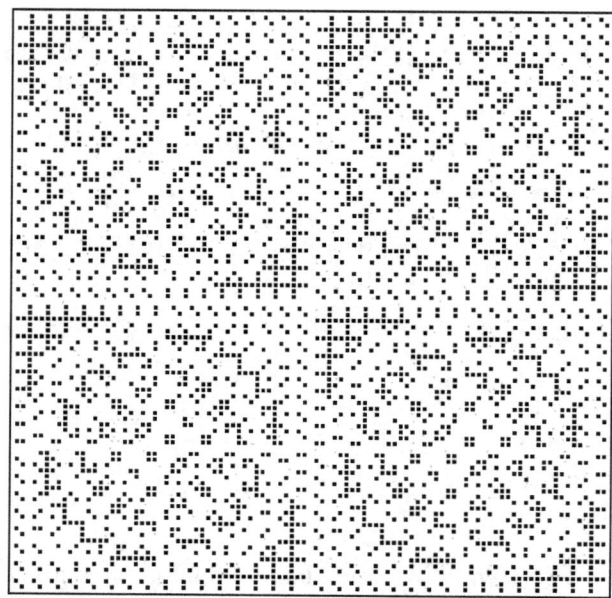

Table 18.10   A 100 by 100 multiplication table, MOD 50 showing multiples of 3.

Similarly, 96 x 54 = 5184 and 5184 MOD 100 = 84 is a multiple of 3; but, 5184 MOD 50 = 34, and 34 is not a multiple of 3; therefore, even though both of the previous tables show multiples of 3, a MOD 100 table is different from a MOD 50 table.

Sum of Squares Tables

There are also other MOD tables that we can create that have similar patterns to the ones we just considered. In this next set of examples we'll create a sum of squares table. To do this, we take the numbers along the top and the left side, and we square them before adding them together and placing them in the table. The following is a ten-row by ten-column sum of squares table.

*	0	1	2	3	4	5	6	7	8	9	10
0	0	1	4	9	16	25	36	49	64	81	100
1	1	2	5	10	17	26	37	50	65	82	101
2	4	5	8	13	20	29	40	53	68	85	104
3	9	10	13	18	25	34	45	58	73	90	109
4	16	17	20	25	32	41	52	65	80	97	116
5	25	26	29	34	41	50	61	74	89	106	125
6	36	37	40	45	52	61	72	85	100	117	136
7	49	50	53	58	65	74	85	98	113	130	149
8	64	65	68	73	80	89	100	113	128	145	164
9	81	82	85	90	97	106	117	130	145	162	181
10	100	101	104	109	116	125	136	149	164	181	200

Table 18.11   A 10 by 10 sum of squares table.

Now, if we perform a MOD 10 operation on each entry in the table, the table becomes:

*	0	1	2	3	4	5	6	7	8	9	10
0	0	1	4	9	6	5	6	9	4	1	0
1	1	2	5	0	7	6	7	0	5	2	1
2	4	5	8	3	0	9	0	3	8	5	4
3	9	0	3	8	5	4	5	8	3	0	9
4	6	7	0	5	2	1	2	5	0	7	6
5	5	6	9	4	1	0	1	4	9	6	5
6	6	7	0	5	2	1	2	5	0	7	6
7	9	0	3	8	5	4	5	8	3	0	9
8	4	5	8	3	0	9	0	3	8	5	4
9	1	2	5	0	7	6	7	0	5	2	1
10	0	1	4	9	6	5	6	9	4	1	0

Table 18.12   The 10 by 10 sum of squares table after performing a MOD 10 operation on each entry.

Again, we see patterns beginning to emerge within the table. And again, as we look at combinations of numbers as well as individual numbers themselves, we can see quite a variety of patterns. The following pattern is created when the multiples of 3 are highlighted.

*	0	1	2	3	4	5	6	7	8	9	10
0				9	6		6	9			
1						6					
2				3		9		3			
3	9		3						3		9
4	6										6
5		6	9						9	6	
6	6										6
7	9		3						3		9
8				3		9		3			
9						6					
10				9	6		6	9			

Table 18.13   A MOD 10 sum of squares table showing multiples of 3.

The numbers 3, 4, 5 and 8 create the following pattern:

*	0	1	2	3	4	5	6	7	8	9	10
0			4			5			4		
1			5						5		
2	4	5	8	3				3	8	5	4
3			3	8	5	4	5	8	3		
4			5						5		
5	5			4				4			5
6			5						5		
7			3	8	5	4	5	8	3		
8	4	5	8	3				3	8	5	4
9			5						5		
10			4			5			4		

Table 18.14   The MOD 10 sum of squares table showing 3, 4, 5 and 8.

Again, if we let the numbers appear as dots, we can show much larger tables (and larger patterns). And, as mentioned earlier, as we show more rows and columns of the table, we are also able to see even more interesting and complex patterns.

The following table has 100 columns and rows. It performs a MOD 50 operation on the sum of squares table. The highlighted numbers are multiples of 4.

Table 18.15   Sum of squares, MOD 50, showing multiples of 4.

The method of creating these patterns is the same for each figure. We start with a sum of squares table, perform a MOD operation on the numbers within the table, and then highlight one or more numbers and/or multiples of numbers within the table. The parameters that vary from table to table are the number of rows and columns, the MOD value and the numbers that are highlighted. The following tables are some of my favorites:

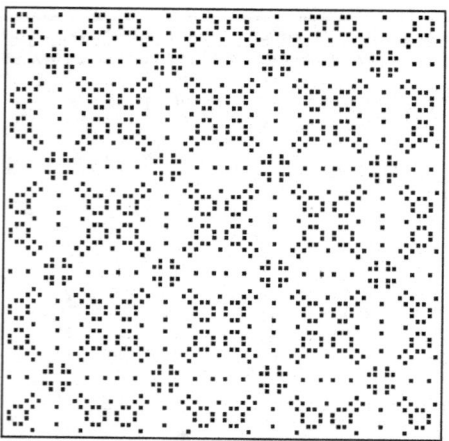

Table 18.16   Sum of squares table showing 72 rows and columns, using the MOD 36 operator where the multiples of 5 are highlighted.

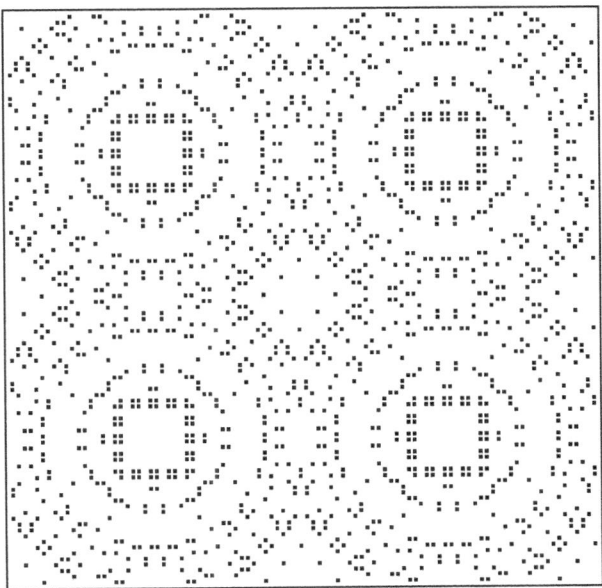

Table 18.17   Sum of squares table showing 98 rows and columns, using the MOD 49 operator where the multiples of 6 are highlighted.

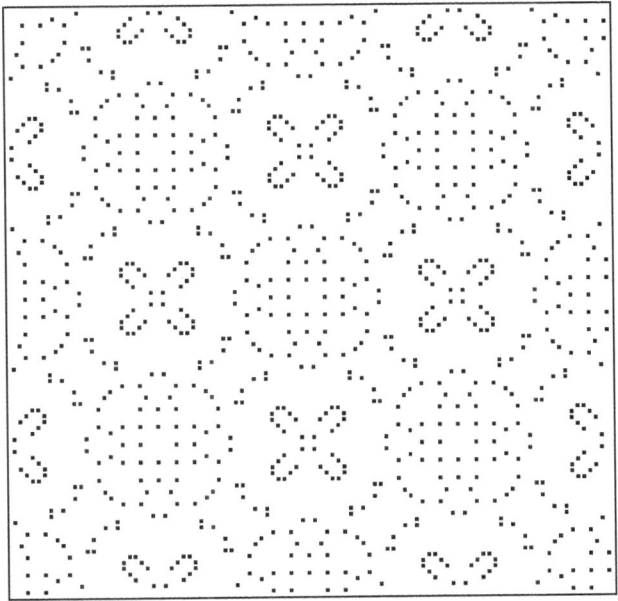

Table 18.18   Sum of squares table, showing 100 rows and columns, using the MOD 50 operator where the multiples of 9 are highlighted.

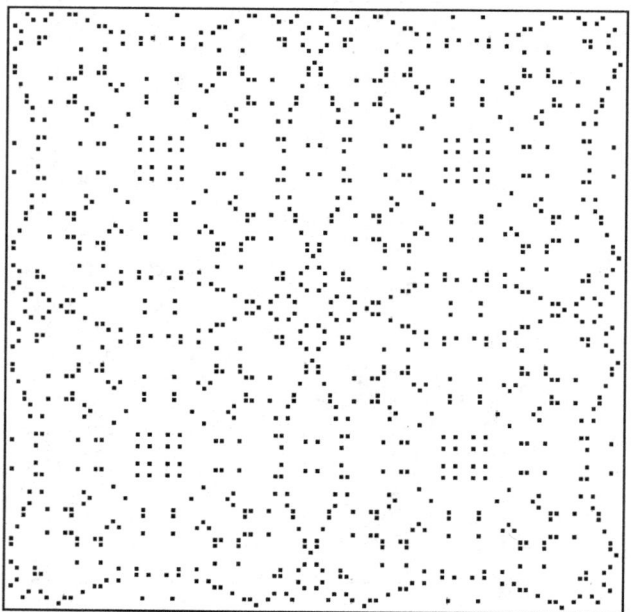

Table 18.19 Sum of squares table, showing 102 columns and rows, using the MOD 51 operator where the multiples of 10 are highlighted.

Difference of Squares Tables

There are an endless number of tables that we can create, each with their own set of patterns. We'll conclude this chapter by briefly looking at one other set of patterns. These patterns are created from the difference of squares table.

A difference of squares table is similar to the sum of squares table in that we take the numbers along the top and the left side, and square them; but this time we subtract one from the other and place the absolute value of that subtraction in the table (in this way all the values in the table will be positive). Here is a ten-row by ten-column difference of squares table.

*	1	2	3	4	5	6	7	8	9	10
1	0	3	8	15	24	35	48	63	80	99
2	3	0	5	12	21	32	45	60	77	96
3	8	5	0	7	16	27	40	55	72	91
4	15	12	7	0	9	20	33	48	65	84
5	24	21	16	9	0	11	24	39	56	75
6	35	32	27	20	11	0	13	28	45	64
7	48	45	40	33	24	13	0	15	32	51
8	63	60	55	48	39	28	15	0	17	36
9	80	77	72	65	56	45	32	17	0	19
10	99	96	91	84	75	64	51	36	19	0

Table 18.20 A 10 by 10 difference of squares table.

Now, if we perform a MOD 10 operation on each entry in the table, the table becomes:

*	1	2	3	4	5	6	7	8	9	10
1	0	3	8	5	4	5	8	3	0	9
2	3	0	5	2	1	2	5	0	7	6
3	8	5	0	7	6	7	0	5	2	1
4	5	2	7	0	9	0	3	8	5	4
5	4	1	6	9	0	1	4	9	6	5
6	5	2	7	0	1	0	3	8	5	4
7	8	5	0	3	4	3	0	5	2	1
8	3	0	5	8	9	8	5	0	7	6
9	0	7	2	5	6	5	2	7	0	9
10	9	6	1	4	5	4	1	6	9	0

Table 18.21   The 10 by 10 difference of squares table after performing a MOD 10 operation on each entry.

If you look closely at this table, (before removing any of the other numbers), you can see several patterns. For example, the 0's make a large X right through the middle of the table, and the 5's make a diamond.

The following table shows the pattern that we get when we leave in the numbers 1, 3, 6, 8, and 9; and remove all other numbers.

*	1	2	3	4	5	6	7	8	9	10
1		3	8				8	3		9
2	3				1					6
3	8				6					1
4					9		3	8		
5		1	6	9		1			6	
6					1		3	8		
7	8			3		3				1
8	3			8	9	8				6
9					6					9
10	9	6	1				1	6	9	

Table 18.22   The 10 by 10 difference of squares table after performing a MOD 10 operation on each entry showing only the numbers 1, 3, 6, 8, and 9.

And various combinations of numbers can create some very interesting patterns.

Of course, if we let dots represent the highlighted numbers, we can increase the number of rows and columns being considered. With that in mind, we'll close this chapter with a look at a few patterns within the difference of squares tables.

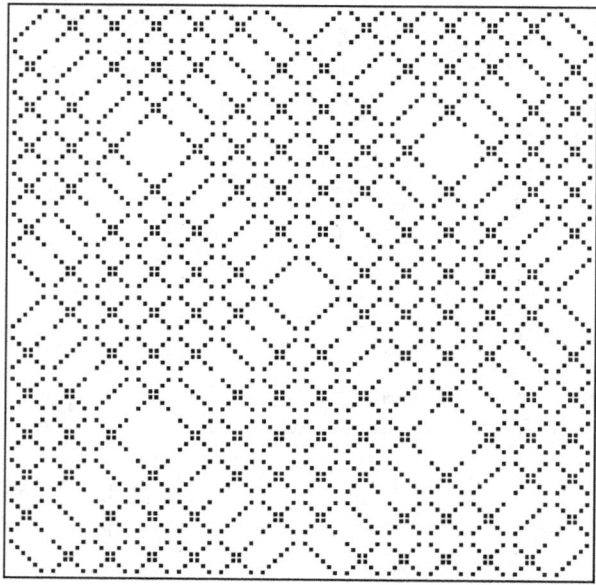

Table 18.23   Difference of squares table, showing 98 columns and rows, using the MOD 49 operator with the multiples of 7 are highlighted.

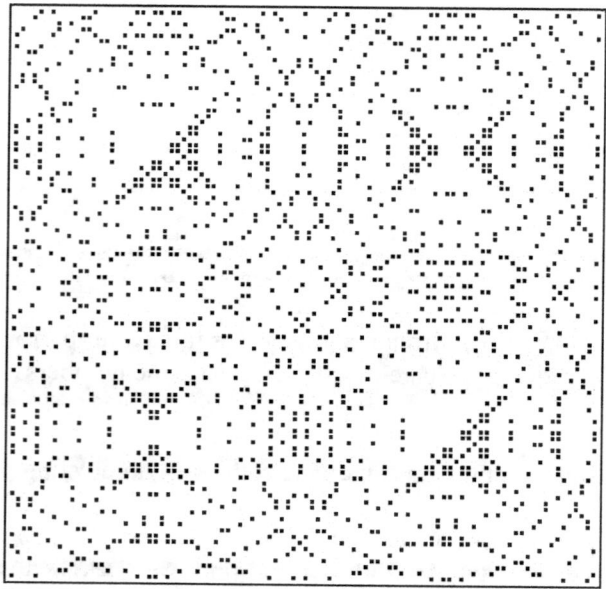

Table 18.24   Difference of squares table, showing 98 columns and rows, using the MOD 49 operator with the multiples of 6 are highlighted.

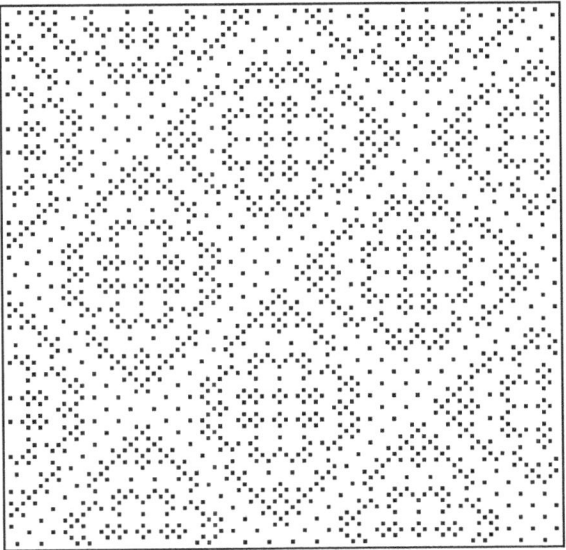

Table 18.25   Difference of squares table, showing 92 columns and rows, using the MOD 92 operator with the multiples of 8 are highlighted.

Table 18.26   Difference of squares table, showing 94 columns and rows, using the MOD 47 operator with the multiples of 2 are highlighted.

Chapter 19
Natural Integer Networks

What Is a Natural Integer Network

If we were to take any number between 0 and 99 and square it, and then look at the two right-most digits (the two least significant digits), we would have some other number between 00 and 99. Now, let's continue this thought a little further: There are one hundred numbers between (and including) 0 and 99. So, if we take a number between 0 and 99, square it, then take the two right-most digits, and square it, and then again take the two right-most digits, and continue doing this over and over again, at some point we will start repeating ourselves. We have to start repeating ourselves because we are working with a closed set of numbers, and because of the way we defined our operation. The numbers we get will always be within our original set. Looking at some examples, we'll see this as it happens. This is what we get when we start with the number 11:

11^2 is equal to 121 where the two right-most digits are 21
21^2 is equal to 441 where the two right-most digits are 41
41^2 is equal to 1681 where the two right-most digits are 81
81^2 is equal to 6561 where the two right-most digits are 61
61^2 is equal to 3721 where the two right-most digits are 21

We started with 11 and went to 21; then 21 went to 41; and 41 went to 81. Next, 81 went to 61, and 61 went to 21. We never made it back to 11, but we did return to a number that we had already seen before (the number 21). And now if we were to continue, we would simply repeat the same sequence of numbers over again within this loop of four numbers. Now let's look at another example. This time we'll start with the number 18:

18^2 is equal to 324 where the two right-most digits are 24
24^2 is equal to 576 where the two right-most digits are 76
76^2 is equal to 5776 where the two right-most digits are 76

In this example, we started with 18 and went to 24; then 24 went to 76; and 76 went to itself. This set of numbers didn't give us a loop; instead, we arrived at what we'll call an attractor, a number that goes to itself.

If we were to do this with every number between 0 and 99, we would find that the numbers 49, 51, and 99 all go to 01 (or just 1). The numbers that end with a 5 (like 15, 35, 45, etc.) all go to 25. The numbers that end with a 0 (like 10, 20, 30, etc.) all go to 00 (or just 0); and the numbers 24, 26, and 74 all go to 76. We could now take this list of numbers that go to other numbers and create a diagram where we place the numbers such as 24, 26, and 74 and show each of them with an arrow pointing to 76. Doing this with all 100 numbers (from 0 to 99) will give us a set of symmetrical patterns that I call a natural integer network. For these squared numbers, this set of patterns looks like this:

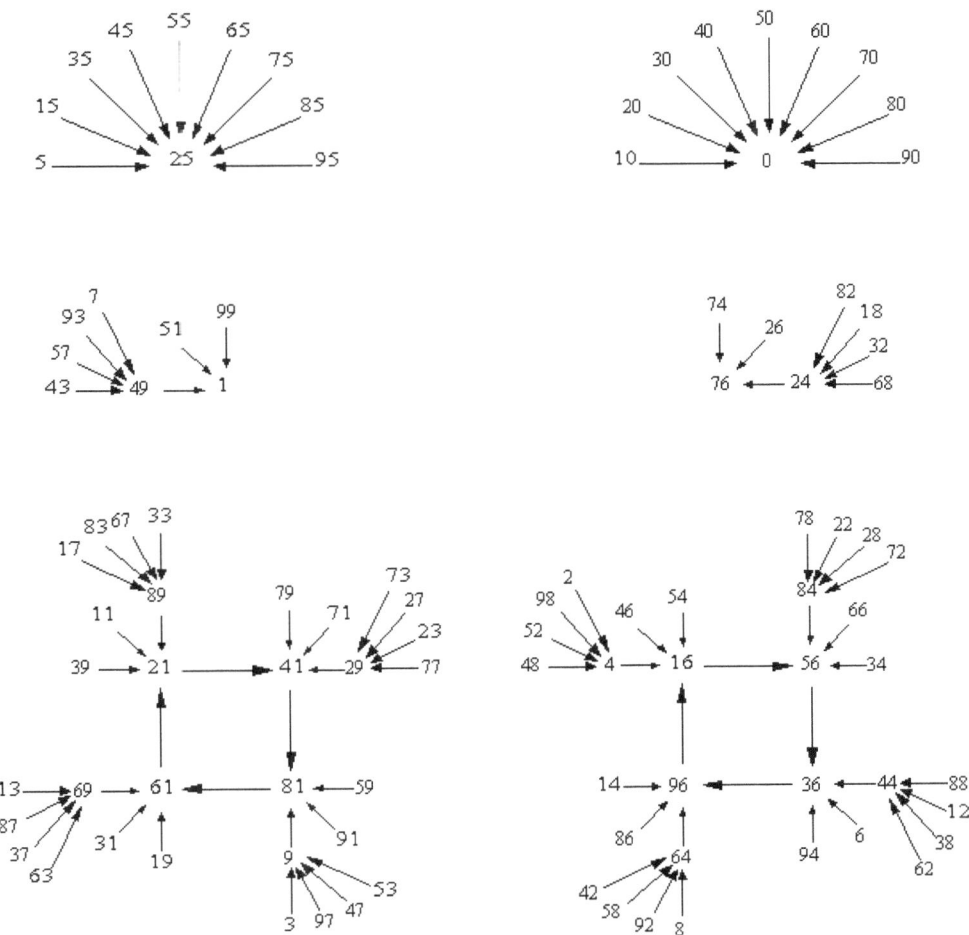

Figure 19.1   The two-digit (or MOD 100) natural integer network diagram for numbers 0 thru 99 squared.

In the figure above, the patterns with odd numbers are on the left, and the even number patterns are on the right. The odd numbers have two attractors, the numbers 1 and 25, and one four-node loop comprised of the numbers 21, 41, 81 and 61. Likewise, the even numbers have two attractors, the numbers 0 and 76, and one four node loop comprised of the numbers 16, 56, 36 and 96.

The odd and even patterns almost look identical, but there is at least one subtle difference between them. If we circle the pairs of numbers that add up to 100 we do see a difference. Disregarding the 0 and 25 attractor-patterns, we see within the odd number patterns that the attractors pair with the non-attractors, while in the even number patterns the attractors pair with the other attractors. For example, in the odd number patterns, 1 and 99 pair with 1 being an attractor and 99 isn't; and 21 and 79 pair with 21 being an attractor and 79 isn't. In the even number patterns, 76 and 24 pair and both are attractors, while 74 and 26 pair and both are not attractors. (See the figure below)

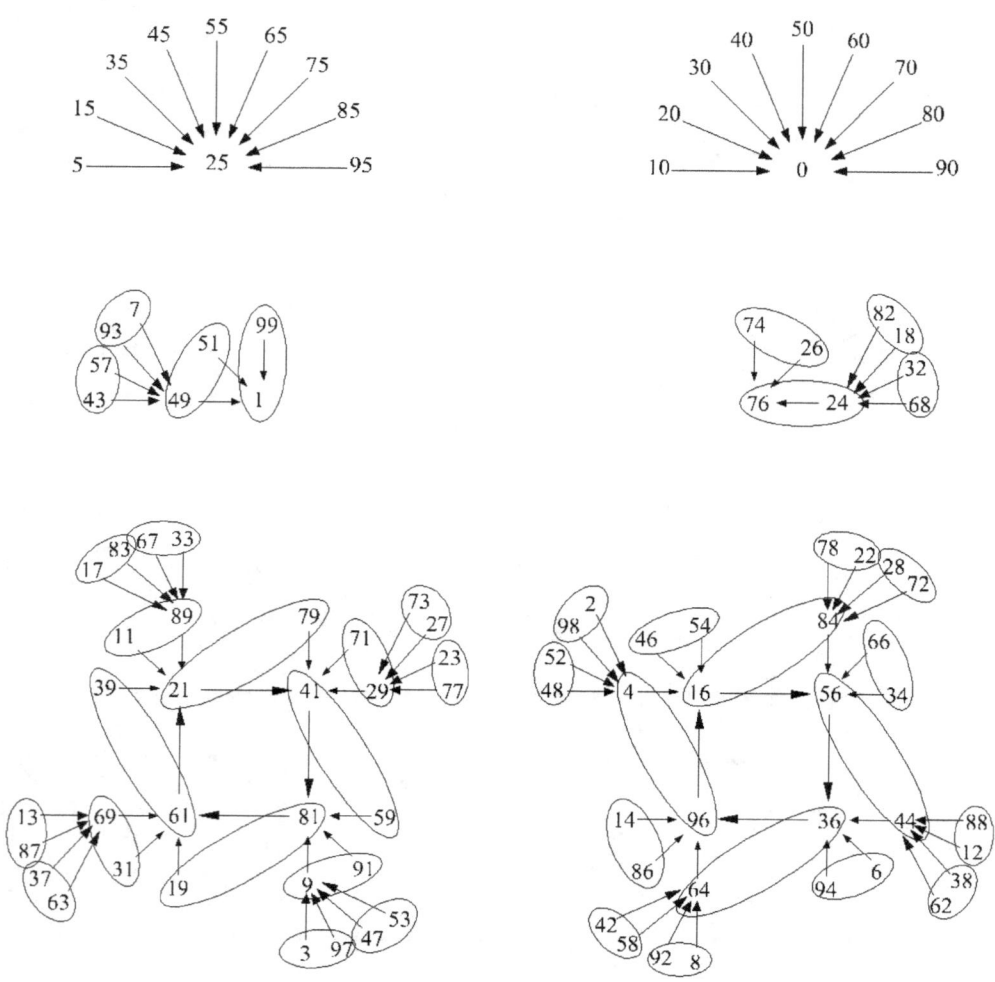

Figure 19.2   The two-digit (or MOD 100) natural integer network diagram for numbers 0 thru 99 squared with pairs circled that add to 100.

This pattern is very interesting, but it makes one wonder if there are more patterns like it? Let's take a look. Instead of squaring the numbers, let's cube them. In other words, we'll take a number between 0 and 99, cube it and then take the two least significant digits for our next number. If we do it for all 100 numbers (from 0 to 99), and create our diagram, we get something that looks like this:

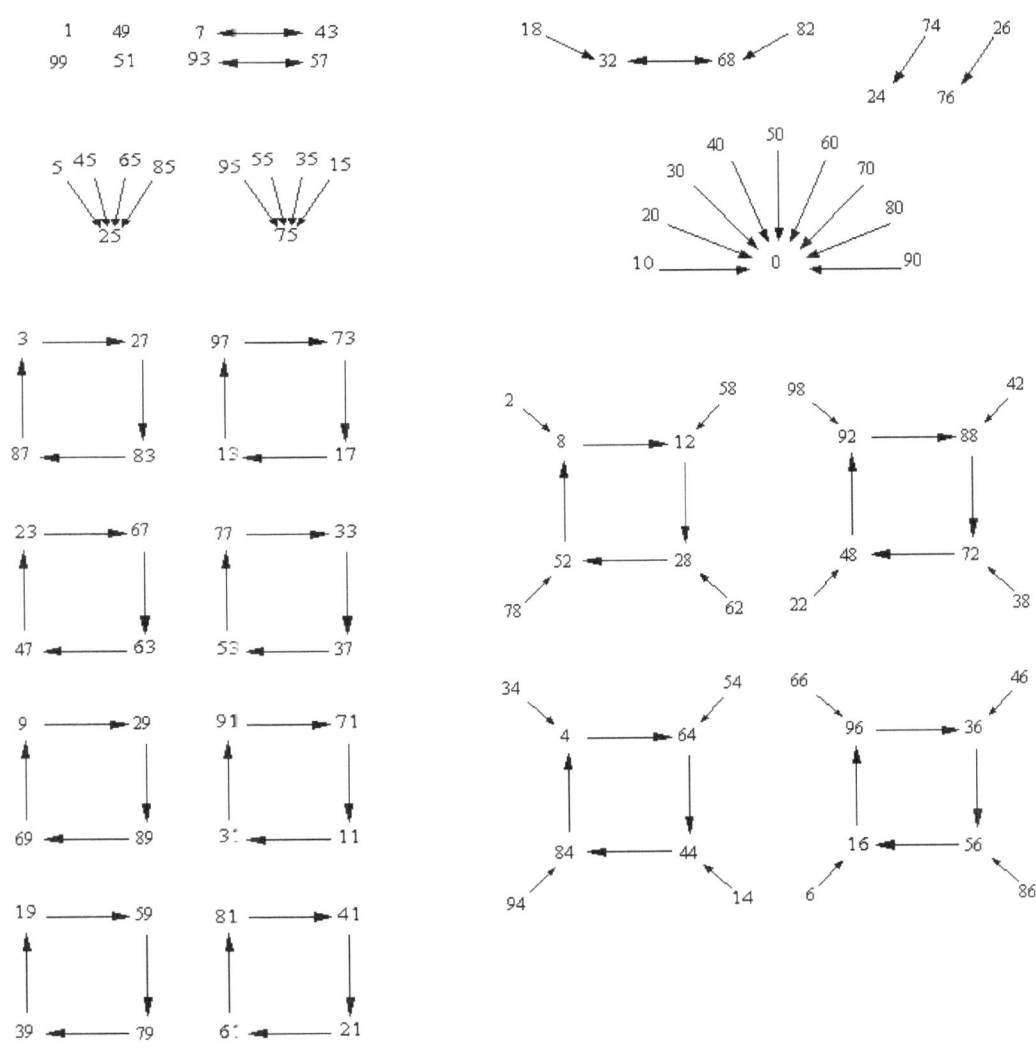

Figure 19.3   The two-digit (or MOD 100) natural integer network diagram for numbers 0 thru 99 cubed.

Again, the odd number patterns are on the left, and the even number patterns are on the right. This time the odd and even patterns are very different from each other. The odd numbers have six attractors, the numbers 1, 49, 51, 99, 25 and 75. There are also two two-node loops (if you want to call them loops) and there are eight four-node loops. On the other hand, the even number patterns have three attractors, one two-node loop, and four four-node loops. Notice that the even number patterns have half as many attractors, two-node loops and four-node loops as compared with the odd number patterns.

This time if we circle the pairs of numbers that add to 100, we find that we require two odd or two even patterns to do this. For example, the odd-number four-node loop of 19, 59, 79 and 39 would be paired with the loop of 81, 41, 21 and 61; while the even four-node loop of 4, 64, 44 and 84 would be paired with the loop of 96, 36, 56 and 16.

There is also another way that we can pair the numbers. We could match numbers together that have a difference of 50. In other words, we would circle 91 with 41, and circle 71 with 21, and so on. With this type of pairing, we again find that we require two patterns for each set of pairs with the odd numbers, but in this case, the even numbers can be paired within their own patterns.

Let's look at a few more patterns. In this next example we'll take each number and raise it to the fourth power and then follow our same MOD 100 process.

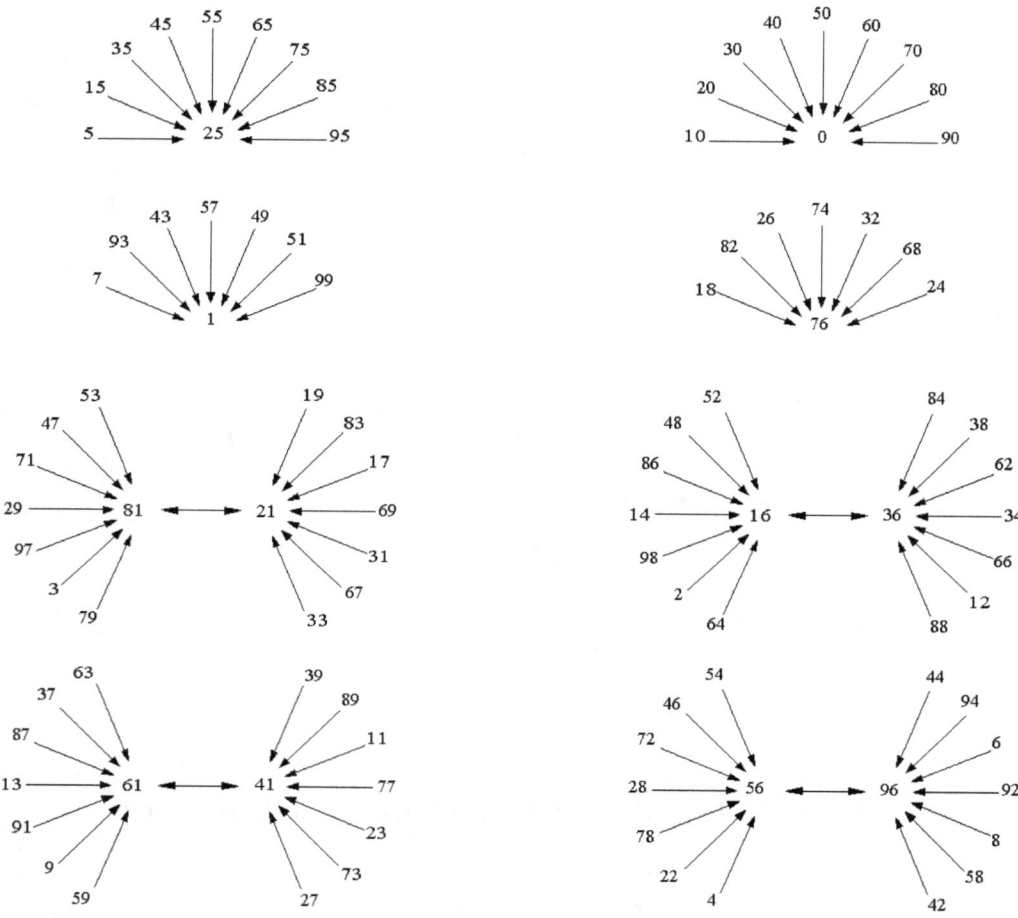

Figure 19.4   The 2-digit (or MOD 100) diagram for 0 thru 99 to the fourth power.

Again, we have another unique diagram where the odd and even number patterns look identical to each other. They each have two attractors and two two-digit loops.

Now if we take the numbers from 0 to 99 and raise them to the fifth power and then follow our process, we get something that looks like the figure below.

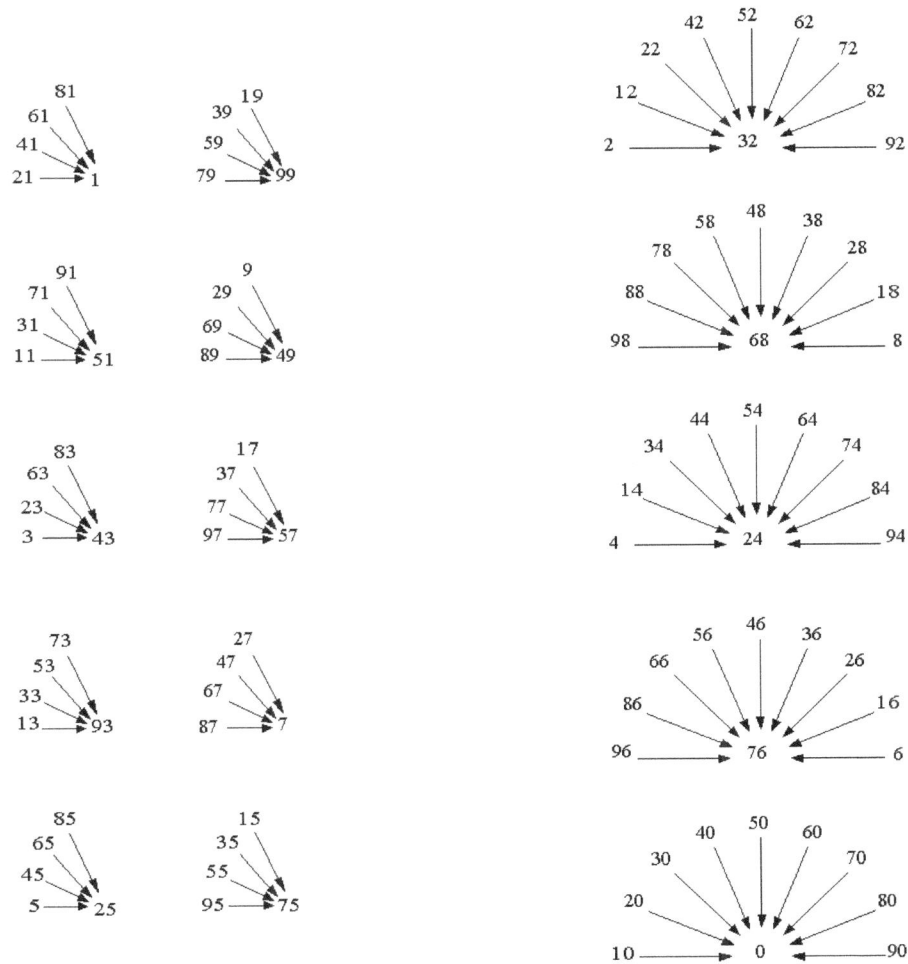

Figure 19.5 The two-digit (or MOD 100) diagram for 0 – 99 to the fifth power.

Even though we only have attractors in this diagram, the odd and even patterns are different. The odd number patterns have 10 attractors while the even number patterns have only 5 attractors. And there are no two-node or four-node loops.

Loops and Attractors

We could continue making diagrams by taking the numbers from 0 to 99 and raising them to the sixth power, the seventh power and so on (these diagrams are included in the appendix): however, in the interest of time and space, I will try to summarize what these diagrams look like.

If we continued making diagrams, they would be unique only until we reached the 21st power. When we take the numbers from 0 to 99 and raise each of them to the 22nd power and then construct the diagram, we find that it is identical to the second power diagram. This is because when you look at the last two digits of every number from 0 to 99 raised to the 22nd power, they are all equal to the last two digits of those same numbers raised to the second power. And after the 22nd power, the patterns repeat; so that the pattern for numbers raised to the 23rd power is identical to the pattern for these numbers raised to the 3rd power. The 24th power is identical to the 4th power and so on.

All of these patterns have some combination of attractors, two-digit loops and/or four-digit loops. Where numbers are raised to an even power, the number of odd-number attractors and loops are equal to the number of even-number attractors and loops. And in fact, these odd-number and even-number patterns appear identical to each other. When the numbers are raised to an odd power, the number of odd attractors and loops are double the number of even attractors and loops. The following table shows the counts of attractors, 2-node loops and 4-node loops for the odd and even numbers for powers 2 through 21.

Power	Odd Numbers			Even Numbers		
	Attractors	2 Node Loops	4 Node Loops	Attractors	2 Node Loops	4 Node Loops
2	2	0	1	2	0	1
3	6	2	8	3	1	4
4	2	2	0	2	2	0
5	10	0	0	5	0	0
6	6	0	0	6	0	0
7	6	2	8	3	1	4
8	2	0	1	2	0	1
9	10	16	0	5	8	0
10	2	0	0	2	0	0
11	22	10	0	11	5	0
12	2	0	1	2	0	1
13	10	0	8	5	0	4
14	2	2	0	2	2	0
15	6	2	0	3	1	0
16	6	0	0	6	0	0
17	10	0	8	5	0	4
18	2	0	1	2	0	1
19	6	18	0	3	9	0
20	2	0	0	2	0	0
21	42	0	0	21	0	0

Table 19.1   The count of attractors and loops as the numbers 0 through 99 are raised to successive powers from the 2nd through the 21st power.

The only misleading information gleaned from this table is that it gives the impression that the figures of certain patterns are identical to each other, when in fact they are only similar. For example, the figures for the second, 8th, 12th, and the 18th powers are all nearly identical to each other; however, these figures only share some common properties with each other, but other than that, they are still unique to each other. The curious reader can create their own diagrams; or they can take a look in the appendix where more of these diagrams can be found.

Other Natural Integer Networks

There are still many other variations that we can perform on our set of two digit numbers to create a limitless number of drawings. For example, let's take a number between 0 and 99, square it and then add one. Looking at the two least significant digits will still give us a number within our set. If we do it for all the numbers from 0 to 99 we get something that looks like Figure 19.6.

Notice that in this diagram we do not have a set of odd number patterns and then a separate set of even number patterns. Instead we have all 100 numbers creating a single pattern. This is because an even number squared plus one goes to and odd number and an odd number squared plus one goes to an even number. And in this case it causes the 100 numbers to create a single pattern.

In figures 19.7, 19.8, and 19.9, we take the numbers between 0 and 99, square them and then add two, four, and six respectively. In each of these figures we have a set of odd patterns, and an identical set of even patterns. It is interesting to see the variety of patterns that can be obtained through simple variations to our generating algorithm.

Figure 19.10 shows the pattern we get if we raise the numbers from 0 to 99 to the 12th power, and add one. Again, we have a diagram consisting of a single pattern using all 100 numbers.

In Figure 19.11, we take the numbers from 0 to 99, square them, and then add that same number again before we take the two least significant digits and repeat the process. In this patterns there aren't any loops; instead, every number goes to an attractor of some kind. And here we notice that all of the attractors are even numbers. This is because an even number squared plus an even number will result in an even number, and an odd number squared plus an odd number will also result in an even number.

Interesting patterns within these patterns can also be seen when we circle pairs of numbers (as we did earlier with the squared two-digit diagram). Except for the numbers that end with a 0 or a 5, I've paired the numbers in the following diagrams so that they are next to (or at least close to) a complement number. In figures 19.6 through 19.10 the numbers are paired so that the number and its complement add to 100. These same numbers also could have been easily arranged so that they have a difference of 50.

In figure 19.11, the numbers are paired so that they add to 99. In this case it isn't a simple matter to group the numbers in pairs so that they add to 100; however, as just mentioned, 99 appears to be the more natural sum. In that figure, it is also possible to pair the numbers so that they have a difference of 50; however, to do so requires the combination of two similar patterns, as with the 56 and 6 attractors, or the 70 and the 20 attractors, along with the other numbers in their respective patterns.

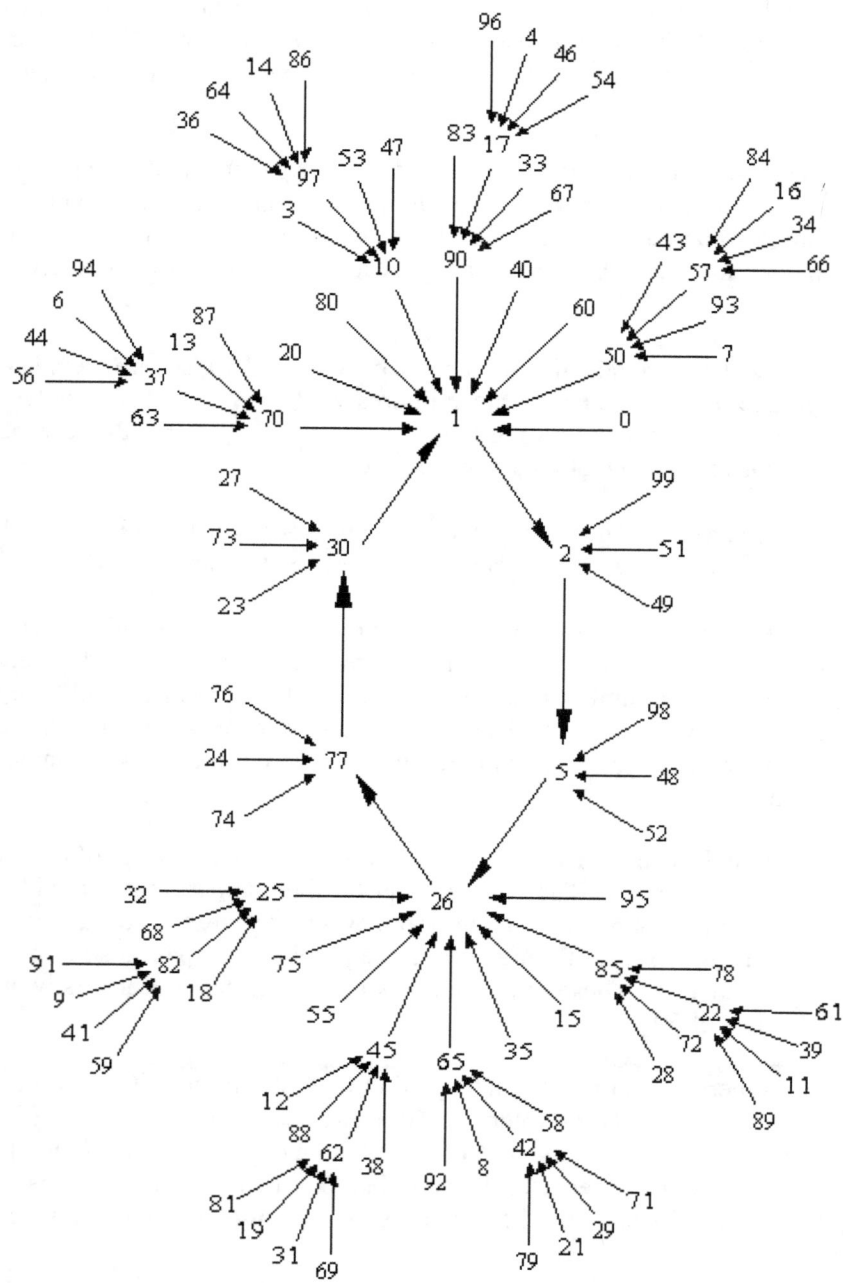

Figure 19.6   The two-digit (or MOD 100) natural integer network diagram for values 0 - 99 squared plus one.

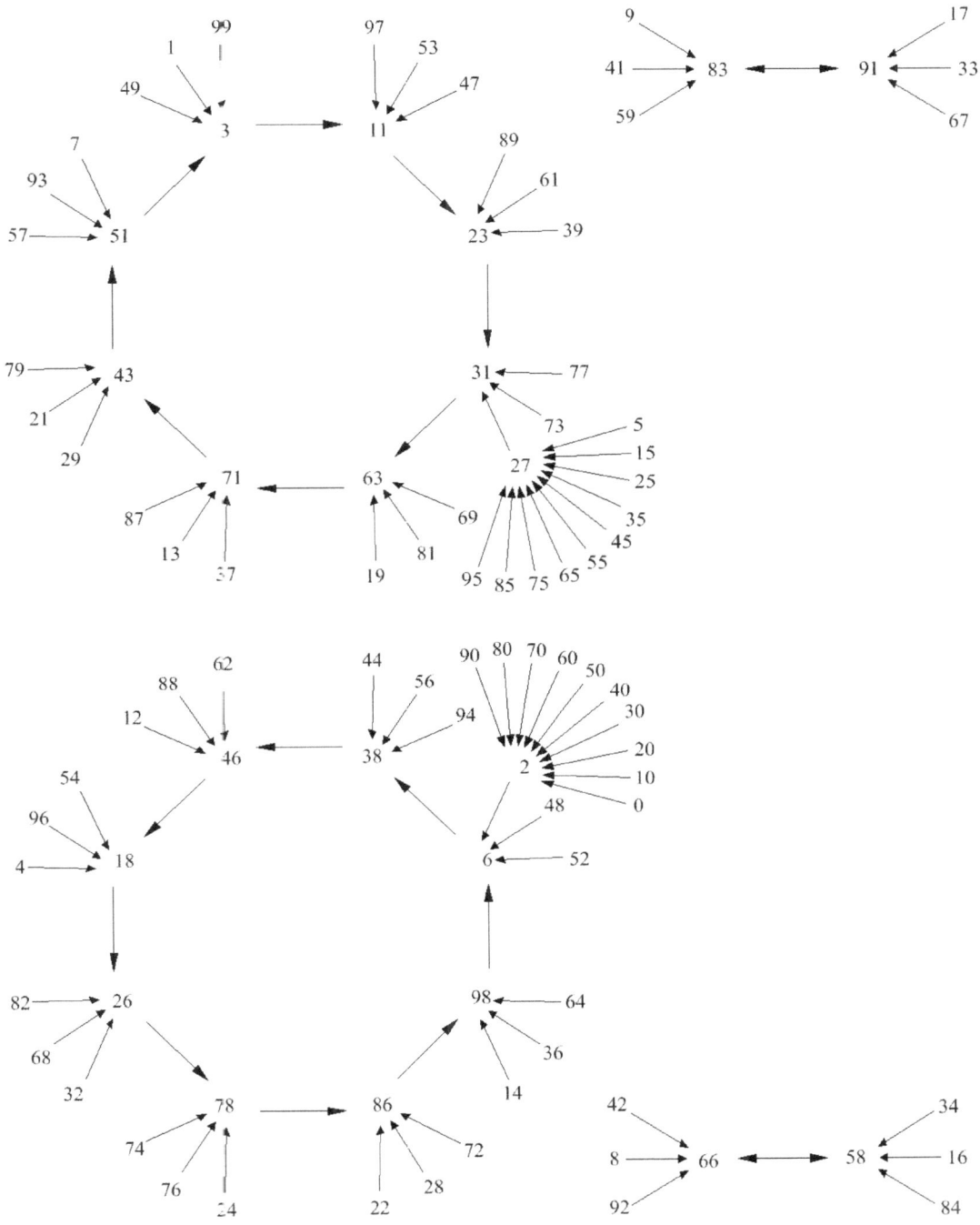

Figure 19.7   The 2-digit (or MOD 100) diagram for the numbers 0 - 99 squared plus two. The odd-number patterns are on top, and the even-number patterns are on the bottom.

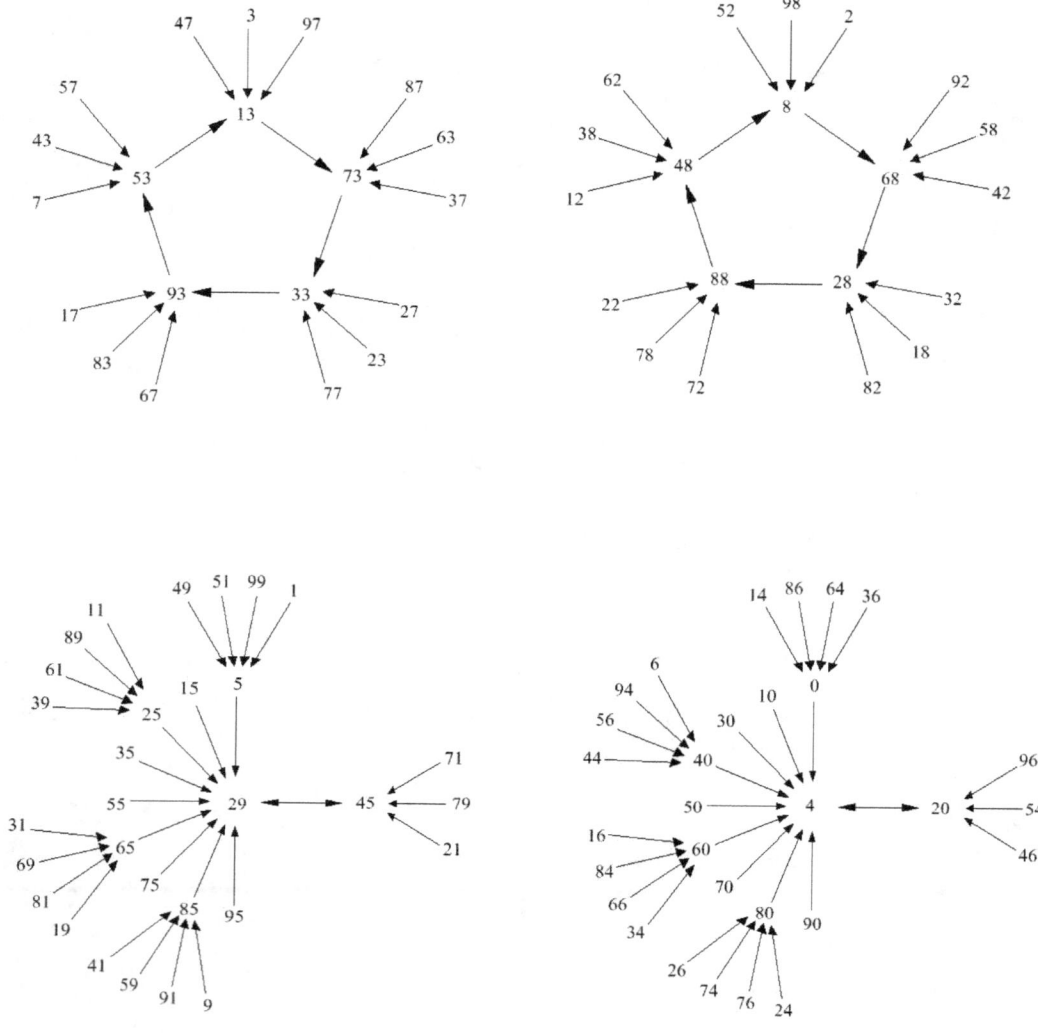

Figure 19.8   The 2-digit (or MOD 100) diagram for the numbers 0 - 99 squared plus four. The odd-number patterns are on the left, and the even-number patterns are on the right.

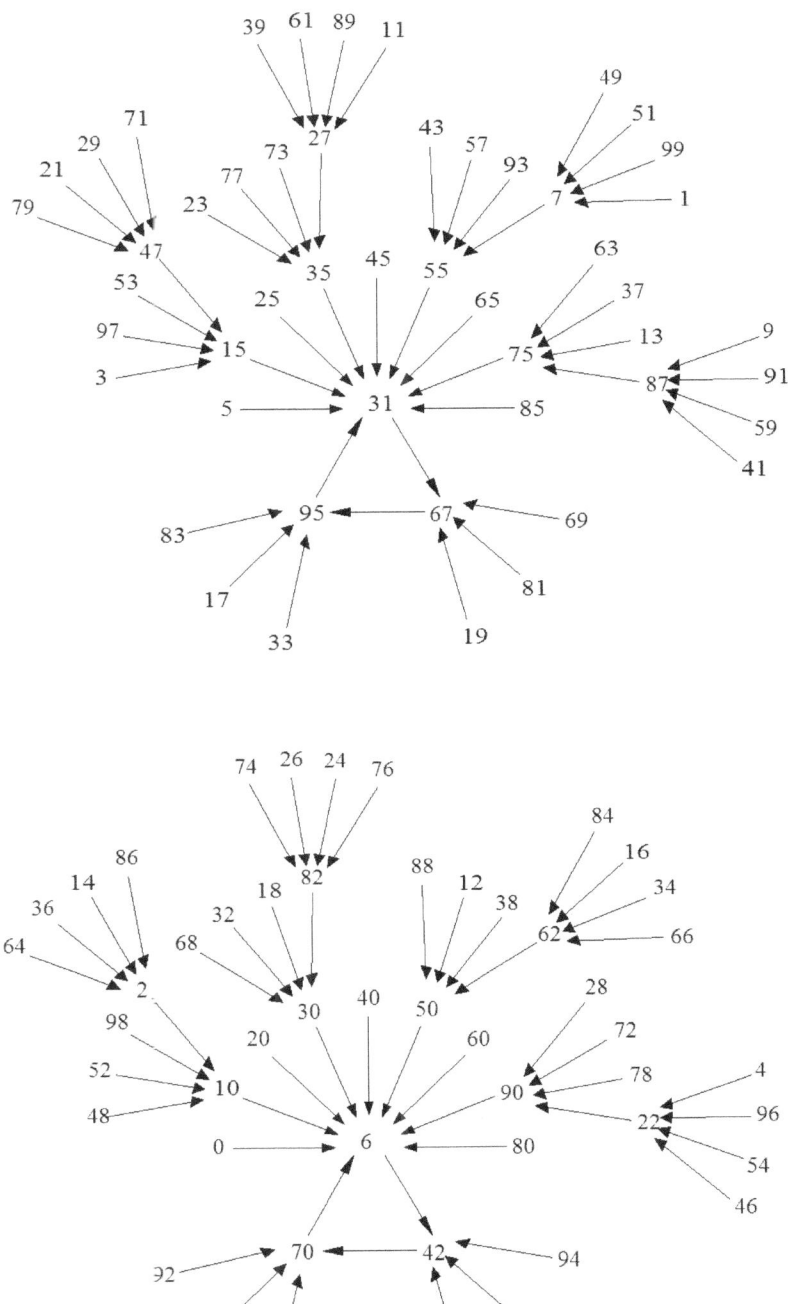

Figure 19.9   The 2-digit (or MOD 100) diagram for 0 - 99 squared plus six. The odd
number pattern is on the top, and the even number pattern is on the bottom.

303

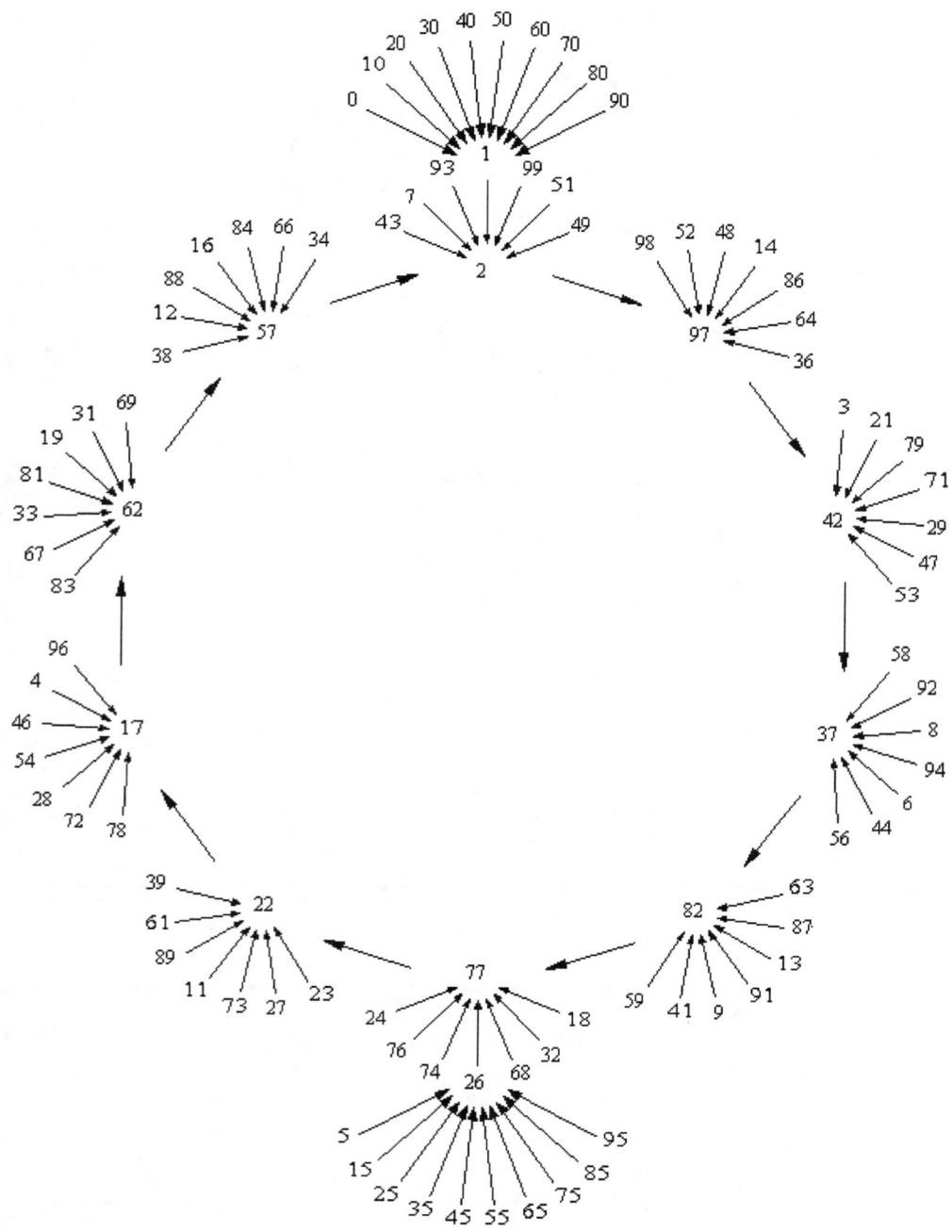

Figure 19.10   The two-digit (or MOD 100) natural integer network diagram for the numbers 0 - 99 raised to the 12th power plus one.

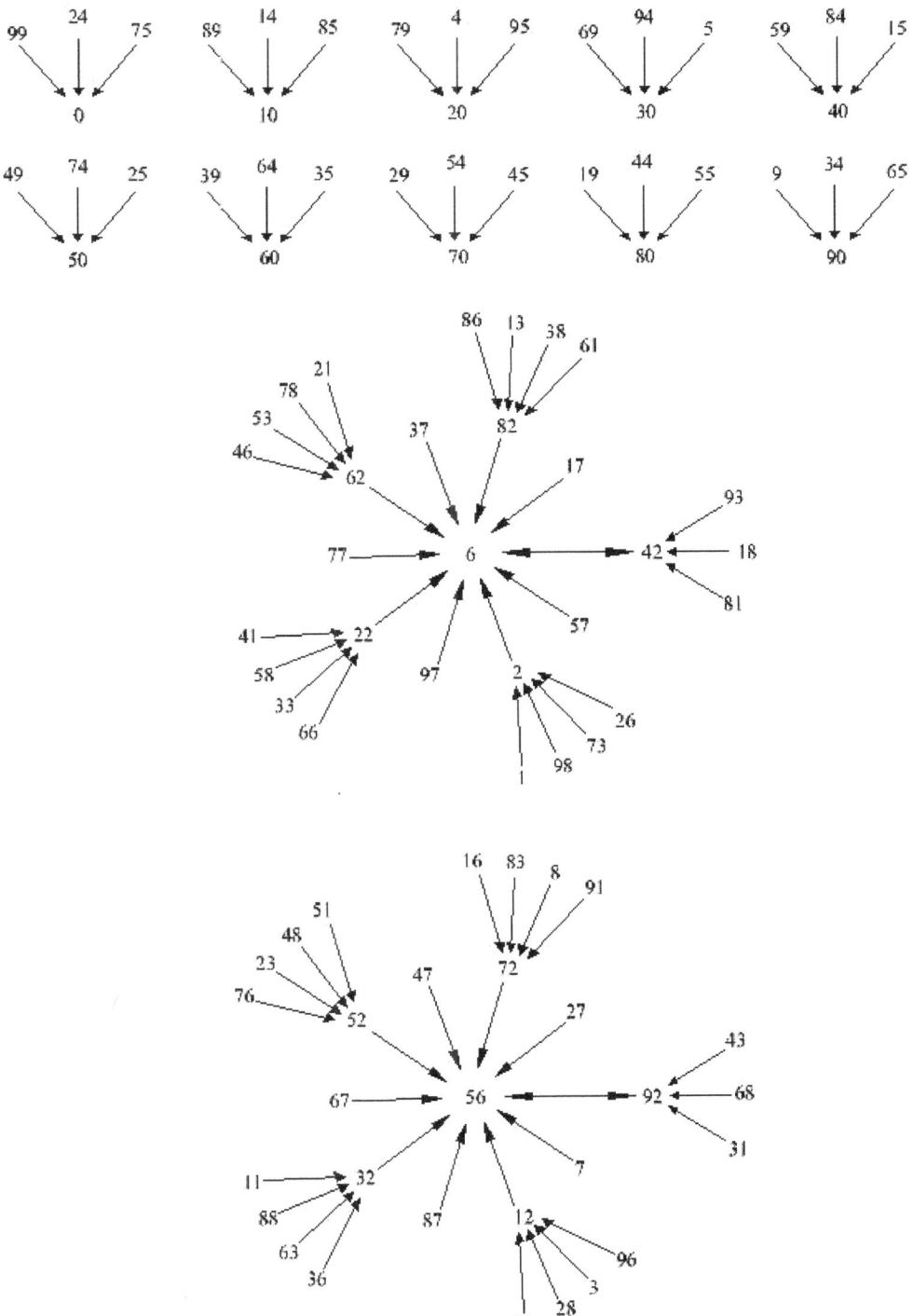

Figure 19.11   The 2-digit (or MOD 100) diagram for the numbers 0 - 99 squared plus that number again (which can be represented by the equation: $x^2 + x$).

Unusual Natural Integer Networks

Up to this point all of the figures that we've looked at appear to have some kind symmetry within the figure, and while that appears to be true in most cases, it isn't true in all cases. The figure below shows the numbers 0 to 99 cubed plus one. It almost looks like the pattern is trying to be symmetrical, but it just doesn't quite make it.

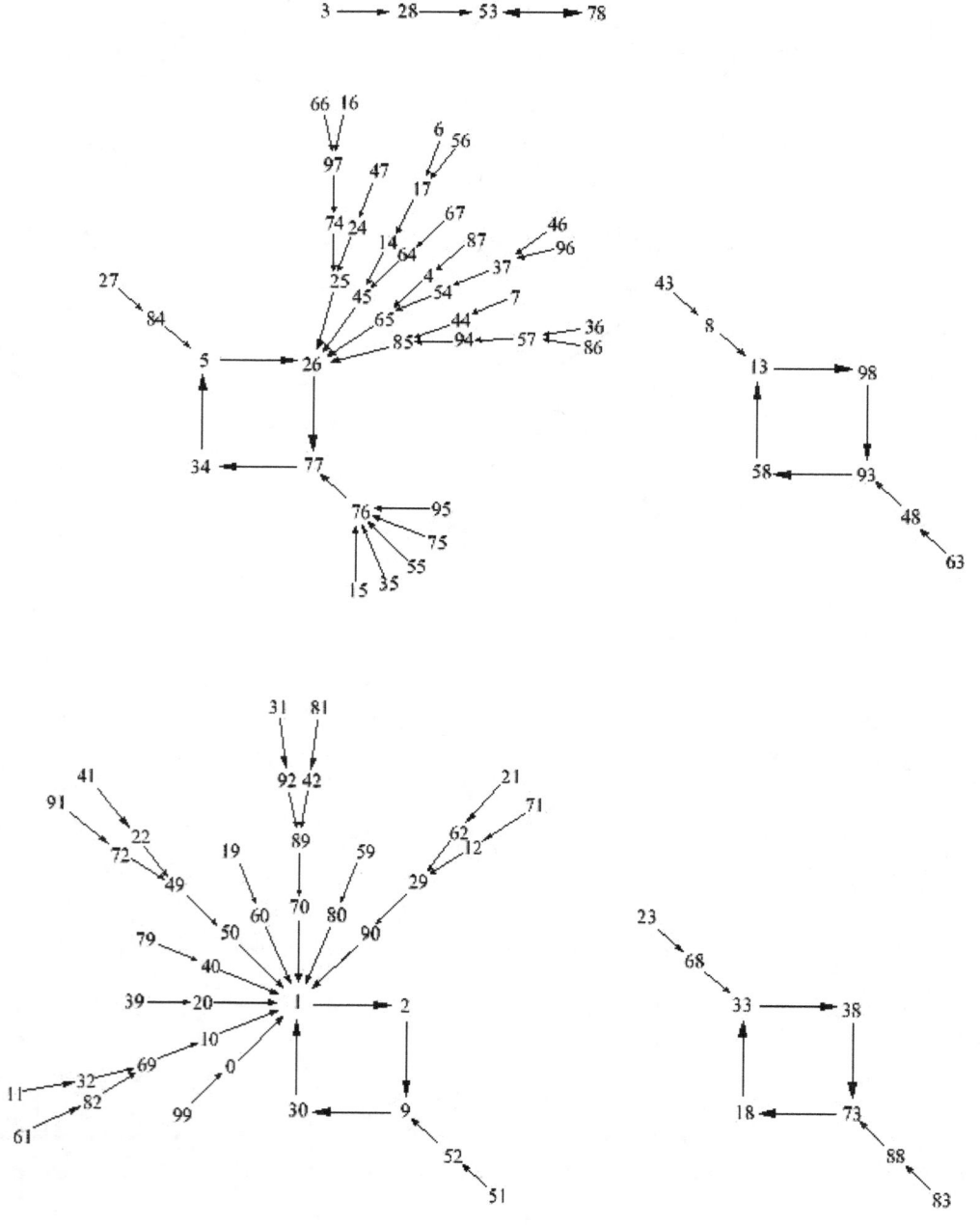

Figure 19.12   The 2-digit (or MOD 100) diagram for the numbers 0 - 99 cubed plus one.

As I examined the lists of numbers that made these previous drawings, I noticed patterns within the lists themselves. The most common pattern is that the numbers would ascend in a certain order, and then descend in reverse order. For example, if we consider the numbers from 0 to 100, looking at the first several two-digit numbers of the squared function, we have 0, 1, 4, 9, 16, 25, etc.; and now if we look at the last several two-digit numbers we see these same numbers in reverse order: ..., 25, 16, 9, 4, 1, 0.

Now, if we were to consider the numbers from 100 to 200, square the numbers, and then look at the last two-digits of these numbers, we would see the same pattern, i.e., the first several two-digit numbers would be 0, 1, 4, 9, 16, 25, etc; and at the end of the range we would see these same numbers in reverse order: ..., 25, 16, 9, 4, 1, 0. This pattern is very consistent, and appears over and over and over again. But this pattern isn't universal. There are exceptions. One of them can be seen when we look at the pentagonal numbers.

If we take pentagonal numbers, and look at the right-most two-digits over the range from 0 to 100, we see an interesting development. The numbers cycle up as we would expect with a 0, 1, 5, 12, 22, 35, 51, ... and then as we approach somewhere around the 60th pentagonal number, we see these same numbers in reverse order (or cycling down). This is a shorter cycle, but other than that, it doesn't seem so unusual. However, the next cycle that starts up is different from the previous cycle. The first few numbers of this second cycle are: 0, 2, 7, 15, 26, 40, ...; and we don't see these numbers cycle back down until we reach the 200th pentagonal number. Then starting with the 200th number we see our first cycle start up again (the numbers 1, 5, 12, 22, etc.)

We should note here that triangular numbers repeat their 2-digit pattern every 200 numbers, as do heptagonal numbers (however, heptagonal numbers don't cycle back down, they just start repeating their cycle over again); so pentagonal numbers aren't unusual for having a 200 number 2-digit pattern. They just appear to be unusual in that they have two unique cycles within that 200 number range.

Remember, that when we look at the two right-most digits of a number, we are doing the same thing as performing a MOD 100 operation on each of the digits. Now, if we were to perform a MOD 50 operation on our pentagonal numbers, we would still find the two cycles with the first cycle again going from the first to the 67th number, and the second cycle going from the 67th number to the 100th number. And then the pattern repeats itself starting with the 101st number.

To sum up what we have so far: When we perform a MOD 100 operation on the pentagonal numbers, we find a pattern that repeats every 200 numbers, and within this pattern we have two unique cycles. When we perform a MOD 50 operation on the pentagonal numbers, we find a pattern that repeats every 100 numbers, and within this pattern we still find two unique cycles.

So, let's experiment just a little more. This time we'll perform a MOD 67 operation on our pentagonal numbers. We find that we still have two unique cycles that repeat; however, this time our pattern repeats every 67 numbers. In this case we have a pattern that is in sync with the MOD number.

Now, if we were to draw the natural integer network from our list of MOD 100 or MOD 50 pentagonal numbers, we would see patterns that leave much to be desired. However, when we draw the network from our list of MOD 67 numbers, we get the following pattern.

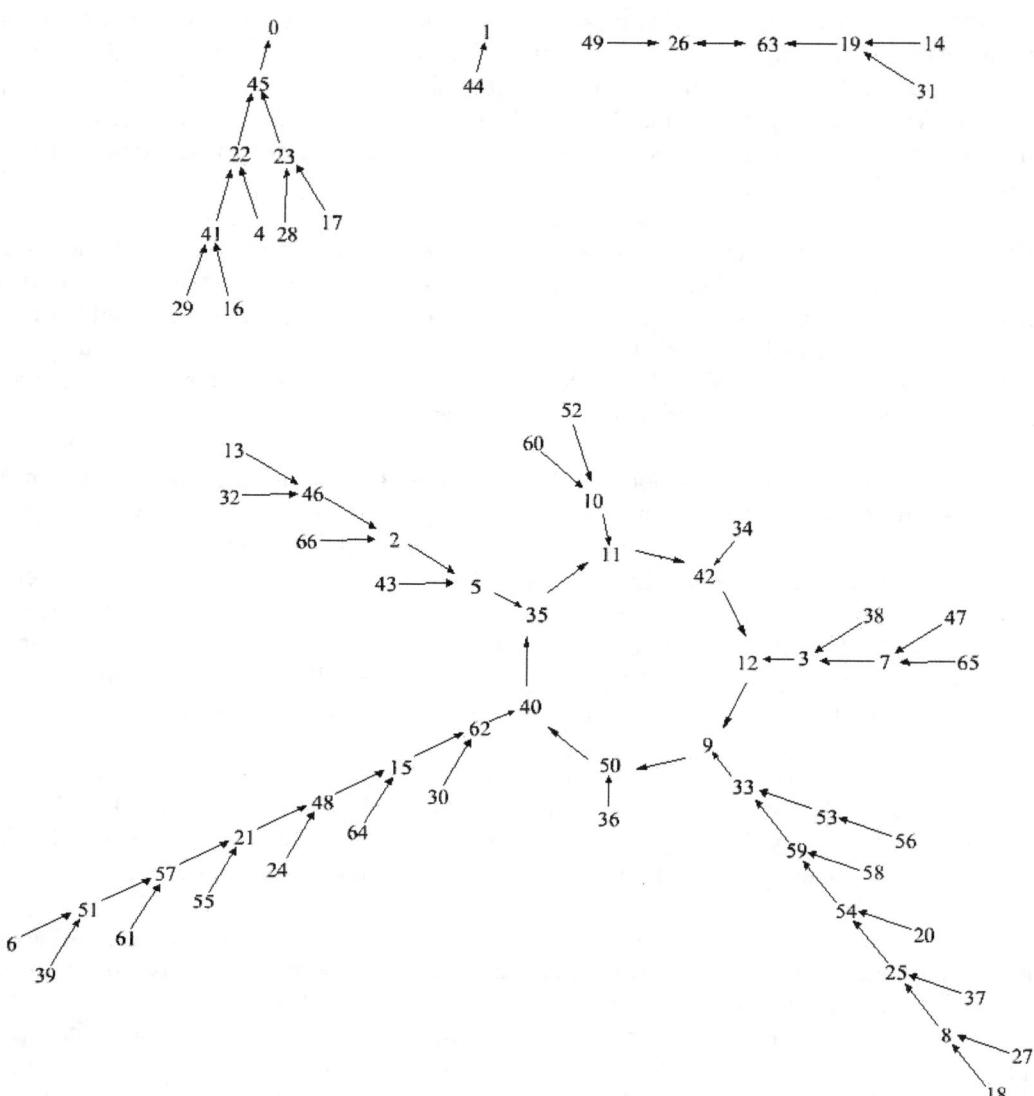

Figure 19.13   These are the first 67 pentagonal numbers operated on by the MOD 67 function.

You may think that this pattern also leaves much to be desired, however, the pattern above is very interesting. It has two attractors, one 2-node loop, and one 7-node loop; and it turns out that this pattern isn't that unique. Let's continue with our experimenting.

If we now perform a MOD 267 operation on our list of pentagonal numbers, we again find that our pattern is in sync with the MOD number; however, this time we only have one cycle. And this set of numbers cycles up with the same numbers of the first cycle from previous sets (i.e., 1, 5, 12, 22, 35), and cycles down with the number from the second cycle (40, 26, 15, 7, 2). Drawing the network gives us the following set of three figures.

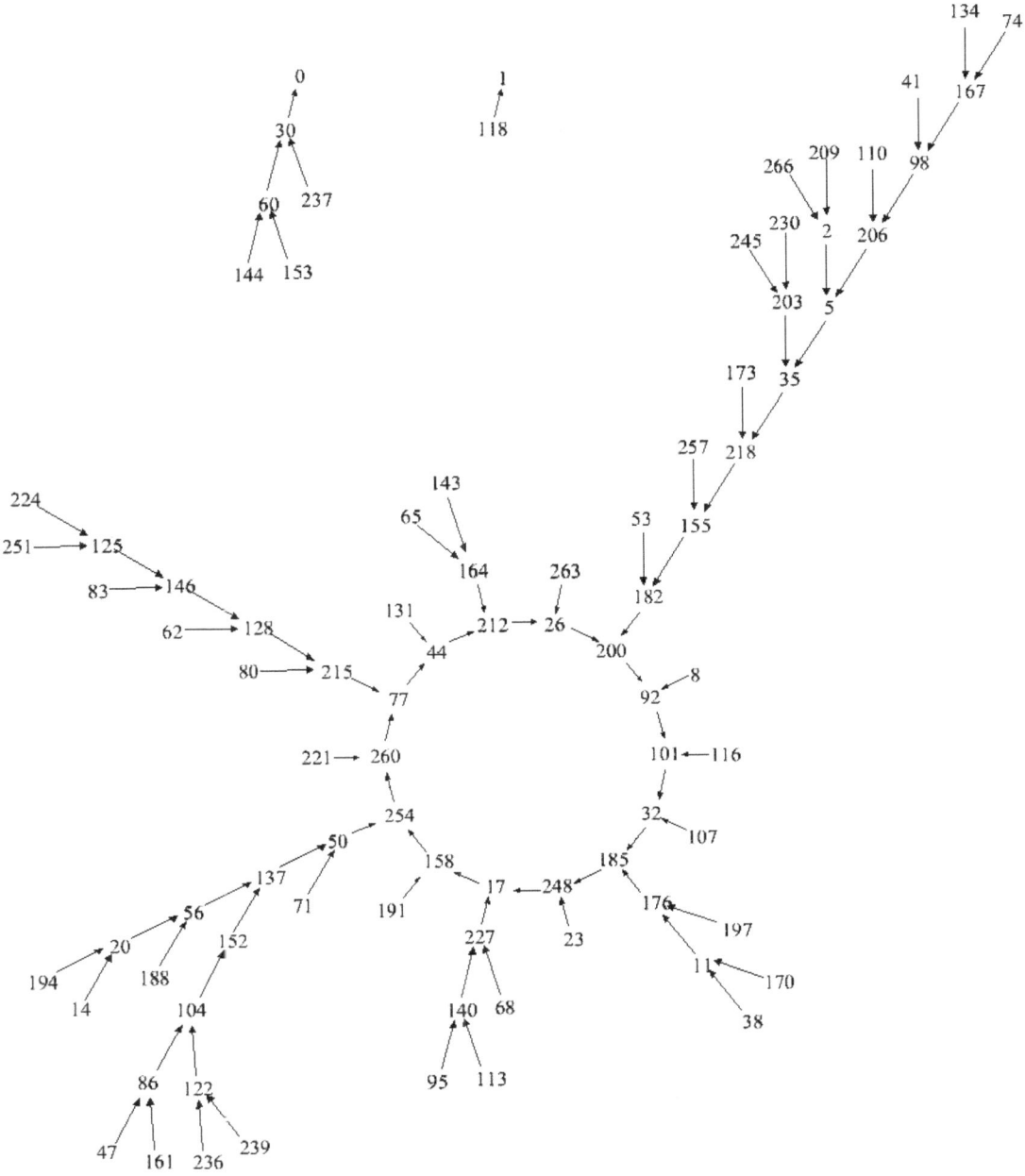

Figure 19.14   This is Plate 1 of the first 267 pentagonal numbers operated on by the MOD 267 function.

These three figures belong to the same network drawing and are divided into Plates 1, 2, and 3 only because this makes it easier to examine this network.

The natural integer network for the pentagonal numbers with a MOD 267 operation performed on them shows six attractors, and three 14-node loops. The six attractors are 0, 1, 89, 90, 178, and 179.

309

Note that the matching of the attractors with the 14-node loops in the plates is purely arbitrary.

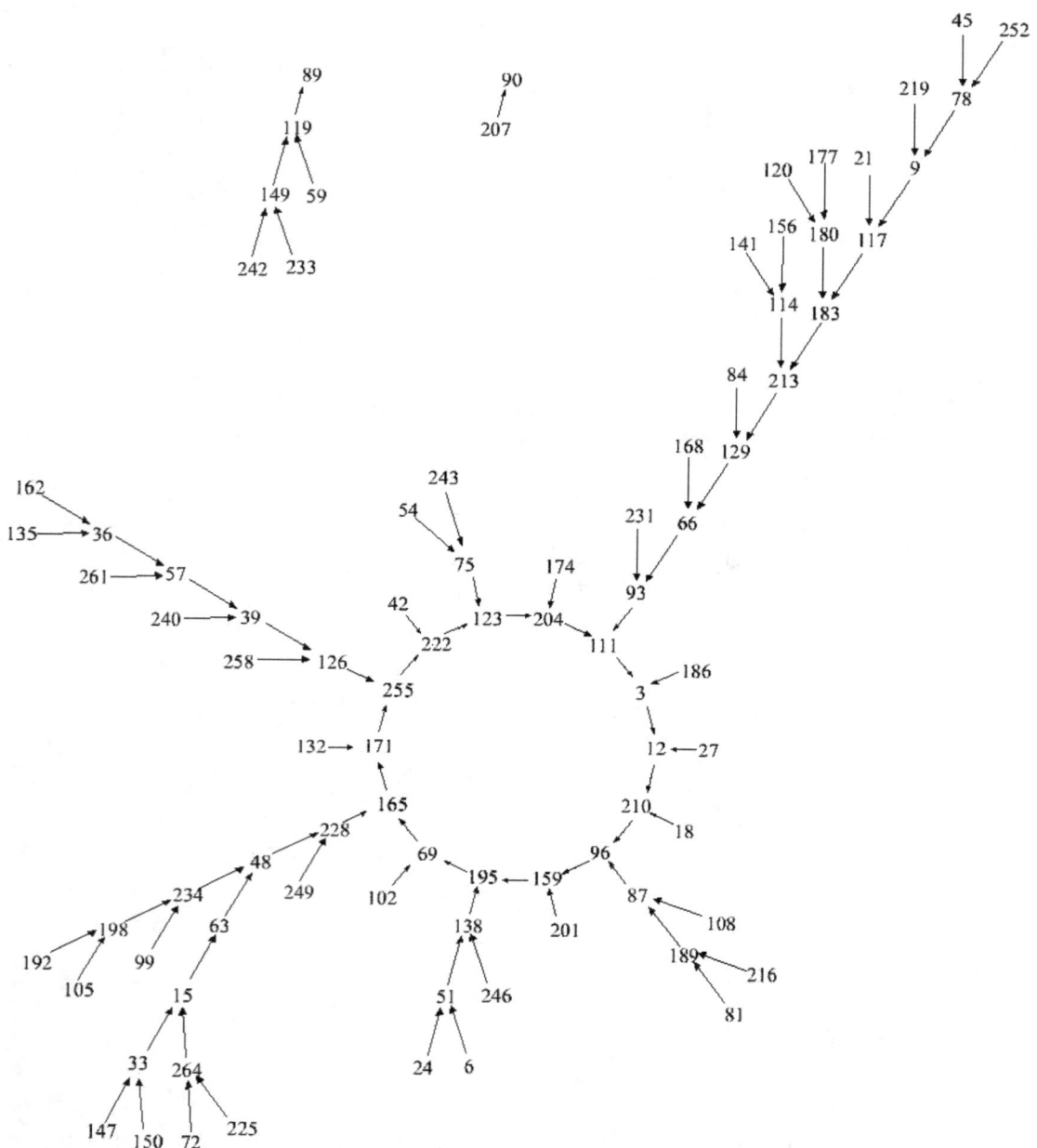

Figure 19.15   This is Plate 2 of the first 267 pentagonal numbers operated on by the MOD 267 function.

In the three plates of this network, we find matching patterns. For example, the attractors can be paired with their adjacent numbers. If we do this, we see that the lower number has a similar structure between the three plates, as does the attractor with the higher number. We can easily see that the 14-node loops all share an identical structure when compared with each other between the three plates.

We can also go back and compare these structures with the structure of the MOD 67 diagram. Again, we find many similarities.

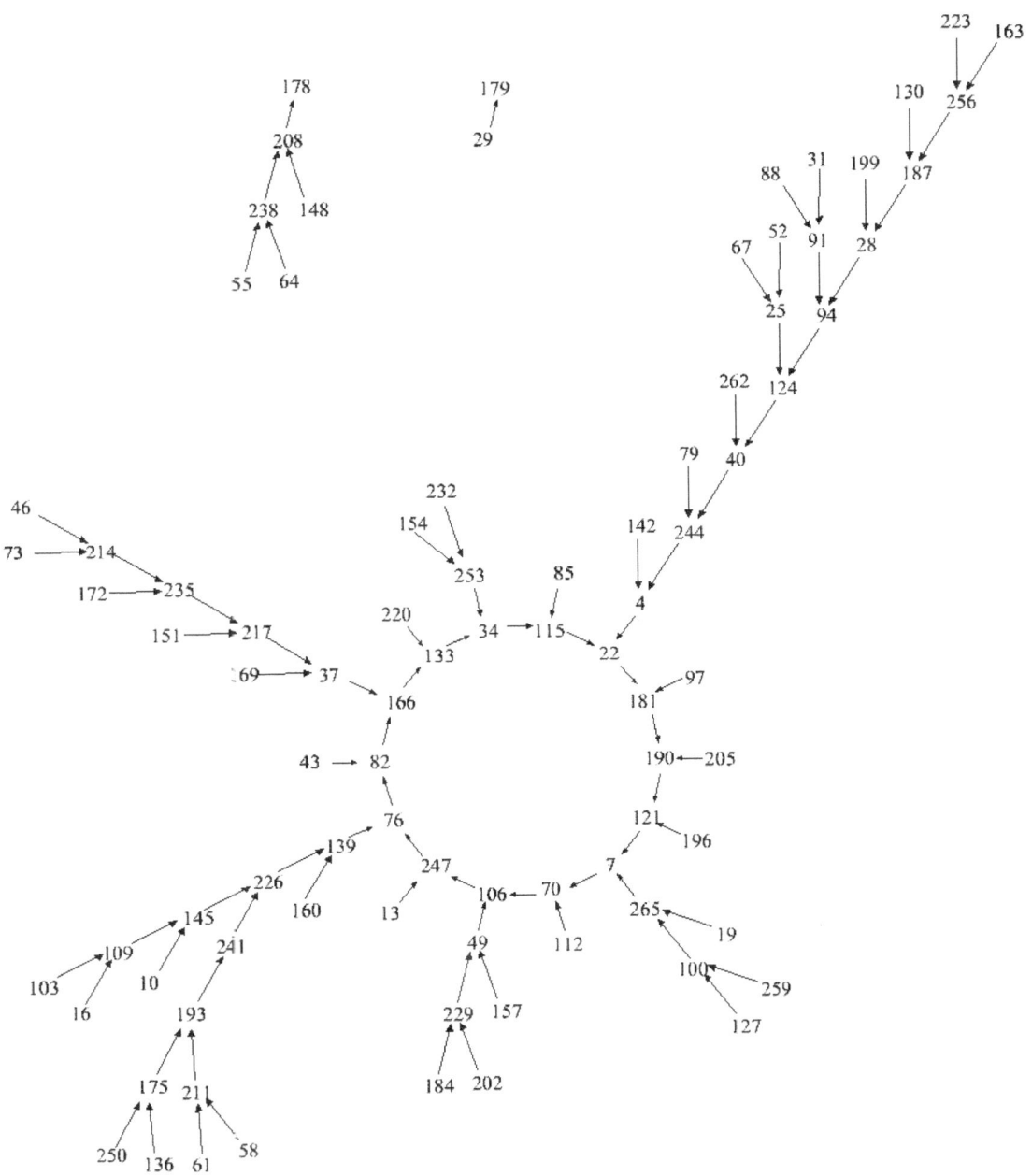

Figure 19.16   This is Plate 3 of the first 267 pentagonal numbers operated on by the MOD 267 function.

311

And the patterns continue. We have barely even scratched the surface of the many possibilities. For example, we don't need to limit ourselves to just the two-digit numbers, and as we just saw, we don't need to limit ourselves to just the MOD 100 operator. One avenue that can be pursued is to take the numbers from 0 to 999 and square them and then look at the three least significant digits (this is the same as performing a MOD 1000 operation on the squared numbers); or we could take the numbers from 0 to 9999 and square them and then look at the four least significant digits.

For example, toward the beginning of this chapter, we saw that with the 2-digit numbers there are two odd attractors, 1 and 25, and two even attractors, 0 and 76. If we now examine 3-digit numbers there are again two odd attractors, 1 and 625, and two even attractors 0 and 376. With 4-digit numbers have two odd attractors, 1 and 0625 (or just 625) and two even attractors, 0 and 9376; and 5-digit numbers also have two odd attractors, 1 and 90625, and two even attractors, 0 and 09376 (or just 9376). These attractors are shown in the top part of the following table.

	2-Digit Numbers	3-Digit Numbers	4-Digit Numbers	5-Digit Numbers
Attractors Odd	1 25	1 625	1 625	1 90625
Attractors Even	0 76	0 376	0 9376	0 9376
4-Node Loop Odd	21 41 81 61	201 401 801 601	2001 4001 8001 6001	20001 40001 80001 60001
4-Node Loop Even	16 56 36 96	176 976 576 776	1376 3376 7376 5376	29376 49376 89376 69376

Table 19.2   A listing of 2-digit through 5-digit numbers showing the values of odd and even attractors as well as the values of the odd and even 4-node loops

The table above also shows that along with the 2-digit numbers, the 3-digit, 4-digit and 5-digit numbers also all have even and odd 4-node loops. For example, if we look at the 3-digit numbers and took 201 and squared it we would get 40401. The right-most 3-digits are 401. Squaring that gives us 160801 with the right-most 3-digits equal to 801. Continuing this process would give us 601 and then the next iteration brings us back to 201. The values of these 4-node loops for the 2-digit through 5-digit numbers are shown in the table above.

In fact, as we examine the 3-digit numbers more closely, we see that they also have an odd and even 20-node loop. We also see that the 4-digit and 5-digit numbers also have odd and even 20-node loops. And it doesn't stop there, 4-digit and 5-digit numbers each have an odd and even

100-node loop; and 5-digit numbers have an odd and even 500-node loop. These corresponding loops are summed up in the following table.

	2-Digit Numbers	3-Digit Numbers	4-Digit Numbers	5-Digit Numbers
Attractors				
Odd	Yes	Yes	Yes	Yes
Even	Yes	Yes	Yes	Yes
4-Node Loop				
Odd	Yes	Yes	Yes	Yes
Even	Yes	Yes	Yes	Yes
20-Node Loop				
Odd	No	Yes	Yes	Yes
Even	No	Yes	Yes	Yes
100-Node Loop				
Odd	No	No	Yes	Yes
Even	No	No	Yes	Yes
500-Node Loop				
Odd	No	No	No	Yes
Even	No	No	No	Yes

Table 19.3   A listing of 2-digit through 5-digit numbers showing their respective loop structures.

From some of the work I've done, as more digits are considered, the patterns of numbers approaching the nodes also become more complex although they still maintain many symmetries within themselves, as well as share similar structures with their original two-digit patterns.

In the next chapter we will continue the exploration of these networks; however, due to the vast number of possibilities, we will limit ourselves to only a comparatively few attractors. (In fact, we will see that we can call these attractors by another name. They are also known as automorphic numbers).

Chapter 20
Automorphic Numbers and Natural Integer Networks

Automorphic Numbers

The numbers 0, 1, 5 and 6 have a unique property. When squared, the least significant (right-most) digit is the same as the original number. Of course zero squared is equal to zero and one squared is equal to one, so no surprise there. Five squared gives us 25 which has a five as the least significant digit, and six squared yields 36, whose least significant digit is six. Because these numbers, when squared, generate themselves in this way, they are called automorphic.

Of the first ten single-digit numbers (the numbers 0 through 9) four of them are automorphic. Now, if we look at two-digit numbers (the numbers 00 through 99), we find again that there are only four numbers that are automorphic. They are the numbers 00, 01, 25 and 76. The 00 (or just 0) and the 01 (or just 1) are obvious; however, the other two numbers are starting to become a little more interesting. Here we notice that 25 squared gives us 625 which has 25 as the two right-most digits, and 76 squared gives us 5776 which has 76 as the two right-most digits.

Continuing on with three-digit numbers (the numbers 000 through 999), once again we find that there are only four automorphic numbers. They are 000, 001, 625 and 376. And if we look at the four-digit numbers 0000 through 9999, again we find that there are only four numbers that are automorphic. They are 0000, 0001, 0625 and 9376. By now, we can see that we are always going to have a 0 and 1 as two of the automorphic numbers. They are considered trivial. However, the other two numbers, the numbers that end with a 5 and a 6, have some interesting properties. The following table lists the automorphic numbers that end with a 5 and a 6. This table shows these numbers as the number of digits considered increases from one to seven.

Number of Digits	The 5 Number	The 6 Number	Sum of 5 and 6 Numbers
1	5	6	11
2	25	76	101
3	625	376	1001
4	0625	9376	10001
5	90625	09376	100001
6	890625	109376	1000001
7	2890625	7109376	10000001

Table 20.1   The "5" and "6" automorphic numbers for digits 1 through 7.

One of the first characteristics we see is that as the number of digits increases, each automorphic number retains its previous automorphic number. For example, the automorphic number 9376 contains the previous automorphic number which was 376; and this number contains the previous automorphic number, which was 76.

Also, the pattern of the sums of each pair of "5" and "6" numbers is equal to some power of 10 plus 1. If we consider the two-digit numbers, their sum is equal to $10^2 + 1$, or 101. The sum of the three-digit numbers is equal to $10^3 + 1$, or 1001. And as we look at more digits, the sum is equal to 10 raised to a power plus one, where the power is equal to the number of digits in the "5" or "6" number.

Another property that isn't quite so obvious is that if we take the "5" number and square it, the result has the next digit that should be added to the left, for the next higher number. For example, the one-digit automorphic number is 5; and when we square the 5 we get 25, and 25 is the two-digit automorphic number. Then, squaring 25 gives us 625, and 625 is the three-digit automorphic number. Likewise, 625 squared is 390625, and the number 0625 is the four-digit automorphic number. In this case it also has the five-digit automorphic number, but just to be certain, we can square 390625. This gives us 152587890625, and the last five-digits are the next automorphic number (which is the number 90625).

We can continue this approach indefinitely where each time we square the "5" number we find the next digit in the automorphic number sequence. However, this property only works with the "5" number. It won't work with the "6" number. For example, 6 squared is 36, but the two-digit "6" number is 76. Therefore, the way to find a particular "6" automorphic number is to subtract the corresponding "5" number from the $10^x + 1$ number. Doing so gives us the corresponding "6" number. With this knowledge we have the tools we need to find any automorphic number that we desire. Here are 50 digits of the two automorphic numbers:

$$57423423230896109004106619977392256259918212890625$$

$$42576576769103890995893380022607743740081787109376$$

And because each number contains the previous numbers (as mentioned above), by knowing the 50-digit automorphic numbers, we also automatically know all of the previous automorphic numbers.

Automorphic Numbers in Other Bases

The automorphic numbers that we've looked at to this point are all in base 10. Now, we'll consider some automorphic numbers in other bases. This automorphic property depends on the base that the numbers are written in. The "5" and "6" numbers only work in base 10. Altogether, base 10 numbers have four automorphic numbers, which are 0, 1, a "5" number and a "6" number. And it appears that all bases have the numbers 0 and 1 as automorphic numbers. However, not all bases have additional automorphic numbers. For example, none of the prime number bases have additional automorphic numbers outside of 0 and 1.

In fact, the only bases under and including base 21 that have automorphic numbers (in addition to the numbers 0 and 1) appear to be bases 6, 10, 12, 14, 15, 18, 20 and 21. Not only are the prime number bases missing from this list but so are bases that are a power of a prime number, such as the bases that are the powers of two, and the powers of three.

The additional automorphic numbers in these other bases share most of the same properties as the "5" and "6" automorphic numbers in base 10. They always come in a pair such that if you add them together they are equal to $10^x + 1$ in their respective base (again where x is equal to the number of digits being considered). However, only the even bases listed above share the property that if you square the odd automorphic number, you can use this result to find the next digit needed to be placed in front of the current number.

315

The following tables show the automorphic numbers in bases 6, 12, 14, 15, 18, 20 and 21 (the table showing the base 10 automorphic numbers was presented earlier in this chapter). The following table is a brief listing of the base 6 automorphic numbers:

Number of Digits	The 3 Number	The 4 Number	Sum of 3 and 4 Numbers
1	3_6	4_6	11_6
2	13_6	44_6	101_6
3	213_6	344_6	1001_6
4	0213_6	5344_6	10001_6
5	50213_6	05344_6	100001_6
6	350213_6	205344_6	1000001_6
7	1350213_6	4205344_6	10000001_6

Table 20.2   Automorphic numbers in base 6 for digits 1 through 7.

This is a brief listing of the automorphic numbers in base 12:

Number of Digits	The 9 Number	The 4 Number	Sum of 9 and 4 Numbers
1	9_{12}	4_{12}	11_{12}
2	69_{12}	54_{12}	101_{12}
3	369_{12}	854_{12}	1001_{12}
4	8369_{12}	3854_{12}	10001_{12}
5	08369_{12}	$b3854_{12}$	100001_{12}
6	$a08369_{12}$	$1b3854_{12}$	1000001_{12}
7	$5a08369_{12}$	$61b3854_{12}$	10000001_{12}

Table 20.3   Automorphic numbers in base 12 for digits 1 through 7.

These are the automorphic numbers in base 14:

Number of Digits	The 7 Number	The 8 Number	Sum of 7 and 8 Numbers
1	7_{14}	8_{14}	11_{14}
2	37_{14}	$a8_{14}$	101_{14}
3	$c37_{14}$	$1a8_{14}$	1001_{14}
4	$0c37_{14}$	$d1a8_{14}$	10001_{14}
5	$a0c37_{14}$	$3d1a8_{14}$	100001_{14}
6	$aa0c37_{14}$	$33d1a8_{14}$	1000001_{14}
7	$7aa0c37_{14}$	$633d1a8_{14}$	10000001_{14}

Table 20.4   Automorphic numbers in base 14 for digits 1 through 7.

316

The following is a brief listing of the automorphic numbers in base 15:

Number of Digits	The 6 Number	The a Number	Sum of 6 and a Numbers
1	6_{15}	a_{15}	11_{15}
2	86_{15}	$6a_{15}$	101_{15}
3	$a86_{15}$	$46a_{15}$	1001_{15}
4	$da86_{15}$	$146a_{15}$	10001_{15}
5	$bda86_{15}$	$3146a_{15}$	100001_{15}
6	$4bda86_{15}$	$a3146a_{15}$	1000001_{15}
7	$d4bda86_{15}$	$1a3146a_{15}$	10000001_{15}

Table 20.5   Automorphic numbers in base 15 for digits 1 through 7.

The following is a brief listing of the automorphic numbers in base 18:

Number of Digits	The 9 Number	The a Number	Sum of 9 and a Numbers
1	9_{18}	a_{18}	11_{18}
2	49_{18}	da_{18}	101_{18}
3	249_{18}	fda_{18}	1001_{18}
4	1249_{18}	$gfda_{18}$	10001_{18}
5	$e1249_{18}$	$3gfda_{18}$	100001_{18}
6	$4e1249_{18}$	$d3gfda_{18}$	1000001_{18}
7	$a4e1249_{18}$	$7d3gfda_{18}$	10000001_{18}

Table 20.6   Automorphic numbers in base 18 for digits 1 through 7.

And these are the first few automorphic numbers in base 20:

Number of Digits	The 5 Number	The g Number	Sum of 5 and g Numbers
1	5_{20}	g_{20}	11_{20}
2	$b5_{20}$	$8g_{20}$	101_{20}
3	$6b5_{20}$	$d8g_{20}$	1001_{20}
4	$b6b5_{20}$	$8d8g_{20}$	10001_{20}
5	$ab6b5_{20}$	$98d8g_{20}$	100001_{20}
6	$1ab6b5_{20}$	$i98d8g_{20}$	1000001_{20}
7	$21ab6b5_{20}$	$hi98d8g_{20}$	10000001_{20}

Table 20.7   Automorphic numbers in base 20 for digits 1 through 7.

And these are the first few automorphic numbers in base 21:

Number of Digits	The 7 Number	The f Number	Sum of 7 and f Numbers
1	7_{21}	f_{21}	11_{21}
2	$g7_{21}$	$4f_{21}$	101_{21}
3	$7g7_{21}$	$d4f_{21}$	1001_{21}
4	$h7g7_{21}$	$3d4f_{21}$	10001_{21}
5	$6h7g7_{21}$	$e3d4f_{21}$	100001_{21}
6	$86h7g7_{21}$	$ce3d4f_{21}$	1000001_{21}
7	$j86h7g7_{21}$	$1ce3d4f_{21}$	10000001_{21}

Table 20.8   Automorphic numbers in base 21 for digits 1 through 7.

Remember that with bases above base 10, we let a = 10, b = 11, c = 12, d = 13, e = 14, f = 15, g = 16, h = 17, i = 18, j = 19, and k = 20. It is interesting to note that with bases 6, 10, 14, and 18, the automorphic numbers are consecutive numbers, in that for base 6 there is a 3 number and a 4 number. Base 10 has a 5 and a 6 number; base 14 has a 7 and an 8 number; and base 18 has a 9 and a 10 number (with 10 represented by the letter a).

Automorphic Numbers and Prime Numbers

Let's briefly review again how automorphic numbers are found. In each case (in each base), we took a range of numbers, one at a time, and squared them, and then looked at the right most digits (the least significant digits) to see if the number generated itself. For the one-digit numbers in base 10, we took the numbers 0 through 9, one at a time, squared them, and then performed a Mod 10 operation on them, and found that 0, 1, 5, and 6 were automorphic. In the other bases, we basically did the same thing; for example, in base 14, we took the numbers 0 through 13, squared them, and then performed a Mod 14 operation on those numbers to find that 0, 1, 7, and 8 were automorphic.

For the two-digit numbers in base 14, we took the numbers 0 through $14^2 - 1$, squared each of them, and then performed a Mod 100_{14} operation on those numbers to find that 0_{14}, 1_{14}, 37_{14}, and $a8_{14}$ are automorphic. That worked great in base 14; however, we could have done the same thing for the numbers in base 14, but work in base 10 by taking the numbers 0 through 195 (where 195 is equal to $14^2 - 1$), squaring them, and then performing a Mod 196 operation on those numbers to find that 0, 1, 49, and 148 are automorphic. Then we could have converted 49 and 148 to base 14, and we would have seen that they are equal to 37_{14}, and $a8_{14}$ respectively. The point is that we can convert all of our numbers to whatever base in which we are working, and do all of our calculations in that base; or more simply, we can do what was described above, and perform all of our calculations in base 10, and still find equivalent results.

In other words, we can do this with any number greater than one and find automorphic numbers for that number. For example, we'll use 188 as our Mod number such that we take the numbers 0 through 187, square each of them, and then perform a Mod 188 operation on those numbers to find that 0, 1, 48, and 141 are automorphic. And if we use the number 189 as our Mod number, we take the numbers 0 through 188, square each of them, and then perform a Mod 189 operation on these numbers to find that 0, 1, 28, and 162 are the automorphic numbers. This seems pretty

318

straight forward for the numbers 188 and 189; however, our results become a little more interesting when we look at 190 and 191. Using 190 as our Mod number, and following the same procedure we find that there are eight automorphic numbers, namely 0, 1, 20, 76, 95, 96, 115, and 171. And then when we use 191 as our Mod number, we find that there are only two automorphic numbers, namely 0 and 1. Obviously, there appears to be some underlying mechanism at work here, but what could it be? Let's take a closer look.

To begin with, we recognize immediately that 191 is a prime number. Earlier in this chapter we saw that prime number bases, and powers of prime number bases only had 0 and 1 as their automorphic numbers. It now becomes apparent that any time we perform a Mod operation using a prime number (or a power of a prime number) as the Mod operator that we will only find 0 and 1 as the automorphic numbers.

The numbers 188 and 189 share the characteristic that they each have two distinct prime factors while 190 has three distinct prime factors. The number 188 has the factors 2^2 and 47, while 189 has the factors 3^3 and 7. When we break 190 into its factors we find that it has the factors 2, 5, and 19. This pattern becomes even more apparent when we look at lists of numbers, their automorphic numbers, and their prime factors.

Number	Automorphic Numbers	Prime Factors
2:	0, 1	2
3:	0, 1	3
4:	0, 1	2^2
5:	0, 1	5
6:	0, 1, 3, 4	2, 3
7:	0, 1	7
8:	0, 1	2^3
9:	0, 1	3^2
10:	0, 1, 5, 6	2, 5
11:	0, 1	11
12:	0, 1, 4, 9	2^2, 3
13:	0, 1	13
14:	0, 1, 7, 8	2, 7
15:	0, 1, 6, 10	3, 5
16:	0, 1	2^4
17:	0, 1	17
18:	0, 1, 9, 10	2, 3^2
19:	0, 1	19
20:	0, 1, 5, 16	2^2, 5
21:	0, 1, 7, 15	3, 7
22:	0, 1, 11, 12	2, 11
23:	0, 1	23
24:	0, 1, 9, 16	2^3, 3
25:	0, 1	5^2
26:	0, 1, 13, 14	2, 13
27:	0, 1	3^3
28:	0, 1, 8, 21	2^2, 7
29:	0, 1	29
30:	0, 1, 6, 10, 15, 16, 21, 25	2, 3, 5

List 20.1   A listing of numbers, their automorphic numbers, and their prime factors.

The list above shows the number, its automorphic numbers, and the prime factors for the numbers 2 through 30. All the prime numbers and powers of a prime number only have one distinct prime factor, and two automorphic numbers (0 and 1); while all other numbers less than 30 have two distinct prime factors, and four automorphic numbers. The number 30 is the first number that we run across that has three distinct prime factors, and eight automorphic numbers.

The list above has the beginnings of an interesting pattern that can easily be verified. The number 210 is the first number that has four distinct prime factors, and it has 16 automorphic numbers.

Number	Automorphic Numbers	Prime Factors
210:	0, 1, 15, 21, 36, 70, 85, 91, 105 106, 120, 126, 141, 175, 190, 196	2, 3, 5, 7

Again, all the prime numbers and powers of a prime number below 210 only have one distinct prime factor, and two automorphic numbers. All other numbers either have two or three distinct prime factors, and respectively, four or eight automorphic numbers.

The first number with five distinct prime factors is 2310, and here we see the next step in the pattern. The number 2310 has five distinct prime factors, and 32 automorphic numbers. Similarly, all the prime numbers and powers of a prime number below 2310 only have one distinct prime factor, and two automorphic numbers (again, 0 and 1). All other numbers either have two, three, or four distinct prime factors, and respectively, 4, 8, or 16 automorphic numbers.

Number	Automorphic Numbers	Prime Factors
2310:	0, 1, 210, 231, 330, 385, 441, 540, 561, 595, 616, 715, 771, 826, 925, 946, 1155, 1156, 1365, 1386, 1485, 1540, 1596, 1695, 1716, 1750, 1771, 1870, 1926, 1981, 2080, 2101	2, 3, 5, 7, 11

The first number with six distinct prime factors is 30030, and the first number with seven distinct prime factors is 510510; and in each case, as the number of prime factors increases by one, the number of automorphic numbers doubles (from the previous number). The number 30030 has 64 automorphic numbers, and the number 510510 has 128 automorphic numbers.

Number	Automorphic Numbers	Prime Factors
30030:	0, 1, 715, 1365, 1716, 2080, 2640, 2926, 3081, 4005, 4291, 5005, 6006, 6370, 6721, 6930, 7371, 7645, 8086, 8295, 8646, 9010, 10011, 10725, 11011, 11935, 12090, 12376, 12936, 13300, 13651, 14301, 15015, 15016, 15730, 16380, 16731, 17095, 17655, 17941, 18096, 19020, 19306, 20020, 21021, 21385, 21736, 21945, 22386, 22660, 23101, 23310, 23661, 24025, 25026, 25740, 26026, 26950, 27105, 27391, 27951, 28315, 28666, 29316	2, 3, 5, 7, 11, 13

Of course, an interesting ramification to all of this is that we can easily check whether or not a number is prime or a power of a prime by simply looking for automorphic numbers. If an

320

automorphic number above one is found, than the number in question isn't a prime number; and if no automorphic number is found, it is a prime or a power of a prime.

Attractors and Automorphic Numbers

Now let's return to base 10, and look at some graphic patterns. We'll begin with the numbers one through nine. As mentioned earlier, the single digit automorphic numbers are 0, 1, 5 and 6. But what happens with the other numbers, namely the numbers 2, 3, 4, 7, 8 and 9? Let's consider the odd numbers first. If we take the 3 and square it, we get 9; and then if we square the 9 we get 81. The right-most digit is 1 and squaring it gives us 1 again. What about the 7? If we square it, we get 49. Then if we take the right-most digit, which is 9, and square it we get 81; and taking the right-most digit and squaring that gives us our automorphic number again. Diagramming this relationship shows the 3 and the 7 going to 9, and the 9 going to 1. Because of this, we could say that not only is 1 automorphic, but it is also an attractor – there are other numbers that go towards the number 1 as we perform our square/MOD operation on the various numbers.

We see the same thing with the even numbers. Squaring the 2 gives us 4, and squaring the 4 gives us 16. The right-most digit is 6, which is one of our even automorphic numbers. Likewise, squaring 8 gives us 64, and the right-most digit is 4, which if we square and take the right-most digit leads us to the 6 again. Diagramming this relationship shows the 2 and the 8 going to 4 and the 4 going to the 6. The number six is another attractor.

And what about the numbers 0 and 5? We could call them attractors because they do go to themselves; however, when considering the single digit numbers (the numbers 0 through 9) there are no other numbers that go to them. Therefore, it would be more appropriate to say that they are simply automorphic.

Now, let's look at the two digit attractors. They are the numbers 0, 1, 25 and 76.

First, we notice that all the numbers that end with a five (like 95, 85, 75, etc.) go to the number 25. (Squaring a number like 95 or 85 gives us a number where the two right-most digits are equal to 25.) Likewise, all the numbers that end with a zero (like 10, 20, 30, etc.) go to the number 0. (Squaring a number like 90 or 80 gives us a number where the two right-most digits are equal to 00, which we simply show as 0.)

The pattern of numbers that go to the 1 is more complex. We find that we have four odd numbers that go to 49, and then the 49 along with two other odd numbers go to the 1. Similarly, when we consider the even numbers we have four even numbers that go to 24, and then the 24 along with two other even numbers go to the 76.

It is interesting to note that the patterns of numbers that go to the 0 and the 25 are similar to each other. And likewise, the patterns of numbers that go to the 1 and 76 are similar to each other. (This can be seen in the figure below.)

Thus we have eight numbers each going to the 1 and 76 attractors (including the numbers 1 and 76); and ten numbers each going to the 0 and 25 attractors (again including the numbers 0 and 25). Therefore, out of the 100 two-digit numbers (the numbers 0 through 99), 36 of those numbers go to attractors. The other 64 numbers find themselves within loops, as we saw in the previous chapter.

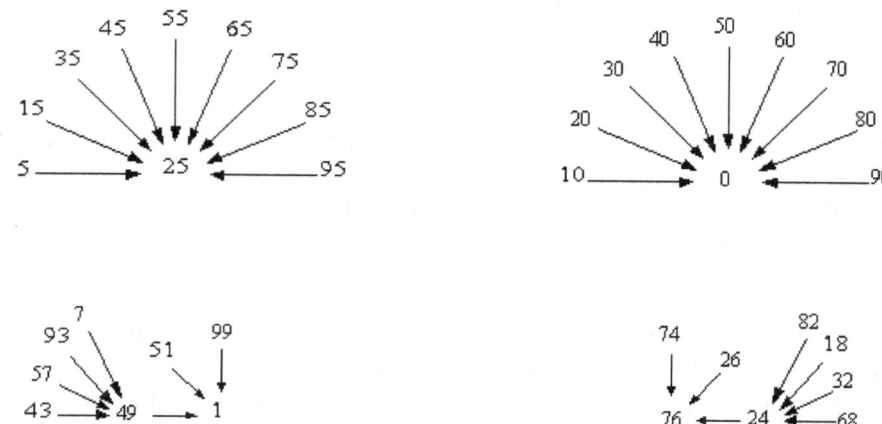

Figure 20.1   Two-digit structures for the 0, 1, 25 and 76 attractors.

The patterns of numbers that go to the 1 and 6 numbers seem to have more structure than the patterns of numbers that go to the 0 and the 5 numbers; therefore, for the remainder of this section we will focus our attention on the 1 and 6 number patterns.

Even though we didn't draw the one-digit patterns for the 1and the 6 attractors, it was evident that their structures were very similar to each other. Likewise, when we draw the diagrams for the two-digit patterns for the 1 and the 6 attractors (in the figure above), we again see that their structures are practically identical to each other.

Now, if we compare the three-digit patterns for the 1 and 6 attractors, we see that their structures are very different from each other. For the number 1 attractor, starting at the outer tier, we have eight numbers that go to a single number, and then that number along with six other numbers goes to the one. In the case of the 6-number (which is actually 376), again starting with the outer tier, we have three sets of four numbers that each go to a number, and then those three numbers go to the 6-number.

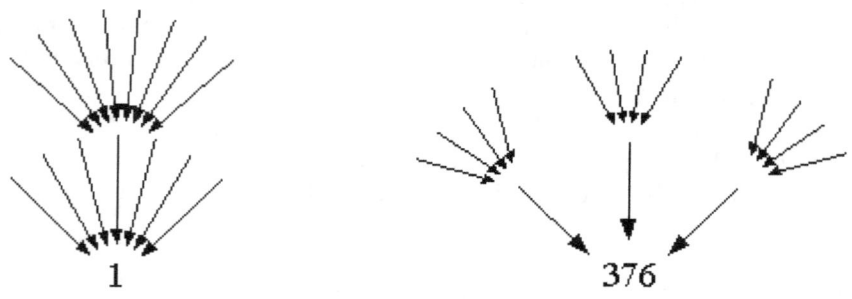

Figure 20.2   Three-digit structures for the 1 and 376 attractors.

In the diagram above we didn't show the actual numbers (except for the attractors themselves). Instead, the numbers are represented as arrows. From this point on the numbers become too large and cumbersome to show within the diagrams. If we tried, it would distract from the structure that we are trying to examine; therefore, for the remaining diagrams in this section, we will represent these numbers simply as arrows, and only show the number that represents the attractor.

The three-digit structures were different from each other, but when we look at the four-digit structures, we see that they are again identical between the 1 and the 6 attractor patterns. Each pattern has three sets of eight numbers on the outer tier that go to a number, and then those three numbers along with four other numbers go to the attractor.

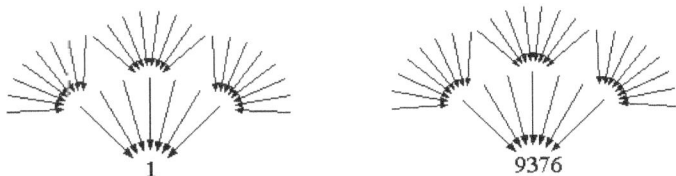

Figure 20.3 Four-digit structures for the 1 and 9376 attractors.

At this point it is interesting to note that each pattern is a continuation of the previous pattern. In each case, the structure from the one-digit pattern carries over to the two-digit pattern. And the structure of the two-digit pattern carries over to the three-digit pattern, which in turn carries over to the four-digit pattern. And even though the three-digit patterns were different between the 1 and the 6 attractors, we can still see the previous patterns of each within the four-digit structure.

Now, as we look at the five-digit structures, we see once again that they are different from each other. And, it is from this point on that the patterns don't appear to have identical structures with each other ever again; and in fact, after this diagram, they don't even appear to be similar any more. Yet, in each case, we can still see the previous structure in each subsequent pattern.

The five-digit patterns add another tier to both structures; and all the new numbers are within this new tier. In the case of the 1-attractor there are four sets of eight numbers in the outer tier that go to four numbers in one set of eight in the next tier. The rest of the pattern is identical to the previous four-digit structure. With the 6-attractor there are two sets of 16 numbers in the outer tier that go to two numbers in one set of eight in the next tier. Again, the rest of the pattern is identical to the previous four-digit structure. The figure below is a side-by-side comparison of the two five-digit patterns. The 1-attractor pattern is on the left, and the 6-attractor pattern is on the right.

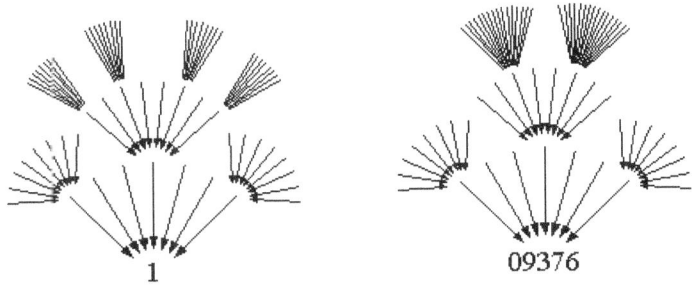

Figure 20.4 Five-digit structures for the 1 and 09376 attractors.

The six-digit structure for the 1-attractor is shown below. By adding another tier, this structure is starting to spread out more. The outer tier of this new pattern adds 64 numbers in eight sets of eight. Four of these sets go to one set of eight in the next tier, and the other four sets go to another set of eight in the same tier. The rest of this structure is identical to the five-digit structure of the 1-attractor. The figure below is the six-digit structure for the 1-attractor.

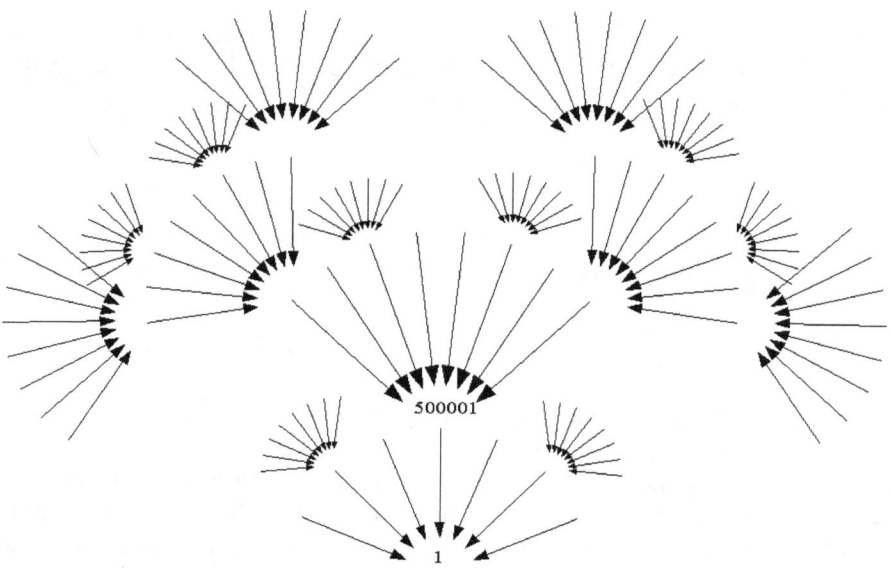

Figure 20.5   Six-digit structure for the 1 attractor.

Notice also within the structure above that there are never more than eight numbers that go to another number. This is a characteristic that appears to be true for all larger-digit structures of the 1-attractor. (See the appendix for a listing of the actual numbers that go to the one-attractor, for 2-digit numbers through 6-digit numbers.)

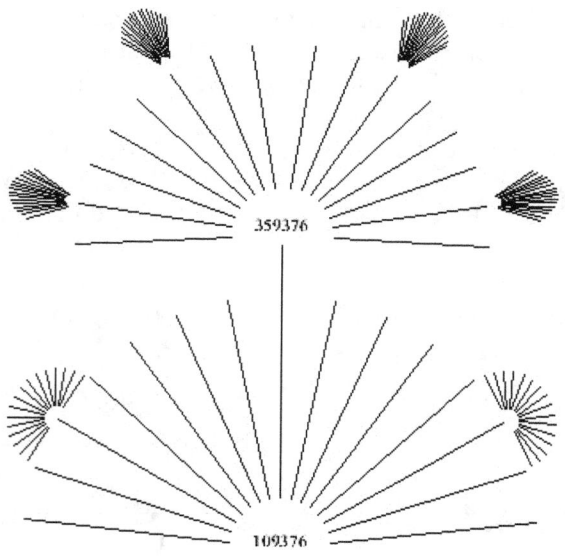

Figure 20.6   Six-digit structure for the 109376 attractor.

In contrast, the six-digit structure for the 6-attractor remains more compact. This structure did not add another tier as we added another digit. And, like the 1-attractor, this structure also added 64 numbers; however, unlike the 1-attractor, these 64 numbers were distributed throughout all the tiers (see the figure above). The outer tier has four sets of 16 numbers going to a single set of 16 numbers at the next tier. At this level there are three sets of 16 numbers going to the inner-most tier, and this inner-most tier now has 15 numbers going to the attractor. The previous structure can also be seen in this structure. (Notice also that at this point we've removed the arrowheads from our lines on the 6-attractor.)

The seven-digit structure for the 1-atrtractor is shown below. Notice that the seven-digit structure for the 1-attractor again adds another tier.

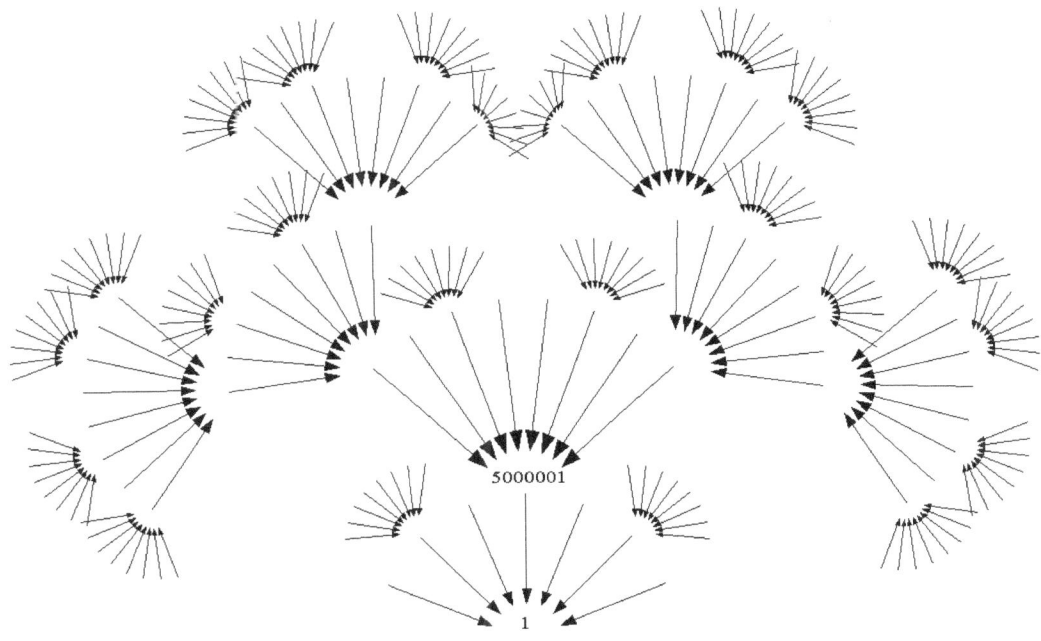

Figure 20.7   Seven-digit structure for the 1 attractor.

The outer tier of this pattern adds 128 numbers in 16 sets of eight with four of these sets going to one set of eight in the next tier, four more sets of eight going to another set of eight, a third set of four going to another set of eight, and the fourth set of four sets of eight going to still another set of eight. The rest of this structure is identical to the six digit structure of the 1-attractor. Again we see within this structure that there are never more than eight numbers that go to another number.

Meanwhile, the seven-digit structure for the 6-attractor continues to become more compact. This time there are instances of 32 numbers going to a single number while in other places there are still sixteen numbers going to a single number.

The seven-digit structure (in the figure below) for the 6-attractor (the value of the attractor is 7109376) is also very unique in another way. Up until now, each of these structures has been symmetrical. However, the seven-digit structure for the 6-attractor is not symmetrical. No matter how you draw it, it is a little off-balance. In the diagram below, there are two nodes that have 32 numbers going into them; however, only one of those nodes has additional numbers going into it. Compared to the symmetry of the previous diagrams for both the 1 and the 6-attractors, this diagram seems out of place. However, as we shall see in the next set of diagrams, the eight-digit diagram for the 6-attractor is symmetrical once again.

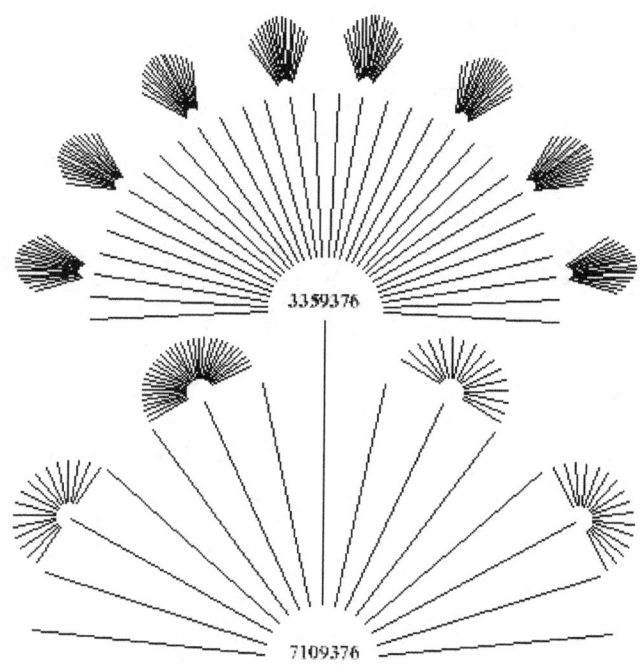

Figure 20.8   Seven-digit structure for the 7109376 attractor.

In the figure below we show the eight-digit structure of the one-attractor, and then the figure after that shows the eight-digit structure of the 6-attractor. You'll notice that I finally removed the arrowheads from the figure of the one-attractor (I did this several figures ago on the 6-attractor). Also, again keep in mind that each of the lines in these figures represents a number, and the place where the numbers come together represents a node.

As we look closely at the figure of the one-attractor, we see that over 95% of the numbers in this diagram funnel through the number 50000001 on their way to the number 1. In contrast, the 6-attractor has only about two-thirds of its numbers funnel through the number 93359376 on their way to the 87109376-attractor.

Notice also that the one-attractor has up to six tiers. In other words, there are some numbers that must pass through five other numbers before they reach the number one. In contrast, the 6-attractor has only three tiers. In this case, there are at most two other numbers that the outer numbers must reach to get to the 87109376-attractor.

326

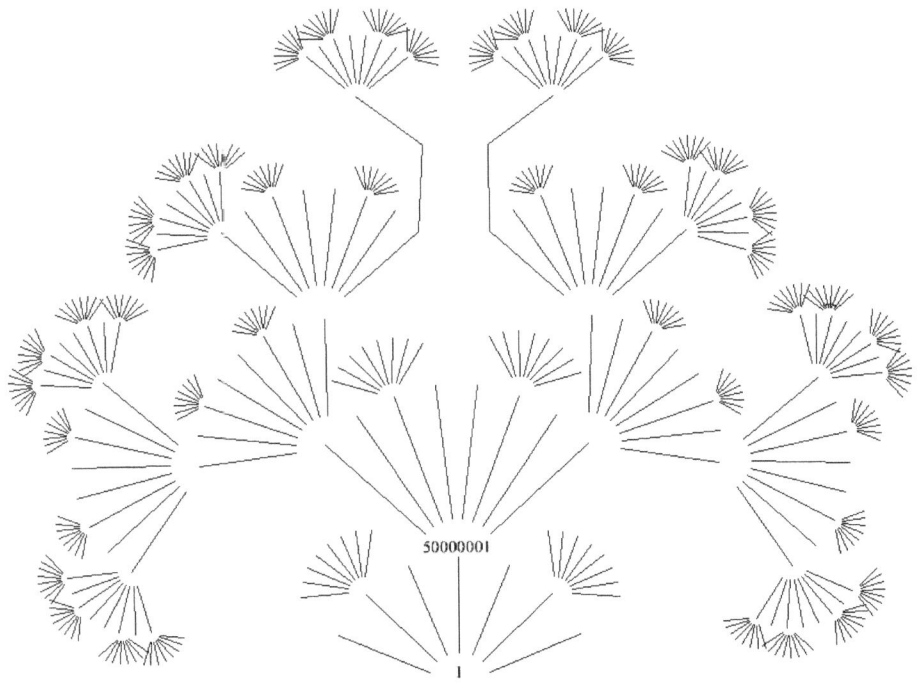

Figure 20.9   Eight-digit structure for the 1 attractor.

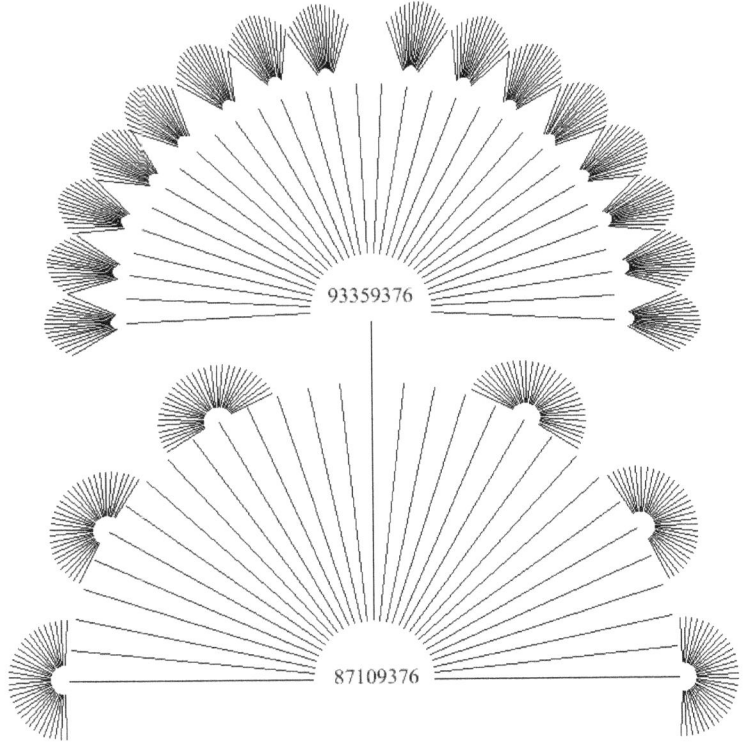

Figure 20.10   Eight-digit structure for the 87109376 attractor.

Attractor Counts

Another way that we can analyze these diagrams is by counting the number of numbers that ultimately feeds into each attractor. If we return and count these numbers from the preceding drawings, we generate the following table:

Number of Digits	Attractor	Count of Numbers Feeding It		Attractor	Count of Numbers Feeding It
1	1	4		6	4
2	1	8		76	8
3	1	16		376	16
4	1	32		9376	32
5	1	64		09376	64
6	1	128		109376	128
7	1	256		7109376	256
8	1	512		87109376	512

Table 20.9   Counts of the numbers that feed into the 1 and 6 attractors in base 10 for digits 1 through 8.

We see in the table above that the same amount of numbers feed into the 1-attractor as feed into the 6-attractor. We also see that as we increase the digits, the count doubles at each level. Therefore, it would be natural to assume that this doubling continues indefinitely; however, after examining attractor counts in other bases, and finding that this is not so with several other bases, it makes one wonder whether this also might be the case in base 10 also.

Attractor Counts in Other Bases

As mentioned earlier in the chapter, every base has 0 and 1 as attractors. The table below shows the attractor counts for the number 1 in bases 2 through 12. In other words, the table shows the number of numbers (the count) that ultimately feeds to the number one in each respective base.

The table below shows us many interesting characteristics of the 1-attractor for the various bases. The odd bases have a constant amount of numbers that feed into the 1 attractor. For example, with base 5, we see that there are four numbers that feed to the 1. And this number stays constant as we consider more digits.

The even bases are also interesting. The number of numbers that feeds to the 1-attractor either doubles, quadruples or increase by some other power of two as we consider more digits. Bases that are only powers of two (bases 2, 4, and 8) have all their odd numbers feed to the 1-attractor.

The column on the left shows the bases considered (bases 2 through 12), while the heading to each column show the number of digits being considered for that base. For example, in base 10, when we look at five digits, there are 64 numbers that go to the number 1. (The appendix contains a more extensive listing of the following table.)

Base\Digits	2	3	4	5	6	7	8
2	2	4	8	16	32	64	128
3	2	2	2	2	2	2	2
4	8	32	128	512	2048	8192	½ (4^8)
5	4	4	4	4	4	4	4
6	4	8	16	32	64	128	256
7	2	2	2	2	2	2	2
8	32	256	2048	16384	½ (8^6)	½ (8^7)	½ (8^8)
9	2	2	2	2	2	2	2
10	8	16	32	64	128	256	512
11	2	2	2	2	2	2	2
12	16	64	256	1024	4096	16384	½ (16^8)

Table 20.10   Counts of the numbers that feed to the 1 attractor in bases 2 thru 12.

Notice that the counts in the odd bases are either 2 or 4. This means that there are only two numbers (or four numbers) that go to the number one when squared. And this remains true whether you are looking at 2 digits, 3 digits, or more digits. On the other hand, within the even bases, the count always starts at some power of two, and then increases by some power of two as more digits are considered.

This table shows some very interesting properties of these attractors. It isn't very difficult to write a software program that counts the number of numbers that feed to an attractor; however, at some point you begin to either push the limits of available computing time; or the size limits of integers on your PC. Here caution must be exercised because as you begin to approach these limits, errors can be introduced into your data, and hence into your results. Therefore, some of these questions must remain unanswered (at least for a little while) while I wait on technology to catch up with my questions (or until I write a more sophisticated program that can handle larger integers and larger integer ranges within a reasonable amount of time).

Chapter 21
Orbits within Mandelbrot and Julia Set Fractals

The Mandelbrot fractal, as do many other fractal patterns, contains attractors and loops within the image. We will look at some of these within this chapter, but to understand the concepts better, let's begin by briefly explaining how the overall pattern is created.

Building a Mandelbrot Fractal

The Mandelbrot fractal is created on a complex number plane. This plane is represented on a graph similar to any other x-y, two-dimensional graph, except in this case, the x axis represents real numbers, while the y axis represents imaginary numbers. And just as every point on a regular graph has an x and a y coordinate; every point on a complex graph has a real and an imaginary component. These points are represented as complex numbers where each number can be written as a + bi, where "a" is the real part, and "bi" is the imaginary part. In this chapter, we'll let capital letters, such as Z, represent an imaginary number so that each Z is equal to some a + bi.

To create the Mandelbrot fractal, we take the equation $Z_{n+1} = Z_n^2 + C$ where Z and C are complex numbers, and enter every point on the graph into this equation. The Z is a variable and the C is a constant, and in fact, C is equal to the initial Z value for each point considered.

You'll notice that we have a Z on both sides of the equal sign of our equation. As we take each point and enter it into the equation on the right side of the equal sign, we get a result for the left side. We then take this result, and enter it back into the equation on the right side of the equal sign to get a new result for the left. We continue this process again and again. The C value is set equal to the initial Z value as we start this process for each point, and it stays set at this same value until we finish the set of iterations. The iterative process continues either until Z goes to infinity or until we reach a pre-determined repetition limit. Computer programs that generate Mandelbrot fractals have both of these checks built into them.

Of course, going to infinity is a vague description of how we'll stop the iterative process. In order to implement this process, we'll need something a little more concrete. To check for infinity, we'll simply check to see if both the real part and the imaginary parts are greater than 4. If they are, we can stop our process because in actuality, if both are greater than 4, then after a few more iterative steps, the process does quickly go to infinity.

As for the predetermined repetition limit, it is an upper limit on the number of iterations that we are willing to try. In other words, if we haven't reached infinity by some predetermined number of iterations, then we'll use this count to break out of our iterative loop, and go on to the next point.

Now, to actually generate the beautiful fractal pattern, the program selects a point and counts how many times it cycles through this iterative process and then assigns a color to that point based on the number of iterations. The program does this for every point on the graph, and in this way we generate our fractal image.

Calculating a value for every point on the graph sounds like a lot of tedious math, but then that's why computers were made. And depending on the speed of your computer and the region of the fractal you are trying to create, the fractal can take anywhere from several seconds to several minutes (or even hours) to generate.

The following figure shows the Mandelbrot fractal. This fractal has been described as a snowman on its side with various other snowmen, snowballs, knobs and strands attached to the perimeter.

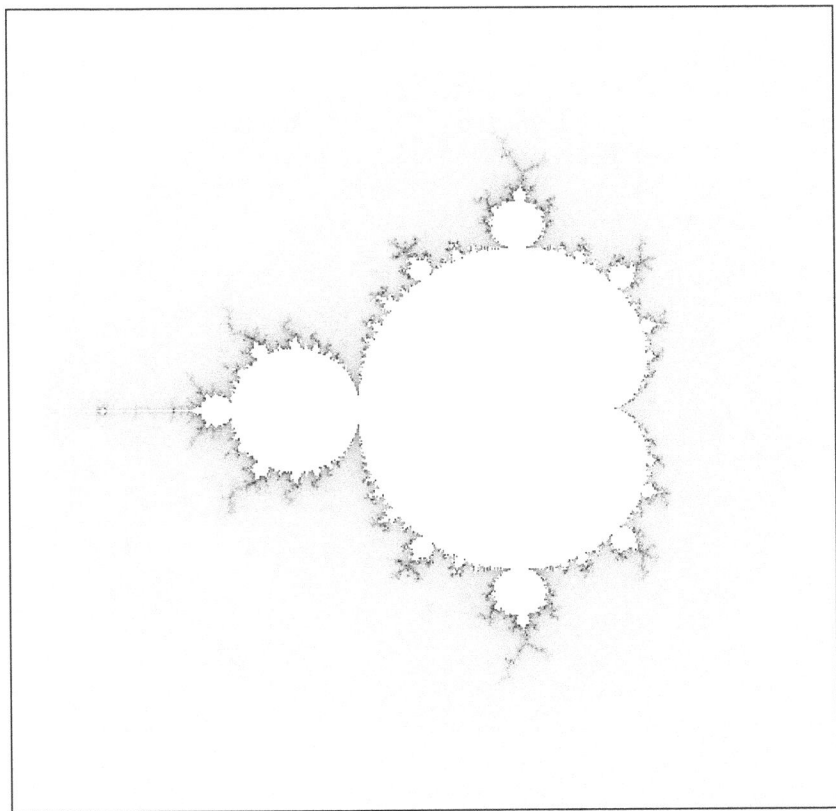

Figure 21.1   The Mandelbrot Fractal.

It is at the perimeter between the upper limit count and going to infinity where all the "action" occurs. If we magnify various regions of the perimeter, we find intricate designs and amazing details as the pattern continues to repeat itself at deeper levels.

However, as interesting as the perimeter is, we're going to look at the part of the fractal inside the perimeter. Most computer programs that create fractal images let you select the maximum number of iterations allowed within that image. This number typically varies anywhere from 50 to 5000 (or more). Almost all of the points that exceed the maximum number of iterations are inside the center region of the fractal.

Orbits Within the Mandelbrot Fractal

So, why do some points exceed the maximum number of iterations? Let's look at our equation:

$$Z_{n+1} = Z_n^2 + C$$

The fractal equation squares a complex number and then adds another complex number to determine a result, which is then used as the new number to go through the process again. In some cases, these points approach a single point as they continue through this iterative process (they approach an attractor); while at other times they find themselves in a loop, where they cycle through the same set of points over and over. In the following figures, we will select various start points and see what kind of pattern results as the complex number either works its way to an attractor, or finds itself in a loop. The path that each point traces is called the orbit of that point.

We can divide the area within the perimeter of the fractal into two categories. One category could be considered the "central core" while the knobs attached to the central core would be the second category. It appears that if we select a starting point within the central core, that we will eventually move to an attractor. While if we select a starting point within one of the knobs (attached to the core), we will find ourselves within a loop.

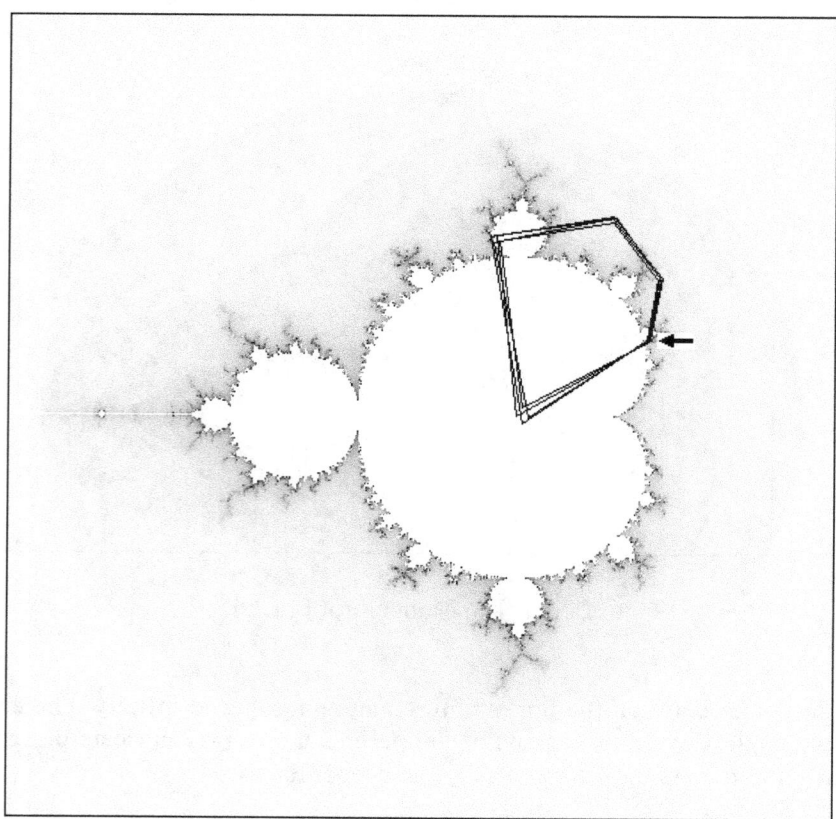

Figure 21.2   A five-point loop pattern within the fractal.

In the figure above, we selected a starting point in one of the knobs. (The arrow shows the starting point.) Then as we iterate through the formula (and create the orbit of that point), we find ourselves in a five-point loop. From tests that I have done, it appears that any point selected within this particular knob would then become part of some five-point loop. And selecting a point within other knobs would give us a three-point loop, a four-point loop, and so on. For example, if we start at one of the highest knobs within the fractal, we find ourselves in a six-point loop. (see the figure below, And again, the arrow shows the starting point.)

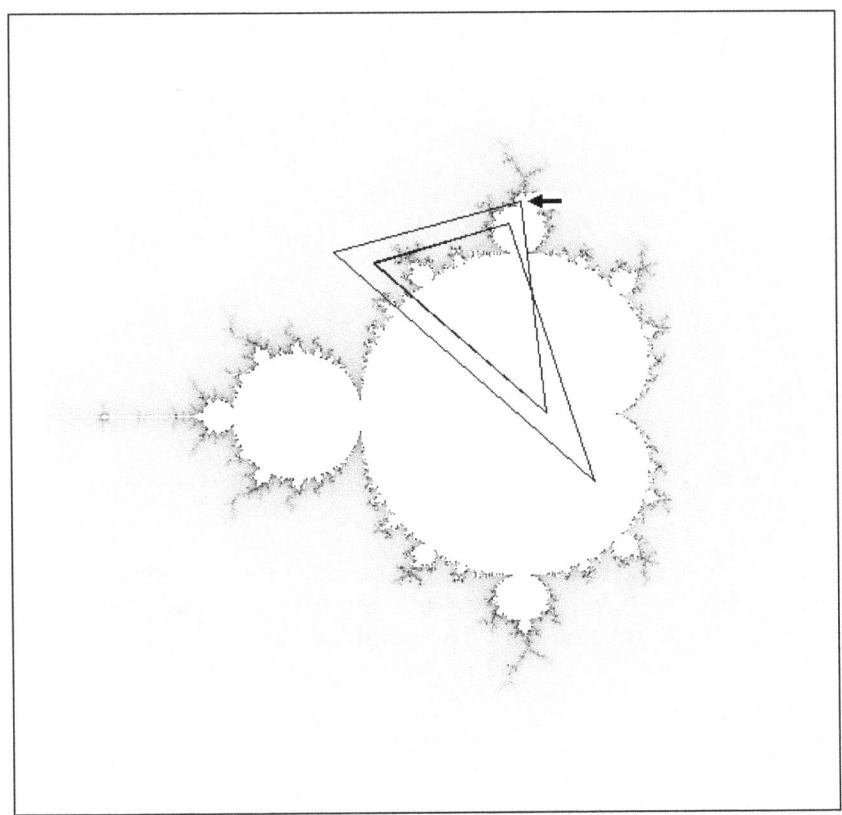

Figure 21.3   A six point loop pattern within the fractal.

Attractors within the Mandelbrot Fractal

If we select a starting point within the central core of the fractal, and then iterate through the Mandelbrot equation, we find ourselves slowly moving toward an attractor. And it appears that there are various ways that we can move to that attractor.

For example, if the start point is on the left side of the core of the fractal, the iterative pattern will make a star pattern as it zeroes in on the attractor, while if we select a start point on the right side of the fractal, the iterative pattern will spiral to the attractor. The figure below shows one of these attractors where the starting point is on the left side of the core of the fractal. The arrow shows the starting point; and from there, we can see how the orbit creates a star pattern as it successively get smaller and smaller. This series of operations is slowly working its way to a single point at the center of the star.

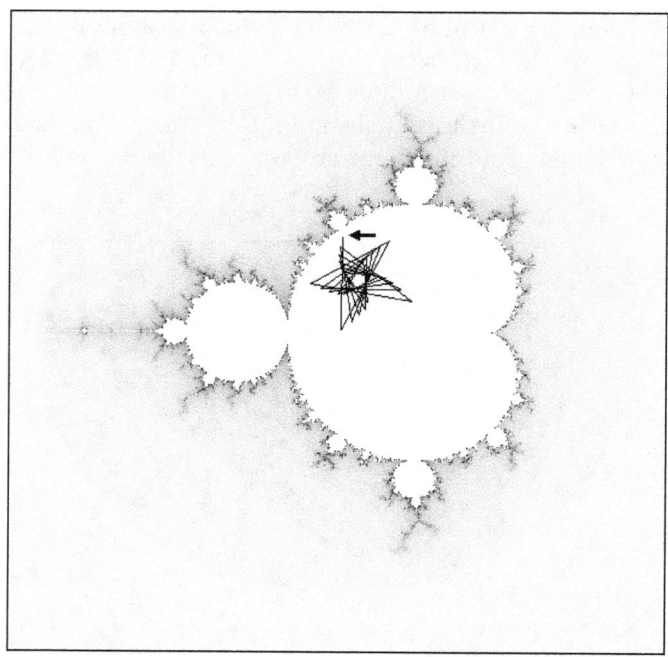

Figure 21.4   A star pattern approaching a single attractor.

In the next figure we selected a different start point and we see another interesting star pattern as the iterative process slowly works its way to a single point. Again, there is a small arrow in the diagram showing the start point. This diagram shows about 15 iterations in the pattern.

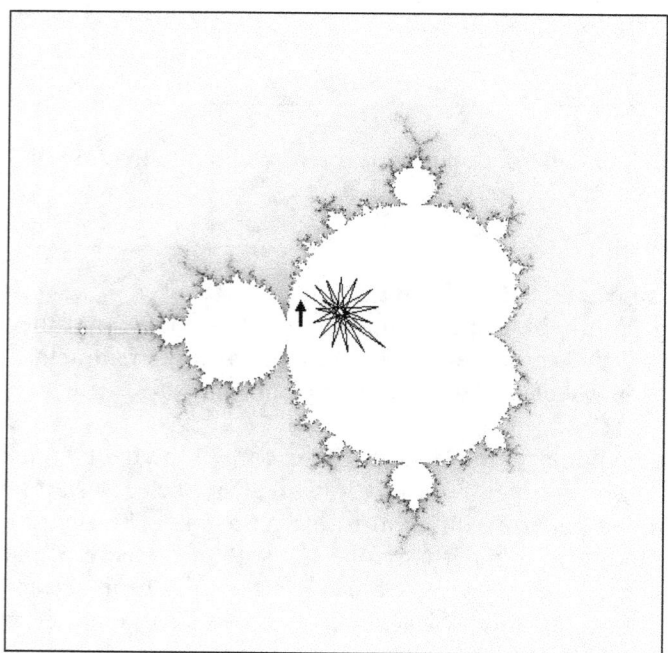

Figure 21.5   Another star pattern approaching a single attractor.

These orbits move very slowly to the attractor. The star pattern can easily go through hundreds of iterations (or more) before you find yourself approaching a central point. It is a different story as we move to the other side of the fractal core, and select a point there. Start points on this side of the fractal follow an iterative process that spirals into a single attractor.

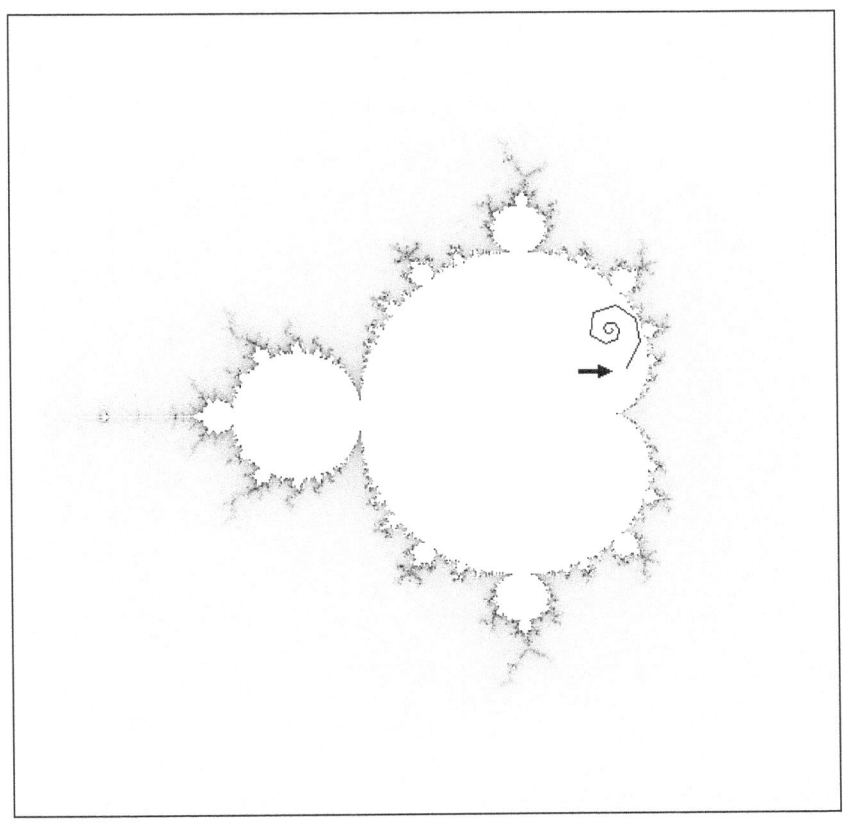

Figure 21.6   A spiral pattern approaching a single attractor.

Any start point selected on the right side of the fractal will spiral into a single attractor. And it appears that each start point spirals in to its own attractor. Selecting several start points all lead to different attractors. It therefore appears that there are an infinite number of attractors, with each attractor dependent on the initial value.

This begs the question of what happens when we use the attractor from one set of iterations as the start point to the next set of iterations? And then what happens if we continue this process over and over again. It turns out that the spirals become smaller and smaller, and they appear to approach a single point within the fractal.

The following figure shows a zoomed-in image of the Mandelbrot fractal. Within the image we see the successive orbits where each attractor became the start point for the next set of iterations. The arrow shows the initial start point on the upper right side of the fractal. (This initial point was randomly chosen.)

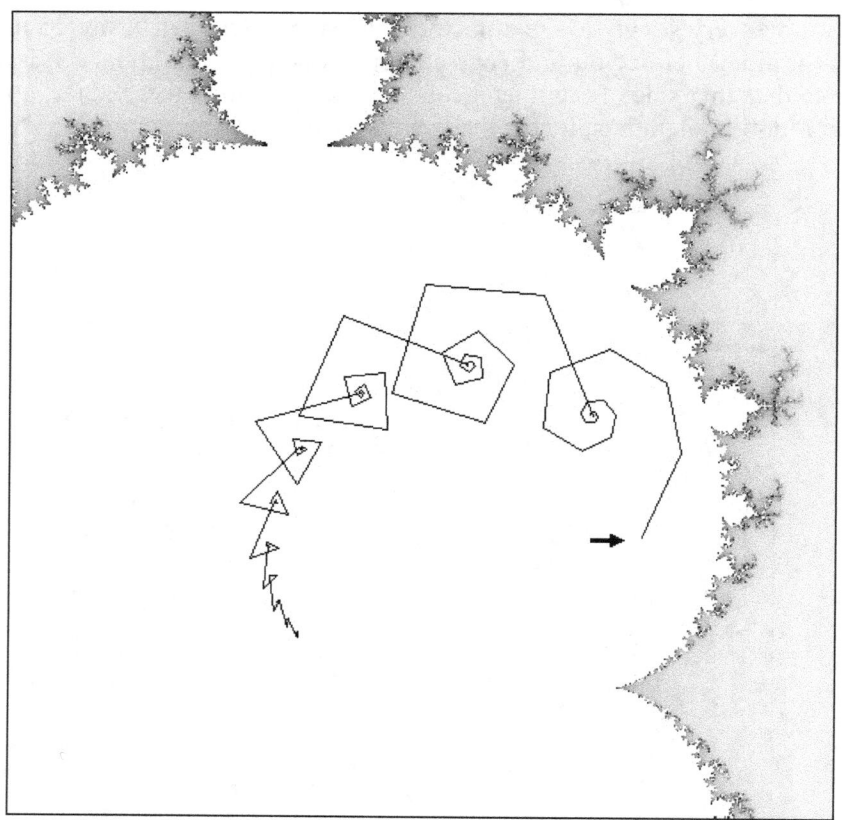

Figure 21.7   A spiral pattern where the attractor of one set of iterations became the start
point for the next iteration set.

Now, if we were to do this process for other points, we would find that they all appear to move
toward the same point. And it doesn't matter where we start within the fractal, all the points
eventually move toward the same final point.

In the next figure we randomly selected four different start points. Three of these points are on
the right side of the fractal core, and one is on the left side. With these three points on the right
we can easily see each set of iterations spiral to their individual attractor. This attractor is then
used as the start point for the next set of iterations. After several repetitions (of orbital sets), we
find that they are all moving to the same point.

The fourth initial point was randomly selected on the left side of the fractal core. Here we see a
star pattern working its way to a single attractor. This attractor is then used as the start point for
the next set of iterations. Again, after going through this process several times, we find the set of
start points working their way to a single attractor. (The arrows in the figure below show the
four initial random start points.)

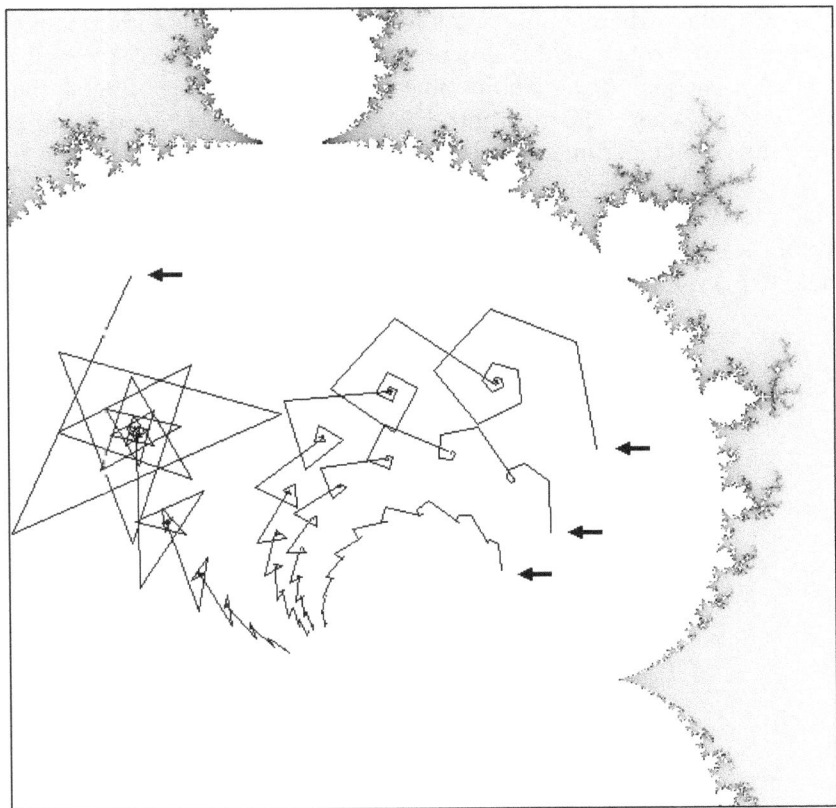

Figure 21.8   A spiral pattern where the attractors from four different orbits become the start points for the next set of orbits.

So, what is the point that they all appear to be going to? The single point that all of these orbits appear to move to is the point 0 + 0i.

Julia Set Fractals

Julia Set fractals are built in the same way as the Mandelbrot fractals; in fact, they use the same equation as the Mandelbrot fractal ($Z_{n+1} = Z_n^2 + C$) with one difference, that difference being the value of the constant, C. For the Mandelbrot fractal, the C was set equal to the initial Z value of each point considered, and it didn't change throughout the iterative process. Then as the next point was considered, the C value was set to the value of this new point, and then again, it was kept constant throughout the iterative process. In this way, each point within the Mandelbrot fractal was evaluated with its own C value.

For Julia Set fractals, we set C to some initial value before we start building the fractal, and then use that same value while the entire fractal is being generated. In other words, the C value doesn't change at any time while the fractal image is being built.

Because of this difference, changing the C value for each image will give us an entirely different fractal each time. In fact, there is a relation between the Mandelbrot fractal, and the C values used to create Julia Set fractals.

If we select a C value where C is equal to some point well within the perimeter of the Mandelbrot fractal, we create a Julia Set image made of a single entity (or blob). If the C value is selected so that it is equal to some point outside of the Mandelbrot fractal, the Julia Set image will consist of many islands. The most intricate Julia Set fractals are created from C values that correspond to points on the perimeter (or boundary) of the Mandelbrot fractal.

The Julia Set fractal in the next figure uses a C value equal to 0.24 + 0.53i. This value corresponds with a point on the Mandelbrot fractal along the upper right-side boundary of the fractal and next to one of the knobs on that fractal.

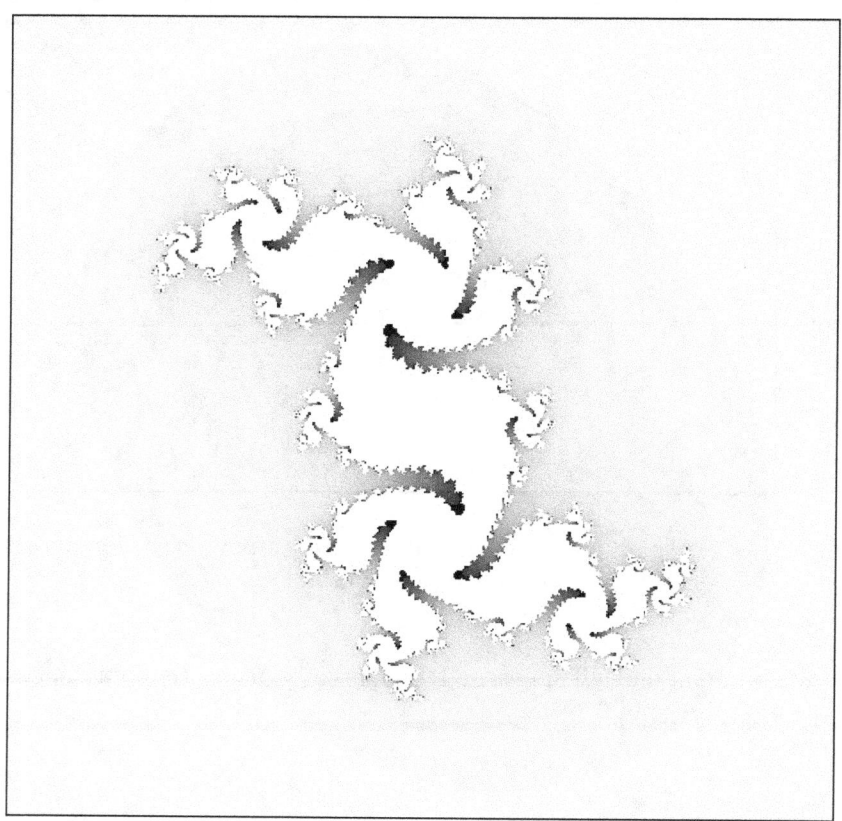

Figure 21.9   Julia Set fractal where C is equal to 0.24 + 0.53i.

Orbits Within the Julia Set Fractals

Selecting a start point within a knob on the Mandelbrot fractal will create a set of points that look like a loop. Julia Set fractals that correspond with knobs on the Mandelbrot fractal also have an internal structure where the orbits also go to a loop. In the following figure we take the same Julia Set fractal that we created above, and we select a start point within the fractal. Now, as we iterate through the equation, we quickly find ourselves in a four-node loop-type pattern. The loop-type pattern hasn't reached a stable configuration, so it is slowly expanding.

In the subsequent figure, we select a different start point within the same fractal, and this time we find the orbit quickly settling into a four-node loop. (The arrows point to the start point in each of these figures.)

Figure 21.10   Julia Set fractal with the orbit settling into an expanding four-node loop.

Figure 21.11   The same Julia Set fractal with a different start point where the orbit is settling into a four-node loop.

As mentioned earlier, changing the C value for the Julia Set fractal also changes the appearance of the fractal. The following Julia Set fractal has a C value equal to -0.37 + 0.65i.

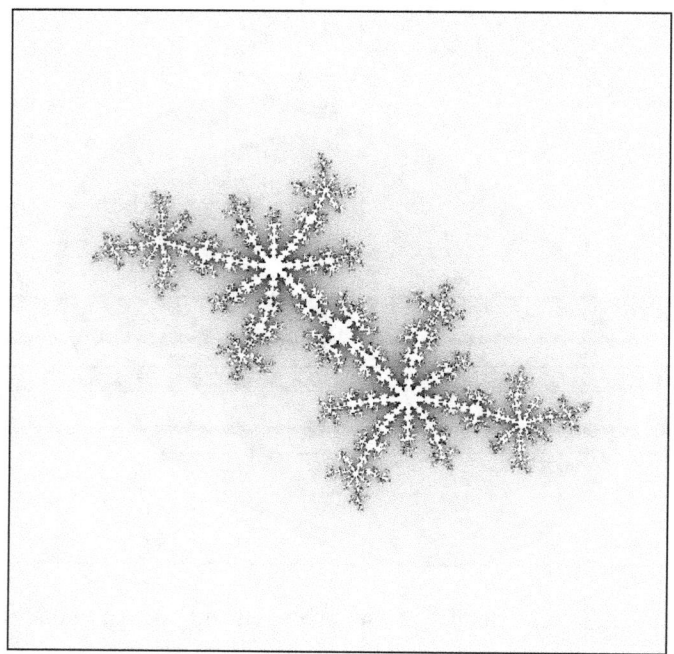

Figure 21.12   Julia Set fractal where C is equal to -0.37 + 0.65i.

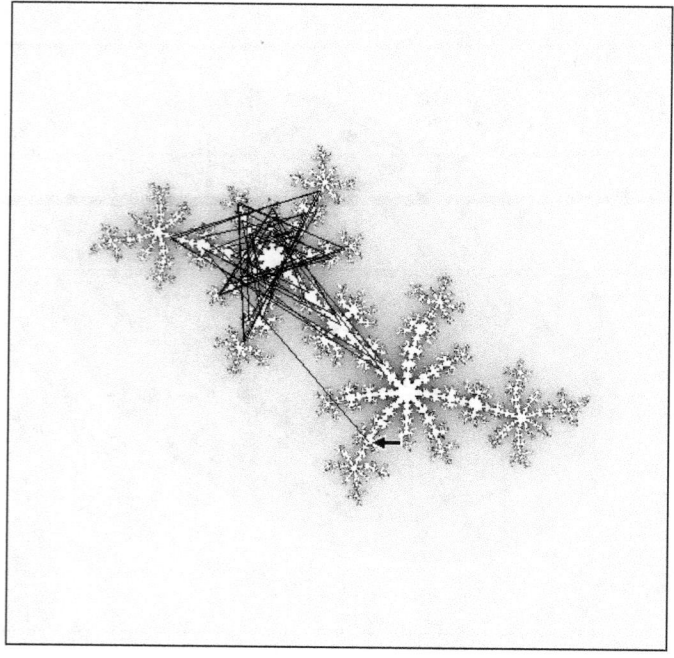

Figure 21.13   The orbit pattern for this Julia Set fractal.

The orbit pattern in the figure above is very interesting in that it goes to the center of the upper left part of the fractal and then each iteration slowly takes it out (away) from the center until it reaches some point, then it jumps back into the center and slowly starts to work its way back out again. This pattern continues over and over again within this fractal.

Attractors Within the Julia Set Fractals

As mentioned earlier, if the C value for the Julia Set fractal is chosen so that it corresponds to the central core of the Mandelbrot fractal, we get a Julia Set fractal that looks something like the blob-figure below.

Figure 21.14   Julia Set fractal where C is equal to $0.2284 + 0.1833i$.

This figure doesn't look very exciting as far as fractals go; however if we select a start point within the fractal and iterate through the equation several times, we find that it goes to a single attractor. In fact, it doesn't matter where we start within the fractal, after several iterations, we find ourselves going to the same point.

The following figure shows a start point near the edge of the fractal; and the figure after that shows five different start points all going to the same attractor point.

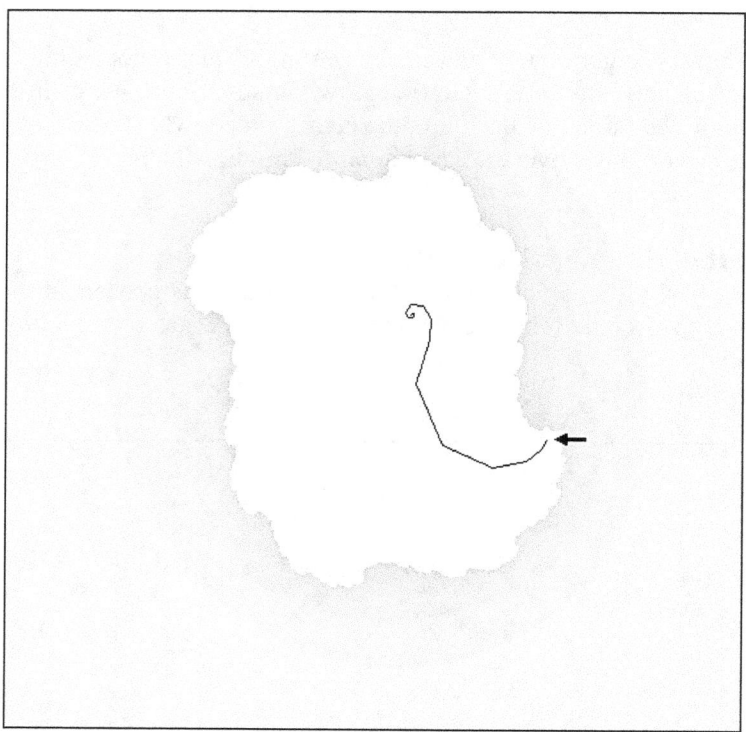

Figure 21.15   Julia Set fractal showing the orbit from a single start point.

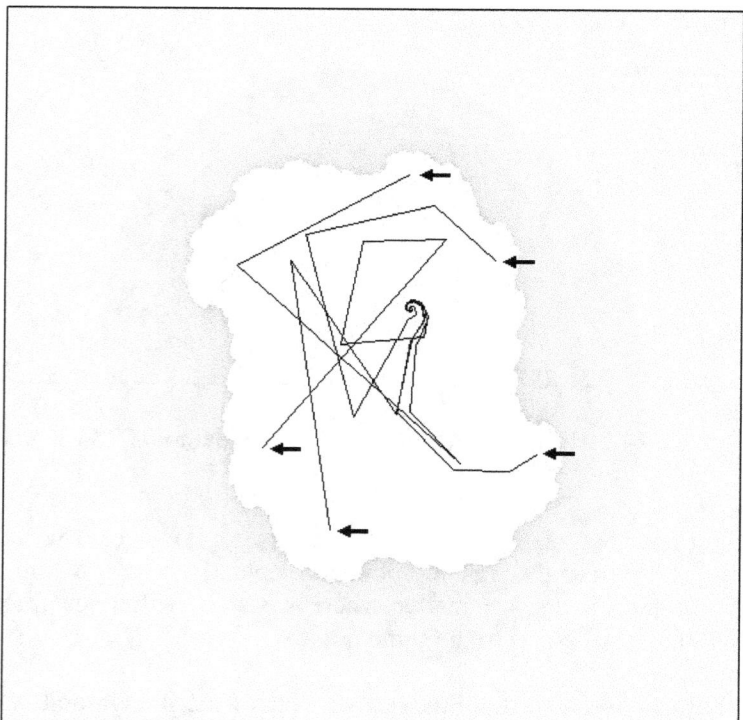

Figure 21.16   Julia Set fractal showing the orbits from five different start points all going to the same attractor.

The attractor point for this fractal is equal to 0.179 + 0.2855i. (The corresponding C value used to create this fractal was 0.2284 + 0.1833i.) While each Julia Set fractal has its own attractor point, the attractor point changes as the C value changes. The following is a small list of C values, and the corresponding attractor point for that C value. (Note that the image of each of these fractals isn't very much different than the images shown in the three figures above; and for this reason, and due to a lack of anything really noteworthy to look at, the fractals that correspond with these C values will not be shown.) Here is the list:

C Value	Attractor Point
-0.2 - 0.2i	-0.1865 + 0.1457i
-0.1 - 0.2i	-0.1136 + 0.1630i
0.0 - 0.2i	-0.0339 + 0.1873i
0.1 - 0.2i	0.0528 + 0.2236i
-0.2 - 0.1i	-0.1749 + 0.0741i
-0.1 - 0.1i	-0.0975 + 0.0837i
0.0 - 0.1i	-0.0095 + 0.0981i
0.1 - 0.1i	0.0936 + 0.1230i
-0.2 + 0.0i	-0.1708 + 0.0i
-0.1 + 0.0i	-0.0916 + 0.0i
0.0 + 0.0i	0.0 + 0.0i
0.1 + 0.0i	0.1127 + 0.0i
-0.2 - 0.1i	-0.1749 - 0.0741i
-0.1 - 0.1i	-0.0975 - 0.0837i
0.0 - 0.1i	-0.0095 - 0.0981i
0.1 - 0.1i	0.0936 - 0.1230i
-0.2 - 0.2i	-0.1865 - 0.1457i
-0.1 - 0.2i	-0.1136 - 0.1630i
0.0 - 0.2i	-0.0339 - 0.1873i
0.1 - 0.2i	0.0528 - 0.2236i

Chapter 22
Other Perspectives of the Mandelbrot Fractal

The Polarity Image

There are still other ways to view a Mandelbrot fractal. One way is to check the polarity of the final point when it meets its exit criteria. Let me explain what I mean by that. For most fractal images, the color of each point is determined by the iteration count. However, in the figure below, the color of each pixel is determined by the + or − value of the last point considered.

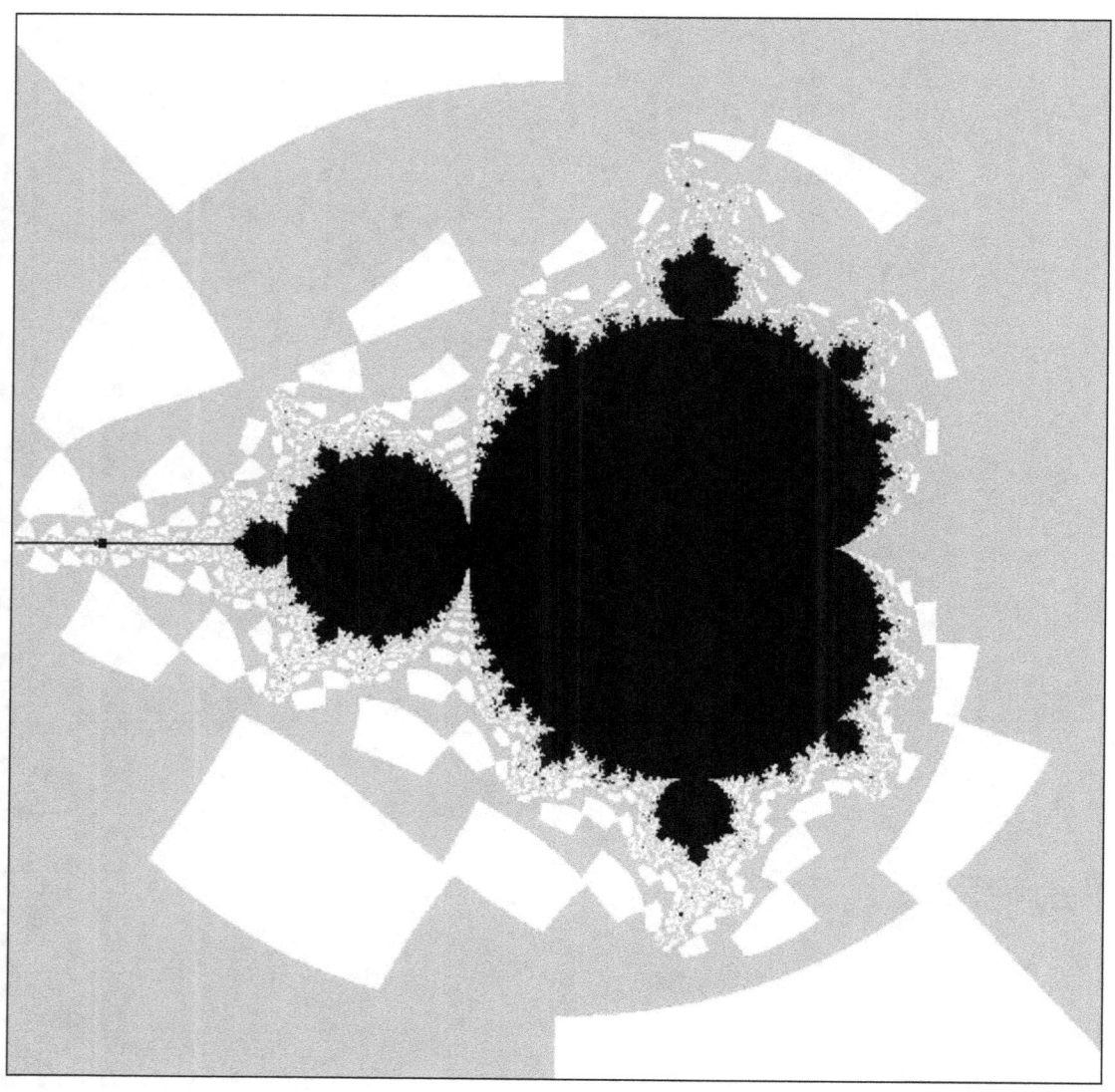

Figure 22.1   A polarity image of the Mandelbrot fractal.

344

The + or − value of the last iterative point is referred to as the polarity of that point. If both the real and the imaginary part of the point are negative, then the point was assigned the white color. If either the real and/or the imaginary part are positive, then the point is assigned the gray color. In the figure above, the points that were assigned black are points that exceeded the iteration count.

However, just because a point exceeds its iteration count is no reason not to give it a polarity color. In other words, we can do the same thing for the internal part of the fractal that we did for the external part. In the figure below, if both the real and the imaginary part of the last point are negative, then the pixel is assigned the black color; otherwise the pixel is given the dark gray color.

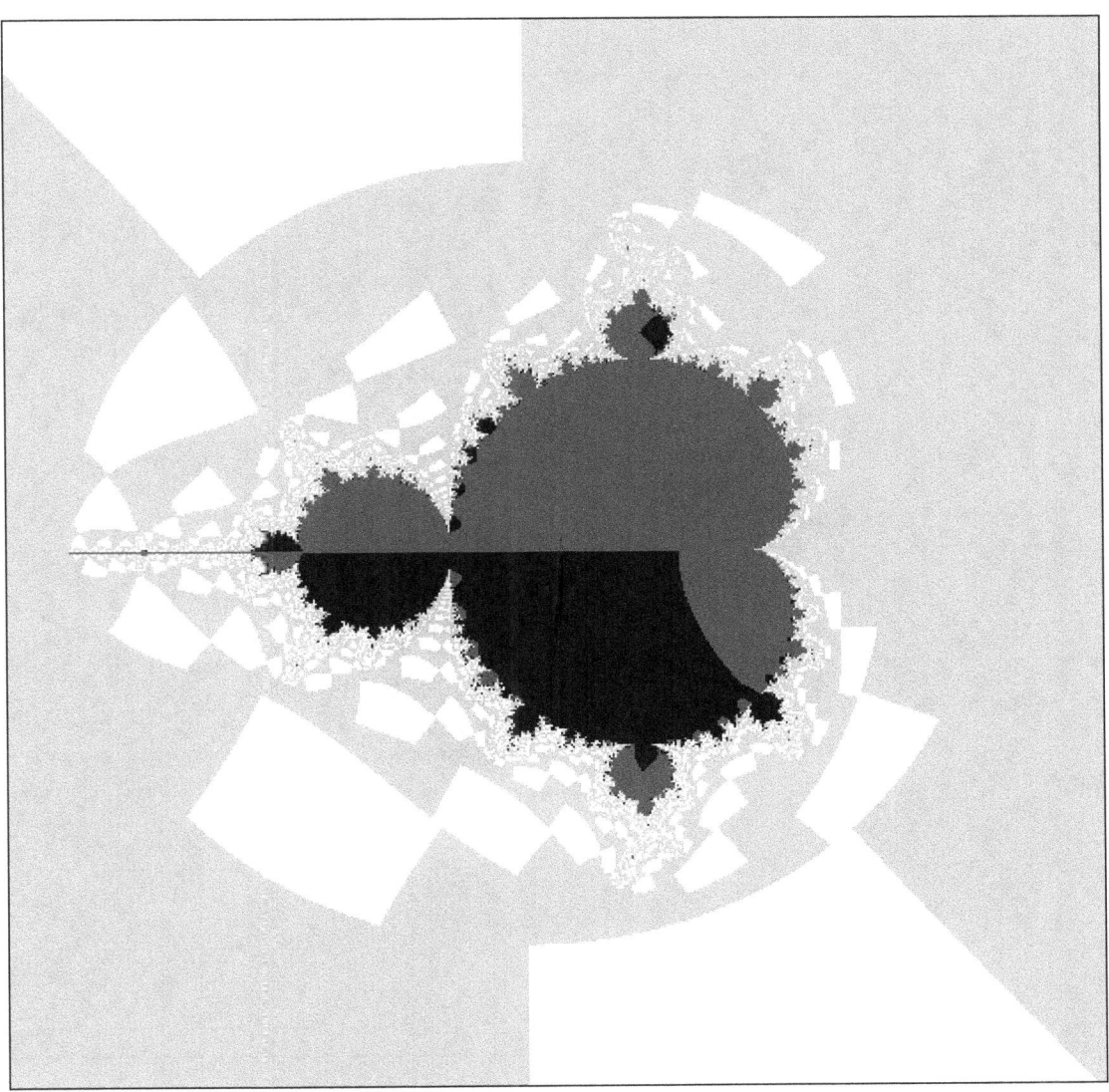

Figure 22.2   A polarity image of the Mandelbrot fractal after 50 iterations.

In the previous chapter we saw that when the initial point was selected from the central core of the fractal that those values would iterate to an attractor (either through a star pattern or a spiral pattern). However, initial points selected from the knobs would loop through several points before repeating again. Points within these loops could be either positive or negative as the fractal cycled through their values.

The image above shows the polarity of the final value after 50 iterations; and because of this looping characteristic, we would expect the polarity diagram to be just a little different after 51 iterations. The figure below shows the polarity image of the Mandelbrot fractal after 51 iterations. Note that the central core hasn't really changed that much; however, it is at the knobs attached to the central core where we find most of the variety.

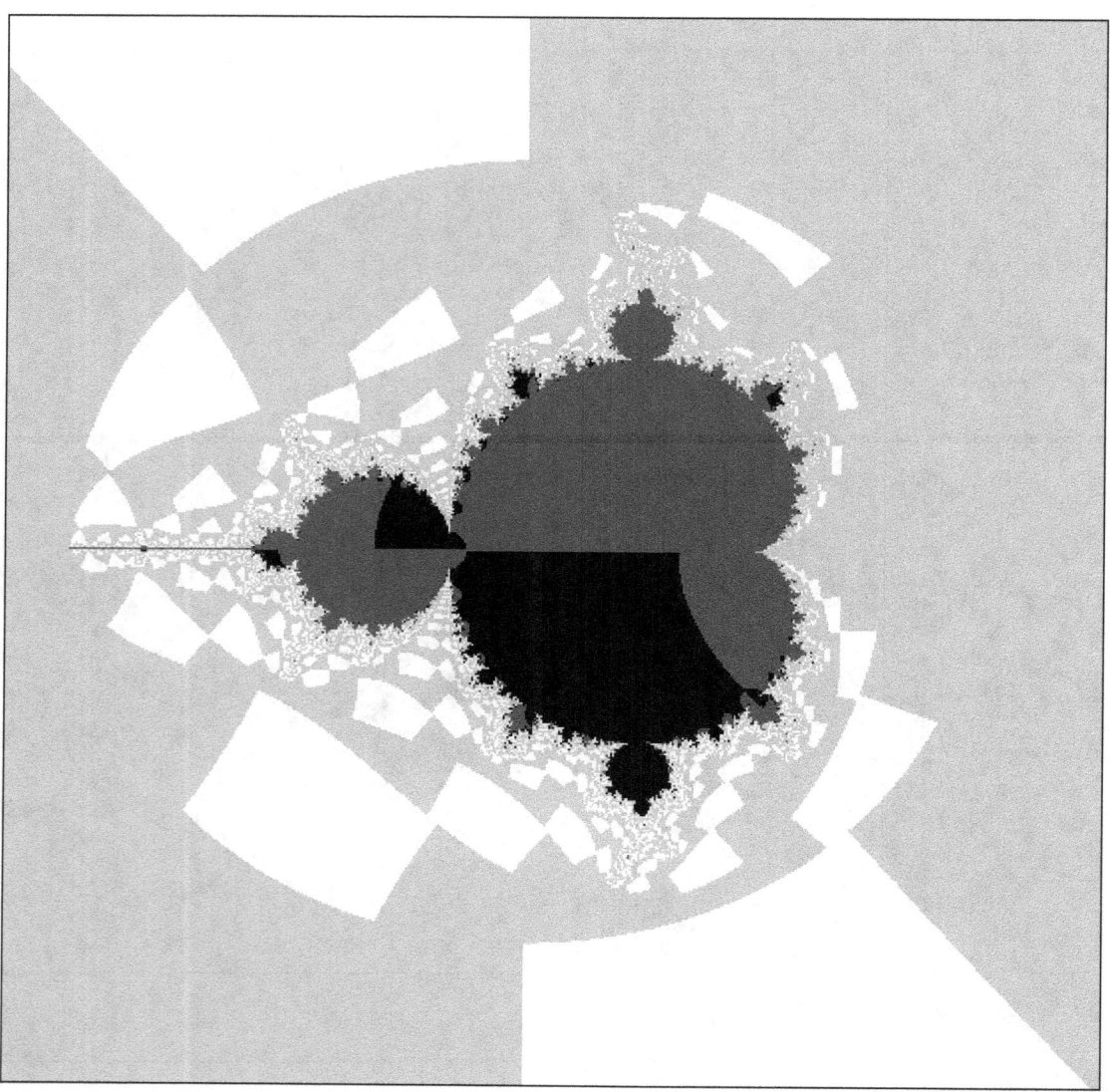

Figure 22.3   A polarity image of the Mandelbrot fractal after 51 iterations.

And this variety becomes more apparent as we consider other values for the maximum iteration count. The figure below is a side-by-side comparison of the Mandelbrot fractal after 50, 51, 52, and 53 iterations.

Keep in mind that we shouldn't see any variation in the figure for points outside of the perimeter. These points are iterating to a very large number (infinity), and if a particular point takes 27 iterations before it passes our infinity check in one diagram, then it will in every diagram.

There also isn't very much difference in the core itself. These values are going to attractors, and the closer they actually are to that attractor, the less likely they are to vary from diagram to diagram.

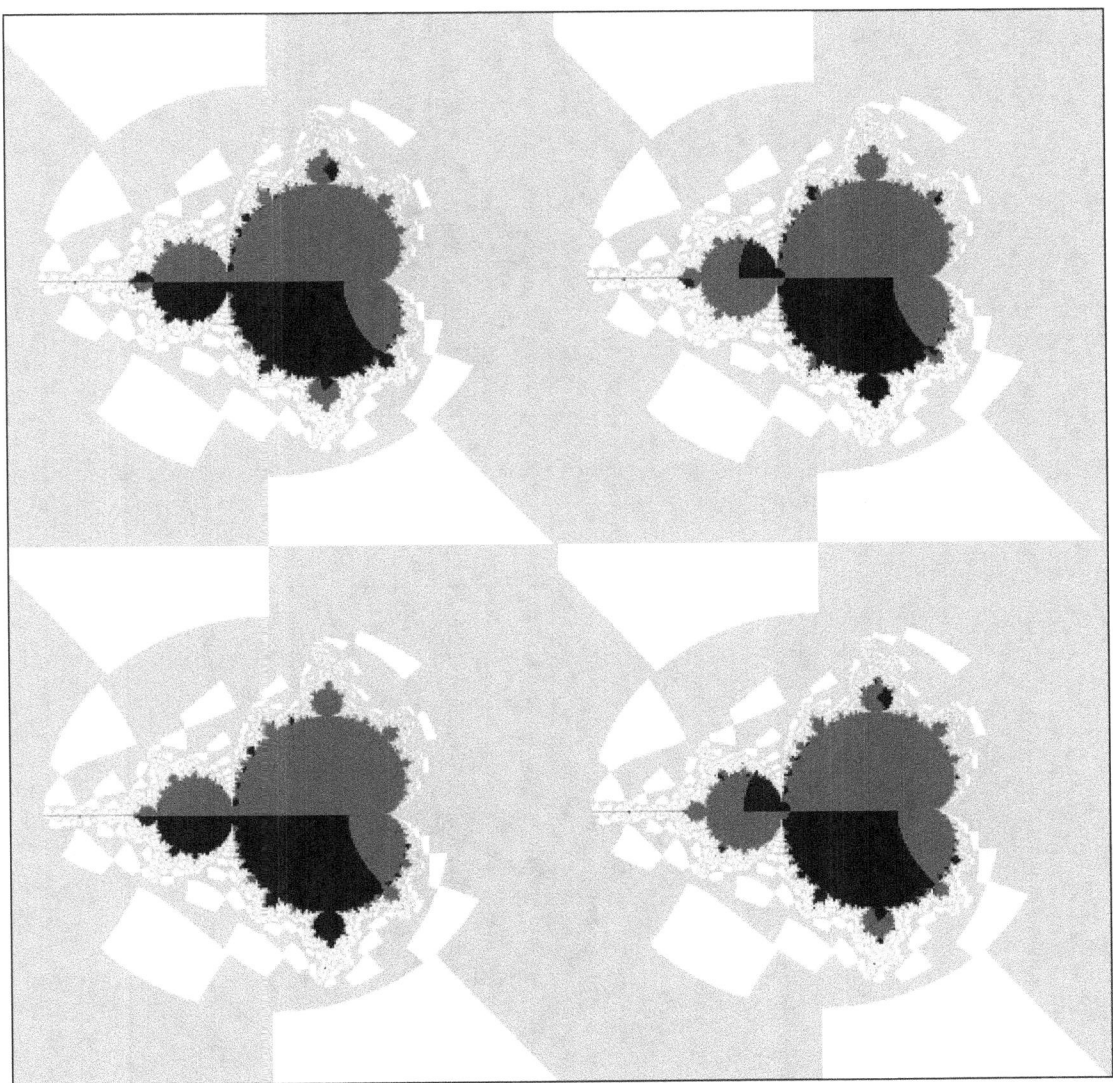

Figure 22.4   A polarity image of the Mandelbrot fractal after 50, 51, 52, and 53 iterations. (The sequence goes from left to right, and from top to bottom.)

The majority of the differences appear within the knobs attached to the central core. If we zoom in on one of the knobs, we can see the differences a little better. The next two figures are a close up of one of the knobs. The first shows that knob after 50 iterations, and the second shows that same knob after 51 iterations.

Since these next figures are a more close-up look, the perimeter also is in more detail; and just as we would expect, the polarity coloring is the same within the two figures for points lying outside the perimeter.

Figure 22.5   A polarity image of one of the knobs of the Mandelbrot fractal after 50 iterations.

Figure 22.6   A polarity image of the same knob of the Mandelbrot fractal after 51 iterations.

The next diagram is a side-by-side comparison of this same knob after 50, 51, 52, and 53 iterations.

Figure 22.7   A polarity image of a knob attached to the Mandelbrot fractal after 50, 51, 52, and 53 iterations. (The sequence goes from left to right, and from top to bottom.)

From what we've seen in the previous chapter, as well as what we've seen so far in this chapter, we can assure ourselves that there is more going on within these fractals than just a simple division between points going to infinity, and points going to some attractor or some kind of a loop.

Variations with the Equations

There are still other variations to consider, for example, what about variations to the equations themselves. This alone opens the door to an infinite number of possibilities. We won't take the time to consider even a fraction of these, but we will look at a few basic variations.

In the previous chapter, we discussed that the original Mandelbrot fractal was generated from the equation: $Z_{n+1} = Z_n^2 + C$. The Z and C are complex numbers, and in this equation, the Z is a variable, and the C is a constant. In fact, the C is set to the initial Z value as we begin each set of iterations. A set of iterations consists of starting with some Z and C value, plugging it into the right side of the equation, and determining a new value for Z (which is shown as the result on the left side of the equality). This new value for Z is then plugged back into the right side of the equation (the C value isn't reset at this time), and a newer value for Z is determined. This continues until either Z goes to some large value, or until we reach a maximum iteration count.

Now, let's change the equation so that instead of squaring the Z value, we cube it. Our new equation becomes: $Z_{n+1} = Z_n^3 + C$, and this is the image that this equation creates:

Figure 22.8   The Mandelbrot Fractal using the equation: $Z_{n+1} = Z_n^3 + C$

The following four figures show the Mandelbrot fractal with Z raised to the fourth, fifth, sixth, and seventh powers. These figures give us an idea of how the fractal image changes as the powers continue to increase.

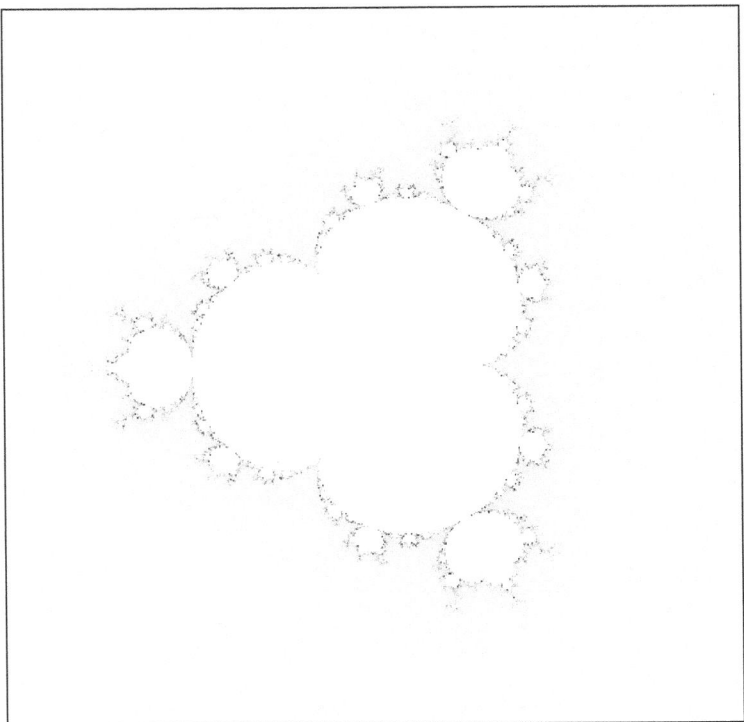

Figure 22.9   The Mandelbrot Fractal using the equation: $Z_{n+1} = Z_n^4 + C$

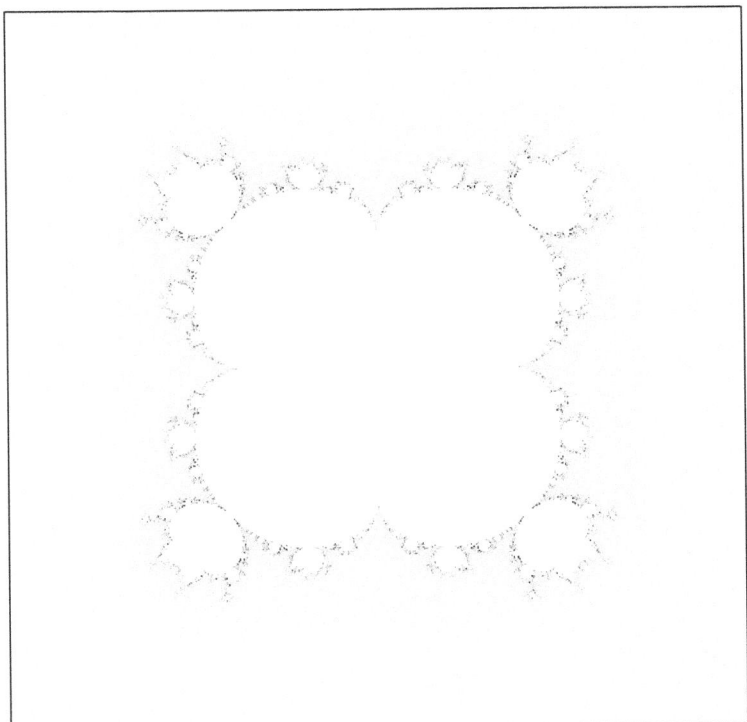

Figure 22.10   The Mandelbrot Fractal using the equation: $Z_{n+1} = Z_n^5 + C$

Figure 22.11   The Mandelbrot Fractal using the equation: $Z_{n+1} = Z_n^6 + C$

Figure 22.12   The Mandelbrot Fractal using the equation: $Z_{n+1} = Z_n^7 + C$

Polarity Diagrams of These Variations

Without belaboring this subject anymore, the following five figures show the polarity diagrams after 50 iterations of the Mandelbrot variations that we just saw.

Figure 22.13   The polarity diagram of the $Z_{n+1} = Z_n^3 + C$ Mandelbrot Fractal.

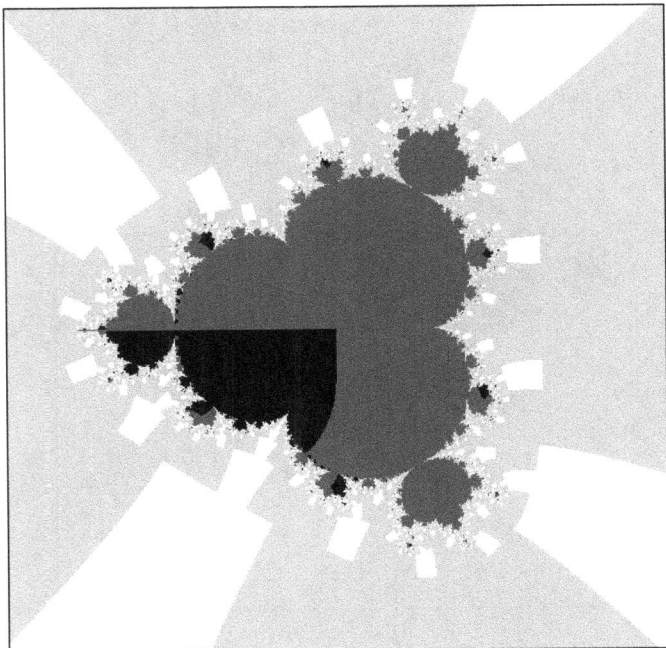

Figure 22.14   The polarity diagram of the $Z_{n+1} = Z_n^4 + C$ Mandelbrot Fractal.

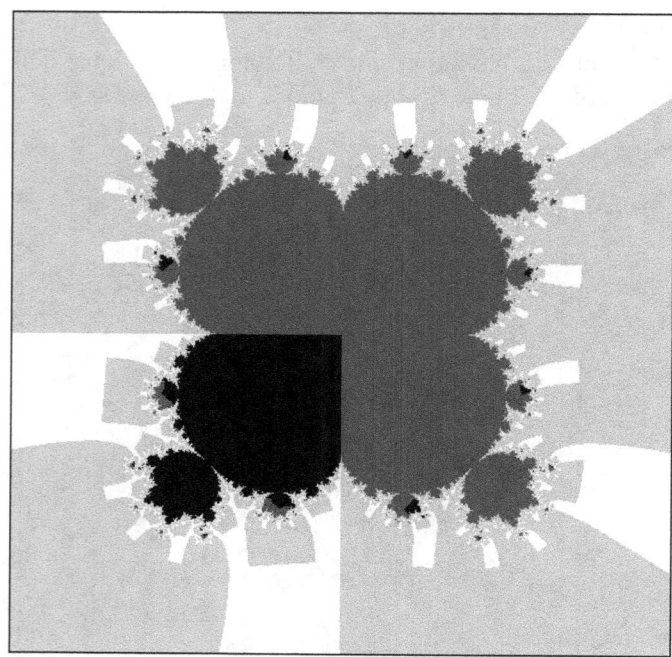

Figure 22.15   The polarity diagram of the $Z_{n+1} = Z_n^5 + C$ Mandelbrot Fractal.

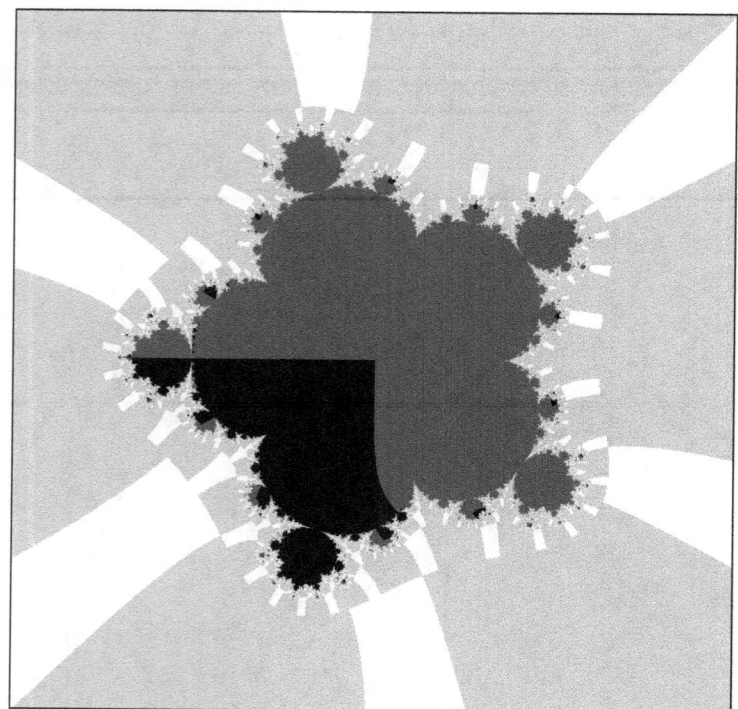

Figure 22.16   The polarity diagram of the $Z_{n+1} = Z_n^6 + C$ Mandelbrot Fractal.

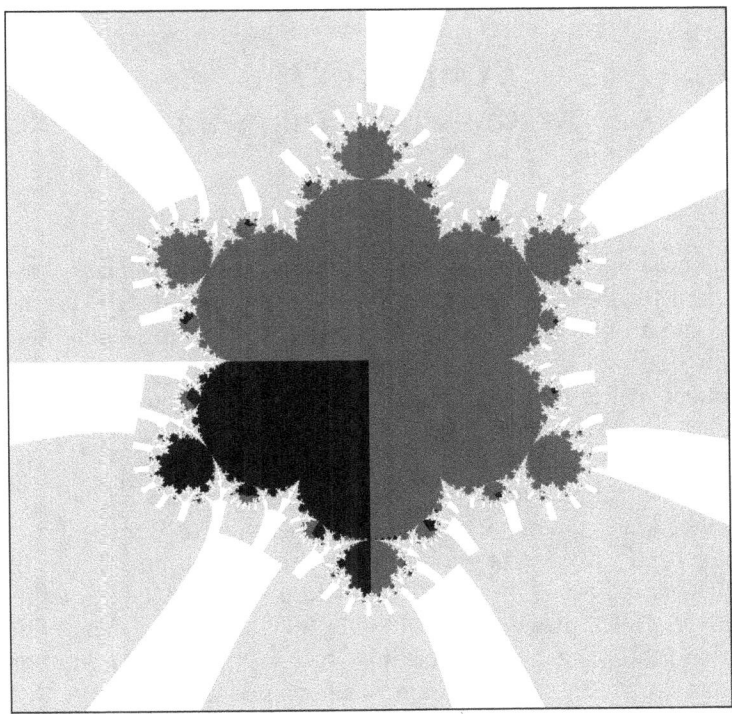

Figure 22.17   The polarity diagram of the $Z_{n+1} = Z_n^7 + C$ Mandelbrot Fractal.

Again, the polarity is determined from the + or − value of the last iterative point considered. Outside the perimeter if both the real and the imaginary part of the point are negative, then the point was assigned the white color. If either the real and/or the imaginary part are positive, then the point was assigned the light-gray color. Inside the perimeter if both the real and the imaginary part of the point are negative, then the point was assigned the black color; otherwise the pixel was given the dark-gray color.

And there are still other variations we could consider within these polarity diagrams. For example, we can see even more detail if we allow even more colors (or more shades of gray). We could allow one color when the real part is positive and the imaginary part is positive; a second color for a positive real and negative imaginary; a third color for a negative real and positive imaginary; and a fourth color for a negative real and negative imaginary. And of course we would do this for points outside of the perimeter as well as points within the perimeter. The possibilities are truly limitless.

Chapter 23
Lindenmayer-Systems (also known as L-Systems)

Lindenmayer Systems create some very interesting fractal patterns. They work like this: Start with a straight line; then for the first iteration replace the straight line with a pattern of straight lines. For the second iteration, repeat the process again by replacing each straight line with the same pattern to create a second, more detailed pattern. This process can continue indefinitely, making each subsequent pattern more complex than the previous while at the same time maintaining a semblance of the previous pattern.

We can see this process in the sequence of diagrams in the figure below. The first diagram shows the initial straight line. Diagram two replaces the straight line with an apparent square sine wave. This square sine wave starts with a line in the same orientation as the initial line. It then makes a 90° left turn, places a line, a 90° right turn, places a line, another 90° right turn, places two lines, a 90° left turn, places a line, another 90° left turn, places a line, and then ends with a 90° right turn and the placement of the final line in the same orientation as the original line. Where we had one line in the first diagram, we have now replaced it with eight lines in the second diagram.

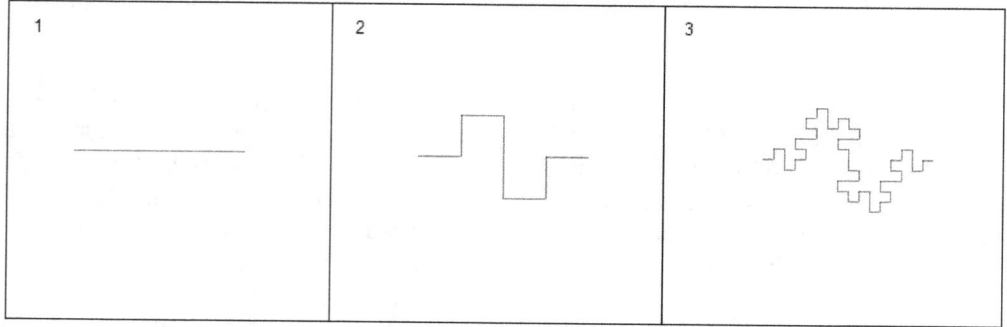

Figure 23.1   Three sequences in a Lindenmayer System

The third diagram replaces each straight line from the second diagram with the same square sine wave. In essence, each iteration replaces each previous straight line with eight new lines. (The image is also scaled down as each diagram is created. If the same scale were used throughout the iterative sequence, the later diagrams would quickly become too large to show in a reasonable manner.)

Defining the Rules

We can write this sequence of patterns shown above as a set of rules. We'll say that each line segment is represented by some letter (alpha-character), such as an A; a 90° left turn is represented as a plus (+), and a 90° right turn as a minus (-). We can now define the figure shown above with the following set of rules:

Rule 1:   Start with A

Rule 2:   For each iteration, make the following replacement:
$$A = A + A - A - AA + A + A - A$$

Turn Rules: + = 90° left turn
                    – = 90° right turn

With these rules, we now write our three diagrams from the figure above like this:

Start with A

The first iteration is very straight-forward. We have the A that is replaced with the sequence of A's from Rule 2:

$$A + A - A - AA + A + A - A$$

However, the next iteration is a little more complicated, and looks something like the following (because we again replace each A on the left with A + A – A – AA + A + A – A from Rule 2):

$$A+A - A - AA+A+A - A = (A+A - A - AA+A+A - A) + (A+A - A - AA+A+A - A) -$$
$$(A+A - A - AA+A+A - A) - (A+A - A - AA+A+A - A)$$
$$(A+A - A - AA+A+A - A) + (A+A - A - AA+A+A - A) +$$
$$(A+A - A - AA+A+A - A) - (A+A - A - AA+A+A - A)$$

Both sides of the equality have the pattern, which is A + A – A – AA + A + A – A; except, on the right side of the equal sign, I have placed parentheses around each A, and then replaced that A with the pattern as defined in Rule 2. Also, keep in mind that each plus (+) represents a 90° left turn, and each minus (–) represents a 90° right turn. Therefore, when we replace an A, we replace it with an entire sequence of parameters that will repeat the same image on an ever-increasing scale. As you can see, the text version of the pattern can become very messy and involved after several iterations.

Alternate Initial Patterns

Since we can define our starting pattern, we can start with other patterns besides a single straight line. For example, we can get a pattern that looks more complete if we start with a closed loop of some kind. The following figure shows what happens when we start with a square instead of a straight line. Note that except for rule 1, our second rule and the turn rules in the following pattern are the same as they were in the previous pattern.

Rule 1:   Start with A + A + A + A
Rule 2:   For each iteration, make the following replacement:
$$A = A + A - A - AA + A + A - A$$

Turn Rules: + = 90° left turn
                    – = 90° right turn

357

Diagram 1 in the figure below is the initial condition. The next three diagrams show the three iterations after the initial condition. Notice again that each straight line from the previous iteration is replaced with a square sine wave.

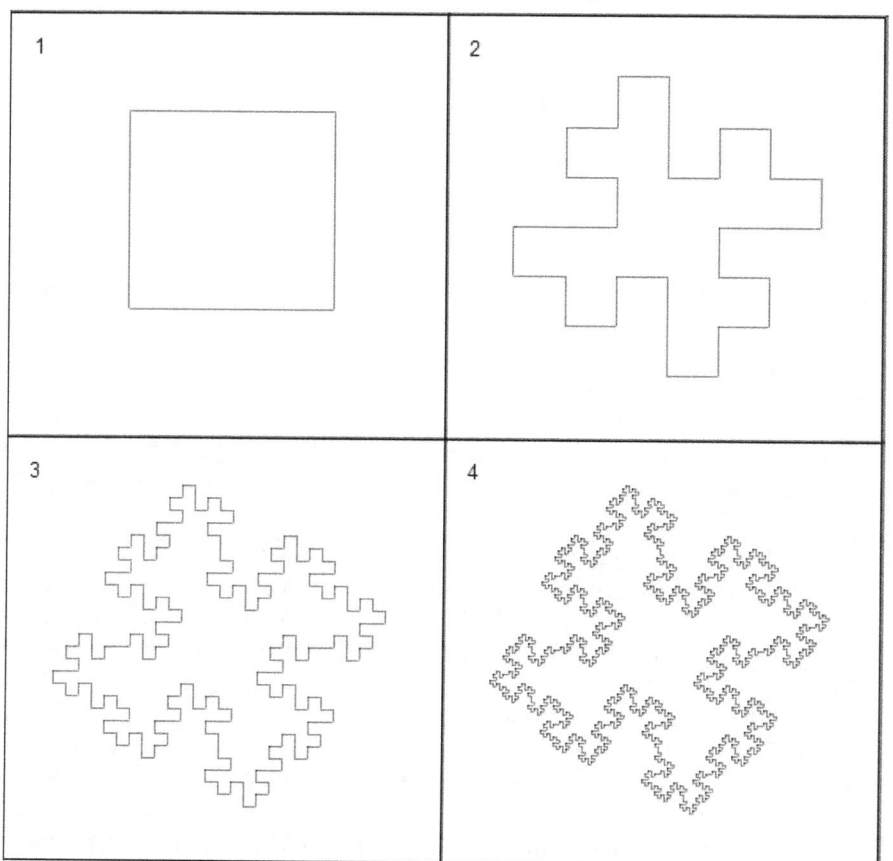

Figure 23.2 Four sequences of a square sine wave in a Lindenmayer System.

After several iterations, these diagrams can become very complex. Yet at the same time each succeeding pattern maintains a semblance with its preceding pattern. Let's look at a few more sets of rules and see what kinds of patterns we can generate.

In this next figure we'll again start with a straight line; but this time, we'll change our turn rules a little so that each iteration will replace each straight line with a spike (triangle) in the middle of the line. Our set of rules will look like this:

Rule 1:   Start with A
Rule 2:   For each iteration: $A = A + A -- A + A$

Turn Rules: $+ = 72°$ left turn
                      $- = 72°$ right turn

The following figure shows the pattern that these rules generate:

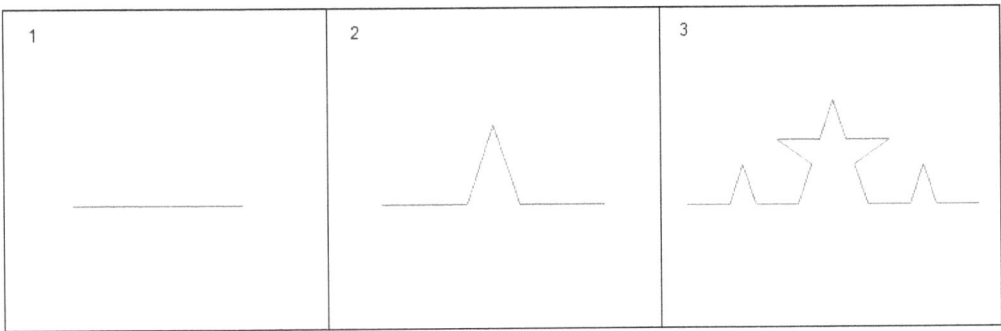

Figure 23.3   Three sequences in a Lindenmayer System

And by changing the first rule so that we start with a five-sided closed loop, we get the following sequence of diagrams (Figure 24.4):

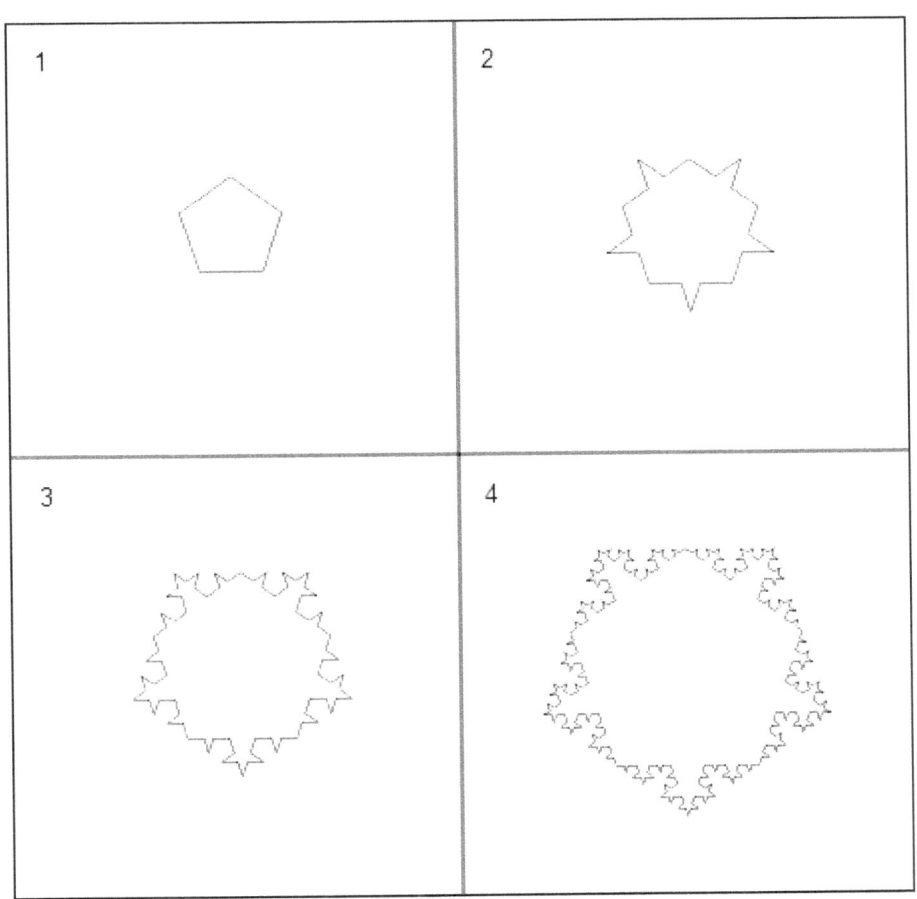

Figure 23.4   Four sequences of the triangle pattern in a Lindenmayer System.

359

In the figure above, we simply changed the initial rule so that we started with a closed loop. Also notice that the turn rules define 72° right and left turns. For this reason, we chose five sides for our initial condition so as to close the loop. Therefore, Rule 1 is defined as:

Rule 1:   Start with $A + A + A + A + A$

The other rules (Rule 2 and the turn rules) remained unchanged.

For the figure below, I took the set of rules from the figure above, and changed the +'s and −'s from Rule 2, so that Rule 2 now reads as:

Rule 2:   For each iteration: $A = A - A + + A - A$

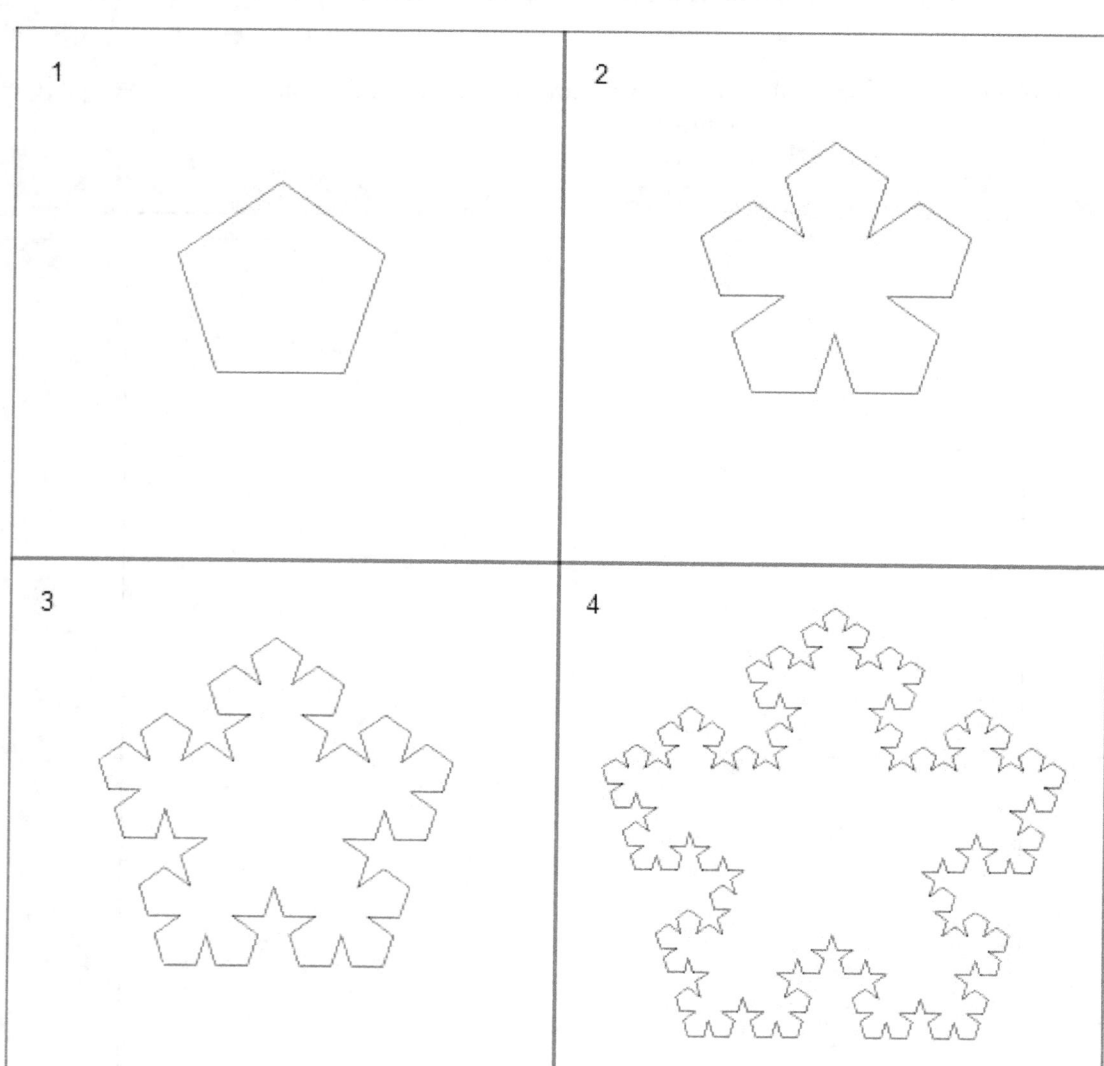

Figure 23.5   Four sequences of the inverted triangle in a Lindenmayer System

By changing Rule 2 like this, the points are now inward instead of outward. And even though this is a very subtle change in the rule, it makes a big difference in the pattern as more sequences are considered.

Of course, by making the initial condition even more complex, yet keeping everything else unchanged we can create something like the figure below. In this example Rule 1 is defined as:

Rule 1: Start with A+A+A+A+A – – – A+A+A+A+A – – – A+A+A+A+A – – –
A+A+A+A+A – – – A+A+A+A+A

Rule 2 goes back to:

Rule 2: For each iteration: A = A + A – – A + A

And this is the sequence of figures that is generated:

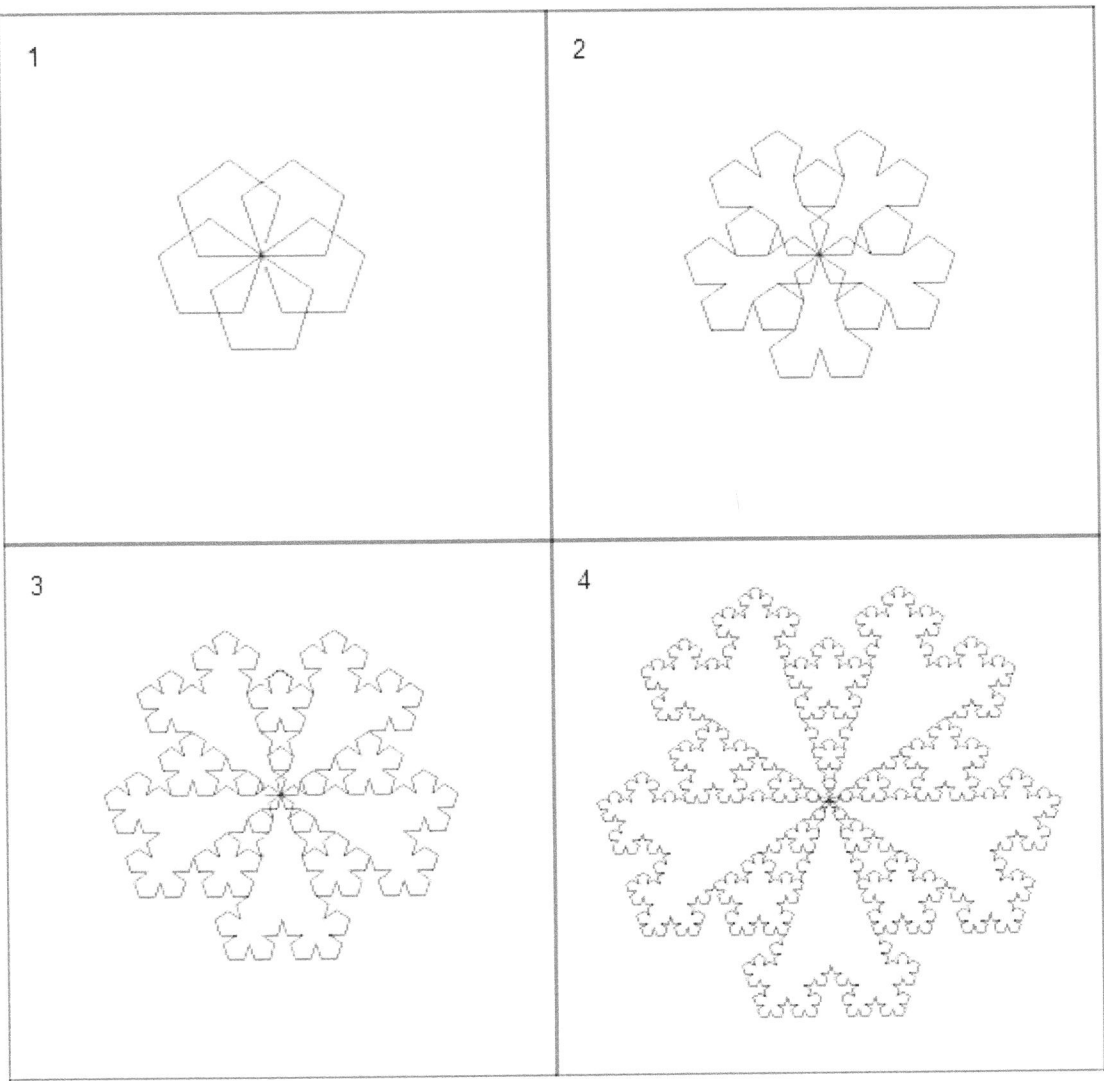

Figure 23.6 Four sequences from a complex initial pattern.

Here is another pattern. Again, we start with a straight line; then for the first iteration, we'll replace the straight line with a set of lines that make a "U" shape. This "U" shape will actually consist of a straight line, a 90 degree right turn, two straight lines, a 90 degree left turn, two straight lines, another 90 degree left turn, two more straight lines, and then a right turn followed by a single straight line. Here are the rules in our abbreviated form:

Rules 1:   Start with A

Rule 2:   For each iteration, make the following replacements
$$A = A - AA + AA + AA - A$$

Turn Rules: $+$ = 90° left turn
                        $-$ = 90° right turn

The following figure shows our initial line, and the next three iterations:

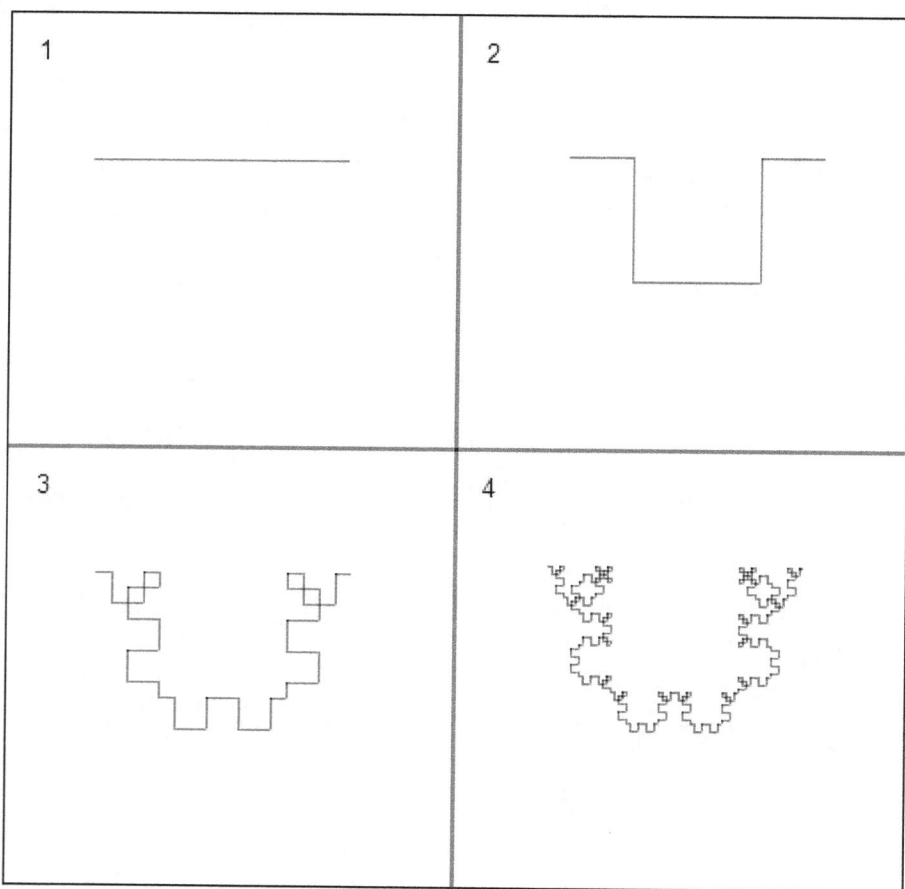

Figure 23.7   The initial line and the next three iterations of the "U" shape.

This pattern is starting to generate another interesting pattern. In the later iterations we have one part of the pattern overlapping another part of the pattern. This becomes even more evident when we begin with a closed loop (a square), instead of a single line. The following figure uses the same replacement rule and turn rules as the previous figure, with the difference being that in this case we are starting with a square for Rule 1. Here are the Rules:

Rule 1:   Start with $A - A - A - A$
Rule 2:   For each iteration, make the following replacements
$$A = A - AA + AA + AA - A$$

Turn Rules: $+ = 90°$ left turn
                $- = 90°$ right turn

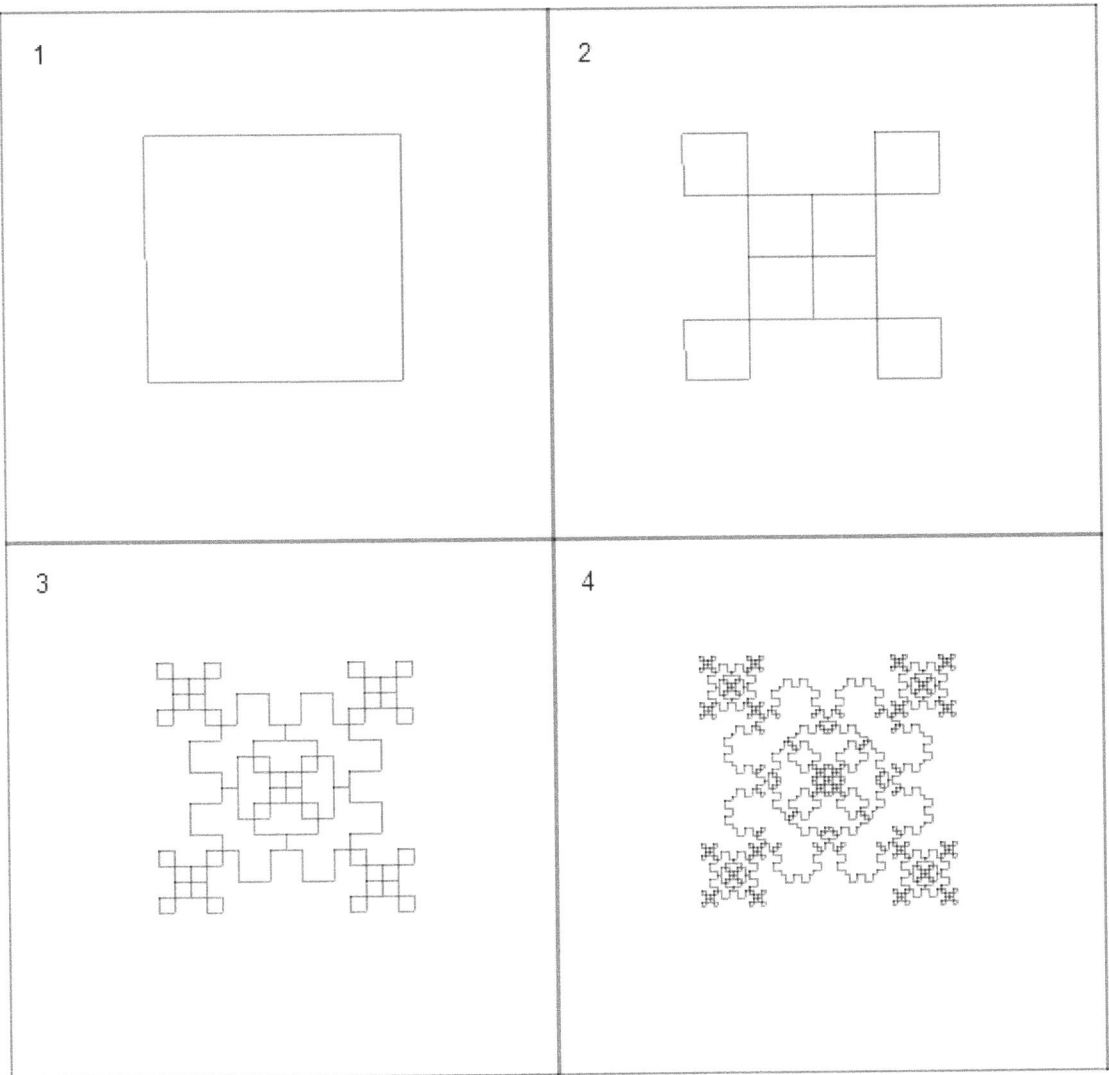

Figure 23.8   The initial square and the next three iterations of the "U" shape.

After three iterations, we can see a complex pattern starting to emerge. Notice how these patterns have a fractal quality to them. We can also see previous patterns imbedded in the succeeding patterns. And each iteration creates an even more complex pattern than the previous. After one more iteration we have the following:

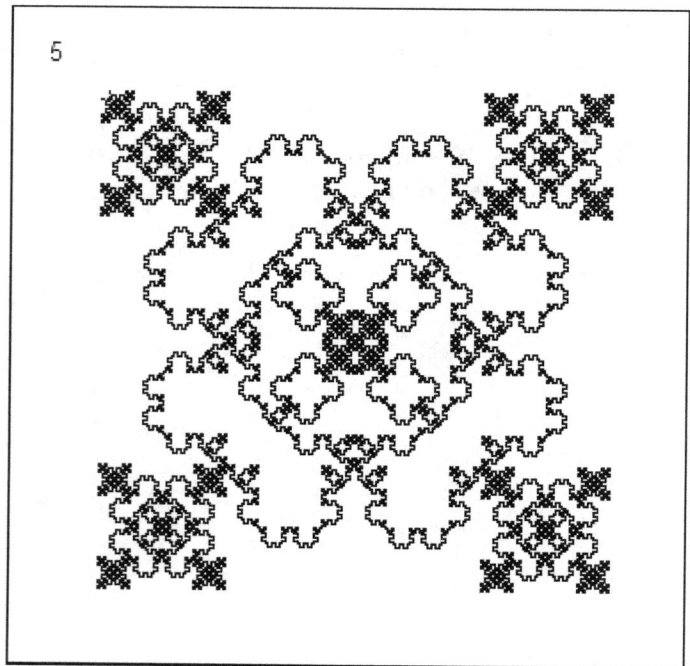

Figure 23.9 The fifth sequence of the closed "U" shaped pattern.

More Complex Lindenmayer-Systems

There are other ways that we can add complexity to our Lindenmayer-Systems. In this next example we will create an A definition and a B definition under rule 2. In this example, both the A and the B represent segments that are the same length; however, the A definition defines one replacement pattern while the B definition defines a second replacement pattern. These are the rules for our next pattern:

Rule 1:   Start with A
Rule 2:   For each iteration, make the following replacements
$$A = B - A - B$$
$$B = A + B + A$$

Turn Rules: $+ = 60°$ left turn
                   $- = 60°$ right turn

We start with an A; then during the first iteration that A becomes $B - A - B$. For the next iteration the pattern becomes $(A + B + A) - (B - A - B) - (A + B + A)$. Even though we started with just an A, after a few iterations we are thoroughly mixing the A's and B's together. This is what our pattern looks like with the start, and the first three iterations:

364

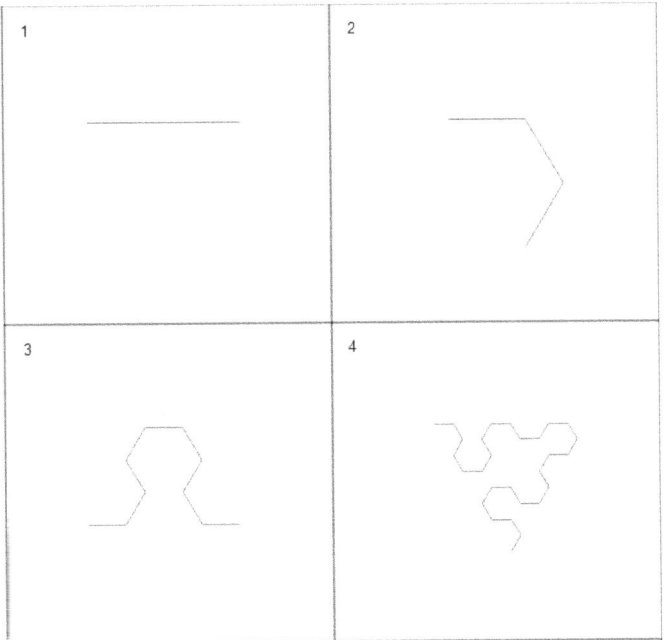

Figure 23.10 A Lindenmayer System composed of both A and B replacements.

These first three iterations show only the beginning of the pattern. As we look at the next four iterations, the pattern becomes more pronounced, and easy to recognize.

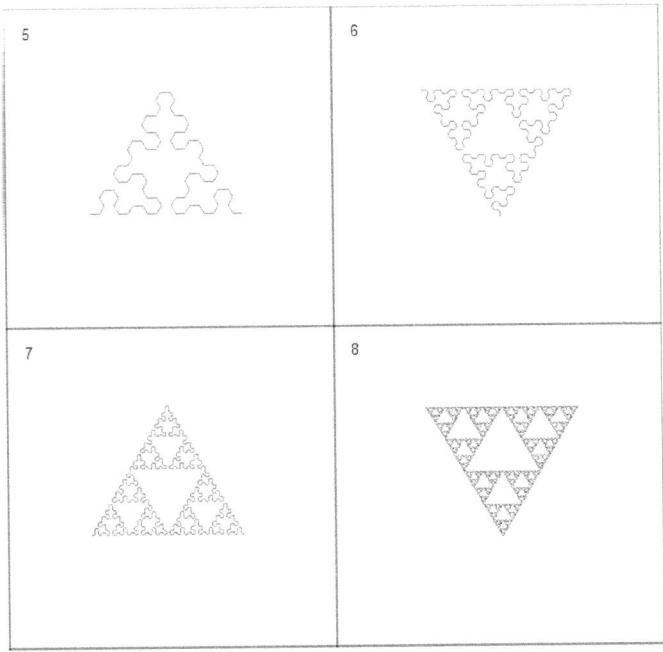

Figure 23.11   A Sierpinski triangle emerges from this Lindenmayer-System.

These rules will produce a Sierpinski triangle. And this was starting with a straight line. If we start with a six sided loop (so that Rule 1 becomes A + A + A + A + A + A), we develop a snowflake pattern during the first few iterations, and this snowflake pattern then evolves into a Sierpinski snowflake. The following figure shows the initial pattern and the first three iterations.

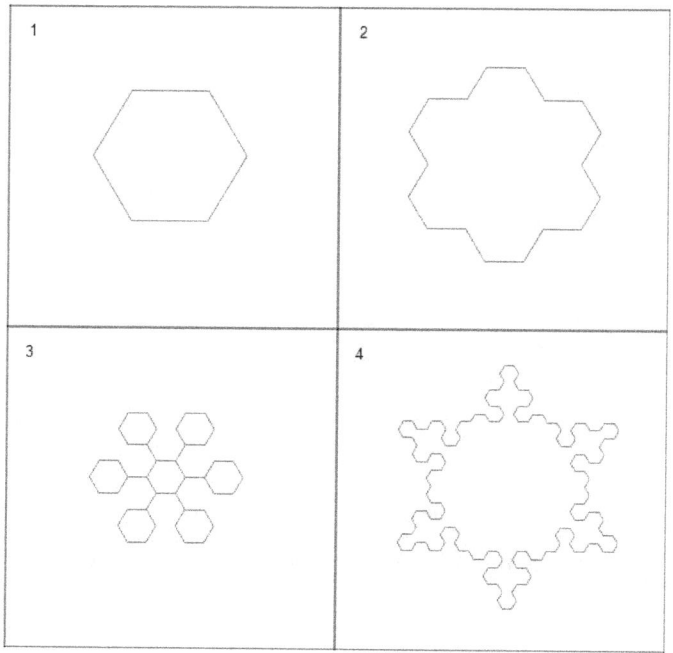

Figure 23.12   A snowflake pattern emerges when we begin with a closed loop.

The next four iterations bring out more of the Sierpinski snowflake pattern.

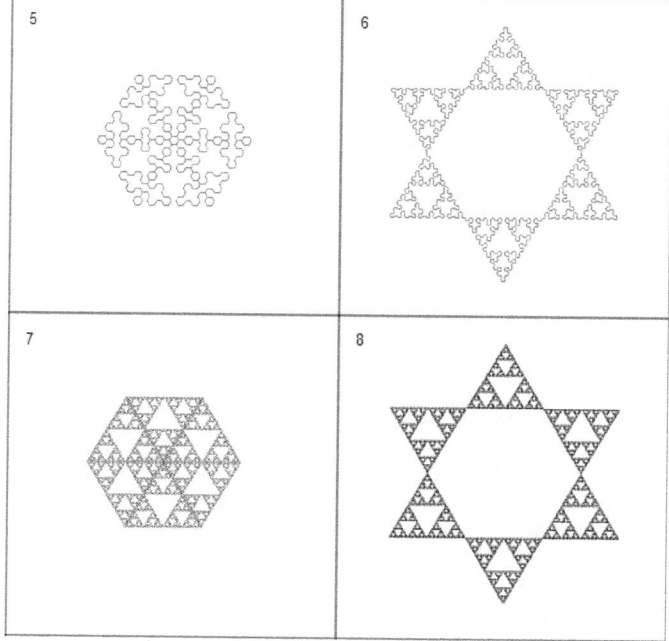

Figure 23.13   A Sierpinski snowflake emerges when we begin with a closed loop.

We will now look at another Lindenmayer pattern. This diagram also uses an A and a B definition under rule 2. Again, both A and B represent segments that are the same size; they just define different replacement patterns. The unique thing about this pattern is that even though we will be starting with only a single straight line, the iterative process will still create a square pattern. Here are the rules for our sequence of patterns:

Rule 1:   Start with A
Rule 2:   For each iteration, make the following replacements
$$A = A + A - A - A - B + A + A + A - A$$
$$B = BBB$$

Turn Rules: $+ = 90°$ left turn
                $- = 90°$ right turn

And here is the sequence of figures that these rules generate:

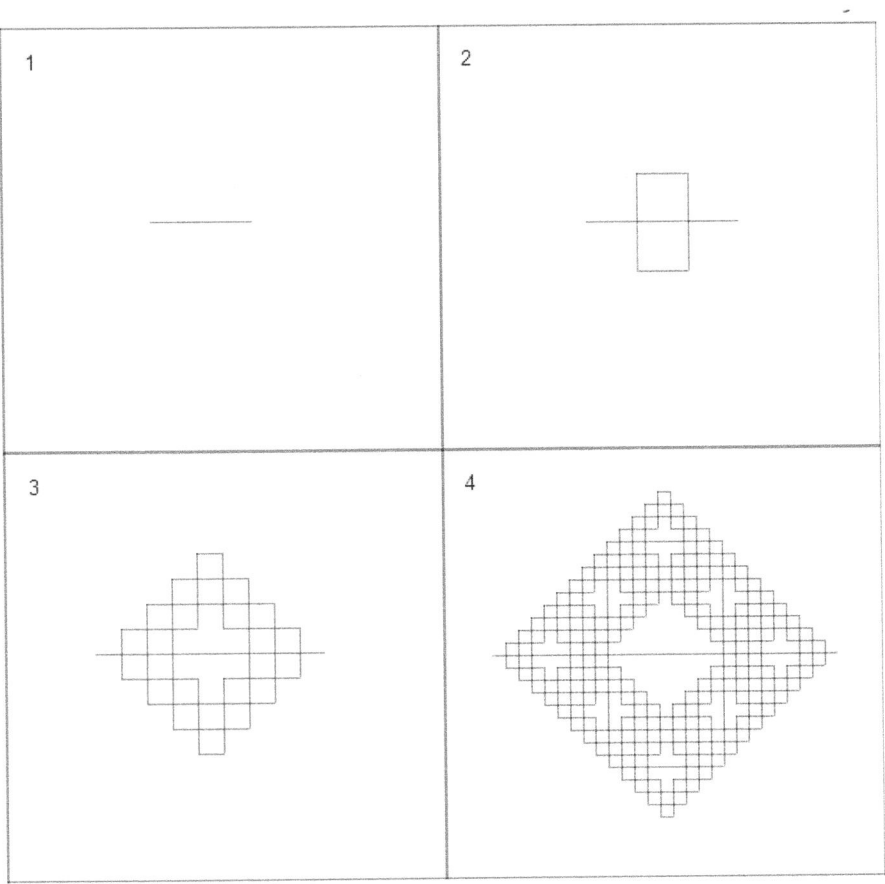

Figure 23.14   The initial line and the next three iterations of a Lindenmayer square pattern.

367

By the third iteration the pattern that is emerging is starting to become clear. After three more iterations the pattern is very pronounced. This is what we have:

Figure 23.15   The sixth sequence of a Lindenmayer square pattern.

And, you may have noticed that this pattern has a striking resemblance to a Sierpinski Square that we saw in an earlier chapter.

Even More Complex Lindenmayer-Systems

There are still other ways that we can add complexity to our Lindenmayer-Systems. Not only can we have A and B definitions under rule 2, but we can also define a space forward and a space backward. The space operator will allow us to move forward or backward the length of A (or B) without drawing a line segment.

The first L-System that we'll consider in this section will be a before-and-after sequence. The diagram below is just a regular L-System without any space forward or space backward operators. The diagram after this one will be practical identical to this one except we'll also include a few carefully positioned backspaces and forward spaces within rule 2. Here are the rules and images for the first sequence:

Rule 1:   Start with $A - A - A - A - A$
Rule 2:   For each iteration, make the following replacements
            $A = A - A - A + A + A + A + A - A - A - A + A$

Turn Rules: $+ = 72°$ left turn
                $- = 72°$ right turn

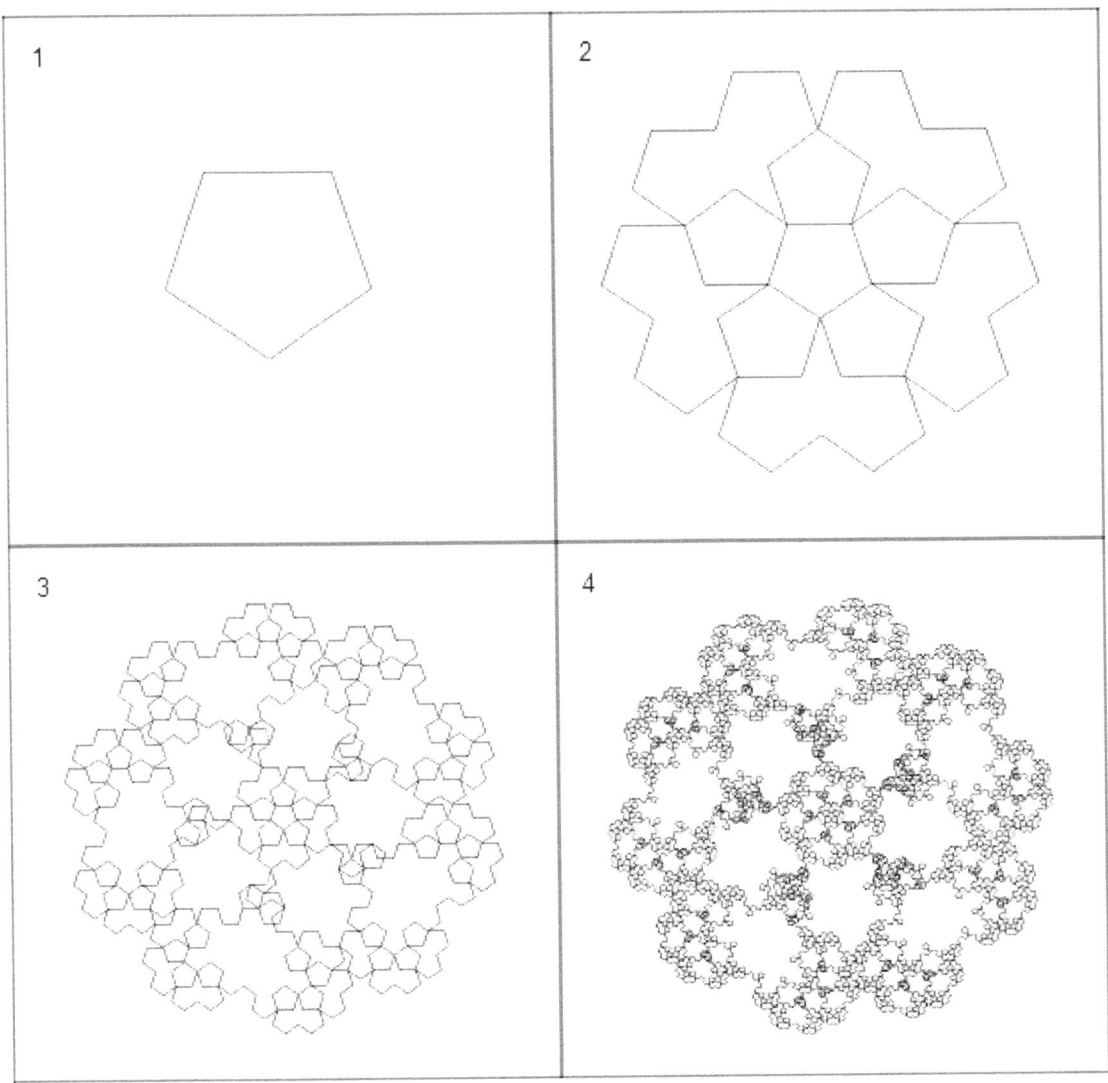

Figure 23.16   The initial pentagon and the next three iterations of a simple Lindenmayer pattern.

As just mentioned, the pattern below is the same as the previous pattern except that a few backspaces have been included in rule 2. Also note that rule 2 below shows both rules: the A rule from the previous pattern and the new A rule for the pattern below. Here are the rules and images for this modified sequence:

Rule 1:   Start with $A - A - A - A - A$

Rule 2:   For each iteration, make the following replacements
(instead of $A = A - A -\ A + A + A +\ A + A - A -\ A - A + A$)
we'll have $A = A - A - <A + A + A + <A + A - A - <A - A + A$

Turn Rules: $+ = 72°$ left turn
$- = 72°$ right turn

Space Rules: $> =$ go forward one length (without drawing a line)
$< =$ go backward one length (without drawing a line)

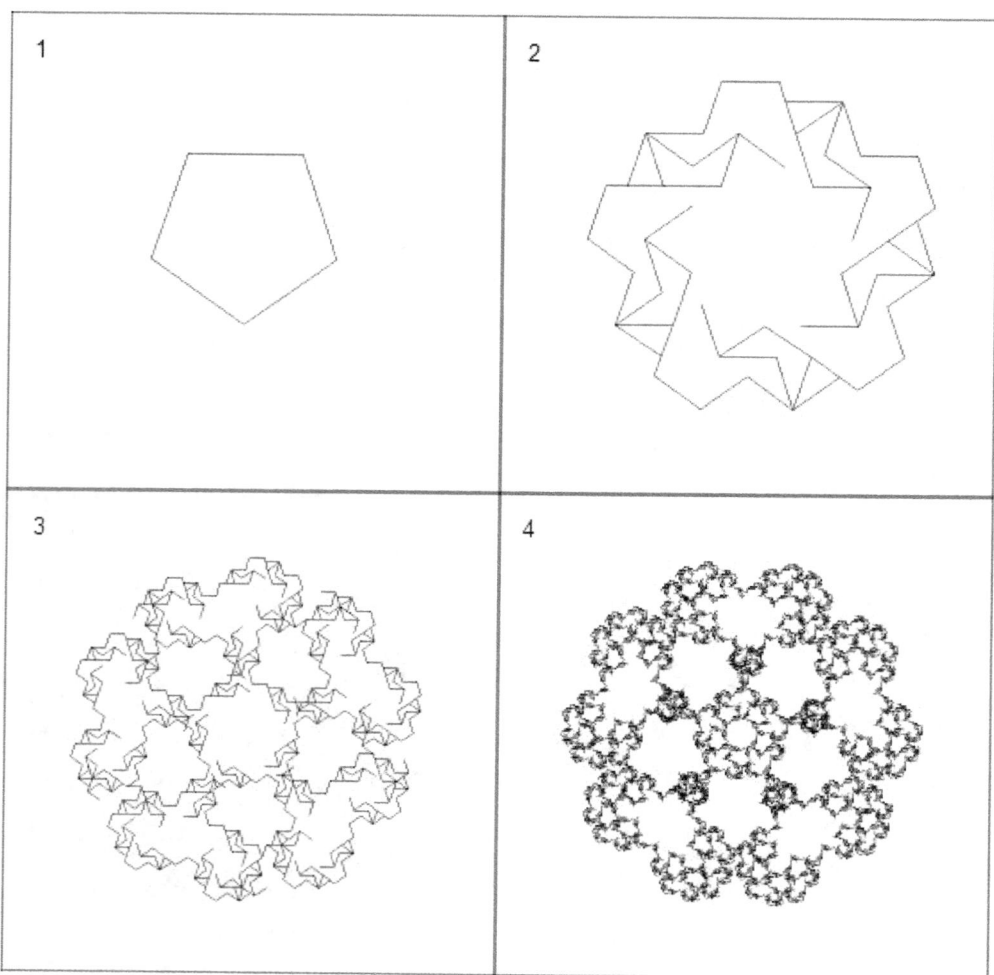

Figure 23.17   The initial pentagon and the next three iterations of a more complex Lindenmayer pattern with backspaces.

The two rules that were added are space rules. They allow us to add a space of length A without drawing a line. The greater than symbol (>) will move us forward one length and the less than symbol (<) will move us backward one length. Of course, with these extra rules we now have even more freedom to create some amazing patterns. The pattern below starts with an octagon, and then uses a combination of A and B rules as well as forward and backward rules.

Rule 1:   Start with $A + A + A + A + A + A + A + A$

Rule 2:   For each iteration, make the following replacements

$$A = B - AB - >> BB$$
$$B = A + > BA + << AA$$

Turn Rules: + = 45° left turn
                     − = 45° right turn

Space Rules: > = go forward one length (without drawing a line)
                     < = go backward one length (without drawing a line)

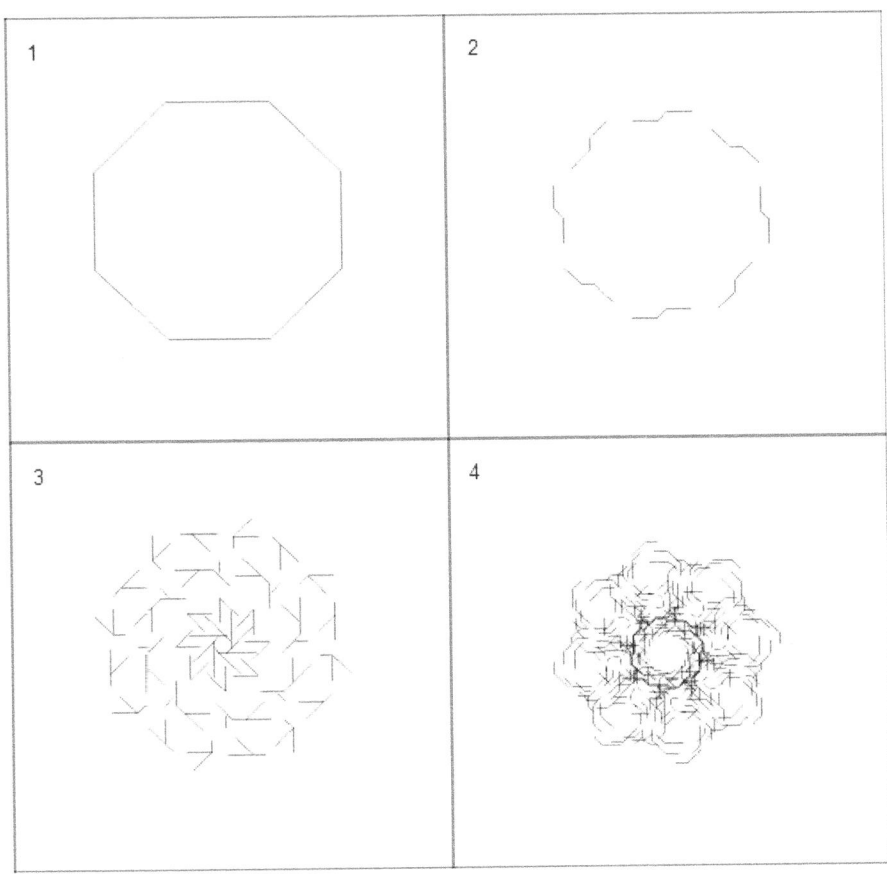

Figure 23.18   The initial octagon and the next three iterations of an even more complex Lindenmayer pattern with A and B rules as well as forward spaces and backspaces.

371

This next pattern we'll consider starts with a square, and then, with each successive iteration, creates a larger square that covers more and more area. This pattern is a plane-filling pattern. There are no holes or gaps left within the pattern as the pattern is being created, and none of the lines overlap. The pattern itself is rather plain (pun intended), but the construction of the pattern is not. Here is the rule set that defines this pattern.

Rule 1:   Start with $A - A - A - A$
Rule 2:   For each iteration, make the following replacements
$$A = A - A + A + A + A - A - A - A + A$$

Turn Rules: $+ = 90°$ left turn
                $- = 90°$ right turn

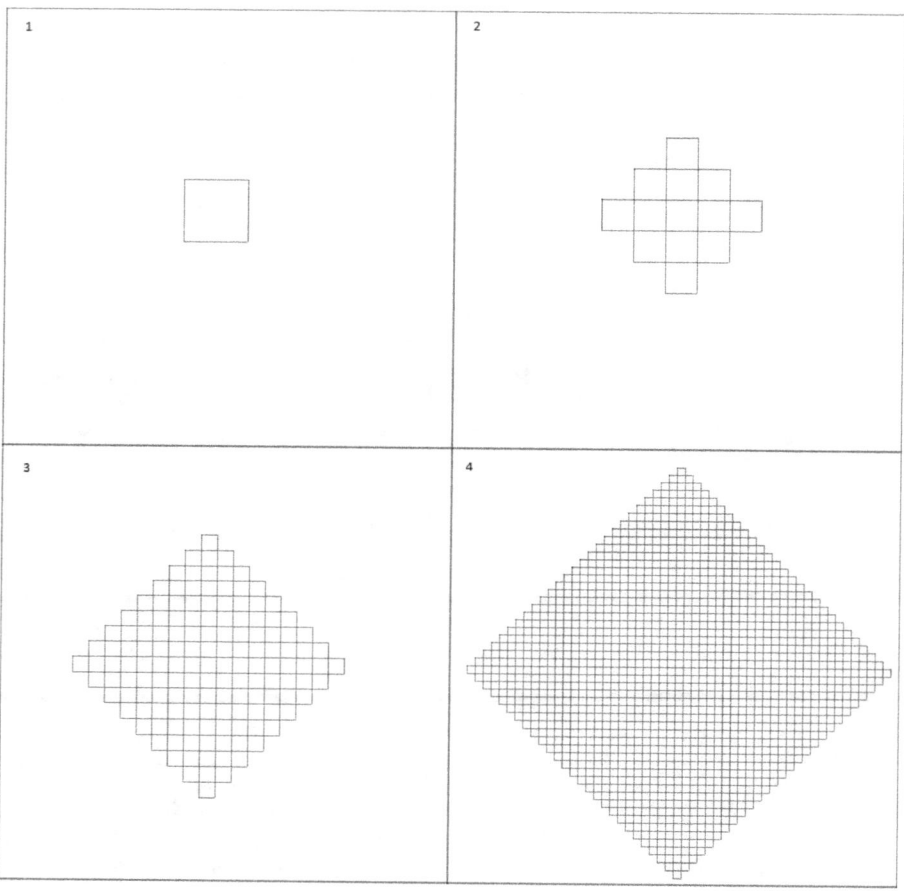

Figure 23.19   The initial square and the next three iterations of a plane-filling Lindenmayer pattern. This pattern can be created with just an A definition or with A and B definitions.

The pattern above also has the added characteristic in that it is possible to create this pattern in terms of just an A definition under rule 2, or in terms of an A and a B definition under rule 2. Not all patterns have this characteristic; however, there are many that do. Here is the rule set that uses both an A and a B under rule 2:

Rule 1: Start with A – A – A – A
Rule 2: For each iteration, make the following replacements
$$A \;=\; B - B + A + A + A - A - A - B + B$$
$$B \;=\; A - A + B + B + B - B - B - A + A$$

Turn Rules: + = 90° left turn
– = 90° right turn

Notice how the A and B definitions under rule 2 complement each other. The following figure roughly shows how this plane-filling pattern constructs itself. (Notice that the plane isn't so plain.)

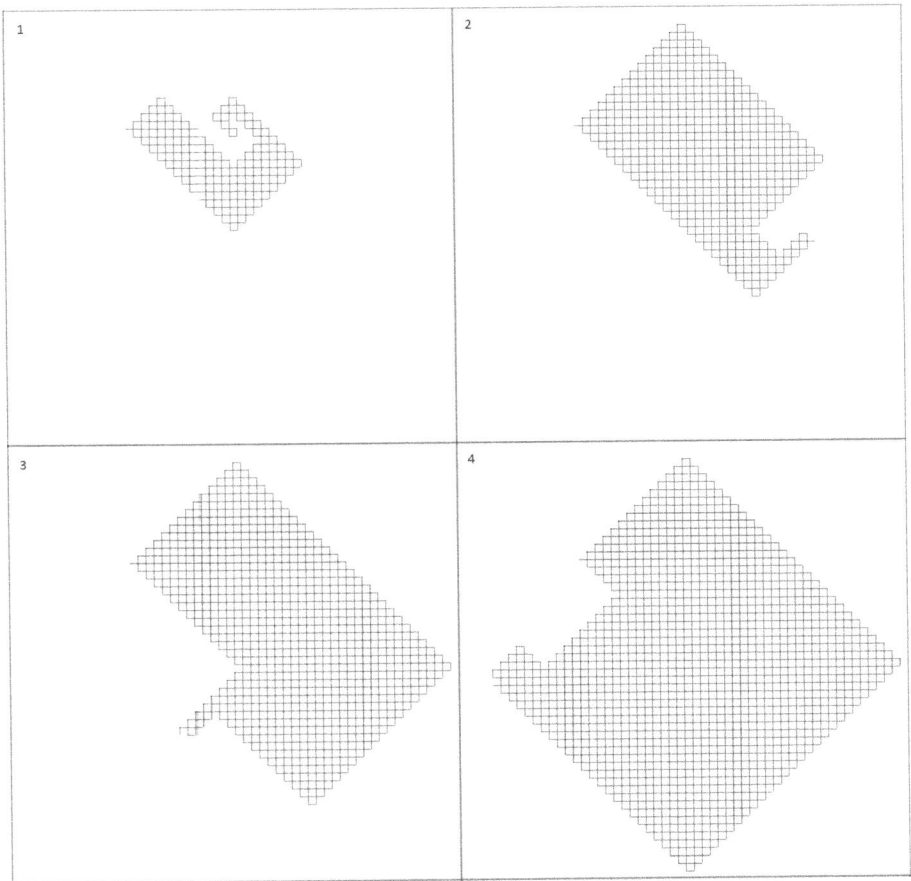

Figure 23.20   A sequence of images showing how the plane-filling pattern constructs itself.

As I mentioned above, it is possible to take several kinds of patterns and under rule 2 create only an A definition, or an A and a B definition. The following pattern is another example of this. In this next example, I have placed both number 2 rules next to each other so that it is easier to compare them with each other. Again, notice how the A and B definitions complement each other.

373

Rule 1:   Start with A + A + A + A
Rule 2:   For each iteration, make the following replacements
           A = AA + A + A + AA + AAA + AA + A + A + AA
Or
Rule 2:   For each iteration, make the following replacements
           A = AA + B + B + AA + AAA + AA + B + B + AA
           B = BB + A + A + BB + BBB + BB + A + A + BB

Turn Rules: + = 90° left turn
                   − = 90° right turn

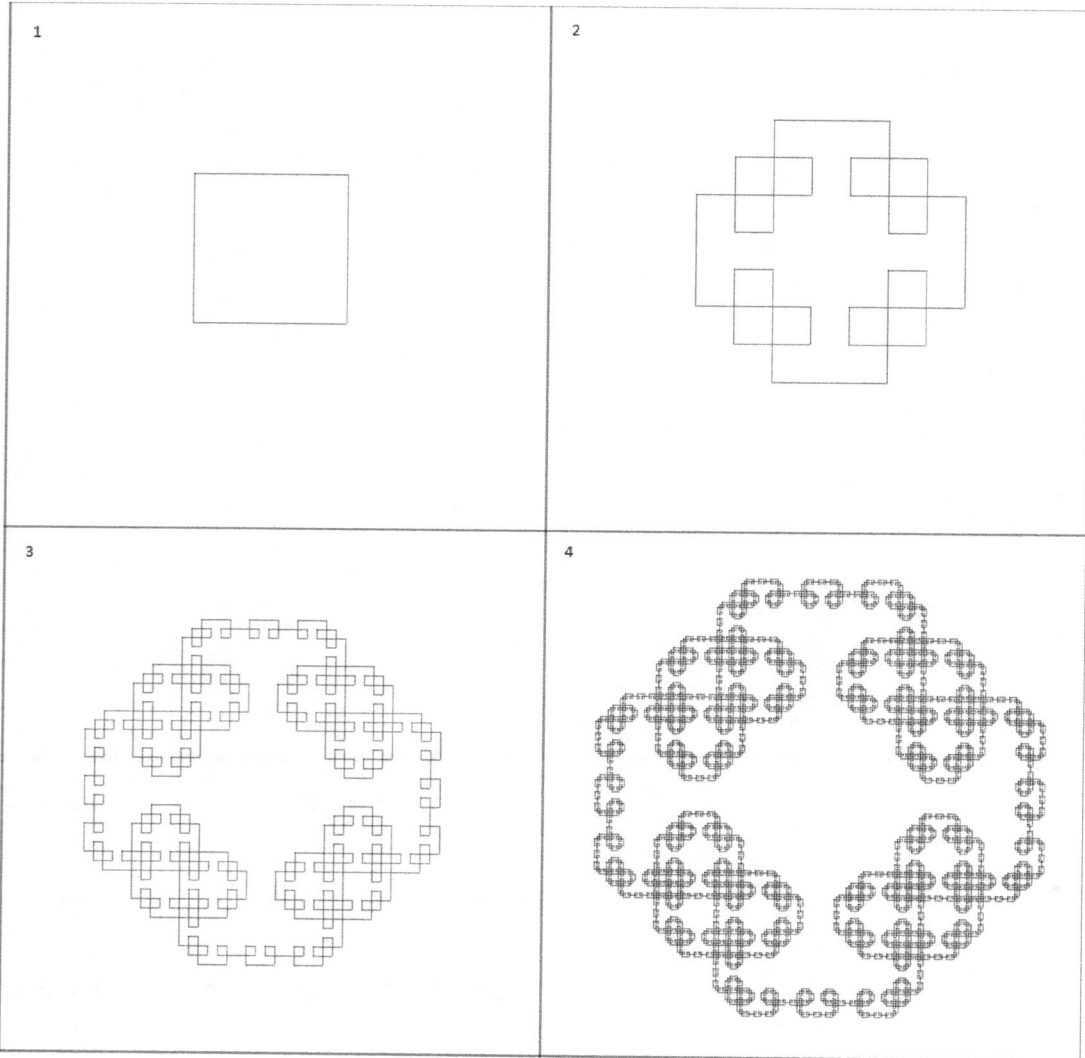

Figure 23.21   This is another Lindenmayer pattern that can be created with either an A rule or with A and B rules.

And finally we'll end this chapter with a pine bough pattern that we create with a combination of A and B rules, turn rules, and backward rules. Note that we don't show the first image in the sequence below (the first image is just a straight line). Here are the rules and sequence of images for the pine bough pattern. (Additional Lindenmayer rules and patterns can be found in the Appendix.)

Rule 1:   Start with A

Rule 2:   For each iteration, make the following replacements

$$A = AB + AA << - BB <<<$$
$$B = BA - BB << + AA <<<$$

Turn Rules: $+ = 30°$ left turn
$- = 30°$ right turn

Space Rules: $> = $ go forward one length (without drawing a line)
$< = $ go backward one length (without drawing a line)

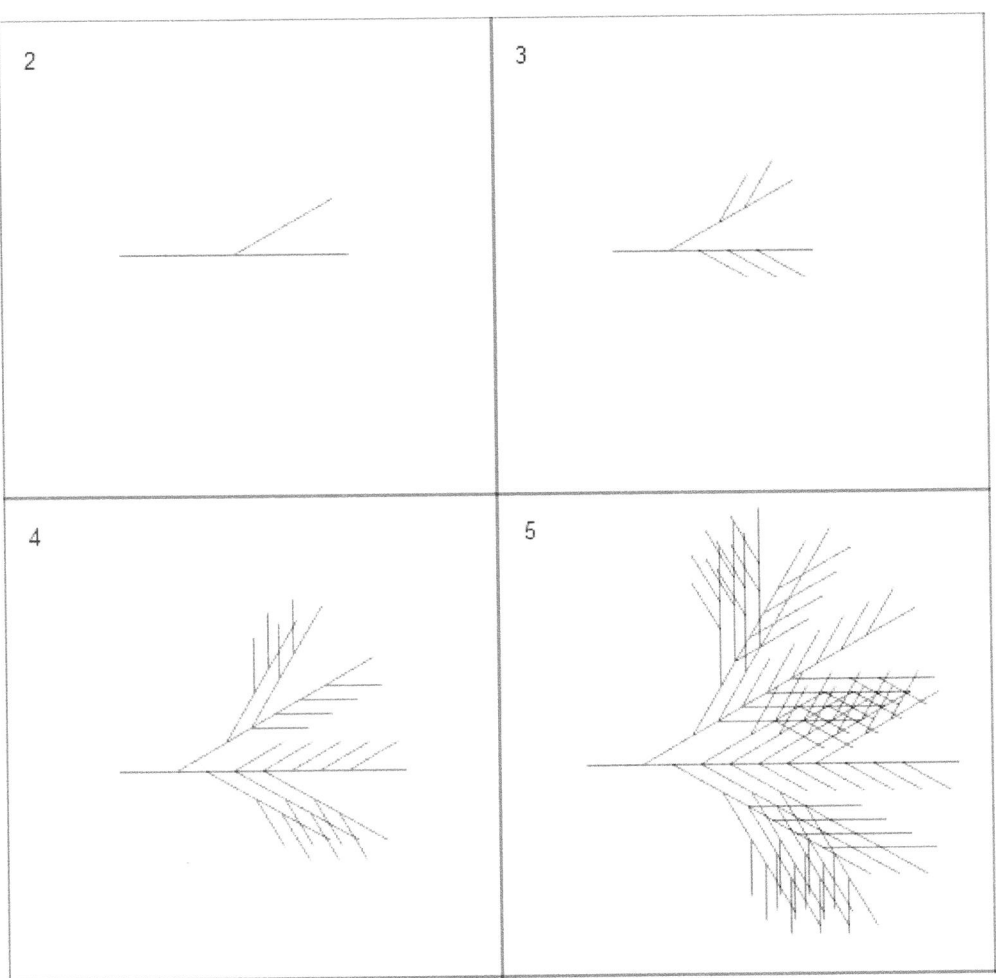

Figure 23.22   The next four iterations of a Lindenmayer pattern that has the appearance of a pine bough.

Chapter 24
Math Illusions, Magic, and Games

A Mind Reading Trick

Mathematics has found its major application in Science, Engineering and Business, but it has also found some unusual and unexpected uses. One of these is in the field of magic. Many magicians spend hours practicing the hand coordination and other illusionary skills required for their trade. However, the nice thing about mathematical magic is that if you follow the steps precisely, the magic will work itself. There is no need to practice hand coordination (which is nice for those of us who are dextrally challenged). Let's look at an example:

> Think of a number between 1 and 10. Got it? Now double it. Add 10 to the result, and then divide this new result by 2. Now, subtract the original number you thought of, and your answer is 5. Right? Of course I'm right!

If you followed along with several friends, you'll notice that it doesn't matter what number you start with, all of you will get 5 as your final answer. This is an example of a self-working trick. You don't need to know the how or why of the mathematics behind the magic, and you most certainly don't need any hand or eye coordination to perform it. Instead, just follow the steps, and you'll get the same answer.

However, if you really want to impress your friends, you'll need to change this trick so that you get a different result each time you do it. (And by varying the results, it will not only help you understand the math behind the trick, but it will also give you more of an appearance of a professional magician.) Let's look at each step individually.

1. Ask the person to think of a number between one and ten (actually, they can use any number, but since they probably will be doing all the math in their head, it's easier if they begin with a smaller number).
2. Ask the person to double the number they are thinking of.
3. Ask them to add 10 to their number.
4. Now divide their result by 2.
5. Subtract the original number they were thinking of.

Notice how steps one and five are the opposite of each other, they cancel each other out. In step one you ask one or more people to think of a number between one and ten, and then in step five you tell them to subtract their original number. Likewise, steps two and four cancel each other. In step two you ask them to double their number, and in step four you ask them to divide their number by 2. Since these steps cancel each other, the secret to this magic trick lies in step three. The secret is that the final result will be equal to half of whatever you tell the persons (or persons) to add in step three. In our example, I asked you to add 10. The final result at the end of the trick was equal to 5. If I had asked you to add 8 in step three, then by the end of step five, the result would have been 4.

Knowing this secret, now you need to embellish the act. For example, when I get to step three, I usually tell them to add a couple of numbers, like 7 and then 5. Then by the time I get to step five, I know the number they are thinking of is 6 (which is half of 7 + 5). Since I now know the number in their mind, at this point I add a few more steps of my own. Like I might tell them to multiply the number by 4 and then divide it by 8. Then square it, add 7 and take the square root. At this point, sometimes the person can see that you are toying with them, and they are even more amazed. They can tell that you know what the number is that they are thinking of and that you are leading them along; and most important, they wonder how you did it.

A Mind Reading Trick Explained with Binary Numbers
Here's another trick that can be just as amazing. Prepare four cards beforehand with the following numbers on each card.

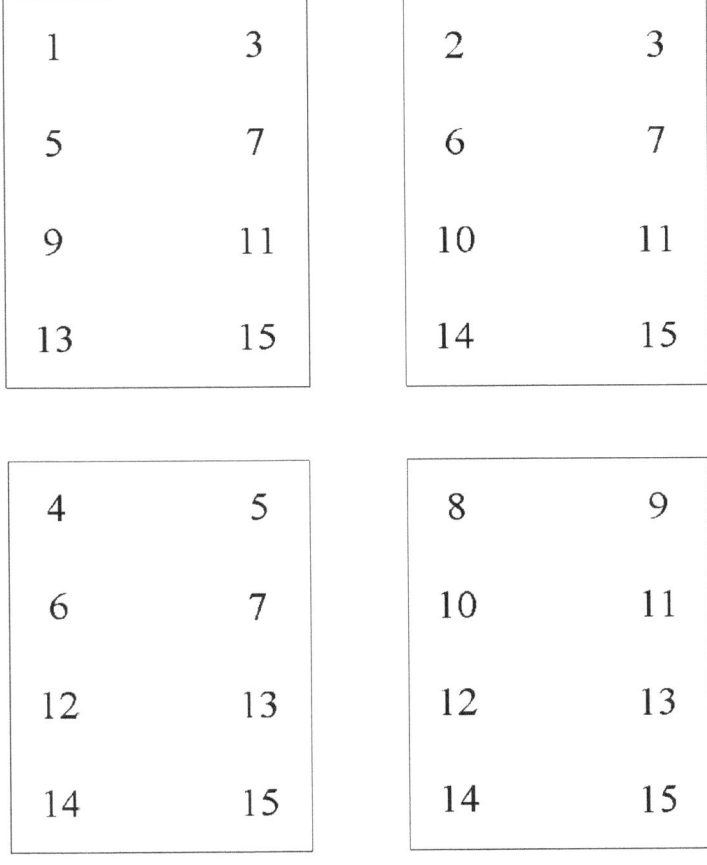

Figure 24.1   Numbered cards used for mind reading.

Notice that the first card has the numbers 1, 3, 5, 7, 9, 11, 13 and 15. The second has the numbers 2, 3, 6, 7, 10, 11, 14 and 15. On the third card place the numbers 4, 5, 6, 7, 12, 13, 14, 15; and on the fourth card place the numbers 8, 9, 10, 11, 12, 13, 14 and 15. Each card has eight numbers, and it more or less looks like the numbers are random. (See figure 25.1)

To perform the trick, you hand the four cards to a friend, and tell that person to select a number between 1 and 15, and then hand back all the cards that have that number on it. As he (or she) hands back the cards, you quickly glance at each card and then place it face down on the table.

Now you begin your act (because you've already figured out what the number is that they're thinking of). You act like the cards are talking to you, and that you can feel the vibration of the numbers reverberating through your entire being (just don't get too carried away). After a minute or two of this, tell them what the number is. They'll be amazed, and if they've handed you the right cards, you'll be right every time.

So, how does this trick work? The secret lies in the numbers that are placed on the four cards. If we write the numbers 1 through 15 in base two, and include the zeroes, we can represent each number as a four digit number. The cards are created from the columns of the base 2 representation of the numbers 1 through 15.

Base 10	Base 2
1	0 0 0 1
2	0 0 1 0
3	0 0 1 1
4	0 1 0 0
5	0 1 0 1
6	0 1 1 0
7	0 1 1 1
8	1 0 0 0
9	1 0 0 1
10	1 0 1 0
11	1 0 1 1
12	1 1 0 0
13	1 1 0 1
14	1 1 1 0
15	1 1 1 1

The numbers on the first card correspond to the numbers that have a one in the right-most column under the base 2 heading. Therefore, the first card has the numbers 1, 3, 5, 7, 9, 11, 13 and 15 on it. Likewise, the numbers on the second card correspond with the 1's in the next column to the left. Every 1 in this column has its corresponding number placed on the second card. This gives us a card with the numbers 2, 3, 6, 7, 10, 11, 14 and 15 on it. The numbers on the third card correspond with the next column to the left, giving us the numbers 4, 5, 6, 7, 12, 13, 14 and 15. And the numbers on the fourth card correspond with the left-most column and include the numbers 8, 9, 10, 11, 12, 13, 14 and 15. These numbers can be placed in any order on the card; however, it helps to place the numbers in some kind of order, usually with the lowest number somewhere near the top. Notice also that the lowest number on the first card is 1. The lowest number on the second card is 2; on the third card it is 4 and on the fourth card it is 8.

Now, to perform the trick, you simply add the lowest number of each card that is handed to you. As an example, say the person you gave the cards to, hands back the first, second and fourth cards. The lowest number on each of these cards is 1, 2 and 8. Therefore, the number they are thinking of is equal to 1 + 2 + 8, which is 11. (You can check for yourself that the 11 is located on those three cards.)

As you can see, this trick is very easy to do, and most people will be very amazed when you perform the trick. Especially, if you only glance at the cards handed to you as you place them face down on the table.

There are also other variations to this trick. One alternative is to tell the person to hand back the cards that don't have the number they are thinking of on it. To perform this trick, you then subtract from 15 the lowest number of each card that is handed to you. Using our previous example, if they were thinking of the number 11, the only card that doesn't have an 11 on it is the card with the 4 as the lowest number. They would hand this card to you, you subtract the 4 from 15, and tell them the number they are thinking of, which is 11.

The Tertiary Sort, A Third Mind Reading Trick

This is a card trick that uses a sort routine to zero in on a selected card. It is very easy to perform, and it doesn't require any manual dexterity to do it. Start by laying out 27 cards in three columns. Lay the cards out so that each card is at least partially visible, yet at the same time the three columns remain very distinct.

Ask a volunteer to select a card, but to only tell you which column it is in. Now collect all the cards, making sure to collect the column with the selected card so that it ends up on top of the deck. Now, lay out the cards in three separate columns again, dealing one card per column until all 27 cards are in the 3 columns. Again ask the volunteer to point to the column that has his selected card. Again, gather the cards such that the column containing the selected card is again on top of the deck. Lay out the three columns one more time, and have the volunteer point to the column one more time. This time as you gather the three columns, and place the selected column on top of your deck, the card that your volunteer is thinking of will be the top card.

What we have done is perform a tertiary sort on the cards. By going through this routine three times, the desired card has moved from somewhere inside the mix of cards to the top card. If you wanted to use the full deck of cards, you can, but you need to repeat the column-selecting process one additional time to account for the additional cards. However, I have found that with the additional cards and the additional steps, the trick becomes just a little too long. It works best with no more than 27 cards, and going through the column-selecting process three times.

A Fourth Mind Reading Trick

With this next trick it is possible for your volunteer to do the mathematics in his head; however, I would recommend that you give him (or her) a pencil and a piece of paper. Ask your volunteer to choose a number between 10 and 99 (it needs to be a two digit number), and to write this number down on the piece of paper without telling you what the number is. Now, ask the volunteer to add the two digits together and then subtract that sum from their original number. Next, take the leading digit of this result, increase it by one, and divide it into the current number. After performing this last step, the number that your volunteer will have is 9 (it will always be 9). And from there you can lead them to whatever final number you wish, and then tell them the number in their mind. Let's look at a couple of examples.

Suppose your volunteer chooses 53 as their initial number. The first step is to add these two digits together (the 5 and the 3) and then to subtract that result from the original number. 5 + 3 is equal to 8, and subtracting that from 53 gives us 45. Now, if we take the leading digit (which is the 4), increase it by one, and then divide it into the current number we will have 45 divided by 5 which will give us 9.

If your volunteer choose 78 as their initial number, the first thing you would have them do is add the 7 and 8 together and then subtract that sum from the original number. 7 + 8 is equal to 15, and subtracting that from 78 gives us 63. Now we take the leading digit (which is the 6) and increase it by one, and then divide it into the current number. This means that we will have 63 divided by 7 which will again give us 9.

Even though you don't know what the initial number was that you started with, you will always end up with the number 9 after performing these steps. From here you can tell your volunteer that the result that they have is 9, or you could embellish your act a little and tell them to add 7 and take the square root; or subtract 4 and double it, or whatever you want.

So how does this "mind reading trick" actually work? We are using a property of the number 9 in base 10. In an earlier chapter, we saw that you can determine whether a number is divisible by 9 by adding together the digits of the number. If that result is divisible by 9, then so is the original number. There is actually a little more to that property: if the sum of the digits isn't divisible by 9, then whatever remainder you get from that sum (when dividing by 9) is the same remainder that you would get if you divided 9 into the original number. Therefore, if you subtract that sum from the original number, you will always end up with a number that is a multiple of 9.

The real trick is to figure out what number you need to divide into the multiple of 9 so that you end up with a 9 as your result. With two digit numbers, it is easy to know what that number would be – it will always be equal to one more than the leading digit. And that is how this trick works.

A Mathematical Illusion

It's usually impossible to legally make a sum of numbers equal to whatever we want; however, sometimes we can take a proof, follow what appears to be a logical process, and still come to a wrong conclusion. For example, here's an interesting little proof that shows that 1 is equal to 2. See if you can find the flaw in our logic. We start by defining a equal to b:

$$a = b \qquad \text{define a equal to b}$$
$$a^2 = ab \qquad \text{multiply both sides by a}$$
$$2a^2 = a^2 + ab \qquad \text{add an } a^2 \text{ to both sides}$$
$$2a^2 - 2ab = a^2 - ab \qquad \text{subtract 2ab from both sides}$$
$$2a(a - b) = a(a - b) \qquad \text{factor each side of the equality}$$
$$2a = a \qquad \text{divide by (a - b), the common factor}$$
$$2 = 1 \qquad \text{divide by a − how did we get this?}$$

All of our steps were valid, or at least they appeared to be; so how did we arrive at this wrong conclusion?

If we let "a" and "b" equal some number, and then followed the proof through, we see that both sides of the equality remain equal to each other until we divide by (a - b). At that point the two sides became unequal to each other. Did you notice that with both "a" and "b" equal to each other, dividing by (a - b) is the same as dividing by zero. Division by zero is undefined in mathematics. It can lead to unexpected results. Anything could happen when you divide by zero, and in our example, something did happen. Dividing by zero caused the two sides to become unequal, thus causing 1 to appear to be equal to 2. A variation to this proof goes like this:

$$
\begin{aligned}
x &= a & &\\
x^2 &= ax & &\text{multiply both sides by x}\\
x^2 - a^2 &= ax - a^2 & &\text{subtract } a^2 \text{ from both sides}\\
(x + a)(x - a) &= a(x - a) & &\text{factor both sides}\\
x + a &= a & &\text{divide both sides by } (x - a)\\
x &= 0 & &\text{x equals 0, but we started with x equal to a}
\end{aligned}
$$

Once again, all of the steps all valid except when we divide both sides by $(x - a)$. And actually, this exercise becomes very instructive if we change it just a little, and then follow the exact same steps. Let's look at the first proof again, but this time we'll say that a is equal to b plus some small infinitesimal amount that we will call i. Now let's see what happens:

$$
\begin{aligned}
a &= b + i & &\text{define a equal to } b + i\\
a^2 &= ab + ai & &\text{multiply both sides by a}\\
2a^2 &= a^2 + ab + ai & &\text{add an } a^2 \text{ to both sides}\\
2a^2 - 2ab &= a^2 - ab + ai & &\text{subtract 2ab from both sides}\\
2a(a - b) &= a(a - b) + ai & &\text{factor each side of the equality}\\
2a &= a + ai/(a - b) & &\text{divide by } (a - b), \text{ the common factor}\\
2 &= 1 + i/(a - b) & &\text{divide by a, and we're not quite done}
\end{aligned}
$$

From our initial definition we said that $a = b + i$; therefore, we can conclude that $a - b = i$. When we make that substitution into the last line, we get:

$$
\begin{aligned}
2 &= 1 + i/i & &\text{substitute i for } a - b, \text{ and simplify}\\
2 &= 1 + 1 & &\text{now that looks right}
\end{aligned}
$$

We see from the sequence above that if b is ever so slightly smaller than a, then when we divide by $(a - b)$ we're not dividing by zero, and therefore we don't create a situation where one side of the equality becomes unequal to the other.

Here is another mathematical illusion, which is just as interesting. In this illusion, the problem arises when we take the square root of both sides of the relationship. Using the method outlined in this false proof, we can practically prove any two adjacent numbers are equal to each other. In this example we'll show that 4 is equal to 5; and since we are trying to prove that 4 is equal to 5, we start this proof with the negative product of 4 and 5, and set it equal to itself.

$$
\begin{aligned}
-20 &= -20 & &\text{-20 is set equal to -20}\\
16 - 36 &= 25 - 45 & &\text{use } 4^2 \text{ and } 5^2 \text{ to create}\\
4^2 - 4*9 &= 5^2 - 5*9 & &\quad\text{equivalent expressions}\\
4^2 - 4*9 + 81/4 &= 5^2 - 5*9 + 81/4 & &\text{complete the square on}\\
4^2 - 2*4*(9/2) + (9/2)^2 &= 5^2 - 2*5*(9/2) + (9/2)^2 & &\quad\text{both sides of the relation}\\
(4 - 9/2)(4 - 9/2) &= (5 - 9/2)(5 - 9/2) & &\text{show the squared factors}\\
(4 - 9/2)^2 &= (5 - 9/2)^2 & &\text{rewrite each side as the } (\text{factor})^2\\
4 - 9/2 &= 5 - 9/2 & &\text{take the square root}\\
4 &= 5 & &\text{simplify, and we get 4 equals 5}
\end{aligned}
$$

Again, all the steps appear to be valid; however, we run into problems when we take the square root of both sides. Right before we take the square root, the left side is equal to $(-0.5)^2$ while the right side is equal to $(+0.5)^2$. As long as both sides are squared, the two sides are equal to each other, but when we take the square root of each side is where they lose their equality.

A Geometric Illusion, Part 1

Now, we'll look at a geometric "proof" that shows a rectangle with an area of 64 square inches is equal to another rectangle with an area of 65 square inches; and yet both rectangles are made from the same pieces. We begin by creating two right triangles, both the same size. Make the two triangles so that one leg is 3 inches long, and the other is 8 inches long. If you use a regular sheet of paper, you should be able to cut them both out of a single piece of paper.

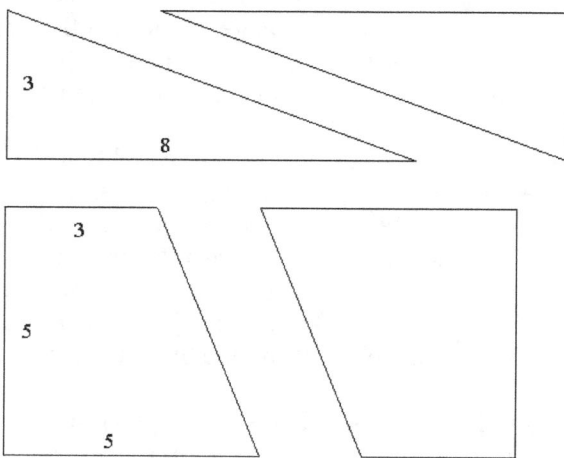

Figure 24.2   Two right triangles and two right trapezoids.

Next, we'll make two right trapezoids, again, both the same size. These trapezoids have a 3 inch base and a 5 inch base. The height of the trapezoid is also 5 inches; and the trapezoid is such that the angles on one side are right angles. Again, if you use a regular sheet of paper, you should be able to cut both of these pieces out of a second single piece of paper.

Take the two triangles, turn one over and put them together and make a 3" x 8" rectangle. Then take the two trapezoids, turn one over and put them together to make a 5" x 8" rectangle. If we take the first rectangle, and place it above the second, we have an 8" x 8" square, which covers an area of 64 sq. in.

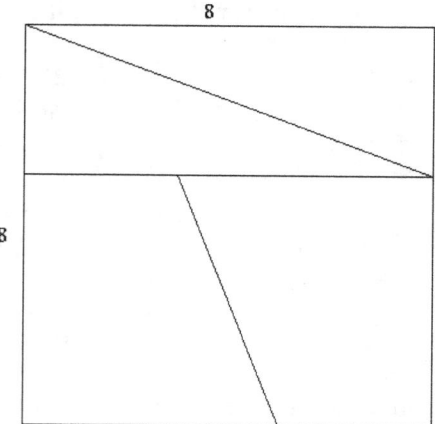

Figure 24.3   The triangles and trapezoids arranged to form a square with an area of 64 sq. in.

Now take each triangle and pair it with a trapezoid. Place the 3" sides of each object (a trapezoid and a triangle) next to each other to form a larger triangle. Each new triangle has a base of 13" and a height of 5". Turn one triangle/trapezoid pair over and fit it together with the other triangle/trapezoid pair. We now have a 13" x 5" rectangle, but this has an area of 65 sq. in. So where did the extra square inch come from?

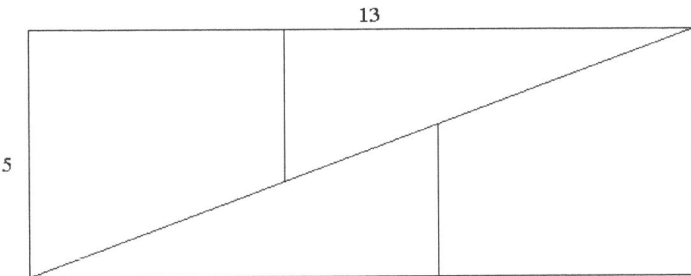

Figure 24.4   The triangles and trapezoids arranged to form a rectangle with an area of 65 sq. in.

If you carefully cutout and carefully layout the pieces, you'll see that the triangle and trapezoid, when put together, don't quite make a collinear edge along the main diagonal. Therefore, when these larger triangles are matched together to make a rectangle, there is an area through the center of the rectangle that leaves a small gap (the black area in the figure below). This is where the unaccounted square inch resides. Of course, if you perform this as a magic trick, you won't carefully layout the pieces, and it becomes very difficult for anyone to find that extra square inch.

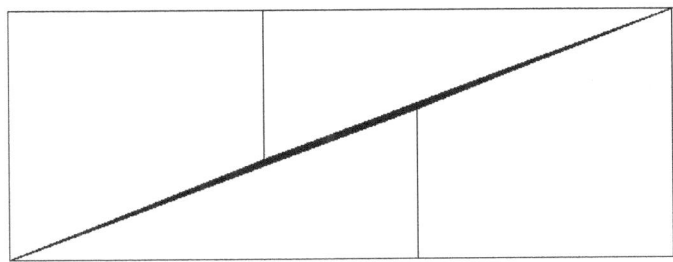

Figure 24.5   The darkened area is where the unaccounted square inch resides.

Did you notice the dimensions used to make the triangles and trapezoids in the figures above? If we list the dimensions in ascending order (and only show each number once), they are 3, 5, and 8. These are all Fibonacci numbers. In fact, we could have made our triangles and trapezoids bigger simply by using larger Fibonacci numbers for the dimensions. However, there is a little more to this geometric illusion.

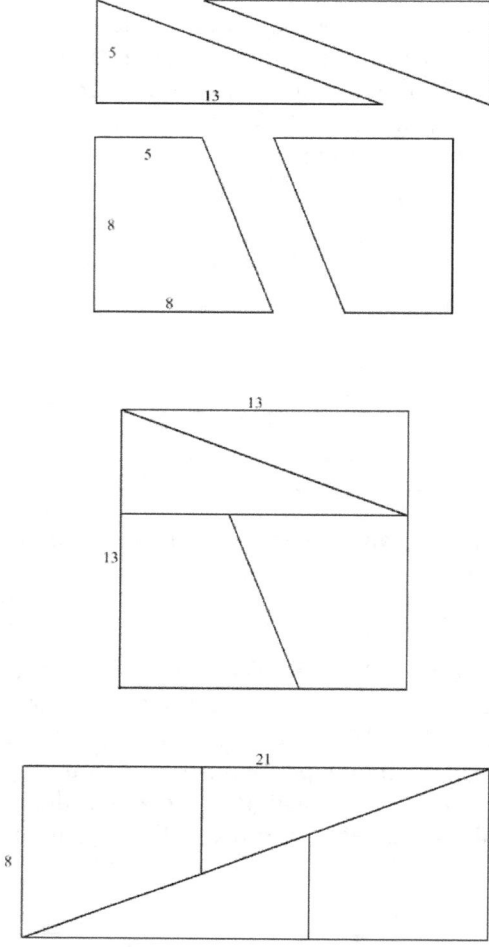

Figure 24.6   The square and rectangle made from triangles and trapezoids with dimensions using the Fibonacci numbers 5, 8, and 13.

The number 8 is the sixth Fibonacci number. Squaring that gives us 64 (which is the area of the square). The 5 and the 13 are on either side of the 8 in the Fibonacci sequence. Multiplying those two numbers together give us 65 (which is the area of the rectangle), and which is one more than the area of the square. If we had used 5, 8, and 13 as our dimensions for the triangles and trapezoids (instead of 3, 5, and 8), then when we put them together as a square, we would have a square with sides equal to 13, and an area of 169. The rectangle made from those same triangles and trapezoids would have dimensions of 8 by 21, and an area of 168. This time the area of the square is one more than the area of the rectangle. Therefore when you assemble the pieces together to form the rectangle, the pieces overlap just a little along the diagonal of the rectangle. The figure below shows this illusion with the larger dimensions.

Therefore, if you would like to create your own geometric illusion, you have the option of doing it with the square one unit larger than the rectangle, or with the rectangle one unit larger than the square. By selecting three consecutive Fibonacci numbers where the first number of the sequence is an even-place Fibonacci number (i.e., 3, 8, 21, 55, etc.) then the area of the square will be one

384

less than the area of the rectangle. On the other hand, by selecting three Fibonacci numbers where the first number is an odd-place Fibonacci number (i.e., 5, 13, 34, 89, etc.) then the area of the square will be one more than the area of the rectangle. The figure below shows the Fibonacci dimensions of the triangles and trapezoids.

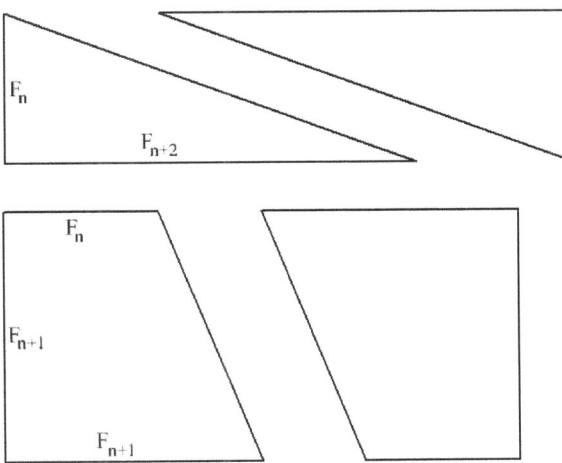

Figure 24.7   The Fibonacci dimensions of the triangles and trapezoids used in this geometric illusion.

A Geometric Illusion, Part 2
This next geometric illusion shows two configurations of a 5 x 13 triangle. Both configurations are made from the same four pieces; however, in the second configuration there is an extra square inch that isn't accounted for in the first configuration. The triangles look like they should have the same area, but in actuality, they don't.

It is possible to begin to see the problem when we calculate the areas of these triangles and then compare them with each other. The overall triangle (in both cases) is 13 inches along the base, with a height equal to 5 inches. Thus the area for the overall triangle (in both cases) is ½(13)(5) which is equal to 65/2 or 32 ½ square inches.

Now, if we look at the areas of the individual pieces, and add them together, we arrive at different numbers. In both of the larger triangles, the P and Q pieces make a rectangle. In the top triangle (in the figure below), the area of the PQ pieces is equal to 15 in^2, and in the bottom triangle, the P and Q pieces form a rectangle with an area equal to 16 in^2 (which includes the 1 in^2 hole). Each of the larger triangles are also comprised of two smaller triangles, where one of these smaller triangles has an area equal to 12 in^2 and the other is equal to 5 in^2. When we add these areas together in the top, larger triangle, the total area is equal to 32 in^2. Then when we add these areas together in the bottom, larger triangle, the total area equal to 33 in^2.

So, what we actually have is that the area of the triangle should be equal to ½ (13)(5) or 32 ½ square inches, but when we add up the areas in the two configurations below, we either get an area of 32 square inches or 33 square inches.

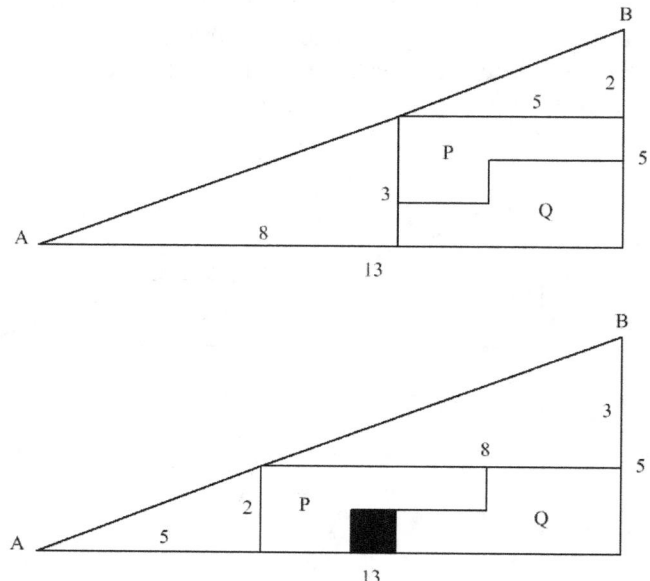

The solution to this conundrum becomes clear when we draw a straight line between A and B within each of the configurations (see the figure below). In the top configuration, piece P doesn't quite reach line AB, while in the bottom configuration, piece P extends past line AB.

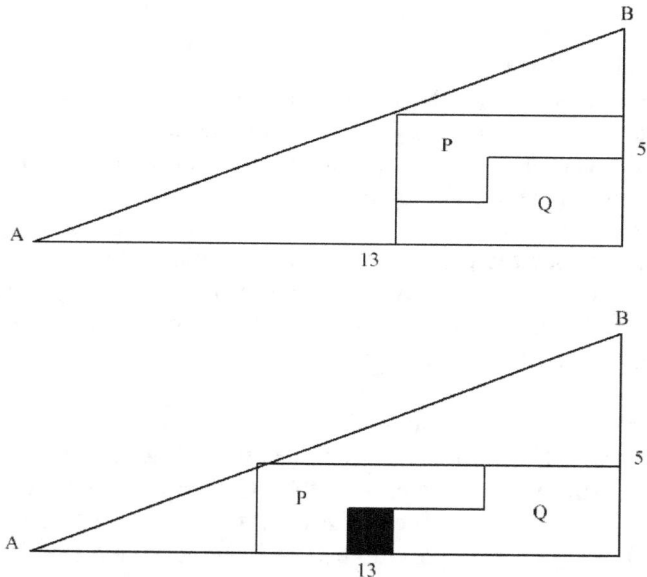

Now, going back to the actual pieces, if we calculate the slope of the hypotenuses for the three triangles, we can see that their slopes are not collinear (yet we assume that they are when they are laid out in the two configurations). The hypotenuse of the smaller triangle has a slope of 2:5, the hypotenuse of the larger triangle has a slope of 3:8, and the hypotenuse of the overall triangle has a slope of 5:13. These slope ratios are close to each other; in fact, they are close enough that if you made a full scale model of these four pieces, and then loosely laid them out in both configurations, side AB would look collinear, and it would be difficult to find where that extra square inch within pieces P and Q rectangles comes from and goes to between the two different configurations.

Notice also that the dimensions used to make these three triangles are 2, 3, 5, 8, and 13; all of which are consecutive Fibonacci Numbers. (The smaller triangle has legs with lengths equal to 2 and 5, larger triangle has legs with lengths equal to 3 and 8, and the overall triangle has legs with lengths equal to 5 and 13. Knowing this, similar constructs can be made with larger triangles with dimensions using other consecutive Fibonacci Numbers.)

As we saw in both of the illusions above, these geometric illusions use Fibonacci numbers for the dimensions of the several triangles and trapezoids. And there are still many other mathematical tricks and illusions that depend on the properties of a number (like the number nine), or the properties of a geometric shape (like a Mobius strip). While we could go on, we will end this brief chapter with a look at a few number games.

Four 4's

There are many games in mathematics; some are games of logic and reasoning, others use algebraic skills, but all require so degree of thinking. Some are solitaire type games that can be played by yourself while others can be played by two or more people. In this section we'll look at some interesting number games. This first one can be played alone or with a group.

An interesting activity is to see how many numbers you can create from four fours. The rules are simple. You can add, subtract, multiple, divide or use any math symbols, anywhere and as many times as you want, but the only numbers you can use are four fours (no more and no less).

$$0 = 44 - 44$$
$$1 = 44 / 44$$
$$2 = (4*4) / (4+4)$$
$$3 = (4+4+4) / 4$$
$$4 = (\text{Sqrt}(4)) * (\text{Sqrt}(4)) + (4-4)$$
$$5 = [(4*4) + 4] / 4$$
$$6 = 4+4 - 4 / (\text{Sqrt}(4))$$
$$7 = 4+4 - 4 / 4$$
$$8 = (4*4) - (4+4)$$
$$9 = 4+4 + 4 / 4$$
$$10 = [(4*4)+4] / (\text{Sqrt}(4))$$
$$11 = 44 / (\text{Sqrt}(4*4))$$
$$12 = 4*4 - \text{Sqrt}(4*4)$$
$$13 = 4! / (\text{Sqrt}(4)) + 4 / 4$$
$$14 = 4*4 - 4 / (\text{Sqrt}(4))$$
$$15 = 4*4 - 4 / 4$$
$$16 = (4^4)/(4*4)$$
$$17 = 4^{(\text{Sqrt}(4))} + 4/4$$
$$18 = 4*4 + 4 / (\text{Sqrt}(4))$$
$$19 = 4! - 4 - 4 / 4$$
$$20 = ((4!/4)*4) - 4$$
$$21 = 4! - 4 + 4 / 4$$
$$22 = 4*4 + 4 + \text{Sqrt}(4)$$
$$23 = 4! - \text{Sqrt}(4) + 4 / 4$$
$$24 = 4! / (\text{Sqrt}(4)) + 4! / (\text{Sqrt}(4))$$
$$25 = 4! + \text{Sqrt}(4) - 4 / 4$$

Starting with zero, you should be able to create every number up to and including one hundred, and even beyond. Most numbers can be created in more than one way. This is a nice activity to do as a group project (you'll be surprised at the different perspectives you get from a group). But I've also enjoyed doing this alone (like the time I was on a backpacking trip with the scouts in Yellowstone, and I found myself stuck in my tent one afternoon during a heavy rain storm). The listing above are some values I came up with for the numbers 0 thru 25.

Of course, if you get hung up, maybe you need to be a little more creative. After all, the rules are simple, and because of their simplicity, it leaves a lot of room for some alternative possibilities. For example, consider these options that can be used for just one or two of the four fours:

$$\cos(4-4) = 1$$
$$Sq(4) = 16$$
$$Cu(4) = 64$$
$$Tri(4) = 10, \text{ where } Tri(4) \text{ is the 4}^{\text{th}} \text{ triangular number.}$$

By combining our options, we could have $Sq(Tri(4)) = 100$. Of course, this adds a level of complexity to the game (which may or may not be a bad thing); however, the simpler we keep the rules, the more amazing the results become.

Five 5's

The four 4 problem is challenging enough on its own, but how about five 5's. The rules are the same as with the four 4's, only this time there are five 5's. How far can you go with this set of numbers? I'll give you the first 10 to start:

$$0 = Sqrt(5*5) - (5*5) / 5$$
$$1 = 55 / 5 - (5+5)$$
$$2 = (5+5) / 5 + (5-5)$$
$$3 = (5*5 - (5+5)) / 5$$
$$4 = (5+5+5+5) / 5$$
$$5 = Sqrt(5+5+5+5+5) \text{ or } 5+5-5+5-5$$
$$6 = 5+5 / 5 + (5-5)$$
$$7 = 5 + 5 / 5 + 5 / 5$$
$$8 = 5 + Sqrt(5+5 - 5 / 5)$$
$$9 = 5! / 5 - (5+5+5)$$
$$10 = 5*5 - (5+5+5)$$
$$..., \text{ etc.}$$

Do you get the idea? Now how many more can you do?

There are still several other variations to this game. For example, you can use the numbers 1, 2, 3, 4 and 5 and do the same thing. Again, here are my results for the numbers 0 through 10 to get you started with this set:

$$0 = (5 + 1) / 3 - 4 / 2$$
$$1 = 3*4 - 5*2 - 1$$
$$2 = (5 + 4 + 1) / (3 + 2)$$
$$3 = 5 - 4 + 3 - 2 + 1$$
$$4 = (5 + 1) / (4 + 2) + 3$$
$$5 = 5 + 4 / 2 - (3 - 1)$$
$$6 = (5*4 - 2) / (3*1)$$
$$7 = Sqrt(5 + 3 + 1) + Sqrt(4) + 2$$
$$8 = Sqrt(5*3 + 1) + Sqrt(4) + 2$$
$$9 = 5 + 3 + 1 + Sqrt(4) - 2$$
$$10 = 5 + 3 + 1 + (Sqrt(4)) / 2$$
..., etc.

The possibilities are limitless, and there is nothing wrong with developing a few variations of your own.

The 7 Game

An interesting game that's fun to play in a group is the seven game. This game is played best with a group of about 5 to 8 people. This game is easy to explain, but it can be a challenge to play. To begin with, seat everyone in a circle. Then start a rhythmic beat by clapping your lap, clapping your hands and finally snapping your fingers. The first person starts by saying "1" while snapping their fingers. The next time the group snaps their fingers, the next person says "2", and so on. Each time you complete a rhythmic cycle and snap your fingers, the next person in the circle says the next number. However, when you get to a number that has a 7 in it, you say
"pickle" instead of the number. If the number is a multiple of 7 you say "pie". And if the number is both a multiple of 7 and has a seven in it, you say "pickle pie".

So, how far do you go? I would recommend just trying to get to a hundred. However, if your group gets good at this, you might try some variations. I've played it a few times where we've actually counted up to one hundred, and then backwards back down to one (but I won't say whether we actually really made it back to one).

Epilogue

When Antonio[1] finished speaking, he knew he had just revealed many of the pearls, rubies, and sapphires relating to the many patterns, relationships, and symmetries within the world of numbers. The storm still raged on, but the crew sat in a stunned silence, mesmerized by the magnificent mathematical marvels they had seen and heard.

It was the captain who finally broke the silence when he turned to Antonio and said, "Antonio, have you gone mad? All I asked for was a story, and instead, you gave us all this mathematical mumbo-jumbo.

"Dark and stormy night or not, you've been marauding on this maritime vessel for far too many months. I don't want to hear any more marvels of Math coming from your mouth."

Antonio paused for a moment, and then he replied, "Maybe, we could discuss Magic Squares some other night? Maybe, when the storm has calmed down a bit?"

The captain paused for a moment and then incredulously said, "You already mentioned magic squares in the chapter about Sums of Squares and Higher Powers. You couldn't possibly have more to say about that could you?"

Antonio calmly replied, "Oh yes, there's more; so much, much more . . ."

The End

(The music begins to crescendo as the camera fades away from Antonio. The captain throws up his arms in disgust while waves continue crashing over the sides of the ship. The storm rages on as the captain, in a rage, storms off to his quarters. The credits start rolling.)

[1] - See the last few paragraphs of the introduction for our introduction to Antonio.

Appendix 1
Palindrome Numbers whose Squares are also Palindromes
(Note that all these squares have an odd number of digits.)

2-Digit Numbers:

The square of	11 is	121
The square of	22 is	484

Middle numbers of the squares are: 2 8
First (and last) numbers are: 1 4

3-Digit Numbers:

The square of	101 is	10201
The square of	111 is	12321
The square of	121 is	14641
The square of	202 is	40804
The square of	212 is	44944

Middle numbers of the squares are: 2 3 6 8 9
First (and last) numbers are: 1 1 1 4 4

4-Digit Numbers:

The square of	1001 is	1002001
The square of	1111 is	1234321
The square of	2002 is	4008004

Middle numbers of the squares are: 2 4 8
First (and last) numbers are: 1 1 4

5-Digit Numbers:

The square of	10001 is	100020001
The square of	10101 is	102030201
The square of	10201 is	104060401
The square of	11011 is	121242121
The square of	11111 is	123454321
The square of	11211 is	125686521
The square of	20002 is	400080004
The square of	20102 is	404090404

Middle numbers of the squares are: 2 3 6 4 5 8 8 9
First (and last) numbers are: 1 1 1 1 1 1 4 4

6-Digit Numbers:

The square of	100001	is	10000200001
The square of	101101	is	10221412201
The square of	110011	is	12102420121
The square of	111111	is	12345654321
The square of	200002	is	40000800004

Middle numbers of the squares are: 2 4 4 6 8
First (and last) numbers are: 1 1 1 1 4

7-Digit Numbers:

The square of	1000001	is	1000002000001
The square of	1001001	is	1002003002001
The square of	1002001	is	1004006004001
The square of	1010101	is	1020304030201
The square of	1011101	is	1022325232201
The square of	1012101	is	1024348434201
The square of	1100011	is	1210024200121
The square of	1101011	is	1212225222121
The square of	1102011	is	1214428244121
The square of	1110111	is	1232346432321
The square of	1111111	is	1234567654321
The square of	2000002	is	4000008000004
The square of	2001002	is	4004009004004

Middle numbers of the squares are: 2 3 6 4 5 8 4 5 8 6 7 8 9
First (and last) numbers are: 1 1 1 1 1 1 1 1 1 1 4 4

8-Digit Numbers:

The square of	10000001	is	100000020000001
The square of	10011001	is	100220141022001
The square of	10100101	is	102012040210201
The square of	10111101	is	102234363432201
The square of	11000011	is	121000242000121
The square of	11011011	is	121242363242121
The square of	11100111	is	123212464212321
The square of	11111111	is	123456787654321
The square of	20000002	is	400000080000004

Middle numbers of the squares are: 2 4 4 6 4 6 6 8 8
First (and last) numbers are: 1 1 1 1 1 1 1 1 4

392

9-Digit Numbers:

The square of 100000001 is 10000000200000001
The square of 100010001 is 10002000300020001
The square of 100020001 is 10004000600040001
The square of 100101001 is 10020210401202001
The square of 100111001 is 10022212521222001
The square of 100121001 is 10024214841242001
The square of 101000101 is 10201020402010201
The square of 101010101 is 10203040504030201
The square of 101020101 is 10205060806050201
The square of 101101101 is 10221432623412201
The square of 101111101 is 10223454745432201
The square of 110000011 is 12100002420000121
The square of 110010011 is 12102202520220121
The square of 110020011 is 12104402820440121
The square of 110101011 is 12122232623222121
The square of 110111011 is 12124434743442121
The square of 111000111 is 12321024642012321
The square of 111010111 is 12323244744232321
The square of 111101111 is 12343456865434321
The square of 111111111 is 12345678987654321
The square of 200000002 is 40000000800000004
The square of 200010002 is 40004000900040004

Middle numbers of the squares are: 2 3 6 4 5 8 4 5 8 6 7 4 5 8 6 7 6 7 8 9 8 9
First (and last) numbers are: 1 1 1 1 1 1 1 1 1 1 1 1 1 1 1 1 1 1 1 1 4 4

10-Digit Numbers:

The square of 1000000001 is 1000000002000000001
The square of 1000110001 is 1000220014100220001
The square of 1001001001 is 1002003004003002001
The square of 1001111001 is 1002223236323222001
The square of 1010000101 is 1020100204020010201
The square of 1010110101 is 1020322416142230201
The square of 1011001101 is 1022123226223212201
The square of 1011111101 is 1022345658565432201
The square of 1100000011 is 1210000024200000121
The square of 1100110011 is 1210242036302420121
The square of 1101001011 is 1212203226223022121
The square of 1101111011 is 1212445458545442121
The square of 1110000111 is 1232100246420012321
The square of 1110110111 is 1232344458544432321
The square of 1111001111 is 1234323468643234321
The square of 2000000002 is 4000000008000000004

Middle numbers of the squares are: 2 4 4 6 4 6 6 8 4 6 6 8 6 8 8 8
First (and last) numbers are: 1 1 1 1 1 1 1 1 1 1 1 1 1 1 1 4

Appendix 2
Non-Palindrome Numbers Whose Squares are Palindromes
(Note that almost all of these squares have an odd number of digits.)

2-Digit Numbers:

The square of	26 is	676

3-Digit Numbers:

The square of	264 is	69696	
The square of	307 is	94249	
The square of	836 is	698896	< -- 6 digit

4-Digit Numbers:

The square of	2285 is	5221225
The square of	2636 is	6948496

5-Digit Numbers:

The square of	22865 is	522808225
The square of	24846 is	617323716
The square of	30693 is	942060249

6-Digit Numbers:

The square of	798644 is	637832238736	< -- 12 digit

7-Digit Numbers:

The square of	1042151 is	1086078706801
The square of	1109111 is	1230127210321
The square of	1270869 is	1615108015161
The square of	2012748 is	4051154511504
The square of	2294675 is	5265533355625
The square of	3069307 is	9420645460249

8-Digit Numbers:

The square of	11129361 is	123862676268321
The square of	12028229 is	144678292876441
The square of	12866669 is	165551171155561
The square of	30001253 is	900075181570009

Appendix 3
Continuous Fractions of Square Root Numbers

$\sqrt{1}$ = 1
$\sqrt{2}$ = 1.414213562373 = [1; 2, 2, 2, 2, 2, 2, 2, 2, 2, 2, 2, 2, 2, 2, ...]
$\sqrt{3}$ = 1.732050807569 = [1; 1, 2, 1, 2, 1, 2, 1, 2, 1, 2, 1, 2, 1, 2, ...]
$\sqrt{4}$ = 2
$\sqrt{5}$ = 2.2360679775 = [2; 4, 4, 4, 4, 4, 4, 4, 4, 4, 4, 4, 4, 4, 4, ...]
$\sqrt{6}$ = 2.449489742783 = [2; 2, 4, 2, 4, 2, 4, 2, 4, 2, 4, 2, 4, 2, 4, ...]
$\sqrt{7}$ = 2.645751311065 = [2; 1, 1, 1, 4, 1, 1, 1, 4, 1, 1, 1, 4, 1, 1, ...]
$\sqrt{8}$ = 2.828427124746 = [2; 1, 4, 1, 4, 1, 4, 1, 4, 1, 4, 1, 4, 1, 4, ...]
$\sqrt{9}$ = 3
$\sqrt{10}$ = 3.162277660168 = [3; 6, 6, 6, 6, 6, 6, 6, 6, 6, 6, 6, 6, 6, 6, ...]
$\sqrt{11}$ = 3.316624790355 = [3; 3, 6, 3, 6, 3, 6, 3, 6, 3, 6, 3, 6, 3, 6, ...]
$\sqrt{12}$ = 3.464101615138 = [3; 2, 6, 2, 6, 2, 6, 2, 6, 2, 6, 2, 6, 2, 6, ...]
$\sqrt{13}$ = 3.605551275464 = [3; 1, 1, 1, 1, 6, 1, 1, 1, 1, 6, 1, 1, 1, 1, ...]
$\sqrt{14}$ = 3.741657386774 = [3; 1, 2, 1, 6, 1, 2, 1, 6, 1, 2, 1, 6, 1, 2, ...]
$\sqrt{15}$ = 3.872983346207 = [3; 1, 6, 1, 6, 1, 6, 1, 6, 1, 6, 1, 6, 1, 6, ...]
$\sqrt{16}$ = 4
$\sqrt{17}$ = 4.123105625618 = [4; 8, 8, 8, 8, 8, 8, 8, 8, 8, 8, 8, 8, 8, 8, ...]
$\sqrt{18}$ = 4.242640687119 = [4; 4, 8, 4, 8, 4, 8, 4, 8, 4, 8, 4, 8, 4, 8, ...]
$\sqrt{19}$ = 4.358898943541 = [4; 2, 1, 3, 1, 2, 8, 2, 1, 3, 1, 2, 8, 2, 1, ...]
$\sqrt{20}$ = 4.472135955 = [4; 2, 8, 2, 8, 2, 8, 2, 8, 2, 8, 2, 8, 2, 8, ...]
$\sqrt{21}$ = 4.582575694956 = [4; 1, 1, 2, 1, 1, 8, 1, 1, 2, 1, 1, 8, 1, 1, ...]
$\sqrt{22}$ = 4.690415759823 = [4; 1, 2, 4, 2, 1, 8, 1, 2, 4, 2, 1, 8, 1, 2, ...]
$\sqrt{23}$ = 4.795831523313 = [4; 1, 3, 1, 8, 1, 3, 1, 8, 1, 3, 1, 8, 1, 3, ...]
$\sqrt{24}$ = 4.898979485566 = [4; 1, 8, 1, 8, 1, 8, 1, 8, 1, 8, 1, 8, 1, 8, ...]
$\sqrt{25}$ = 5
$\sqrt{26}$ = 5.099019513593 = [5; 10, 10, 10, 10, 10, 10, 10, 10, 10, 10, 10, 10, 10, ...]
$\sqrt{27}$ = 5.196152422707 = [5; 5, 10, 5, 10, 5, 10, 5, 10, 5, 10, 5, 10, 5, ...]
$\sqrt{28}$ = 5.291502622129 = [5; 3, 2, 3, 10, 3, 2, 3, 10, 3, 2, 3, 10, 3, 2, ...]
$\sqrt{29}$ = 5.385164807135 = [5; 2, 1, 1, 2, 10, 2, 1, 1, 2, 10, 2, 1, 1, 2, ...]
$\sqrt{30}$ = 5.477225575052 = [5; 2, 10, 2, 10, 2, 10, 2, 10, 2, 10, 2, 10, 2, 10, ...]
$\sqrt{31}$ = 5.56776436283 = [5; 1, 1, 3, 5, 3, 1, 1, 10, 1, 1, 3, 5, 3, 1, ...]
$\sqrt{32}$ = 5.656854249492 = [5; 1, 1, 1, 10, 1, 1, 1, 10, 1, 1, 1, 10, 1, 1, ...]
$\sqrt{33}$ = 5.744562646538 = [5; 1, 2, 1, 10, 1, 2, 1, 10, 1, 2, 1, 10, 1, 2, ...]
$\sqrt{34}$ = 5.830951894845 = [5; 1, 4, 1, 10, 1, 4, 1, 10, 1, 4, 1, 10, 1, 4, ...]
$\sqrt{35}$ = 5.9160797831 = [5; 1, 10, 1, 10, 1, 10, 1, 10, 1, 10, 1, 10, 1, 10, ...]
$\sqrt{36}$ = 6
$\sqrt{37}$ = 6.082762530298 = [6; 12, 12, 12, 12, 12, 12, 12, 12, 12, 12, 12, 12, 12, ...]
$\sqrt{38}$ = 6.164414002969 = [6; 6, 12, 6, 12, 6, 12, 6, 12, 6, 12, 6, 12, 6, 12, ...]
$\sqrt{39}$ = 6.244997998398 = [6; 4, 12, 4, 12, 4, 12, 4, 12, 4, 12, 4, 12, 4, 12, ...]
$\sqrt{40}$ = 6.324555320337 = [6; 3, 12, 3, 12, 3, 12, 3, 12, 3, 12, 3, 12, 3, 12, ...]
$\sqrt{41}$ = 6.403124237433 = [6; 2, 2, 12, 2, 2, 12, 2, 2, 12, 2, 2, 12, 2, 2, ...]
$\sqrt{42}$ = 6.480740698408 = [6; 2, 12, 2, 12, 2, 12, 2, 12, 2, 12, 2, 12, 2, 12, ...]
$\sqrt{43}$ = 6.557438524302 = [6; 1, 1, 3, 1, 5, 1, 3, 1, 1, 12, 1, 1, 3, 1, ...]
$\sqrt{44}$ = 6.633249580711 = [6; 1, 1, 1, 2, 1, 1, 1, 12, 1, 1, 1, 2, 1, 1, ...]
$\sqrt{45}$ = 6.708203932499 = [6; 1, 2, 2, 2, 1, 12, 1, 2, 2, 2, 1, 12, 1, 2, ...]
$\sqrt{46}$ = 6.782329983125 = [6; 1, 3, 1, 1, 2, 6, 2, 1, 1, 3, 1, 12, 1, 3, ...]
$\sqrt{47}$ = 6.855654600401 = [6; 1, 5, 1, 12, 1, 5, 1, 12, 1, 5, 1, 12, 1, 5, ...]
$\sqrt{48}$ = 6.928203230276 = [6; 1, 12, 1, 12, 1, 12, 1, 12, 1, 12, 1, 12, 1, 12, ...]
$\sqrt{49}$ = 7
$\sqrt{50}$ = 7.071067811865 = [7; 14, 14, 14, 14, 14, 14, 14, 14, 14, 14, 14, 14, 14, ...]

$\sqrt{51}$ = 7.141428428543 = [7; 7, 14, 7, 14, 7, 14, 7, 14, 7, 14, 7, 14, 7, 14, ...]
$\sqrt{52}$ = 7.211102550928 = [7; 4, 1, 2, 1, 4, 14, 4, 1, 2, 1, 4, 14, 4, 1, ...]
$\sqrt{53}$ = 7.280109889281 = [7; 3, 1, 1, 3, 14, 3, 1, 1, 3, 14, 3, 1, 1, 3, ...]
$\sqrt{54}$ = 7.34846922835 = [7; 2, 1, 6, 1, 2, 14, 2, 1, 6, 1, 2, 14, 2, 1, ...]
$\sqrt{55}$ = 7.416198487096 = [7; 2, 2, 2, 14, 2, 2, 2, 14, 2, 2, 2, 14, 2, 2, ...]
$\sqrt{56}$ = 7.483314773548 = [7; 2, 14, 2, 14, 2, 14, 2, 14, 2, 14, 2, 14, 2, 14, ...]
$\sqrt{57}$ = 7.549834435271 = [7; 1, 1, 4, 1, 1, 14, 1, 1, 4, 1, 1, 14, 1, 1, ...]
$\sqrt{58}$ = 7.615773105864 = [7; 1, 1, 1, 1, 1, 1, 14, 1, 1, 1, 1, 1, 1, 14, ...]
$\sqrt{59}$ = 7.681145747869 = [7; 1, 2, 7, 2, 1, 14, 1, 2, 7, 2, 1, 14, 1, 2, ...]
$\sqrt{60}$ = 7.745966692415 = [7; 1, 2, 1, 14, 1, 2, 1, 14, 1, 2, 1, 14, 1, 2, ...]
$\sqrt{61}$ = 7.810249675907 = [7; 1, 4, 3, 1, 2, 2, 1, 3, 4, 1, 14, 1, 4, 3, ...]
$\sqrt{62}$ = 7.874007874012 = [7; 1, 6, 1, 14, 1, 6, 1, 14, 1, 6, 1, 14, 1, 6, ...]
$\sqrt{63}$ = 7.937253933194 = [7; 1, 14, 1, 14, 1, 14, 1, 14, 1, 14, 1, 14, 1, 14, ...]
$\sqrt{64}$ = 8
$\sqrt{65}$ = 8.062257748299 = [8; 16, 16, 16, 16, 16, 16, 16, 16, 16, 16, 16, 16, 16, ...]
$\sqrt{66}$ = 8.124038404636 = [8; 8, 16, 8, 16, 8, 16, 8, 16, 8, 16, 8, 16, 8, 16, ...]
$\sqrt{67}$ = 8.185352771872 = [8; 5, 2, 1, 1, 7, 1, 1, 2, 5, 16, 5, 2, 1, 1, ...]
$\sqrt{68}$ = 8.246211251235 = [8; 4, 16, 4, 16, 4, 16, 4, 16, 4, 16, 4, 16, 4, 16, ...]
$\sqrt{69}$ = 8.306623862918 = [8; 3, 3, 1, 4, 1, 3, 3, 16, 3, 3, 1, 4, 1, 3, ...]
$\sqrt{70}$ = 8.366600265341 = [8; 2, 1, 2, 1, 2, 16, 2, 1, 2, 1, 2, 16, 2, 1, ...]
$\sqrt{71}$ = 8.426149773176 = [8; 2, 2, 1, 7, 1, 2, 2, 16, 2, 2, 1, 7, 1, 2, ...]
$\sqrt{72}$ = 8.485281374239 = [8; 2, 16, 2, 16, 2, 16, 2, 16, 2, 16, 2, 16, 2, 16, ...]
$\sqrt{73}$ = 8.544003745318 = [8; 1, 1, 5, 5, 1, 1, 16, 1, 1, 5, 5, 1, 1, 16, ...]
$\sqrt{74}$ = 8.602325267043 = [8; 1, 1, 1, 1, 16, 1, 1, 1, 1, 16, 1, 1, 1, 1, ...]
$\sqrt{75}$ = 8.660254037844 = [8; 1, 1, 1, 16, 1, 1, 1, 16, 1, 1, 1, 16, 1, 1, ...]
$\sqrt{76}$ = 8.717797887081 = [8; 1, 2, 1, 1, 5, 4, 5, 1, 1, 2, 1, 16, 1, 2, ...]
$\sqrt{77}$ = 8.774964387392 = [8; 1, 3, 2, 3, 1, 16, 1, 3, 2, 3, 1, 16, 1, 3, ...]
$\sqrt{78}$ = 8.831760866328 = [8; 1, 4, 1, 16, 1, 4, 1, 16, 1, 4, 1, 16, 1, 4, ...]
$\sqrt{79}$ = 8.888194417316 = [8; 1, 7, 1, 16, 1, 7, 1, 16, 1, 7, 1, 16, 1, 7, ...]
$\sqrt{80}$ = 8.944271909999 = [8; 1, 16, 1, 16, 1, 16, 1, 16, 1, 16, 1, 16, 1, 16, ...]
$\sqrt{81}$ = 9
$\sqrt{82}$ = 9.055385138137 = [9; 18, 18, 18, 18, 18, 18, 18, 18, 18, 18, 18, 18, 18, ...]
$\sqrt{83}$ = 9.110433579144 = [9; 9, 18, 9, 18, 9, 18, 9, 18, 9, 18, 9, 18, 9, 18, ...]
$\sqrt{84}$ = 9.165151389912 = [9; 6, 18, 6, 18, 6, 18, 6, 18, 6, 18, 6, 18, 6, 18, ...]
$\sqrt{85}$ = 9.219544457293 = [9; 4, 1, 1, 4, 18, 4, 1, 1, 4, 18, 4, 1, 1, 4, ...]
$\sqrt{86}$ = 9.273618495496 = [9; 3, 1, 1, 1, 8, 1, 1, 1, 3, 18, 3, 1, 1, 1, ...]
$\sqrt{87}$ = 9.327379053089 = [9; 3, 18, 3, 18, 3, 18, 3, 18, 3, 18, 3, 18, 3, 18, ...]
$\sqrt{88}$ = 9.380831519647 = [9; 2, 1, 1, 1, 2, 18, 2, 1, 1, 1, 2, 18, 2, 1, ...]
$\sqrt{89}$ = 9.433981132057 = [9; 2, 3, 3, 2, 18, 2, 3, 3, 2, 18, 2, 3, 3, 2, ...]
$\sqrt{90}$ = 9.486832980505 = [9; 2, 18, 2, 18, 2, 18, 2, 18, 2, 18, 2, 18, 2, 18, ...]
$\sqrt{91}$ = 9.539392014169 = [9; 1, 1, 5, 1, 5, 1, 1, 18, 1, 1, 5, 1, 5, 1, ...]
$\sqrt{92}$ = 9.591663046625 = [9; 1, 1, 2, 4, 2, 1, 1, 18, 1, 1, 2, 4, 2, 1, ...]
$\sqrt{93}$ = 9.643650760993 = [9; 1, 1, 1, 4, 6, 4, 1, 1, 1, 18, 1, 1, 1, 4, ...]
$\sqrt{94}$ = 9.695359714833 = [9; 1, 2, 3, 1, 1, 5, 1, 8, 1, 5, 1, 1, 3, 2, ...]
$\sqrt{95}$ = 9.746794344809 = [9; 1, 2, 1, 18, 1, 2, 1, 18, 1, 2, 1, 18, 1, 2, ...]
$\sqrt{96}$ = 9.797958971133 = [9; 1, 3, 1, 18, 1, 3, 1, 18, 1, 3, 1, 18, 1, 3, ...]
$\sqrt{97}$ = 9.848857801796 = [9; 1, 5, 1, 1, 1, 1, 1, 1, 5, 1, 18, 1, 5, 1, ...]
$\sqrt{98}$ = 9.899494936612 = [9; 1, 8, 1, 18, 1, 8, 1, 18, 1, 8, 1, 18, 1, 8, ...]
$\sqrt{99}$ = 9.949874371066 = [9; 1, 18, 1, 18, 1, 18, 1, 18, 1, 18, 1, 18, 1, 18, ...]
$\sqrt{100}$ = 10

Appendix 4
Listing of the First 50 Fibonacci Numbers

1	121393
1	196418
2	317811
3	514229
5	832040
8	1346269
13	2178309
21	3524578
34	5702887
55	9227465
89	14930352
144	24157817
233	39088169
377	63245986
610	102334155
987	165580141
1597	267914296
2584	433494437
4181	701408733
6765	1134903170
10946	1836311903
17711	2971215073
28657	4807526976
46368	7778742049
75025	12586269025

Appendix 5
Listing of the First 50 Lucas Numbers

3	439204
4	710647
7	1149851
11	1860498
18	3010349
29	4870847
47	7881196
76	12752043
123	20633239
199	33385282
322	54018521
521	87403803
843	141422324
1364	228826127
2207	370248451
3571	599074578
5778	969323029
9349	1568397607
15127	2537720636
24476	4106118243
39603	6643838879
64079	10749957122
103682	17393796001
167761	28143753123
271443	45537549124

Appendix 6
Polygonal Numbers

Listing of the First 100 Triangular Numbers

1	351	1326	2926
3	378	1378	3003
6	406	1431	3081
10	435	1485	3160
15	465	1540	3240
21	496	1596	3321
28	528	1653	3403
36	561	1711	3486
45	595	1770	3570
55	630	1830	3655
66	666	1891	3741
78	703	1953	3828
91	741	2016	3916
105	780	2080	4005
120	820	2145	4095
136	861	2211	4186
153	903	2278	4278
171	946	2346	4371
190	990	2415	4465
210	1035	2485	4560
231	1081	2556	4656
253	1128	2628	4753
276	1176	2701	4851
300	1225	2775	4950
325	1275	2850	5050

Where:
$$T_1 = 1 = 1$$
$$T_2 = 1 + 2 = 3$$
$$T_3 = 1 + 2 + 3 = 6$$
$$T_4 = 1 + 2 + 3 + 4 = 10$$
$$T_5 = 1 + 2 + 3 + 4 + 5 = 15$$
$$T_6 = 1 + 2 + 3 + 4 + 5 + 6 = 21$$
… etc …

Or
$$T_n = \tfrac{1}{2}n(n + 1)$$ Where T_n is the nth triangular number.

Listing of the First 100 Square Numbers

1	676	2601	5776
4	729	2704	5929
9	784	2809	6084
16	841	2916	6241
25	900	3025	6400
36	961	3136	6561
49	1024	3249	6724
64	1089	3364	6889
81	1156	3481	7056
100	1225	3600	7225
121	1296	3721	7396
144	1369	3844	7569
169	1444	3969	7744
196	1521	4096	7921
225	1600	4225	8100
256	1681	4356	8281
289	1764	4489	8464
324	1849	4624	8649
361	1936	4761	8836
400	2025	4900	9025
441	2116	5041	9216
484	2209	5184	9409
529	2304	5329	9604
576	2401	5476	9801
625	2500	5625	10000

Where:
$$S_1 = 1 \qquad\qquad = 1$$
$$S_2 = 1 + 3 \qquad\qquad = 4$$
$$S_3 = 1 + 3 + 5 \qquad\qquad = 9$$
$$S_4 = 1 + 3 + 5 + 7 \qquad\qquad = 16$$
$$S_5 = 1 + 3 + 5 + 7 + 9 \qquad\qquad = 25$$
$$S_6 = 1 + 3 + 5 + 7 + 9 + 11 \qquad\qquad = 36$$

… etc …

Or

$$S_n = \tfrac{1}{2}n(2n + 0) = n^2 \qquad \text{Where } S_n \text{ is the } n^{th} \text{ square number.}$$

Listing of the First 100 Pentagonal Numbers

1	1001	3876	8626
5	1080	4030	8855
12	1162	4187	9087
22	1247	4347	9322
35	1335	4510	9560
51	1426	4676	9801
70	1520	4845	10045
92	1617	5017	10292
117	1717	5192	10542
145	1820	5370	10795
176	1926	5551	11051
210	2035	5735	11310
247	2147	5922	11572
287	2262	6112	11837
330	2380	6305	12105
376	2501	6501	12376
425	2625	6700	12650
477	2752	6902	12927
532	2882	7107	13207
590	3015	7315	13490
651	3151	7526	13776
715	3290	7740	14065
782	3432	7957	14357
852	3577	8177	14652
925	3725	8400	14950

Where:

$$P_1 = 1 \qquad\qquad = 1$$
$$P_2 = 1 + 4 \qquad\qquad = 5$$
$$P_3 = 1 + 4 + 7 \qquad\qquad = 12$$
$$P_4 = 1 + 4 + 7 + 10 \qquad\qquad = 22$$
$$P_5 = 1 + 4 + 7 + 10 + 13 \qquad = 35$$
$$P_6 = 1 + 4 + 7 + 10 + 13 + 16 = 51$$

… etc …

Or

$$P_n = \tfrac{1}{2}n(3n - 1) \qquad \text{Where } P_n \text{ is the } n^{th} \text{ pentagonal number.}$$

Appendix 7
Continuous Fractions of Triangular Roots

$^{t}\sqrt{1}$ = 1

$^{t}\sqrt{2}$ = 1.561552812809 = [1; 1, 1, 3, 1, 1, 3, 1, 1, 3, 1, 1, 3, 1, 1, 3, ...]

$^{t}\sqrt{3}$ = 2

$^{t}\sqrt{4}$ = 2.372281323269 = [2; 2, 1, 2, 5, 2, 1, 2, 5, 2, 1, 2, 5, 2, 1, 2, ...]

$^{t}\sqrt{5}$ = 2.701562118716 = [2; 1, 2, 2, 1, 5, 1, 2, 2, 1, 5, 1, 2, 2, 1, 5, ...]

$^{t}\sqrt{6}$ = 3

$^{t}\sqrt{7}$ = 3.274917217635 = [3; 3, 1, 1, 1, 3, 7, 3, 1, 1, 1, 3, 7, 3, 1, 1, ...]

$^{t}\sqrt{8}$ = 3.531128874149 = [3; 1, 1, 7, 1, 1, 7, 1, 1, 7, 1, 1, 7, 1, 1, 7, ...]

$^{t}\sqrt{9}$ = 3.772001872659 = [3; 1, 3, 2, 1, 1, 2, 3, 1, 7, 1, 3, 2, 1, 1, 2, ...]

$^{t}\sqrt{10}$ = 4

$^{t}\sqrt{11}$ = 4.216990566028 = [4; 4, 1, 1, 1, 1, 4, 9, 4, 1, 1, 1, 1, 4, 9, 4, ...]

$^{t}\sqrt{12}$ = 4.424428900898 = [4; 2, 2, 1, 4, 4, 1, 2, 2, 9, 2, 2, 1, 4, 4, 1, ...]

$^{t}\sqrt{13}$ = 4.62347538298 = [4; 1, 1, 1, 1, 9, 1, 1, 1, 1, 9, 1, 1, 1, ...]

$^{t}\sqrt{14}$ = 4.815072906367 = [4; 1, 4, 2, 2, 4, 1, 9, 1, 4, 2, 2, 4, 1, 9, 1, ...]

$^{t}\sqrt{15}$ = 5

$^{t}\sqrt{16}$ = 5.1789083458 = [5; 5, 1, 1, 2, 3, 2, 1, 1, 5, 11, 5, 1, 1, 2, 3, ...]

$^{t}\sqrt{17}$ = 5.35234995536 = [5; 2, 1, 5, 5, 1, 2, 11, 2, 1, 5, 5, 1, 2, 11, 2, ...]

$^{t}\sqrt{18}$ = 5.520797289396 = [5; 1, 1, 11, 1, 1, 11, 1, 1, 11, 1, 1, 11, 1, 1, ...]

$^{t}\sqrt{19}$ = 5.684658438426 = [5; 1, 2, 5, 1, 5, 2, 1, 11, 1, 2, 5, 1, 5, 2, 1, ...]

$^{t}\sqrt{20}$ = 5.844288770225 = [5; 1, 5, 2, 2, 1, 2, 2, 5, 1, 11, 1, 5, 2, 2, 1, ...]

$^{t}\sqrt{21}$ = 6

$^{t}\sqrt{22}$ = 6.152067347825 = [6; 6, 1, 1, 2, 1, 3, 1, 2, 1, 1, 6, 13, 6, 1, 1, ...]

$^{t}\sqrt{23}$ = 6.300735254368 = [6; 3, 3, 13, 3, 3, 13, 3, 3, 13, 3, 3, 13, 3, 3, ...]

$^{t}\sqrt{24}$ = 6.446221994725 = [6; 2, 4, 6, 1, 2, 1, 1, 1, 2, 1, 6, 4, 2, 13, ...]

$^{t}\sqrt{25}$ = 6.588723439379 = [6; 1, 1, 2, 3, 6, 1, 3, 1, 6, 3, 2, 1, 1, 13, 1, ...]

$^{t}\sqrt{26}$ = 6.7284161474 = [6; 1, 2, 1, 2, 6, 1, 6, 2, 1, 2, 1, 13, 1, 2, 1, ...]

$^{t}\sqrt{27}$ = 6.865459931328 = [6; 1, 6, 2, 3, 4, 1, 1, 1, 1, 1, 4, 3, 2, 6, 1, ...]

$^{t}\sqrt{28}$ = 7

$^{t}\sqrt{29}$ = 7.132168761237 = [7; 7, 1, 1, 3, 3, 1, 1, 7, 15, 7, 1, 1, 3, 3, 1, ...]

$^{t}\sqrt{30}$ = 7.26208734813 = [7; 3, 1, 4, 2, 2, 1, 1, 1, 7, 7, 1, 1, 1, 2, 2, ...]

$^{t}\sqrt{31}$ = 7.38986691903 = [7; 2, 1, 1, 3, 2, 1, 7, 5, 7, 1, 2, 3, 1, 1, 2, ...]

$^{t}\sqrt{32}$ = 7.515609770941 = [7; 1, 1, 15, 1, 1, 15, 1, 1, 15, 1, 1, 15, 1, 1, ...]

$^{t}\sqrt{33}$ = 7.63941029805 = [7; 1, 1, 1, 3, 2, 2, 3, 1, 1, 1, 15, 1, 1, 1, 3, ...]

$^{t}\sqrt{34}$ = 7.761355820929 = [7; 1, 3, 5, 3, 1, 15, 1, 3, 5, 3, 1, 15, 1, 3, 5, ...]

$^{t}\sqrt{35}$ = 7.88152730712 = [7; 1, 7, 2, 3, 1, 2, 1, 1, 2, 1, 3, 2, 7, 1, 15, ...]

$^{t}\sqrt{36}$ = 8

$^{t}\sqrt{37}$ = 8.116843969807 = [8; 8, 1, 1, 3, 1, 3, 1, 1, 8, 17, 8, 1, 1, 3, 1, ...]

$^{t}\sqrt{38}$ = 8.232124598286 = [8; 4, 3, 4, 17, 4, 3, 4, 17, 4, 3, 4, 17, 4, 3, 4, ...]

$^{t}\sqrt{39}$ = 8.345903006477 = [8; 2, 1, 8, 5, 1, 3, 1, 1, 2, 2, 1, 1, 3, 1, 5, ...]

$^{t}\sqrt{40}$ = 8.458236433584 = [8; 2, 5, 2, 17, 2, 5, 2, 17, 2, 5, 2, 17, 2, 5, 2, ...]

$^{t}\sqrt{41}$ = 8.569178573609 = [8; 1, 1, 3, 8, 1, 3, 1, 1, 1, 3, 1, 8, 3, 1, 1, ...]

$^{t}\sqrt{42}$ = 8.678779875343 = [8; 1, 2, 8, 1, 5, 4, 2, 2, 1, 1, 1, 1, 2, 2, 4, ...]

$^{t}\sqrt{43}$ = 8.787087810503 = [8; 1, 3, 1, 2, 3, 2, 1, 3, 1, 17, 1, 3, 1, 2, 3, ...]

$^{t}\sqrt{44}$ = 8.894147114028 = [8; 1, 8, 2, 4, 4, 2, 8, 1, 17, 1, 8, 2, 4, 4, 2, ...]

$^{t}\sqrt{45}$ = 9

$^{t}\sqrt{46}$ = 9.104686356149 = [9; 9, 1, 1, 4, 3, 1, 1, 1, 1, 1, 3, 4, 1, 1, 9, ...]

$^{t}\sqrt{47}$ = 9.208243919474 = [9; 4, 1, 4, 19, 4, 1, 4, 19, 4, 1, 4, 19, 4, 1, 4, ...]

$^{t}\sqrt{48}$ = 9.310708435174 = [9; 3, 4, 1, 1, 2, 1, 2, 1, 1, 4, 3, 19, 3, 4, 1, ...]

$^{t}\sqrt{49}$ = 9.4121138008 = [9; 2, 2, 2, 1, 9, 4, 1, 5, 1, 4, 9, 1, 2, 2, 2, ...]

$^{t}\sqrt{50}$ = 9.51249219725 = [9; 1, 1, 19, 1, 1, 19, 1, 1, 19, 1, 1, 19, 1, 1, ...]

$\sqrt[t]{51}$ = 9.611874208078 = [9; 1, 1, 1, 1, 2, 1, 3, 3, 9, 1, 4, 6, 1, 1, 6, ...]
$\sqrt[t]{52}$ = 9.710288928331 = [9; 1, 2, 2, 4, 1, 2, 9, 1, 5, 1, 9, 2, 1, 4, 2, ...]
$\sqrt[t]{53}$ = 9.807764064044 = [9; 1, 4, 4, 1, 19, 1, 4, 4, 1, 19, 1, 4, 4, 1, 19, ...]
$\sqrt[t]{54}$ = 9.904326023342 = [9; 1, 9, 2, 4, 1, 2, 1, 1, 1, 6, 3, 3, 6, 1, 1, ...]
$\sqrt[t]{55}$ = 10
$\sqrt[t]{56}$ = 10.094810050209 = [10; 10, 1, 1, 4, 1, 3, 2, 2, 1, 1, 2, 2, 3, 1, 4, ...]
$\sqrt[t]{57}$ = 10.188779163216 = [10; 5, 3, 2, 1, 2, 1, 6, 2, 1, 1, 10, 10, 1, 1, ...]
$\sqrt[t]{58}$ = 10.281929326424 = [10; 3, 1, 1, 4, 1, 4, 1, 1, 3, 21, 3, 1, 1, 4, 1, ...]
$\sqrt[t]{59}$ = 10.374281585466 = [10; 2, 1, 2, 21, 2, 1, 2, 21, 2, 1, 2, 21, 2, 1, ...]
$\sqrt[t]{60}$ = 10.465856099731 = [10; 2, 6, 1, 4, 1, 1, 1, 1, 1, 1, 4, 1, 6, 2, 21, ...]
$\sqrt[t]{61}$ = 10.556672193748 = [10; 1, 1, 3, 1, 10, 3, 1, 1, 2, 5, 7, 5, 2, 1, 1, ...]
$\sqrt[t]{62}$ = 10.646748404804 = [10; 1, 1, 1, 4, 1, 10, 3, 10, 1, 4, 1, 1, 1, 21, ...]
$\sqrt[t]{63}$ = 10.736102527122 = [10; 1, 2, 1, 3, 1, 2, 1, 21, 1, 2, 1, 3, 1, 2, 1, ...]
$\sqrt[t]{64}$ = 10.824751652906 = [10; 1, 4, 1, 2, 2, 2, 10, 1, 10, 2, 2, 2, 1, 4, ...]
$\sqrt[t]{65}$ = 10.912712210513 = [10; 1, 10, 2, 5, 4, 2, 1, 1, 1, 1, 2, 4, 5, 2, ...]
$\sqrt[t]{66}$ = 11
$\sqrt[t]{67}$ = 11.086630226257 = [11; 11, 1, 1, 5, 3, 1, 2, 7, 2, 1, 3, 5, 1, 1, ...]
$\sqrt[t]{68}$ = 11.172617529929 = [11; 5, 1, 3, 1, 5, 23, 5, 1, 3, 1, 5, 23, 5, 1, ...]
$\sqrt[t]{69}$ = 11.257976016305 = [11; 3, 1, 7, 11, 1, 1, 1, 2, 3, 1, 1, 5, 3, 5, 1, ...]
$\sqrt[t]{70}$ = 11.342719282327 = [11; 2, 1, 11, 5, 1, 5, 11, 1, 2, 23, 2, 1, 11, 5, ...]
$\sqrt[t]{71}$ = 11.426860441877 = [11; 2, 2, 1, 11, 4, 1, 2, 5, 1, 1, 1, 1, 5, 2, 1, ...]
$\sqrt[t]{72}$ = 11.510412149464 = [11; 1, 1, 23, 1, 1, 23, 1, 1, 23, 1, 1, 23, 1, 1, ...]
$\sqrt[t]{73}$ = 11.593386622448 = [11; 1, 1, 2, 5, 1, 1, 1, 5, 2, 1, 1, 23, 1, 1, 2, ...]
$\sqrt[t]{74}$ = 11.675795661886 = [11; 1, 2, 11, 1, 5, 5, 1, 11, 2, 1, 23, 1, 2, 11, ...]
$\sqrt[t]{75}$ = 11.757650672131 = [11; 1, 3, 7, 1, 11, 2, 1, 1, 1, 3, 2, 5, 1, 2, 4, ...]
$\sqrt[t]{76}$ = 11.838962679253 = [11; 1, 5, 4, 1, 3, 3, 3, 1, 4, 5, 1, 23, 1, 5, 4, ...]
$\sqrt[t]{77}$ = 11.919742348374 = [11; 1, 11, 2, 5, 1, 2, 1, 2, 2, 1, 2, 1, 5, 2, ...]
$\sqrt[t]{78}$ = 12
$\sqrt[t]{79}$ = 12.079745625409 = [12; 12, 1, 1, 5, 1, 3, 2, 1, 7, 1, 2, 3, 1, 5, 1, ...]
$\sqrt[t]{80}$ = 12.158988901172 = [12; 6, 3, 2, 4, 1, 1, 1, 2, 1, 1, 12, 12, 1, 1, ...]
$\sqrt[t]{81}$ = 12.237739202857 = [12; 4, 4, 1, 5, 1, 1, 3, 1, 2, 2, 2, 8, 12, ...]
$\sqrt[t]{82}$ = 12.316005617976 = [12; 3, 6, 12, 1, 1, 1, 12, 6, 3, 25, 3, 6, 12, 1, ...]
$\sqrt[t]{83}$ = 12.393796958228 = [12; 2, 1, 1, 5, 1, 5, 1, 1, 2, 25, 2, 1, 1, 5, 1, ...]
$\sqrt[t]{84}$ = 12.471121771073 = [12; 2, 8, 6, 2, 1, 2, 1, 1, 3, 1, 2, 1, 12, 4, 4, ...]
$\sqrt[t]{85}$ = 12.5479883507 = [12; 1, 1, 4, 1, 2, 2, 3, 1, 12, 3, 1, 1, 1, 5, 1, ...]
$\sqrt[t]{86}$ = 12.624404748407 = [12; 1, 1, 1, 1, 1, 25, 1, 1, 1, 1, 1, 25, 1, 1, ...]
$\sqrt[t]{87}$ = 12.700378782444 = [12; 1, 2, 2, 1, 25, 1, 2, 2, 1, 25, 1, 2, 2, 1, ...]
$\sqrt[t]{88}$ = 12.775918047352 = [12; 1, 3, 2, 6, 5, 6, 2, 3, 1, 25, 1, 3, 2, 6, 5, ...]
$\sqrt[t]{89}$ = 12.851029922819 = [12; 1, 5, 1, 2, 2, 12, 1, 12, 2, 2, 1, 5, 1, 25, ...]
$\sqrt[t]{90}$ = 12.925721582098 = [12; 1, 12, 2, 6, 4, 3, 8, 1, 1, 1, 3, 1, 4, 1, 1, ...]
$\sqrt[t]{91}$ = 13
$\sqrt[t]{92}$ = 13.073871960498 = [13; 13, 1, 1, 6, 3, 1, 2, 1, 1, 1, 2, 1, 3, 6, 1, ...]
$\sqrt[t]{93}$ = 13.147344063956 = [13; 6, 1, 3, 1, 2, 4, 5, 4, 2, 1, 3, 1, 6, ...]
$\sqrt[t]{94}$ = 13.220422734012 = [13; 4, 1, 1, 6, 3, 3, 1, 1, 1, 1, 13, 9, 13, 1, ...]
$\sqrt[t]{95}$ = 13.293114224134 = [13; 3, 2, 2, 3, 27, 3, 2, 2, 3, 27, 3, 2, 2, 3, ...]
$\sqrt[t]{96}$ = 13.365424623862 = [13; 2, 1, 2, 1, 3, 1, 8, 2, 5, 13, 1, 2, 6, 1, 1, ...]
$\sqrt[t]{97}$ = 13.437359864766 = [13; 2, 3, 2, 27, 2, 3, 2, 27, 2, 3, 2, 27, 2, 3, ...]
$\sqrt[t]{98}$ = 13.508925726122 = [13; 1, 1, 27, 1, 1, 27, 1, 1, 27, 1, 1, 27, 1, 1, ...]
$\sqrt[t]{99}$ = 13.580127840329 = [13; 1, 1, 2, 1, 1, 1, 1, 1, 2, 1, 1, 27, 1, 1, 2, ...]
$\sqrt[t]{100}$ = 13.650971698085 = [13; 1, 1, 1, 6, 2, 2, 2, 1, 2, 1, 4, 1, 13, 3, ...]

Appendix 8
Selected Pascal's Triangles with Highlighted Multiples

150 rows of Pascal's Triangle showing multiples of 8

150 rows of Pascal's Triangle showing multiples of 16

150 rows of Pascal's Triangle showing multiples of 9

150 rows of Pascal's Triangle showing multiples of 27

405

150 rows of Pascal's Triangle showing multiples of 58

150 rows of Pascal's Triangle showing multiples of 74

406

150 rows of Pascal's Triangle showing multiples of 86

150 rows of Pascal's Triangle showing multiples of 93

407

Appendix 9
Napier Bones

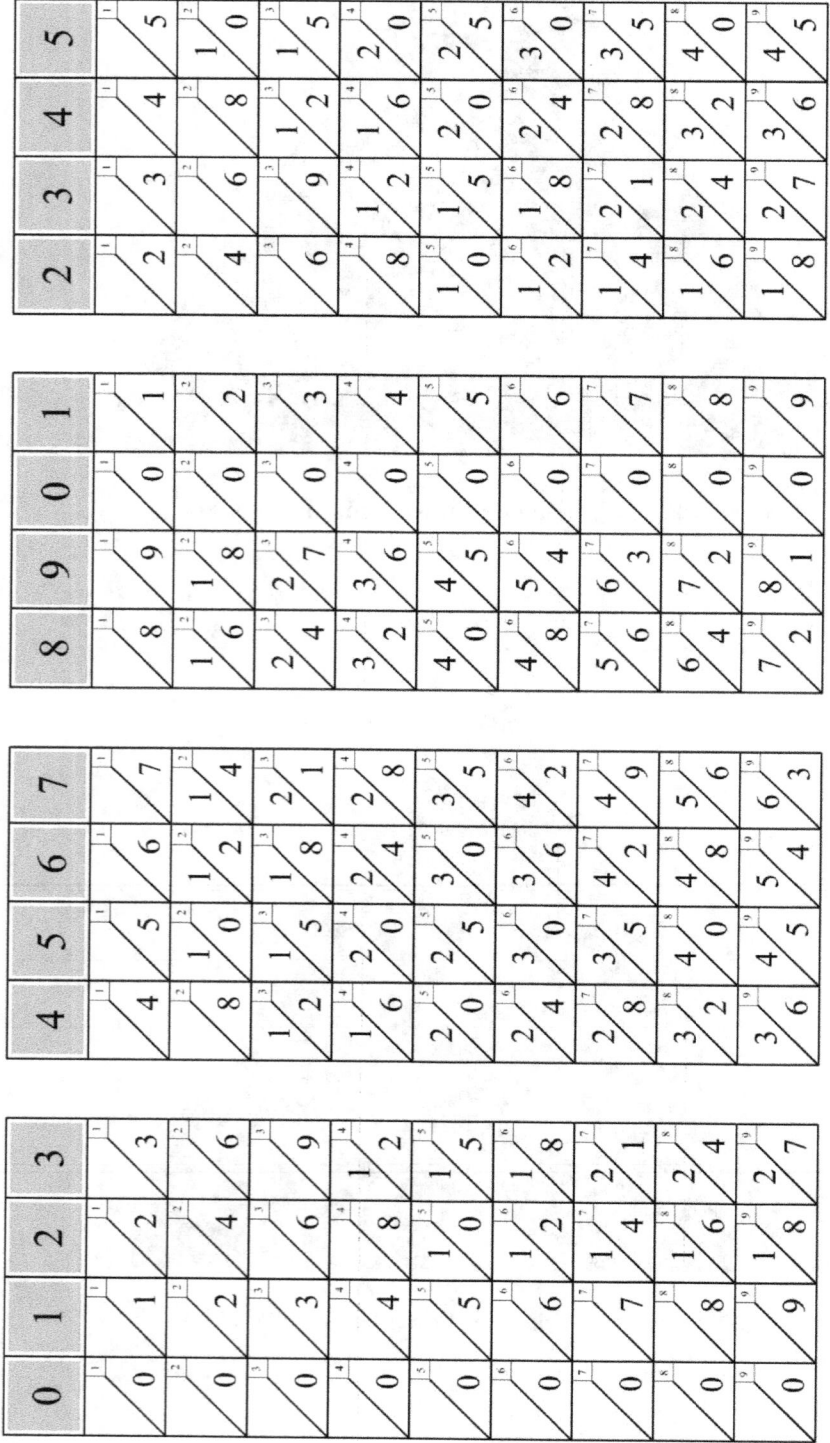

These templates can be used to create a set of Napier Bones. Copy them, cut them out, and then glue them around an appropriately sized square dowel.

Appendix 10
Pythagorean Triples

These are the first 100 primitive Pythagorean Triples (ordered in such a way that the hypotenuse increases from a smaller number to a larger number):

3	4	5
5	12	13
8	15	17
7	24	25
20	21	29
12	35	37
9	40	41
28	45	53
11	60	61
16	63	65
33	56	65
48	55	73
13	84	85
36	77	85
39	80	89
65	72	97
20	99	101
60	91	109
15	112	113
44	117	125
88	105	137
17	144	145
24	143	145
51	140	149
85	132	157
119	120	169
52	165	173
19	180	181
57	176	185
104	153	185
95	168	193
28	195	197
84	187	205
133	156	205
21	220	221
140	171	221
60	221	229
105	208	233
120	209	241
32	255	257
23	264	265
96	247	265
69	260	269
115	252	277
160	231	281
161	240	289

68	285	293
136	273	305
207	224	305
25	312	313
75	308	317
36	323	325
204	253	325
175	288	337
180	299	349
225	272	353
27	364	365
76	357	365
252	275	373
135	352	377
152	345	377
189	340	389
228	325	397
40	399	401
120	391	409
29	420	421
87	416	425
297	304	425
145	408	433
84	437	445
203	396	445
280	351	449
168	425	457
261	380	461
31	480	481
319	360	481
44	483	485
93	476	485
132	475	493
155	468	493
217	456	505
336	377	505
220	459	509
279	440	521
92	525	533
308	435	533
341	420	541
33	544	545
184	513	545
165	532	557
276	493	565
396	403	565
231	520	569
48	575	577
368	465	593
240	551	601
35	612	613
105	608	617
336	527	625
100	621	629

Appendix 11
Listing of the First 100 Prime Numbers

2	101	233	383
3	103	239	389
5	107	241	397
7	109	251	401
11	113	257	409
13	127	263	419
17	131	269	421
19	137	271	431
23	139	277	433
29	149	281	439
31	151	283	443
37	157	293	449
41	163	307	457
43	167	311	461
47	173	313	463
53	179	317	467
59	181	331	479
61	191	337	487
67	193	347	491
71	197	349	499
73	199	353	503
79	211	359	509
83	223	367	521
89	227	373	523
97	229	379	541

Appendix 12
Varying Table Widths Showing Prime Numbers

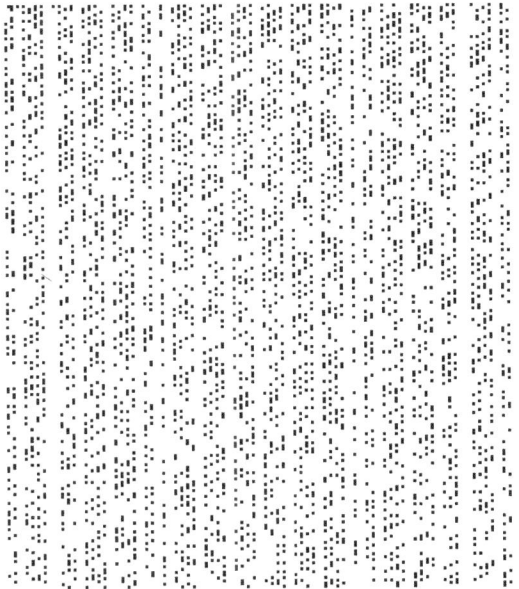

Table of primes with a width of 170 columns and 200 rows, containing 3638 primes out of 34,000 numbers shown/checked. The prime factors of 170 are 2, 5, 17. (The prime numbers in the tables in this appendix are represented as black dots).

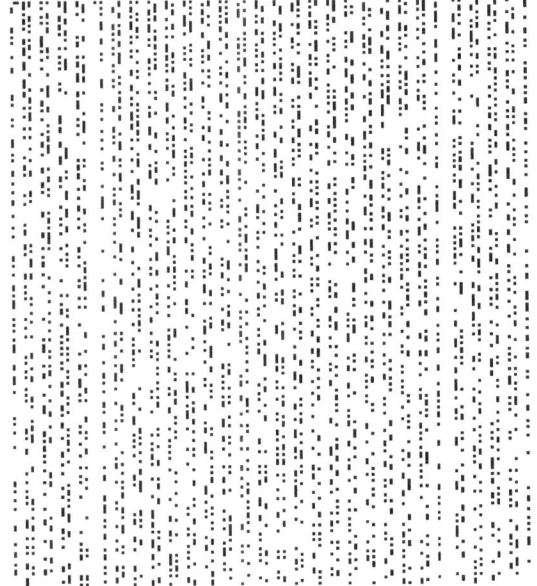

Table of primes with a width of 174 columns and 200 rows, containing 3715 primes out of 34,800 numbers shown/checked. The prime factors of 174 are 2, 3, 29.

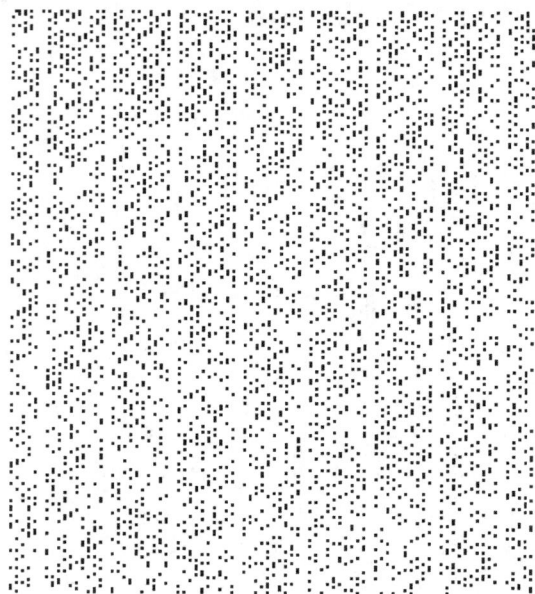

Table of primes with a width of 176 columns and 200 rows, containing 3751 primes out of 35,200 numbers shown/checked. The prime factors of 176 are 2, 2, 2, 2, 11.

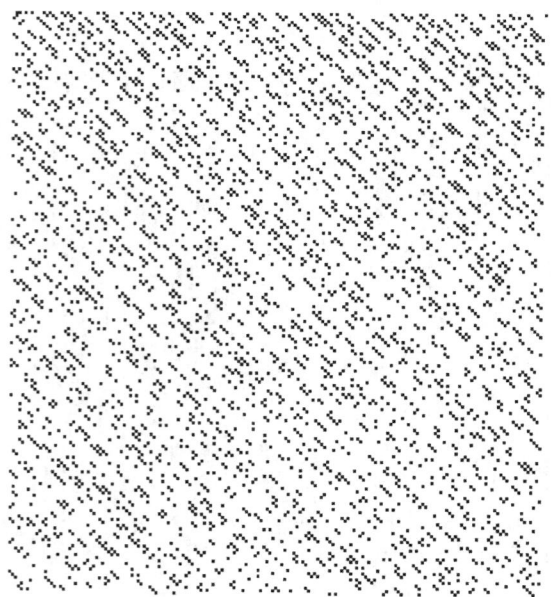

Table of primes with a width of 179 columns and 200 rows, containing 3802 primes out of 35,800 numbers shown/checked. 179 is a prime number.

414

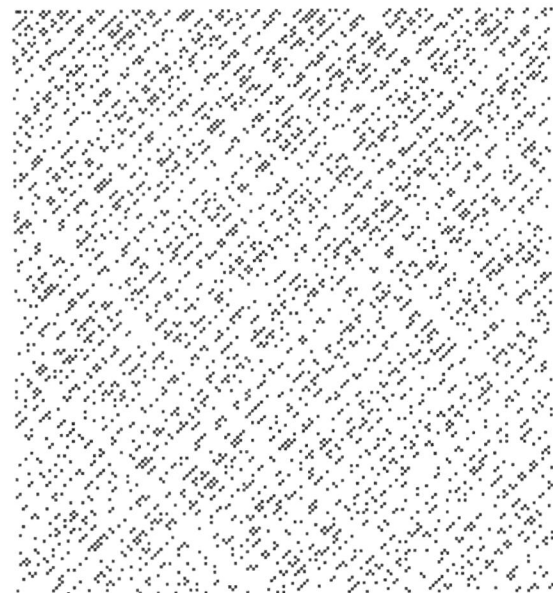

Table of primes with a width of 180 columns and 200 rows, containing 3824 primes out of 36,000 numbers shown/checked. The prime factors of 180 are 2, 2, 3, 3, 5.

Table of primes with a width of 181 columns and 200 rows, containing 3842 primes out of 36,200 numbers shown/checked. 181 is a prime number.

415

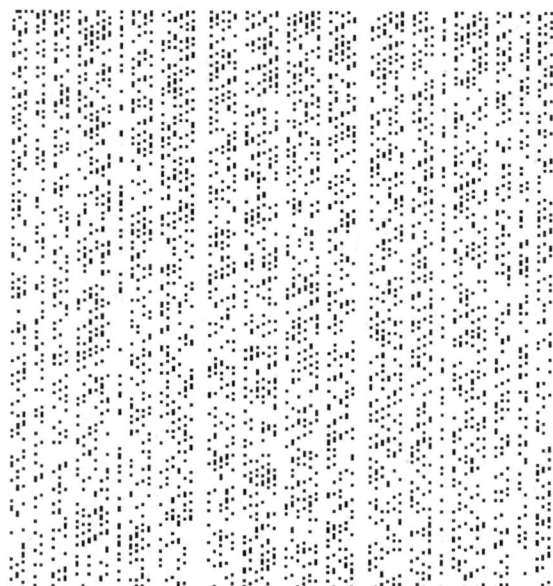

Table of primes with a width of 182 columns and 200 rows, containing 3861 primes out of 36,400 numbers shown/checked. The prime factors of 182 are 2, 7, 13.

Table of primes with a width of 186 columns and 200 rows, containing 3941 primes out of 37,200 numbers shown/checked. The prime factors of 186 are 2, 3, 31.

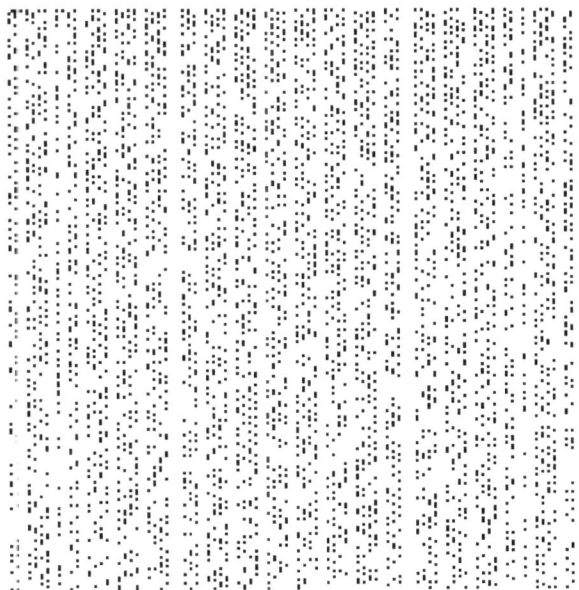

Table of primes with a width of 190 columns and 200 rows, containing 4017 primes out of 38,000 numbers shown/checked. The prime factors of 190 are 2, 5, 19.

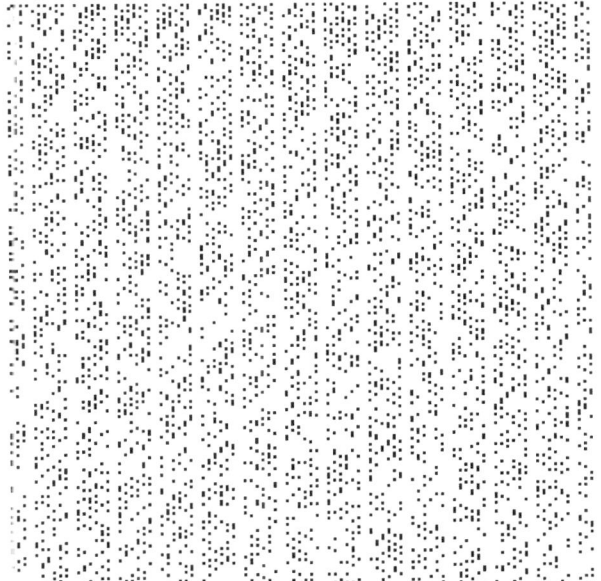

Table of primes with a width of 196 columns and 200 rows, containing 4127 primes out of 39,200 numbers shown/checked. The prime factors of 196 are 2, 2, 7, 7.

417

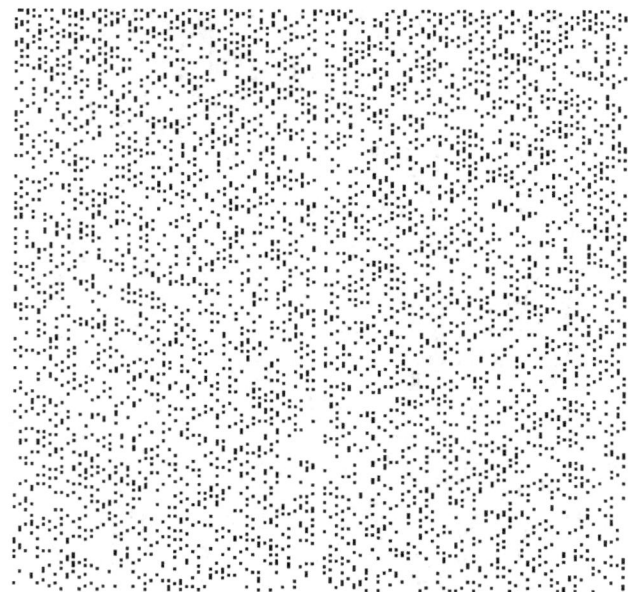

Table of primes with a width of 206 columns and 200 rows, containing 4311 primes out of 41,200 numbers shown/checked. The prime factors of 206 are 2, 103.

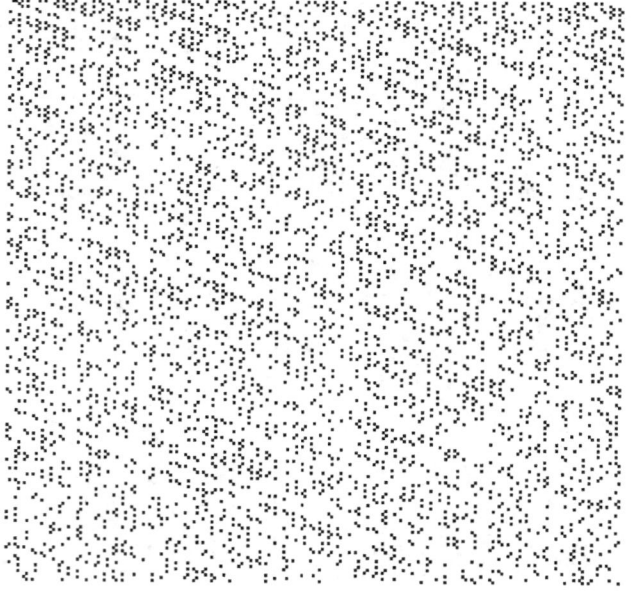

Table of primes with a width of 207 columns and 200 rows, containing 4332 primes out of 41,400 numbers shown/checked. The prime factors of 207 are 3, 3, 23.

418

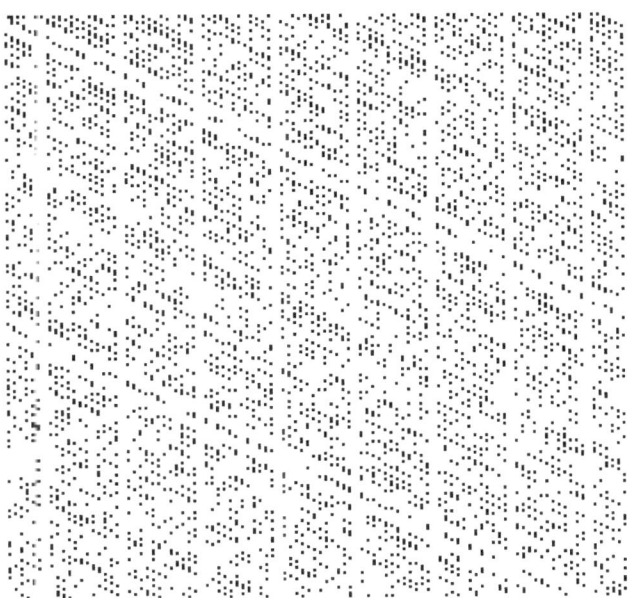

Table of primes with a width of 208 columns and 200 rows, containing 4349 primes out of 41,600 numbers shown/checked. The prime factors of 208 are 2, 2, 2, 2, 13.

Table of primes with a width of 209 columns and 200 rows, containing 4369 primes out of 41,800 numbers shown/checked. The prime factors of 209 are 11, 19.

Appendix 13
Listing of the First 100 Squares MOD 100

1	1	26	76	51	1	76	76
2	4	27	29	52	4	77	29
3	9	28	84	53	9	78	84
4	16	29	41	54	16	79	41
5	25	30	0	55	25	80	0
6	36	31	61	56	36	81	61
7	49	32	24	57	49	82	24
8	64	33	89	58	64	83	89
9	81	34	56	59	81	84	56
10	0	35	25	60	0	85	25
11	21	36	96	61	21	86	96
12	44	37	69	62	44	87	69
13	69	38	44	63	69	88	44
14	96	39	21	64	96	89	21
15	25	40	0	65	25	90	0
16	56	41	81	66	56	91	81
17	89	42	64	67	89	92	64
18	24	43	49	68	24	93	49
19	61	44	36	69	61	94	36
20	0	45	25	70	0	95	25
21	41	46	16	71	41	96	16
22	84	47	9	72	84	97	9
23	29	48	4	73	29	98	4
24	76	49	1	74	76	99	1
25	25	50	0	75	25	100	0

Appendix 14
Listing of the First 100 Cubes MOD 100

1	1	26	76	51	51	76	76
2	8	27	83	52	8	77	33
3	27	28	52	53	77	78	52
4	64	29	89	54	64	79	39
5	25	30	0	55	75	80	0
6	16	31	91	56	16	81	41
7	43	32	68	57	93	82	68
8	12	33	37	58	12	83	87
9	29	34	4	59	79	84	4
10	0	35	75	60	0	85	25
11	31	36	56	61	81	86	56
12	28	37	53	62	28	87	3
13	97	38	72	63	47	88	72
14	44	39	19	64	44	89	69
15	75	40	0	65	25	90	0
16	96	41	21	66	96	91	71
17	13	42	88	67	63	92	88
18	32	43	7	68	32	93	57
19	59	44	84	69	9	94	84
20	0	45	25	70	0	95	75
21	61	46	36	71	11	96	36
22	48	47	23	72	48	97	73
23	67	48	92	73	17	98	92
24	24	49	49	74	24	99	99
25	25	50	0	75	75	100	0

Appendix 15
Natural Integer Networks (Loop Diagrams)

This diagram lists the numbers 0 thru 99 raised to the 6th power, and then looks at the two right-most digits as the next number in the network.

Odd Number Patterns   Even Number Patterns

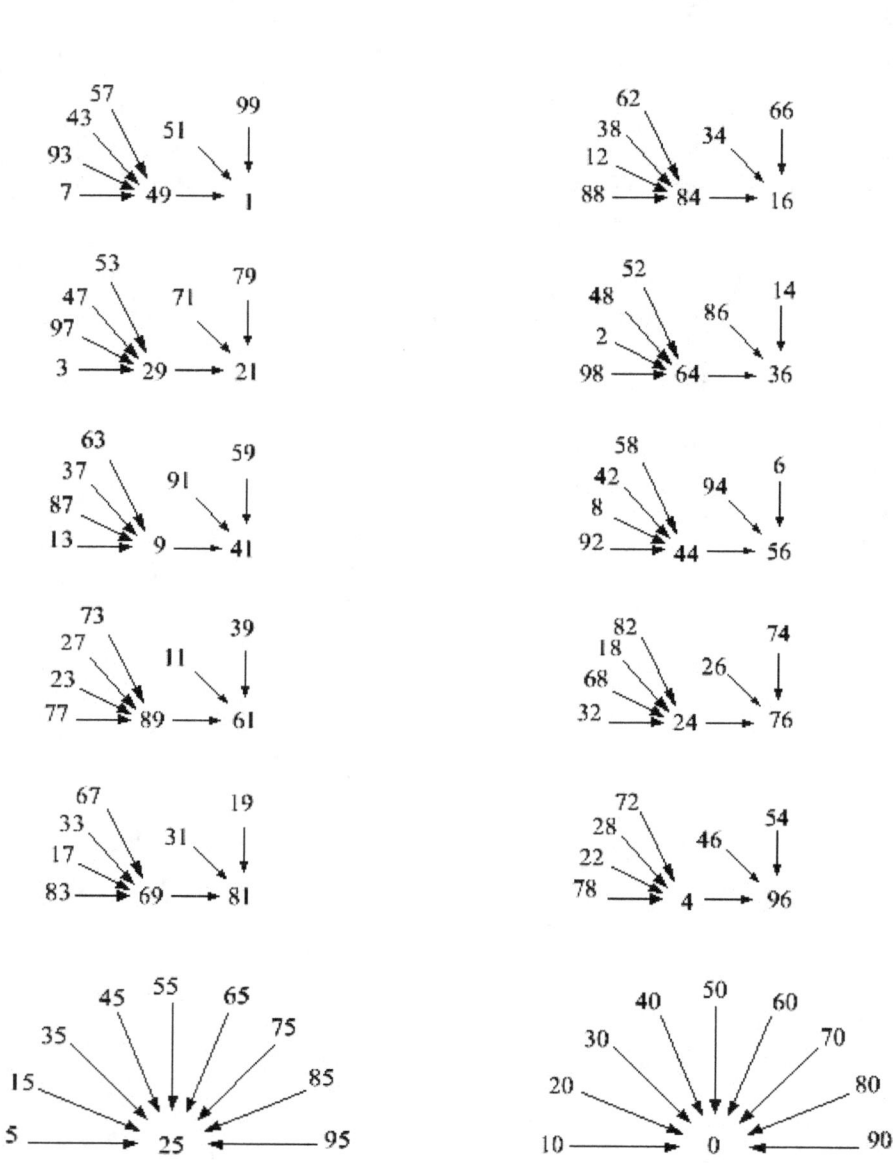

Attractors: 0, 1, 16, 21, 25, 36, 41, 56, 61, 76, 81, 96

Pairs add to 100 (Odd and even patterns are different)

This diagram lists the numbers 0 thru 99 raised to the 7th power, and then looks at the two right-most digits as the next number in the network.

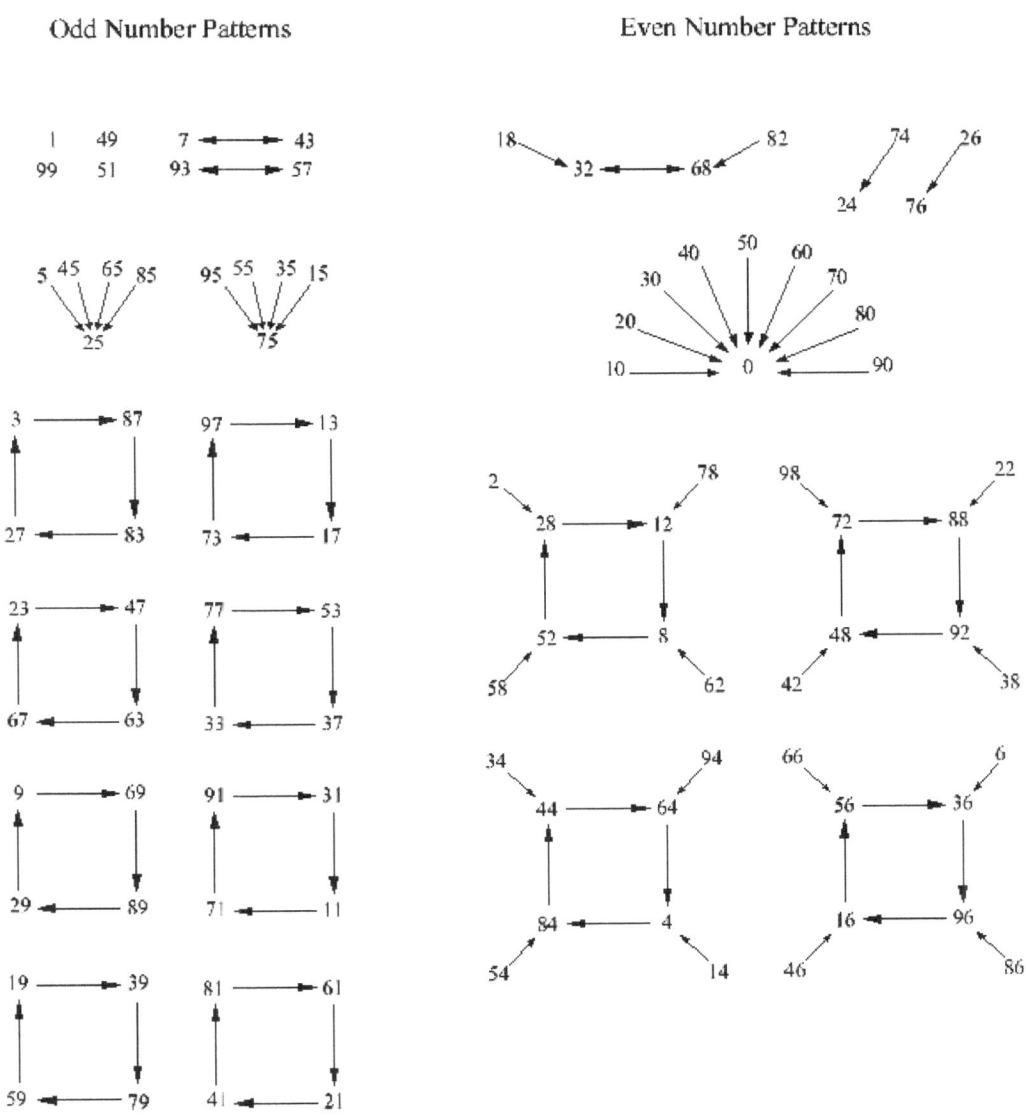

Odd Number Patterns

Even Number Patterns

Pairs of numbers add to 100; however,
Two sets are required to pair the numbers.

423

This diagram lists the numbers 0 thru 99 raised to the 8th power, and then looks at the two right-most digits as the next number in the network.

Odd Number Patterns   Even Number Patterns

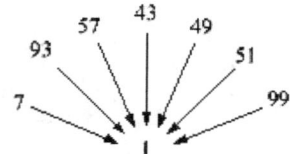

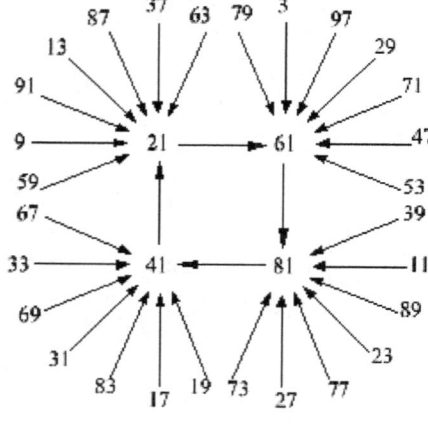

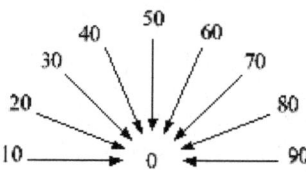

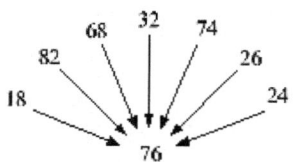

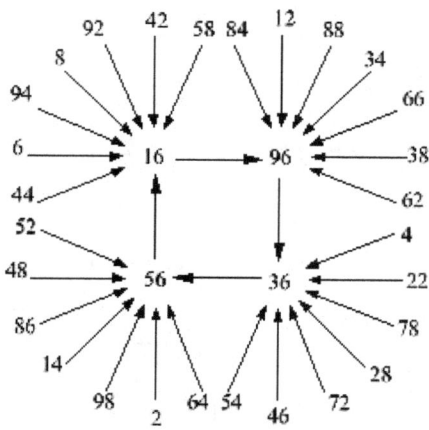

Attractors: 0, 1, 25, 76
Pairs add to 100 within their own patterns.
Even and Odd patterns are identical.

This diagram lists the numbers 0 thru 99 raised to the 9th power, and then looks at the two right-most digits as the next number in the network.

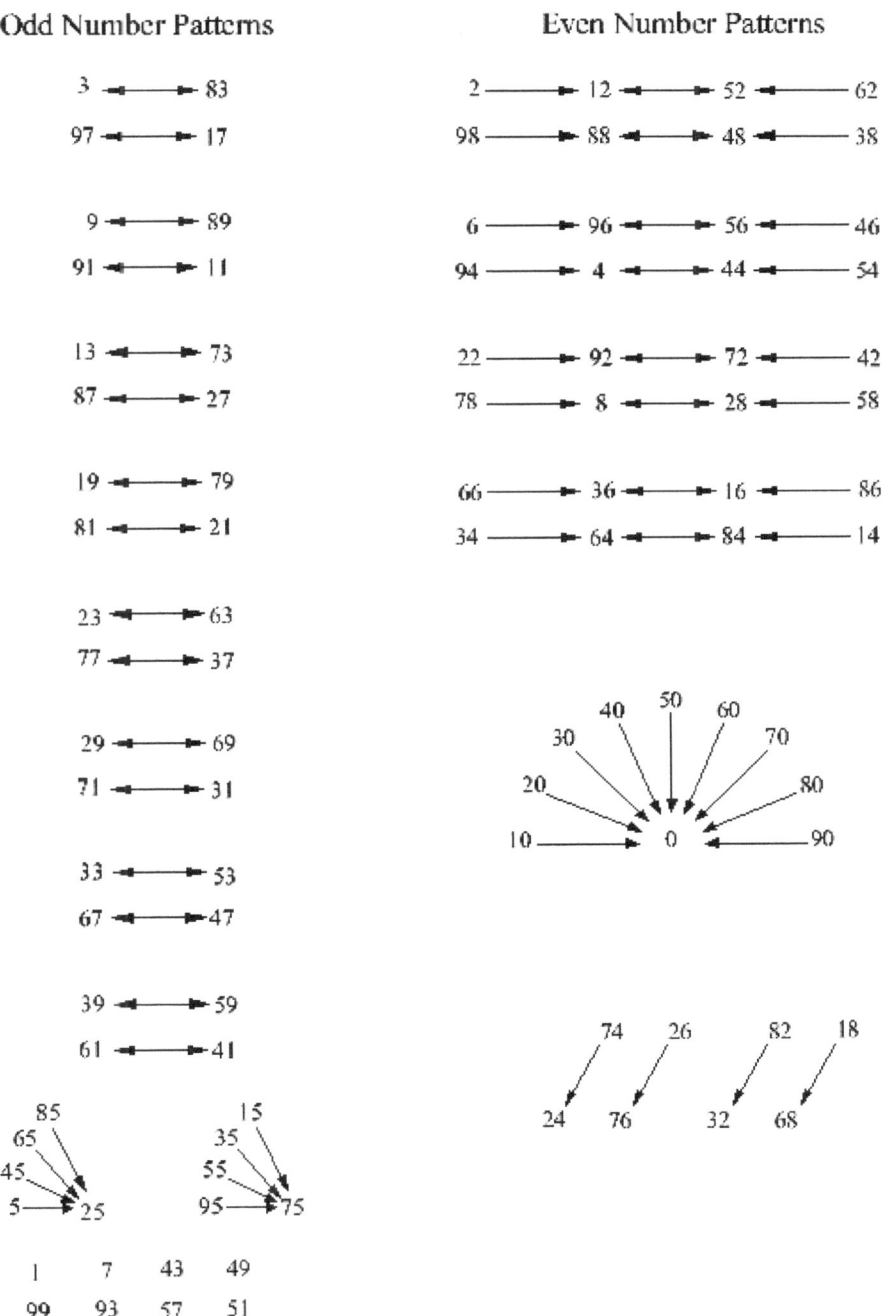

Odd Number Patterns

3 ⟷ 83
97 ⟷ 17

9 ⟷ 89
91 ⟷ 11

13 ⟷ 73
87 ⟷ 27

19 ⟷ 79
81 ⟷ 21

23 ⟷ 63
77 ⟷ 37

29 ⟷ 69
71 ⟷ 31

33 ⟷ 53
67 ⟷ 47

39 ⟷ 59
61 ⟷ 41

85
65
45
5 → 25

15
35
55
95 → 75

1 7 43 49
99 93 57 51

Even Number Patterns

2 → 12 ⟷ 52 ⟷ 62
98 → 88 ⟷ 48 ⟷ 38

6 → 96 ⟷ 56 ⟷ 46
94 → 4 ⟷ 44 ⟷ 54

22 → 92 ⟷ 72 ⟷ 42
78 → 8 ⟷ 28 ⟷ 58

66 → 36 ⟷ 16 ⟷ 86
34 → 64 ⟷ 84 ⟷ 14

40 50 60
30   70
20   80
10 → 0 ← 90

74 26 82 18
24 76 32 68

Attractors: 0, 1, 7, 24, 25, 32, 43, 49, 51, 57, 68, 75, 76, 93, 99
Pairs add to 100; however, two sets are required.

425

This diagram lists the numbers 0 thru 99 raised to the 10th power, and then looks at the two right-most digits as the next number in the network.

Odd Number Patterns   Even Number Patterns

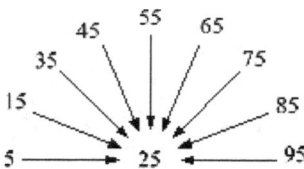

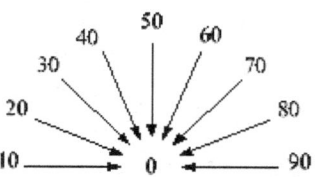

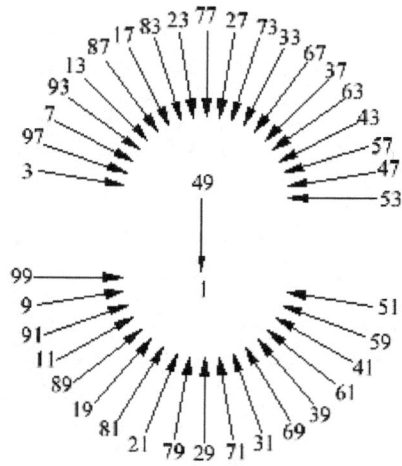

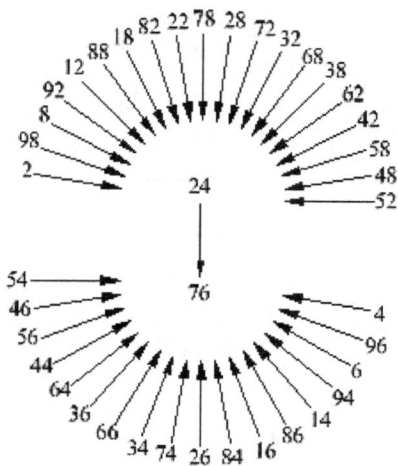

Attractors: 0, 1, 25, 76
Pairs add to 100, within each pattern, but
Patterns are not identical.

426

This diagram lists the numbers 0 thru 99 raised to the 11th power, and then looks at the two right-most digits as the next number in the network.

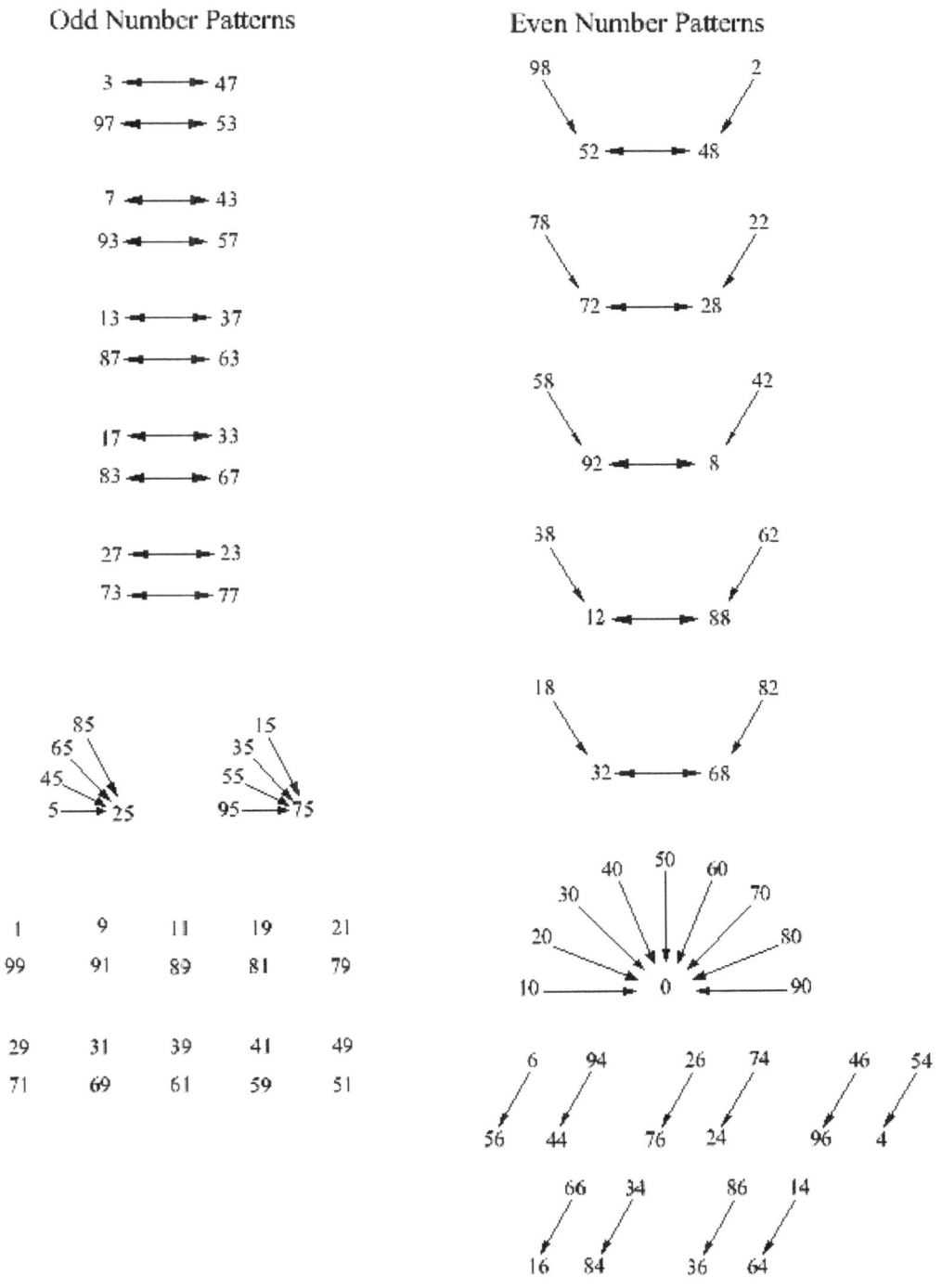

Odd Number Patterns

Even Number Patterns

Attractors: 0, 1, 4, 9, 11, 16, 19, 21, 24, 25, 29, 31, 36, 39, 41, 44, 49, 51, 56, 59, 61, 64, 69, 71, 75, 76, 79, 81, 84, 89, 91, 96, 99
Two sets are required to pair the numbers to 100.

This diagram lists the numbers 0 thru 99 raised to the 12th power, and then looks at the two right-most digits as the next number in the network.

Odd Number Patterns

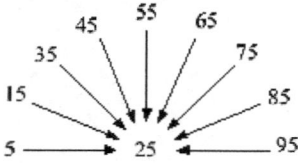

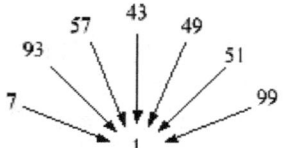

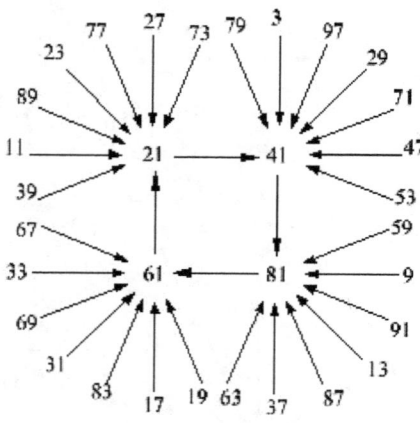

Even Number Patterns

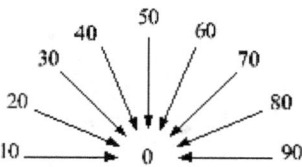

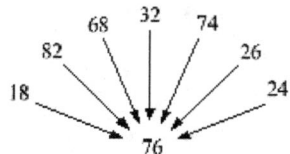

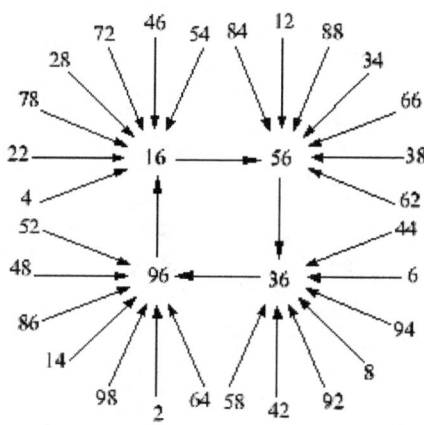

Attractors: 0, 1, 25, 76
Pairs add to 100 within their own patterns.
Even and Odd patterns are identical.

This diagram lists the numbers 0 thru 99 raised to the 13th power, and then looks at the two right-most digits as the next number in the network.

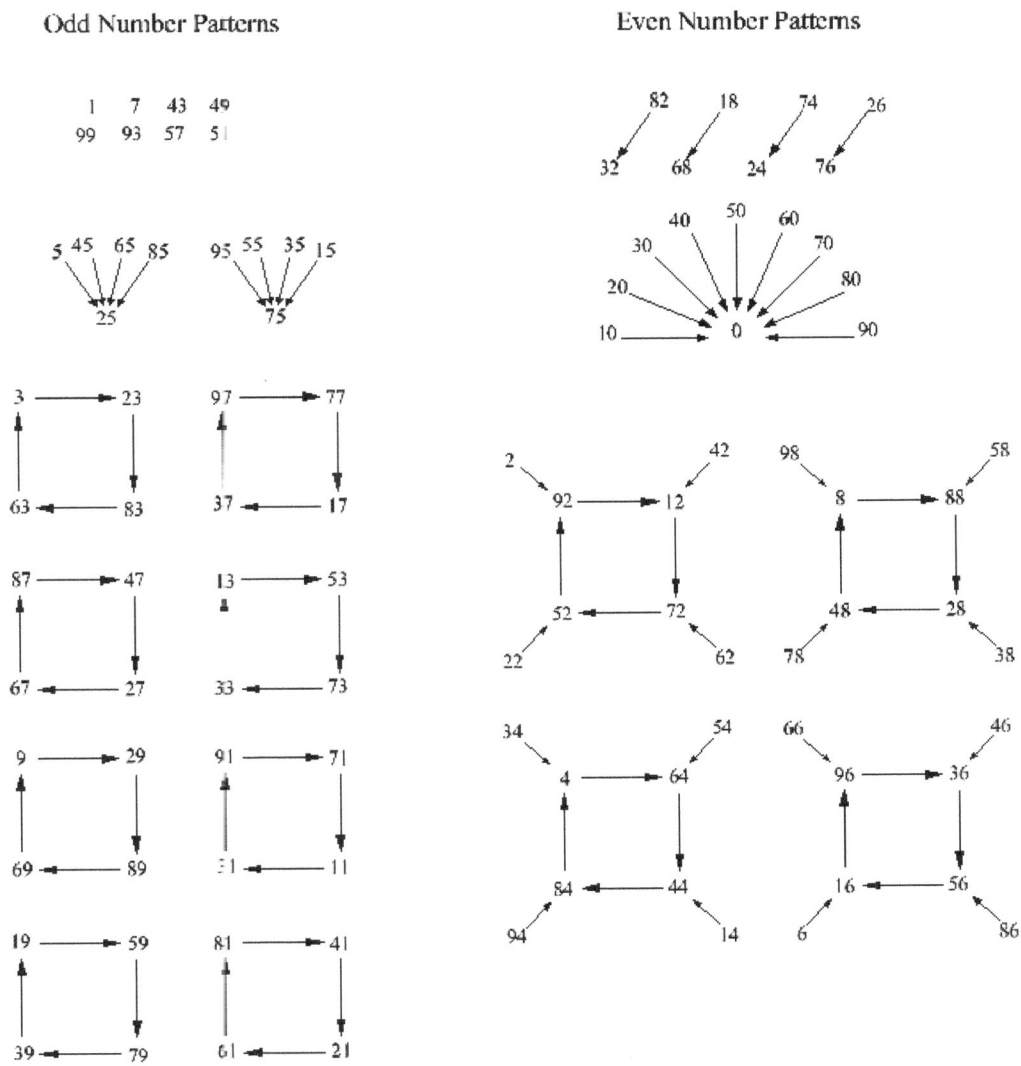

Odd Number Patterns

Even Number Patterns

Attractors: 0, 1, 7, 24, 25, 32, 43, 49, 51, 57, 68, 75, 76, 93, 99
Pairs add to 100; however,
Two sets are required to pair the numbers.

429

This diagram lists the numbers 0 thru 99 raised to the 14th power, and then looks at the two right-most digits as the next number in the network.

Odd Number Patterns   Even Number Patterns

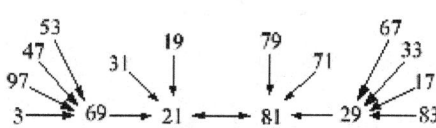

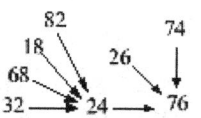

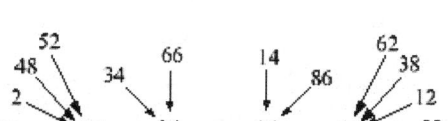

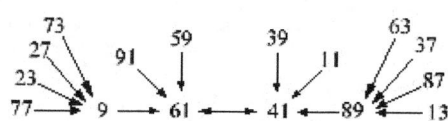

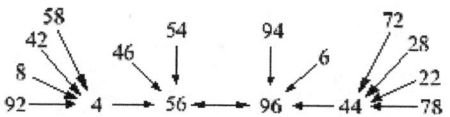

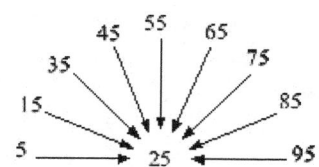

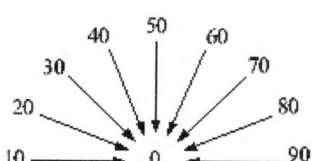

Attractors: 0, 1, 25, 76

Pairs add to 100 (Note differences between odd and even patterns)

This diagram lists the numbers 0 thru 99 raised to the 15th power, and then looks at the two right-most digits as the next number in the network.

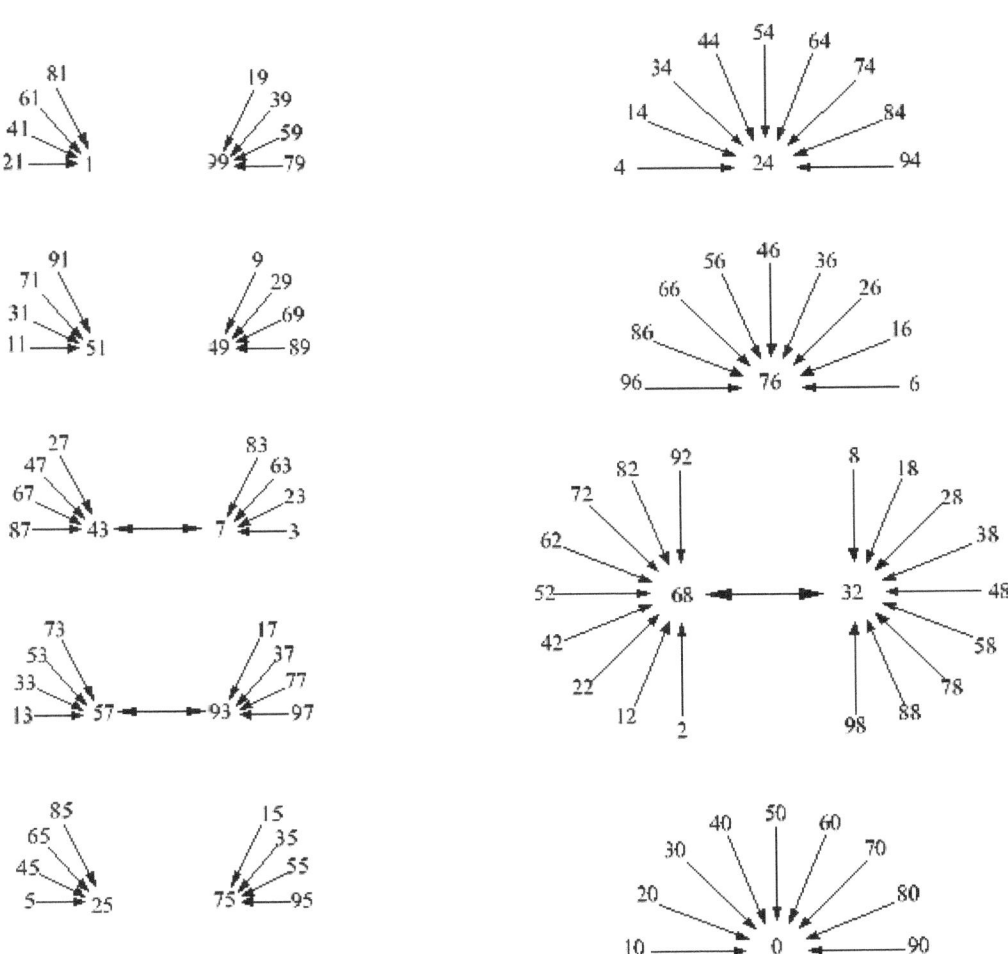

Odd Number Patterns   Even Number Patterns

Attractors: 0, 1, 24, 25, 49, 51, 75, 76, 99
Two patterns required for pairs to add to 100

431

This diagram lists the numbers 0 thru 99 raised to the 16th power, and then looks at the two right-most digits as the next number in the network.

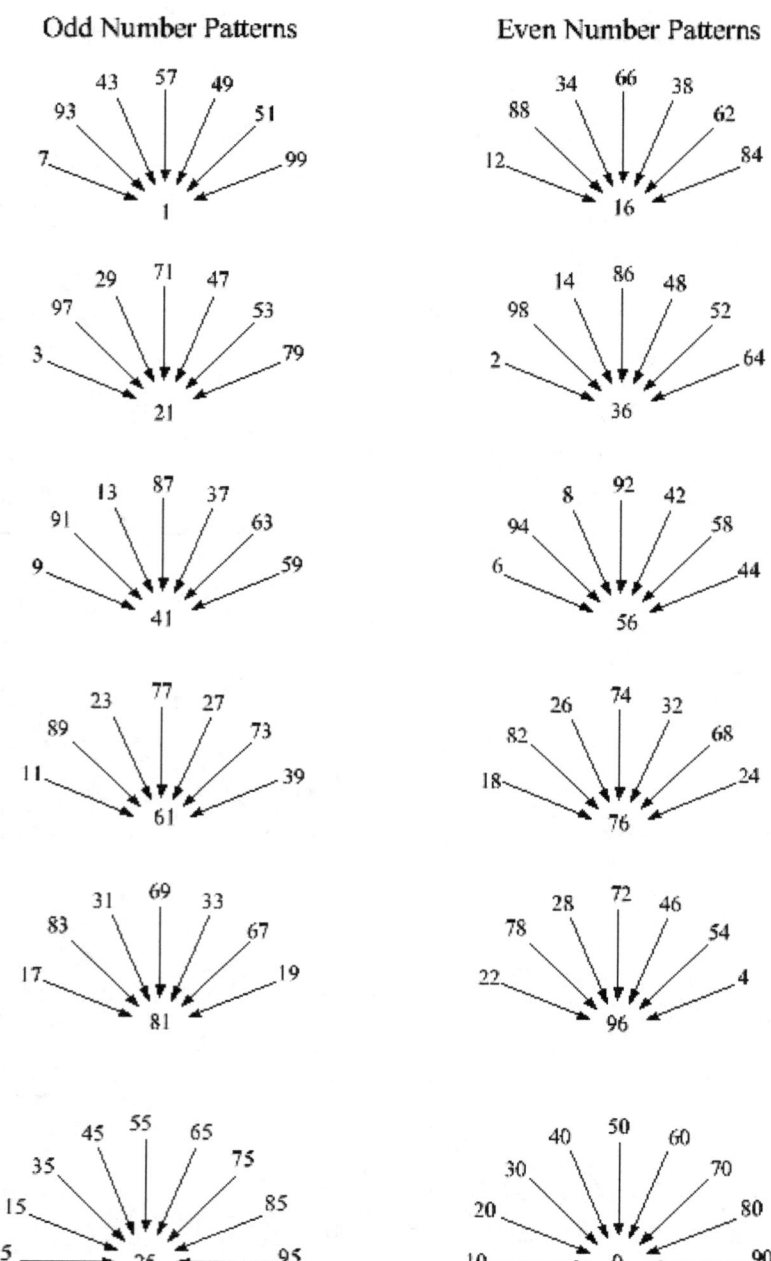

Odd Number Patterns   Even Number Patterns

Attractors: 0, 1, 16, 21, 25, 36, 41, 56, 61, 76, 81, 96
Pairs add to 100, odd and even patterns are identical.

This diagram lists the numbers 0 thru 99 raised to the 17th power, and then looks at the two right-most digits as the next number in the network.

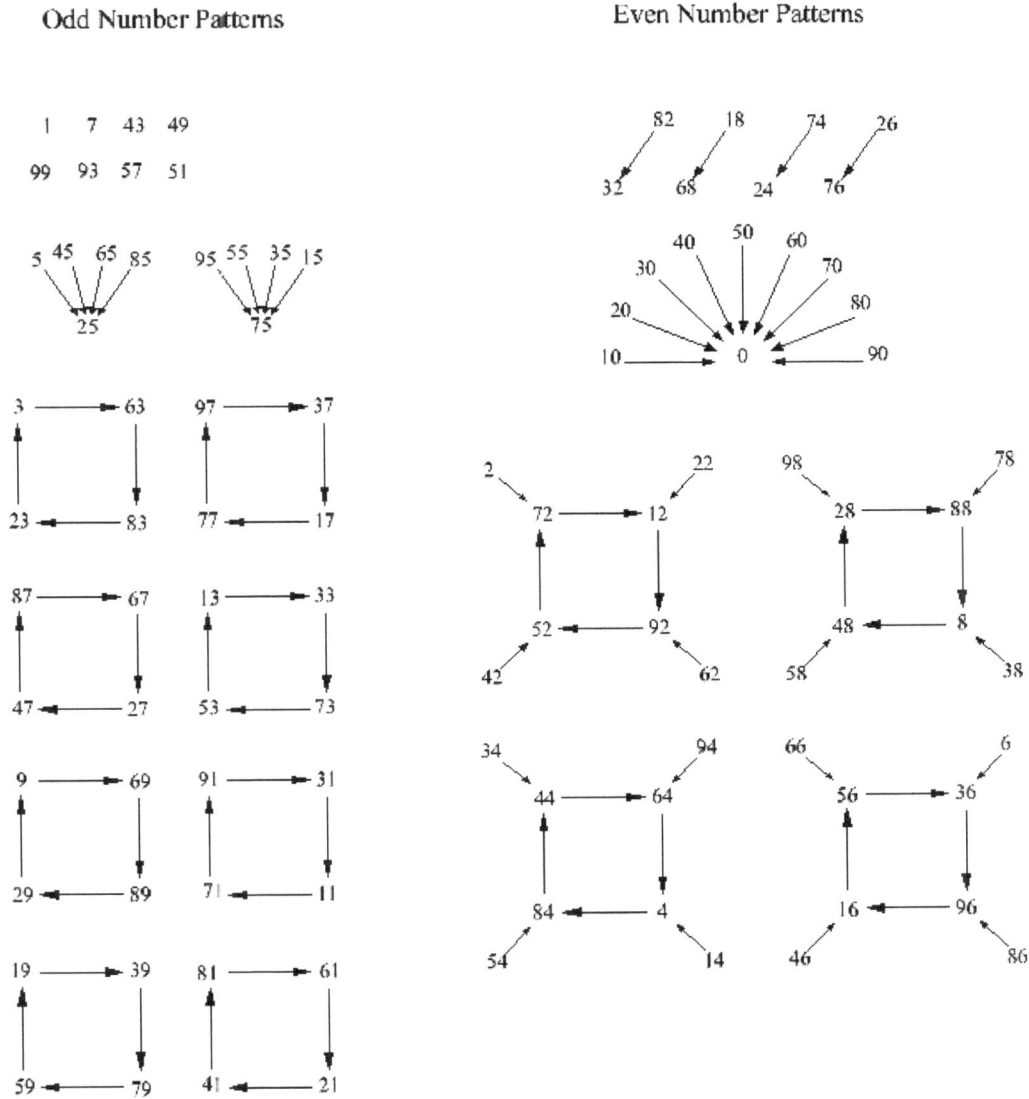

Odd Number Patterns

Even Number Patterns

Attractors: 0, 1, 7, 24, 25, 32, 43, 49, 51, 57, 68, 75, 76, 93, 99
Pairs add to 100
Two sets are required to pair numbers.

433

This diagram lists the numbers 0 thru 99 raised to the 18th power, and then looks at the two right-most digits as the next number in the network.

Odd Number Patterns   Even Number Patterns

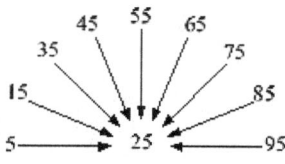

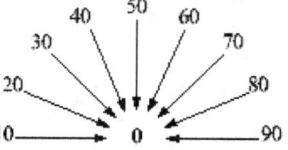

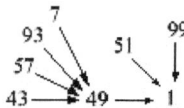

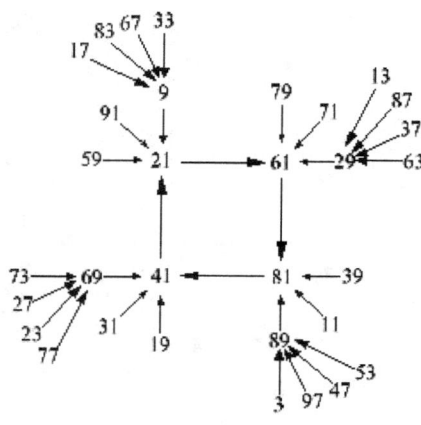

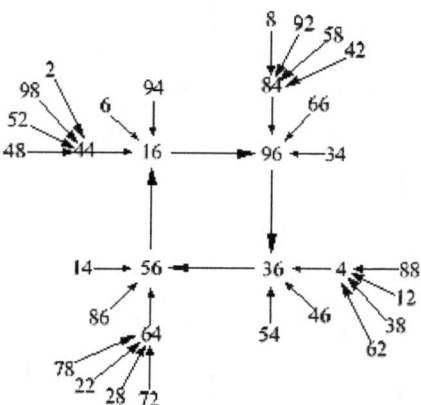

Attractors: 0, 1, 25, 76
Pairs add to 100, odd and even patterns are different.

This diagram lists the numbers 0 thru 99 raised to the 19th power, and then looks at the two right-most digits as the next number in the network.

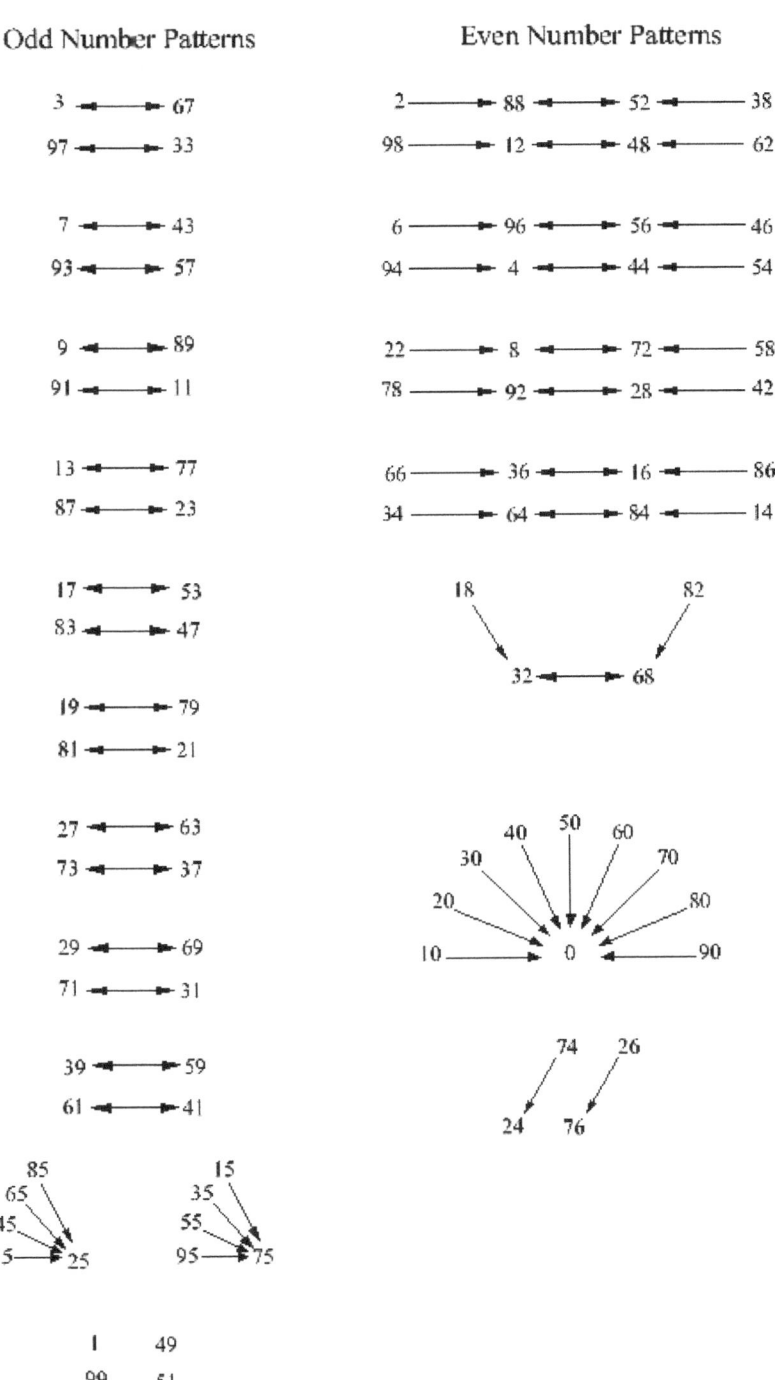

Odd Number Patterns

3 ← → 67
97 ← → 33

7 ← → 43
93 ← → 57

9 ← → 89
91 ← → 11

13 ← → 77
87 ← → 23

17 ← → 53
83 ← → 47

19 ← → 79
81 ← → 21

27 ← → 63
73 ← → 37

29 ← → 69
71 ← → 31

39 ← → 59
61 ← → 41

85
65
45
5 → 25

15
35
55
95 → 75

1   49
99   51

Even Number Patterns

2 → 88 ← → 52 ← → 38
98 → 12 ← → 48 ← → 62

6 → 96 ← → 56 ← → 46
94 → 4 ← → 44 ← → 54

22 → 8 ← → 72 ← → 58
78 → 92 ← → 28 ← → 42

66 → 36 ← → 16 ← → 86
34 → 64 ← → 84 ← → 14

18   82
32 ← → 68

40 50 60
30   70
20   80
10 → 0 ← 90

74   26
24   76

Attractors: 0, 1, 24, 25, 49, 51, 75, 76, 99
Pairs from two patterns add to 100

This diagram lists the numbers 0 thru 99 raised to the 20th power, and then looks at the two right-most digits as the next number in the network.

Odd Number Patterns

Even Number Patterns

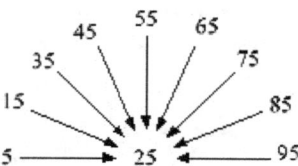

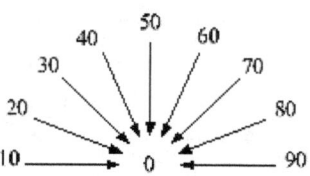

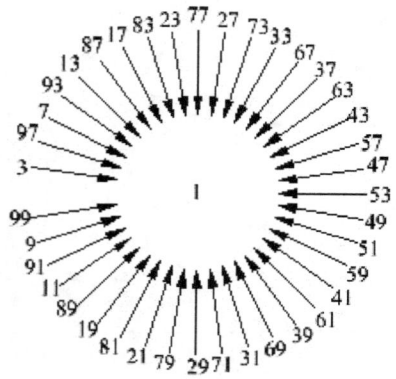

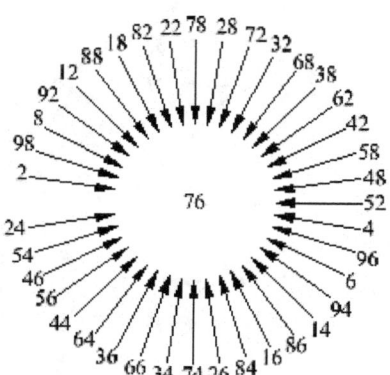

Attractors: 0, 1, 25, 76

Pairs add to 100, odd and even patterns are identical.

This diagram lists the numbers 0 thru 99 raised to the 21st power, and then looks at the two right-most digits as the next number in the network.

Odd Number Patterns

1	3	7	9
99	97	93	91

11	13	17	19
89	87	83	81

21	23	27	29
79	77	73	71

31	33	37	39
69	67	63	61

41	43	47	49
59	57	53	51

Even Number Patterns

Attractors: 0, 1, 3, 4, 7, 8, 9, 11, 12, 13, 16, 17, 19, 21, 23, 24, 25, 27, 28, 29, 31, 32, 33, 36, 37, 39, 41, 43, 44, 47, 48, 49, 51, 52, 53, 56, 57, 59, 61, 63, 64, 67, 68, 69, 71, 72, 73, 75, 76, 77, 79, 81, 83, 84, 87, 88, 89, 91, 92, 93, 96, 97, 99

Pairs add to 100, two patterns are required.

Appendix 16
Automorphic Numbers for Even Bases 22 through 30

All bases have 0 and 1 as automorphic numbers; however, bases that are a prime number or some power of a prime number only have 0 and 1 as their automorphic numbers. Therefore, we won't need a table to show that bases 23, 25, 27, and 29 have 0 and 1 as their automorphic numbers. The following tables show the automorphic numbers for bases 22, 24, 26, 28, and 30 where the number of digits ranges from 1 to 6 digits in their respective bases.

The following is a brief listing of the base 22 automorphic numbers (in base 22):

Number of Digits	The b Number	The c Number	Sum of b and c Numbers
1	b_{22}	c_{22}	11_{22}
2	$5b_{22}$	gc_{22}	101_{22}
3	$85b_{22}$	dgc_{22}	1001_{22}
4	$185b_{22}$	$kdgc_{22}$	10001_{22}
5	$d185b_{22}$	$8kdgc_{22}$	100001_{22}
6	$8d185b_{22}$	$d8kdgc_{22}$	1000001_{22}

The following is a brief listing of the base 24 automorphic numbers (in base 24):

Number of Digits	The 9 Number	The g Number	Sum of 9 and g Numbers
1	9_{24}	g_{24}	11_{24}
2	$L9_{24}$	$2g_{24}$	101_{24}
3	$0L9_{24}$	$n2g_{24}$	1001_{24}
4	$d0L9_{24}$	$an2g_{24}$	10001_{24}
5	$4d0L9_{24}$	$jan2g_{24}$	100001_{24}
6	$e4d0L9_{24}$	$9jan2g_{24}$	1000001_{24}

The following is a brief listing of the base 26 automorphic numbers (in base 26):

Number of Digits	The d Number	The e Number	Sum of d and e Numbers
1	d_{26}	e_{26}	11_{26}
2	$6d_{26}$	je_{26}	101_{26}
3	$g6d_{26}$	$9je_{26}$	1001_{26}
4	$1g6d_{26}$	$o9je_{26}$	10001_{26}
5	$h1g6d_{26}$	$8o9je_{26}$	100001_{26}
6	$3h1g6d_{26}$	$m8o9je_{26}$	1000001_{26}

438

The following is a brief listing of the base 28 automorphic numbers (in base 28):

Number of Digits	The 8 Number	The L Number	Sum of 8 and L Numbers
1	8_{28}	L_{28}	11_{28}
2	$q8_{28}$	$1L_{28}$	101_{28}
3	$aq8_{28}$	$h1L_{28}$	1001_{28}
4	$aaq8_{28}$	$hh1L_{28}$	10001_{28}
5	$daaq8_{28}$	$ehh1L_{28}$	100001_{28}
6	$idaaq8_{28}$	$9ehh1L_{28}$	1000001_{28}

Base 30 has six automorphic numbers in addition to 0 and 1. The following is a brief listing in base 30 of the automorphic numbers (each of the three tables show a pair of automorphic numbers):

Number of Digits	The 6 Number	The p Number	Sum of 6 and p Numbers
1	6_{30}	p_{30}	11_{30}
2	$j6_{30}$	ap_{30}	101_{30}
3	$2j6_{30}$	rap_{30}	1001_{30}
4	$b2j6_{30}$	$irap_{30}$	10001_{30}
5	$Lb2j6_{30}$	$8irap_{30}$	100001_{30}
6	$6Lb2j6_{30}$	$n8irap_{30}$	1000001_{30}

Number of Digits	The a Number	The L Number	Sum of a and L Numbers
1	a_{30}	L_{30}	11_{30}
2	$3a_{30}$	qL_{30}	101_{30}
3	$13a_{30}$	sqL_{30}	1001_{30}
4	$h13a_{30}$	$csqL_{30}$	10001_{30}
5	$oh13a_{30}$	$5csqL_{30}$	100001_{30}
6	$7oh13a_{30}$	$m5csqL_{30}$	1000001_{30}

Number of Digits	The f Number	The g Number	Sum of f and g Numbers
1	f_{30}	g_{30}	11_{30}
2	$7f_{30}$	mg_{30}	101_{30}
3	$q7f_{30}$	$3mg_{30}$	1001_{30}
4	$1q7f_{30}$	$s3mg_{30}$	10001_{30}
5	$e1q7f_{30}$	$fs3mg_{30}$	100001_{30}
6	$fe1q7f_{30}$	$efs3mg_{30}$	1000001_{30}

Appendix 17
Listing of Automorphic Numbers and Prime Factors

The following is a listing in base 10 of the numbers 6 to 110, along with that number's automorphic numbers and prime factors. Prime numbers and numbers that are a power of a prime number only have 0 and 1 as their automorphic numbers, and therefore are excluded from this list.

Number	Automorphic Numbers	Prime Factors of the Number
6:	0, 1, 3, 4	2, 3
10:	0, 1, 5, 6	2, 5
12:	0, 1, 4, 9	2^2, 3
14:	0, 1, 7, 8	2, 7
15:	0, 1, 6, 10	3, 5
18:	0, 1, 9, 10	2, 3^2
20:	0, 1, 5, 16	2^2, 5
21:	0, 1, 7, 15	3, 7
22:	0, 1, 11, 12	2, 11
24:	0, 1, 9, 16	2^3, 3
26:	0, 1, 13, 14	2, 13
28:	0, 1, 8, 21	2^2, 7
30:	0, 1, 6, 10, 15, 16, 21, 25	2, 3, 5
33:	0, 1, 12, 22	3, 11
34:	0, 1, 17, 18	2, 17
35:	0, 1, 15, 21	5, 7
36:	0, 1, 9, 28	2^2, 3^2
38:	0, 1, 19, 20	2, 19
39:	0, 1, 13, 27	3, 13
40:	0, 1, 16, 25	2^3, 5
42:	0, 1, 7, 15, 21, 22, 28, 36	2, 3, 7
44:	0, 1, 12, 33	2^2, 11
45:	0, 1, 10, 36	3^2, 5
46:	0, 1, 23, 24	2, 23
48:	0, 1, 16, 33	2^4, 3
50:	0, 1, 25, 26	2, 5^2
51:	0, 1, 18, 34	3, 17
52:	0, 1, 13, 40	2^2, 13
54:	0, 1, 27, 28	2, 3^3
55:	0, 1, 11, 45	5, 11
56:	0, 1, 8, 49	2^3, 7
57:	0, 1, 19, 39	3, 19
58:	0, 1, 29, 30	2, 29

Number	Automorphic Numbers	Prime Factors of the Number
60:	0, 1, 16, 21, 25, 36, 40, 45	2^2, 3, 5
62:	0, 1, 31, 32	2, 13
63:	0, 1, 28, 36	3^2, 7
65:	0, 1, 26, 40	5, 13
66:	0, 1, 12, 22, 33, 34, 45, 55	2, 3, 11
68:	0, 1, 17, 52	2^2, 17
69:	0, 1, 24, 46	3, 23
70:	0, 1, 15, 21, 35, 36, 50, 56	2, 5, 7
72:	0, 1, 9, 64	2^3, 3^2
74:	0, 1, 37, 38	2, 37
75:	0, 1, 25, 51	3, 5^2
76:	0, 1, 20, 57	2^2, 19
77:	0, 1, 22, 56	7, 11
78:	0, 1, 13, 27, 39, 40, 52, 66	2, 3, 13
80:	0, 1, 16, 65	2^4, 5
82:	0, 1, 41, 42	2, 41
84:	0, 1, 21, 28, 36, 49, 57, 64	2^2, 3, 7
85:	0, 1, 35, 51	5, 17
86:	0, 1, 43, 44	2, 43
87:	0, 1, 30, 58	3, 29
88:	0, 1, 33, 56	2^3, 11
90:	0, 1, 10, 36, 45, 46, 55, 81	2, 3^2, 5
91:	0, 1, 14, 78	7, 13
92:	0, 1, 24, 69	2^2, 23
93:	0, 1, 31, 63	3, 31
94:	0, 1, 47, 48	2, 47
95:	0, 1, 20, 76	5, 19
96:	0, 1, 33, 64	2^5, 3
98:	0, 1, 49, 50	2, 7^2
99:	0, 1, 45, 55	3^2, 11
100:	0, 1, 25, 76	2^2, 5^2
102:	0, 1, 18, 34, 51, 52, 69, 85	2, 3, 17
104:	0, 1, 40, 65	2^3, 13
105:	0, 1, 15, 21, 36, 70, 85, 91	3, 5, 7
106:	0, 1, 53, 54	2, 53
108:	0, 1, 28, 81	2^2, 3^3
110:	0, 1, 11, 45, 55, 56, 66, 100	2, 5, 11

Appendix 18
Table Showing the Counts of Numbers that Feed the 1 Attractor for Bases 2 thru 32, and Digit Counts from 2 to 10

This is a more extensive table of the one found at the end of chapter 20. This table shows the count of numbers that when squared repeatedly, will feed into the number 1. The number of digits is listed along the top of the table, the base is listed along the left side of the table.

Digits / Base	2	3	4	5	6	7	8	9	10
2	2	4	8	16	32	64	128	256	512
3	2	2	2	2	2	2	2	2	2
4	8	32	128	512	2048	8192	$\frac{1}{2}(4^8)$	$\frac{1}{2}(4^9)$	$\frac{1}{2}(4^{10})$
5	4	4	4	4	4	4	4	4	4
6	4	8	16	32	64	128	256	512	1024
7	2	2	2	2	2	2	2	2	2
8	32	256	2048	16384	$\frac{1}{2}(8^6)$	$\frac{1}{2}(8^7)$	$\frac{1}{2}(8^8)$	$\frac{1}{2}(8^9)$	$\frac{1}{2}(8^{10})$
9	2	2	2	2	2	2	2	2	2
10	8	16	32	64	128	256	512	1024	2048
11	2	2	2	2	2	2	2	2	2
12	16	64	256	1024	4096	16384	2^{16}	2^{18}	2^{20}
13	4	4	4	4	4	4	4	4	4
14	4	8	16	32	64	128	256	512	1024
15	8	8	8	8	8	8	8	8	8
16	128	2048	32768	$\frac{1}{2}(16^5)$	$\frac{1}{2}(16^6)$	$\frac{1}{2}(16^7)$	$\frac{1}{2}(16^8)$	$\frac{1}{2}(16^9)$	$\frac{1}{2}(16^{10})$
17	16	16	16	16	16	16	16	16	16
18	4	8	16	32	64	128	256	512	1024
19	2	2	2	2	2	2	2	2	2
20	32	128	512	2048	8192	32768	2^{17}	2^{19}	2^{21}
21	4	4	4	4	4	4	4	4	4
22	4	8	16	32	64	128	256	512	1024
23	2	2	2	2	2	2	2	2	2
24	64	512	4096	32768	2^{18}	2^{21}	2^{24}	2^{27}	2^{30}
25	4	4	4	4	4	4	4	4	4
26	8	16	32	64	128	256	512	1024	2048
27	2	2	2	2	2	2	2	2	2
28	16	64	256	1024	4096	16384	65536	2^{18}	2^{20}
29	4	4	4	4	4	4	4	4	4
30	16	32	64	128	256	512	1024	2048	4096
31	2	2	2	2	2	2	2	2	2
32	512	16384	$\frac{1}{2}(32^4)$	$\frac{1}{2}(32^5)$	$\frac{1}{2}(32^6)$	$\frac{1}{2}(32^7)$	$\frac{1}{2}(32^8)$	$\frac{1}{2}(32^9)$	$\frac{1}{2}(32^{10})$

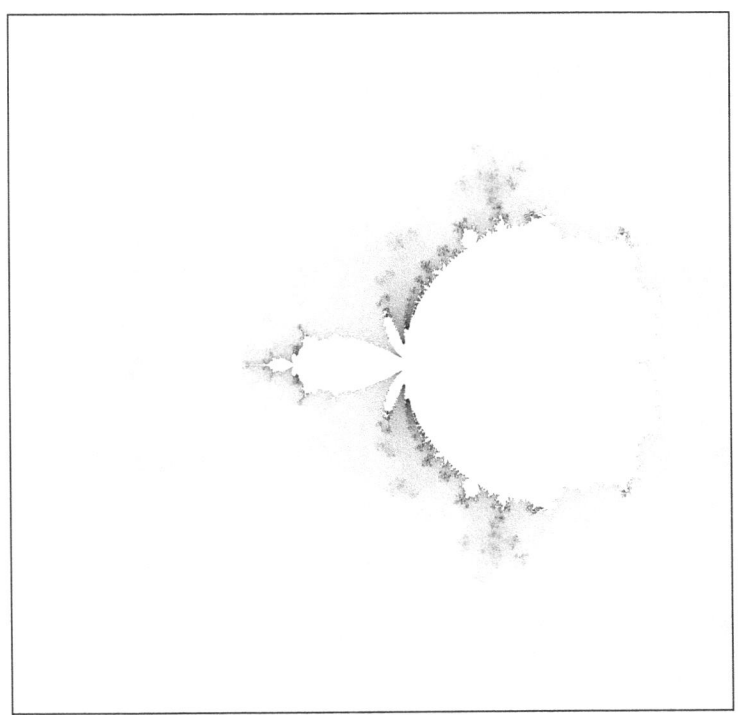

Standard and polarity diagrams of the $Z_{n+1} = Z_n^2 + Z_n + C$ Mandelbrot Fractal.

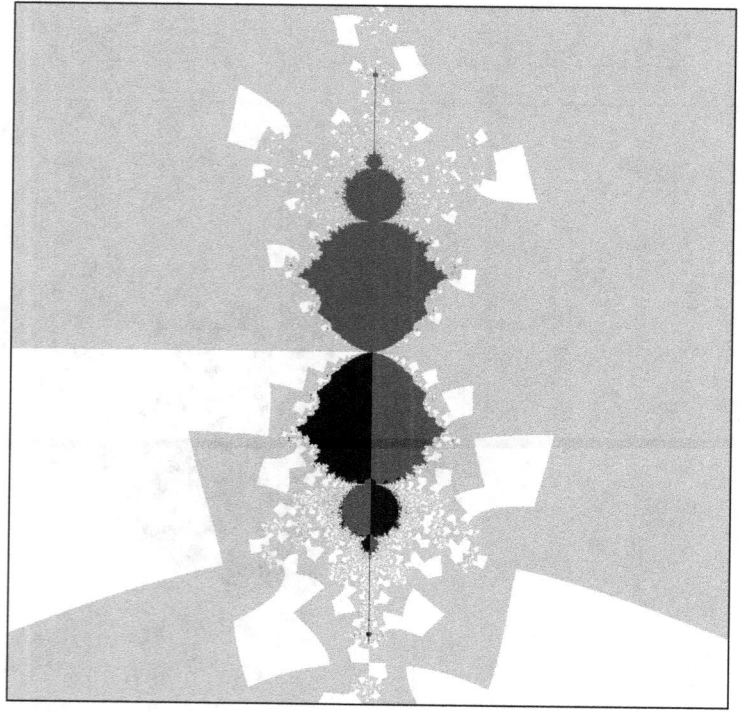

Standard and polarity diagrams of the $Z_{n+1} = Z_n^3 + Z_n + C$ Mandelbrot Fractal.

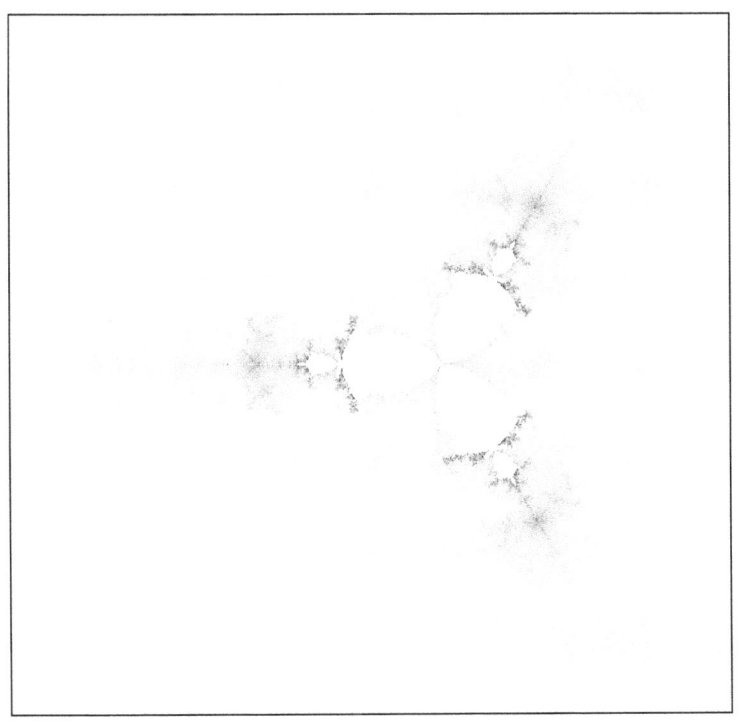

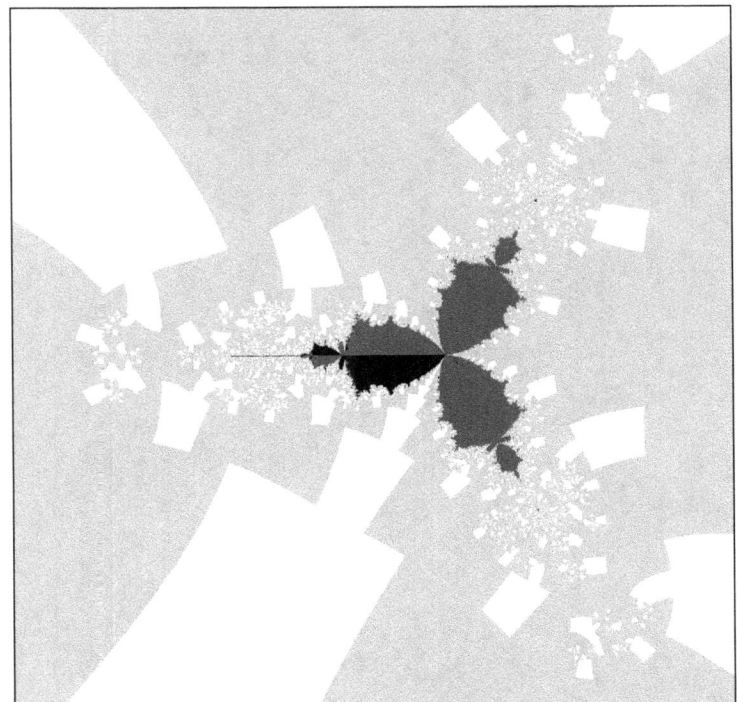

Standard and polarity diagrams of the $Z_{n+1} = Z_n^4 + Z_n + C$ Mandelbrot Fractal.

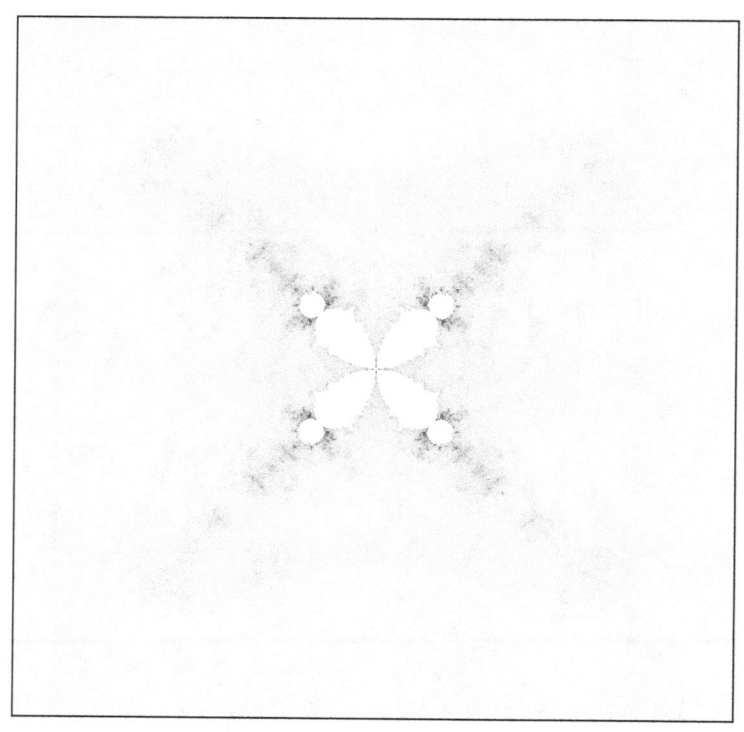

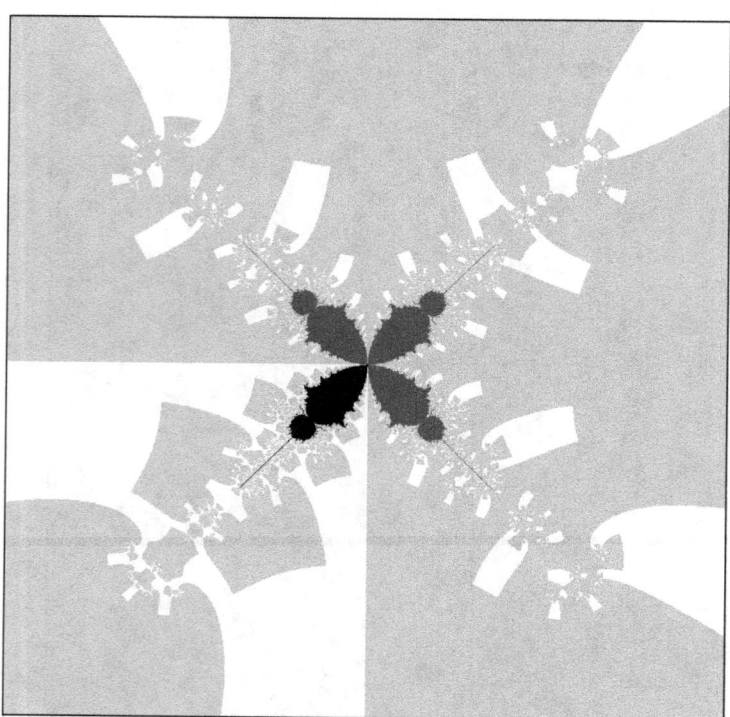

Standard and polarity diagrams of the $Z_{n+1} = Z_n^5 + Z_n + C$ Mandelbrot Fractal.

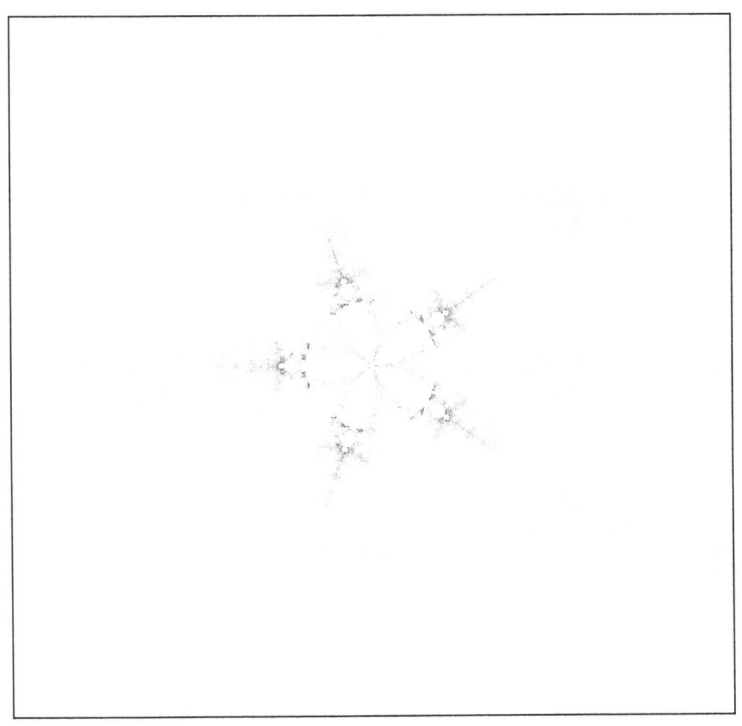

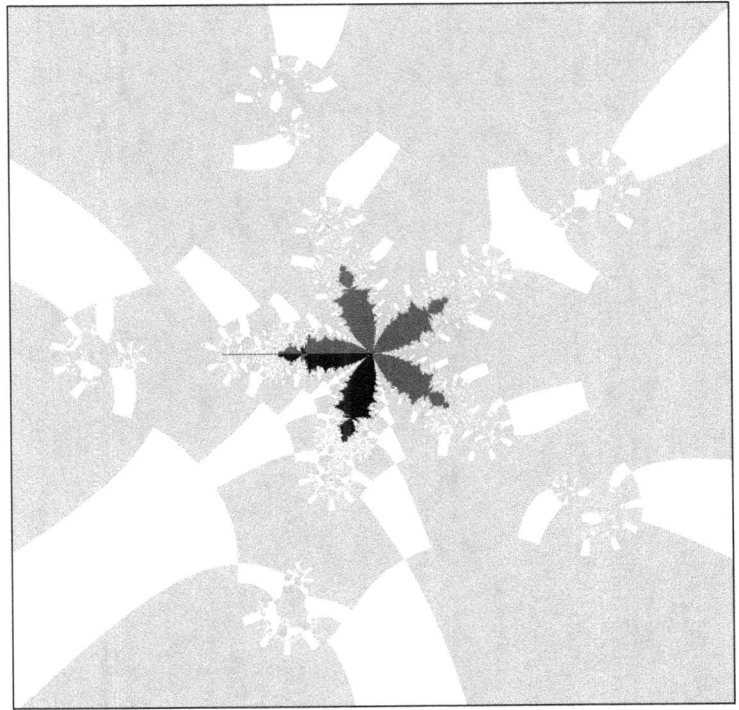

Standard and polarity diagrams of the $Z_{n+1} = Z_n^6 + Z_n + C$ Mandelbrot Fractal.

Standard and polarity diagrams of the $Z_{n+1} = Z_n^7 + Z_n + C$ Mandelbrot Fractal.

Appendix 20
Selected Lindenmayer Systems (L-Systems)

Rule 1:   Start with A – A – A
Rule 2:   For each iteration, make the following replacements
            A = A – A + A + A – A – A + A

Turn Rules: + = 120° left turn
                     – = 120° right turn

Space Rules: > = go forward one length (without drawing a line)
                     < = go backward one length (without drawing a line)

449

Rule 1:   Start with A + A + A + A
Rule 2:   For each iteration, make the following replacements
             A = AA + A + A + AA + AA + A – A

Turn Rules: + = 90° left turn
                     – = 90° right turn

Space Rules: > = go forward one length (without drawing a line)
                     < = go backward one length (without drawing a line)

450

Rule 1:   Start with A – A – A – A – A – A
Rule 2:   For each iteration, make the following replacements
            A = A + + A A – – A A – – A A + + A

Turn Rules: + = 60° left turn
                     – = 60° right turn

Space Rules: > = go forward one length (without drawing a line)
                     < = go backward one length (without drawing a line)

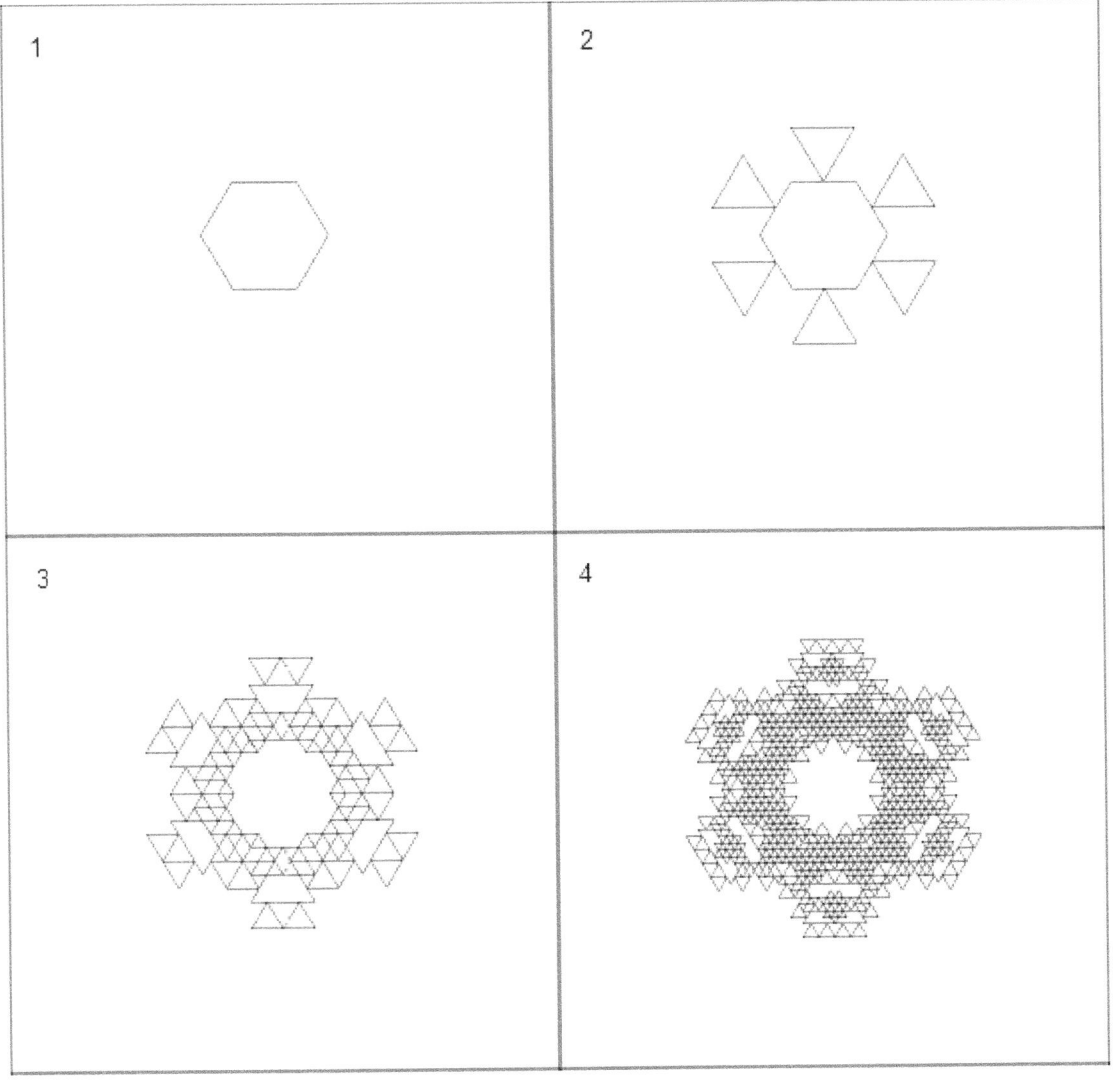

Rule 1:   Start with A + A + A + A + A — — — A + A + A + A + A — — — A + A + A +
           A + A — — — A + A + A + A + A — — — A + A + A + A

Rule 2:   For each iteration, make the following replacements
           A = A — — A + A + A — — A

Turn Rules: + = 72° left turn
                   — = 72° right turn

Space Rules: > = go forward one length (without drawing a line)
                   < = go backward one length (without drawing a line)

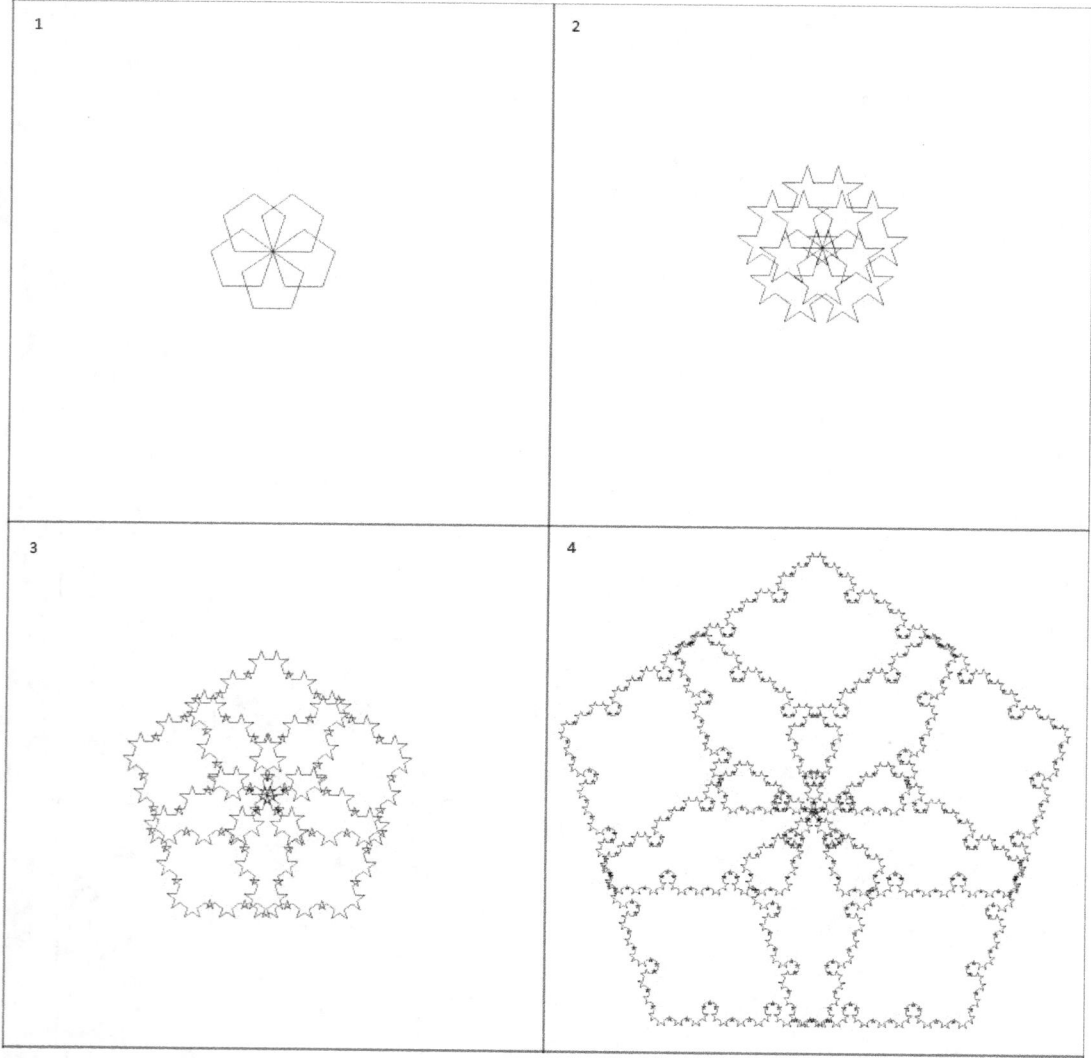

452

Rule 1:   Start with A – A – A – A – A – A
Rule 2:   For each iteration, make the following replacements
             A = A – A – – A + A + A + + + A – A – – A + A

Turn Rules: + = 60° left turn
                      – = 60° right turn

Space Rules: > = go forward one length (without drawing a line)
                      < = go backward one length (without drawing a line)

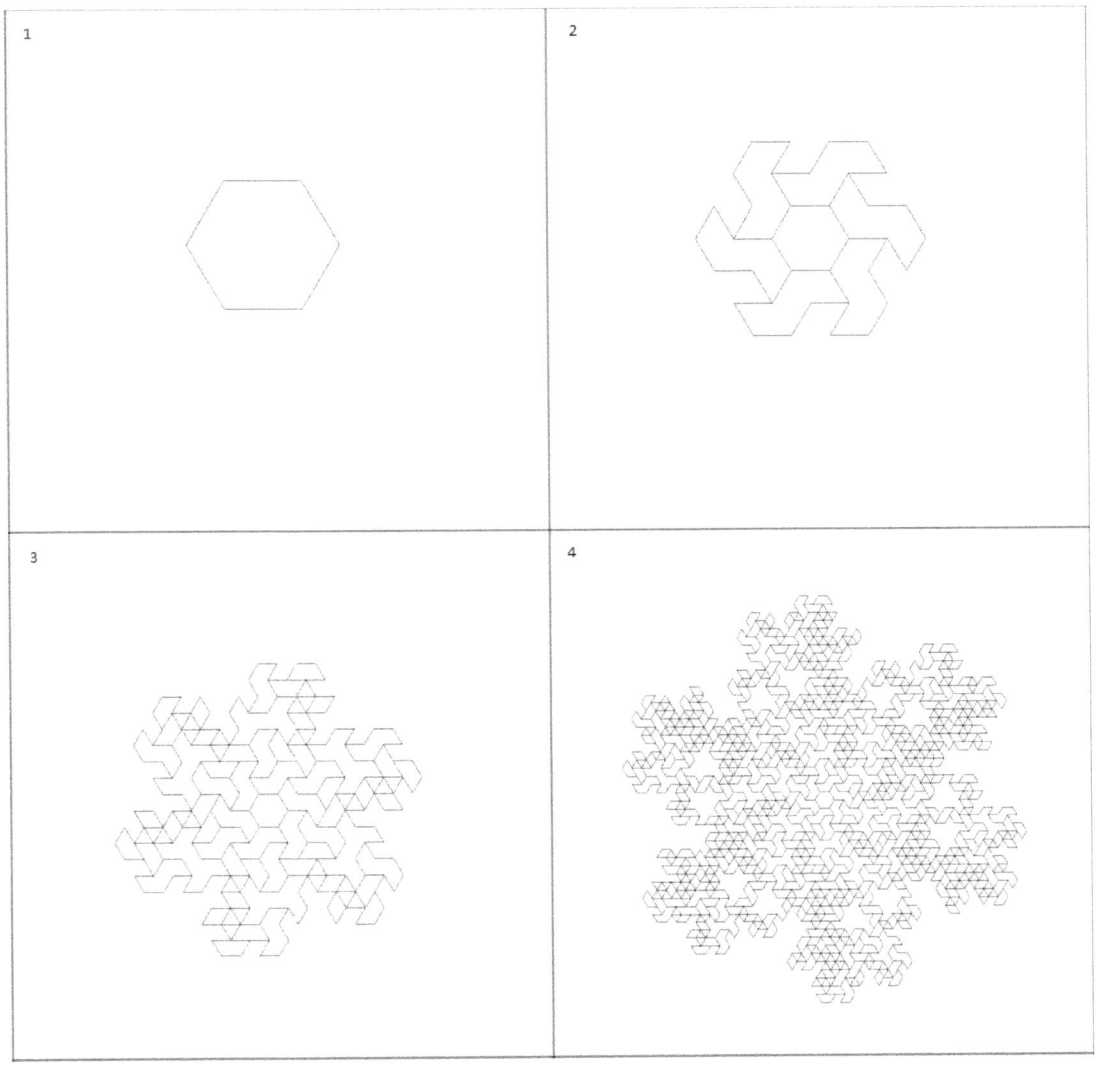

453

Rule 1:   Start with A – A – A – A – A – A – A – A
Rule 2:   For each iteration, make the following replacements
             A = A – – – A + < A + + < A + + A – – – A + A

Turn Rules: + = 45° left turn
                   – = 45° right turn

Space Rules: > = go forward one length (without drawing a line)
                   < = go backward one length (without drawing a line)

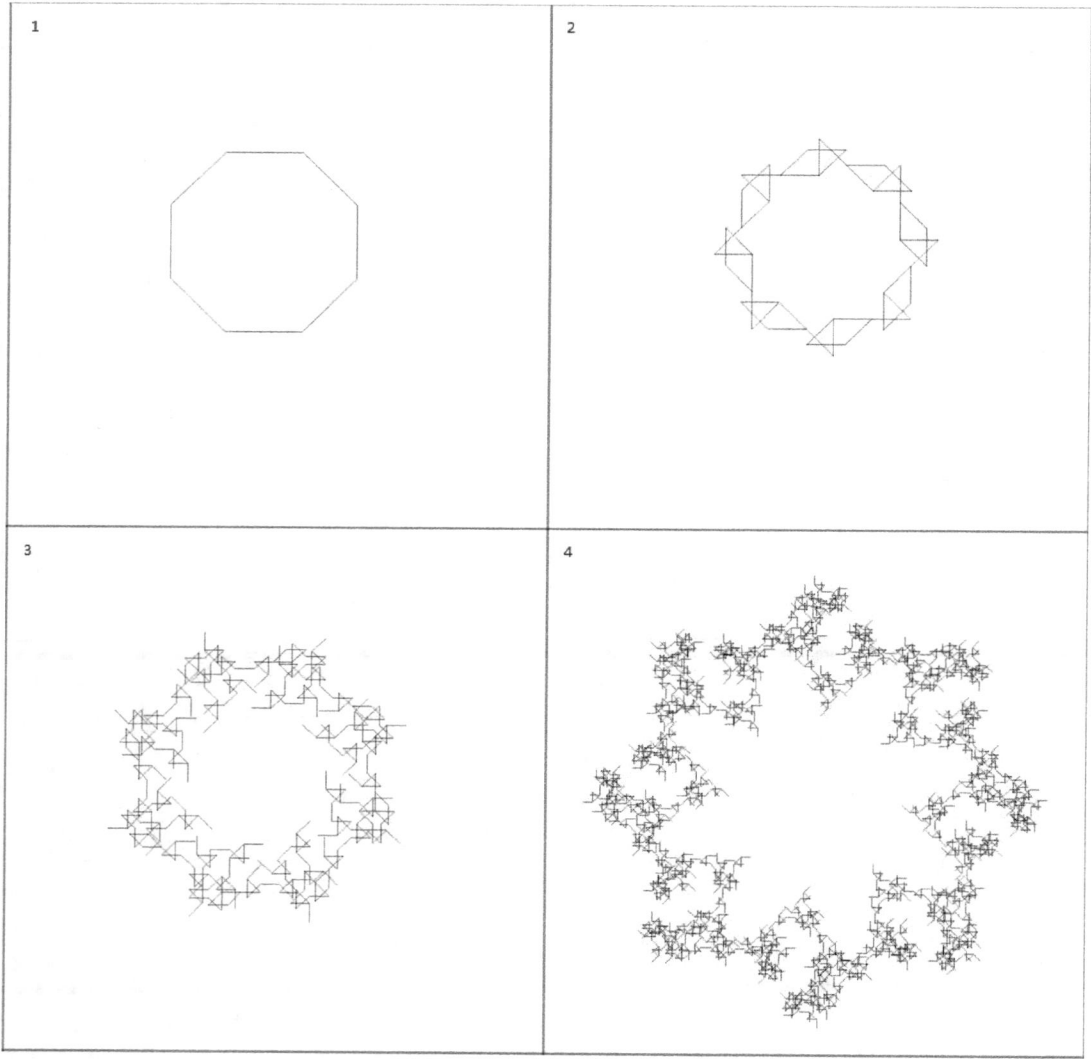

Rule 1:   Start with A – A – A – A – A – A – A – A
Rule 2:   For each iteration, make the following replacements
            A = A – – – A + + + AA + + + A – – – A

Turn Rules: + = 45° left turn
                   – = 45° right turn

Space Rules: > = go forward one length (without drawing a line)
                   < = go backward one length (without drawing a line)

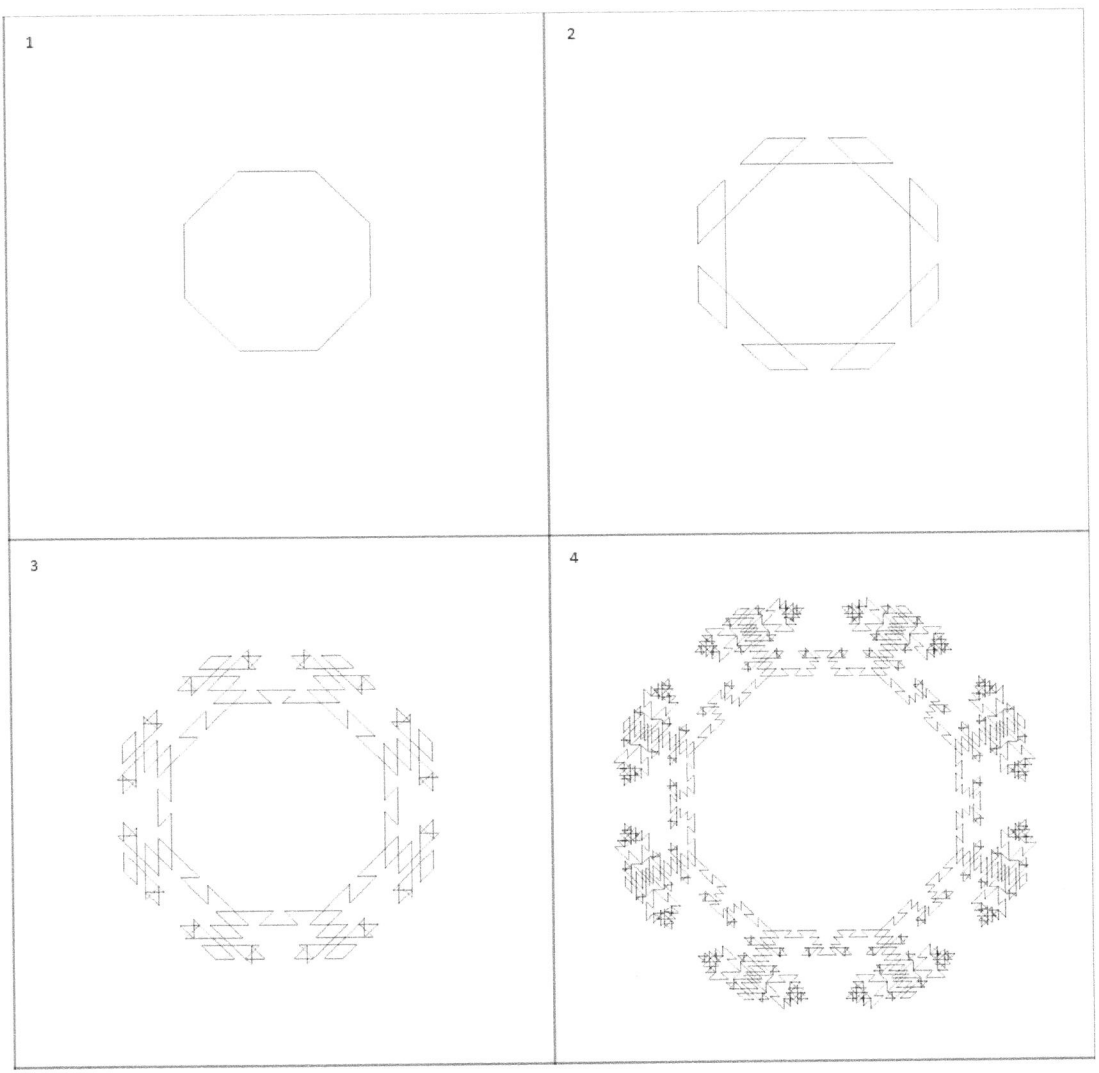

Rule 1:   Start with A − − A − − A − − A
Rule 2:   For each iteration, make the following replacements
           A = A − − − A + + + AA + + + A − − − A

Turn Rules: + = 45° left turn
                     − = 45° right turn

Space Rules: > = go forward one length (without drawing a line)
                     < = go backward one length (without drawing a line)

Rule 1:   Start with A – A – A – A
Rule 2:   For each iteration, make the following replacements
                   A = A + AA – BB – AA + A
                   B = AAA

Turn Rules: + = 90° left turn
                       – = 90° right turn

Space Rules: > = go forward one length (without drawing a line)
                       < = go backward one length (without drawing a line)

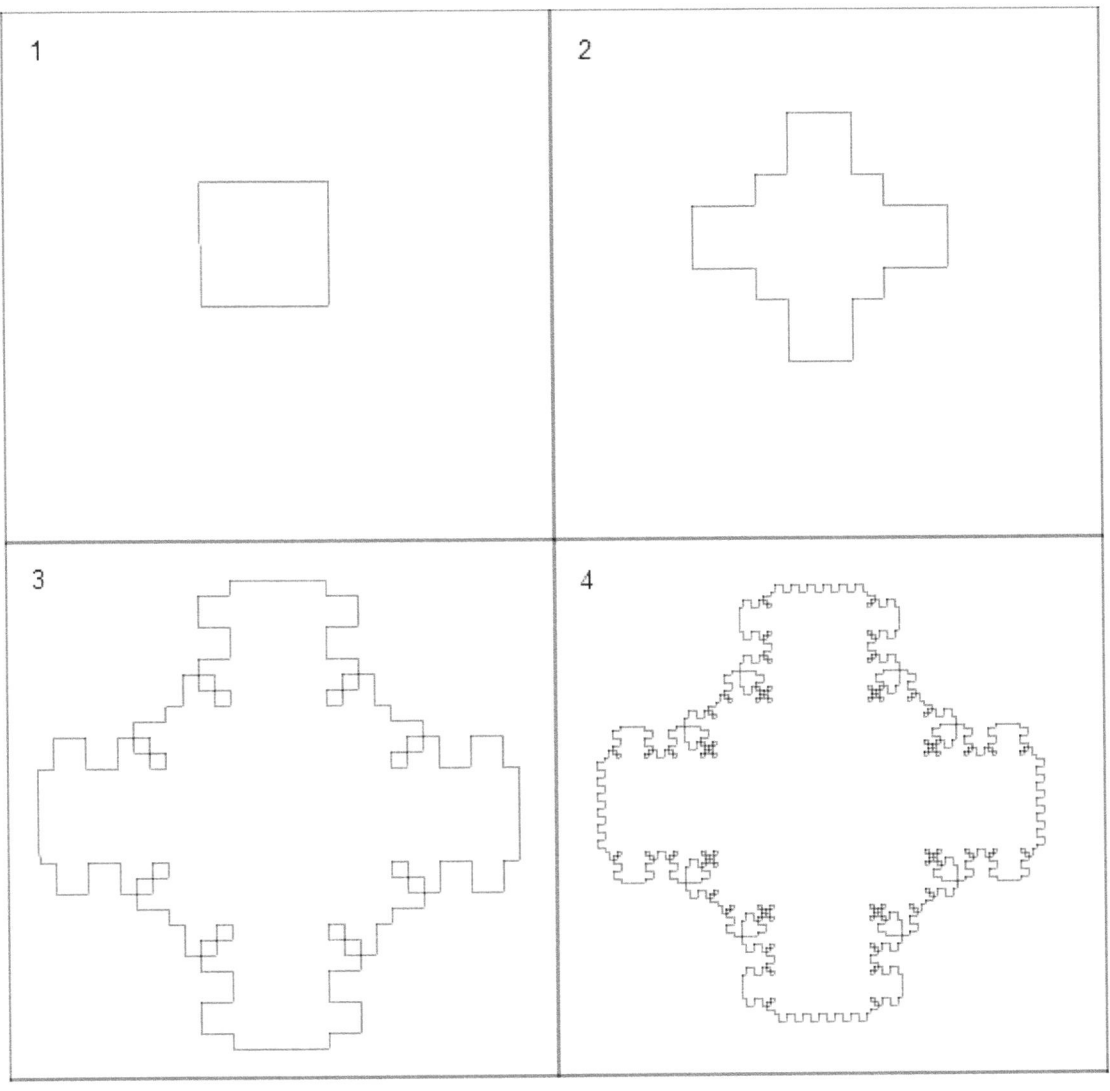

Rule 1:   Start with A – A – A – A – A – A – A – A
Rule 2:   For each iteration, make the following replacements
          A = B – B – A + A + A – B – B
          B = A + A + B – B – B + A + A

Turn Rules: + = 45° left turn
                   – = 45° right turn

Space Rules: > = go forward one length (without drawing a line)
                   < = go backward one length (without drawing a line)

Rule 1:   Start with A
Rule 2:   For each iteration, make the following replacements
             A = A – A < + A + A < – A < <

Turn Rules: + = 30° left turn
                     – = 30° right turn

Space Rules: > = go forward one length (without drawing a line)
                     < = go backward one length (without drawing a line)

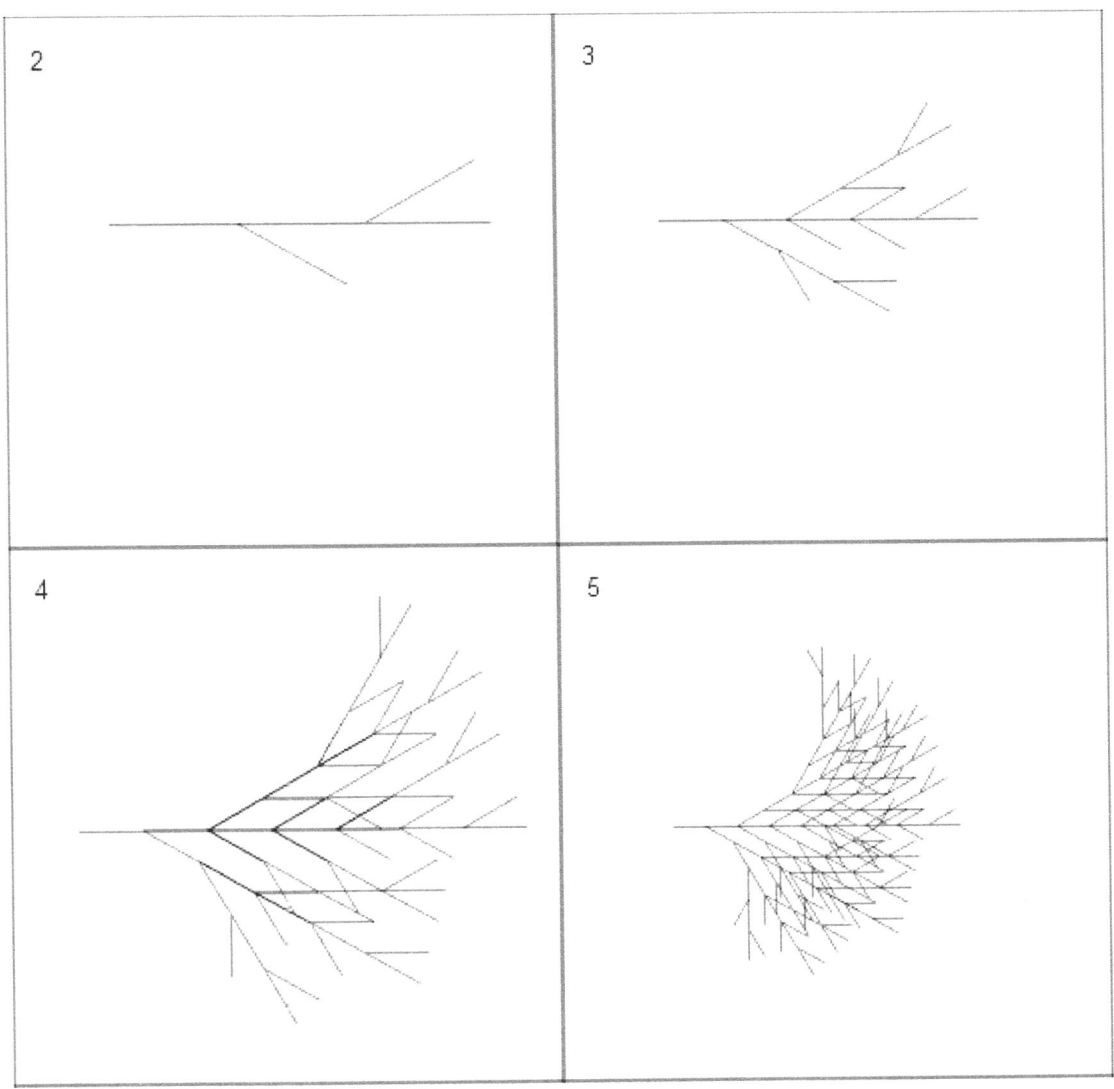

459

Rule 1:   Start with A
Rule 2:   For each iteration, make the following replacements
$$A = AB + AA << -- BB << + A <<$$
$$B = BA - BB << ++ AA << - B <<$$

Turn Rules: $+ = 45°$ left turn
    $- = 45°$ right turn

Space Rules: $> =$ go forward one length (without drawing a line)
    $< =$ go backward one length (without drawing a line)

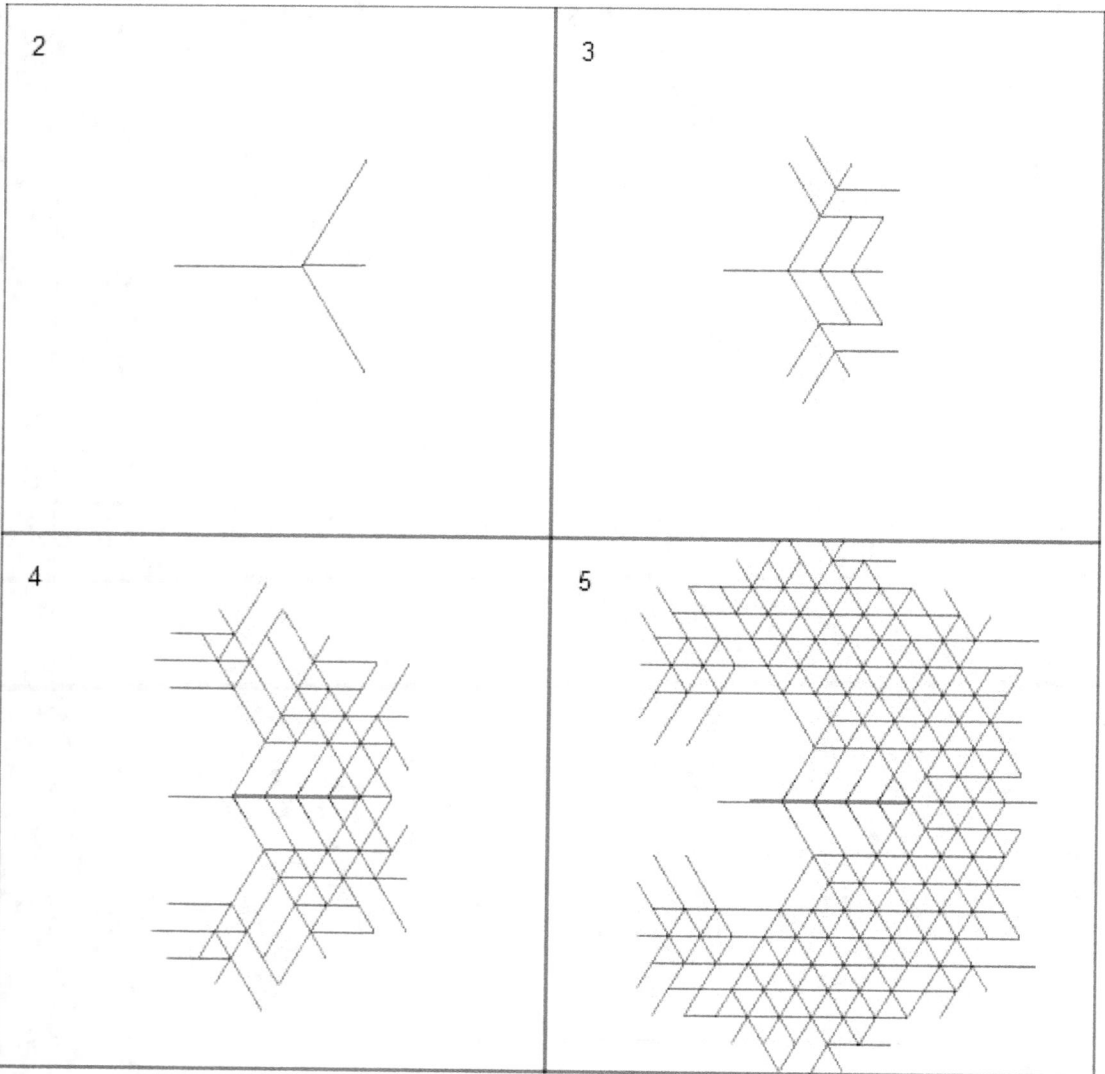

460

Additional Reading

Mathematical Recreations, by Maurice Kraitchik, Dover, 1953
(originally published in 1942 by W. W. Norton and Company)

Mathematics Magic and Mystery, by Martin Gardner, Dover, 1956

Recreations in the Theory of Numbers, by Albert H. Beiler, Dover, 1966

Mathematical Circus, by Martin Gardner, Vintage Books, 1968

The Unexpected Hanging, by Martin Gardner, Simon & Schuster, 1969

Gotcha, Paradoxes to Puzzle and Delight, by Martin Gardner, W. H. Freeman and Company, 1982

The Divine Proportion, H.E. Huntley, Dover, 1970

The Fractal Geometry of Nature, by Benoit B. Mandelbrot, W. H. Freeman and Company, 1977

Wheels, Life and Other Mathematical Amusements, by Martin Gardner, W. H. Freeman and Company, 1983

Dictionary of Curious and Interesting Numbers, by David Wells, Penguin Books, 1986

Time Travel, by Martin Gardner, W. H. Freeman and Company, 1988

Excursions in Number Theory, by C. Stanley Ogilvy and John T. Anderson, Dover, 1988

Exploring the Geometry of Nature, by Edward Rietman, Windcrest Books, 1989

The Joy of Mathematics by Theoni Pappas, Wide World Publishing/Tetra, 1989

Fractal, Chaos, Power Laws, Minutes from an Infinite Paradise, by Manfred Schroeder, W. H. Freeman and Company, 1991

Mazes for the Mind, by Clifford A. Pickover, St. Martin's Press, 1992

Concrete Mathematics, by Ronald L. Graham, Donald E. Knuth, and Oren Patashnik, Addison-Wesley, 1994

The Mathematical Universe, by William Dunham, Wiley, 1994

www.ingramcontent.com/pod-product-compliance
Lightning Source LLC
Chambersburg PA
CBHW080835120626
46553CB00009B/2436